THE ROUGH GUIDE TO

Norfolk & Suffolk

written and researched by

Martin Dunford and Phil Lee

ROUGH
GUIDES

D0176888

roughguides.com

Contents

Introduction to
Norfolk and Suffolk

Jutting out into the North Sea above London, the counties of Norfolk and Suffolk form an incredibly diverse region that is the missing link between southeast England and the North, stretching from the marshy banks of the Orwell estuary near Felixstowe right up to the Wash beyond King's Lynn. Like Britain's southwest corner, Norfolk and Suffolk feel like a place apart from the rest of the country: they're not on the way to anywhere and, unusually in a densely populated country like England, they boast few truly large urban centres. The two regional capitals, Norwich and Ipswich, are thriving and enticing places, especially Norwich with its cathedral and ancient centre, but beyond here it is a region of small market towns and idyllic villages scattered across untouched ancient landscapes and farms, with a skyline punctured by medieval church towers that seems hardly to have changed in centuries.

The key to Norfolk and Suffolk's charm is that they're within easy reach of the capital and the Midlands yet far enough off the beaten track to retain a rural quality that's rare this far south in England. Both counties have become a little more discovered over the past two or three decades – parts of the north Norfolk coast are firm Chelsea tractor territory, and Southwold and Aldeburgh have always been genteel – but the landscape remains either wild and uncultivated or given over to solid arable farmland, and there are few concessions to urban ways. **Suffolk** is the gentler of the two counties, smaller, more refined and less remote, although there are pockets that are about as rural as Britain ever gets, and its coast is a truly wild and unspoilt mix of heath, marsh and dune that feels quite separate from the rest. **Norfolk** is Suffolk's big brother, larger, rawer and much more diverse than people imagine, with landscapes ranging from the sandy forests and heathlands of the Brecks (the driest region in Britain) to the haunting wetlands of the Broads and the dunes and long sandy beaches of the north and east coasts.

ABOVE WINDMILL ON THE BROADS **RIGHT** ST PETER & ST PAUL, SWAFFHAM

Where to go

Norwich, Norfolk's capital and home to a third of its population, has one of the country's finest Gothic cathedrals and a lovely old centre whose pubs, restaurants and shops could keep you entertained for days. Beyond here, **King's Lynn** and **Great Yarmouth** are old ports fallen on hard times mostly, but not without their charms, especially King's Lynn, whose perfectly preserved quayside harks back to its days as a member of the Hanseatic League; Great Yarmouth has great beaches and a range of kiss-me-quick attractions in an intriguing mixture of run-down port and shabby seaside town. East of Norwich, the glorious expanse of the **Broads** remains one of the county's prime attractions, great for boating and watersports but also a unique source of wildlife. It blends almost imperceptibly into the beautiful beaches and dunes of the **east coast**, most appealing around **Winterton**, **Horsey** and **Waxham**, although these days the **north coast**, between the old-time seaside resorts of **Cromer** and **Hunstanton**, draws the bulk of the crowds, an odd mixture of bijou businesses and wild coastline whose charms coalesce around fine beaches like **Holkham Bay**, seaside hubs such as **Wells** and **Blakeney** and handsome Georgian towns like **Holt**. Central and western Norfolk is less well known, home to the mysterious expanse of field and dykes that is Norfolk's portion of the **Fens**, worth visiting not only for the unique watery landscape but also for its back-of-beyond villages and birdwatching centres such as Welney. The iconic cathedral of **Ely**, actually in Cambridgeshire, is the Fens' one truly unmissable sight. Central Norfolk revolves around the marvellous woody heaths of **Breckland**, an intensely rural area punctuated by lovely villages such as **Castle Acre** and the intriguing small towns of **Swaffham**, **Wymondham** and **Thetford**. To the south, Norfolk blends into Suffolk along

THE GLORY DAYS

It's not just the landscape that marks out Norfolk and Suffolk. This is one of England's most historic regions, and the cradle of its medieval prosperity, when it was the richest part of the British Isles, growing fat on the proceeds of the weaving industry, which nurtured wool towns like Lavenham and North Walsham, the ports of Ipswich and of course Norwich, and the now almost vanished communities of Dunwich and Worstead. It was the most densely populated part of England at this time, and you can feel the history all around, whether it's in the church towers that puncture the horizon in every direction – Norfolk has a greater concentration of medieval churches than anywhere on earth – or the otherwise ordinary town centres whose grand monuments and oversized churches hark back to more prosperous times. Most of the region's churches are kept unlocked too, which makes it easy to base a trip around the best ones (see box, p.31).

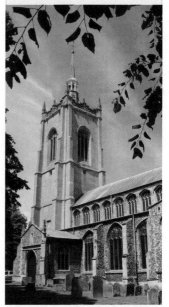

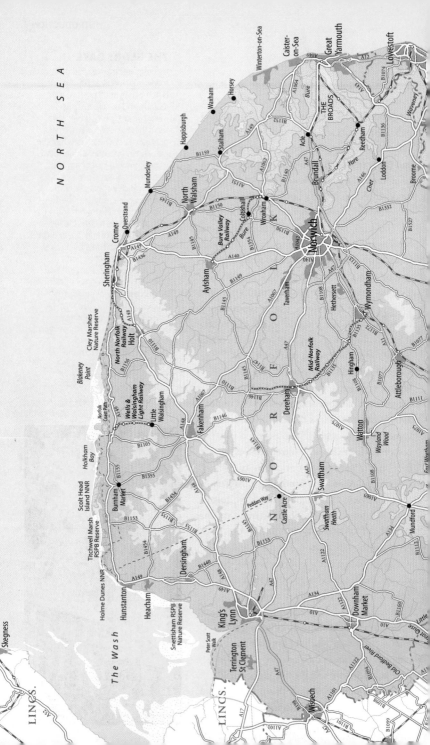

the **Waveney Valley**, where **Diss** is a worthwhile target, and, as the southernmost point on the Broads, **Beccles** – in Suffolk – bridges the gap between the two counties.

Suffolk's greatest attractions are not in **Ipswich**, its capital, but it's a more enticing town than you might think, and a base for visiting **Constable Country**, a string of bucolic villages famously inhabited – and painted – by the English landscape painter. Inland, Suffolk's former glories are evoked in the old wool towns of **Lavenham** and **Bury St Edmunds** – the latter an evocative and historic destination – while to the north, on the far side of the A12, the **Suffolk coast** up to the old fishing port of **Lowestoft** is home to some of the region's most alluring resorts in **Aldeburgh** and **Southwold**, and, north of Ipswich, one of its most attractive provincial centres in **Woodbridge**. The coast in between is unspoilt and in places wild, with a couple of RSPB reserves and some glorious stretches of marsh, heath and woodland that feel a world away from anywhere.

When to go

There's never a bad **time to go** to Norfolk and Suffolk, but they're best when the weather is likely to be warm and dry and the crowds at their most comfortable, in May, June, early July and early September. Late July and throughout August can be busy, especially on the Broads and at the coast, although many of the beaches are so big that they can accommodate the crowds. Both counties are drier than much of England, so spring and autumn can be nice – April and September are the peak months for spotting migratory birds. Even during winter you'll find enough sunny days to make a trip worthwhile, with October to January often the best time to see seals and for spotting waterfowl. Even if the weather is bad, there are loads of rainy-day activities and places to hunker down for good food and drink.

THEY ARE FROM ROUND HERE

As essentially backwater counties, it can be a challenge to name many famous East Anglians, but the region actually punches above its weight in the celebrity firmament.

Benjamin Britten Born in Lowestoft, long-time resident of Aldeburgh, and perhaps the greatest twentieth-century English composer.

Bill Bryson The best-selling travel writer and adoptive native of Norfolk lives near Wymondham and never misses an opportunity to speak up for the county.

Brian Eno The record producer was born and still lives in Woodbridge when not hobnobbing with Davids Byrne and Bowie, U2 and… Belinda Carlisle.

Stephen Fry The twitter-addicted national treasure was born in Reepham and is still a resident of the county.

Bernard Matthews Famed for his "turkey twizzlerrs", Matthews oversaw his Norfolk turkey empire until his death in 2010.

George Orwell So Suffolk-bred he named himself after its major river (he was born Eric Blair) and wrote several of his early books at the family home in Southwold.

Alan Partridge Steve Coogan's creation deliberately stereotypes the parochial nature of East Anglia. His career peaked with his own show on Radio Norwich.

W.G. Sebald The Anglo-German writer and UEA academic adopted East Anglia as his own. He died in 2001 and is buried in the churchyard at Framingham Earl.

Delia Smith The TV chef (see p.50) is the majority shareholder of Norwich FC, but – whisper it! – she lives in Suffolk.

Tim Westwood The Radio One DJ was perhaps the inspiration for TV's Ali G, but he comes from – oh dear – Lowestoft.

Author picks

We've spent a lot of time in Norfolk and Suffolk, and we're keen on all aspects of both counties, from the obvious heavyweight sights to their many hidden corners. What follows is a selection of some of the things that for us make Norfolk and Suffolk unique and fascinating places to visit.

Paddling your own canoe The Broads are glorious for all kinds of boating, but there's nothing quite like travelling by canoe through their remoter reaches. (p.66).

A swift half A multitude of breweries and brilliantly sited pubs mean that both counties are the perfect places to construct a trip not only around tasting the local brews but also feasting on locally sourced food – two things you can easily do at Woodforde's brewery (p.71)and its next door pub, the *Fur and Feather* (p.74).

Among the ruins The counties' prominence in the Middle Ages means that you usually can't go far without encountering the remnants of a medieval priory or abbey, most often in an evocatively ruined state, for example at Castle Acre (p.196), Leiston (p.255), Snettisham (p.161), Baconsthorpe (p.140) and Binham (p.137).

Flippers and feathers Wildlife alone is a reason to visit both counties: otters have returned to the Broads and the region is home to more than a quarter of Britain's rarest species; you can spot seals on the north and east coasts; and lots of rarely seen birds at a range of reserves, like those at Minsmere (p.258), Titchwell (p.156), Strumpshaw Fen (p.111) and Cley Marshes (p.134).

A coastal stroll The Norfolk Coast Path nudges its way along the coast, exploring its marshes, dunes and bays – lovely walking, and easy too (p.123).

Our author recommendations don't end here. We've flagged up our favourite places – a perfectly sited hotel, an atmospheric café, a special restaurant – throughout the guide, highlighted with the ★ symbol.

FROM TOP LOCAL OYSTERS AT ORFORD; BINHAM PRIORY; OTTER; NORFOLK COAST PATH SIGN

things not to miss

It's not possible to see everything that Norfolk and Suffolk have to offer in one trip – and we don't suggest you try. What follows, in no particular order, is a selective taste of the region's highlights, from beautiful beaches and outstanding nature reserves to splendid stately homes and tasty local treats. All highlights have a page reference to take you straight into the guide, where you can find out more.

1 MESSING ABOUT IN BOATS

Pages 66–67

Kick back under the endless sky on the Broads, with only the creak of the rigging and the swish of the water for company. Bliss.

2 BIRDWATCHING

Page 322

Both Norfolk and Suffolk have some of the best RSPB reserves in the country – flocks of avocets like these are a common sight.

3 EAST RUSTON VICARAGE GARDEN

Page 89

North Norfolk's most glorious and inventive garden; visiting is like walking around a restless horticultural brain.

4 ORFORD NESS

Page 246

Orford itself feels like the end of the road, but take a boat on to Orford Ness to really experience the eerie wildness of the Suffolk Coast.

5 ST HELEN'S, RANWORTH

Page 72

The "Cathedral of the Broads" is a typical Norfolk church, with some beautiful original features. But the view over Broadland from its tower is a rare bonus.

6 LOCAL BREWS

Page 26

East Anglia is home to a growing collection of excellent local breweries, some of which you can visit, and most of which sell their wares in local pubs and make a showing at summer beer festivals.

7 NORWICH CATHEDRAL

Page 39

This is where the county's medieval glories reach their peak.

8 HOLT'S SHOPS

Page 142

Handsome Holt is as prosperous and well-heeled a county town as you'll find, and it shows in a fantastic array of independent local shops.

9 WINTERTON-ON-SEA

Page 100

Winterton beach is lovely, but yomping across the vast area of dunes behind is even better.

10 BLAKENEY SEAL-SPOTTING

Page 137

There are seals all along the Norfolk Coast, but a boat trip or walk out to Blakeney Point is the best way to spot them.

9

10

11 BURY ST EDMUNDS
Page 299

One of the most historic provincial towns in England , with an elegant Georgian centre and a host of attractions around.

12 SOUTHWOLD PIER
Page 262

If you like your seaside piers low-key and traditional, this is the country's best.

13 THETFORD FOREST
Page 208

Miles of cycle and footpaths take you to every last corner of this huge area of woodland, the largest in the country. Perfect for kids of all ages.

14 DUNWICH HEATH
Page 258

Dunwich Heath and the nearby Minsmere RSPB Reserve provide some of the best walking and wildlife in both counties, and are among the most enticing spots on the glorious Suffolk Coastal Path.

15 BLICKLING HALL
Page 75

One of the country's finest Jacobean houses, and with an evocative "Downton Abbey" period interior.

16 HORSEY MERE AND WINDMILL
Page 98
A focus for adventures on land and water, with the Mere and its wonderful drainage mill looking out across to the coastal dunes.

17 IPSWICH WATERFRONT
Page 223
Dockland areas all over the country have been restored, but none as successfully as this one.

18 CROMER CRABS
Page 126
Crab meat dressed and eaten from the half shell with a touch of lemon and pepper is a delicious Norfolk snack.

19 ALDEBURGH FESTIVAL
Page 254
Britten's local summer arts festival has been a huge success, and its venue, on the edge of Suffolk's marches, is delightful.

20 BEWILDERWOOD
Page 79
An eco-friendly theme park that is rightly popular.

21 CONSTABLE COUNTRY
Page 278
This ravishing and unchanged landscape inspired the painter's best-known work.

22 HOLKHAM BAY
Page 146
The ultimate flat and sandy Norfolk beach, with the sea almost invisible at low tide.

Itineraries

These suggested itineraries cover the best of what the region has to offer, whether it's medieval churches, outdoor activities, beaches or just enjoying the countryside. There's no need to follow them slavishly but we hope they give you a taste of the richness and diversity of the region.

A WEEK IN NORFOLK

You could spend a month in Norfolk and still find something new. However, if you have just a week this selection of places to stay takes in the best of what the county has to offer.

❶ Norwich There's no better place to start a tour of Norfolk than its capital, which is one of the country's truly great cathedral cities. **See p.36**

❷ Swaffham You wouldn't stay here for the town itself, but it has a great hotel and is a good base for Breckland's northern reaches, Castle Acre and even parts of the Fens. **See p.186**

❸ Wells-next-the-Sea An enticing seaside town, with none of the airs and graces of other parts of the north coast, and the best base for Holkham beach. **See p.144**

❹ North Walsham The town is nothing special but it has a nice boutique hotel and is close to some of the best places on the east coast, including Norfolk's most enticing garden at East Ruston. **See p.88**

❺ Horning One of north Norfolk's most picturesque villages, and with a couple of good places to sleep and eat too – a great place from which to explore the northern Broads. **See p.78**

❻ Diss South Norfolk at its most low-key, but that's exactly why you might come here, plus it's a springboard for the sights of the beautiful Waveney Valley. **See p.210**

A WEEK IN SUFFOLK

It's a small county packed full of interest – if time is tight, this makes an enjoyable week.

❶ Bury St Edmunds There's no more appealing town in the country, and few better introductions to Suffolk. **See p.299**

❷ Constable Country The countryside and villages of the Stour valley have a timeless beauty even if you don't give two hoots for the painter. **See p.278**

❸ Woodbridge and the Deben estuary The small-town charms of Woodbridge make it a great overnight stop, and there's plenty to explore in the nearby area, from ancient Sutton Hoo to the lovely landscapes and villages of the Deben River. **See p.237**

❹ Aldeburgh and Snape A cut above most seaside towns, with some excellent hotels and restaurants and as cool a vibe as you ever get in Suffolk, plus the attraction of annual festivals of arts and food at nearby Snape Maltings. **See p.248**

❺ Southwold With its pier and sandy beach, and genteel high street with plenty of good places to eat, it's no surprise that a beach hut in Southwold can cost tens of thousands. Luckily you can stay at one of several comfortable hotels and B&Bs. **See p.260**

❻ Beccles One of the most handsome small towns in the region, and the gateway to the southern Broads too, with a picturesque riverside and boats to rent. **See p.116**

MEDIEVAL EAST ANGLIA

❶ **Wymondham Abbey** The ruins of the abbey and its church are a magnificent reminder of this tiny town's past significance – a very Norfolk phenomenon. **See p.199**

❷ **Castle Acre** This picturesque village is full of medieval treasures, from its ruined priory and magnificent church to its eponymous castle; a great place to stay the night. **See p.194**

❸ **Oxborough** The church has some of the finest pre-Reformation devotional carving in England, and the hall is magnificent. **See p.194**

❹ **King's Lynn** King's Lynn's waterfront looks much the same as the day the Hanseatic League disbanded. **See p.166**

❺ **Castle Rising** Norfolk's most imposing medieval castle, its ruins tower over the surrounding fields and marshes. **See p.163**

❻ **Binham Priory** Just outside Blakeney, these are some of the most substantial priory ruins in the county – quite a claim in Norfolk. **See p.137**

THE GREAT OUTDOORS

❶ **Cley Marshes Nature Reserve** Norfolk's oldest reserve is one of the county's best places to watch migrating birds and rare waterfowl, including bitterns and marsh harriers. **See p.134**

❷ **Horsey and Waxham** Gorgeous spots, both, with wild walks and plenty of opportunities for spotting seals and their pups. **See p.97 & 98**

❸ **The Electric Eel, How Hill** An hour-long boat tour with knowledgeable guides takes you through high reeds and tiny inlets. **See p.82**

❹ **The Canoe Man** Joining one of his nature or bushcraft trails is a real adventure, and a great way to see the Broads and the best of its wildlife too. **See p.66**

❺ **Thetford Forest** The forest isn't that old, but it offers fantastic opportunities to hike, bike and even race huskies along its miles of well-defined trails. **See p.208**

❻ **Minsmere** There's no better place in Suffolk to spot birds in a delightful landscape. **See p.258**

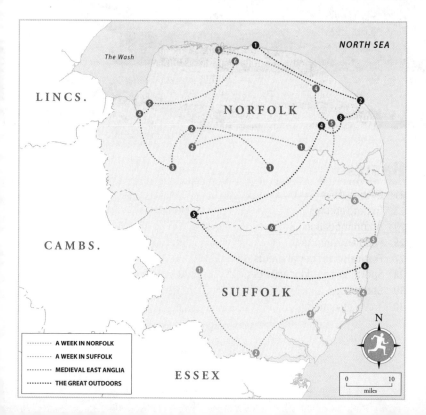

A WEEK IN NORFOLK
A WEEK IN SUFFOLK
MEDIEVAL EAST ANGLIA
THE GREAT OUTDOORS

BOAT ON ALDEBURGH BEACH

Basics

Getting there

By road and rail, Norfolk and Suffolk are within easy striking distance of London and the Midlands, though neither county possesses a motorway, so journey times can be a little longer than you might expect. For international travellers, the obvious – and usually least expensive – way to reach either county is to fly into London and catch the train from there, but there are two regional airports – Norwich, in Norfolk, with a limited range of short-haul flights, and London Stansted, just fifteen miles or so southwest of Suffolk, with a wider range of flights, again largely short-haul. It's also easy to reach Norfolk and Suffolk by train from mainland Europe via London St Pancras station and there are two ferry routes to Harwich, just south of Ipswich – one from Esbjerg, the other from the Hook of Holland.

By car from around the UK

By car, the fastest route from London is the **A12** for Ipswich and most of Suffolk, the **M11** then the **A11** for Norwich and most of Norfolk. Coming from the Midlands, the **A52/A17** will bring you to King's Lynn as will the much faster **A47**, whereas Suffolk is best reached from the Midlands via the **A1/A14**. The region's worst traffic jams are generally in Norwich, where the ring road can be a real pain, on the notorious single carriageway section of the A11 just south of Thetford (though this is now scheduled to be widened), and during the summer season, the A149 between King's Lynn and Hunstanton.

By train

There are two main-line train services from **London** to Norfolk and Suffolk, one from London **King's Cross** to **Cambridge**, **Ely** and **King's Lynn**, the other from London **Liverpool Street** to **Colchester**, **Ipswich** and **Norwich**. Journey times are fairly short – King's Cross to King's Lynn takes about 1hr 30min, Liverpool Street to Norwich 1hr 50min. There are also two main **east–west train lines**, one from Ipswich to Bury St Edmunds, Newmarket, Ely and Cambridge, the other from Peterborough to Ely, Thetford and Norwich. There are connecting trains to Peterborough from the likes of Leicester and Birmingham as well as a cross-country train that runs from Liverpool to Norwich via Manchester,

Sheffield, Nottingham and Peterborough. Nottingham to Norwich takes about 2hr 30min; it's a somewhat epic 5hr from Liverpool. For information on routes, **timetables** and fares, contact National Rail Enquiries (☎0845 748 4950, Ⓦnationalrail.co.uk).

The key to getting the best **fares** is to book early, bearing in mind that most journeys will be cheaper – often much cheaper – in off-peak periods, characteristically Monday to Friday 10/10.30am to 3/3.30pm and all day Saturday and Sunday. As a sample fare, a single from London to Norwich can cost as little as £21 and as much as £60.

If the ticket office at your departure station is closed and/or there is no ticket machine, you can buy your ticket on the train. Otherwise, **boarding without a ticket** will render you liable to paying the full fare plus, possibly, a surcharge. Note also that on Sundays, engineering work can add hours – literally – onto even the shortest journey.

From Europe, **Eurostar trains** (Ⓦeurostar .com) run roughly hourly to London St Pancras from Lille (1hr 20min), Paris (2hr 15min) and Brussels (2hr), with connections running into these three cities from all over Europe with Thalys (Ⓦthalys .com) providing some of the speediest services. To get from London St Pancras to Norfolk and Suffolk by train, you can either walk across to London King's Cross station (for King's Lynn) or take the underground to Liverpool Street station (for Ipswich and Norwich).

By bus

National Express (Ⓦnationalexpress.com), the UK's largest long-distance bus (or coach) operator, doesn't make much of a showing in Norfolk or Suffolk, though it does run fast and frequent buses from **London Victoria** coach station to **Norwich** with fares from as little as £3. Neither does its main rival, **Megabus** (Ⓦmegabus.com), do much better with only two routes, London to **Norwich** (UEA) and London to **Thetford**. To plan a journey, contact **Traveline** (Ⓦtraveline.info), whose website carries comprehensive bus timetable details.

By plane

For travellers from **mainland Europe** and **Ireland**, the handiest airports for Norfolk and Suffolk are **London Stansted** (STN; Ⓦstanstedairport.com) and **Norwich** (NWI; Ⓦwww.norwichairport.co.uk). London Stansted, which is convenient for Norfolk and more especially Suffolk, has a particularly wide choice, and Norwich airport weighs in with around twenty European cities. **Norwich airport** is located about four miles northwest of the city centre along the A140. There are regular buses (journey time 20min) to the city centre from the airport's Park and Ride, but the taxi fare is only about £6. From **London Stansted**, there are regular long-distance buses to Thetford, Norwich and Ipswich as well as hourly trains to Cambridge and Ely for onward connections to Norfolk and Suffolk.

Long-haul destinations arrive at either London Gatwick or London Heathrow – and from London it's a short(ish) train journey onto Norfolk and Suffolk (see p.21).

By ferry from mainland Europe

Drivers have a choice of **ferry** routes. The cheapest services are on the short, cross-Channel hops from the French ports of Calais, Boulogne and Dunkerque to Dover, but this leaves a longish drive to Suffolk and Norfolk via – or rather round – London. The most convenient port for both Norfolk and Suffolk is **Harwich**, in Essex, and there are regular ferries to Harwich from Esbjerg with DFDS (Ⓦdfdsseaways.co.uk) and Hook of Holland with Stena Line (Ⓦstenaline.co.uk). Fares vary enormously according to the date, time and length of stay. The sailing time from Esbjerg to Harwich is about 16hr, 9hr from the Hook.

Getting around

In both Norfolk and Suffolk, all the larger towns and villages are readily accessible by train or bus, but out in the sticks the smaller places can be a real hassle to reach if you don't have your own transport.

By train

The train network in Norfolk and Suffolk is reasonably dense with two south–north main lines originating in London, one linking **Cambridge**, **Ely** and **King's Lynn**, the other **Ipswich** and **Norwich** and points in between. There are also two main east–west lines, one connecting Norwich with **Thetford** and Ely, the other running from Ipswich to **Bury St Edmunds**, **Newmarket** and Ely. Among several branch lines, the most useful are those from Norwich to **Cromer** and **Sheringham**; **Marks Tey** to **Sudbury**; and Norwich to **Great Yarmouth**. The bulk of these services are operated by **National**

Express East Anglia (Ⓦnationalexpresseastanglia .com), though the London to King's Lynn route falls to **First Capital Connect** (Ⓦfirstcapitalconnect .co.uk).

The essential first call for information on routes, timetables, fares and special offers is **National Rail Enquiries** (Ⓦnationalrail.co.uk), and it's always worth booking in advance. National Express East Anglia also offers several sorts of Ranger and Rover tickets. The details are really rather complicated, but one of the more comprehensible is the **Anglia Plus One Day Pass**, which permits unlimited travel for just £15 per adult plus up to four children for just £2 each. The **Anglia Plus Three Days in Seven Pass** is in the same vein and costs £30 per adult. There's no need to book in advance for either of these passes – just turn up and go. There are also several sorts of nationwide railcard, which entitle the bearer to substantial discounts. These include the **16–25 Railcard** for people aged between 16 and 25 (and full-time students of any age) and the **Senior Railcard** for those over 60.

By bus

A small army of local bus companies combines to serve most of the region's towns and villages most of the time, though as a general rule, the smaller the place the harder it is to reach. The main exception is the **Norfolk Coasthopper** (Ⓦwww .coasthopper.co.uk) which provides an exemplary service among the villages that lie dotted along the north Norfolk coast from Hunstanton to Cromer (see p.122). To plan a journey in either Norfolk or Suffolk, contact **Traveline** (Ⓦtraveline.info).

By car or motorbike

At risk of stating the obvious, the easiest way to explore Norfolk and Suffolk is by car. **Scenic routes** abound and although the coast attracts most of the attention, the region's inland villages can be delightful as can the rolling countryside. This is also one part of England where there are no motorways and instead you'll be mostly glued to the region's **"A" roads**, sometimes dual carriageway, but mostly not, which can add time to any journey but tend to give it more character. With the exception of Norwich, where hold-ups are fairly common, traffic congestion is rarely a problem, though the main "A" roads north from London do get clogged on the weekend as does the A149 along the north Norfolk coast. Neither should you underestimate the **weather**: much to the chagrin of many locals,

TWENTY OF THE BEST PLACES TO STAY

NORFOLK

Beechwood Hotel North Walsham. See p.90

Berney Arms Barton Bendish. See p.179

Congham Hall near King's Lynn. See p.143

The Crown, Wells. See p.147

Gothic House Norwich. See p.52

Rose & Crown Snettisham. See p.162

Ship Hotel Brancaster. See p.159

Titchwell Manor Hotel Titchwell. See p.158

White Horse Brancaster Staithe. See p.155

SUFFOLK

Bildeston Crown Bildeston. See p.293

The Crown, Westleton. See p.259

The Crown Woodbridge. See p.241

Great House Hotel Lavenham. See p.291

Ickworth Hotel Horringer. See p.305

Ocean House B&B Aldeburgh. See p.252

Old Cannon B&B Bury St Edmunds. See p.305

The Old Rectory Campsea Ashe. See p.243

Salthouse Harbour Ipswich. See p.225

Swan Hotel Lavenham. See p.291

Swan Hotel Southwold. See p.265

driving conditions can deteriorate quickly during rain, snow, ice, fog and high winds. BBC Radio Five Live (693 or 909 AM nationwide) and local stations feature regularly updated traffic bulletins, as does the Highways Agency website (Ⓦhighways .gov.uk).

Be aware that **speed limits** are not always marked, but you are expected to know (and obey) them: 20 miles per hour in residential streets, 30 or 40mph in built-up areas, 60mph on out-of-town single carriageway roads (often signed by a white circle with a black diagonal stripe), 70mph on dual carriageways. Speed cameras are commonplace.

Vehicle rental

Car rental is usually cheaper arranged in advance through one of the multinational chains. Costs vary considerably, so it's well worth rooting around for a deal, but you can expect to pay around £30 per day, £50 for a weekend or from £150 per week. You can sometimes find deals under £20 per day, though you'll need to book well in advance for the least expensive rates and be prepared for extra charges, primarily damage excess waiver (CDW). Few companies will rent to drivers with less than one year's experience and most will only rent to people between 21 and 75 years of age. Rental cars will be manual (stick shift) unless you specify otherwise.

Just Go (Ⓣ01582 842888, Ⓦjustgo.uk.com), can rent quality **motorhomes** sleeping four to six people, equipped with full bathrooms, kitchenette and bike racks, for £300–1000 per week, depending on the season.

Cycling

Precious few people would choose to get around East Anglia by **cycling** on the main "A" roads –

there's simply too much traffic – but the region's quieter "B" roads and country lanes are of much more appeal, especially as the National Cycle Network (see p.29) sustains many miles of cycling route in both counties. **Off-road** cyclists must stick to bridleways and byways designated for their use.

Accommodation

Accommodation in Norfolk and Suffolk covers everything from motorway lodges and budget guesthouses through to deluxe country retreats and chic boutique hotels. Atmospheric old buildings – former coaching inns in towns, converted mansions and manor houses in rural areas – offer oodles of historic atmosphere, but everywhere you should try to book ahead in the summer season when vacant rooms can get thin on the ground. If you're stuck, the local tourist office will almost invariably lend a helping hand by booking a room on your behalf.

A nationwide **grading system** awards stars to hotels, guesthouses and B&Bs. There's no hard and fast correlation between rank and price, never mind aesthetic appeal, but the grading system does lay down minimum levels of standards and service.

Hotels

Hotels vary wildly in size, style, comfort and price. The starting price for a one-star establishment is around £60 per night for a double/twin room, breakfast usually included; two- and three-star hotels can easily cost £80–100 a night, while

ACCOMMODATION PRICES

For all **accommodation** reviewed in the Guide, we provide sample prices for high season (roughly July–Sept). In hotels and B&Bs, we give the lowest price for one night's stay in a double or twin room, for hostels it's the price of a bed in dorm accommodation (and of a double room if available), and on campsites the cost of two people with a tent. Note, however, that special deals and discounts, especially midweek (and online), are legion.

four-and five-star properties will be around – £150–200 a night – considerably more in country-house hotels. Many city hotels offer cut-price **weekend rates** to fill the rooms whereas seaside and resort hotels almost always charge more on the weekend and an increasing number insist on a minimum two-night stay on the weekend too.

Almost everywhere, standards are improving with Flying Kiwi Inns (Ⓦ flyingkiwiinns.co.uk) being the stand-out **mini-chain**: its owner, an industrious New Zealander Chris Coubrough, has already revitalized half a dozen Norfolk country pubs both decoratively and gastronomically and more will no doubt follow. Marco Pierre White has recently bought a small chain that straddles both counties; there's the Suffolk-based chain that runs the excellent *Crown* at Woodbridge and a handful of other properties on the Suffolk Coast.

At the other end of the scale, both counties have a smattering of **budget chain hotels** with

EIGHT GREAT CAMPSITES

Alde Garden Saxmundham.
See p.257
Beeston Regis Holiday Park West Runton. See p.132
Clippesby Hall Thurne, Suffolk.
See p.92
Deepdale Backpackers & Camping Burnham Deepdale. See p.155
High Sand Creek Campsite Stiffkey.
See p.139
Nature's Path Yaxham. See p.198
Orchard Campsite Wickham Market.
See p.244
Walnut Farm Waxham. See p.98

Premier Inn (Ⓦ premierinn.com) and Travelodge (Ⓦ travelodge.co.uk) being two big names; these offer no-frills accommodation – breakfast is charged extra – from as little as £40 per double if booked in advance.

B&Bs and guesthouses

B&Bs and **guesthouses** are often a great option for travellers looking for character and a local experience: the best – with fresh, house-proud rooms, hearty home-cooked food and a wealth of local knowledge – can match or beat a hotel stay at any price. At its simplest, a B&B (bed-and-breakfast) is a private house with a couple of bedrooms set aside for paying guests. Larger establishments with more rooms, particularly in resorts, style themselves **guesthouses**, but they are pretty much the same thing. Don't assume that a B&B is no good if it is ungraded in official listings as some places simply choose not to enter into a grading scheme: in countryside locations, for instance, some of the best accommodation can be found in **farmhouses** whose facilities may technically fall short of official standards. Many village **pubs** also offer B&B accommodation. Standards vary widely – some are great, others truly awful – but at best you'll be staying in a friendly spot with a sociable bar on hand, and you'll rarely pay more than £80 a room.

Single travellers should note that many B&Bs and guesthouses don't have single rooms, and sole occupancy of a double or twin room will normally be charged at seventy or eighty percent of the standard rate.

Hostels

The **Youth Hostel Association** (YHA; Ⓦ yha.org.uk) has two hostels in Norfolk – one at Wells and one at Sheringham – and another in Suffolk, at Blaxhall, near Aldeburgh. All three offer bunk-bed accommodation in dormitories and smaller rooms of two, four or six beds. Each of them also has a reasonable range of facilities, including a kitchen, and the overnight rate is around £20 per person. The YHA is affiliated to the global network of **Hostelling International** (Ⓦ hihostels.com). If you're already an HI member, you qualify for the YHA's standard rates. Otherwise, you must pay a supplement of £3 a night (£1.50 for under-18s) – or you can join HI in person at any hostel or online for £16 a year (£10 for under-26s). Family deals are also available.

Camping

There are scores of **campsites** in Norfolk and Suffolk, ranging from rustic, family-run places to large sites with laundries, shops and sports facilities. Costs range from around £5 per adult at the simplest sites up to around £20 per tent (including two adults) in the most sought-after locations. Many campsites also offer accommodation in static **caravans**, which are mostly large and well equipped, and a few have a selection of chalet-style (wooden) huts. *The Rough Guide to Camping in Britain* has detailed reviews of the best campsites, including several in Norfolk and Suffolk, or you might check out ⓦ camping andcaravanningclub.co.uk. **Camping rough** is frowned upon just about everywhere.

Self-catering accommodation

Self-catering is a big deal in the tourist industries of both Norfolk and Suffolk with literally hundreds of properties – usually **cottages** – rented out either all year or just during the season. Traditionally, the minimum rental period is a week, but there's more flexibility in the market than there used to be and weekend lets are now far from uncommon. Expect to pay around £300 a week for a small cottage in an out-of-the-way location, maybe three times that for a larger property in a popular spot.

SELF-CATERING RENTAL COMPANIES

Best of Suffolk ☎ 01728 638962, ⓦ bestofsuffolk.co.uk.
Exemplary and extremely efficient lettings agency offering a wide range of upmarket properties all over Suffolk with a particular concentration of places along the coast. Hard to beat.

Landmark Trust ☎ 01628 825925, ⓦ landmarktrust.org.uk. A preservation charity that owns eleven historic properties in Norfolk and Suffolk, each of which has been creatively converted into holiday accommodation. One particular highlight is the restored Martello tower at Aldeburgh.

National Trust ☎ 0844 800 2070, ⓦ nationaltrustcottages .co.uk. The NT owns 35 cottages, barns, houses and farmhouses in Norfolk and Suffolk, mostly set in their own gardens or grounds and mostly of some historical interest or importance.

Norfolk Country Cottages ☎ 01603 871872, ⓦ norfolkcottages .co.uk. Well-established lettings agency with a large portfolio of properties, everything from large manor houses through to cosy flint cottages in every part of the county, but especially on the coast.

Rural Retreats ☎ 01386 701177, ⓦ ruralretreats.co.uk.
Upmarket agency with eighteen properties in Norfolk and Suffolk, mostly sympathetically modernized old cottages.

A TOP TEN NORFOLK AND SUFFOLK RESTAURANTS

Bank House King's Lynn. See p.172
Bildeston Crown Bildeston. See p.294
Bure River Cottage Horning. See p.81
The Crown Woodbridge. See p.242
Elm Hill Brasserie Norwich. See p.54
Great House Lavenham. See p.292
Market Bistro King's Lynn. See p.174
The Ostrich Castle Acre. See p.196
Strattons Swaffham. See p.193
Titchwell Manor Hotel Titchwell. See p.159

Food and drink

Changing tastes have transformed Norfolk and Suffolk's food and drink over the last decade. Great importance is now placed on "ethical" eating – principally sourcing products locally and using organic ingredients. Good-quality, moderately priced restaurants can now be found almost everywhere and the majority are independently owned with barely a chain in sight. The East Anglian pub has wrung the changes too: the traditional village boozer is on the wane and although lots of rural pubs have closed, scores have reinvented themselves, sprucing up their decor and serving both real ales and excellent food.

In turn, this culinary transformation means that there are now enough (gastro-)pubs and restaurants demanding top-quality ingredients to support scores of local food suppliers. Free-range Suffolk pork and Cromer crabs (see box, p.126) are obvious and widespread examples, but other memorable specialities include Brancaster and Stiffkey oysters and mussels and Norfolk samphire. In many pubs and restaurants, locally sourced food ties in with a well-considered "**Modern British**" menu that features old favourites – steak-and-kidney pies – with more adven-

---

OPENING TIMES

We've given the **opening times** of all the pubs, restaurants and cafés we list throughout the text. In the case of pubs they refer to the hours they serve food, though most will of course be open outside of those times.

LOCAL BEERS, CIDERS AND JUICES

Adnams Ⓦadnams.co.uk. The ultimate successful local brewer, rooted in the heart of its Suffolk community yet producing a wide range of great draft and bottled beers. They have a great county-wide chain of classy beer and wine shops too.

Aspall Ⓦwww.aspall.co.uk. Based at Aspall Hall and run by the eighth generation of the Chevalier family, Aspall ciders are another fine example of a brilliant Suffolk product that has gone national. Great cider, apple juice and vinegar.

Beeston Brewery Ⓦbeestonbrewery .com. Small brewer based in Beeston, near Dereham, that produces half a dozen ales, from the light, easy-drinking Afternoon Delight to the heavier and stronger Norfolk Black Strong Stout.

Blackfriar's Ⓦblackfriars-brewery.co.uk. Based in Great Yarmouth since 2004, and mostly supplying local pubs with their excellent range of half a dozen beers and seasonal specials.

Brandon Brewery Ⓦbrandonbrewery .co.uk. It's only been going since 2005, but this Breckland brewer is prolific, producing over a dozen diverse ales from its Suffolk base.

Calvors Brewery Ⓦcalvors.co.uk. This Suffolk producer is one of the youngest East Anglia breweries, and uniquely concentrates on pure English lager, from its headquarters just north of Ipswich. You can find its beers in shops and pubs all over Suffolk, as well as the odd Norfolk location.

Cliff Quay Brewery Ⓦcliffquay.co.uk. This small Ipswich-based brewer supplies outlets around the city and half a dozen places outside with its range of four regular ales and innumerable seasonal brews.

Earl Soham Brewery Ⓦearlsohambrewery. co.uk. One of the best-established Suffolk brewers, whose Victoria Bitter can be found in many a decent Suffolk pub.

Greene King Ⓦwww.greeneking.co.uk. This well-known brewery has been going for 200 years and hardly needs an introduction if you've been into a pub anywhere in Britain over the past two decades. But its beers are reliably good, and it's still based in its original Bury St Edmund's home.

Humpty Dumpty Brewery
Ⓦhumptydumpty.typepad.com. This Norfolk brewer is based in a large shed in Reedham, and produces a wide and delicious range of

ales despite being a relatively small affair. Their shop (see p.110) sells their own products, alongside brews from Belgium and local ciders.

Iceni Brewery Ⓦicenibrewery.co.uk. This small brewery on the edge of Thetford Forest brews a huge range of beers considering its size. The best place to buy them is at their tiny shop (see p.210), but you can find them at local farmers' markets.

James White Ⓦwww.jameswhite.co.uk. This fantastic rural Suffolk business has a royal warrant for its apple and other juices. Its fresh-pressed russet juice is a joy.

Mauldon's Ⓦmauldons.co.uk. At over 200 years old this is one of Suffolk's best-established brewers, but it remains a microbrewer at heart, producing five draft ales and three bottled beers at its home in Sudbury. You can sample its wares at its own local, the *Brewery Tap* (see p.284).

St Peter's Brewery Ⓦstpetersbrewery .co.uk. Based just outside Bungay, St Peter's was started about fifteen years ago not by a brewer but an expert in brands. They brew some great beers, and they're available at their on-site shop and restaurant (see p.214), and decent pubs across Norfolk and Suffolk.

Spectrum Brewery Ⓦspectrumbrewery. co.uk. This small brewer to the south of Norwich won't win any prizes for branding or design, but its beers are decent, and they do a wide range for such a small concern. Plus they claim to be East Anglia's only truly organic brewery.

Tipples Ⓦtipplesbrewery.com. With a name like Jason Tipple, he really had to start his own brewery, and he now produces half a dozen or so bottled ales from his Acle HQ, as well as plenty of seasonal specials and so-called experimental ales – "Hey Pesto!" anyone?

Wagtail Brewery Ⓦwagtailbrewery.com. This great Norfolk brewery's ales can be found all over the county and a little bit beyond, both on draft and in bottles.

Wolf Brewery Based just outside Attleborough since 1995, this is one of the best-established Norfolk microbreweries, producing four draft ales and a whole slew of bottled varieties.

Woodforde's Ⓦwww.woodfordes.co.uk. Based in the heart of the Broads, Woodforde's supplies pubs all over Norfolk and Suffolk, and most people swear by at least one of its five or so draft beers and bottled equivalents.

turous concoctions – crab in a beetroot sauce for example. One casualty of the change has been the **teashop** or **tearoom**: once there were scores, now there are a handful, their decline assured by the irresistible rise of the gastropub and, in the larger towns, the chain-outlet coffee bars such as *Costa* and *Caffè Nero*.

Festivals and special events

Festivals are something of a growth industry in the UK and East Anglia is no exception with lots of towns and villages designing new special-interest shindigs each and every year – not surprising, really, when you consider, for example, the roaring success of Southwold's Latitude music festival, which only started in 2006. These new concoctions are grafted onto more established festivals, ranging from the agricultural delights of the Royal Norfolk Show to the studied gentility of the Aldeburgh Festival. The calendar below picks out some of the best, but for detailed local listings either contact the appropriate tourist office (see p.33) or go to Ⓦfestivalsuffolk.com and Ⓦvisitnorfolk.co.uk.

JANUARY–MARCH

Shrove Tuesday The last day before Lent – in Feb or March depending on the year. Known as "Pancake Day", this is when the English get down to some serious pancake eating. In 2011, an ancient Pancake Day tradition was revived in Dereham with the ringing of church bells and Felixstowe holds the record for the largest number of pancakes tossed in the shortest amount of time (349 tosses in 2 minutes). Also celebrated with a Mardi Gras parade in Great Yarmouth.

APRIL

High Tide Festival Four days in late April/early May; Ⓦ hightide.org.uk. Enterprising festival showcasing newly written plays plus workshops, panel debates and films. Held in Halesworth, Suffolk.

MAY

Broads Outdoors Festival 2nd week of May; Ⓦ outdoorsfestival .co.uk. Guided walks, jazz boats, wildlife tours – a host of things to do on and off the water in the Broads.
Folk on the Pier Three days in early May; Ⓦ deckchairproductions.co.uk. Held in Cromer, this ambitious music festival celebrates all things folk with concerts, gigs and workshops. Acoustic folk, folk rock, blues and world music are all represented and performances feature an international cast of artists.

Norfolk & Norwich Festival Two weeks in May; Ⓦ nnfestival .org.uk. This is Norwich's premier arts festival with a particular emphasis on music, especially jazz, contemporary and classical, plus oodles of theatre and dance. Features an international cast of performing artists.
Bury St Edmunds Festival Two weeks in late May; Ⓦ buryfestival.co.uk. Small-town cultural knees-up with jazz, theatre, film, classical music and street theatre.

JUNE

Suffolk Show Two days in early June; Ⓦ www.suffolkshow.co.uk. Folksy/rural celebration of the best of Suffolk's agricultural trade, with a special emphasis on skilled craftsmen, animals and local produce. Held on the Suffolk Showground on the edge of Ipswich.
Three Rivers Race Horning, first Sat in June; Ⓦ threeriversrace .org.uk. For some this is the major sailing event of the summer, a sort of Norfolk Broads Le Mans, lasting right through the night and with over 100 yachts in contention.
Aldeburgh Festival Two and a half weeks in June; Ⓦ aldeburgh.co.uk. Suffolk jamboree of classical music with a worldwide reputation. Established by Benjamin Britten in 1948. Book early to avoid disappointment. Core performances are held at the Snape Maltings, just outside Aldeburgh. See p.250.
Royal Norfolk Show Two days in late June/early July, Ⓦ www.royalnorfolkshow.co.uk. The largest agricultural show in England showcases all things farming – from crops to livestock and beyond. Hearty sports and hearty, locally produced food too. Held on the Norfolk Showground, Dereham Road, on the edge of Norwich.

JULY

Latitude Festival Four days in mid-July; Ⓦ latitudefestival .co.uk. Relatively new music festival that has quickly become one of England's best, featuring several hundred performers with add-ons in the shape of comedy, theatre, dance, poetry and cabaret. Held in Henham Park just outside Southwold. Headline acts in recent years have included Suede, The Waterboys, The Cribs and The National. See p.266.
The Shakespeare Festival Five days in mid-July; Ⓦ cathedral .org.uk. Top-ranking Shakespearean performances held in the cloisters of Norwich cathedral – great setting.
Holt Festival Last week of July; Ⓦ holtsummerfestival.org. Attracting a well-heeled crew, this week-long festival features all the performing arts, from dance, poetry, literature and street theatre through to comedy and contemporary music.

AUGUST

Cromer Carnival One week in mid-Aug; Ⓦ cromercarnival .co.uk. Family fun and entertainment culminating in an impressive Carnival Parade and a whopping firework display.
Voewood Festival Holt; Ⓦ voewoodfestival.com. Yet another literary festival, but this one is growing, and attracts lot of big names to the fantastic Arts & Crafts venue of Voewood House, just outside Holt.

SEPTEMBER

Heritage Open Days Three days in mid-Sept; Ⓦ heritageopendays.org.uk. A once-a-year opportunity to peek inside dozens of buildings that don't normally open their doors to the public. Coordinated by English Heritage; the properties concerned are dotted all over the region.

Yare Navigation Race Brundall; Ⓦ coldhamhallsailingclub .co.uk. The biggest Norfolk Broad cruiser event on the southern Broads, with around 80 yachts racing between Brundall and Breydon Water.

OCTOBER

Norwich Beer Festival Late Oct; Ⓦ norwichcamra.org.uk. Six days of happy, hoppy stupefaction in St Andrew's Hall. CAMRA buffs abound.

Halloween Oct 31. All Hallows' Eve. In the last decade, British kids have taken to the mock horror of Halloween like ducks to water, parading round in ghoulish disguises mainly copied from the USA. Expect to be tricked-or-treated.

NOVEMBER

Aldeburgh Poetry Festival Three days in early Nov; Ⓦ thepoetrytrust.org. The Poetry Trust is one of the UK's leading poetry organizations and it has steered this festival into becoming a big poetic deal, attracting a wide range of new and established poets.

Bonfire Night Nov 5. In 1605, Guy Fawkes tried to blow up Parliament in the Gunpowder Plot, but for better or worse he failed and was subsequently executed for his pains. The English have celebrated Fawkes's failure ever since with bonfires and fireworks in every corner of the land. Traditionally, an effigy of Fawkes was burnt on the bonfire, though nowadays it's as likely to be a heartily disliked celebrity. Celebrated with particular gusto in Norwich at both Earlham Park and the Norfolk Showground.

DECEMBER

New Year's Eve Dec 31. Much carousing in the region's town and cities; more genteel tipsiness in the country.

Sports and outdoor activities

The average East Anglian may love his or her spectator sports, but most of the action takes place in England's big cities, well away from Norfolk and Suffolk, with two main exceptions – one football, the other horse racing. For participants, Norfolk and Suffolk offer a battery of outdoor activities, with three of the most popular being walking, cycling and beach-combing – or just lying on the beach and going in for a dip now and again. Sailing is popular too, both on the coast and on the Norfolk Broads (see box, p.66–67), and birdwatching is a major pastime as well (see p.322).

Spectator sports

Football games between Ipswich and Norwich, excite intense local rivalry, though Norwich (see p.58) were promoted to the Premier League in 2011, leaving Ipswich (see p.221) behind in the Championship and, as a result, regular league fixtures between them are no more – at least for the time being. The other spectator sport hereabouts is **horse racing**, principally in horse-mad Newmarket (see p.308), which is home to two – flat – **racecourses**. They hold several meetings a year between April and October, including the Guineas festival in May, which takes in two of the five classics on the flat racing calendar, the 1000 Guineas and the 2000 Guineas. There is also flat racing in Great Yarmouth (see p.107) during the same period, and National Hunt racing at Fakenham, from April to December (see p.142).

Walking

Norfolk and Suffolk are neither rugged nor especially wild, but their easy, rolling landscapes, long coast, rich birdlife and wide skies have combined to make them a very popular **walking area**. Almost all of the region's many tourist offices have details of local rambles, most of which are easily accomplished in a day and are physically undemanding, especially as clearly signed footpaths abound. General details of local walks are given in this guide and the region also possesses one of England's busiest **National Trails** (Ⓦ nationaltrail.co.uk), the **Peddars Way/ Norfolk Coast Path**. This waymarked path and track separates into two clearly defined sections, the less-used portion being the 46-mile Peddars Way, which stretches north from Suffolk's Knettishall Heath Country Park, following the route of an old Roman road as far as Holme-next-the-Sea on the Norfolk coast. The second section is the 44-mile Norfolk Coast Path, which ambles east along the coast from Holme-next-the-Sea to Cromer. Only a minority of walkers undertake the whole caboodle with most opting for short(ish) hikes, especially along the Norfolk Coast Path where the **Norfolk Coasthopper** bus (Ⓦ www .coasthopper.co.uk) provides excellent public transport, making round trips easy and convenient. Other long-distance routes include the sixty-mile **Stour Valley Path**, linking Dedham Vale with Sudbury and Newmarket; the fifty-mile **Suffolk Coast and Heaths Path**, which follows the coat from Felixstowe to Lowestoft; the 56-mile

Weavers' Way, an inland route between Cromer and Great Yarmouth; the twenty-mile-long **Paston Way**, from North Walsham to Cromer; the 70-mile **Angles Way**, from just beyond Diss to Great Yarmouth; and the 35-mile **Wherryman's Way**, a riverine route connecting Norwich with Great Yarmouth. There are also paths that start outside but finish up in Norfolk or Suffolk, like the **Fens Rivers Way**, which starts in Cambridge and runs right up the Ouse and its tributaries to King's Lynn. There's just one designated national park in the region – **The Broads** (Ⓦ broads-authority .gov.uk).

It almost goes without saying that even for a fairly short hike you need to be properly equipped. The East Anglian climate is relatively benign, but the weather is very changeable and on the coast in particular the wind can be bitingly chill. As for maps, walkers almost invariably stick to **Ordnance Survey** maps (OS; Ⓦ ordnancesurvey.co.uk), either in the Explorer (1:25,000) or the Landranger series (1:50,000). These can be used in conjunction with the companionable **Wilfrid George maps**, simple sketch maps showing items of interest and potential walking routes. These are available at most major tourist offices – for example Lavenham and Cromer – and cost around £2; they don't cover all of Norfolk and Suffolk, but they do cover the most visited bits of both.

Cycling

The UK's **National Cycle Network** (Ⓦ sustrans.org .uk) is made up of 10,000 miles of signed cycle routes, a third on traffic-free paths (including disused railways and canal towpaths), the rest mainly on country roads. In Norfolk and Suffolk, NCN cycle routes loop their way through both counties, dropping by all the major towns - Norwich, Ipswich, Bury St Edmunds, Thetford etc – and a battery of villages. **Sustrans** produces an excellent series of waterproof maps (1:100,000) to help you on your way. There's also the **Norfolk Coast Cycleway**, following quiet roads and lanes from King's Lynn to Great Yarmouth; detailed maps of the route, which is a regional route of the Sustrans Hull to Harwich route, are produced by the Norfolk Coast Partnership (Ⓦ norfolkcoastaonb.org.uk) and are also available at larger tourist offices. In addition, most local tourist offices stock a range of **cycling guides**, with maps and detailed route descriptions, and have details of local cycle rental companies,

---

TOP FIVE SANDY BEACHES

Cromer See p.124
Holkham Bay See p.146
Holme-next-the-Sea See p.157
Southwold See p.260
Wells-next-the-Sea See p.144

---

though these are not as plentiful as you would perhaps imagine. Expect to pay around £10–15 per day, with discounts for longer periods; you may need to provide credit card details, or leave a passport as a deposit.

Beaches

The elongated coastline of Norfolk and Suffolk boasts long stretches of golden sand interspersed with mud flats and salt marsh, shingle and pebble. Everywhere, the sea disappears into the distance at low tide, possibly to the frustration of bathers, but to the delight of kids who can nose around the tide pools, observe the lugworms casting up their coils and watch (or catch) the crabs. Perhaps the eeriest part of the coast is between Hunstanton and King's Lynn, where The Wash empties into the ocean creating a mass phalanx of treacle-mud that attracts birds by the thousand and birdwatchers by the score. A number of beaches are currently recipients of **Blue Flag** quality awards, including Hunstanton, Cromer, Sea Palling, Southwold and Lowestoft.

Sailing and watersports

Most visitors to the Norfolk and Suffolk seaside are content with bucket and spade, deckchair and ice cream, but others are after more activity with sailing exercising an enduring appeal. Among the resorts of the north Norfolk coast, Blakeney is the apple of the sailor's eye, though here you will need your own boat, whereas, just along the coast at Brancaster Staithe, the Sailcraft Sea School (Ⓦ www .northshoresport.co.uk) organizes training sessions and rents out boats. There's also surfing with The Glide Surf School in Cromer (Ⓦ glidesurfschool .co.uk); windsurfing at Hunstanton with Hunstanton Watersports (Ⓦ hunstantonwater sports.com); and all sorts of nautical activity at the NT's Brancaster Millennium Activity Centre (Ⓦ nationaltrust.org.uk). Away from the coast, the Broads are extraordinarily popular with boaters too, and here boat rental is easy and straightforward (**see box, p.66–67**), whether you're a keen sailor –

LOCAL FOOD HEROES: GREAT PRODUCERS, DELIS AND FARMSHOPS

Blythburgh Pork ⓦ freerangepork.co.uk
Booja-Booja. Dairy-free confectionery
ⓦ boojabooja.com
Cley Smokehouse Cley. See p.136
Denver Mill Denver. See p.178
Drove Farm Orchards Near Holme-next-the-Sea. See p.157
Emmett's Peasenhall. See p.257
Farm to Fork & Fish Horstead. See p.74
Food Safari Saxmundham. See p.257
Gurneys Fish Shop Burnham Market. See p.155

Jimmy's Farm Ipswich. See p.224, 228
Lawson's Aldeburgh. See p.253
Norfolk Farmhouse Ice Cream
ⓦ norfolkfarmhouseicecream.co.uk
Pinney's Orford. See p.247
Revetts Wickham Market. See p.244
Richardson's Smokehouse Orford. See p.247
Suffolk Food Hall Ipswich. See p.228
Tavern Tasty Meats ⓦ taverntasty.co.uk
Wiveton Hall near Cley. See p.135
Woodbridge Fine Food Co 2A New St Woodbridge. ⓦ woodbridgefinefoodcompany.co.uk

---

there is no better place in the country for safe yet demanding **sailing** – a **canoeist** (the reedy wetlands of the Broads is ideal canoeing country) or you just want to do as most people do and pootle around in a **motor cruiser.**

Shopping

Homogenization may be the name of the game in most of the UK, but in Norfolk and Suffolk small, independent shops have survived – even flourished – in substantial numbers with Norwich leading the retail resistance.

Many of the region's towns and larger villages have, for example, a weekly **market**, where local produce is a particular highlight – this is, after all, a predominantly agricultural region – and Country Markets (ⓦ www.country-markets.co.uk) has detailed listings of what's on and where. There's also a veritable battery of specialist **food shops** in the prime tourist zones with the north Norfolk and Suffolk coasts in the forefront. It's here on the coast you'll find a goodly number of fishmongers with the good old Cromer crab clinging onto many a gastronomic headline. **Farm shops** are a feature of the region too, as well as roadside stalls selling the freshest of fruit and veg – Norfolk strawberries can taste absolutely wonderful.

Furthermore, some of the more prosperous towns – like Holt, Burnham Market and Long Melford – have a good range of **independent retailers** selling books, antiques and designer clothes, but these tend to be on the pricey side except in Norwich, which excels in bargain-basement specialist shops selling everything from vintage clothes to ancient furniture.

Travel essentials

Costs and passes

By comparison with the rest of western Europe, England in general and Norfolk and Suffolk in particular are competitively priced, less so in comparison with North America, Australia and New Zealand. If you're camping or hostelling, using public transport, buying picnic lunches and eating in pubs and cafés your **minimum expenditure** will be around £35/US$55/€40 per person per day. Couples staying in B&Bs, eating at mid-range restaurants and visiting some attractions should anticipate roughly £70/US$110/€80 per person, while if you're renting a car, staying in hotels and eating well, budget for £120/US$185/€135 each – but double that figure if you choose to stay in stylish deluxe hotels or grand country houses.

Many of the region's **historic attractions** are owned and/or operated by either the **National Trust** (ⓦ nationaltrust.org.uk) or **English Heritage** (ⓦ www.english-heritage.org.uk), whose properties are denoted throughout this book with "NT" or "EH". Most of the lesser, smaller sites are free, but all the more prestigious locations attract a hefty-ish admission charge of about £7 and up. If you plan to visit more than half a dozen places owned by either, it's worth considering an annual membership – you can join online or in person at any staffed attraction. There are several different sorts of membership, but a standard, adult, year-long pass currently costs between £38 and £50 (NT), £46 (EH). Non-UK residents can, on the other hand, buy a **Great British Heritage Pass** (3/7/15/30 days £39/69/89/119; ⓦ britishheritagepass.com), which gives free entry to over six

---

NORFOLK AND SUFFOLK'S BEST CHURCHES

The Abbey, Wymondham See p.199
Binham Priory church, Binham See p.137
Holy Trinity, Blythburgh See p.264
Holy Trinity, Long Melford See p.286
St Edmund Southwold See p.261
St Helen Ranworth See p.72
St Margaret, Cley-next-the-Sea See p.134
St Margaret, King's Lynn See p.169
St Mary, Bury St Edmunds See p.301
St Mary, Stoke-by-Nayland See p.281

St Mary, Thornham Parva See p.298
St Michael, Framlingham See p.244
St Nicholas, Blakeney See p.136
St Nicholas , Salthouse See p.132
St Peter Mancroft , Norwich See p.47
St John, Oxborough See p.194
St Peter & St Paul, Lavenham See p.290
St Peter & St Paul, Salle See p.76
St Peter & St Paul, Swaffham See p.190
Walpole St Peter See p.175

---

hundred cultural and historic attractions, including National Trust and English Heritage properties. Family discounts are available and you can buy it online and from travel agents in your home country.

A number of **stately homes** are still in private hands and these charge substantial entry fees – £11 for Holkham Hall, £8.80 for Houghton Hall – whereas the region's privately owned museums and art **galleries**, of which there are a fair number, charge modest admission fees starting from as little as £2. Norfolk and Suffolk are short of publicly owned museums and art galleries, but admission to them is either free or reasonably priced. Churches are usually free, but the big cathedrals – primarily Ely and Norwich – charge.

Throughout this book, admission prices quoted are the full adult rate, unless otherwise stated. Concessionary rates – generally half-price – for **senior citizens**, under-26s, and **children** (aged 5–17) apply almost everywhere, from tourist attractions to public transport; you'll need official ID as proof of age. Children under 5 are rarely charged. Full-time **students** are often entitled to discounts too via an ISIC (International Student Identity Card; ⓦisic.org).

Gay and lesbian travellers

England offers one of Europe's most diverse and accessible **lesbian and gay** scenes, but most of the action is in the big cities, which tends to leave most of Norfolk and Suffolk high and dry with the notable exception of Norwich. Countrywide listings and news can be found at ⓦpinkpaper .com and in the glossy magazine *Gay Times* (ⓦgaytimes.co.uk). For information and links, go to ⓦgaybritain.co.uk and ⓦgaytravel.co.uk. The age of consent is 16.

Health

Citizens of all EU and EEA countries are entitled to free medical treatment within the UK's National Health Service (NHS), on production of their **European Health Insurance Card** (EHIC). The same applies to those Commonwealth countries that have reciprocal healthcare arrangements with the UK – for example Australia and New Zealand. Everyone else will be charged and should, therefore, take out their own medical insurance. However, EU/EEA citizens may also want to consider private health insurance, both to cover the cost of items not within the EU/EEA scheme and to enable them to seek treatment within the private sector. No inoculations are currently required for entry into Britain.

For medical advice 24 hours a day, call **NHS Direct** (☎0845 4647, ⓦnhsdirect.nhs.uk). Their website is packed with useful information, and also has directories of doctors' surgeries. Otherwise, minor issues can be dealt with at the surgery of any local **doctor**, also known as a **GP** (General Practitioner), whereas medical emergencies are treated in hospital at 24hr "**A&E**" (accident and emergency) – or "**Casualty**" – sections; note that not all hospitals have A&E facilities. You can either make your own way to the nearest A&E or call an ambulance on ☎999.

Maps

There's a bewildering variety of road maps, but the best – or at least the clearest – are those produced by **A-Z Maps** (ⓦa-zmaps.co.uk), whose excellent and competitively priced A-Z Super Scale Britain (1:100,000) has inset maps of Norwich and Ipswich too. The same company also publishes a wide range of detailed city street maps, including maps of Norwich and Ipswich (both at 1:16000), and

ROUGH GUIDES TRAVEL INSURANCE

Rough Guides has teamed up with WorldNomads.com to offer great **travel insurance** deals. Policies are available to residents of over 150 countries, with cover for a wide range of **adventure sports**, 24hr emergency assistance, high levels of medical and evacuation cover Roughguides. com users can take advantage of their policies online 24/7, from anywhere in the world – even if you're already travelling. And since plans often change when you're on the road, you can extend your policy and even claim online. Roughguides.com users who buy travel insurance with WorldNomads.com can also leave a positive footprint and donate to a community development project. For more information go to ⓦ**roughguides.com/shop**.

produces county maps for both Norfolk and Suffolk (1:17000), each of which has literally dozens of village and town street maps. For hiking you'll need Ordnance Survey maps (see p.29).

Newspapers

There are lots of local newspapers in Norfolk and Suffolk, but the best coverage of regional news, scandal and gossip is provided by the **Eastern Daily Press**, which covers all of Norfolk as well as north Suffolk. The other regional daily is the **East Anglian Daily Times**, which covers Ipswich and the rest of Suffolk; and both papers publish a monthly magazine on Norfolk and Suffolk respectively, full of the usual glossy ads, lifestyle and property articles. The major local newspaper for Norwich and its surroundings is the **Norwich Evening News**, while the **Evening Star** does the same job for Ipswich and around.

Opening hours

Opening hours for most businesses, shops and offices are Monday to Saturday 9am to 5.30 or 6pm, with many shops, especially in the popular tourist areas, also open on Sundays, generally 10.30 or 11am until 4/5pm. Big supermarkets have longer hours (except on Sundays), sometimes round the clock. Some towns have an **early-closing day** (usually Wednesday) when most shops close at 1pm. **Banks** are usually open Monday to Friday 9am–4pm, and Saturday 9am–12.30pm or so. You can usually get fuel any time of the day or night in larger towns and cities, but in rural areas keep an eye on the petrol gauge.

USEFUL NUMBERS

Domestic operator ☎ 100
International operator ☎ 155

Phones

With the irresistible rise of the mobile phone, public **payphones** are increasingly thin on the ground, especially in the countryside. Where they have survived, they take coins (minimum charge 40p) and some also accept credit cards. Otherwise, the English have taken to **mobile phones** like ducks to water, but outside of the towns in both Norfolk and Suffolk network coverage is frustratingly patchy.

The UK mobile network is on the 900/1800 MHz band - the band common to the rest of Europe, Australia and New Zealand (but not North America). Phoning UK **directory enquiries** is inordinately expensive; instead look online at ⓦbt.com. Business and service numbers are searchable at ⓦyell.com.

Smoking

Smoking is banned in all enclosed public spaces, including restaurants, cafés, pubs and offices, and on all public transport. Hotel rooms that are designated specifically as smoking rooms are exempt – but the vast majority of hotels and B&Bs impose smoking bans throughout their premises anyway. All of this means that smokers have taken to the great outdoors, though quite a few pubs have created sheltered outside areas specifically for them – and some are even heated.

Time zones

The UK is on **Greenwich Mean Time** (GMT), five hours ahead of US Eastern Standard Time, eight hours ahead of US Pacific Standard Time, ten hours behind Australian Eastern Standard Time and twelve hours behind New Zealand. There are, however, variations during the changeover periods involved in daylight saving. The UK operates **daylight saving**, moving its clocks forward one hour on the last Sunday in March and one hour back on the last

PUBLIC HOLIDAYS

New Year's Day January 1
Good Friday Variable March/April
Easter Monday Variable March/April
May Day Bank Holiday First Monday in May
Spring Bank Holiday Last Monday in May
Summer Bank Holiday Last Monday in August
Christmas Day December 25
Boxing Day December 26
(If Jan 1, Dec 25, or Dec 26 fall on a Sat or Sun, the next weekday becomes a public holiday).

Sunday in October. During this summer period, the UK is on **British Summer Time** (BST).

Tourist information

The body promoting inbound tourism to the UK is **VisitBritain** (Ⓦvisitbritain.com), with offices worldwide and a comprehensive website. Its partner agency VisitEngland operates under the branding "**Enjoy England**" (Ⓦenjoyengland.com) – another excellent source of general information. The work of these two agencies is supplemented by a network of regional tourist boards with **East of England** (Ⓦvisiteastofengland.com) covering – among several other counties – Norfolk and Suffolk. Their work is supplemented by two county organizations – **Choose Suffolk** (Ⓦchoosesuffolk .com) and **Visit Norfolk** (Ⓦvisitnorfolk.co.uk).

There are also tourist offices in all the larger towns – Ipswich, Norwich, Sudbury et al – and some villages and coastal resorts like Cromer and Aldeburgh. Staff here will often be able to book local accommodation and sell guidebooks, maps and hiking leaflets. Details of all these local tourist offices are in this guide. There is a scattering of specialist information centres too, like those advising on the Broads National Park and those attached to all the larger nature reserves.

Travellers with disabilities

Generally speaking, Norfolk and Suffolk have reasonably good facilities for **travellers with disabilities**. All new public buildings – including museums, galleries and cinemas – must provide wheelchair access, train stations and airports are fully accessible, and many buses have easy-access boarding ramps. In the towns, kerbs and signalled crossings have usually been dropped, but in the villages this remains something of a rarity – indeed in many places there's no pavement at all. More positively, the number of accessible hotels and restaurants is growing, and reserved parking bays are commonplace. One useful point of reference is **Tourism for All** (Ⓦwww.tourismforall.org.uk) with generic advice, listings and information.

Travelling with children

If you're **travelling with children**, facilities in Norfolk and Suffolk are up to par with the rest of the UK. Breastfeeding is allowed in all public places, including restaurants, cafés and public transport, and baby-changing rooms are available widely, including in malls and train stations. Under-5s aren't charged on public transport or at attractions and 5 – 16-year-olds usually get a fifty-percent discount. Children aren't allowed in certain licensed (that is, alcohol-serving) premises – though this doesn't apply to restaurants, and many pubs have family rooms or beer gardens where children are welcome. As for pastimes, children can spend hour after hour on the beach, building sandcastles, catching crabs and going for a paddle, but there is a scattering of specific attractions too – we've listed eight of the best (see box, below). For more general advice, check Ⓦtravellingwithchildren.co.uk and Ⓦbabygoes2 .com for tips and ideas.

EIGHT GREAT FAMILY ATTRACTIONS

Bewilderwood near Horning. See p.79
Brancaster Millennium Activity Centre Brancaster. See p.156
Dinosaur Adventure near Norwich. See p.59
Fritton Lake near Great Yarmouth. See p.109
Gressenhall Farm & Workhouse East Dereham. See p.197
Merrivale Model Village Great Yarmouth. See p.105
Under the Pier Show Southwold. See p.262
West Stow Country Park and Anglo-Saxon Village West Stow. See p.304

Norwich

PLANTATION GARDEN

1

Norwich

Partly because it's tucked away in a corner of England far away from the nearest motorway, Norwich is often misunderstood. Neither has the city done well in popular culture – mention the city to the average Briton and you're likely to hear about Delia Smith, the revered but distinctly staid television chef and writer; Bernard Matthews, the turkey king who famously described his birds in a full flourish of the Norfolk dialect as "bootiful"; and Alan Partridge, the laughably inept presenter of Radio Norwich, as played by the comedian Steve Coogan. By such stereotypes images are made, but in fact Norwich is a go-ahead place with a sound and diverse economy, a flourishing cultural life, a major university, a lively restaurant and bar scene, and, for a small city, a surprisingly varied range of independent shops.

As for sights and attractions, pride of place goes to the beautiful **cathedral** and the imposing **castle**, but the city's hallmark is its **medieval churches**, thirty or so squat flintstone structures with sturdy towers and sinuous stone tracery round the windows. Many are no longer in regular use and are now in the care of the Norwich Historic Churches Trust (ⓦ norwich-churches.org), whose excellent website describes each church in detail and gives opening times.

And finally, as the capital of Norfolk, Norwich lies at the hub of the region's **transport network**, serving as a useful base for visiting the Broads and as a springboard for the north Norfolk coast.

Brief history

Norwich boasts a long and distinguished **history**. It was one of the five largest cities in Norman England, serving a vast hinterland of **East Anglian** cloth producers, whose work was brought here by river and then exported to the Continent. The city's isolated position beyond the Fens meant that it enjoyed closer links with the Low Countries than with the rest of England – it was, after all, quicker to cross the North Sea than to go cross-country to London. The local textile industry, based on **worsted cloth** (named after the nearby village of Worstead), was further enhanced by an influx of Flemish and Huguenot weavers, who made up more than a third of the population in Tudor times. By 1700, Norwich was the second richest city in the country after London. With the onset of the Industrial Revolution, however, Norwich lost ground to the northern manufacturing towns – the city's famous mustard company, **Colman's**, remains one of its few industrial success stories – but there again this helped preserve much of the ancient street plan and many of the city's older buildings. Norwich's relative isolation has also meant that the **population** has never swelled to any great extent and today, with just 140,000 inhabitants, it remains an easy and enjoyable city to negotiate.

NORWICH CASTLE

Highlights

❶ Norwich Cathedral Without doubt the city's most magnificent building, a stirringly beautiful medieval structure of imposing grace and elegance. **See p.39**

❷ Plantation Garden This delightful garden, hidden away in a wooded dell, is a charming surprise. **See p.47**

❸ Norwich Castle Museum and Gallery The castle may be something of an architectural disappointment, but not the exquisite collection of Norwich School paintings, which are simply superb. **See p.48**

❹ The Sainsbury Centre for Visual Arts There's money in those supermarkets and the Sainsbury family have turned a portion of their profits into this well-endowed collection **See p.51**

❺ Gothic House Smashing B&B, arguably the city's best and certainly the most distinctive – all at a very reasonable price. **See p.52**

❻ Cinema City Excellent art-house cinema with an extraordinarily imaginative programme. **See p.56**

❼ Norwich Puppet Theatre Simply brilliant puppet theatre, whose performances cater for children and adults alike. **See p.56**

HIGHLIGHTS ARE MARKED ON THE MAP ON P.38

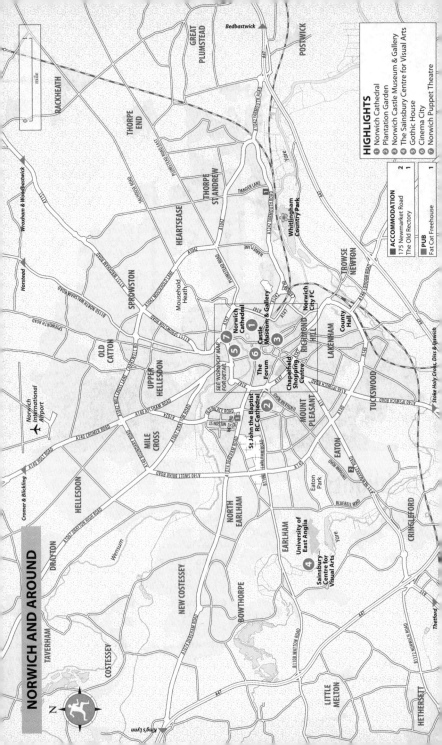

NORWICH AND AROUND

HIGHLIGHTS

1. Norwich Cathedral
2. Plantation Garden
3. Norwich Castle Museum & Gallery
4. The Sainsbury Centre for Visual Arts
5. Gothic House
6. Cinema City
7. Norwich Puppet Theatre

ACCOMMODATION
175 Newmarket Road — 2
The Old Rectory — 1

PUB
Fat Cat Freehouse — 1

N

Bedbastwick

GREAT PLUMSTEAD

POSTWICK

RACKHEATH

THORPE END

THORPE ST ANDREW

HEARTSEASE

Wroxham & Woodbastwick

Horsted

SPROWSTON

Whitlingham Country Park

TROWSE NEWTON

Mousehold Heath

Norwich International Airport

OLD CATTON

UPPER HELLESDON

Norwich Cathedral

Castle Museums & Gallery

Norwich City FC

County Hall

RICHMOND HILL

LAKENHAM

The Forum

Chapelfield Shopping Centre

Cromer & Blickling

MILE CROSS

TUCKSWOOD

Stoke Holy Cross, Diss & Ipswich

St John the Baptist RC Cathedral

MOUNT PLEASANT

HELLESDON

DRAYTON

EATON

Eaton Park

BLUEBELL ROAD

CRINGLEFORD

NORTH EARLHAM

EARLHAM

University of East Anglia

Sainsbury Centre for Visual Arts

Wensum

Yare

NEW COSTESSEY

BOWTHORPE

TAVERHAM

King's Lynn

COSTESSEY

LITTLE MELTON

HETHERSETT

Thetford

mile

1

FESTIVALS

For a smallish city, Norwich punches well above its weight when it comes to **festivals**. Calendar highlights include:

The Spring Literary Festival ⓦ uea.ac.uk. At the University of East Anglia, and attracting a heavy-duty bunch of writers and intellectuals, whose lectures and workshops spread over almost two months beginning in February.

Norfolk & Norwich Festival ⓦ nnfestival .org.uk. Held over two weeks in May, this is Norwich's premier arts festival, featuring an international cast of jazz, classical and world musicians plus lots, lots more.

The Shakespeare Festival ⓦ cathedral .org.uk. Five days of Shakespearean performances held in the cloisters of the cathedral during July.

The Autumn Literary Festival ⓦ uea .ac.uk. At the University of East Anglia. Similar to the Spring Festival but beginning in late September.

Norwich Beer Festival ⓦ norwichcamra .org.uk. Six days of hoppy satisfaction in St Andrew's Hall in October.

The city centre

Nestling within a sweeping bend of the River Wensum, Norwich's irregular street plan can make **orientation** difficult. There are, however, three obvious landmarks to help you find your way – the cathedral with its giant spire, the Norman castle on its commanding mound and the distinctive clock tower of City Hall. The **cathedral** and the **castle** are the city's premier attractions and the latter also holds one of the region's most satisfying collections of fine art.

The cathedral

The Close, NR1 4EH • Daily 7.30am–6.30pm • Free, but £5 donation requested • ☎ 01603 218300, ⓦ cathedral.org.uk

Of all the medieval buildings in Norwich, it's the **cathedral** that fires the imagination, a mighty, sand-coloured structure finessed by its prickly octagonal spire, which rises to a height of 315ft, second only to Salisbury Cathedral in Wiltshire. From the front, the cathedral looks no more than imposing, but from the south – from the Lower Close (see p.44) – the full intricacy of the design becomes apparent, the thick curves of the flying buttresses and the rounded sweep of the ambulatory chapels – unusual in an English cathedral – set against the straight symmetries of the main trunk. The cathedral is entered via the **Hostry**, a glassy, well-proportioned visitor centre located just to the right of the main doors. There are often modest displays of local art here, both secular and religious, plus a café whose attractive modern architecture is rather better than the food.

The nave

The interior of the cathedral is pleasantly light thanks to a creamy tint in the stone and the clear-glass windows of much of the **nave**, where the thick pillars are a powerful legacy of the Norman builders who began the cathedral in 1096. The nave's architectural highlight is the **ceiling**, a finely crafted affair whose delicate and geometrically precise fan vaulting is adorned by several dozen roof bosses recounting

GUIDED WALKING TOURS

Bookable at the tourist office (see p.52), the city's Blue Badge Guides run a programme of **guided walking tours** that take in all the leading sights, seasoned with anecdotes (April–Oct between 3 weekly and once daily; 90min; £4). The programme also includes themed walks – "In the footsteps of Nelson" and so forth – but these cost a pound or two more and last a little longer (May–Sept 5–6 weekly). For more ideas on Norwich walks, go to ⓦ www.visitnorwich.co.uk

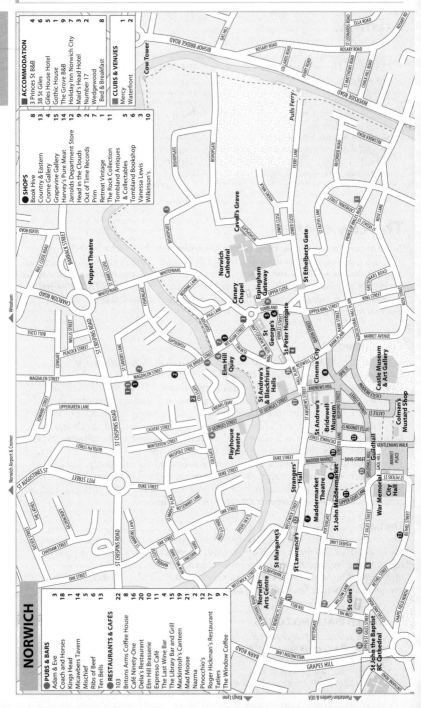

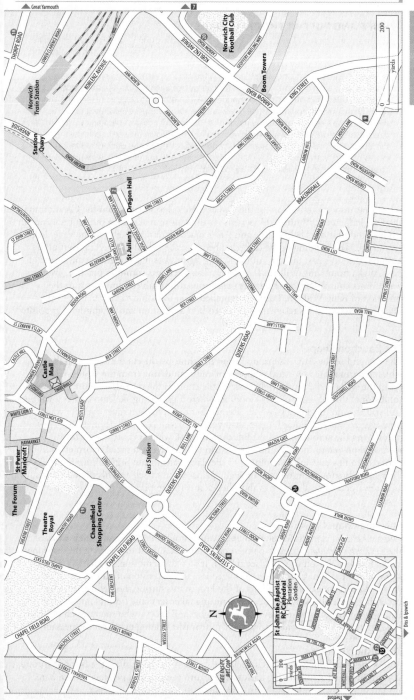

1

– from east to west – the story of the Old and New Testaments from the Creation to the Last Judgement. Without binoculars it's difficult to make these out, but a mirror in front of the altar does help a little and a touch-screen terminal, also in the nave, helps even more. The building of the cathedral began at the behest of a certain **Herbert de Losinga**, the city's first bishop. An interesting figure, Losinga bought the bishopric of East Anglia from King William II in 1091. This itself was common practice, even if it was against church law, but Losinga's conscience still troubled him. Much to the irritation of King William, Losinga hightailed it off to Rome to do penance to the Pope, who accepted his resignation, granted him absolution and promptly re-appointed him as bishop – what an obliging pontiff.

The Bauchon Chapel

The east end of the nave is separated from the choir by the choir screen, or pulpitum, which is surmounted by a real whopper of an organ dating from the 1940s. Close by, set in the wall on the south (right) side of the choir, is the cathedral's most interesting **tombstone**, that of one Thomas Gooding, where a grimacing skeleton carries a warning "All you that do this place pass bye. Remember death for you must dye. As you are now even so was I. And as I am so shall you be". From poor old Thomas, it's a few paces along the ambulatory to the **Bauchon Chapel**, which is noteworthy for its memorial plaque to the MP Thomas Buxton (1786–1845), a social reformer who played a leading role in the abolition of the slave trade in the British Empire in 1807. Thereafter, Buxton went on to campaign against slavery itself and his tireless efforts were rewarded when slavery was abolished across the empire just over twenty years later.

St Luke's Chapel

The next chapel along is **St Luke's Chapel**, which holds the cathedral's finest work of art, the *Despenser Reredos*, a superb painted panel commissioned to celebrate the crushing of the Peasants' Revolt of 1381 (see p.316). It's a naive, emotionally charged painting showing the Passion, Crucifixion, Resurrection and Ascension of Christ, but it only survived the iconoclastic attentions of the Protestants during the Reformation by becoming a plumber's worktable. The painting takes its name from Henry le Despenser (c.1341–1406), otherwise known as the "Fighting Bishop", who spent much of his time warring in France and England when he wasn't beating down on the peasantry.

The bishop's throne

Across the aisle from St Luke's Chapel, and encased by the choir, is the **bishop's throne**, a sturdy stone structure dating back to the eighth century and possibly moved here

1

from the long-gone cathedral at Dunwich in Suffolk (see p.258). Norman bishops were barons as much as religious leaders, and to emphasize their direct relationship with the Almighty they usually put their thrones behind the high altar. Most were relocated during the Reformation, but this one occupies its original position. The bishop of Norwich also had a spiritual prop: a flue runs down from the back of the throne to a reliquary recess in the ambulatory, the idea being that divine essences would be transported up to him to help him do his job.

The cloisters

Accessible from the south aisle of the nave are the cathedral's beautifully preserved **cloisters**. Built between 1297 and 1450, and the only two-storey cloisters left standing in England, they contain a remarkable set of sculpted bosses, similar to the ones in the main nave, but here they are close enough to be scrutinized without binoculars. The carving is fabulously intricate and the dominant theme is the Apocalypse, but look out also for the bosses depicting Green Men, originally pagan fertility symbols.

Norwich School and the Upper Close

In front of the cathedral's main doors stands the medieval **Canary Chapel** (no public access). This is the original building of **Norwich School**, whose blue-blazered pupils are often visible during term-time – the rambling school buildings are adjacent. A statue of the school's most famous boy, **Horatio Nelson** (see p.154), faces the chapel, standing beside a cannon, telescope in hand, in a suitably maritime pose that does not quite stand up to close examination: poor old Nelson would appear to have lost his original nose and the new snout is too big by far. The statue is on the green of the cathedral's **Upper Close**, which is itself guarded by two ornate and imposing medieval gates, Erpingham and, a hundred yards or so to the south, **Ethelbert**. The **Erpingham gate** is perhaps the more interesting, dating from the 1420s and named after Thomas Erpingham, who had it built to celebrate his safe return from the Battle of Agincourt, where he commanded the archers – his kneeling figure with sword at his side is on the gable.

The Edith Cavell memorial

Beside the Erpingham gate is a memorial to **Edith Cavell**, a local woman whose heroic exploits were once famous across the British Empire. A nurse in occupied Brussels during World War I, Cavell was shot by the Germans in 1915 for helping allied prisoners to escape, a propaganda disaster for the Kaiser exacerbated by Cavell's stoic bravery: the night before her execution, she famously declared "Standing as I do, in view of God and eternity, I realize that patriotism is not enough, I must have no hatred or bitterness towards anyone". Cavell was initially buried in Brussels, but after the war she was re-interred in Norwich – her grave is outside the cathedral ambulatory.

The Lower Close and a river walk

Just beyond the Upper Close, extending east towards the river, is the pedestrianized **Lower Close**, where attractive Georgian and Victorian houses flank a scattering of wispy silver birches. Straight on from the Close, the main footpath continues east to the city's medieval watergate and the adjacent **Pull's Ferry**, a good-looking, seventeenth-century flint structure named after the last ferryman to work this stretch of the river. It's a picturesque spot and from here (during daylight hours) you can wander along the riverbank path either south to the train station or north to Bishopgate, then back to Tombland (see opposite). Beyond Bishopgate, the path continues north and then west along the river to Elm Hill (see opposite) and St George's Street. On the way you pass **Cow Tower**, a 50ft-high, brick watchtower with arrow slits and gun ports where the bishop's retainers collected river tolls. This is one of the few surviving pieces of

Norwich's fortified walls, which once stretched for over two miles, surrounding the city and incorporating thirty such circular towers and ten defensive gates. Up until the 1790s, the gates were closed at dusk and all day on Sundays.

Tombland

The Erpingham and Ethelbert gates face out onto **Tombland**, a wide and busy thoroughfare whose name derives from the Saxon word for an open space. On the west side stands **St George's** (Tues–Thurs 9am–noon; free), an attractive, mostly fifteenth-century flint church with an impressive clock tower. Entry is via the south porch, whose carved bosses include one showing St George standing on a dragon, and although the interior is largely Victorian, the church holds a splendid Jacobean pulpit. Behind the organ there's also the **tomb** of a long-forgotten city father, the splendidly named Alderman Anguish, who kneels with his wife flanked by their offspring, five of whom carry skulls representing those children who predeceased him.

Elm Hill and St Peter Hungate

At the north end of Tombland, fork left into Wensum Street and cobbled **Elm Hill**, more a gentle slope than a hill, soon appears on the left. Priestley, in his *English Journey* of 1933, thought this part of Norwich to be overbearingly Dickensian, proclaiming "it difficult to believe that behind those bowed and twisted fronts there did not live an assortment of misers, mad spinsters, saintly clergymen, eccentric comic clerks, and lunatic sextons." In summer you can hardly move for tourists, but the quirky half-timbered houses still appeal and while you're here take a look at **Wright's Court**, down a passageway at no. 43, one of the few remaining enclosed courtyards which were once a feature of the city. Elm Hill quickly opens out into a triangular square centred on a plane tree, planted on the spot where the eponymous elm tree once stood. It then veers left up to **St Peter Hungate** (Thurs–Sat 10am–4pm; £3; Ⓦnorfolkchurches.co.uk), a standard-issue, fifteenth-century flint church whose bare and bleak interior now holds a (very) modest display of stained glass retrieved from several local churches.

The Halls: St Andrew's and Blackfriars

St Andrews Hall Plain, NR3 1AU • Mon–Sat 9am–5pm • Free • ☎ 01603 628477, Ⓦ standrewshall.co.uk

Just west of Tombland, **Blackfriars Hall** and, on the left, **St Andrew's Hall**, are two adjoining buildings which share the same entrance and were originally the chancel and nave, respectively, of a Dominican monastery church: typical of a medieval friary church, the nave was used for the lay congregation, the smaller chancel by the friars alone. Imaginatively recycled, **The Halls** are now used for a variety of public events, including concerts, but the whole complex is looking a little frayed at the edges and a much needed revamp is promised. The Halls display a large collection of civic paintings, mostly indeterminate bishops and aldermen, but in Blackfriars is a splendid **portrait of Nelson**, shown in all his maritime pomp and completed three years before his death by one of his friends, **William Beechey** (1753–1839), a talented artist who made a name for himself painting the most powerful men and women of the age.

St Andrew's church and the Bridewell

St Andrews St, NR3 1AU • Late March to late Oct Thurs 2.30–4.30pm, also Sun 11.30am–12.30pm • Free • ☎ 01603 498821, Ⓦ standrewsnorwich.org

Opposite The Halls, up the slope and across the street, stands **St Andrew's church**, a large and impressive structure equipped with a handsome square tower and massive

1

windows, which render the nave light and airy. The highlight of the interior are the two alabaster tombs of the **Suckling Chapel**, one of Robert Suckling (d.1589), the other of John Suckling (d.1613), another member of the clan, who is depicted in his favourite suit of armour with his wife lying beside him kitted out in her fanciest Elizabethan dress. From the church, it's a few yards up Bridewell Alley to **The Bridewell**, a city museum that is closed for a major refurbishment. It's devoted to the history of the city and its inhabitants, but given the current level of government spending cuts, it's questionable as to whether the museum will actually reopen at all.

Strangers' Hall

Charing Cross, NR2 4AL • Wed–Sat 10.30am–4pm • £3.50 • ☎ 01603 667 229, ⊛ museums.norfolk.gov.uk

Strangers' Hall is the city's most unusual attraction. Dating back to the fourteenth century, it's a veritable rabbit warren of a place stuffed with all manner of bygones including ancient fireplaces, oodles of wood panelling, a Regency music room and a Georgian dining room. Allow an hour or so to explore its nooks and crannies, though the most impressive room, the **Great Hall**, with its church-like Gothic windows, old portrait paintings and rickety staircase, comes right at the beginning. The hall is named after the Protestant refugees who fled here from the Spanish Netherlands to avoid the tender mercies of the Inquisition in the 1560s; at the peak of the migration, these "Strangers" accounted for around a third of the local population.

St Benedict's and Upper St Giles streets

One of Norwich's most pleasing thoroughfares is **St Benedict's Street**, lined with restaurants and shops and flanked by no less than three medieval **churches**, all of which have been decommissioned. From east to west, these are **St Lawrence's**, where there are textile stalls exhibiting local work; **St Margaret's**, now with very mediocre art displays; and **St Swithin's**, which has been turned into the Norwich Arts Centre (see p.56).

From here, a sequence of narrow lanes lead up from St Benedict's Street to **Pottergate**, which looks like it hasn't changed much for years, its trail of old houses meandering prettily out towards Cow Hill, another old and attractive street that scuttles up to the dinky little shops and stores clustering **Upper St Giles Street** with the massive bulk of the Catholic cathedral looming across the ring road. Much more appealing is the **church of St Giles** (no fixed opening times), an especially handsome structure mostly dating from the fifteenth century. Built of flint, but with a fancy stone porch, the church has a wide and high nave topped off by a splendid hammer-beam roof, but the furnishings and fittings are largely Victorian.

The Catholic Cathedral of St John the Baptist

Unthank Rd, NR2 2PA• Daily 7.30am–7.30pm • Free • ☎ 01603 624615, ⊛ sjbcathedral.org.uk

Towering over the ring road opposite Upper St Giles Street is the **Catholic Cathedral of St John the Baptist**, a huge clunker of a building constructed at the end of the nineteenth century in an exuberant flourish of the neo-Gothic style. The fifteenth Duke of Norfolk footed the bill, appropriately as the Norfolks have long been one of England's leading Catholic families, and the cathedral was built on the site of what had been the old city prison. Aesthetically, it's a very cold building whose most appealing feature, apart perhaps from its sheer bulk, is its stained-glass windows. The architect, George Gilbert Scott (1811–1878) was famous for his Gothic Revival churches, but he died while work was in progress here in Norwich and the cathedral was completed by his brother, John Oldrid Scott.

The Plantation Garden

4 Earlham Rd, NR2 3DB • Daily 9am–6pm, or dusk if earlier • £2 • ☎ 01603 621 868, ⓦ plantationgarden.co.uk

Below the Catholic cathedral, the **Plantation Garden** is a simply delightful spot, where mature trees overhang a sweet little dell, complete with a fancy stone stairway that leads up to the cutest of thatched cabins (a glorified garden shed) with a pagoda-style water fountain as an added decorative bonus. The gardens date from the late nineteenth century when a local businessman, one Henry Trevor, turned the medieval chalk quarry immediately behind and below the Cathedral of St John the Baptist into an ornate garden. Sadly, within the space of a few years it had been forgotten and was overgrown. In the 1980s, however, the garden was re-discovered, cleared and turned into the version you see today.

St John Maddermarket

Pottergate, NR2 1DR • April–Oct Tues–Fri 11am–3pm; Nov–March Wed & Fri 11am–2pm • Free • ⓦ visitchurches.org.uk

St John Maddermarket, on Pottergate, is one of thirty medieval churches standing within the boundaries of the old city walls. Most are redundant and are rarely open to the public, but this is one of the more accessible, courtesy of dedicated volunteers from the Churches Conservation Trust. Apart from the stone trimmings, the church – which is named after **madder**, the yellow flower the weavers used to make red vegetable dye – is almost entirely composed of flint rubble, the traditional building material of east Norfolk, an area chronically short of decent stone. The exterior is a good example of the Perpendicular style, a subdivision of English Gothic which flourished from the middle of the fourteenth to the early sixteenth century and is characterized by straight vertical lines – as you might expect from the name – and large windows framed by flowing, but plain, tracery. By comparison, the interior is something of a disappointment, its furnishings and fittings thoroughly remodelled at the start of the twentieth century, though there's compensation in a trio of finely carved Jacobean tombstones.

Outside, the arch under the church tower leads through to the Maddermarket Theatre, built in 1921 in the style of an Elizabethan playhouse (see p.56).

The Market Place

Norwich Market, Market Place, NR2 1NH • Mon–Sat 8am–5.30pm • ☎ 01603 213537, ⓦ norwich-market.co.uk

Norwich **Market Place** has long been the site of one of the country's largest open-air markets, with over 190 stalls selling everything from bargain-basement clothes to local mussels and whelks. Three very different but equally distinctive buildings oversee the market's stripy awnings, the oldest of them being the fifteenth-century **Guildhall**, a capacious flint and stone structure begun in 1407. Opposite, commanding the heights of the Market Place, is **City Hall**, an austere brick pile with a landmark clock tower built in the 1930s in a Scandinavian style – it bears a striking resemblance to Oslo's city hall. Three large bronze doors provide some decorative intricacy here as each is carved with six small reliefs depicting historical scenes and local industry, from the ravages brought on the city by the Black Death and the coming of the Danes to a girl at a silk loom and a man at a machine filling tins with mustard. In front of City Hall is a **war memorial**, designed by Edwin Lutyens in the 1930s, and beside it is **The Forum**, a large, flashy, glassy structure completed in 2001 and now home to the city's main library, **Fusion**, an enormous digital screen gallery, and the tourist office (see p.52).

St Peter Mancroft

Market Place, NR2 1NH • Mon–Sat 10am–3pm • Free • ⓦ norwich-churches.org

On the south side of the Market Place is Norwich's finest church, **St Peter Mancroft**, whose long and graceful nave leads to a mighty stone tower, an intricately carved affair

1

NORWICH'S RENAISSANCE MAN: THOMAS BROWNE

St Peter Mancroft is the final resting place of **Thomas Browne** (1605–1682), a doctor, philosopher and naturalist who is little known today but was once a major figure, renowned for his *Religio Medici* ("The Religion of a Doctor"), a combined religious testament and intellectual dalliance with digressions into everything from alchemy to astrology. Predictably, the Catholics didn't like Browne's freewheeling ways and the Pope put the book on his *Index Librorum Prohibitorum* ("List of Prohibited Books"). Browne's tomb is just in front of the church's high altar and is marked by a **memorial plaque** commissioned by his wife, who lies buried close by. This isn't without its ironies: Browne wanted to be cremated, railing against the potential indignities of burial – "to be knaved out of our graves, to have our skulls made drinking bowls and our bones turned into pipes, are tragicall abominations excaped by burning burials". And so it proved: Browne's skull was extracted from his grave to be kept on display in a doctor's surgery for almost a century; it was only put back in 1922.

---

surmounted by a spiky little spire. The church once delighted John Wesley, who declared "I scarcely ever remember to have seen a more beautiful parish church", a fair description of what remains an exquisite example of the Perpendicular with the slender columns of the nave reaching up towards the delicate groining of the roof. Completed in 1455, the open design of the nave was meant to express the mystery of the Christian faith with light filtering in through the stained-glass windows in a kaleidoscope of colours. Some of the original glass has survived, most notably in the east window, which boasts a cartoon strip of biblical scenes from the Virgin nursing the baby Jesus, through to the Crucifixion and Resurrection.

Gentlemen's Walk and the Royal Arcade

Just below St Peter Mancroft stands the *Sir Garnet Wolseley* pub, sole survivor of the 44 alehouses that once crowded the Market Place – and stirred the local bourgeoisie into endless discussions about the drunken fecklessness of the working class. Just below the pub is **Gentlemen's Walk**, the city's main promenade, which runs along the bottom of the Market Place, and this in turn leads to the **Royal Arcade**, an Art Nouveau extravagance from 1899. The arcade has been beautifully restored to reveal the swirl of the tiling, ironwork and stained glass, though it's actually the eastern entrance, further from Gentlemen's Walk, which is the fanciest section. Inside the arcade, at no. 15, is **Colman's Mustard Shop**, which is often referred to as a museum – it isn't, unless, that is, you count a few display boards explaining the history of mustard in general and the Colman's company in particular.

The Castle Museum and Art Gallery

Castle Meadow, NR1 3JU • Mon–Sat 10am–4.30pm, Sun 1–4.30pm; July–Sept till 5pm • £6.20 • ☎ 01603 493625, ⓦ museums.norfolk .gov.uk

Glued to the top of a grassy mound right in the centre of town – with a modern shopping mall drilled into its side – the stern walls of **Norwich Castle**, replete with their conspicuous blind arcading, date from the twelfth century. To begin with they were a reminder of Norman power and then, when the castle was turned into a prison, they served as a grim warning to potential law-breakers. Now thoroughly refurbished, the castle holds the **Castle Museum and Art Gallery**, which is divided into three zones. The **Art and Exhibitions zone** is the pick, scoring well with its temporary displays and boasting an outstanding selection of work by the **Norwich School**, whose leading figures were John Crome – aka "Old Crome" – and John Sell Cotman (see box, opposite). Both have a gallery to themselves – though their paintings are dotted across the whole of the zone – and, helpfully, there's also a gallery given over to those Dutch painters

THE CITY CENTRE **NORWICH** 49

1

THE NORWICH SCHOOL

Often neglected, frequently ignored, the **Norwich Society of Artists** – now usually referred to as the **Norwich School** – was founded in 1803 by two local, self-taught painters, **John Crome** (1768–1821) and **Robert Ladbrooke** (1770–1842). Both men were working class – Crome was the son of a weaver – which partly accounts for their ambitious, even earnest, statement of purpose "[the Society was to enquire] into the rise, progress and present state of painting, architecture and sculpture, with a view to point out the best methods…[of attaining]…greater perfection". A popular man, Crome soon attracted other like-minded artists to the Society, which organized its first exhibition in 1805 to great acclaim. Crome was the most talented member of the Society by a long chalk, his vigorous, vital paintings of the Norfolk countryside greatly influenced by both the realism of Dutch seventeenth-century painters and that of his contemporary, Suffolk's John Constable: like Constable, for example, Crome painted identifiable species of trees rather than the generalized versions of his artistic predecessors.

After Crome's death, the prolific **John Sell Cotman** (1782–1842) became the Society's leading light, holding the group together until it fell apart after he left Norwich for London in the early 1830s. Cotman churned out etchings, engravings and oil paintings by the rack load, but it is for his **watercolours** that he is best remembered, each displaying a precise tone and line, the hallmarks of his technique. Cotman's early watercolours are restrained, sometimes austere, but later he began to mix rice-paste into his palette, which allowed him to work in a heavier, more flamboyant style.

At the time, the Norwich Society was hard-pressed to find a patron – and all of the members struggled with money – but, curiously enough, it was the purchasing power of a later tycoon and art collector, the mustard baron **Jeremiah James Colman** (1830–98), that kept the Norwich School out of the artistic limelight: he snaffled up all their best work for his private collection, though in fairness he did bequeath many of his paintings to the city of Norwich in the 1880s.

who influenced them. Fine examples of the work of Crome include his elegiac *Norwich River: Afternoon* and the lonely-looking *A Road with Pollards*.

Mixed up with the paintings of the Norwich School is the work of a string of leading English painters, including **Thomas Gainsborough**'s (see p.282) glossy portrait of a local MP, *Sir Harbord Harbord*; **William Hogarth**'s (1697–1764) *Francis Matthews Schutz in his Bed* with poor old Francis suffering from the most terrible of hangovers; and several paintings by **Alfred Munnings** (see p.280), one of England's most traditional painters whose speciality was horses – or rather sentimental visions of them as in *The Horse Fair* and *Sunny June*.

Natural History and Castle and History zones

The castle's **Natural History zone** has a small army of stuffed animals, mostly from Norfolk, and the catch-all **Castle and History zone** has child-friendly displays on the Vikings, Anglo-Saxon life and customs, the early British warrior queen Boudicca, and the Egyptians, with half a dozen "mummies" thrown in for good measure. The Castle and History zone also includes the **castle keep**, though this is no more than a shell, its gloomy walls rising high above a scattering of local archeological finds. More unusual is a bloated model dragon, known as Snap, which was paraded round town on the annual guilds' day procession – a folkloric hand-me-down from the dragon St George had so much trouble finishing off. To see more of the castle, join one of the regular guided tours (£2.20 extra) that explore the battlements and the dungeons.

Royal Norfolk Regimental Museum

Market Ave, NR1 3JQ – or access via the Castle Museum • Tues–Sat 10am–4.30pm • £3.50 • ☎ 01603 493650, ⓦ museums.norfolk.gov.uk

A long, dark (and one-way) stairway leads down from the Castle Museum to the **Royal Norfolk Regimental Museum**, which tracks through the history of the regiment

1

with the aid of some excellent old photos, though at time of writing the future of this museum is under review and there's a strong chance the collection may be moved into the Castle Museum.

The Dragon Hall

115–123 King St, NR1 1QE • Mon–Fri 10am–4pm & Sun noon–4pm • £5 • ☎ 01603 663922, ⓦ dragonhall.org

East of the castle, King Street possesses one or two surprises, beginning with **Dragon Hall**, an extraordinarily long, half-timbered showroom built for the cloth merchant Robert Toppes in the fifteenth century, which has been bowed and bent by age. You get a good impression of the building from the outside, but enthusiasts can pop in to have a closer look at the roof – there's nothing much else to see.

St Julian's

St Julian's Alley, NR1 3QD • Daily 7.30am–6pm • Free • ☎ 01603 622509, ⓦ julianofnorwich.org

A right turn opposite the Dragon Hall up St Julian's Alley leads off King Street to **St Julian's Church**, whose round stone tower witnesses its Saxon origins. The interior is a modest affair, but the adjoining chapel was formerly a monastic cell, which served as the retreat of St Julian, a Norwich woman who took to living here after experiencing visions of Christ in 1373. Her mystical *Revelations of Divine Love* – written after twenty years' meditation on her visitations – was the first widely distributed book written by a woman in the English language, and has been in print ever since.

Carrow Bridge and around

King Street runs down to **Carrow Bridge**, where you'll spy the ruins of two medieval boom towers, which once formed part of the city's defences – with the concrete terraces of **Norwich City football ground** looming just behind (see p.58); the famed cookery writer Delia Smith, is the majority shareholder of the club (see box, below) and it's here she has a restaurant (see p.54).

DELIA SMITH

Without doubt, the gastronomic guru **Delia Smith** (born 1941) has done more to change the face of British cooking than anyone else. Raised in Surrey, Smith left school at 16 without a single O-Level to her name, trying her hand at hairdressing and working in a travel agency before getting a job as a washer-upper at *The Singing Chef*, a tiny restaurant in Paddington, London. It was here that she began to help with the cooking beginning a meteoric rise that saw her appointed as the cookery writer for the *Daily Mirror*'s magazine in 1969 – in the same year as one of her cakes appeared on the cover of the Rolling Stones' album, *Let It Bleed*. In 1972, she became the cookery columnist for the *Evening Standard*, but it was her **TV appearances** that really made her name, beginning in the mid-1970s with *Family Fare* and as the resident cook on BBC East's regional programme *Look East*. Smith's easy, modest style and relaxed presentation made her trusted and liked by millions of Brits – so much so that by the 1990s, the mention of a particular ingredient in one of her recipes, either on TV or in one of her cookery books, could jump-start sales to an extraordinary extent– the so-called "**Delia-effect**". In 2003, Smith announced her retirement from television, though she did do further stints in 2008 and 2010, by which time she had sold around 21 million of her cookbooks.

Smith and her husband, Michael Wynn-Jones, live near Stowmarket in Suffolk (see p.294). They were already season ticket holders at **Norwich City FC** when they were invited to invest in the club, which had fallen on hard times. They became majority shareholders in the football club in 1996, a position they retain, though they appear to be keen to sell up should the right offer be made.

From the boom towers, a **riverside walk** follows the Wensum round to the **train station**, a large and handsome structure of red brick and stucco that looks a little like a French château. Completed in 1886, it had a moment of cinematic fame when it featured in Joseph Losey's 1971 film *The Go-Between*.

The University of East Anglia (UEA)

Earlham Rd beside the B1108 • Open access • ☎ 01603 456161, ⓦ uea.ac.uk • Bus #25 or #35 (from Castle Meadow) or #25 from the train station

The **University of East Anglia (UEA)** occupies a sprawling, semi-rural campus on the western outskirts of the city beside the B1108. The university enrolled its first students in 1963, but from small and surprisingly humble beginnings, it soon administered a major cultural shock to what was then a sleepy Norwich. In the early 1970s, UEA students were conspicuous for their radicalism, uniting together in their flares, Afghan coats, bangles, beads and beards to occupy the university buildings in a series of **mass sit-ins**. The reasons were complex, but although there was certainly a political edge (the Miners' Strike, Vietnam), it was just as much to do with personal freedoms: in 1969, for example, University cleaners still had to report students who had overnight "guests". Those radical days are long gone, but you can still get a sense of how adventurous a place it was once if you wander the elevated walkways to UEA's most distinctive buildings, **Norfolk Terrace and Suffolk Terrace**, halls of residence built in the shape of **ziggurats** to an inspired design by Denys Lasdun (1914–2001).

The Sainsbury Centre for Visual Arts

UEA, NR4 7TJ • Tues–Sun 10am–5pm • Free except for temporary exhibitions • ☎ 01603 593199, ⓦ scva.ac.uk

For the casual visitor today, UEA's key attraction is the **Sainsbury Centre for Visual Arts**, which occupies a large, shed-like building designed by Norman Foster at the western end of the campus. The centre is named after its original benefactor, the supermarket king Robert Sainsbury (1906–2000), who began collecting fine and applied art in the 1930s. He gifted 300 pieces to the Centre in 1973, since when the collection has quadrupled in size. Well lit and beautifully presented, key pieces include a *Mother & Child* by **Henry Moore**, a bronze cast of **Edgar Degas**'s famous *Little Dancer*, a *Torso in Metal* by Jacob Epstein, and several sketches by **Picasso**. There is also a platoon of paintings by **Francis Bacon** (1909–92), most memorably an *Imaginary Portrait of Pope Pius XII* and *Study of a Nude*. In 1955, Bacon also painted the portrait of his friend/ sponsor Robert Sainsbury, though it's hard not to think he approached this commission with his tongue firmly in his cheek – it looks as if someone has just poked Sainsbury in the eye. From the ground floor, the permanent collection continues on two mezzanine levels, where there are several **Henry Moore** sketches and a cabinet of tiny Roman figurines, but pride of place here goes to a strangely unsettling *Bucket Man* sculpture by John Davies (b.1946). Other parts of the centre are devoted to an ambitious programme of temporary exhibitions and a reserve, holding paintings and sculptures that can be viewed, but are not on display as such.

ARRIVAL AND DEPARTURE · NORWICH

By plane Norwich airport (ⓦ norwichairport.co.uk) is located about four miles northwest of the city centre along the A140. There are regular buses (journey time 20min) to the city centre from the airport's Park and Ride; a taxi fare is only about £6.

By train Norwich train station is on the east bank of the River Wensum, 10min walk from the centre along Prince of

Wales Rd. For journey planning, by bus or train, consult ⓦ www.travelineeastanglia.org.uk.

Destinations Bury St Edmunds (hourly; 1hr, change at Stowmarket); Cambridge (hourly; 1hr 20min); Cromer (hourly; 45min); Ely (2 hourly; 1hr); Great Yarmouth (hourly; 35min); Ipswich (every 30min; 40min); King's Lynn (hourly; 1hr 30min, change at Ely); London, Liverpool St (every

30min; 1hr 50min); London Stansted airport (hourly; 1hr 40min, change at Ely); Sheringham (hourly; 1hr); Stowmarket (hourly; 30min); Thetford (2 hourly; 30min).

By bus Long-distance buses mostly terminate at the Surrey Street Station, from where it's about 10min walk north to the city centre, though some services also stop in the centre on Castle Meadow.

Destinations Blakeney (hourly; 2hr); Cromer (2–3 hourly; 1hr 10min); Great Yarmouth (2 hourly; 45min); Holt (hourly; 1hr 20min); King's Lynn (2 hourly; 1hr 50min); London Victoria (2hr; 4hr 30min); Sheringham (hourly; 1hr

30min); Swaffham (2 hourly; 1hr 15min); Wisbech (2hourly; 2hr 20min).

By car From whichever way you approach Norwich, you'll eventually hit the inner ring road, which gives ready access to every part of the city centre, though the traffic can get badly snarled up. There are a dozen or so car parks with one of the largest and most convenient being next to the Castle at the Castle Mall shopping centre. The myriad lanes and alleys of central Norwich – never mind the one-way system and the pedestrianized zones – make driving complicated so once you've arrived it's best to explore on foot.

GETTING AROUND AND INFORMATION

Almost all of the key attractions are within easy walking distance of each other and where they aren't – as in the case of the University – it's easy enough to hop on a bus.

By bus The largest local bus company, serving the city and much of Norfolk, is First (☎0845 6020121, ⓦfirstgroup .com). There are bus stops all over the city centre, but the greatest concentration is on Castle Meadow.

By boat From April until late September, City Boats (☎01603 701701, ⓦcityboats.co.uk) operates cruises through Norwich along the River Wensum, starting at Station Quay near the train station and proceeding to Elm

Hill Quay near the cathedral (1 daily, but weekends only in June; 20min; £5, £8 return). The same company also offers longer cruises out from Norwich and into the Norfolk Broads.

Tourist office In the glassy Forum building overlooking the Market Place (April–Oct Mon–Sat 9.30am–6pm, Sun 10.30am–4.30pm; Nov–March Mon–Sat 9.30am–5.30pm; ☎01603 213999, ⓦvisitnorwich.co.uk).

ACCOMMODATION

Norwich has enough **accommodation** to suit every budget, but the city's most distinctive offering is its **B&Bs**, two of which are perfectly delightful. Apart from convenience, there's no compelling reason to stay in the city centre, but, if you do choose to stay there, aim for the two most appealing areas – near the cathedral or north of the River Wensum in the vicinity of Colegate.

B&BS

3 Princes St B&B 3 Princes St, NR3 1AZ ☎01603 662693, ⓦ3princes-norwich.co.uk. Great location, up a narrow lane yards from the cathedral, this B&B looks pretty dour from the outside – it occupies a plain red-brick Georgian terraced house that was once a rectory – but the four, en-suite rooms inside are attractively furnished in pastel shades, and three of them have views over Blackfriars Hall (see p.45). **£85**

38 St Giles 38 St Giles St, NR2 1LL ☎01603 662944, ⓦ38stgiles.co.uk. Billing itself as a cross between a B&B and a hotel, this deluxe establishment has five en-suite rooms of varying size and description, but they all have silk curtains, top-whack bedding and Bang & Olufsen TVs. Breakfasts feature home-made bread, freshly baked croissants, fresh fruit and cereals – with the option of a full English instead. It's in a handy location too, a few yards from the Market Place, on the first floor above other premises. **£140**

★ **Gothic House** King's Head Yard, Magdalen St, NR3 1JE ☎01603 631879, ⓦgothic-house-norwich.com. This particularly charming B&B occupies a slender, three-storey Georgian house down a little courtyard off Magdalen St. The interior has been meticulously renovated in a period

style with plates, prints, curios and paintings liberally distributed throughout. The two, salon-style bedrooms are reached via the most charming of spiral staircases. and although not en suite, this really is no inconvenience. Highly recommended – and the host is a gold mine of information too. Single **£65**, doubles **£95**

★ **The Grove B&B** 59 Bracondale, NR1 2AT ☎01603 622053, ⓦthegrovenorwich.co.uk. In a large Victorian villa, this outstanding – and outstandingly friendly – B&B has three rooms, each of which is decorated in an extremely attractive version of period style, complete with comfy brass beds and a scattering of antiques and bygones. All the rooms are en suite but the toilet is in an adjoining room. The breakfasts are cooked to order, and very tasty they are as well. *The Grove* has a very quiet setting on a ridge above the football ground and is reached down a long wooded drive. (If using Sat Nav, the postcode will usually deliver you to Ice House Lane just north of the private drive leading to the B&B.) **£85**

Number 17 Colegate, NR3 1BN ☎01603 764486, ⓦnumber17norwich.co.uk. Family-run guesthouse with eight, en-suite rooms decorated in a brisk, modern style with solid oak flooring; there are two larger family rooms as

1

well. Wi-fi throughout and home-cooked breakfasts, which – if the sun is out – can be taken in the courtyard. Good location too, in one of the nicest parts of the centre. **£78**

Wedgewood Bed & Breakfast 42 St Stephens Rd, NR1 3RE ☎01603 625 730, ⓦwedgewoodhouse.co.uk. In a large Victorian house just off the inner ring road to the southwest of the city centre, this comfortable B&B has half a dozen well-maintained en-suite rooms. Wi-fi, parking and home-cooked breakfasts, plus a warm welcome. **£60**

HOTELS

Giles House Hotel 41 St Giles St, NR2 1JR ☎01603 275180, ⓦstgileshousehotel.com. This deluxe hotel, Norwich's fanciest, occupies a handsome Edwardian building designed in a sort of grand French imperial style by George Skipper, for many years the city's leading architect and the man responsible for the Royal Arcade (see p.48). The exterior, with its columns and balustrade, is impressive – perhaps overly so – and each of the 24 rooms beyond is different, though most combine new, sometimes adventurous pastel shades with retro flourishes. **£130**

Holiday Inn Norwich City Carrow Rd, NR1 1HU ☎0870 8901000, ⓦholidayinn.com. Holiday Inns are, of course, fairly commonplace, but this one is especially good with large and extremely comfortable rooms, equipped with all mod cons, and a spacious public area on the ground floor. The decor is modern-minimalist throughout, and the buffet breakfast is top-ranking. However, what really distinguishes this hotel is its location – it adjoins Norwich City football ground and the best rooms have panoramic views of the football pitch. There's only a small premium charge of £25 on match days, but if you're visiting when Norwich FC are at home to regional rivals Ipswich ("The Tractor Boys"), then you won't get a room for love nor money. **£90**

Maid's Head Hotel Tombland, NR3 1LB ☎01603 209955, ⓦmaidsheadhotel.co.uk. Not everyone's cup of tea perhaps, but this chain hotel is delightfully idiosyncratic – a rabbit warren of a place with all sorts of architectural bits and pieces, from the mock-Tudor facade to the ancient, wood-panelled bar, though there is also a clumpy modern extension. The rooms are mostly large and very comfortable in a standard-issue sort of way, and the location, bang in the centre opposite the cathedral, can't be beat. If you are a light sleeper, you should avoid those rooms that overlook the street especially on the weekend as local drunks wend their not-so-merry way home. **£130**

Old Rectory Hotel 103 Yarmouth Rd, Thorpe St Andrew, NR7 0HF ☎01603 700772, ⓦoldrectorynorwich.com. In a handsome, ivy-clad Georgian villa, this relaxing hotel holds eight commodious, en-suite rooms. The five rooms in the main house are decorated in a modern and very relaxing rendition of country house style, those in the Coach House annexe are more modern. The grounds are extensive and there's an outside pool, but in the winter guests gather round the open fire. Outstanding breakfasts and wi-fi, plus a smart dining room/restaurant where the food is first-rate with due emphasis given to local, seasonal ingredients – try, for example, the roasted, wild breast of woodpigeon salad. The hotel is located close to the River Yare on the A1242, a couple of miles east of Norwich train station. **£125**

EATING

Until fairly recently, eating out in Norwich hardly set the pulse racing, but things are very much on the move with a string of first-rate **cafés** and **restaurants** opening up in the city centre and its immediate environs. Several – including the *Mad Moose* and *Mackintosh's Canteen* – are owned and operated by a local mini-chain, Animal Inns, who, since they established themselves in the 1990s, have done much to raise gastronomic standards – and expectations. The only problem is Sundays, when most cafés and restaurants are closed.

CAFÉS

103 103 Unthank Rd, NR2 2PE ☎01603 610 047. This excellent café-restaurant, located just outside the centre in a part of the city that is particularly popular with academics, offers a creative menu with all sorts of international flourishes – from Vietnam to Valencia. A blues meets R&B and soul soundtrack adds to the atmosphere, but come early if you want to get a seat at the weekend when the place is jam-packed. Mains average £8–10. Mon–Sat 8.30am–10pm & Sun 9am–6pm.

Britons Arms Coffee House 9 Elm Hill, NR3 1HN ☎01603 623367. Home-made quiches, tarts, cakes and scones plus pies and salads in a quaint Elm Hill thatched house with a terraced garden. There's a roaring open fire in winter too – very cosy. Mon–Sat 9.30am–5pm.

Café Ninety-One 91 Upper St Giles St, NR2 1LT ☎01603 627422. Fancy and very cosy little café in a former sweet shop, where much of the old wood panelling has survived in perfect nick. Sells a tasty range of home-made cakes and snacks – try the scones. Mon–Fri 9am–5.30pm, Sat & Sun 9am–4pm.

Expresso Café 12 St George's St, NR3 1BA ☎01603 768 881. Pleasant and pleasantly decorated café that does a good line in coffee. The snacks and sandwiches are really rather pedestrian, but at least the place is an independent. Mon–Sat 7am–5.30pm & Sun 9am–4pm.

The Window Coffee 25 Wensum St, NR3 1LA ☎07913 672 491. Odd little place – "little" being the operative word as it's billed as the smallest coffee shop in world. Occupying the window of what was once a shop, they sell excellent coffee and cakes with a smile. Tues–Fri 8am–3pm & Sat 9am–3pm.

1

RESTAURANTS

Delia's Restaurant (☎ 01603 218704) and **Yellows American Bar & Grill** (☎ 01603 218209), both at Norwich City Football Club, Carrow Rd, NR1 1JE. Delia Smith's smart hometown restaurant as well as her more fan-orientated *Yellows* are down at the football ground – no surprise there then, given her keen interest in Norwich Football Club. It's a blessing: most football fans are condemned to eat grotty fast-food, but not here, where fans can get good tucker at *Yellows American Bar & Grill* or stump up extra to go to *Delia's Restaurant*, though this is only open on Friday and Saturday evenings and it's a three-course, £35 set meal only. *Yellows* do the finest burger in town – no mistake. Yellows: Sun–Wed 11.30am–10.30pm, Thurs–Sat 11.30am–11pm, kitchen till 9/10pm respectively; Delia's: Fri & Sat 6.30–11.30pm.

★ **Elm Hill Brasserie** 2 Elm Hill, NR3 1HN ☎ 01603 624847. This intimate, one-room bistro-brasserie, housed in an old shop, offers an inventive menu with a full dash of French flair. Daily specials, written on a blackboard, are well considered and reasonably priced at around £14 per main course. Mon–Sat 12.30–2.30pm & 5.45–10.30pm, Sun noon–6pm.

★ **The Last Wine Bar** 76 St George's St, NR3 1AB ☎ 01603 626626. Imaginatively converted old shoe factory, a couple of minutes' walk north of the river, holding a relaxed and very amenable wine bar in one section and an excellent restaurant in the other. The food is firmly modern British, with the likes of braised lamb shank with carrots and parsnips in a rosemary jus (around £14). Mon–Sat noon–2.30pm, plus Mon–Fri 5pm–12.30am & Sat 6pm–12.30am, but kitchen closes 10.30pm.

The Library Bar and Grill 4a Guildhall Hill, NR2 1JH ☎ 01603 616606. One of the city's more unusual restaurants, *The Library* is housed – as indeed the name would suggest – in the old records library. It's a clever recycling of an old building, but not entirely successful – when the restaurant is busy, as it often is, the place is a bit of a barn. However, the menu is very good, imaginative and often locally sourced, featuring the likes of braised venison and chestnut pie with sweet and sour red cabbage and new potatoes. It's reasonably priced too – with mains from as little as £12. One of a small, family-run chain that includes *Pinocchio's* (see opposite); it's located just off the Market Place, behind the Guildhall. Mon–Fri noon–2pm & 6–10pm, Sat noon–10pm & Sun noon–3pm.

Mackintosh's Canteen Unit 410, Chapelfield Plain, NR2 1SZ ☎ 01603 305280. A member of "Animal Inns", a small local chain, this busy, bustling place is named after the

chocolate factory – Mackintosh's – that was demolished a few years ago to be replaced by the *Canteen* and the adjoining Chapelfield shopping centre. Decorated in sharp, modern style, the *Canteen* comprises a café downstairs and a restaurant up above. At both, the menu is resolutely British – though there's a bit more choice upstairs – and everything is extremely fresh. Try the home-made beefburger – it's delicious. Mains hover around £12. Mon–Fri 10am–midnight, Sat & Sun 9am–midnight.

Mad Moose 2 Warwick St, NR2 3LD ☎ 01603 627687. In a residential area just north of the city centre, this large and very popular spot is a pub downstairs and a restaurant up above – as per *Mackintosh's Canteen* (it's in the same mini-chain). The bar menu is very gastro, there's a wide range of local brews, and *The Moose* is justifiably proud of its locally sourced, home-made food. Start off with the Norfolk asparagus, marinated chicken and wild mushroom salad and you can't go far wrong. Main courses from £13. Daily noon–11pm.

★ **Nazma** 15 Magdalen St, NR3 1LE ☎ 01603 618701. Many locals swear this is the city's best Indian restaurant – and they're almost certainly right. The menu covers all the classics, each prepared from scratch with the freshest of ingredients, but it's particularly strong on Bangladeshi cuisine. The decor is smart, modern and very appealing too. Mains average around £9, slightly less for takeaway. Daily noon–2.30pm & 6pm–midnight.

Pinocchio's 11 St Benedict's St, NR2 4PE ☎ 01603 613318. There's not much finesse here at this (broadly) Italian restaurant, but the portions are generous, the menu is inexpensive, and the place itself, which inhabits what was once a general store, is alive with conversation – with vibrant decor to match. Pizzas from £9. Tues–Sat noon–2pm & 5–11pm.

Roger Hickman's Restaurant 79 Upper St Giles St, NR2 1AB ☎ 01603 633522. Impeccable service, attractive decor and a sometime inspirational menu are the hallmarks of this stylish restaurant, the choicest in town. The menu is every inch modern British and conscientious efforts are made to source ingredients locally – try, for example, the pan-fried John Dory with braised fennel, mussel and saffron casserole and deep-fried squid. Two-course set meal £30, half that at lunchtimes. Tues–Sat noon–2.30pm & 7–10pm.

Tatlers 21 Tombland, NR3 1RF ☎ 01603 766670. Enticing contemporary restaurant – all plain-wood floors and deep-red walls – where they stick to local, seasonal ingredients when they can. The portions are a little nouvelle, but there's a good wine cellar to compensate. Try the wood pigeon. Mon–Sat noon–2pm & 6.30–10pm, Sun noon–3pm & 6.30–10pm.

DRINKING AND NIGHTLIFE

Norwich literally heaves with **pubs** and although many have been badly treated by the developers with ersatz themes and tacky copycat decor, a goodly number have bucked the trend. Some have maintained their traditional appearance, others

CLOCKWISE FROM TOP GOTHIC HOUSE (P.52); KING'S HEAD (P.56); NORWICH MARKET (P.47) >

1

have survived by offering a wide range of real ales, and yet others have ventured into the idiosyncratic-meets-surreal. As for **clubs**, Norwich cannot really compete with its big-city British rivals, but it does muster a handful of places, where locals gather, all high-heels, short skirts and short-sleeved shirts, no matter what the weather.

PUBS

Adam & Eve Bishopgate, NR3 1RZ A rabbit warren of a place, there's been a pub here on this site for seven hundred years and it's still a popular spot for the discerning drinker with a changing range of real ales and an eclectic wine list supplied by Adnams. Daily 11am–11pm.

Coach and Horses 82 Thorpe Rd, NR1 1BA. Boisterous boozer attracting a youthful crew, not least because of the three big-screen TVs and the inexpensive bar food. It's also home to the small-time Chalk Hill Brewery, who make a first-class range of ales – knock your socks off with their Old Tackle brew (at 5.6%). Daily 11am–11pm.

Fat Cat Freehouse 49 West End St, NR2 4NA ☎ 01603 624 364. Award-winning pub with a friendly atmosphere and a fantastic range of well-kept, top-quality draft ales. Also sells a great range of bottled beers, ciders and perries, and there's takeaway if you don't want to hang around. The pub is located to the northwest of the city centre off the Dereham Rd. Daily 11am–11pm.

★ **Kings Head** 42 Magdalen St, NR3 1JE. The perfect drinkers' pub with precious little in the way of distraction – there are certainly no one-armed bandits here – but instead there is an outstanding selection of real ales supplemented by an equally impressive, international range of bottled beers with Belgium leading the alcoholic charge. In two smallish rooms, so you may need to be assertive to get served. Daily 11am–11pm.

Micawbers Tavern 92 Pottergate, NR2 1DZ. Lodged in an old beamed building on one of the city's prettiest streets, this friendly and busy pub is a local par excellence, featuring an outstanding range of guest ales on draft. There's home-cooked food and Sports TV too. Daily 4pm–late.

Mischief 8 Fye Bridge St, NR3 1HZ. The counterfoil to the

Ribs of Beef just across the bridge, *Mischief* has dispensed with any claim to comfort with its plain furniture and bare wooden floors – this is youthful drinking territory make no mistake, and students come here by the seminar load. Daily 11am–11pm.

Ribs of Beef 24 Wensum St, NR3 1HY. There's been a pub here for hundreds of years and the present incarnation is a lively, friendly kind of place that makes a play for the couple rather than the group – witness the comfy chairs and the thick carpet. Has a very likeable riverside mini-terrace too. Daily 11am–11pm.

Ten Bells 74 St. Benedict's St, NR2 4AR. Weird and wonderful place that attracts a weird and wonderful clientele, who hunker down among the crusty old sofas and the rickety chairs with barely a light to illuminate proceedings. As you might expect, lots of students love the vibe. In an old building at the junction of St Benedict's St and Ten Bells Lane. Daily 11am–11pm.

CLUBS AND VENUES

Mercy 82 Prince of Wales Rd, NR1 1NJ ☎ 01603 627666, ⓦ mercynightclub.com. Very large and very flashy nightclub with a thunderous sound system, acres of neon lighting and massive, heaving dancefloors. Subtle it isn't – good fun it is. Wed–Sat 9.30pm till the wee hours.

Waterfront 139–141 King St, NR1 1QH ☎ 01603 632717, ⓦ waterfrontnorwich.com. This happening club and alternative music venue, which occupies what was once an old beer bottling plant, showcases some great bands, both big names and local talent, and offers club and DJ nights too. Run by the University of East Anglia's student union. Fri & Sat from 9pm, plus additional gigs.

ENTERTAINMENT

★ **Cinema City** Suckling House, St Andrew's St, NR2 4AD ☎ 0871/9025724, ⓦ picturehouses.co.uk. Easily the best cinema in town, featuring the very best of new releases plus themed evenings and cult and classic films. Also has live feeds from, for example, the New York Met, a Kids' Club and regular late-night horror films, billed as "Friday Frighteners".

Maddermarket St John's Alley, off Pottergate, NR2 1DR ☎ 01603 620917, ⓦ maddermarket.co.uk. With a long and distinguished pedigree, this amateur theatre company offers an interesting range of modern theatre mixed up and in with the classics. The building is interesting too – it's in the style of an Elizabethan theatre.

Norwich Arts Centre St Benedict's St, NR2 4PG ☎ 01603 660352, ⓦ norwichartscentre.co.uk. Adventurous venue

with a varied programme of film and comedy, dance and art exhibitions, theatre and music. Performances are held in St Swithin's, a recycled medieval church, which is attached to a café and box office. Open Wed–Sun from noon.

Norwich Playhouse St George's St, NR3 1AB ☎ 01603 598598, ⓦ norwichplayhouse.co.uk. Opened in the mid-1990s, this enterprising and popular venue offers a varied programme, featuring everything from dance, cabaret, stand-up comedy and celebrity chit chats to rock and pop concerts, ballet and panto.

Norwich Puppet Theatre Church of St James, Whitefriars, NR3 1TN ☎ 01603 629921, ⓦ puppettheatre.co.uk. This long-established puppet theatre company has an outstanding reputation for the quality of its puppets and the excellence of its performances, with recent shows including *Thumbelina* and *The Frog Princess*. Some performances are aimed at young children – who are simply enraptured – others are for adults. Children's tickets cost £5, £7 for adults. The company is housed in a deconsecrated medieval church beside the busy Whitefriars roundabout.

Norwich Theatre Royal Theatre St, NR2 1RL ☎01603 630000, ⓦtheatreroyalnorwich.co.uk. Recently revamped and renovated, this 1300-seater Art Deco theatre is the city's major performance venue. It casts its artistic net wide, but for the most part it's mainstream stuff with a large helping of classical music thrown in for good measure.

SHOPPING

For a small city, Norwich does extremely well for independent shops, selling everything from vintage clothing and old vinyls to chichi fashion and fine art. Attempting to capitalize on this, the narrow lanes and alleys between the Market Place and St Benedict's St have been designated the **Norwich Lanes** (ⓦnorwichlanes.co.uk), though in fact this excludes what is arguably the city's most diverting shopping strip, **Magdalen Street**, which is neither neat nor pretty, but it does hold a real rag tag and bob tail of great little shops. Of course, Norwich has its fair share of multinational shopping chains and these are at their ritziest in the **Chapelfield Shopping Centre** (ⓦchapelfield.co.uk), beside the inner ring road.

Book Hive 53 London St, NR2 1HL ☎01603 219268, ⓦthebookhive.co.uk. Norwich's only independent bookshop, the award-winning Book Hive is a stylishly decorated affair with two large floors crammed with books. There's a café, a children's book room, easy chairs, and – best of all – knowledgeable, interested staff. They also host events here – book launches, signings, kids' workshops and so forth. Mon 10am–5.30pm Tues–Sat 9.30am–5.30pm.

Country & Eastern The Old Skating Rink, 34 Bethel St, NR2 1NR ☎01603 663890, ⓦcountryandeastern. co.uk. One of Norwich's most distinctive shops, this barn-like store, lodged in what was once the city skating rink, offers all sorts of Eastern stuff, from Buddha statues and delicately carved Burmese wall panels to rugs, Thai jewellery and Indian paintings. Apparently, the owners make regular trips to Asia to source the material and take pains to patronize small, independent craftsmen and women. Mon–Sat 9.30am–5pm.

Crome Gallery 34 Elm Hill, NR3 1HG ☎01603 622827, ⓦcromegallery.co.uk. One of the prettiest streets in Norwich, Elm Hill has a fair smattering of fine art and antique shops, but this is perhaps the most diverting, selling vintage maps and sketches, plus a good selection of local land - and seascapes, both antique and modern. They offer a picture framing service too and mount temporary art exhibitions. Mon–Sat 10am–5pm.

Grapevine Gallery 109 Unthank Rd, NR2 2PE ☎01603 760660, ⓦgrapevinegallery.co.uk. Well-regarded gallery featuring the work of over 200 artists and craftsfolk, many of whom are local. Paintings often take pride of place, but jewellery, ceramics and glassware are particularly popular too, and there's a specialist fine and applied art library. Prices range from the unbearable to the reasonable. Tues–Sat 10am–5.30pm.

Harvey's Pure Meat 63 Grove Rd, NR1 3RL ☎01603 621930, ⓦpuremeat.org.uk. There are several good butchers in Norwich, but this is the best with a great pedigree of sourcing their organic meat locally to the highest welfare standards with no chemicals or drugs. They do cured meats too – ham, bacon etc – but their particular speciality is game – pheasant, partridge, grouse, hare, woodcock and snipe. Mon–Fri 7am–5pm & Sat 7am–4pm.

Head in the Clouds 13 Pottergate, NR2 1DS ☎01603 620479, ⓦheadintheclouds.info. Peering into the window of this "head shop", you can be forgiven for thinking you've been beamed back into the 1970s, a land of flared trousers, bangles, beads and Afghan coats – and it's true, as the owner proudly proclaims, that nothing much has changed here for several decades. So, stock up on your incense sticks, badges, pipes and vintage hippy clothes. Real groovy, man. Mon–Sat 9.30am–5.30pm & Sun 11am–4.30pm.

Jarrolds Department Store London St, NR2 1JF ☎01603 660661, ⓦjarrold.co.uk. A Saturday shopping trip to Jarrolds has been a popular outing for many a local for many a year. Perhaps surprisingly, Jarrolds has remained independent and its flagship premises, here on London St, covers all the retail bases from sports to travel, arts and crafts to PCs, wedding gifts to fashion. Mon, Wed & Fri 9am–5.30pm, Tues 9.30am–5.30pm, Thurs 9am–9pm, Sat 9am–6pm, Sun 10.30am–4.30pm.

Out of Time Records 4 Magdalen St, NR3 1LH ☎01603 610139, ⓦoutoftimerecords.co.uk. Something of an institution, this long-established shop groans and heaves with records, tapes and CDs, a veritable Aladdin's cave of all things audio. As such, it reflects the enthusiasms of its owner, Eric White, who first opened his doors way back in 1986. There's lots of rock memorabilia on sale here too, plus a mail order service. Mon–Sat 10am–5pm.

Prim 14 St Benedict's St, NR2 4AG ☎01603 766261, ⓦprimvintagefashion.com. Inventive, creative and often delightful vintage clothes shop, complete with a gold-mirrored old cocktail bar, that sells an enjoyable range of 1930s to 1980s clothing and accessories. The women's stuff is on the ground floor, the men's in the basement – dig

1

those skinny ties, braces and belts. Mon–Sat 10am–6pm.

Retreat Vintage 26 Magdalen St, NR3 1HU ☎07766 397 807. Norwich has a good line in secondhand and vintage clothes shops and this is one of the best, offering a wide selection of women's dresses, coats, blouses, skirts, shoes, belts and handbags from the 1920s to the 1980s. There's a smaller men's section as well. Mon 11am–5pm, Tues–Sat 10.30am–5.30pm & Sun noon–4pm.

The Rock Collection 14–16 Lower Goat Lane, NR2 1EL ☎01603 625 055, ⓦrockcollection.co.uk. Alternative street- and club-wear store specializing in niche collections from rockabilly to rave via punk and goth. Featured designers include Darkside, Cyberdog, Criminal Damage, Famous Stars and Straps, Living Dead Souls, Phaze, Hell Bunny, Alchemy Gothic, Poizen Industries, SDL, Stargazer Make-up, New Rock, Lowlife, Directions Hair Dye, Rock & Rebellion and Wildcat Body Jewellery. They also play host to the occasional band signing. Mon–Sat 9.30am–5.30pm, Sun 10.30am–4.30pm.

Tombland Antiques & Collectables 14 Tombland, NR3 1HF ☎01603 619129, ⓦnorwichonline.co.uk. Yards from the cathedral, this is perhaps the most enjoyable of Norwich's several antique shops, its series of ancient rooms ideal browsing territory. A number of dealers display here, filling a long series of glass cabinets with their assorted baubles and trinkets, from jewellery and coins through to ceramics and pewterware. Tues–Sat 10am–5pm.

Tombland Bookshop 8 Tombland, NR3 1HF ☎01603 490000, ⓦtomblandbookshop.co.uk. In an attractive, fifteenth-century building close to the cathedral, this secondhand and antiquarian bookshop is just ideal – its bookshelves well organized and arranged, the whole caboodle permeated by that lovely and distinctive smell of old books. As they say themselves "From belly-dancing to Bauhaus, botany to bee-keeping there will be a book for the keen collector or the serendipitous reader" – though a particular specialism is East Anglian history. Mon–Sat 9.30am–5pm.

Vanessa Lewis 23 Wensum St, NR3 1LA ☎07905 186 198, ⓦvanessalewis.net. Outside of London, independent dressmakers are thin on the ground, but here in Norwich Vanessa Lewis steers a chic and distinctive course, specializing in Audrey Hepburn-inspired pencil skirts and shift dresses, though she dabbles in more contemporary stuff too. Thurs 10am–6pm, Fri 10am–5pm & Sat 10am–5.30pm.

Wilkinson's 5 Lobster Lane, NR2 1DQ ☎01603 625121, ⓦwilkinsonsofnorwich.com. There's something really refreshing about this independent tea and coffee merchant, who take great care to buy the best of the crop and then sell it here in these attractive old premises. Mon–Sat 9am–5.30pm.

DIRECTORY

Car rental There are several car rental firms at both the airport and in the city centre – try Europcar (ⓦeuropcar .co.uk), Hertz (ⓦhertz.co.uk) or easyCar (ⓦeasycar .com).

Football Norwich City Football Club – The Canaries – play at their stadium on Carrow Rd, near the train station (ⓦcanaries.co.uk).

Library The main city library is in the Forum building just behind the Market Place (Mon–Fri 9am–8pm & Sat 9am–5pm; ☎01603 774774).

Post office There's a central post office inside the Castle Mall Shopping Centre (Mon–Sat 9am–5.30pm).

Taxis There are several taxi stands in the city centre with one of the busiest being in front of the Guildhall, on the Market Place. Alternatively, call Beeline Taxis on ☎01603 633333.

Around Norwich

In every direction, Norwich's suburbs fade into the open countryside beyond, where a network of country lanes mazes across farmland to connect a string of tiny, little villages. Within easy striking distance of the city centre, both **Mousehold Heath** and **Whitlingham Country Park** offer good walking and, a little further afield, are two theme parks designed for kids – **Animal Ark** and **Dinosaur Adventure**.

THE BOUDICCA WAY

The **Boudicca Way** (ⓦboudiccaway.co.uk) is a long-distance **footpath**, which runs the forty-odd miles south from Norwich to Diss (see p.210), starting and finishing at the two main-line train stations. For most of its course, it runs parallel with the **A140**, itself an old Roman road, passing through a string of pretty little villages set amid quiet countryside.

Mousehold Heath

Spreading over a hilly parcel of land just to the northeast of the city centre, **Mousehold Heath** once extended east almost as far as The Broads. The remaining heath was bequeathed to the city council in 1880, but by then its character had begun to change with the open heathland rapidly disappearing beneath a covering of scrub and woodland as locals stopped grazing their animals and collecting their winter fuel here. Plans are afoot to extend the patches of remaining heathland, but in the meantime most of the area is wooded, its dips and dells explored on a network of **footpaths**, several of which begin beside **Gurney Road**, which cuts right across the heath. The heath does support a varied wildlife, but the particular highlight is the spring gathering of mating frogs around **Vinegar Pond**.

Whitlingham Country Park

Whitlingham Lane, Trowse, NR14 8TR • Visitor centre: in the old flint barn: April–Dec daily 10am–2pm & 2.30–4pm • ☎ 01603 632307, ⓦ whitlinghamec.co.uk

Stretching out along the southern bank of the River Yare just to the east of the city centre, **Whitlingham Country Park** is one of the city's most popular attractions, its assorted woods, meadows and wetland crisscrossed by easy footpaths. It's also home to an **Outdoor Education Centre**, where the emphasis is on all things watery, from canoeing and kayaking through to sailing and windsurfing.

Animal Ark

Fakenham Rd, Great Witchingham, NR9 5QS • Tues–Sun 10am–5pm or dusk • £6.50, children aged 3–14 £5.50 • ☎ 01603 872274, ⓦ theanimalark.org • Six miles northwest of Norwich on the A1067

Aimed at kids, **Animal Ark** is a popular attraction that holds a selection of farm animals plus lots of pets in its "Pets' Pavilion", from the very likeable – rabbits, guinea pigs, cockatiels and budgies – to the less so – rats, mice and ferrets. There's also an adventure area for climbing, racing, swinging and sliding as well as go-karts and a zip wire.

Dinosaur Adventure

Weston Park, Lenwade, NR9 5JW • Daily: late March to late July 9.30am–5pm; late July to mid-Sept 10am–6pm; mid-Sept to Oct 9.30am–5pm; Nov to late March 9.30am–4pm • £9.95, £10.95 in peak season, under-15s £10.95, £12.95, under-3s free • ☎ 01603 876310, ⓦ dinosauradventure.co.uk

The **Dinosaur Adventure** theme park occupies a sprawling, partly wooded site about twenty minutes' drive northwest of Norwich via the A1067. Apart from the petting animals, there are lots of "prehistoric" adventures geared for kids, whether it be along the Neanderthal Walk or in the Lost World Amazing Adventure. Don't expect too much in the way of subtlety.

The Broads and northeast Norfolk

THE RIVER ANT AND HOW HILL (P.82)

The Broads and northeast Norfolk

Generally known as the Broads, the pancake-flat region between Norwich and Norfolk's east coast and reaching down into northern Suffolk is a haunting, sometimes eerie wilderness of lake and river, reedbed and marsh, huge skies and distant horizons, cut only by windmills and the gaff-rigged sails of far-off yachts. Three rivers – the Yare, Waveney and Bure and their various tributaries, notably the Thurne and Ant in the north, and the Chet in the south – meander across these flatlands, converging on Breydon Water before flowing into the sea at the old port and seaside resort of Great Yarmouth.

In places these rivers swell into wide expanses of water called "broads", which were long thought to be natural lakes. In fact they're the result of several centuries of extensive peat cutting in an area where peat was a valuable source of energy and wood was scarce. The pits flooded when sea levels rose in the thirteenth and fourteenth centuries to create the Broads, and this is now the largest wetland area in the country (and one of the most important in Europe), a haven for bird- and wildlife. You can see grebes, herons and if you're lucky a kingfisher or two; you might also catch a glimpse of the rare swallowtail butterfly, which is unique to the area, and it's not unusual to spot an otter poking its whiskered snout out of the water.

It's a beautiful area, and has been popular as a tourist destination for the best part of a century. However, during the 1970s and 1980s the Broads' delicate ecological balance was under threat: the careless use of fertilizers poisoned the water and phosphates and nitrates encouraged the spread of algae; the decline in reed cutting – previously in great demand for thatching – made the broads partly un-navigable; and the enormous amount of pleasure boat traffic began to erode the banks. National Park status was accorded to the area in 1988, and it is tightly regulated by the **Broads Authority** (⊕ broads-authority.gov .uk), which has jurisdiction over much of the riverside and marshland and maintains a series of information centres throughout the region. At any of these, you can pick up a free copy of the annual *Broadcaster*, a useful guide to the Broads as a whole.

The Broads break neatly down into the **Northern Broads** and **Southern Broads**. The Northern Broads is the busier of the two, focused on big boating centres like **Wroxham** and popular villages like **Horning**, **Acle** and **Potter Heigham**, and boasting the largest two broads, **Barton Broad** and **Hickling Broad**. To get to the Southern Broads, you have to pass through Great Yarmouth, which puts a lot of people off, and as a result the Yare and Waveney rivers are for the most part free of the summertime congestion you get further north. **Reedham** and **Brundall** are the two main boating centres here, and you can follow the river all the way into Norwich, although you should also consider heading way south to **Oulton Broad**, on the fringes of **Lowestoft** in Suffolk.

EAST RUSTON VICARAGE GARDEN

Highlights

❶ Horning This is the classic Broadland village – with a great location on a bend in the Bure, good restaurants and one of the region's best riverside pubs. **See p.78**

❷ Bewilderwood Tom Blofeld's magical Broads fantasyland for kids is very easy to reach, and great fun. **See p.79**

❸ Electric Eel, How Hill One of several wildlife trips you can take into the reedy heartland of the Broads, but maybe the best. **See p.82**

❹ East Ruston Vicarage Garden There are lots of beautiful gardens in Norfolk, but if you only have time to visit one, make it this – a garden fantasy created from scratch over the last three decades. **See p.89**

❺ Horsey Windpump Visit the windmill, sail on or walk around Horsey Mere, and take in the seal colonies of the nearby coast. **See p.98**

❻ Winterton-on-Sea The best beach settlement along this stretch of coast, with golden sands, wonderful dunes, a beach café and a nice village pub. **See p.100**

HIGHLIGHTS ARE MARKED ON THE MAP ON P.64

THE BROADS AND NORTHEAST NORFOLK

HIGHLIGHTS
1 Horning
2 Bewilderwood
3 Electric Eel, How Hill
4 East Ruston Vicarage Garden
5 Horsey Windpump
6 Winterton-on-Sea

0   2
miles

N

2

FOOTPATHS AND CYCLE TRAILS

If you're not getting out on the water (see box, p.66) you need to at least take some advantage of the region's network of **footpaths** and **cycle trails**. There are a number of bike rental points dotted around the region, and walkers might consider dipping into the 56-mile **Weavers' Way**, which winds through some of the best parts of the Broads on its way from Cromer to Great Yarmouth, or the 35-mile **Wherryman's Way**, which skirts Breydon Water from Great Yarmouth, and then follows the Yare as far as Whitlingham Country Park on the edge of Norwich (see p.109). And of course there are any number of shorter options, including several boardwalked paths through nature reserves and along the edges of the most scenic broads and rivers. There is also a plan to link the Bure, Ant and Thurne rivers with a brand new foot- and cyclepath, the Three Rivers Way – see ⓦ threeriversway.org.uk.

BIKE RENTAL

The Canoe Man Wroxham. See p.66
Broadland Cycle Hire Bewilderwood, Horning, NR12 8JW ☎07887 480331, ⓦ norfolkbroadscycling.co.uk
Clippesby Hall Hall Lane, Clippesby, NR29 3BL ☎01493 367800, ⓦ clippesby.com
Riverside Tearooms The Green, Stokesby ☎01493 750470, ⓦ stokesby.org.uk
Sea Palling Cycle Hire Waxham Barn, NR12 0EE ☎01692 598592, ⓦ norfolkbicyclehire.co.uk
Waveney River Centre Staithe Rd, Burgh St Peter, NR34 0BT ☎01502 677343, ⓦ waveneyrivercentre.co.uk

RIVERSIDE PATHS AND BOARDWALKS

Barton Broad See p.80
Carlton Marshes See p.270
Cockshoot Broad See p.72
Filby Broad See p.99
Hickling Broad See p.84
How Hill See p.84
Horsey Mere See p.98
Ranworth Broad See p.72
Rockland Broad See p.114
Salhouse Broad See p.71

Finally there's the **east coast**, which has more to it than the seaside tack and low-level deprivation of **Great Yarmouth**, Norfolk's largest port and resort, and overall is a refreshingly unpretentious antidote to Norfolk's better-known north coast. The Broads landscape blends seamlessly into the coast around **Horsey** and **Waxham**, while small-scale resorts like **Winterton**, **Mundesley** and **Overstrand** boast great Blue Flag beaches and sumptuous dunes, although the ongoing problem of coastal erosion – at its worst around the village of **Happisburgh** – means that much of this beautiful landscape is under threat.

Wroxham and around

Straddling the River Bure at one of its few crossing points, the small town of **WROXHAM** styles itself as the "capital of the Broads", and with good reason – it's home to more boatyards than anywhere else in the area and is dependent on the boating industry to survive; it also makes a good base for visiting some of the most picturesque Broadland villages in the surrounding area, notably Salhouse and Ranworth. It's not a very attractive place in truth, made up of two villages: **Wroxham** proper, on the south side of the river, and **Hoveton**, on the north. The latter is home to the bulk of the town centre and most facilities, including the main town moorings and pretty riverside park, and perhaps Wroxham's most famous attraction, **Roys** – "the largest village store in the world", whose department store, supermarket, garden centre, toy shop and various other dependencies make up most of the town's commercial activity.

2

MESSING ABOUT IN BOATS

The best way to appreciate the fragile beauty of the Broads is to get out on the water. Naturally there are many ways of doing just that: **motor cruisers** are the most popular option, but you can also rent a **sailing boat** or a **canoe**, or take any number of **guided boat trips**. The Broads are above all the perfect place for a spot of novice boating. You don't need any experience – at least if you opt for engine rather than sail, which is what most people do. Not surprisingly, it's crowded in peak season, but the area has a tardis-like ability to absorb visitors, and even in the height of summer it's possible to escape to somewhere that feels like the middle of nowhere, with only – if you're sailing – the creak of your sheets and the swish of the water for company. Better yet, get out in a canoe and explore the smaller waterways that aren't so easily navigable by larger craft.

BOAT TRIPS

Broads Tours, Wroxham See p.67
Electric Eel, How Hill See p.82
Gentleman Jim, Rollesby Broad
See p.100
Ranworth Broad trips See p.72
Liana, Hoveton See p.68

Ross's Rivertrips, Horsey Mere
See p.99
Southern Comfort, Horning See p.78
Visitor Centre, Hickling Broad See p.84
Waveney Princess, Oulton Broad
See p.270

BOAT RENTAL

Barnes Brinkcraft Riverside Rd, Wroxham, NR12 8UD ☎ 01603 782625, ⓦ barnesbrinkcraft.co.uk. Wroxham-based family firm offering motor cruisers, day boats and even canoes.

Blakes ☎ 0844 856 7060, ⓦ blakes.co.uk. Boating holidays specialist, with a special focus on the Broads cruising, and bases in Wroxham, Ludham and Reedham.

★ **The Canoe Man** 10 Norwich Rd, Wroxham, NR12 8RX ☎ 01603 499177, ⓦ thecanoeman.com. The Canoe Man brings originality and adventure to the Broads, with a whole range of mainly canoe-based activities, taking in straight canoe rental from a range of locations (see opposite), guided canoe trails, bushcraft experiences and teepee canoe trips. They also have bikes for rent from their office by the bridge in Wroxham. A great place to start any discovery of Broadland.

Ferry Marina Horning, NR12 8PS ☎ 01692 631111, ⓦ ferry-marina.co.uk. Cruisers by the week or day from this versatile and reliable Horning marina outfit.

They also rent holiday cottages, and have various other facilities – a pool, café and fish and chip shop among them.

Herbert Woods Broads Haven, Potter Heigham, NR29 5JD ☎ 01692 670711, ⓦ herbertwoods.co.uk. Motor cruisers and day boats from one of the pioneers of Broads tourism, based in Potter Heigham. Holiday cottages too.

Hoseasons ☎ 0844 847 1356, ⓦ hoseasons.co.uk. The largest selection of motor cruisers available for rent on the Broads, from bases in Wroxham, Stalham, Acle Brundall and Beccles.

Hunter's Yard Horsefen Rd, Ludham, NR29 5DG ☎ 01692 678263, ⓦ huntersyard.co.uk. Based at Womack Staithe in Ludham, this yard has a wonderful collection of classic, gaff-rigged Broads yachts and half-decker sailing boats for rent by the day. It also offers skippered sails to give you a taster, runs RYA and youth courses.

Martham Boats Cess Rd, Martham, NR29 4RF ☎ 01493 740249, ⓦ marthamboats.com. Specialists

Church of St Mary

Wroxham, NR12 8NX • ⓦ wroxham.churchnorfolk.com

Tucked away on its own, south of the river, just off the main road into town, Wroxham's church of **St Mary** is – unusually for a Broadland church – often kept locked, and in any case its most distinctive feature is on the outside: a magnificent Norman doorway, stained blue, which the architectural historian Nikolaus Pevsner described as "barbaric and glorious", though it's hard to see if the outer doors are closed. In any case, it's a peaceful spot – quite unlike anywhere else in Wroxham.

in both classic wooden Broads motor cruisers and sailing yachts, as well as half-deckers and cruisers for rent by the day, and canoes too.

Norfolk Broads Direct The Bridge, Wroxham, NR12 8RX ☎01603 782207, ⓦnorfolkbroadsdirect.co.uk. Cruisers by the week from this Wroxham-based stalwart.

Norfolk Broads Yachting Company Southgates Boatyard, Lower St, Horning, NR12 8PF ☎01692 631330, ⓦnorfolk-broads.com. One of the best places to go if you want to rent a proper old-fashioned Broads sailing boat on the Northern Broads.

Posh Boats ☎01508 499167, ⓦposhboats.co.uk. Wroxham-based boatyard that does what it says on the tin – motor cruisers that are a cut above the old tubs you see most of the time on the Broads. As such it's more expensive, but it might just be worth it.

Richardson's The Staithe, Stalham, NR12 9BX ⓦrichardsonsboatingholidays.co.uk. Long-standing family-run firm that rents motor cruisers by the week from its Stalham base.

Sanderson Marine Riverside, Reedham, NR13 3TE ☎01493 700242, ⓦsandersonmarine.co.uk. Reedham-based firm with around a dozen motor cruisers for rent – perfect for exploring the Southern Broads.

Swancraft Riverside, Brundall, NR13 5PL ☎01603 712362, ⓦswancraft.co.uk. Brundall-based boat rental and boatbuilding business that has about fifteen motor cruisers of varying shapes and sizes.

Whispering Reeds Staithe Rd, Hickling, NR12 0YW ⓦwhisperingreeds.net. Great, family-run boatyard and boatbuilder on Hickling Broad that does motor cruiser, dinghy and canoe rental by the day and the week.

DAY BOATS AND CANOES

Bank Boats Staithe Cottage, Wayford Bridge, NR12 9LN ☎01692 582457, ⓦbankboats.co.uk. Boat and canoe rental.

Broads Tours The Bridge, Wroxham, NR12 8RX ☎01603 782207, ⓦbroadstours.co.uk

The Canoe Man 10 Norwich Rd, Wroxham NR12 8RX

☎01603 499177, ⓦthecanoeman.com. Canoe rental from Wroxham, Horning, Buxton, Fairhaven Gardens, Beccles.

Ferry Marina Ferry Rd, Horning, NR12 8PS ☎01692 631111, ⓦferry-marina.co.uk or ⓦwww.daycruisers.co.uk. Day boat rental (see p.80).

Fineway The Rhond, Hoveton, NR12 8UE ☎01603 782309, ⓦfinewayleisure.co.uk. Boat rental.

JB Boats 106 Lower St, Horning, NR12 8PF ☎01692 631411 ⓦjbboats.co.uk

Ludham Bridge Boatyard Johnson St, Ludham Bridge, NR29 5NX ☎01692 631011, ⓦludhambridgeboats.co.uk

Phoenix Repps Staithe Boatyard, Potter Heigham, NR29 5JD ☎01692 670460, ⓦphoenixfleet.com. Canoe and boat rental.

Rowancraft Big Row, Geldeston, NR34 0LY ☎01508 518598 ⓦrowancraft.com

Sutton Staithe Boatyard Sutton Staithe, NR12 9QS ☎01692 581653, ⓦsuttonstaitheboatyard.co.uk

Waveney River Centre Staithe Rd, Burgh St Peter, NR34 0BT ☎01502 677343, ⓦwaveneyrivercentre.co.uk or ⓦwww.daycruisers.co.uk. Boats and canoes.

Whispering Reeds Staithe Rd, Hickling, NR12 0YW ☎01692 598314, ⓦwhisperingreeds.net. Boats and canoes.

SAILING FOR PEOPLE WITH DISABILITIES

Nancy Oldfield Trust Irstead Rd, Neatishead, NR12 8BJ ☎01692 630572, ⓦnancyoldfield.org.uk

Sailability Oulton Broad ☎01502 573556, ⓦwaveneysailability.co.uk

USEFUL GENERAL WEBSITES

ⓦwww.broads-authority.gov.uk
ⓦwww.enjoythebroads.com
ⓦwww.discoverthebroads.com
ⓦwww.norfolkbroads.com

Church of St John

Horning Rd, NR12 8NX • ⓦHovetonStJohn.churchnorfolk.com

North of the river, Hoveton's church of **St John**, on the Horning Road, is in a much less peaceful position than St Mary's, but is more likely to be open. A small church, it has an ancient intimacy all of its own. Inside, you'll find a fifteenth-century beamed roof and some fifteenth-century stained glass details in the windows of the nave (though its red-brick tower is a Victorian addition). The most distinctive feature, however, are the many memorials to the Blofeld family (see box, p.69), on whose estate the church stands.

2

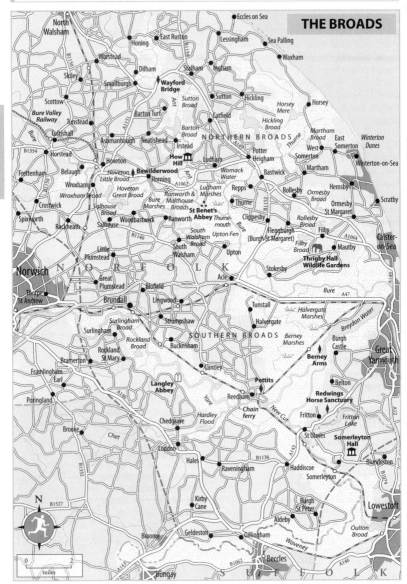

The Liana

April–Oct 4 daily: 11am, noon, 2pm & 3pm • £7, family tickets £17 • Tickets and info from the Broads Information Centre in Hoveton (see p.73)

This small, Edwardian-style boat used to be based down in Beccles; now it plies the waters between Hoveton and Belaugh several times a day – a pleasant, hour-long journey that takes in one of the most scenic stretches of the Bure. Bear in mind it only takes eight people – you may need to book.

THE NAME'S BLOFELD, HENRY BLOFELD...

The **Blofelds** have been major players around these parts for many years, and among others have produced the genial cricket commentator Henry Blofeld, and his nephew Tom, who lives at nearby Hoveton House (no relation to Hoveton Hall) and is responsible for the Bewilderwood books and children's theme park (see p.79). Intriguingly, Tom Blofeld's grandfather John was something of a mystic and practising Buddhist who lived in China for years. He was at school with Ian Fleming and is believed to have been the inspiration for the eponymous Bond villain.

Church of St Peter

St Peter's Lane, NR12 8RL • Ⓦ HovetonStPeter.churchnorfolk.com

Hoveton's other church, **St Peter**, is just off the Stalham road on the Hoveton Hall estate, on the northern outskirts of the village, an unusual step-gabled building, built of red brick and with a thatched roof, and full of memorials to the Buxton family – the current incumbents of Hoveton Hall.

Hoveton Hall Gardens

Off Stalham Rd, NR12 8RJ • Mid-April to mid-Sept daily 10.30am–5pm • Guided tours first Wed of the month at 11am, guided wildlife tours third Wed of the month at 11am • £6.50, children £3, family tickets £17 • ☎ 01603 782558, Ⓦ hovetonhallgardens.co.uk

On the northern outskirts of Hoveton, just past St Peter's church a mile or so up the Stalham road, **Hoveton Hall Gardens** are a delightful and diverse fifteen acres in the grounds of a Georgian house. They're beautiful in May and June, when there's a fine display of azaleas and rhododendrons, while midsummer sees the old walled gardens turn into a riot of colour. Gorgeous lakeside and woodland walks take in a puzzle trail for kids, a makeshift bird hide and a recently restored early nineteenth-century glasshouse. There's also a decent little café and plant sales next door.

Wroxham Barns

Tunstead Rd, NR12 8QU • Daily 10am–5pm • Farm entry £3.95 • ☎ 01603 783762, Ⓦ wroxham-barns.co.uk

Just outside Hoveton, **Wroxham Barns** is a successful development that has plenty for children and adults alike – various craft shops and galleries, a fine food store, garden centre and a microbrewery, Uncle Stuart's, selling its products direct (along with other local beers). It's also home to a small "junior farm" with goats, sheep, cows, pigs and donkeys to pet and feed, a funfair during summer and school holidays, and an excellent restaurant which is arguably the area's best bet for lunch (see p.73).

Wroxham Broad

On the edge of Wroxham, **Wroxham Broad**, reached by taking **The Avenue**, is one of the largest of the broads, and great for sailing, at its best during several annual **Wroxham Regattas**, organized by the Norfolk Broads Yacht Club – one of the area's most venerable sailing establishments – in the far corner of the Broad.

Belaugh

Between Wroxham and Coltishall, the riverside village of **BELAUGH** lies at the end of a winding side road off the main road, a peaceful spot with a handful of free moorings and the church of **St Peter** high above the river, in which what's left of a medieval rood screen shows ten of the eleven loyal Disciples.

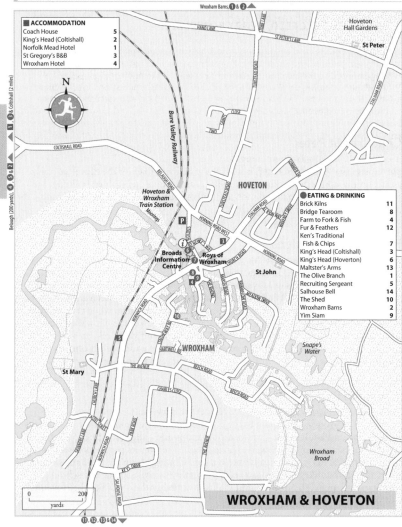

ACCOMMODATION

Coach House	5
King's Head (Coltishall)	2
Norfolk Mead Hotel	1
St Gregory's B&B	3
Wroxham Hotel	4

EATING & DRINKING

Brick Kilns	11
Bridge Tearoom	8
Farm to Fork & Fish	4
Fur & Feathers	12
Ken's Traditional Fish & Chips	7
King's Head (Coltishall)	3
King's Head (Hoveton)	6
Maltster's Arms	13
The Olive Branch	1
Recruiting Sergeant	5
Salhouse Bell	14
The Shed	10
Wroxham Barns	2
Yim Siam	9

WROXHAM & HOVETON

Coltishall

Just three miles upriver from Wroxham, the sprawling village of **COLTISHALL** really represents the westernmost fringe of the Broads proper (the river is not navigable beyond this point by commercial craft). It's a pleasant place, once a centre for boatbuilding, its public **staithe** (with plenty of free moorings) fringed by green meadows and close to *King's Head* (see p.74). Just past here, the thatched church of **St John the Baptist** has a light whitewashed interior, full of stained glass and grand memorials, beyond which is the heart of the village and a bridge over the river, which separates Coltishall from its sister village of Horstead. Here you'll find both the excellent *Recruiting Sergeant* pub and a good local farm shop (see p.74).

Salhouse and Salhouse Broad

NR13 6RX• Moorings £6, canoes £10/hr • ☎ 01603 722775, ⓦ salhousebroad.org.uk

The village of **SALHOUSE** gathers around its **pub**, *The Salhouse Bell*, at which you can eat and drink well (see p.74), and from where you can make the ten-minute walk to the car park and signposted trail down to **Salhouse Broad**, an easy stroll that finishes up at one of the prettiest of the smaller northern Broads – no more than a wider stretch in the Bure really, shielded from the main body of the river by stands of trees. There are moorings on the bank, and riverside paths lead around the wooded hill just above and down to a small children's playground by the shore. There are **canoes** for rent here, and **rough camping** is also possible by the Broad if you get permission first.

All Saints church

Bell Lane, NR13 6HD • Mon–Sat 9.30am–4.30pm • ⓦ salhouse.churchnorfolk.com

Like so many Norfolk churches, Salhouse's **All Saints** is a mile or so outside the village, on the Wroxham road, a thatched affair with a squat fifteenth-century tower that was never finished (hence its shape), although the main body of the church is at least two centuries older than this. Inside is a dark, cosy church with a number of curious features, including a wrought-iron hourglass on the pulpit, presumably to prevent the priest from droning on too long, and a rood screen topped – for once – by its "rood" or cross; behind it take a look at the sixteenth-century "sacring" bell, which used to be rung to celebrate Mass – only one of two in the country still *in situ*.

Hoveton Great Broad

April–Sept 10am–5pm • Free

On the north bank of the Bure, across the river from Salhouse Broad, **Hoveton Great Broad** is a protected area, and can only be accessed from the river, and visited on foot by following a laid-out nature trail. The trail is only about half a mile long and is well marked, winding through the woodland and swamp around the broad, and it represents one of the best chances you'll get of seeing a swallowtail butterfly, not to mention dragonflies and various bird species like woodpeckers and kingfishers. You can reach Hoveton Great Broad with your own boat or by taking a **ferry** from Salhouse Broad (Thurs & Sun every hour 10am–4pm; £3 return, children £1).

Woodbastwick

WOODBASTWICK is one of the prettiest villages in the area, with a nucleus of thatched cottages around a green, overlooked by the thatched church of **St Fabian and St Sebastian**, which has a nice churchyard and was refashioned inside in the nineteenth century by George Gilbert Scott.

Woodforde's Brewery

Woodbastwick, NR13 6SW • Mon–Fri 10am–4.30pm, Sat & Sun 11am–4.30pm • £10 • ☎ 01603 720353, ⓦ www.woodfordes.co.uk

For most people Woodbastwick's main draw is **Woodforde's** brewery, one of the best known and most successful of Norfolk's many independent brewers. The brewery is on the edge of the village, next to the *Fur and Feather* pub (see p.74); you can visit its **shop and visitor centre** and join one of their excellent tours, which take you through the brewing process and give you a brief tasting at the end. Wherry is their standard bitter, and very good it is too, kept on tap at many pubs in the area, but they also do a range of other beers, including the light and refreshing Sundew and the fearsomely strong Headcracker.

The ferry to Horning and Cockshoot Broad

Horning ferry: available on demand April–Sept daily Mon–Sat 10am–5pm; Oct–March daily except Wed & Sun 10am–5pm • £2 adults, £1 children • ☎ 01692 63056, ⓦ horningferry.co.uk

It's a short walk from the centre of Woodbastwick through the Bure Marshes down to the south bank of the Bure River, where you can either cross the river to Horning by way of the **foot ferry,** or follow the boardwalked path along the river and up the picturesque Cockshoot Dyke for fifteen minutes or so to the NWT-managed **Cockshoot Broad,** a wonderfully secret spot, viewable from a bird hide and known for its water lily beds, which are home to schools of buzzing damsel - and dragonflies during high summer.

Ranworth

Situated on the southern side of **Malthouse Broad** (Ranworth Broad is next door, and not accessible to ordinary boats), the village of **RANWORTH** has free moorings on its staithe, where there's also a car park, café and shop, a NWT information office, and, across the road, a pub, the *Maltsters Arms* (see p.74).

St Helen

Ranworth, NR13 6HT • Mid-March to Oct Mon–Fri 10.30am–4.30pm, Sat & Sun 2–5pm; Nov to mid-March Sat & Sun 2–5pm • ⓦ broadsideparishes.org.uk

Ranworth is best known for its church of **St Helen,** the so-called "Cathedral of the Broads" for both its treasures and the marvellous views from the top of its 100ft bell tower, though it's a strenuous climb up steep and irregular steps, with a couple of ladders at the top to negotiate as well. Inside, the font, bang in front of the entrance, dates from the building's foundation in the eleventh century. The rest is mainly fifteenth-century, and its most impressive feature is the rood screen at the opposite end of the nave, painted with saints and with the rose of Ranworth on the back. Just in front is a similarly ancient lectern, decorated with the symbol of St John the Evangelist on one side and a fifteenth-century verse on the other, although it normally supports the so-called *Antiphony*, kept in a display case to the right of the entrance – a late fifteenth-century illuminated service book that is in fantastic condition.

Malthouse and Ranworth Broads

Visitor centre April–Oct daily 10am–5pm; Nov–March Sat & Sun only • ☎ 01603 270479

Small open boats (£6) make regular one-hour trips from Ranworth staithe across Malthouse Broad and into adjoining Ranworth Broad, which is an NWT nature reserve, dropping you off at the informative **visitor centre** and viewing gallery built out into the water there. There are less frequent trips, also run by the NWT, up the Bure River to Cockshoot Broad for £12 (see above). You can of course also reach Ranworth Broad and visitor centre on foot – take the boarded path from the staithe or off the road that winds behind St Helen's church.

ARRIVAL AND INFORMATION

WROXHAM AND AROUND

By boat There are free moorings on the southern (Wroxham) side of the river, and also on the Hoveton side, in the direction of Coltishall, where there's a nice riverside park.

By train Wroxham is 15min by train from Norwich: Wroxham–Hoveton station, on the Bittern line between Norwich and Sheringham, is on the edge of the village on

---

BURE VALLEY RAILWAY

Just across the road from Wroxham's main-line station on the edge of town, the **Bure Valley Railway** runs from Wroxham up to Aylsham, taking in Coltishall, Brampton and Buxton along the way. You can also walk or cycle the **Bure Valley Path,** which shadows the rail line – and for some of the way the river.

the Coltishall road, on the far side of Roys car parks. Connections include Salhouse Worstead, North Walsham and Cromer. You can also get to Coltishall, Buxton and Aylsham on the Bure Valley Railway (see opposite).

By bus Buses from Norwich stop on the main road, outside Roys, as do buses on to Horning, Ludham and Great Yarmouth.

Broads Information Centre Station Rd, Hoveton, NR12 8UR (April–Oct daily 9am–5pm; ☎01603 782281).

ACCOMMODATION

WROXHAM AND HOVETON

Coach House 96 Norwich Rd, NR12 8RY ☎01603 784376, ⓦcoachhousewroxham.co.uk. Well-located, cosy B&B on the Wroxham side of the river, just 5min from the centre of town, with three bedrooms – one double, two twins – and including a really good breakfast. **£70**

St Gregory's B&B 11 Stalham Rd, Hoveton, NR12 8DG ☎01603 784319, ⓦstgregoryswroxham.co.uk. Local artist Chris Hutchins' place is a home from home in the heart of Hoveton with a double and a twin-bedded room, both en suite, excellent breakfasts and free wi-fi. Both the house and the rooms are lovely, and Chris and Sue and their Jack Russell will make you very comfortable. Hard to fault really. **£65**

Wroxham Hotel The Bridge, Hoveton, NR12 8AJ ☎01603 782061, ⓦarlingtonhotelgroup.co.uk /wroxham. Nicer than it looks from the outside, with eighteen en-suite rooms, some of which have balconies overlooking the river. **£98.50**

COLTISHALL

King's Head 26 Wroxham Rd, Coltishall, NR12 7EA ☎01603 737426, ⓦwww.kingsheadcoltishall.co.uk. Four en-suite double rooms above the pub (see p.74), well located by the riverside green in Coltishall. Reasonable sizes, and fairly recently refurbished. Breakfast included. **£75**

Norfolk Mead Hotel Church Loke, Coltishall ☎01603 737531, ⓦnorfolkmead.co.uk. You couldn't ask for a more peaceful location than the one enjoyed by this comfortable Georgian hotel right on the Bure, down a long lane off the main road through Coltishall. Its nine rooms are spacious and beautifully furnished, with very large bathrooms. Grassy water meadows stretch down to the river and the hotel's private moorings, close to which is pitched one of The Canoe Man's teepees (see p.66). There's an outdoor pool, and the public areas are squashily relaxing, as if you were lazing around in a (rich) friend's country house for the weekend – plus there's a cosy bar and classy restaurant. Includes breakfast. **£150**

EATING AND DRINKING

WROXHAM AND HOVETON

Bridge Tearoom The Bridge, Hoveton, NR12 8DA ☎01603 781817. Right by the bridge, this greasy-spoon café does a good line in big breakfasts and hot lunches. Mon–Sat 8.45am–4.45pm.

Ken's Traditional Fish and Chips Norwich Rd, Hoveton, NR12 8DA ☎01603 783739. Hungry sailors make a beeline for Ken's famous chippy – just a takeaway, and nothing special to look at, but renowned for the lightness of its batter and the tastiness of its chips. Expect to queue. Daily 11.30am–2.30pm & 4.30–7.45pm.

King's Head Station Rd, Hoveton, NR12 8UR ☎01603 782429. Hoveton village centre's only pub, next door to Roys department store, and decent enough, with a Sunday carvery and other food served daily. Mon–Sat 10am–11pm, Sun noon–10.30pm.

The Shed The Peninsula, Staitheway Rd, Wroxham, NR12 8TH ☎01603 781952, ⓦtheshedwroxham.co.uk. Hard to find among the riverside cottages but well worth searching out, this ramshackle joint has comfy chairs and pine tables, a pool table, and shows live sport on its big screens, and has a vast range of real ales on tap, including many of the best local breweries as well as others from farther afield. It does sandwiches, but its main food offering is a choice of deliveries from a selection of local takeaways. Sit outside to best appreciate its riverside location. Daily noon–11pm.

Wroxham Barns Tunstead Rd, Wroxham, NR12 8QU ☎01603 777106, ⓦwroxhambarns.co.uk. One of the best places to eat in and around Wroxham, with an excellent restaurant that will do just a coffee and a cake or a sandwich or a full lunch from a list of specials – think Brancaster mussels, smoked haddock and bacon chowder, rare breed sausage and mash or grilled fillet of sea bass – all made using local ingredients. Daily 10am–5pm.

Yim Siam 3 Riverside Centre, Wroxham, NR12 8AJ ☎01603 7811133, ⓦyimsiam.co.uk. Really good, authentic Thai food, in a place you wouldn't expect to find it, tucked away in a shopping precinct in the centre of Hoveton. Starters form £4.95, mains from £8.95. Well worth a visit, and they do takeaways too. Tues–Sun noon–3pm & 5.30–11pm.

TUNSTEAD

The Olive Branch Market St, NR12 8AH ☎01603 737555, ⓦolivebranchnorfolk.org.uk. As well as a short menu of meat dishes, this friendly restaurant, right in the centre of Tunstead, the next village north from Hoveton, has great fish and seafood mains (local mussels, sea bass, bouillabaisse) for £16–18 and does a daily three-course set menu for £14.50. It also has a good coffee shop and patisserie next door Restaurant. Tues–Sat noon–3pm & 6–9.30pm, Sun noon–3pm; coffee shop: Tues–Fri 9am–4pm, Sat & Sun 10am–4pm.

2

2

COLTISHALL AND HORSTEAD

Farm to Fork & Fish Norwich Rd, Horstead, NR12 7EE ☏01603 266129, ⓦfarmtoforkandfish.co.uk. Great farm shop with deli, butcher's and fishmonger's counter, and fantastically fresh local produce. Tues–Fri 8am–6pm, Sat 8am–4pm.

King's Head 26 Wroxham Rd, Coltishall, NR12 7EA ☏01603 737426, ⓦkingsheadcoltishall.co.uk. The focus is on food in this friendly pub, right by the village staithe, and in fact it's one of two good places to eat in Coltishall/Horstead with most mains going for around £15; try the calves' liver, or sea bass with scallops. It has rooms upstairs too (see p.73), and serves an excellent breakfast as well as lunch and dinner every day. Daily 8am–10am, noon–2.30pm & 6–9pm.

★ **Recruiting Sergeant** Norwich Rd, Horstead, NR12 7EE ☏01603 737077, ⓦrecruitingsergeant.co.uk. In Coltishall's adjoining village of Horstead, this is one of the best places hereabouts for good, gastropub food, with a great choice of daily specials around the £15 mark – hearty cooking that's deliberately simple and contemporary: skate wing, lamb shanks, smoked haddock with spinach or just burgers or fish and chips. The atmosphere is relaxed, with a roaring fire in winter and outside tables in summer, but the food and service is of restaurant standard – and worth the trip to Coltishall alone. Mon–Sat noon–2pm & 6.30–9pm, Sun noon–9pm.

SALHOUSE AND LITTLE PLUMSTEAD

Brick Kilns Norwich Rd, NR13 5JH ☏01603 723043, ⓦthebrickkilns.co.uk. This distinctive pink-washed pub is a good local that focuses on food, and has the unusual distinction of serving a full menu of vegan and vegetarian options, as well as all the usual pub standards and a good array of fish. Most mains go for around £9–12, although some steaks and fish dishes cost more, and the food is pretty good. Daily noon–2.15pm & 6–9.30pm.

Salhouse Bell 3 Lower St, NR13 6RW ☏01603 721141, ⓦsalhousebell.co.uk. Nice village local, very friendly, and with a wide-ranging menu, taking in everything from steak-and-ale pie, chicken dishes, burgers, steaks and fish and chips, plus a handful of veggie options. Mains £10–12. Open daily – food daily except Mondays.

WOODBASTWICK

Fur & Feather Slad Lane, NR13 6HQ ☏01603 720003, ⓦthefurandfeatherinn.co.uk. A large, well-run family-friendly establishment that naturally serves Woodforde ales as well as cooking up some handsome pub grub, some of it using the beer as an ingredient. Mon–Fri & Sun 10am–9pm, Sat 10am–9.30pm.

RANWORTH

Maltster's Arms Hill Drive, NR13 6AB ☏01603 270900, ⓦthemaltsters.com. This village pub has been serving the sailors who pitch up here for years with food that's nothing special but filling enough from about £7.95 – stick to the home-made curries and pub classics. Mon–Sat noon–2pm & 6–8pm, Sun noon–3pm.

Aylsham and around

The market town of **AYLSHAM** is not really part of the Broads, but it is the terminal for the Bure Valley Railway (see p.72) from Wroxham. It's a pleasant enough place, and like most Norfolk towns, life revolves around the **marketplace**, home to a twice-weekly market and overlooked by the *Black Boys Inn*. There's not much to see apart from the considerable attraction of **Blickling Hall**, a couple of miles to the north of the town centre, but the town is one of nine "**cittaslow**" communities in the UK (Ludlow in Shropshire was the first), an offshoot of Italy's Slow Food movement, designed to promote local food and food producers. As a result, it's a big venue for the Eastern Daily Press's **Norfolk Food Festival** in September, and other events around town.

St Michael and All Angels

Church Terrace, NR11 6BZ • ⓦaylshamparishchurch.co.uk

On the far side of Aylsham's Market Place, the church of **St Michael and All Angels** was built in the early part of the fifteenth century under John of Gaunt (Aylsham was one of his dominions) on the proceeds of the town's linen trade. It sports a font carved with symbols of the Evangelists and the lower part of a rood screen painted with various saints, some of them defaced during the Reformation, both of which are contemporary with the building.

Bure Valley Railway

Aylsham Station, NR11 6BW • Aylsham–Wroxham £8 single, £12 return, family return £32 • ☎ 01263 733858, ⓦ bvrw.co.uk

Five minutes' walk south from the Market Place, Aylsham's station is home to the **Bure Valley Railway** – an old-fashioned train line that runs from Aylsham down to Wroxham in the heart of the Broads, taking in Buxton, Brampton and Coltishall along the way. Engines are either steam- or diesel-powered, and the nine-mile trip to Wroxham takes 45 minutes. If you don't want to take the train you can walk or cycle the **Bure Valley Path**, which shadows the rail line – and the river – all the way.

2

Blickling Hall

Blickling, NR11 6NF • Park daily all year; house mid-Feb to mid-July & early Sept to Oct Wed–Sun 11am–5pm; mid-July to early Sept Mon & Wed–Sun 11am–5pm; gardens, shop, restaurant: Jan to mid-Feb Thurs–Sun 11am–4pm; mid-Feb to Oct daily 10am–5.30pm; Nov & Dec Wed–Sun 11am–4pm; bike rental April–Oct Sat & Sun 10am–5.30pm • £10.75, gardens only £7.25; NT • ⓦ nationaltrust.org.uk/main/w-blickling-estate

Built by Sir Henry Hobart in 1629, on the site of a mansion that once belonged to the Boleyn family, **Blickling Hall** is a mixed bag – it's a superb example of a Jacobean mansion from the outside, while its interior is furnished in the style of an Edwardian country house, dating from when it was the residence of the British ambassador to Washington, Lord Lothian (who bequeathed it to the National Trust in 1940). It's his portrait that oversees the dining room, laid out for dinner, but there are also examples of the Hobart family coat of arms, surmounted by the family bull – above the main entrance and on the ceiling of the Great Hall, for example. For the most part it's an "upstairs-downstairs" type of experience: the tour takes in the servants' quarters downstairs, where you can listen to recordings of staff who worked here in 1930 – the footman, cook, gardener – while upstairs there is a series of bedrooms, state-of-the-art 1930s bathrooms, and most impressively the **Long Room**, almost 130ft long and now a library with some ten thousand books, although it was built to suit a more modern purpose – for Sir Henry to keep fit when the weather was poor. There's also the so-called **Great Room**, which is home to a tapestry given to Sir Henry by Catherine the Great that was so large that the room had to be built around it. Two **Gainsborough portraits** – of the second earl and his wife – hang on either side of the fireplace.

The **grounds** of Blickling Hall incorporate formal gardens, extensive woodlands, a lake and the weird, pyramid-like mausoleum of the second earl. There's also a café and shop, although the best **place to eat** is the *Buckingham Arms*, right outside the Hall (see p.77).

Wolterton Park

Wolterton Hall, NR11 7LY • Hall: mid-May to Oct Fri 2–5pm; park all year daily 9am–dusk • Hall £5, car park £2 • ⓦ manningtongardens.co.uk

Built for Horatio Walpole, the brother of Britain's first prime minister, in the early 1700s, **Wolterton Park**, just outside the village of Erpingham about four miles north of Aylsham, has been empty for much of the last two centuries, and is a rather forlorn sight these days. You can visit during the summer months, and it usually hosts an exhibition highlighting the family's collection of paintings – although it's the grounds that are the real attraction, with miles of waymarked paths that lead around the lake and past the ruined tower of the estate's ruined church, and eventually to another Walpole property, Mannington Hall, to which the Walpoles decamped in the nineteenth century.

Mannington Gardens

Mannington Hall, NR11 7BB • June–Aug Wed–Fri 11am–5pm; May & Sept Sun noon–5pm • £5 • ⓦ manningtongardens.co.uk

Originally a fifteenth-century moated manor house, **Mannington Hall**, just north of the village of Itteringham, remains the home of Lord and Lady Walpole– the descendants of the first British prime minister. As such you can only visit the grounds. But what grounds they are, with amazing roses, fern gardens, woodland and wildflower meadows, a lake, and miles of trails that link up with the Walpoles' sister estate, Wolterton Hall, about a mile away to the east. There are lots of plants on sale, too.

Alby Craft Centre

Cromer Rd, Erpingham, NR11 7QW • Tues–Sun & bank hol Mon 10am–5pm; gardens April–Nov Tues–Sun & bank hol Mon 10am–4pm • Garden £3 • ☎ 01263 761590, ⓦ albycrafts.co.uk

About five miles north of Aylsham, just outside Erpingham on the main road to Cromer, **Alby Crafts Centre** is a collection of cottages and farm buildings that have been converted into creative studios and galleries, home to a thriving complex of artists and craftspeople making and selling their products direct to the public, along with a gallery, tearoom and gift shop. It's worth a stop and a browse, particularly during summer when they open the gardens to the public – four acres of strikingly planted beds and borders set around several ponds and a small area of woodland.

St Agnes, Cawston

Cawston, NR10 4AG • Daily 9am–5pm or dusk • ⓦ st-agnes.org.uk

Straddling the Aylsham road, the modest village of **CAWSTON** holds one of the county's most lauded churches, **St Agnes**, whose sturdy tower, built on the profits of the wool trade, rises high above a dinky flint entry porch and a long line of gargoyles. The interior holds an especially fine hammerbeam roof, decorated with a solemn band of angels who are positioned as if they are on medieval diving boards.

Booton

A couple of miles south of Cawston, a handful of houses make up **BOOTON**, where in the nineteenth century Whitwell Elwin made his mark as the local clergyman, writing copious letters to Charles Darwin about evolution – the post office even allocated him his own postbox – and organizing the construction of an unusual-to-bizarre Gothic Revival church, **St Michaels's**, whose slender twin towers poke high into the sky. Close inspection reveals all sorts of fancy details – there's even a minaret – but the church is no longer in use and is rarely open.

Reepham

Reepham train station, Whitwell Rd, NG10 4GA • Sat & Sun 10am–5pm • Free • ☎ 01603 871694, ⓦ whitwellstation.com

Heading west from Cawston, it's a short drive to **REEPHAM**, whose neat and trim marketplace is at its liveliest on Wednesday, its market day. The town holds a particularly attractive assortment of Georgian buildings, mostly red brick trimmed with stone, and it even had its own **train station**, which has been lovingly returned to its 1930s appearance by a dedicated team of volunteers. The station is as good a place as any to join the **Marriott's Way,** a 21-mile walking and cycling trail that follows the former railway track between Norwich and Aylsham.

St Peter and St Paul, Salle

The Street, Salle, NR10 4SE • Daily 9am–5pm or dusk • ⓦ norfolkchurches.co.uk

From Reepham, it's a mile and a half north to **SALLE** – pronounced Saul – where wide fields and a gentle trail of agricultural cottages edge one of Norfolk's finest churches, **St Peter and St Paul**, a fifteenth-century extravagance, whose top-quality stone was paid for by the wool of the sheep that used to graze near here in their hundreds. Two feathered angels wave censers above the west door and inside the finest feature is the chancel roof, supported on the wings of 160 angels. Look out also for the elaborate carving of the armrests and seats in the nave, a veritable menagerie of all things late medieval, from dragons and Green Men through to squirrels, swans and dolphins.

Heydon

In a county of rambling old villages, **HEYDON**, two miles north of Salle, has an entirely different air, its huddle of red-brick cottages neatly arranged around the village green at the behest of the local lord of the manor – for this is an estate village *par excellence*. The owners of the estate, the Bulwers, still live next door in Heydon Hall (no public access), a large mansion dating from the fifteenth century and surrounded by a strollable **park**. Just in case anyone forgot who was in control, the village church of **St Peter and St Paul**, just beside the green, possesses a large and imposing manorial pew, but its main item of interest are the medieval murals on the north wall. These are badly weathered, but you can still make out the three living and three dead figures – painted to remind the congregation of their mortality.

ARRIVAL AND INFORMATION

By train You can reach Aylsham from the Broads proper by way of the quaint Bure Valley Railway, (see p.72) which runs from Wroxham via Coltishall and other villages to a station 5min walk south of the town centre.

By bus Aylsham lies on the main bus line between Norwich and Sheringham (daily except Sun, every 30min).

Tourist office In the station (Jan–Easter & Oct–Dec daily except Wed & Sat 10am–2pm; Easter–Sept daily 10am–4.30pm; ☎01263 733903).

ACCOMMODATION

Black Boys Market Place, NR11 6EH ☎01263 732122, ⊛blackboyshotel.co.uk. If you want to stay in Aylsham, this is the best place, a dog-friendly hotel whose five rooms are traditionally – and comfortably – furnished. Breakfast not included. **£65**

Buckingham Arms Blickling, NR11 6NF ☎01263 732133, ⊛bucksarms.co.uk. Right outside Blickling Hall, this welcoming pub has three comfortable and atmospheric rooms upstairs equipped with four-posters and private bathrooms. **£100**

★ **Saracen's Head** Wolterton, near Erpingham, NR11 7LZ ☎01263 768909, ⊛saracenshead-norfolk .co.uk. This Georgian inn is well situated for both the north Norfolk coast, the Broads and east coast, and has six nicely turned-out en-suite double bedrooms, with plug-in free internet access. The location – "in the middle of nowhere but centre of everywhere", say the owners Tim and Janie – feels very remote despite its convenience, and nothing is too much trouble. It also has a great restaurant (see p.78). **£95**

EATING AND DRINKING

All Things Nice 9 High St, Cawston, NR10 4AE ☎01603 871246. In the centre of this village, this popular deli sells a good line in pies, pasties and baguettes. Takeaway or eat in at the handful of tables. Mon–Sat 9am–5pm.

Black Boys Market Place, NR11 6EH ☎01263 732122, ⊛blackboyshotel.co.uk. Comfy hotel bar, and the restaurant is pretty good too, as you would expect from the people who also own the *Recruiting Sergeant* pub down the road in Coltishall (see p.74) – with starters from £6.95 and classic English mains (chargrilled pheasant, steak-and-kidney pudding, game pie, several fish options) for £10.95–14.95. Mon–Sat noon–2pm & 6–9pm, Sun noon–9pm.

Buckingham Arms Blickling, NR11 6NF ☎01263 732133, ⊛bucksarms.co.uk. This inevitably caters mainly for visitors to Blickling Hall, but retains something of the feel of a local pub. The food is high quality and local, with posh ciabatta sandwiches, sausage and mash and more adventurous choices like chicken-and-chorizo casserole for £7.95 to £12.95. It also does roasts on Sundays, "pie and a pint" nights on Mondays, and fish and chip suppers on Thursdays. Mon–Fri noon–2pm & 6.30–9pm, Sat noon–2.30pm & 6.30–9pm, Sun noon–2.30pm.

Earle Arms The Street, Heydon, NR11 6AD ☎01263 587376. This traditional country pub, with its beamed ceilings, open fires and wood panelling, offers a good range of draft beers plus bar food and snacks. Mains from £10. Tues–Sat noon–3pm & 6–11pm, Sun noon–11pm; kitchen: Tues–Sun noon–2pm & 6–8.30pm.

The Goat Inn Long Rd, Skeyton, NR10 5DH ☎01692 538600, ⊛skeytongoatinn.co.uk. A nice country pub that's only a few miles east of Aylsham but feels more or less in the middle of nowhere, which makes its mix of good company and food all the more alluring. A large beer garden too, and a field for camping out the back. Mon–Fri noon–2pm & 6–11pm, Sat & Sun noon–11pm.

★ **Saracen's Head** Wolterton, near Erpingham, NR11 7LZ ☎01263 768909, ⍟saracenshead-norfolk.co.uk. This revitalized country inn has lovely rooms (see p.77) and a great ground floor restaurant, serving inventive, seasonal and above all locally sourced food – indeed the menu tells you just how far the ingredients have travelled. Choose from portobello mushrooms with Binham Blue cheese or ham hock terrine to start, and skate wing or slow-cooked belly of pork to follow. Or just have a drink in the bar or the courtyard out the back. Tues–Sun noon–2.15pm & 6.30–8.30pm;

Oct–June closed Tues lunchtimes.

Walpole Arms The Common, Itteringham, NR11 7AR ☎01263 587258, ⍟thewalpolearms.co.uk. Just outside Aylsham, and a mile or so from Blickling Hall, Itteringham's village pub is a good place for a drink (the bar remains pubby and welcoming), a snack or pub lunch – think a half pint of prawns, fish and chips or corned-beef-hash cake – or a proper dinner in its more formal yet still moderately priced restaurant, with excellent steaks, mussels, duck and veggie options (like squash ravioli). It's also the home of the David Adlard cookery school (⍟davidadlardcookeryschool.co.uk) which runs courses with well-known local chefs. Mon–Fri noon–2pm & 6–9pm, Sat noon–11pm, Sun noon–9pm.

Horning and around

Just three miles downriver from Wroxham, the village of **HORNING** hugs a right-angle bend in the river but is an altogether different kettle of fish from its neighbour – equally focused on the water and the boat industry, with a long main street that leads down to boatyards and a large marina, but one of the prettiest villages on the Broads, with a buzzy vibe that attracts visitors year-round to its handful of pubs, restaurants and cafés.

The main focus is the shops and village green, and the adjacent staithe, next to which *The Swan* pub (see p.81) looks out over Horning Reach and the marshes opposite. Once you've wandered along by the river and around the village's two greens, you've more or less seen Horning, although the village extends for another mile or so east. You can wander along Horning's straggling main street, which follows the river past numerous dykes and riverfront holiday homes, to Ferry Marina, down a turning to the right, where there are more moorings where you can watch the boats coming and going while having have a drink at the *Ferry Inn*. You can rent a boat here, or take the foot ferry across to the far bank, where a boarded path leads to Cockshoot Broad (see p.72).

St Benedict

Church Rd, NR12 8PZ • ⍟horning.churchnorfolk.com.

About half a mile beyond the turn-off to Ferry Marina, a right turn by the village school leads to Horning's parish church of **St Benedict**, which enjoys a peaceful location by the river, and is worth popping into to see its fourteenth-century font, ancient priest's door and carved choir stalls, and a scale model of St Benet's Abbey (see p.80) just inside the entrance. Perhaps the most enjoyable thing, though, is the path that leads from the churchyard down to the church's own staithe – a marvellously tranquil spot among the reed beds, where you can picnic and wave at the cruisers as they chug past.

THE SOUTHERN COMFORT

Just beyond the *Swan* pub, the **Southern Comfort** (Lower St, Horning, HR12 8AA; March–Nov sailings 3–4 times a day; £7, family tickets £20.40; ☎01692 630262 , ⍟southern-comfort.co.uk) Mississippi-style riverboat sets sail several times a day in the season for Malthouse Broad and other points east, a ninety-minute round-trip, with relaxed and informative commentary and a comfily old-fashioned bar downstairs serving drinks and snacks.

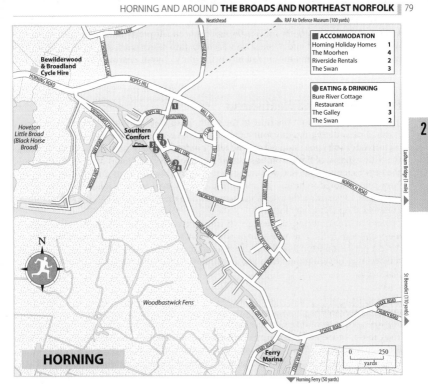

HORNING

Bewilderwood

Horning Rd, NR12 8JW • Mid-March to Oct roughly daily 10am–5.30pm, but opening times are complex – check the website • Adults and children over 105cm £11.50, children 92–105cm £8.50, children under 92cm free • ☎ 01692 783900, ⓦ bewilderwood.co.uk

Just outside Horning, off the main Wroxham road, **Bewilderwood** is one of the newest and biggest local attractions, a homespun theme park based on a series of books by local author Tom Blofeld. It's the reedy, watery world of the Broads brought to life, both a land of make-believe based on characters in the books and an over-sized adventure playground, with rope bridges and ladders, treehouses and zip wires, all connected by boardwalks, forest paths and boats. It's pretty popular in summer, and might be worth avoiding on bank holiday weekends, but its mixture of spooky fantasy and adventure has something for kids of all ages, and there's a wittiness to the whole thing that's refreshing and fun. It has a policy of sustainability too, with everything made of wood, rope and other ecologically sound resources, though the undeniable wholesomeness of it all harks back to an age before such things seemed important.

RAF Air Defence Radar Museum

RRH Neatishead, NR12 8YB • April–Oct Tues & Thurs 10am–5pm; year-round second Sat of each month 10am–5pm • £5, free guided tours on the hour • ☎ 01692 631485, ⓦ radarmuseum.co.uk

Just north of Horning (a 15min walk from the village if you're on foot), RAF Neatishead shut down in 2004, but the buildings host the **RAF Air Defence Radar Museum**, a labyrinth of rooms and corridors that was a key centre of operations during World War II, and during the Cold War years too. There are rooms devoted to the Battle of Britain and a replica of the operations room at Neatishead in 1942, but the highlight is undoubtedly the Cold War operations room, which monitored most of the

UK's airspace in the 1950s and 1960s and has been left pretty much as it was then, with banks of screens and a board on which operatives mastered the art of writing backwards. Next door a room remembers the glory days of nearby RAF Coltishall, which closed in 2006.

Barton Broad and Neatishead

The River **Ant** runs from the Bure in the south up to **Wayford Bridge** (see p.87) to the north, a meandering roughly four-mile stretch that is one of the region's most picturesque. You could stop off at **How Hill** or **Irstead** staithes (see p.82), before reaching the wide expanse of **Barton Broad**, second largest of the Broads and recently dredged of the heavy silt and algae that was clogging it up as both a waterway and wildlife zone. Now fully restored to health, it's a beautiful spot: by boat you can follow the channel of Lime Kiln Dyke off to the left all the way down to the village of **NEATISHEAD**, where there is a shop and a cosy locals' pub – the *White Horse* (see opposite).

There are free moorings about 425yds from the centre of the village, left off the main road, and also half a mile or so further on at **Gay's Staithe**. Across the road from here is the car park for **Barton Boardwalk**, a ten-minute walk away across the fields – which is the best way of seeing the broad and its wildlife on foot, from various viewing platforms.

Alderfen Broad

Daily dawn–dusk • Free • ⓦ www.norfolkwildlifetrust.org.uk

You can do a good and pretty easy circular walk from Neatishead down to the picturesque **Alderfen Broad**, an NWT-run nature reserve, about half a mile to the south. A path winds from a small jetty through the trees around its western edge, after which you can pick up the road that heads back north towards Neatishead – maybe an hour's walk in all.

St Benet's Abbey

St Benet's Rd, Ludham • Always open • Free • ⓦ www.norfarchtrust.org.uk/stbenets

Along the river from Horning, just past the junction with the River Ant, you can visit the ruins of **St Benet's Abbey**, which date back to the twelfth century, although they are dwarfed by the remains of the windmill a local farmer built behind the abbey gatehouse six centuries later. There are moorings here for boats, or you can reach the ruins by taking the path a mile or so across the marshy fields from Hall Common Road to the north – or at a pinch taking your car down the muddy farm track. The abbey feels isolated even today, but it was even more so before the surrounding marshes were drained, when it was, in effect, situated on an island. The abbey was originally a Saxon foundation that prospered throughout the Middle Ages, when it was the greatest landowner hereabouts, until the mid-sixteenth century and the Dissolution. It's still a sacred site and the bishop of Norwich has celebrated worship here every year since the 1930s. Nonetheless it remains a bleak spot, and you need a fair amount of imagination to re-imagine the thriving monastic life that once was based here.

ARRIVAL AND INFORMATION   HORNING AND AROUND

By bus Buses between Norwich and Stalham, taking in Wroxham, Ludham and Potter Heigham on the way, stop on the main road, Ropes Hill, just outside the village, and run roughly every hour

By boat There are free moorings outside the *Swan* and at the village staithe next door, and on the opposite side of

the river (though you'll need to cadge a lift off someone if you want to get to the shops or the pub). There are also moorings at Ferry Marina, a 15min walk from the centre (the ones outside the *Ferry Inn* cost £10 overnight if you don't eat at the pub and the ones on the opposite bank are free); there are washing facilities, a café, fish and chip shop and even a swimming pool in the Helska complex in the marina. Finally there are a couple at Horning church staithe, half a mile further on – a wonderfully peaceful spot but with no facilities at all.

Cycle rental Broadland Cycle Hire Bewilderwood, NR12 8JW ☎07887 480331 ⓦ norfolkbroadscycling.co.uk. Bikes from £15/day, £55/week; also does rental by half-day or 2hr. They rent kids bikes, tandems, baby seats, child trailers, etc, and they have a second outlet at Ludham Bridge (see p.83), three miles east, as well as lots of maps and suggestions for local cycle routes.

ACCOMMODATION

★ **The Moorhen** 45 Lower St, NR12 8AA ☎01692 631444, ⓦ themoorhenhorning.co.uk. Horning is a great base for the Broads, and it's an added bonus that it has this really great B&B in the heart of the village, where David and Christine Batley offer a warm welcome, four very nicely furnished en-suite rooms and a fantastic breakfast. They also have a self-catering bunk-bedded cabin in the garden that sleeps four. Discounts for stays of three nights or more. __£70__

The Swan 10 Lower St, NR12 8AA ☎01692 630316, ⓦ www.vintageinn.co.uk/theswaninnhorning. Not much character but perfectly good en-suite rooms above the pub. The best rooms overlook the river. Good breakfasts, too. __£56__

Self-catering There are tons of options around the village, many of them available through either Horning Holiday Homes, 1 Lower St (☎01692 630507, ⓦ horningholidayhomes.co.uk), or Riverside Rentals, 17 Lower St (☎01692 631177, ⓦ www.riverside-rentals. co.uk). Or rent the writer of this guide's beautiful holiday cottage at 61 Lower St (☎01692 631210, ⓦ gablecottagehorning.com).

EATING AND DRINKING

HORNING

★ **Bure River Cottage Restaurant** 27 Lower St, NR12 8AA ☎01692 631241, ⓦ burerivercottagerestaurant .co.uk. Right opposite the pub in the centre of the village, this excellent fish restaurant run by a husband-and-wife team has a blackboard menu featuring changing specials like Brancaster mussels, pan-fried sea bream and fantastic locally smoked salmon. Not especially cheap – starters go for £5–8, mains £12–16 – but one of the best places to eat for miles around. Tues–Sat 6–9.30pm.

★ **The Galley** 43 Lower St, NR12 8AA ☎01692 630088. Fantastic deli, again run by a husband-and-wife team who specialize in high-quality produce (try the sausage rolls or home-made "Hornish" pasties) that's perfect for picnics and on-board lunches. They also have a next-door café serving coffee, sandwiches and light lunch dishes. Daily 10am–6pm.

The Swan 10 Lower St, Horning NR12 8AA ☎01692 630316, ⓦ vintageinn.co.uk/theswaninnhorning. A cosy and welcoming place that does decent, reasonably priced food all day (starters £4–6, mains £8–12) –and its outside terrace enjoys one of the best riverside views too. It also has accommodation. Daily noon–9pm.

NEATISHEAD

White Horse The Street, NR12 8AD ☎01692 630828. Good local village pub that serves hearty food every day in its bar or neat-as-a-pin next-door dining room – gammon steaks, burgers, home-made curry. Mains around £8–10. Daily noon–2pm & 6–9pm.

Ludham and around

About three miles east of Horning, **LUDHAM** is a quiet Broadland village which clusters around a bend in the main road. It's home to a pub and tearooms, and has a good village shop – **Throwers** (☎01692 678248, ⓦ throwers.co.uk). It also has free moorings at **Womack Staithe**, five minutes' walk away just outside the village, at the end of a long inlet of the Thurne River, and there are nice walks to be done in the marshes roundabouts.

Ludham Bridge

The main road from Horning to Ludham crosses the River Ant at **Ludham Bridge**, where there's a straggle of houses, a couple of shops and a gallery, free moorings and a boatyard. You can follow a footpath north along the river for about a mile and a half and double back to *The Dog* **pub** on the main road (see p.83) – perhaps an hour's walk in all. *The Dog* also has a small **campsite** during the summer months.

2

EDWARD SEAGO

Ludham was the home of the artist **Edward Seago** (1910–74), not exactly a household name nowadays, but an accomplished painter of oils and watercolours that depict the Broads and other parts of Norfolk. He was a favourite of the royal family's, in particular the Queen Mother, to whom he donated two paintings a year. He lived at the **Dutch House**, down Staithe Road on the left, and created a wonderful garden there that stretches down to Womack Water and is open to the public on selected days during June and July under the National Gardens Scheme or by appointment (☎01692 678225, ⓦngs.org.uk).

St Catherine

High St, NR29 5AB • ⓦ ludham.churchnorfolk.com

The main thing to see in Ludham is the church of **St Catherine**, for once bang in the centre of the village, a late fifteenth-century building with a wooden beamed roof and a painted rood screen that is one of the finest in the county – beautifully preserved, with its ranks of saints on one side and arms of Queen Elizabeth I on the other, added hastily on her accession to the throne in 1558. In the north aisle, the mangled old alms chest is roughly contemporary with the rood screen, while the font, at the back of the church, is late fifteenth-century, carved with figures of the Evangelists and images of wild men and – unusually – wild women, clad in skins and carrying clubs.

How Hill

Norfolk Broads Study Centre, NR29 5PG • ☎ 01692 67855, ⓦ how-hill.org.uk

Just outside Ludham, the Arts and Crafts-style mansion of **How Hill** was designed and built by architect Thomas Boardman in 1904 as his family home, and enjoys an enviable position perched on a hummock overlooking the River Ant and the adjoining woods and marshes. These days it's occupied by the How Hill Trust, which runs all sorts of residential courses pertaining to Broadland – on birds and wildlife, art, gardens and walks – and oversees the extensive grounds and gardens.

Toad Hole Cottage

How Hill • April, May & Oct Mon–Fri 10.30am–1pm & 1.30–5pm, Sat & Sun 10.30am–5pm; June–Sept daily 9.30am–6pm • Free

You can walk parts of How Hill's grounds on various loops, or just follow the river downstream, but the one building on the estate that's open to the public is **Toad Hole Cottage**, a marshman's cottage down near the river that was occupied until the early twentieth century, after which it was used as a playhouse by the Boardman children (it was the Boardman brood who named it). It was restored in the 1980s and is beautifully and authentically kept in the style of the marshfolk that would have occupied it in the eighteenth century, with a stocked larder and living room with wood-burning stove and various tools for reed-cutting, eel-catching and rabbit-foraging. The two upstairs bedrooms have hot water bottles to combat the

THE ELECTRIC EEL

How Hill's Toad Hole Cottage has a little shop and Broads Information Centre that sells tickets for trips on board the **Electric Eel** (April, May & Oct Sat & Sun hourly 11am–3pm; June–Sept daily hourly 10am–5pm; £7, family tickets £17; ☎01692 756096), which leaves from the staithe just beyond. These last just under an hour and are an absolute delight, taking you deep into the marshes on the far side of the Ant, a beautiful trip through narrow channels and dykes fringed by high reeds. You get out to walk (or sometimes wade) to nearby Reedham Water, where you can spot birds from a hide, and the guide provides binoculars and lots of background on the wildlife and unique vegetation you can see.

ART IN LUDHAM

Ludham is home to a couple of local **artists' studios** which are open to the public – that of **Linda Matthews**, an ex-police officer who retired here a decade ago and now runs a gallery at Ludham Bridge (Tues–Fri 10am–5pm, Sat 10am–2pm; ☎07961 813885, ⓦlhm-artworks. co.uk); she paints scenes of Broadland, Norfolk and France in oils and watercolours and also runs day and weekend courses in painting and drawing – ⓦpaintncanvasholidays.co.uk.

The other local studio is **Grove Farm Gallery**, north of Ludham just off the road to Catfield (Wed–Sat 10am–4pm; ☎01692 670679, ⓦgrovefarmgallery.co.uk), the home and studio of S.F. Clarke, who paints scenes of the Broads (along with Scotland and Canada) in oil and watercolours. His place also has a wonderful garden that alone is worth the trip.

2

winter winds off the reedbeds, and the picture on the living room mantelpiece is of the last person to occupy the house, along with his wife and two children, until his death in 1910.

ARRIVAL AND INFORMATION

LUDHAM AND AROUND

By bus Buses from Hoveton, Horning and Potter Heigham stop in the centre of the village.

By boat Ludham's staithe, with free moorings, is a 5min walk from the village centre at the head of Womack Water,

where there is also a shop and other facilities.

Cycle rental Broadland Cycle Hire (see p.81) has a branch behind the Ludham Bridge Stores.

ACCOMMODATION

Hall Farm Cottages Ludham Bridge, NR12 8NJ ☎01692 630385, ⓦhallfarm.com. A beautiful grouping of holiday cottages in a peaceful location well off the main road near Ludham Bridge, and handy for both Horning and Ludham. Dog-friendly too. Half a dozen cottages in all, sleeping anything from two to ten. One week: <u>£400–£1000</u>

How Hill Windmill The Mill House, Ludham, NR29 5PG ☎01692 678575, ⓦnorfolkholidaywindmill.co.uk. Its sails have gone, and it's been thoroughly modernized, but otherwise this early nineteenth-century grain mill makes an atmospheric place to stay, sleeping four in a large living area and two small upstairs bedrooms. One week: <u>£375–575</u>

EATING AND DRINKING

The Dog Johnson St, Ludham Bridge, NR29 5NY ☎01692 630321. The closest pub to Ludham Bridge, and good enough, with a decent selection of ales, food and occasional live music. It also has a small adjacent campsite open in summer. Daily noon–3pm & 6–9pm.

Al Fresco Tea Rooms Norwich Rd, Ludham NR29 5QA ☎01692 678384, ⓦalfrescotearooms.blogspot.com. Right in the centre of the village opposite the church, this is

the place in Ludham for morning coffee, light lunches and afternoon tea and cakes. Good cream teas too. Tues–Fri 10am–4pm, Sat & Sun 11am–5pm.

The King's Arms High St, Ludham NR29 5QQ ☎01692 678386, ⓦkingsarmsludham.co.uk. Right on the bend in the road, the *King's Arms* is both a good locals' pub and a reasonable venue for food, with a very large menu. Mon–Sat 11.30am–midnight, Sun noon–midnight.

Potter Heigham and around

It's a pity, but **POTTER HEIGHAM**, on the Thurne River, is one of the Broads' least attractive villages, split in two by the A149 and with a riverside area (the bit that most people see) dominated by the car parks and unalluring buildings of the various boatyards. Prominent among these is Herbert Woods, who have been based in Potter since 1929, when the youngish Woods took over the family boat building business, and are still thriving today; their purpose-built Broads Haven headquarters can be seen for miles around. Otherwise there's not much to see apart from **Lathams** discount store, which sells pretty much anything you might want, and the village's famous medieval **bridge**, which dates from 1385 and is renowned for being almost impossible to get through without a pilot, or indeed at all at high tide.

St Nicholas

Church Rd, NR29 5LE

The only other structure of note in Potter Heigham is the church of **St Nicholas**, on the edge of the more attractive part of the village, across the A149, a ten-minute walk away from the riverside. It's a thatched building with a distinctive round, crenellated tower and a hammerbeam roof, below which is a series of fourteenth-century wall paintings, including a startlingly naturalistic series depicting the Seven Acts of Mercy. The churchyard is very peaceful, and there are some good circular walks you can do from here, down to the edges of Hickling Broad and back.

Hickling Broad

Hickling Broad Nature Reserve, NR12 0BW • Daily 10am–5pm; visitor centre April–Sept daily 10am–5pm • £4.50 • ☎ 01692 598276, ⓦ www.norfolkwildlifetrust.org.uk/hickling.aspx

Those boating folk who manage to negotiate the bridge at Potter finish up eventually on **Hickling Broad**, the largest broad of all and location of a Norfolk Wildlife Trust-managed nature reserve on its eastern edge. Hickling is the Broads at its very best, a large expanse of water fringed by reed beds which is home to some of the area's best and rarest wildlife – if you're going to see a swallowtail butterfly or a bittern, the odds are it will be here. It's also sublimely peaceful, and getting out on its shallow waters and paddling among its reedy fringes, preferably in a canoe or a rowing boat, is a joy.

You can access the edge of the Broad by way of Staithe Road from the edge of **Hickling village**; there's a car park and moorings here and you can follow the path along the dyke down to a picnic spot by the water, although most people come to this part of the Broad for the sailing club next door or to visit the **Pleasure Boat Inn** on the left.

You can also access the Broad by following the path from the *Pleasure Boat Inn* car park half a mile or so to the **NWT visitor centre** and car park, where you can buy tickets to enter the nature reserve. There are marked tracks through the reserve which take in stretches of reedbed, woodland and of course the banks of the Broad, where there's a bird-hide on stilts. **Boat trips** run from a landing stage down on the Broad and are fantastic, taking you all around the Broad, and visiting a 60ft-high treehouse. By car, the visitor centre and nature reserve are reachable by taking the long muddy track a mile or so down Stubb Road, which leads off from beside the *Greyhound* pub in the centre of the village.

ARRIVAL AND DEPARTURE
POTTER HEIGHAM AND AROUND

By bus Potter Heigham is connected by regular buses with North Walsham, Stalham and Great Yarmouth, and with Ludham, Horning and Hoveton.

By boat There are free moorings either side of the old bridge

at Potter Heigham and in Hickling by the *Pleasure Boat Inn*. If you have a craft wider than about 3m or higher than 2.3m you won't get under Potter's bridge at all. In any case, only try it at low tide and take it very slowly, and head for the central point.

ACCOMMODATION

Red Roof Farmhouse Ludham Rd, Potter Heigham ☎ 01692 670604. Close to the Potter Heigham boatyards,

this spick-and-span B&B has four double bedrooms and two self-catering apartments. **£50**

EATING AND DRINKING

The Greyhound Hickling, NR12 0YA ☎ 01692 598306, ⓦ greyhoundinn.com. Right in the centre of Hickling village, this is a proper village pub, with both a very warm welcome and excellent food – steaks, burgers, fish and chips and suchlike for £7.95 or so, as well as sandwiches and bar snacks. Daily 12.15–2.15pm & 6–8.30pm.

Pleasure Boat Inn Staithe Rd, Hickling, NR12 0YW ☎ 01692 598870, ⓦ thepleasureboat.com. After a period

in the doldrums, this Broadside pub is open again. It enjoys a great location right on the staithe and it serves excellent pub food too, from both a simple bar menu – fish and chips, burgers, ham, egg and chips, home-made pies, ploughman's, filled baguettes – for £8–10, and a slightly more refined evening menu – sea bass, steaks, duck breasts – for around £12. Daily noon–2.30pm & 5.30–8pm.

Stalham and around

A couple of miles east of Wayford Bridge, the centre of **STALHAM** has seen better days, and locals peg its relative demise to the opening of Tesco here a few years ago – after years of being refused planning permission. Despite that the farmers' market is still going strong, twice a month on Saturday mornings at Stalham town hall, and there's a regular general market on Tuesdays in the centre, and the high street is still a fairly attractive stretch and has all the amenities you could need. Like Potter, though, the town is split in two by the A149, with the staithe and boatyards a short walk away on the opposite side of the main road.

St Mary's

High St, NR12 9AU • ⓦ stalhambenefice.org.uk/stalham

Stalham's parish church of **St Mary** has had a stunted tower since its belfry collapsed in the sixteenth century; the bells were sold to the Dutch after this catastrophe, but the ship carrying them went down with all hands and it's said that the bells can still be heard tolling when a storm is forecast. Inside, the church has a lovely fifteenth-century font, carved with images of the Apostles, the Trinity and the baptism of Christ.

The Museum of the Broads

The Staithe, NR12 9DA **Museum** Easter–Oct daily 10.30am–5pm • £4, family tickets £10 **Falcon boat trips** Tues–Thurs on the hour 11am–3pm • £3.50, children £2.50 • ☎ 01692 581681, ⓦ museumofthebroads.org.uk

There are a couple of boatyards, notably Richardsons, across the main road from the centre at Stalham Staithe, close to which the **Museum of the Broads** does a good if somewhat nostalgic job of summarizing the uniqueness of Broadland. You can climb into the cabin of a wherry, while other sheds have displays on the history of the Broads, its wildlife and its tourism, even on Roys of Wroxham (see p.65), and there are plenty of historic craft on display too, including an old commissioner's launch, various reedlighters, dinghies and other sailing vessels. From Tuesdays to Thursdays you can also take a trip on the museum's Victorian steam launch, the *Falcon*.

Sutton

Just south of Stalham, **SUTTON** is a sprawling village with its own staithe, again on the far side of the A149, where there are free moorings and sustenance and **accommodation** at the *Sutton Staithe Hotel* (see opposite), and **canoe rental** from **Sutton Staithe Boatyard** (3hr/£20, 6hr/£30; ☎ 01692 581 653, ⓦ suttonstaitheboatyard.co.uk).

Sutton Pottery

Church Rd, NR12 9SG • Mon–Fri 9am–1pm & 2–6pm • ☎ 01692 580595, ⓦ suttonpottery.com

The main thing to visit in the village is the **Sutton Pottery** where Malcolm Flatman throws – and sells –his own unique style of pots and invites you in to watch, buy and indeed learn to make your own, with regular three-hour lessons and residential courses.

Holy Trinity Church

Ingham, NR12 9AB • ⓦ stalhambenefice.org.uk/ingham

About a mile east of Stalham, there's nothing much to the village of **INGHAM**, but its church of **Holy Trinity** is a beautiful, soaring Gothic building from the early fourteenth century, with a light interior and a number of carved effigy tombs contemporary with the building. One, unfortunately defaced and graffitied, is of one **Roger du Bois** and his wife Margaret, who died in 1300 and 1315 respectively, and another, in the choir, is of Sir Oliver de Ingham, a more flamboyantly posed figure, again rather damaged, oddly nestling on a bed of pebbles, though there's a better example of this in Reepham (see p.76).

Wayford Bridge

Following the River Ant north from Barton Broad takes you eventually to **Wayford Bridge**, the navigable northern limit, where you can rent or buy a canoe from **Bank Boats** (☎01692 582457, ⓦbankboats.co.uk) if you want to go further north on the North Walsham and Dilham Canal (see p.89); only non-powered boats are allowed on the canal up to Honing and Smallburgh.

2

ARRIVAL AND DEPARTURE
STALHAM AND AROUND

By bus Buses link Stalham to Cromer and Great Yarmouth, North Walsham, Wroxham and Norwich.
By boat There are free moorings at Stalham's town

staithe, across the A149 by the Museum of the Broads. There are also free moorings at Sutton Staithe, just off the A149.

ACCOMMODATION

INGHAM
The Swan Sea Palling Rd, Ingham, NR12 9AB ☎01692 581099, ⓦtheinghamswan.co.uk. This ex-pub is now an upscale restaurant with five en-suite rooms, including family rooms (from £85) in the converted stable block next door. Nice rooms, a marvellously peaceful location – and the restaurant is very good too. Breakfast included. **£70**

SUTTON
Sutton Staithe Hotel Sutton Staithe, NR12 9QS ☎01692 583156, ⓦsuttonstaithehotel.co.uk. A good

location right on the staithe and thirteen pleasantly if basically furnished en-suite rooms from, with family rooms for around £80 a night. It also serves food to the hungry boaters moored at the staithe. **£55**

WAYFORD BRIDGE
Wayford Bridge Inn NR12 9LL ☎01692 583259, ⓦmaypolehotels.com/wayfordbridge. This old standby currently has fifteen blandly furnished en-suite rooms, and an unpretentious riverside restaurant. However it was recently acquired by Marco Pierre White so watch this space. **£60**

EATING AND DRINKING

STALHAM
The Mermaid's Slipper The Staithe, NR12 9BY ☎01692 580808. Right by the water at Stalham Staithe, this is perhaps the best place in town to eat, housed in a converted barn and serving a wide-ranging menu of fresh, well-cooked food – everything from seared scallops to Asian curry to fillet steak: it's moderately priced and the service is pretty good. Thurs–Sat noon–2pm & 6–9pm, Sun 12.30–3pm.
Read's Coffeehouse 62–63 High St, NR12 9AS ☎01692 581070, ⓦreadscoffeehouse.co.uk. Busy and friendly café that does excellent coffee, cooked breakfasts, high tea and cakes, sandwiches, quiches and jackets at lunchtime – and even "nibbles" in the evening to which you can bring your own drinks. Lots of knick-knacks for sale, too, and a dozy resident cat. Mon–Sat 9am–4pm.
The Swan Inn 90 High St, NR12 9AU ☎01692 582829, ⓦstalhamswan.co.uk. The heartbeat of Stalham is not Tesco's but the *Swan*, which has been well updated and serves coffees and pastries in the morning and decent pub food at lunchtime and evenings, including a good kids' menu. Free wi-fi. Food served Mon–Fri noon–3pm & 5–8pm, Sat & Sun noon–8pm.

INGHAM
The Swan Sea Palling Rd, NR12 9AB ☎01692 581099, ⓦtheinghamswan.co.uk. This is a pretty serious gastropub with a nice if complicated menu with about half a dozen starters and mains; think Binham blue cheese soufflé followed by pan-roasted wood pigeon and partridge. Prices are moderate to high – starters £6–8.95 and mains £15–20 – but they do good-value two-course lunches for £12, and two-course dinner menus for £16.95 (three courses £21.50). Tues–Sun 11.30am–3pm & 6–11pm.

LESSINGHAM
The Star School Rd, Lessingham, NR12 0DN ☎01692 585510, ⓦthestarlessingham.co.uk. Just outside the village of Lessingham, this is a really friendly pub with a big fireplace in the bar and a more formal restaurant out the back. It specializes in good-quality pub grub – gammon, steaks, Norfolk sausages with mustard mash – for £9–12; always lots of specials on too. Dog-friendly. Tues–Sat noon–2.30pm & 6–9pm, Sun noon–3pm.

North Walsham and around

The small market town of **NORTH WALSHAM** was at the centre of the Norfolk weaving trade in the Middle Ages, its light Walsham cloth bringing huge prosperity to the town in the fourteenth and fifteenth centuries. It's a pleasant if unexciting little place, life as ever revolving around the lead-topped **Market Cross** at the end of the High Street, built in 1602 after a fire gutted most of the town centre. The town has a couple of good places to stay and to eat, which is a bonus because there are a number of attractions in the countryside around – and of course it's only three miles or so from the coast at Mundesley (see p.94).

St Nicholas

Market Place, NR28 9BT • ⓦ saint-nicholas.org.uk

Just off the Market Place are the peaceful precincts of the church of **St Nicholas**, the largest parish church in Norfolk, built on the proceeds of the fourteenth-century wool trade, when its vast rood screen would have filled the width of the building, though now only the bottom painted panels of this survive. There's an elaborate Paston family memorial in the high altar – they once owned a lot of North Walsham, and much else besides in the area (see p.95) – and the interior is impressive for its sheer size, although sadly not much else survives and the once-grand tower is a ruin. However, when it was built it was second in height in the county only to Norwich Cathedral.

The Cat Pottery

1 Grammar School Rd, NR28 1JH • Mon–Fri 9.30am–5pm, Sat 11am–1pm • Free • ☎ 01692 402962

While you're wandering around the centre of North Walsham, look in on the **Cat Pottery**, an eccentric collection of railway paraphernalia and hand-crafted pottery cats (with the odd dog and rabbit thrown in), housed in a ramshackle collection of cottages and outbuildings.

Worstead

Like North Walsham, **WORSTEAD**, about three miles south, was at the heart of Norfolk's medieval wool and weaving trade and was by the standards of the day a large town, and its name survives in the close-textured woollen cloth that originated here. These days it's no more than a small village, but its large church of **St Mary**, right in the centre, epitomizes the wealth and strength of the wool trade, and still boasts a few remnants of its fourteenth-century heyday – a painted rood screen and a beautiful hammerbeam roof, although like North Walsham's church its size is the most notable feature.

Before you move on, have a drink and maybe a bite to eat at the **New Inn**, virtually next door to the church, just off the main square; another good reason to visit is **Worstead Festival** (ⓦ worsteadfestival.org), a music and arts affair that takes over the entire village over a weekend in late July.

Honing

Across the other side of the A149 from Worstead, **HONING** is an attractive village whose church of **St Peter and Paul**, with its elegant high tower, occupies a lovely location on a hill just outside the village, and whose centre is mainly made up of the woods of **Honing Common**. The **North Walsham and Dilham Canal** runs right through its centre, a now disused waterway that was built to extend the navigability of the Ant as far as North Walsham in the early nineteenth century. It was never much of a success and is only properly navigable from Honing down to Smallburgh and Wayford

THE PASTON WAY AND PIGNEYS WOOD

The **Paston Way** footpath starts in North Walsham, from St Nicholas' church, and follows the Mundesley road out of town, east to the coast and then up to Cromer. It's a lovely path and its early stretches provide a good stroll into the countryside beyond North Walsham, following an old railway line to **Pigneys Wood** (wpigneyswood.co.uk) home to a 450-year-old oak tree and a number of marked walking routes and picnic areas. Walking out to here and back is a 2-to-3 mile walk, and should take no more than an hour or so.

2

Bridge, both about three miles south, where you can rent **canoes**, but its banks and bridges make the village an even more appealing spot.

East Ruston Vicarage Garden

East Ruston, NR12 9HN • End March to Oct Wed–Sun & bank hols 2–5.30pm • £7, children £1 • ☎ 01692 650432, ⓦwww .eastrustonoldvicarage.co.uk

The best thing to see in the area around North Walsham is **East Ruston Vicarage Garden**, created by Alan Gray and Graham Robeson in the early 1970s out of nothing. Gray and Robeson have worked miracles with the thirty-acre site, which isn't even well suited to gardening, and their fantasies and themes dominate throughout – a woodland area, overlooked by East Ruston's church, the dry, stony yet lush Arizona garden, several walled and sunken gardens, and the King's Walk, whose yew obelisks lead right up to the vicarage itself. It's everything a garden should be: escapist, calming and always surprising, and so cleverly planned that even its increasing popularity has not diminished its charms, with the crowds easily swallowed up by the garden's nooks and corners. It's easy to get lost but that's part of the joy of the place, and once you've emerged you can enjoy tea and cake at the café and maybe buy a plant or two before you leave.

Bacton Wood

About two and a half miles east of North Walsham, **Bacton Wood** is an ancient piece of woodland now owned by the forestry commission, although many of its indigenous trees have been replaced with evergreens. There are parking spaces among the trees on the corner of Old Hall Road, and several colour-coded trails and cycleways.

Edingthorpe

Half a mile north of Bacton Wood, the hamlet of **EDINGTHORPE** has a unique village church, **All Saints**, occupying a very lonely spot – almost on a hill in fact – just outside the village, and with a newly replaced thatched roof and a tapered round tower that is one of Norfolk's most elegant. Inside is a beautifully bare, whitewashed church full of traces of its age – a damaged but still richly decorated rood screen with paintings of saints and wonderfully delicate tracery and fragments of fourteenth-century wall paintings showing St Christopher and the Seven Acts of Mercy.

Knapton

North of Edingthorpe, just outside Mundesley, the village of **KNAPTON** also has a church worth visiting, **Saints Peter and Paul**, which has a magnificent double hammerbeam roof decorated with angels (not unlike the one in Swaffham), dating from 1503, and which some claim was created from the remains of a shipwreck off nearby Mundesley. It's in perfect condition, and still decorated with 160 figures of angels, apostles and prophets – a stupendous achievement, not only for the completeness of its religious vision but also for the sheer practical skill involved.

Trunch

Three miles north of North Walsham, the small village of **TRUNCH** has a shop and a pub, but is really worth visiting for its church of **St Botolph**, a mainly fourteenth-century building with a wealth of carved features, notably the arms and undersides of the misericords in the choir, and the rather more primitive graffiti on the choir stalls, dating from when this part of the church was used as a schoolroom. As usual the choir is separated form the rest of a church by a rood screen, and this one is very finely carved and painted with good depictions of various saints. There's also a fine hammerbeam roof, decorated with angels, though perhaps not quite as impressive as those in Knapton and Swaffham. The church's most distinctive feature is its font canopy, carved out of oak in 1500, and boasting a wealth of intricate detail – tendrils, fruit, leaves – though the bright paint that would once have covered it has long gone.

ARRIVAL AND DEPARTURE
NORTH WALSHAM AND AROUND

By train North Walsham's station is a short walk from the town centre, just across the A149. It's on the Bittern Line, with connections to Norwich and Hoveton in one direction, and to Cromer and Sheringham in the other.

By bus North Walsham is a hub for a lot of local bus routes – to Norwich, Aylsham, Cromer and Sheringham, Holt, Mundesley, Stalham and Great Yarmouth, and Potter Heigham and Wroxham, among others. Buses stop at the train station, outside Roys department store and other locations around the town centre.

ACCOMMODATION

★ **Beechwood Hotel** Cromer Rd, North Walsham, NR28 0HD ☎ 01692 403231, ⊛ www.beechwood-hotel.co.uk. There's one very good reason to stay in North Walsham, and that's Don Birch and Lindsay Spalding's lovely boutique hotel, whose seventeen very comfortable and traditionally furnished rooms that hark back to the days of Agatha Christie, who was a regular guest here when it was a private house. There's lots of Christie memorabilia, and just a hint of the country house murder mystery about the place, although the easy affability of the place soon kicks this into touch. There's a great restaurant, too (see below), which serves superb all-inclusive breakfasts, and free wi-fi. **£90–150**

Scarborough Hill Hotel Old Yarmouth Rd, North Walsham, NR28 9NA ☎ 01692 402151, ⊛ arlington hotelgroup.co.uk/scarhill/index.aspx. A mile or south of the town centre, this small country house-style hotel is an extremely peaceful place to stay, and although some of its rooms could do with a little TLC, they're large and well furnished, and the public areas have a pleasingly homely feel. It feels miles from anywhere, but North Walsham isn't far away, and the bar is comfortable and the restaurant reasonable. **£75**

EATING AND DRINKING

NORTH WALSHAM

★ **Beechwood Hotel** Cromer Rd, NR28 0HD ☎ 01692 403231, ⊛ www.beechwood-hotel.co.uk. The elegant dining room of the hotel where they serve a "ten-mile" dinner menu, using ingredients sourced no more than ten miles from the hotel. Service is first-class, as is the food – you pick from a fixed-price menu (£36), excellent value for three courses. There's a great wine list too. The menu changes regularly, but if you can try the loin of Norfolk lamb on dauphinoise potatoes or fillet of beef with horseradish mash. Mon–Sat 6.45–8.45pm, Sun noon–2.30pm & 6.45–8.45pm.

Butterfingers 1 Mitre Tavern Yard, NR28 9BN ☎ 01692 500642. Just off Market St, this is the best place in town for cheap lunchtime snacks, sandwiches, jackets, pasta specials, soups – and all-day breakfasts too. Mon–Sat 8.30am–4.30pm.

★ **The Olive Tree** 1 Bacton Rd, NR28 0RA ☎ 01692 404900, ⊛ theolivetreenorfolk.com. Incongruously located in a caravan and chalet park on the edge of town, this restaurant isn't the sort of place to benefit from passing traffic, but features slick presentation and an airy contemporary dining room, which opens onto a swimming pool. Also, of course, there's the food, which is very good, served from either a simple lunch menu – burgers, shepherd's pie, pasta dishes – or a heavier dinner menu, featuring pan-fried sea bass, rib-eye steak, and lots of pasta and risotto dishes for veggies, for around £12.95 a main. Lovely desserts too – try the dark chocolate and orange tart, or the Norfolk cheeseboard. Look out for the all-day summer Saturday barbecues outside on the patio. Tues 6–8.45pm, Wed–Sun 12.45–2.45pm & 6–8.45pm.

EAST RUSTON

Butchers Arms Oak Lane, East Ruston, NR12 9JG ☎ 01692 650237. Great village local right on the green in East Ruston – a peaceful location even at the busiest times. They serve food, and it's a cosy, quirky place, lined with books and selling local home-made jam, as well as their own souvenir Butcher's Arms beer glasses. Daily noon–2pm & 7–8.30pm.

Acle and around

About ten miles east of Norwich on the A47, **ACLE** is the last major stop on the northern Broads before Great Yarmouth. It gives its name to the bridge over the Bure, about half a mile or so north of the town, where there are free moorings and a shop. The town itself (a large village, really) is nothing special, but it enjoys a good location, good not only for boating but also for exploring some of Broadland's most evocative – and flattest – countryside on foot.

2

St Edmund the King and Martyr

The Street, NR13 6QY • ⓦ acle.churchnorfolk.com

Acle's church of **St Edmund the King and Martyr**, in the centre of the town, has a crenellated Saxon round tower, believed to date back to the ninth century, and a thatched roof. Inside, its fifteenth-century font is still partially painted and carved with images of wild men with clubs and the Virgin and Christ, while at the other end of the nave there is a delicate painted rood screen of a similar age. Look out too for the inscription on the north wall of the choir dating back to the plague of 1349, which describes "the black beast plague raging hour by hour".

Thurne

North of Acle, just beyond where the Bure meets the Thurne at Thurne Mouth, the tiny village of **THURNE** sits at the end of a small cutting on the east bank of the river, home to a number of moorings and the **Lion Inn** (see p.93), a family-run pub that's a good spot for a pint and food, and also runs a small shop in summer stocking basic provisions. Thurne is a spot on the **Weavers' Way** and you can follow the river in either direction, either north up to Potter Heigham (see p.83), about three miles away, following the east bank of the Thurne, or the two-mile or so trip south down to Acle Bridge following the Bure. There are free moorings about ten minutes' walk from the village in this direction.

Stokesby

Heading east down the Bure from Acle Bridge towards Great Yarmouth takes you through beautiful countryside of big skies and open, treeless fields; coasting down here on a traditional Broads yacht with the wind behind you on a summer's day is one of the finest experiences of the Broads. About a quarter of the way to Yarmouth, **STOKESBY**, on the north bank of the river, is a pretty riverside village with a pub with a great location in the **Ferry Inn** (see p.93), and free moorings if you eat at the pub.

Upton Broad and Marshes

Upton Broad and Marches, NR13 6EQ • Daily dawn–dusk • ⓦ norfolkwildlifetrust.org.uk

Around three miles north of Acle, the spread-out village of **UPTON** lies to the south of **Upton Broad and Marshes** – managed by the NWT, and viewable on foot by means of a series of well-maintained footpaths. It's one of the best places in the UK to see dragonflies, and offers great walks. **Upton village** itself retains its own pub, the **White Horse**, after a spirited fight by the villagers in the summer of 2010, when they clubbed together to make an offer for the doomed business, thereby persuading the current owners that it was a viable concern.

South Walsham

The small village of **SOUTH WALSHAM**, just west of Upton Fen, is home to a nice pub in the **Ship Inn** (see p.93). North of the village proper and on the far side of

Fairhaven Water Gardens, **South Walsham Broad** is more easily reached on foot from nearby **Pilson Green**. You can park your car by the broad, where there are free moorings and a couple of boatyards, and follow the footpath along Fleet dyke all the way up to the River Bure, and then either come back the same way or continue along the river and link up with the path down to the village of Upton and Upton Fen – a great circular walk that delivers you back to Pilson Green in around two hours.

St Mary and St Lawrence

The Street, South Walsham, NR13 6DQ • ⑲ broadsideparishes.org.uk/churches/south_walsham.htm

Across the road from the *Ship Inn*, the church of **St Mary** is one of two churches on this site that share the same churchyard – the other, **St Lawrence**, has fallen into ruin and its nave is now a fragrant garden. St Mary itself is intact, and is a classic large Gothic Norfolk church, although its stained-glass windows are fine examples of early twentieth-century work.

Fairhaven Water Gardens

School Rd, NR13 6DZ • Daily: March–Nov 10am–5pm; Dec–Feb 10am–4pm • £5.50 • ☎ 01603 270449, ⑲ fairhavengarden.co.uk

Right on the edge of the village of South Walsham, **Fairhaven Water Gardens** provide an easy (and wheelchair-friendly) glimpse of the swampy woodland that makes up so much of the Broadland landscape and is so often inaccessible, with paths that lead through the grounds of the Fairhaven estate. Wooden bridges cross narrow waterways and lead you past a 950-year-old oak, candelabra primulas (in spring) and down to the estate's private section of South Walsham Broad, which you can tour by boat or by canoe – the latter run by the Canoe Man (see p.66). There's a café and bookstore, and a really nice nursery selling all manner of plants.

ARRIVAL AND DEPARTURE   ACLE AND AROUND

By bus Regular buses from Great Yarmouth, Wroxham and Norwich.

By boat There are free moorings at Acle Bridge, where there is also a shop, and moorings on the opposite side of

the river at the *Bridge Inn* pub, who charge £4 (refundable if you eat at the pub). Thurne's moorings are free till 4.30pm, and £3.50 after that.

ACCOMMODATION

Amber Lodge South Walsham Rd, Acle, NR13 3ES ☎ 01493 750377, ⑲ amberlodgeacle.com. Occupying a peaceful building in an old rectory on the far western edge of the village, the *Amber Lodge* has a wide selection of rooms in all categories, ranging from smallish but perfectly acceptable doubles to larger and more sumptuous options for £75, including breakfast and wi-fi. It's not the height of luxury, but is very friendly, and the location is excellent, with lots of good walks nearby, and occasional falconry demonstrations in the fields behind. **£45**

St Margaret's Mill Caister Rd, Acle, NR13 3AX ☎ 01493 752288, ⑲ stmargaretsmill.co.uk. Just outside Acle, Reiki teacher Kevin Daniels runs a small B&B from this converted mill that is designed to encourage peace and contemplation – and strolling around its small stretch of woodland and cow parsley meadows, it's not hard to pick up the vibe. There are just two double rooms, one attached to the main building with its own kitchen and another in a separate cabin in the grounds. Kevin is always open to barter if you want to help around the place – all part of his

desire to encourage creative folk, and those just wanting to escape the pace of modern life. Breakfast included. **£65**

CAMPSITES

★ **Clippesby Hall** Hall Lane, Clippesby, NR29 3BL ☎ 01493 367800, ⑲ clippesby.com. About a mile east of Thurne, this site has secluded pitches for camping, hook-ups for caravans, holiday cottages and lodges, as well as its own pub, a very nice outdoor pool, bike rental and a children's playground – all in all a fantastic spot to explore this part of the Broads, and indeed one of the best campsites in Norfolk. Pitches including tent, car and two adults from **£22.50**

Woodside Farm Thurne, NR29 3BX ☎ 01692 670367, ⑲ woodside-farm.co.uk. Right at the end of the village, this is as peaceful as it gets, a small, fairly basic campsite that caters only for tents, though it does have electrical hook-ups. Ten pitches only so you may want to book in advance. May–Oct only. Tent, car and four adults around **£18**

EATING AND DRINKING

ACLE

Bridge Inn Old Rd, Acle Bridge, NR13 3AS ☎01493 750288, ⓦmaypolehotels.com/bridgeinn. Large pub right by Acle Bridge that has moorings, free wi-fi and a cosy bar and restaurant that does decent food from a large menu – better than you might expect given its size and location. Standards predominate – fish pie, steak-and-ale pie, lasagne, ploughman's – and they also serve breakfast to hungry boat-people during the summer months, but who knows what to expect now the group that owns the place has been taken over by Marco Pierre White. The mooring fee is £4, and is refundable from anything you buy in the pub, and the large garden has plenty to keep the kids amused. Food daily noon–9pm, plus open for breakfast from the end of July to early Sept.

★ **The Hermitage** 64 Old Rd, NR13 3QP ☎0193 750310, ⓦthehermitageseafoodrestaurant.co.uk. It's not much to look at from the outside, but this cosy and popular restaurant is one of the best places to eat fish in the county, served fresh from the harbour at Lowestoft or the north Norfolk coast. Try the seafood medley to start followed by the pan-fried halibut with wild mushrooms or the fresh local dover sole, or just the excellent fish and chips. Great value, too, with starters for £5–6 and most mains £10–15, and the service is excellent. There are also a few good meat and veggie dishes. Mon–Sat 11.30am–2.15pm & 6–9.15pm, Sun noon–2.15pm & 6–9.15pm. Closed Mon & Sun eve outside July & Aug.

STOKESBY

Ferry Inn Riverfront, The Green, NR29 3EX ☎01493 751096, ⓦferryinn.net. A newly refurbished, dog-friendly pub that serves good-quality, well-presented pub food – crab cakes, steak-and-kidney pudding, burgers, fish and chips for £9–10 – and a slightly more adventurous dinner menu, most of it locally sourced, which you can also enjoy outside by the blissfully peaceful river. Overnight

moorings cost £5, which you can claim back if you eat your evening meal in the pub. Food daily from noon.

Riverside Tearooms The Green, NR29 3EX ☎01493 750470. Breakfasts, lunches and cream teas at this long-established and indeed iconic Broads stalwart that uses mainly local produce. Daily 7.30am–6.30pm.

THURNE

Lion Inn The Street, Thurne, NR29 3AP ☎01692 670796, ⓦlion-inn-thurne.co.uk. Nice traditional pub that enjoys a great location right by the staithe in Thurne, where there are lots of moorings owned by the pub. It serves a well-cooked and wholesome menu – good steaks, and a great mixed grill for £16.95, as well as other good-value pub grub mains for under £10; veggie options too. Breakfast daily 8am–10am, lunch noon–2pm, dinner 6–9pm.

UPTON

The White Horse 17 Chapel Rd, NR13 6BT ☎01493 750696, ⓦwhitehorseupton.co.uk. Excellent locals' pub that does good food, including roasts on Sundays, fish and chips on Fridays, and hearty "sailor's breakfasts" if you book in advance. They also host occasional live music. Daily noon–midnight.

SOUTH WALSHAM

Ship Inn 18 The Street, South Walsham, NR13 6DQ ☎01603 270049, ⓦtheshipsouthwalsham.co.uk. Owned by Matthew and Nicola Colchester of *Recruiting Sergeant* fame (see p.74), this is a great village pub that does excellent gastro pub food – daily 11am–3pm during the week, and all day at weekends. A relatively simple menu – half a dozen starters, including belly of pork or seared scallops for £6–7.95 and around ten mains, most around the £12.95 mark; try the haunch of venison or sea bass fillet. Mon–Thurs noon–2pm & 6–9pm, Fri & Sat noon–2pm & 6–9.30pm, Sun noon–9pm.

The east coast

Norfolk's **east coast,** south of Cromer down to Great Yarmouth, is less renowned and as a result much less gentrified than its northern neighbour. But it's no less spectacular, and in some places more so, with long unbroken stretches of dunes, sandy beaches and seal colonies basking in the water just offshore – and its lack of refinement is refreshing if you're fed up with the Chelsea tractors and bijou shops of Burnham Market. Most of the east coast's villages and resorts are little known and feel off the beaten track, though its only large town, Great Yarmouth, is for the most part a sad shadow of its former self as a fishing port and seaside resort. The only drawback is the steady erosion of the sandy cliffs and dunes that is threatening the very existence of some of the villages, with **Happisburgh** the most extreme example of a community that is literally falling into the sea (see p.97).

2

Overstrand and around

You wouldn't know it now, but the village of **OVERSTRAND**, just south of Cromer, was a fashionable resort at the turn of the twentieth century and had a very grand hotel that crumbled into the sea in the 1940s (coastal erosion was a problem even then). It has a good sandy **beach**, and you should take some time to wander through the **Londs**, a tiny quarter of flint cottages and narrow lanes, next to which is the **Pleasaunce**, designed by a young Edwin Lutyens in the 1890s for the heirs to the Flowers brewing fortune and with extensive gardens by Gertrude Jekyll. Today it's in use as a Christian holiday centre. Nearby, on Cliff Road, there's another building by Lutyens, a small red-brick **Methodist church**, and the great man was also responsible for **Overstrand Hall** on the edge of the village.

ARRIVAL AND DEPARTURE   OVERSTRAND AND AROUND

By bus Overstrand is served by two local bus routes, the #35 which links Cromer and Wroxham via Mundesley and North Walsham around four times daily, and a summer-only service which runs from Sheringham.

ACCOMMODATION

OVERSTRAND

Sea Marge Hotel 16 High St, NR27 0AB ☎01263 579579, ⏺seamargehotel.co.uk. A large mock-Tudor masterpiece that was built as a country retreat by a German banker who was deported shortly after its completion due to the outbreak of World War I. It was rescued from serious neglect in the mid-1990s and now has comfy refurbished rooms, a restaurant and public areas and gardens that stretch down to the sea. **£125**

Shoal Cottage 22 Cliff Rd, NR27 0PP ☎01263 576996, ⏺clifftopholidays.co.uk. Clifftop cottage, right next to its sister concern, the *Clifftop Café*, sleeps eight people in four comfy bedrooms, some of which have wonderful views out to sea. One week in high season around **£1000**

White Horse 34 High St, NR27 0AB ☎01263 579237, ⏺whitehorseoverstrand.co.uk. First-class rooms furnished in contemporary style above Overstrand's village pub, all en suite and including an excellent breakfast. **£69**

NORTHREPPS

Northrepps Cottage Nut Lane, NR27 0JN ☎01263 579202, ⏺northreppscottagehotel.co.uk. Just inland from Overstrand, Simon and Deborah Gurney's country hotel has well-furnished and pretty luxurious doubles and a great restaurant, plus a great location, on the Northrepps estate. **£130**

EATING AND DRINKING

OVERSTRAND

Clifftop Café 22 Cliff Rd, NR27 0PP ☎01263 579319. The excellent *Clifftop Café*, above the beach, serves huge breakfasts and full-on lunches for £7.75, as well as crab sandwiches and salads, and has great seaward views. Daily 8am–5pm.

White Horse 34 High St, NR27 0AB ☎01263 579237, ⏺whitehorseoverstrand.co.uk. In the centre of the village, a block back from the sea, this is a good village pub that does excellent food – either pub grub and sandwiches or more exotic options such as rack of lamb or wild halibut fillets. Food served daily noon–2.30pm & 6–9pm.

NORTHREPPS

Reptons Nut Lane, NR27 0JN ☎01263 579202, ⏺northreppscottagehotel.co.uk. Restaurant of the *Northrepps Cottage* hotel, serving a well-chosen short menu based on local ingredients; try the smoked ham hock rillettes or double baked crab and shrimp soufflé to start (around £6), followed by Lowestoft plaice or roast guinea fowl – around £15. Daily noon–2pm & 6.45–9pm.

Mundesley and around

About five miles down the coast from Overstrand, **MUNDESLEY** is a long-standing resort, and another east coast town dealing with the problem of coastal erosion, with a large, virtually derelict hotel perched on the edge of the cliff to prove it. Despite that it's a cheerful place, with a long stretch of mainly sandy (Blue Flag) beach lined by colourful beach huts, which is a very popular spot during summer. There's a tiny **Maritime Museum** in the coastguard station overlooking the beach (Easter & May–Sept daily 11am–1pm & 2–4pm; 50p), with bits and bobs relating to Mundesley and the sea, fishing wrecks and the old lifeboat station. Across the road, **Adventure Island** is an elaborate twelve-hole mini golf course (daily 10am–4pm; £3).

Stow Windmill

Stow Hill, Paston, NR28 9TG • Daily 10am–dusk • £1.50, children 50p • ☎ 01263 720298, ⓦ stowmill.co.uk

Just outside Mundesley, **Stow Windmill** is an early nineteenth-century flour mill that shut down in the 1930s and has been beautifully restored over the past decade by Roger and Andrea Hough, who live in the miller's cottage behind. You can climb up through the mill's various levels by way of a series of vertiginous ladders, taking in lots of photos of the mill through its life, along with displays explaining the purpose of each level. It's beautifully done, the views back across to Mundesley and the sea are lovely, and there's a small shop selling models of the mill and other gifts.

Paston

Just beyond Stow Windmill, the village of **PASTON** is named after the Paston family who were immensely powerful during the Middle Ages, and is still home to a magnificent thatched **barn** that dates from 1581, which was deliberately upstaged by their rivals the Wodehouse family in Waxham (see p.97). Paston's church of **St Margaret** has a number of tomb memorials to family members, one a marble edifice showing a reclining Lady Katherine Paston, who died in 1628, and a much plainer monument to her husband, who died four years later.

ARRIVAL AND INFORMATION   MUNDESLEY AND AROUND

By bus Buses arrive in the village centre, 5min inland from the beach.

Tourist office The visitor centre (Easter–Oct Mon–Sat 10am–4pm, Sun 11am–4pm; ☎ 01263 721070) is in a wooden hut just past the main parade of shops in the inland part of the village.

ACCOMMODATION

Manor Hotel Beach Rd, Mundesley, NR11 8BG ☎ 01263 720309, ⓦ manorhotelmundesley.co.uk. Recently updated red-brick Victorian hotel whose rooms are well equipped if fairly characterless, although some have great views out to sea – and it's dog-friendly. **£100**

EATING AND DRINKING

Beach Café Beach Rd, NR11 8BG ☎ 01263 720608. On – yes – the beach, this popular café does fried breakfasts, sandwiches, fish and chips and other hot lunches. Mid-May to mid-Sept daily 10am–5pm; April to mid-May Sat & Sun only.

Café Lilia 3 Station Rd, NR11 8JH.☎ 01263 722282. In the inland part of the village, this is a popular spot for lunch, serving sandwiches, fry-ups, jackets and roasts on Sunday. Mon–Fri 9am–3pm, Sun 12.30pm–2pm.

Manor Hotel Beach Rd, NR11 8BG ☎ 01263 720309, ⓦ manorhotelmundesley.co.uk. You can eat either from the hotel's excellent pub grub menu in the bar (mains from £6.95) or there's a slightly dowdy restaurant serving steaks and also offering a well-chosen table d'hôte menu – one course £11.95, two courses £16.25, three courses £19.50. Food served noon–3pm & 6–9.30pm.

Happisburgh and around

Unfortunately **HAPPISBURGH** is best known for the fact that it is slowly sliding into the sea. It certainly feels a bit more off the beaten track than other nearby villages – and indeed it is, situated well off the main road and signalled by its red-and-white-striped lighthouse, a famous landmark hereabouts.

St Mary

Church St, NR12 0PN • ⓦ happisburgh.churchnorfolk.com

The main part of Happisburgh village clusters just inland next to the church of **St Mary**, which occupies a commanding position above the sea – and in fact its elegant battlemented tower was a beacon for shipping until the building of the lighthouse. It's unusually large inside, with three aisles and a lovely fifteenth-century octagonal font carved with symbols of the Evangelists – and, in a county not exactly short of appealing churchyards, St Mary's is one of Norfolk's most atmospheric, not least because of the perpetual soundtrack of waves pounding below.

2

Happisburgh Lighthouse

Select spring and summer Sun and bank hol Mon (check website) 11am–4pm • £2 • ⓦ happisburgh.org

The other thing to see in Happisburgh besides the church and beach – and very much the symbol of the village – is the **Lighthouse** on the other side of the village. The UK's only independently run lighthouse, it's still functional and is only open to the public during summer, when you can climb right up to the lantern and enjoy the glorious 360-degree views.

Happisburgh beach

You can reach Happisburgh's **beach** on foot by taking the track from the pub through the clifftop campsite, though to do so underlines the tragedy of Happisburgh, because its once-beautiful sandy beach is now littered with the mangled iron and concrete of the village's flood defences. These have so far failed to stop the sea eroding the crumbling cliffs at a rate of around 30ft a year, and a few hardy souls sit looking out to sea in what were once the front gardens of their homes. Judging by the domestic debris that litters the cliffside immediately below it's hard to see how any of these few properties that are left will survive much longer (see box, opposite).

Cart Gap

There's a better stretch of beach than Happisburgh's – with golden sands and no debris – at **Cart Gap** about a mile south of the village, next to **Eccles-on-Sea**, a huddle of shacks around a small car park, to which they have moved the Happisburgh RNLI lifeboat. There's also a good café just inland, the **Smallsticks Barn**.

ARRIVAL AND DEPARTURE | HAPPISBURGH AND AROUND

By bus Happisburgh is connected to Norwich via Sea Palling, North Walsham, Stalham and Wroxham.

ACCOMMODATION

Hill House Inn Happisburgh, NR12 0PW ☎01692 650004. The village pub has a few rooms upstairs, one of which was occupied by Sir Arthur Conan Doyle when on holiday here, where he was inspired by the landlord's son to write his short story, *The Adventure of the Dancing Men*, in 1903 – a fact confirmed by a blue plaque on the front of the building. **£60**

Manor Caravan Park Happisburgh, NR12 0PW ☎01692 652228. Happisburgh's campsite enjoys a great if exposed location just beyond the pub, though you'll want to keep your children under control as there's no fencing along the cliff edge.

EATING AND DRINKING

Happisburgh Tea Rooms Beach Rd, Happisburgh, NR12 0ES, no phone. Good breakfast and lunches are served at this hardy perennial just above the beach. Try the fresh crab sandwiches. Daily 10am–4pm.

Hill House Inn Happisburgh, NR12 0PW ☎01692 650004. Great pub at the centre of the village, connected to the churchyard by a gate and serving a good range of ales and home-cooked food in its timbered bar or cosy restaurant out the back. The food's basic pub grub, but a cut above the usual, with highlights like suet puddings and

excellent mulligatawny soup. The pub also hosts the very popular summer solstice beer festival every June, with live music and around seventy beers and two dozen ciders available to taste. Daily noon–2.30pm & 7–9.30pm.

Smallsticks Barn Café Cart Gap Rd, NR12 0QL ☎01692 583368. This small café, just outside Happisburgh at Cart Gap, converted from a barn and with a small and sheltered outside courtyard, does breakfast, lunches and excellent cream teas. April–Oct daily 9.30am–4pm; Nov–March Sat & Sun 9.30am–4pm.

Sea Palling and around

A couple of miles south of Eccles-on-Sea, the sandy beach at **Sea Palling** is pretty good, and has Blue Flag status, protected by the artificial reefs of rocks that have been built just offshore as part of the coastal flood defences, and backed by concrete walls set into the dunes. It's not the classiest place along here, with a huddle of tacky shops and snack bars, and arguably the beach is more pristine further south, but it's nice enough if the sun is shining.

HOLDING BACK THE TIDE: THE FUTURE FOR NORFOLK'S EAST COAST

Happisburgh is only the most extreme example of a problem that afflicts a great deal of Norfolk's eastern shore – **coastal erosion**, which since 1992 has claimed around 500ft and also increased vulnerability to **flooding** of low-lying land. There have been a number of major floods in the area over the centuries – a massive one in 1622, another in 1938, which inundated the area around Horsey, and again in 1953, when over 300 people were killed.

Many of the settlements along the coast are protected in some way from the North Sea, either by flood defences (as at Happisburgh), concrete supports on the dunes, which provide a barrier between the sea and the land, or artificial offshore reefs (as at Sea Palling). However, a 2008 **Environment Agency plan** concluded that it was impossible to hold back the sea for more than another twenty to fifty years at most, and that at some point local people had no choice but to submit to the inevitable and let the land flood the area between Happisburgh and Winterton, creating an estuary and consigning six villages, five churches, acres of valuable farmland and around a fifth of the Broads national park to the sea. Centuries ago the land would have looked like this anyway, they argued, and there isn't the money to maintain sea defences indefinitely. Not surprisingly this has affected property prices – and morale – and has led to a storm of protests from residents. **Happisburgh** is already fast, and visibly, disappearing, but **Hickling**, **Waxham** and **Horsey** are just some of the places where homes will be lost underwater if the EA plan is adopted, and there is no compensation for anyone affected. Conservationists have also argued against the salination of part of the UK's most important freshwater wetland. Whatever happens, there is no doubt that climate change means that the sea will be almost impossible to contain entirely, and it seems likely that the landscape around Hickling and along the nearby coast will look very different a century from now.

Across the North Sea, the Netherlands has done a very good job of protecting low-lying and reclaimed land from the sea. However, such efforts need both overwhelming political will and a great deal of money, and these are in much shorter supply in the UK, at least in the relatively off-the-beaten-track rural communities of east Norfolk.

Waxham

A mile or so south of Sea Palling, the beach is better at **Waxham**, where a path cuts through the dunes from behind the village to emerge onto gorgeous golden sands that are relatively untouched by flood defence works, and are backed by a high, dense line of dunes. Walk a little way south and you may be lucky enough to see some of the seal colony that lives nearby.

Waxham Great Barn

Coast Rd, Waxham, NR12 0EE • April–Oct daily 9.30am–5pm • Free • ☎ 01603 629048

Waxham itself is tiny, and centres on **Waxham Great Barn**, a huge sixteenth-century thatched barn, 180ft long, that has been recently restored in Norfolk reed. Built by the influential and wealthy Wodehouse family in the mid-sixteenth century, you can admire its construction during a free audio tour, marvelling at the hubris that induced Thomas Wodehouse to build this giant structure, ostensibly to upstage a rival's barn in nearby Paston (a structure which still stands, and is 24ft shorter). There's also a small café selling sandwiches, cakes and light lunches, and a car park.

St John

Church Rd, Waxham, NR12 0DZ

Thomas Wodehouse died in 1571, and you can see his tomb in the church of **St John**, which is in a state of some disrepair but is nonetheless a beautiful and very peaceful spot, before heading off for a swim and a picnic on the beach.

ARRIVAL AND INFORMATION SEA PALLING AND AROUND

By bus Sea Palling is connected to Happisburgh, North Walsham and Norwich via Stalham and Wroxham.

Cycle rental Sea Palling Cycle Hire is based at Waxham Barn (April–Oct daily 10am–6pm; ☎ 01692 598592,

Ⓦ seapallingcyclehire.co.uk). From £14/day for an adult bike, £20 for tandems, kids' bikes and tag-along kids' (and dogs!) extensions available too.

ACCOMMODATION

Walnut Farm Camping Walnut Farm, NR123 0EG Ⓣ01692 598217, Ⓦwalnutfarmwaxham.co.uk. Small family-run campsite about a mile south of Waxham and a twenty-minute walk from the beach. Very peaceful, dog-friendly and they also rent a static caravan for those who baulk at the idea of erecting a tent. A good alternative to the bigger and busier *Waxham Sands Holiday Park* a bit further south. Pitches from £10

Walnut Yurt Bridge House, Sea Palling Rd, NR12 0TS Ⓣ01692 582463, Ⓦnorfolkyurtholiday.co.uk. If you've ever dreamed of staying in a yurt on the Norfolk coast, miles from anywhere, then Cheryl and Derek's place is for you. It has a double bed and two single futons, so you can live out your Genghis Khan fantasies in style. One week (high season) from £550

EATING AND DRINKING

Reefs Bar Beach Rd, Sea Palling, NR12 0AL Ⓣ01692 598177, Ⓦreefsbar.com. Formerly a pub called the *Lifeboat*, which was destroyed in the floods of 1953 and rebuilt as the *Reefs*, a convivial, dog-friendly shack that serves a basic bar menu and hosts regular live music.

Horsey and around

HORSEY feels like a very remote spot, more of a hamlet than a village really, with a huddle of houses looking out across the marshes to sea, which is no more than a mile away and home to a large colony of seals you can usually ever basking on the shore or bobbing in the waves. As well as visiting **Horsey Windpump**, you can do a circular walk around part of **Horsey Mere** to the village and back, or strike out across the fields and then down to the sea to view the **seal colonies** there – detouring if you like to the **Nelson's Head** pub on the edge of the village (see opposite). The **beach** is reachable in ten minutes by a footpath from the pub, or there's a small car park behind the dunes, at the end of a track off the main road, just north of the village.

All Saint's Church

The Street, NR29 4EF • Ⓦ horsey.churchnorfolk.com

The village's church, **All Saints**, is tucked away on the other side of the main road, and has a thatched roof and round Saxon tower, topped with a later octagonal belfry. There's not much to it inside apart from a late-Gothic rood screen and attached staircase, but it has a tranquil feel that stays with you long after you have left, and its churchyard is another candidate for one of Norfolk's best.

Horsey Windpump

NR29 4EF • March Sat & Sun 10am–4.30pm; April–Oct daily 10am–4.30pm • £2.50; NT • Ⓣ01263 740241, Ⓦnationaltrust.org.uk/main/w-horseywindpump

Stark and proud against the dead flat landscape of the eastern fringes of the Broads (Horsey Mere is the furthest east you can go by boat), **Horsey Windpump**, the 1912 replacement of an earlier drainage mill, is what brings most people here. It's owned by the National Trust and you can climb to the top deck and look out over the Mere and fens, viewing various displays on the way – on the wildlife of the area, Arthur Ransome (who featured Horsey in a number of his stories) and the massive storm of 1938, which flooded most of the land around. Down below, there's a tearoom where you can sit and watch the activity on the boats moored along the cutting.

Horsey Mere

Horsey Mere reaches a watery hand west back into the Broads from Horsey Windpump, a beguiling expanse of water in which John Betjeman documented a magical swim in his poem, *East Anglian Bathe*. There's a good walk around part of the

Mere, following the dyke inland and then around the northern banks before turning north along Waxham New Cut to emerge on the far side of the village at Horsey Corner, where you can follow a track back to the church. You can also see the Mere and its wildlife on one of Ross Warrell's hour-long **riverboat trips**, aboard the *Lady Ann* (May–Sept 5 daily 10am–4pm; £7.50; ☎01692 598135, ⊕rossrivertrips.co.uk), which leave from Horsey Staithe; they also run early-morning bird-spotting trips for the super-keen.

ARRIVAL AND DEPARTURE   HORSEY AND AROUND

By bus Horsey isn't very well connected by public transport; the nearest bus stops are in Sea Palling to the north, which has connections with Wroxham (around 3 daily; 40min), and Martham to the south, which has at least hourly services to Great Yarmouth (55min).
By boat There are free moorings at the Horsey windpump and along the cut to Horsey Mere.

ACCOMMODATION

Horsey Barns The Street, Horsey, NR29 4AD ☎0844 800 2070, ⊕nationaltrustcottages.co.uk. Three beautifully restored timbered barns, owned and run by the National Trust, and perfectly placed too, right in the heart of Horsey, with the *Nelson Head* and footpath to the beach nearby. They sleep between four and six. One week **£800–1000**

EATING AND DRINKING

Nelson Head The Street, Horsey, NR12 8UR ☎01493 393378. Cosy pub on the edge of the village, a fifteen-minute walk across the fields from the windpump, which does excellent food and has various bits of Nelson-related memorabilia decorating its walls. Mon–Thurs noon–2pm & 6–9pm, Fri & Sat noon–2.30pm & 6–9.30pm, Sun noon–2.30pm & 6–9pm.
Poppylands Café Palling Rd, Horsey, NR29 4EQ

☎01493 393393. About 400yd out of Horsey village towards Waxham, this place does good breakfasts, sandwiches and jackets, gammon steaks, fish and chips and the like at lunchtime, and a full, slightly more refined menu in the evening, featuring steaks, salmon and chicken. It's also got a quirky gift and antique shop upstairs and just across the road a path leads down to the beach. Daily noon–3pm & 6–9pm.

Martham and the coast to Great Yarmouth

The large village of **MARTHAM** sits on the far eastern edge of the Broads, and has in fact as much in common with the seas as with the inland waterways of the Broads. It's an attractive if sprawling village, its centre set around a green as picturesque as anywhere in the county, and home to a couple of pubs, shops and other facilities. Its church, **St Mary the Virgin**, is a massive structure, and dominates the flat landscape for miles around. If you're lucky you'll be able to climb the church tower, which is occasionally open during the summer and on special occasions, but if not make do with its classic fifteenth-century interior and rough carved font showing the seven sacraments.

Martham Staithe and Broad

A mile or so outside Martham proper, the **village staithe** is a delightfully peaceful spot: the river is quieter here, as you have to negotiate the bridge at Potter to reach this stretch, and that deters the average boater. The road ends at the waterside, and there's a hand-operated bridge that can get you across to the other side. There are boats for rent by the day (or hourly) at Martham Ferry Boatyard, and just before that there's a stretch of dyke with moorings. You can make a circular walk from here down the Thurne River to **Martham Broad** and back to the village. Back towards the centre of the village, Martham Boats rents cruisers, yachts and canoes by the hour, day, or week.

The Trinity Broads

Just south of Martham, the so-called **Trinity Broads** – Ormesby, Rollesby and Filby Broads (along with the smaller Ormesby Little and Lily Broads) – form a necklace of water that stretches from the edges of Hemsby in the north down to Fleggburgh in

---

SAVE OUR SEALS

Just outside the village on the Martham road, the **Winterton Seal Hospital** rescues sick or injured seals from the beach and nurses them back to health before releasing them back into the wild. It's staffed by volunteers and funded by donations, and hosts occasional open days to highlight their work in more detail. Stop by if you can – it's a worthwhile organization, and needs all the support it can get; go to Ⓦ www.saveourseals.co.uk for contact details and the date of the next open day.

---

the south. They are connected to the river Bure by way of Muck Fleet dyke, but this is not navigable and they are effectively cut off from the main body of the Broads proper. No motor-powered craft are permitted on these Broads, but you can tour part by electric boat, and rowing boat and canoe rental is available, plus there's a sailing club on Rollesby Broad. But for the most part you'll find them quieter and more tranquil than the rest of the northern Broads. The pity is that so little can be accessed on foot.

The Waterside
Just beyond the village of Rollesby, the main A149 crosses between Ormesby and Rollesby Broads, and it's here you'll find the **Waterside** complex, home to a café and restaurant, and boat trips on *Gentleman Jim* (April–Oct daily 11am–5pm; Nov–March Sat & Sun 11am–5pm; £2.75, family tickets £8.50), which take around forty minutes to tour both Rollesby and Ormesby Little Broad just beyond. You can also rent rowing boats or kayaks from £5 an hour.

Thrigby Wildlife Gardens
Filby Rd, Thrigby, NR29 3DR · Daily 10am–dusk · £10.50, children £8.50 · Ⓦ thrigbyhall.co.uk

Thrigby Wildlife Gardens is a rather sweet, homespun little zoo with a conservation agenda. It hasn't got a huge selection of animals, but those it does have are well and humanely housed, and can be viewed from a series of ingeniously constructed walkways, which take you past snow leopards, gibbons and macaques, and a variety of birds, including two white cockatoos – the only survivors of an illegally transported cargo of eight that was confiscated at Heathrow a few years back. There's also a reptile house, with crocs and alligators and snakes, and a "willow pattern" garden, complete with little bridges and Chinese horoscopes, a "natural" playground for children – and of course the obligatory café and gift shop.

Winterton-on-Sea
The small village of **WINTERTON-ON-SEA** is much the best seaside village hereabouts, with a marvellous sandy beach backed by some majestic dunes that stretch halfway to Horsey to the north and offer some strenuous windswept walks. What's more, Winterton is the first point that really feels separate from the depressing tack of Great Yarmouth to the south. It's a lovely spot, and it's not uncommon to see seals basking in the waves offshore – there's a family of thirty or forty or so a little way north – and the dunes are home to terns, natterjack toads and the odd adder or two. There's a (pay) car park and an excellent small café – the *Dunes Café* (see p.102).

ARRIVAL AND DEPARTURE   MARTHAM AND THE COAST TO GREAT YARMOUTH

By bus There are services at least every hour between Martham and Great Yarmouth (55min); they stop on White St, near the village green. Buses run every half an hour to Winterton from Martham.

By boat Martham village staithe is about a mile north of the village, right at the end of the road that ends at the Thurne River, and has some free moorings; there are also moorings on the dyke at West Somerton.

FROM TOP WINTERTON-ON-SEA (P.100); BOATS AT HORSEY WINDPUMP (P.98) >

2

ACCOMMODATION

WINTERTON

Fisherman's Return The Lane, NR29 4BN ☎01493 393305, ⊛fishermansreturn.com. If you want to stay — and there are worse ways of spending a day or two than soaking up the peace of Winterton and its surroundings — try the village pub, which has three en-suite double rooms. **£80**

Hermanus Leisure The Holway, NR29 4BP ☎01493 393216, ⊛hermanusholidays.com. Overlooking the sea, this is a family-run establishment whose unique round

thatched chalets were inspired by a trip to South Africa's Hermanus Bay. There are twelve single roundhouses for couples overlooking the dunes, and a number of double roundhouses and various other bungalows and chalets. The simply furnished one-bedroom chalets ingeniously squeeze a kitchen/sitting room, bedroom and bathroom into a space the size of the average policemen's telephone box. There's an outdoor heated pool, and a bar and restaurant on site, but you're only two minutes' walk from the pub. **£50**

EATING AND DRINKING

WINTERTON

Dunes Café Beach Rd, Winterton, NR29 4AJ ☎01493 394931. At the top of the path down to the beach, this is the perfect beach café, in which Mick and Carmel serve good breakfasts and lunches as well as lovely cakes, sandwiches and ice creams. Daily 10am–4pm.

★ **Fisherman's Return** The Lane, NR29 4BN ☎01493 393305, ⊛fishermansreturn.com. In the village proper, this is a great dog-friendly locals' pub that serves good food and has rooms. Daily noon–2.30pm & 6–9pm.

TRINITY BROADS

Eel's Foot Inn Ormesby St Michael, NR29 3LP ☎01493 730342. This long-established pub enjoys a lovely position overlooking the water of Ormesby Little Broad, serves reasonable pub food and rents rowing boats (£5/hr, £10/half-day, £15/day), but it's looking a little frayed these days, and it can get very busy on summer weekends. Daily noon–3pm & 6–9pm.

Great Yarmouth and around

Not even the greatest apologist for run-down British seaside towns would make much of a case for **GREAT YARMOUTH** – or at least not for spending any amount of time there. And yet it's a hard place to dislike, a once majestic port that supported a fishing fleet of over a thousand vessels, most of them hunting for herring – an industry that thrived from the Middle Ages, when this was one of the country's wealthiest cities. The herring fleet supported Yarmouth until the turn of the twentieth century, when it entered a steep period of decline, just as its days as a seaside resort began to gather momentum, spurred on by the mid-nineteenth-century arrival of the railway. These days it's a faded mixture of the two: a port that barely survives, a so-called heritage quarter that blends tattoo parlours, Polish supermarkets and Elizabethan mansions, and a kiss-me-quick resort that fronts a beautiful stretch of sandy beach. It's not everyone's cup of tea, but there is plenty to see, and as your expectations aren't sky-high, you might just be pleasantly surprised.

The Heritage Quarter

Yarmouth's **Heritage Quarter** is a slightly desperate tourist board epithet for the neighbourhood of fairly run-down social housing and the odd historic attraction sandwiched between the town quay and the seafront. But its few attractions are for the most part worth seeing and it does repay a wander.

Elizabethan House Museum

4 South Quay, NR30 2QH • April–Nov Mon–Fri 10am–4pm, Sat & Sun noon–4pm • £3.50; NT

The edge of Great Yarmouth's Heritage Quarter is marked by the Dutch-looking nineteenth-century town hall, just beyond which the sixteenth-century **Elizabethan House Museum** does a good job of recreating domestic life during Yarmouth's glory years, with period furnishings, a hoard of silver coins and a display on the Civil War

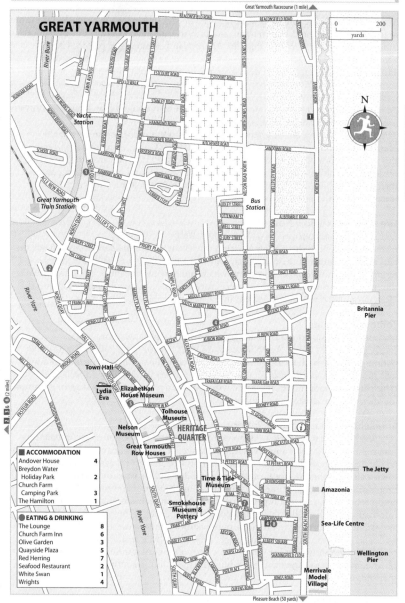

GREAT YARMOUTH

ACCOMMODATION	
Andover House	4
Breydon Water Holiday Park	2
Church Farm Camping Park	3
The Hamilton	1

EATING & DRINKING	
The Lounge	8
Church Farm Inn	6
Olive Garden	3
Quayside Plaza	5
Red Herring	7
Seafood Restaurant	2
White Swan	1
Wrights	4

(Cromwell is said to have spent time here). It's educational and fun, with clothes for the kids to dress up in, and free audio guides.

The Lydia Eva

South Quay, NR30 2QH • Tues–Sun 10am–4pm • Free • ⓦ lydiaeva.org.uk

Moored right by the town hall on South Quay, the **Lydia Eva** joined the Yarmouth fishing fleet in 1930, when the herring industry had already peaked, and lasted less than a decade before being retired to work for the Ministry of Defence. Nonetheless she is the only surviving herring drifter in town, and as such has been restored and is open as a museum, along with her sister ship, the *Mincarlo* in Lowestoft (see p.269). Climb aboard to see the bridge, the engine room and hold, and plenty of illustrated displays and films that do a great job of describing the herring industry when it was at its height.

Nelson Museum

26 South Quay, NR30 2RG • April–Sept Mon–Fri 10am–5pm, Sat & Sun 1–4pm; Jan–March & Oct–Dec Mon–Fri 10am–4pm, Sat & Sun 1–4pm • £3.50 • ☎ 01493 850698, Ⓦ nelson-museum.co.uk

About halfway along South Quay, the **Nelson Museum** is one of the best of the Heritage Quarter's museums, housed in a handsome Georgian mansion and telling the story of Norfolk's most famous son. It focuses on his naval career and love life, his leadership skills, and to some extent his appearance, and is an engaging and imaginative display for the most part, loaded with information and with a few touches that will appeal to kids.

Great Yarmouth Row Houses

South Quay, NR20 2RG • April–Sept noon–5pm • £4.20; EH • ☎ 01493 857900

Immediately behind the Nelson Museum, the **Great Yarmouth Row Houses** provide the best extant example of these distinctive houses, which were originally merchants' residences that lined the narrow alleys which run down to the quay. They were divided into tenements during the eighteenth century, and the port workers crowded into the "Rows"– a period that is well evoked in this small exhibition.

Tolhouse Museum

Tolhouse St, NR30 2SH • April–Oct Mon–Fri 10am–4pm, Sat & Sun noon–4pm • £3.50 • ☎ 01493 858900

Just beyond South Quay, the **Tolhouse Museum** is housed in one of the town's oldest buildings, dating back to the twelfth century. It served for a time as Yarmouth's town hall and later became a prison, and the museum focuses on the ne'r-do-wells and criminals of Yarmouth over the years, with some scary basement cells – again great fun for kids, with good free audio guides.

Smokehouse Museum and Pottery

18–19 Trinity Place, NR30 3HA • May–Oct Mon–Fri 9.30am–5pm; Nov–April Mon–Fri 9.30am–3.30pm • £3 • ☎ 01493 850585

Five minutes' walk from South Quay, the Smokehouse Museum and Pottery, housed in an old herring smokehouse built of ships' masts and timbers up against the medieval town wall, is a fantastic place, run by Ernie Childs and his wife for thirty-odd years and showcasing the innards of the old building along with a treasure-trove of nautical bits and pieces – nets, rudders, ropes, ships-in-bottles, you name it. Ernie is a mine of information on the building and indeed on any aspect of Yarmouth life and history, and will talk you through both, in between painting the sea scenes that hang on the walls and firing the commemorative pots they sell in the gift shop. There are also a couple of constantly running films on the Yarmouth fishing industry and Yarmouth in general, but perhaps best of all is the building itself, infused with the smell of fish and the scent of the sea.

Time and Tide Museum

Blackfriars Rd, NR30 3BX • Mon–Fri: April–Oct 9.30am–5pm; Nov–March 9.30am–3.30pm • £4.80 • ☎ 01493 743930

More or less opposite the Smokehouse Museum, the **Time and Tide Museum** is also housed in an old smokehouse, though it's an altogether slicker affair than its lesser-known rival, with a host of awards to its name. Deservedly so, for it's a great and engaging museum, that also tells the story of the Yarmouth fishing industry and its demise, with exhibits on the smoking and curing process, showing the brine baths and smoke room, another giving a feel for life on board a drifter, and a mock-up of a

Yarmouth street in the nineteenth century, all convincingly documented and dramatized on the audio guide. Upstairs there are displays on the rise of Yarmouth as a seaside resort, the two world wars and the contemporary town and port. All in all a thoughtful and absorbing museum.

The seafront

Great Yarmouth's **seafront** stretches for about a mile north to south along Marine Parade, and is a fairly predictable mix of B&Bs, amusement arcades and cheap restaurants, anchored by the Britannia Pier to the north and the Wellington Pier to the south. It's not unpleasant, and compared to much of the Heritage Quarter feels positively vibrant, but the real attraction is the **beach** beyond, an unbroken strand of golden sand where you can ride donkeys, play crazy golf or just flop.

Sea Life

Marine Parade, NR30 3AH • Daily 10am–3pm • £13.95, children £10, family tickets £40 (25 percent cheaper if booked online) • ☎ 0871 423 2110, Ⓦ visitsealife.com/great-yarmouth

A worthy part of the nationwide family of aquariums, Yarmouth's **Sea Life** has an array of tanks of sharks, rays, penguins, sea horses and lots of fish. It's not a huge attraction, but it's very well done, and the staff are helpful and enthusiastic and on hand to answer questions and deliver regular talks and feeding times.

Merrivale Model Village

Marine Parade, NR30 3JG • End March to end Oct daily from 10am, closing time varies • £6.50, children £4.75, family tickets £20 • ☎ 01493 842097, Ⓦ greatyarmouthmodelvillage.co.uk

Right on the seafront just a few minutes' walk from Sea Life, the **Merrivale Model Village** is great, with paths that wind past all manner of creations – churches hosting weddings, suburban streets witnessing robberies, villages and ruined abbeys. A railway winds through the various buildings and across bridges and through tunnels, past down-at-heel hotels and shopping parades, and when you've had enough you can enjoy a game of mini golf. What could be nicer?

Amazonia

Central Seafront, NR30 3AH • Feb–Nov daily 10am–5pm • £4.99, children £4.50, family tickets £16 • ☎ 01493 842202, Ⓦ amazonia-worldofreptiles.net

Right on the seafront, you can view around seventy different species of reptiles at **Amazonia** – snakes and lizards, crocodiles and alligators, along with spiders, scorpions, tree frogs and cane toads. It's a small display but quite well done, with an emphasis on conservation and an interested and informed staff who will answer any questions you may have.

Pleasure Beach

South Beach Parade, NR30 3EH • July to early Sept daily 11am–6pm; also open selected days and times March–June & Sept–Oct – see website • Tokens £1, each ride 1–3 tokens, unlimited ride wristbands £16.50–19.50, family ticket £60–70 ☎ 01493 844585, Ⓦ pleasure-beach.co.uk

If the beach and its associated attractions begin to pall, you can take in the rides at Yarmouth's **Pleasure Beach** at the far southern end of Marine Parade, where there is a roller coaster, log flume ride and much more besides. And if it's all a bit much and you're after a more sedate seafront experience, the **Pleasure Beach Gardens** just beyond should more or less fit the bill.

ARRIVAL AND INFORMATION   GREAT YARMOUTH

By train Yarmouth's train station is on the edge of the town centre on Acle New Rd, not far from the mouth of

Breydon Water on the far side of the Bure. Trains for Norwich every 30–60min, via Acle, Reedham Brundall and sometimes Berney Arms (see p.108).

By boat The town's rather unprepossessing moorings are on the south side of the river, a 10min walk from the centre of town, at Great Yarmouth Yacht Station, Tar Works Rd ☎01493 842794. They cost £12/night and have a range of facilities – water, electricity, toilets, etc.

By bus Buses stop at the Market Gates Rd Bus Station in the centre of town. There are buses to Norwich and Lowestoft (roughly every 20min; about 45min to both).

Tourist office On the seafront at 25 Marine Parade (Mon–Sat 9.30am–5pm, Sun 10am–5pm; ☎01493 84636, Ⓦgreat-yarmouth.co.uk).

ACCOMMODATION

Yarmouth doesn't have a great choice of accommodation, but look hard and you'll find something to suit, and the town does make a good base for visiting attractions in the surrounding area.

GREAT YARMOUTH

★ **Andover House** 28–30 Camperdown, NR30 3JB ☎01493 8434490, Ⓦandoverhouse.co.uk. Just back from the seafront on the edge of the Heritage Quarter, *Andover House* is a self-styled boutique B&B situated on one of Yarmouth's most elegant streets. It has simply yet stylishly furnished double rooms and a really good restaurant too. £85

The Hamilton 23–24 North Drive, NR30 4EW ☎01493 844662, Ⓦhamilton-hotel.co.uk. The rooms are quite stylish at this updated Yarmouth guesthouse at the northern end of the seafront, and good value. £60

AROUND GREAT YARMOUTH

Breydon Water Holiday Park Butt Lane, Burgh Castle, NR31 9QB ☎0844 770 9350, Ⓦpark-resorts. com/gy. On the western edge of town next door to Burgh Castle Roman fort, this is the best place to camp in the vicinity, with reasonable facilities – a bar and restaurant

and small pool among them. It's also close to good walks by the river and around the fort.

Church Farm Camping Park Church Rd, Burgh Castle, NR31 9QG ☎07979 427121. Small, tucked-away campsite right next to the pub of the same name – very quiet, with fairly basic amenities, but the pub is very close by for food and drink, and its location close by the river is great. Open July & Aug only. Pitch for two adults around £10

Fritton House Church Lane, Fritton, NR31 9HA ☎01493 484008, Ⓦfrittonhouse.co.uk. Right by Fritton Lake, this well-preserved Georgian house has nine large, light-filled and beautifully finished rooms, as well as a two-bedroom suite that would suite a family or two friendly couples. There's access to the lakeside and formal gardens and indeed all the walks around the Somerleyton estate, and a good bar-restaurant (see below), making it quite a blissful place to stay all in all. £120

EATING AND DRINKING

GREAT YARMOUTH

The Lounge Andover House Hotel, 28–30 Camperdown, NR30 3JB ☎01493 8434490. The *Andover House* hotel's restaurant is arguably central Yarmouth's best, a self-consciously slick joint with a short menu that's a mixture of well-presented classics like duck spring rolls, caesar salad and fish and chips, and slightly more adventurous options such as tenderloin of pork with parsnip puree, decorated with shavings, jus and various fussy additions. Overall, though, the food is really good, and moderately priced too, with starters for around £7, mains £14–20, and a good wine list too. Lunch Tues–Sat noon–2pm, dinner Mon–Sat 6.30–9pm.

Olive Garden 42 Regent Rd, NR30 2AJ ☎01493 844641, Ⓦolivegardenrestaurant.co.uk. Restaurant at the seafront end of Regent Rd that specializes in well-presented dishes with a Greek theme – beef stifado, lamb kleftiko, good steaks, fried halloumi, skewered scallops, and lots of meat and fish platters to share. Starters around £3.95, mains from £10.95, but they also do lunch specials for £5.95 and dinner deals for £9.50 before 7pm. Mon

6–9pm, Tues–Thurs 6.30–9.30pm, Fri & Sat 6–10pm.

Quayside Plaza 9 South Quay, NR30 2QH ☎07500 740827. Good café serving breakfasts and lunches – salads, sandwiches and lots of other more substantial options from £6.95, including burgers, steaks, pan-fried sea bass and locally smoked fish served with ratatouille and potatoes. It incorporates a store selling oriental furniture and decorative objects. Mon–Sat 8am–4pm, Sat & Sun 10am–4pm. Also Fri & Sat 7pm–late during summer.

Red Herring 24–25 Havelock Rd, NR30 3HQ ☎01493 853384. Locals' pub in the heart of old Yarmouth, with a good choice of local ales and lots of pictures of old Yarmouth on the walls. There's not the warmest of welcomes, but persevere – after a couple of pints they'll be challenging you to a game of pool.

Seafood Restaurant 85 North Quay, NR30 1JF ☎01493 856009, Ⓦtheseafood.co.uk. Long-running, popular family-run restaurant that serves the freshest fish you could imagine – plus great cheesecake for afters. Mon–Sat noon–1.45pm & 6.30–10.30pm.

Wrights 24 Regent Rd, NR30 2AF ☎01493 842658.

HAVING A FLUTTER

The flat racing season at Great Yarmouth's **racecourse** (☎01493 842 527, ⓦgreatyarmouth-racecourse.co.uk) lasts roughly from mid-April until the end of October, during which time there are meetings every one to two weeks on average. The course is just north of the centre on Jellicoe Rd – follow Marine Parade and its northerly extension, North Drive, for a little over a mile and you're there.

2

Traditional restaurant on the main drag of Regent Rd, that's a good option for lunch, and a cut above most of the places along the seafront, from which it's only five minutes' walk. Try the chicken Maryland, or a steak. Daily 11am–7.30pm.

AROUND GREAT YARMOUTH

Berney Arms Inn Berney Arms, NR30 1SB ☎01493 700303. Right on the riverside path, close to the junction of the Yare and Waveney rivers and only accessible on foot or by water or by train (see p.108), this is as remote a pub as you'll find. The food is nothing special, but it's a cosy, unchanged sort of place, with good ales on tap and a warm welcome to dogs and most humans. Sit outside and watch the world go by on the river.

Church Farm Inn Church Rd, Burgh Castle, NR31 9QG ☎01493 789015, ⓦchurchfarmcountryinn.co.uk. Large, recently renovated pub that enjoys splendid views across the water to Berney Arms, and a large terrace to enjoy its excellent food from too – everything from lentil nut roast to confit of guinea fowl (£9–13), and sandwiches and lighter

fare at lunchtime. Daily noon–2.30pm & 6–9pm.

★ **Fritton House** Church Lane, Fritton, NR31 9HA ☎01493 484008, ⓦfrittonhouse.co.uk. Pleasant hotel bar-restaurant, set in beautiful grounds, whose short menu of half a dozen mains and starters changes daily. Light bites, tapas and sandwiches at lunchtime for £5–6, as well as the handful of hot dishes for around £14.95 that they serve at dinner. Think slow roast belly of pork or pan-fried sea bass, with grilled goat's cheese with beetroot to start. Daily noon–3pm & 6–10pm.

SOMERLEYTON

Duke's Head Slugs Lane, Somerleyton, NR32 5QR ☎01502 730281, ⓦdukesheadsomerleyton.co.uk. Right out by the Waveney at Somerleyton Hall, this is a great place to stop by for lunch if you're out that way, with really good food served from short menus that focus on simple dishes well executed: burgers, fish pie, fish and chips, pasta and so on– all for £10–14. Mon–Sat 11.30am–11pm, Sun noon–10.30pm.

Around Great Yarmouth

There are many who would advise you to avoid staying over in Great Yarmouth, but the fact is there is plenty to see in the **surrounding area** if you do.

Caister-on-Sea

Just north of Yarmouth, there's not much to **CAISTER-ON-SEA**, which is a downbeat extension of its larger neighbour, and home to the town's racecourse. However, its beach is nice enough, fringed with modest dunes and a beach café, and with the **Caister Lifeboat Station** (April–Oct Wed & Sun 10am–3pm; £2) just behind, famous for being one of only two non-RNLI stations in the UK (the other is at Hemsby). There was a notorious lifeboat disaster here in 1901, when the lifeboat was launched for a rescue and then forced back onto the beach by heavy seas and overturned, killing nine of the twelve crew. During an inquest into the incident the survivors were asked why they set out, to which they got the memorable answer: "Caister men never turn back" – which is how the nearby **pub**, on Manor Road, got its name. The thirty turbines of **Scroby Sands Wind Farm** are clearly visible from the beach and provide power to around 40,000 homes, although they don't seem to put off the seals you can often see offshore. The town is also at pains to publicize its Roman connections, and the **Roman Fort**, back towards the main road, although it's a modest set of ruins. The town's other major sight, **Caister Castle** (mid-May to Sept daily except Sat 10am–4.30pm; £9.50), is more interesting, a set of elegantly crumbling ruins just outside the town that hide a vintage car collection that ranges from the first-ever Ford Fiesta to a Lotus that Jim Clark drove in the 1960s.

Hemsby

To the north of Caister, **HEMSBY** is more of the same – seafront tack and caravan parks – but you may want to stop by if you're here during the **Hemsby Herring Festival** at the end of August: a grand term for what is basically the local lifeboat service cooking up herrings on the beach. They're rolled in oats and cooked in beef dripping, and after sampling one of these even Hemsby may begin to seem attractive.

Burgh Castle

Open year-round • Free; EH • ⓦ norfarchtrust.org.uk

Burgh Castle is both a suburb of Yarmouth and the site of Burgh Castle Roman fort, a remarkably intact example of an early fourth-century AD Roman fort, with gaspingly thick walls and the odd parapet to clamber about on. It's in much better shape than its cousin in Caister, with three of its four walls still standing, and its splendid location couldn't be more different, a beautiful, remote spot, overlooking the River Waveney, which spurs off the Yare just beyond Berney Arms and the marshes on the far side. They've built a visitors' car park nearby, but the numbers were never going to reach the level it deserves and you may as well park near the *Church Farm* pub (see p.107) and take in the round-towered church of **St Peter and St Paul** before moving onto the castle just beyond. After that you can walk down to the river and join the Angles Way footpath, taking it back alongside Breydon Water into Yarmouth, or – more appealingly – follow it down past the Burgh Castle marina and *Fisherman's Inn* towards Fritton Lake (see opposite), Somerleyton (see opposite), or all the way to Oulton Broad (see p.270).

Breydon Water

RSPB reserve open year-round • ⓦ rspb.org.uk/reserves/guide/b/berneybreydon

The large expanse of **Breydon Water** forms the barrier between the northern and southern Broads, although it isn't in fact a broad at all, but a wide tidal estuary, where the rivers Yare, Bure and Waveney meet. It's over three miles long and about a mile across, and is very shallow – boats must stick closely to the marked channel or risk running aground. It is one of the Broads' bleakest spots, but is also an RSPB nature reserve, and there is a bird hide on the north shore at the eastern end, which you can reach by following the Weavers' Way footpath from Great Yarmouth train station. You can follow this further along as far as the *Berney Arms* pub and the Berney Arms windmill beyond – a total distance of about five miles.

Berney Arms

Access to windmill on pre-booked tours only • ☏ 01493 857900, ⓦ www.english-heritage.org.uk/daysout/properties/berney-arms-windmill

At the far end of Breydon Water, on the northern bank of the River Yare, the nineteenth-century windmill at **Berney Arms** is a landmark for miles around, and forms the focus of an odd settlement of mill, pub and – across the fields – train station, and not much else. The mill is owned by English Heritage and is open to the public, while the pub (see p.107) is Norfolk's most remote inasmuch as it can only be reached on foot, or by river or train.

As for the **train station**, it's one of the country's most peculiar, and it's a miracle it exists at all: situated on the Wherry Line between Norwich and Yarmouth, it's a request stop that's not near anywhere, even the windmill and pub are about half a mile and a mile or so away respectively, along the Weavers' Way path. The station opened in the mid-nineteenth century, on the insistence of Thomas Trench Berney, who owned the land that the railway company wanted to build their track on. He made it a condition that the station be built here "in perpetuity", and the company had no choice but to comply. After a while it became evident that no one got on or off at Berney Arms, and an agreement was hashed out that trains only stopped three times a week, Berney was paid compensation, and everyone was happy. Now trains stop at Berney Arms daily

---

THE WALK FROM HALVERGATE TO BERNEY ARMS

The most satisfying way to get to Berney Arms isn't in fact by train, but by **walking** from the nearby village of **Halvergate** – about three miles in all, and an easy 45-to 60-minute hike across the marshes following a part of the **Weavers' Way** (see p.65). You can park your car on the farm track just east of the village, and then pick up the path which leads southeast past the disused Mutton's drainage mill – a glorious route on a bright, sunny day. The way is reasonably well marked – make sure you keep to it as at certain times of year the ground can be boggy – and crosses the rail line at Berney Arms station before hitting the river at the windmill; the pub is a few hundred yards northeast along the river from here.

2

– infrequently, but there's plenty to do if you're stuck in between trains. Failing that, you can follow the riverside path all the way down to Reedham, seven miles away, which follows a part of the Wherryman's Way and takes about two and a half hours.

Somerleyton Hall and Gardens

Lowestoft, Suffolk, NR32 5QQ • Mid-April to Sept Thurs & Sun 11.30am–3.30pm; mid-July to Sept also Tues & Wed; Oct gardens, maze and tea rooms only • Hall and gardens £8.95, gardens only £5.50, children £4.95/3.50, family tickets £25 • ☎ 01502 734901, ⓦ somerleyton.co.uk

The Somerleyton estate crosses the border between Norfolk and Suffolk, while the building itself, **Somerleyton Hall**, is a bit of a fake – a grand mock-Jacobean mansion rebuilt in the 1840s for the railway entrepreneur Morton Peto, and since 1862 the home of the Crossley family. Fake or not, it's an impressive dwelling, and if you're lucky enough to coincide with its limited opening times, you can see the great ballroom, the parlour's oak carvings by Grinling Gibbons, the library and the family's collections of paintings and sculpture. Be sure to take in the gardens too, at their best in summer when the herbaceous borders and roses are in flower, but with lots more besides – walled gardens, glasshouses designed by Crystal Palace architect, Joseph Paxton, a super-long pergola and a fantastic, very large maze – all harking back to the estate's Victorian heyday. Down by the river you can see the restored Herringfleet Windmill and enjoy lunch and a pint at the estate's pub, the *Duke's Head* (see p.107).

Fritton Lake

Church Lane, Fritton, NR31 9HA • April–Sept Sat & Sun and school hols 10am–5pm • £8.50, children £4.50 • ☎ 01493 488288, ⓦ somerleyton.co.uk.

Part of the Somerleyton Hall estate, just across the border in Norfolk, **Fritton Lake**, off the main Beccles road, is a huge adventure playground, with slides, sandpits and all the usual attractions, but on a much bigger scale than you may be used to. It also offers rowboats and launch trips on the lake, nature trails around the lake as well as fishing, golf and other activities – some included in the price, some extra.

St Edmund, Fritton

Church Lane, Fritton, NR31 9EZ • ⓦ www.fritton.churchnorfolk.com

On the road to Fritton Lake, Fritton village's round-towered parish church of **St Edmund** is a very ancient church, not far off a thousand years old, perhaps originally a wayside chapel that was enlarged in the fourteenth century. It's a small, simple church, but has a number of Saxon and Norman features, namely an unusually shaped apse, decorated with twelfth- and fourteenth-century fresco fragments depicting St Edmund's martyrdom, a giant fresco of St Christopher carrying Christ on his shoulders, in the nave, and a simple medieval rood screen separating the two.

Redwings Horse Sanctuary

Caldecott Visitor Centre • April–Oct daily 10am–5pm • Free • ☎ 0870 0400033, ⓦ www.redwings.co.uk

Redwings is a nationwide concern and this is its Norfolk base, opposite Fritton Lake between Great Yarmouth and Beccles. Their mission is to rescue horses, ponies and donkeys who have suffered neglect or cruelty and they rescue around 150 animals a year. Visitors can get up close to the animals, watch horse care demonstrations and go on tractor rides, and there's a café and shop. The centre is also dog- and wheelchair-friendly.

St Olaves

A couple of miles northwest of Somerleyton, right by the crossing over the Waveney River, the small village of **ST OLAVES** is an odd mixture: strictly practical down by the river, where boatyards and their sheds aren't especially a pretty sight, while also being an ancient village which grew up around its thirteenth-century **priory**, which was named after an evangelical Norwegian king known for his friendly greeting, "Baptism or Death!" You can wander around what's left of the priory (not much), afterwards taking the weight off at the *Bell* by the river – which claims to be Broadland's oldest pub and serves predictable but good pub food. There are free moorings, too, if you're eating at the pub.

Reedham and around

Set on high ground above the fast-flowing River Yare, **REEDHAM** is probably the most attractive spot on the southern Broads, with a busy and appealing quayside and a handful of pubs and other attractions. It's famous for its swing railway bridge, but otherwise there's no way to cross the river here other than at Reedham's equally famous **chain ferry** a little way upstream, indeed there's no other crossing on the Yare between Norwich and Great Yarmouth.

Pettitts Animal Adventure Park

Church Rd, NR13 3UA • End March to end Oct daily 10am–5pm • Children & adults £9.95 • ☎ 01493 700084, ⓦ pettittsadventurepark.co.uk

Just strolling Reedham's quayside and watching the boats come and go is a pleasant enough way to while away an hour or two, but many people come here for **Pettitts Animal Adventure Park**, up above the quayside on the edge of the village, one of the most significant attractions hereabouts. It was formerly a small farm for kids, where you could pet goats and ponies, and to some extent it still is, with lots of other animals besides – pigs, rabbits, raccoons, some slightly sad owls, many more, including a small reptile house. But the emphasis these days is on the rides: a mini railway loops around most of the site, and there are various fairground attractions, slides and a big adventure playground. Small children will like it well enough, but Disneyworld it ain't.

Humpy Dumpty Brewery

Church Rd, NR13 3TZ • Easter–Oct noon–5pm; Nov & Dec Sat & Sun 12.30–4.30pm • ☎ 01493 701818, ⓦ humptydumpty.typepad.com.

Immediately next door to Pettits, the **Humpy Dumpty Brewery** is a little bit of compensation for the mums and dads who have trudged around Pettits, an excellent small brewery that has been going for just over a decade, and whose wide range of draft and bottled beers are on sale all over East Anglia and the Midlands. On quiet days you may be able to join a brewery tour but otherwise make do with its shop, which as well

---

REEDHAM FERRY

Reedham's **ferry** has operated on this spot since the early seventeenth century, and it still runs year-round (Mon–Fri 7.30am–10pm, Sat & Sun 8am–10pm; cars £3.90, day return £7, motorbikes £2, foot passengers 50p), though at busy times be prepared for a wait – it only takes two cars at a time.

as selling Humpty Dumpty's beers also stocks ales from other Norfolk brewers, local ciders and a few Belgian beers.

St John the Baptist

Church Rd, NR13 3TZ

Reedham's church of **St John the Baptist** is worth popping into to see its modern stained-glass windows – the church was gutted by fire in the 1980s and has been restored since – and various memorials to the Berney family, best of which is the late sixteenth-century tomb showing Henry Berney, kneeling in prayer surrounded by members of his family.

2

ARRIVAL AND DEPARTURE
REEDHAM AND AROUND

By train Reedham's station is in the top part of the village, at the junction of Station Rd and Ferry Rd, and is on the main line between Norwich and Great Yarmouth with connections to Reedham and Acle among other places.
By bus Buses – to Brundall and Acle – leave from the train station.

By boat There are free moorings on the Riverside quay in Reedham, very handy for all the village's facilities, and a lively spot in summer.

ACCOMMODATION

The Pyghtle 26a The Hills, NR13 3AR ☎01493 701262, ⓦreedham-thepyghtle.co.uk. This comfy B&B consists of a kitchen, sitting room and bedroom in a separate part of the house – a bargain, and including breakfast, though you can always self-cater if you prefer. **£50**

Reedham Ferry Touring Park NR13 3HA ☎01493 700999, ⓦreedhamferry.co.uk. Run by the same folk who run the ferry and the *Ferry Inn*, this campsite is handy for Reedham and a good site in its own right, with the pub on its doorstep. Pitches **£13–20**

EATING AND DRINKING

Cupcakes Café 48 Riverside, NR13 3TE ☎01493 700713, ⓦcupcakes-reedham.co.uk. A few doors down from the *Lord Nelson* on the quay, this is a small coffee shop, serving toasted sandwiches, jackets and the like. March–Oct Sat–Wed 10am–4pm.

Lord Nelson 38 Riverside, NR13 3TE ☎01493 701548. ⓦlordnelsonpub.com. Right on the staithe, the *Nelson* is Reedham's most obvious place for a pint, and cosy it is too, with a good selection of real ales and reasonable food. It also puts on live music, and hosts the annual Reedham Beer Festival every August, with around sixty real ales and

ciders, including a good selection from the Humpy Dumpy Brewery. Open for breakfast 7.30am–11.30am, lunch noon–2.30pm and dinner 6–9pm.

The Ship 19 Riverside, NR13 3TQ ☎01493 700287. Festooned with flower baskets, and right by the railway bridge on the river, this has a good choice of pub grub (including a kids' menu and various daily specials), and a good riverfront garden with children's playground. Most mains – lamb shanks, chicken curry, steak pie – go for around £7.95. Daily noon–2.30pm & 6.30–9.30pm.

Brundall and around

BRUNDALL is one of the major boating venues on the Southern Broads, and very easy to reach. Yet it's a disappointing kind of place, strung out along the river, with no real centre other than the area around the train station and the boatyards beyond, where the riverbank is lined with one holiday chalet after another – not one of the Broads' finest moments. You may come to pick up a boat, however, and for one other, unexpected reason: it's home to the region's premier restaurant, *Lavender House*.

Strumpshaw Fen

Strumpshaw Station • Daily: autumn & winter 9am–4pm; spring & summer 9am–5pm • £2.50, children 50p • ☎01603 715191, ⓦrspb .org.uk/reserves/guide/s/strumpshawfen

Just across the railway line on the edge of Strumpshaw village (you park on one side and the fen is on the other), the RSPB reserve of **Strumpshaw Fen** is one of the best places to spot birds in Broadland, and is set up with well-maintained trails that take you through a variety of habitats – woodland, meadows and reedy fenland. There's a hide at the reception, and two others around the reserve, and although sometimes busy it can be glorious, the air rich with birdsong, and the reedbeds and water stretching far into the distance. It's worth taking the path through the woods and then along the river into the fenland area to get the full flavour of the place.

Strumpshaw Steam Museum

Strumpshaw, NR13 4HR • July–Sept daily except Sat 10.30am–3.30pm; May & June Wed & Sun 10.30am–3.30pm, plus assorted Wed & Sun in April • £5, children £2 • ☎ 01603 714535, ⓦ www.strumpshawsteammuseum.co.uk

This family-owned museum just outside the village was opened in the 1950s by Wesley Key and is now run by his grandson William. It displays steam and traction engines – one of the largest collections in the UK – and has a narrow-gauge railway and various countryside trails – not to mention the obligatory gift shop and café. They also host an annual and very well-attended steam rally every late-May bank holiday. Good, homespun fun.

Buckenham Marshes

Buckenham Station • Always open • Free • ☎ 01603 715191, ⓦ rspb.org.uk/reserves/guide/b/buckenham

A little further along the river from Strumpshaw Fen, another RSPB reserve, **Buckenham Marshes**, stretches out to the river from Buckenham train station, where you can park and cross the line and then follow the path to the main hide, which is perfectly placed for the best of the marsh's bird-and wildlife. It's another beautiful spot, although it doesn't quite have the diversity of landscape of its neighbour. It's big on geese, and boasts the only regular winter flock of bean geese in England between November and February, as well as lots of wigeons. Beyond the hide is the river, and you can follow this along through adjacent Cantley Marshes to Cantley (around a 40min walk), where you can pick up the train back.

ARRIVAL AND DEPARTURE   BRUNDALL AND AROUND

By train There are two train stations in Brundall: the main one, down by the river, and Brundall Gardens, the next stop west. Both are on the main line between Norwich and Great Yarmouth, with connections to Reedham and Acle among other places.

By bus Buses stop on Station Rd and connect with Lingwood, Acle, Wroxham and Great Yarmouth, among other destinations.

By boat There are moorings at Brundall bay Marina and free moorings at Church Marsh, opposite the *Ferry House* pub.

ACCOMMODATION

The Station House Station Rd, Lingwood, NR13 4AZ ☎ 01603 715872, ⓦ stationhouseonline.com. At the village between Brundall and Acle, Lingwood's Victorian former train station has been put to good use as a private house and bed and breakfast, with three double rooms. And trains still run on the line, so it's perfect if you're touring without a car. **£55**

EATING AND DRINKING

BRUNDALL
Lavender House 9 The Street, NR13 5AA ☎ 01603 712215, ⓦ thelavenderhouse.co.uk. This lovely thatched restaurant in the centre of the village is reason enough to come to Brundall, the domain of celebrated chef Richard Hughes, and serving an excellent-value three-course menu for £39.95, and a tasting menu for £58. The food is complex

yet hearty, with lots of amuse-bouches and tasters between courses, and a very serious emphasis on Norfolk produce. Menus change regularly but typical dishes include: sea salt-grilled mackerel with beetroot, orange and horseradish crème fraiche followed by roast Gressingham duck, duck confit cake, potato blinis and prune, apple and calvados shallots. All in all one of the county's finest culinary experiences. Tues–Sat 7pm– midnight, plus Fri 12.30–2.30pm.

STRUMPSHAW
Shoulder of Mutton Norwich Rd, NR13 4NT ☎ 01603

712274. Good, unpretentious and friendly locals' pub with a cheapish pub grub menu featuring burgers, gammon steaks and the like. Mon–Sat noon–2pm & 7–9pm, Sun noon–2pm.

Loddon, Chedgrave and around

The adjacent villages of **LODDON** and **CHEDGRAVE** together make up one of the southern Broads' most popular boating destinations – pleasant villages both, although of the two Loddon has most life. There are free moorings at Loddon Staithe, and the main street leads up the hill from here to the main part of the village, where the flint parish church of **Holy Trinity** cuts an imposing presence off the main square (car park, really). The church interior is equally grand, the main feature a beautiful rood screen depicting a number of saints, including, oddly, a panel showing one St William of Norwich – a political addition, for St William was a posthumously canonized child who, it was claimed, was sacrificed by Jews in medieval Norwich and as such became a focus of anti-Semitic feeling at the time.

In Chedgrave, **All Saint's** church is set on a mound above the river, tucked away behind a housing estate, and is unusual in that the roof of its tower is thatched. The building is Norman in origin, with an elaborately carved Norman arched doorway and stained glass from Rouen Cathedral.

The Chet and Hardley Flood

You can reach the River **Chet** by following a path from the main road (next to *Chedgrave House B&B*) that edges past the boatyards to pick up another path that leads along the north bank of the river (you can also reach this from Chedgrave's church). The path leads in about twenty minutes to a thin strand between the river and the wide expanse of **Hardley Flood**, where there's a bird hide, and then continues on to Hardley Cross – basically the marker post between the district of Norwich and Great Yarmouth – and the Yare near Reedham, where it leads off left towards Hardley Marshes and beyond to Langley Dike, which you can follow up to Langley Abbey.

Langley Abbey

Near Loddon, NR14 6DG • Tues–Sat 10am–4pm • £4 • ☎ 01508 480289, ⓦ langleyabbey.co.uk

Two miles north of Chedgrave are the ruins of **Langley Abbey**, a Premonstratensian monastery that was founded in 1195 and dissolved in 1536, shortly after which it was taken over by the Berney family. There's not a great deal left, just a few stretches of wall and a ruined arches, but a couple of buildings are more intact and are given over to exhibitions on the abbey's history, and the abbot's quarters upstairs. It's rather antiseptically restored, however, and the main event is really the shop and the restaurant next door, which sell and serve beef from the abbey's longhorn herd; the restaurant does a celebrated brunch, and sandwiches and salads. You can also stroll down to the free moorings at nearby Langley Dike, and follow the path for ten minutes or so down to the Yare – part of the Wherryman's Way.

Surlingham and Church Marsh Nature Reserve

ⓦ rspb.org.uk/reserves/guide/s/surlingham/index.aspx

North of Loddon, just a few hundred yards from the Yare, **SURLINGHAM** village is pretty enough, and well placed for great walking, but it's most often visited for the

pubs on either side– the *Ferry House* and *Coldham Hall* (see p.116). You can do a relatively easy loop walk, just over a mile in all, starting at the *Ferry House*, following the river and continuing through **Church Marsh Nature Reserve** to Surlingham's small and immaculate church of **St Mary**, with its Norman door and hexagonal topped round tower. Just beyond here, on high ground overlooking the marshes, is the ruined Norman church of **St Saviour**, a gorgeous spot, where local naturalist (and conserver of nearby Wheatfen Broad) Ted Ellis chose to be buried – and who can blame him?

Rockland Broad

Rockland Broad is one of the least-known Broads, but also one of the most beautiful – and characteristic – Broadland's landscapes. The light and the views are glorious, and a well-laid path runs half a mile or so around one side, where you can spot all kinds of birdlife from the hide in its far corner, before continuing on along Fleet Dike, linking the broad with the main river, which you can follow all the way along to the *Beachamp Arms*, opposite Buckenham Marshes on the opposite bank, about a half-an-hour walk – following, in effect, the Wherryman's Way. There are free moorings at Rockland staithe, where the path starts, and a car park, although the *New Inn* opposite has sadly closed down.

Wheatfen Broad

The Ted Ellis Trust, Wheatfen Broad, The Cover, Surlingham, NR14 7AL • ☎ 01508 538036, Ⓦ wheatfen.org.

The area on the far (northern) side of Rockland Broad and Fleet Dike is **Wheatfen Broad**, home to a nature reserve initiated by the naturalist Ted Ellis, who made his home here while he was keeper of the natural history collection at Norwich Castle. He lived in the thatched cottage by the entrance to the reserve, and was one of the most vocal chroniclers and advocates of Broadland's beauty, and the need to preserve it for the future. Since his death in 1986, the marshes and watery channels of Wheatfen have been a nature reserve, with a series of paths down to the river – about an hour's walk there and back – that give you some appreciation of what Ted and his wife Phyllis (who lived here until her death in 2004) saw in this magical place.

St Margaret, Hales

Church Lane Hales, NR14 6QL • Ⓦ visitchurches.org.uk/Ourchurches/Completelistofchurches/St-Margarets-Church-Hales-Norfolk

The church of **St Margaret** just outside the village of **HALES**, a mile or so southeast of Loddon, is typical of the churches in this part of Norfolk, but is perhaps the best. Abandoned in the 1970s due to its remote location and now owned by the Churches Conservation Trust, it's a gorgeous, truly out-there spot, and feels very old indeed, the exterior dominated by the finely carved sandstone shapes and tendrils of its Norman north door. Inside is small and bare, but there are traces of fourteenth-century wall paintings and a fifteenth-century font, carved with lions and roses and angels presenting shields.

Raveningham Hall and Gardens

Raveningham, NR14 6NS • April–Aug Thurs 11am–4pm, plus bank hol Sun & Mon 2–5pm • £4 • ☎ 01508 548152.

About a mile or so east of Hales, nineteenth-century **Raveningham Hall** is the home of the Bacon family, who open their extensive gardens to the public on selected days during summer. The gardens were developed, more or less from scratch, by the mother of the current incumbent, Priscilla Bacon, who lived here for fifty years and created a series of very large herbaceous borders, and replanted and restored the eighteenth-century walled garden, herb garden and rose garden. Since her death in 2000, the Victorian glasshouses have been refurbished and the gardens are dotted with a number of contemporary sculptures – all in all well worth a visit.

St Mary, Haddiscoe

Church Lane, Haddiscoe, NR14 6PB • ⓦ www.haddiscoe.churchnorfolk.com

There's no reason to stop in **HADDISCOE** other than to eat (see p.116) or visit its church of **St Mary**, which occupies a commanding position on high ground on the edge of the village – a round-towered, originally Saxon building but with Norman features, notably the tower windows and the main doorway, which is fringed with decorative carving and is topped by a relief said to depict St Peter. Inside is pretty bare, but it's worth peeking in to see a fine and clear remnant of its original paintwork in the nave – a figure of St Christopher holding Christ.

Burgh St Peter

A few miles southeast of Haddiscoe, the village of **BURGH ST PETER** feels very out of the way, and it is, but just beyond the village the **Waveney River Centre** (see p.67), is a hub of boat and tourist traffic, a complex of moorings (£9/night), campsite and cabins, and with lots of facilities, including a heated indoor pool, a store and a pub – the *Waveney Inn*. Just beyond there's the distinctive ziggurat-like tower of the flint and brick church of **St Mary the Virgin**, a long, thin thatched building whose odd tower was added in 1795 to serve as the local Boycott family mausoleum. The church is intriguing inside too, with a late fourteenth-century font decorated with rosettes and grotesque faces. Interestingly, it was a member of the Boycott family – Charles – who gave the word "boycott" to the English language in the late nineteenth century, when his brutal enforcement of rents and eviction of tenants led to him being ostracized – or "boycotted" – by the local community.

ARRIVAL AND DEPARTURE   LODDON, CHEDGRAVE AND AROUND

By bus The fast #X2 buses between Norwich and Lowestoft, via Beccles, stop in Loddon every half an hour.
By boat There are free moorings at Loddon staithe and a little further up the river at Chedgrave Common, within easy walking distance of the village.

ACCOMMODATION

Chedgrave House Norwich Rd, Loddon, NR14 6HB ☎ 01508 521095, ⓦ chedgrave-house.co.uk. Just before the bridge at Loddon staithe, this is a homely B&B with three double bedrooms, including a very good breakfast. **£60**

Hall Green Farm Norton Rd, Loddon, NR14 6DT ☎ 01508 522039, ⓦ hallgreenfarm.co.uk. Just outside Loddon, this B&B has three very comfortable en-suite double rooms, each decorated with a different theme, in a self-contained converted dairy next door to the main house. Includes free wi-fi and an excellent breakfast, although you have to stay a minimum of two nights at weekends between April and September. **£80**

EATING AND DRINKING

LODDON

★ **Rosie Lee's Tearoom** 37a Bridge St, Loddon, NR14 6NA ☎ 01508 520204. Opposite Loddon staithe, and a bit of local institution, *Rosie Lee's* is a great place for breakfast or lunch, with owner Caroline doing a good line in sandwiches, cakes, and light lunches using the fish fresh from her fishmonger's up the street. She sells work by local artists too. Mon–Sat 7.30am–5pm, Sun 8.30am–5pm.

CHEDGRAVE

White Horse 5 Norwich Rd, Chedgrave, NR14 6ND ☎ 01508 520250, ⓦ whitehorsechedgrave.co.uk. Friendly local pub that's perhaps the town's best place for dinner, with a large menu of burgers, steaks, mussels, lasagne and lots of veggie options – mains around £10.95–13.95. Jackets, baguettes and various sharing platters available at lunchtime too for around £4–5. Daily noon–3pm & 6–9pm.

2

SURLINGHAM

Coldham Hall NR14 7AN ☎01508 538366, ⓦ coldhamhalltavern.co.uk. Recently revamped, *Coldham Hall* sits at the end of a long track through the marshes, a hard-to-reach riverside pub that looks over to the chalets and boathouses of Brundall across the water. It has gastropub pretensions, and a more adventurous menu than its neighbour the *Ferry House*, and overall more of a restaurant feel. Not expensive, with starters around £5, mains £10, from a menu that includes burgers and BLTs alongside fish cakes and Gressingham duck – all well executed. Moorings £10, but redeemable against food purchases; electricity and water £5. Food Mon–Sat noon–3pm & 6–9pm, Sun noon–3pm.

Ferry House 1 Ferry Rd, NR14 7AR ☎01508 538659. Excellent riverside pub, cosy, dog-friendly and family-run, with free moorings and seating outside. It also serves a good menu of pub staples, jackets, baguettes and good home-made soup, with mains from £7.95. Daily noon–4pm & 6.30–9pm.

HADDISCOE

The Crown The Street, NR14 6AA ☎01502 677368, ⓦ thecrownathaddiscoe.co.uk. Refurbished pub whose contemporary lounge-style interior and rattan furniture terrace seem a bit out of place in this part of south Norfolk, but the welcome is friendly and there's a roaring fire in winter, and the food they serve in the bar and restaurant next door is hearty and reliable. Choose from a bar menu of burgers and sandwiches – £5.95 – and a more expensive restaurant menu of steaks, chicken dishes, beef stroganoff, lamb shanks, for £8.95–12.95. Veggie options too. Mon–Fri noon–3pm & 6–9pm, Sat noon–9pm, Sun noon–6pm.

Beccles and around

BECCLES is perhaps the most handsome town along the Waveney valley, and the furthest navigable mooring point for craft on the Broads. Like its close neighbour Bungay (see p.214), it's actually in Suffolk (Norfolk begins immediately across the river), and has the same kind of self-contained, low-key prosperity as its neighbour, with an alluring Georgian centre that's home to the sort of small-scale sights and independent businesses that make visiting East Anglian market towns such a pleasure. It also has a couple of good places to stay and to eat.

St Michael

The Walk, NR34 9AJ • ⓦ www.becclesparish.org.uk

The centre of Beccles sits high above the river, lofty heights only enhanced by the squat sixteenth-century stand-alone tower of the fifteenth-century church of **St Michael the Archangel**, which was built to the east of the church so as to avoid being too near the cliff. The interior was damaged in a fire not long after its completion, and doesn't hold all that much of interest, although it's worth knowing that Nelson's mum and dad were married here in 1749 – they had Horatio nine years later.

Beccles and District Museum

Leman House, Ballygate, NR34 9ND • Tues–Sun 2.15–5pm • Free • ☎01502 715722, ⓦ becclesmuseum.org.uk

A short walk out of the immediate centre, the **Beccles and District Museum**, housed in an eighteenth-century schoolhouse with a garden overlooking the boatyards down below, has the usual civic museum material – agricultural items, prints and photographs, but it's all quite well done, and there's a good model of the town as it looked in the nineteenth century, stuff for kids, and usually a temporary exhibition or two on a local theme.

ARRIVAL AND INFORMATION

BECCLES AND AROUND

By train Beccles is on the main line between Ipswich and Lowestoft and its train station is a 5min walk from the town centre at the junction of Station Rd and George Westwood Way.

By bus Buses stop at the train station and outside Tesco, and the town is well connected to Norwich and Lowestoft by the #X2 (every 30min), which runs via Loddon.

By boat Beccles' town staithe – and free moorings – are a

10min walk from the centre, at the end of Northgate. Day boat-rental is possible from H.E. Hipperson, just across the bridge near the quay, on the road to Gillingham (£18/hr, £86/day; ☎01502 712166). Ferries run upriver to Geldeston (ⓦbigdogferry.co.uk).

Tourist office At Beccles town staithe, north of the centre (daily 9am–5pm; ☎01502 713303); there are toilets and all the usual facilities of a Broadland quayside.

ACCOMMODATION

BECCLES

Saltgate House 5 Saltgate, NR34 9AN ☎01502 710889, ⓦwww.saltgatehouse.co.uk. In a big pale blue townhouse in the heart of town, this family-run B&B has five well-furnished double and twin rooms – the largest at the front but the quietest at the back, overlooking a pretty courtyard garden. Wi-fi throughout, and a bright breakfast room and comfy sitting room and downstairs, where you can interact with the playful resident dog. **£65**

Waveney House Hotel Puddingmoor, NR34 9PL ☎01502 712270, ⓦwaveneyhousehotel.co.uk. A great location by the river, and at heart a historic building, whose creaky sloping floors date back to the sixteenth century, and although the guest rooms are on the bland side,

they're pleasant enough, with everything you might need. The restaurant downstairs is deliberately informal, good for a just a drink or a full meal – both best enjoyed on the outdoor riverside terrace. **£98.50**

GILLINGHAM

The Swan Loddon Rd, NR34 0LD ☎01502 470047, ⓦgillinghamswan.co.uk. Just outside Beccles, over the Norfolk border in the village of Gillingham, the *Swan* is under friendly if slightly chaotic new management, and has fourteen simply furnished rooms in an annexe behind the main building. Run by a part-South African couple, the restaurant has both pub grub classics and a South African menu featuring ostrich, crocodile and springbok steaks. **£60**

EATING AND DRINKING

BECCLES

Baileys 2 Hungate, NR34 9TL ☎01502 710609. A great food shop and deli with a Spanish flavour, which also does lunches – squid with white beans, foccaccia with black pudding for £6–7 – as well as a delicious dinner menu on Friday and Saturday in the restaurant upstairs, with mains like monkfish cod and pork belly confit for £15–17. It's a wine merchant, too, specializing in Spanish wine – ⓦbaileyswines.com. Mon–Thurs 9am–5pm, Fri & Sat 9am–11pm.

Swan House Beccles, NR34 9HE ☎01502 713474, ⓦswan-house.com. A good place for lunches and cream teas, which also serves a bar menu (meatballs, pasta, croques monsieurs, rostis and fried eggs) for £8–9 and dinner mains for £14–16, when you're talking pan-fried sea bass and confit of duck. Contemporary and uncluttered inside, with stripped tables and squashy sofas. Very much at the heart of the Beccles scene, and deservedly so; it runs an artsy film club and various events throughout the summer. Daily 11am–11pm, Sun from noon; lunch noon–2.15pm, dinner 6.45pm–9.30pm, afternoon tea 3–5.30pm.

Twyfords Exchange Square, NR34 9HL ☎01502 710614, ⓦtwyfordscafe.co.uk. This café occupies a former gentlemen's outfitters right in the heart of Beccles, and does great coffee and cakes and lots of sandwiches, including exotic Americana like pulled pork and chicken Maryland. A place to drop into at any time of day, and with a garden out the back that's perfect in summer. Mon–Sat 8.30am–5pm.

BARNBY

Swan Inn Swan Lane, Barnby, NR34 7QE ☎01502 476646, ⓦswaninn-barnby.co.uk. Unpretentious village pub about three miles east of Beccles, which specializes in

fish – indeed it was voted Britain's best pub for seafood a few years back. The large menu is almost exclusively fish- and seafood-based, incorporating everything from grilled sea bass fillets stuffed with crab, and scallops in garlic butter to basic Lowestoft plaice in batter with chips – all very keenly priced at £9.95–11.95. If you're not that hungry try the "Scandinavian toast", a big plate of toast piled high with prawns, salmon, cheese and salad – for £4.95 perhaps the greatest pub food bargain of all time. Mon–Sat noon–2pm & 6–9pm, Sun noon–2pm & 7–9pm.

GELDESTON

The Locks Locks Lane, IP19 8AP ☎01508 518414, ⓦgeldestonlocks.co.uk. Across the border, just outside the nearby village of Geldeston, down a long dirt track, is a Broads pub *par excellence*, right on the river and not even on the national grid. It's remote enough to host regular, loud live music at weekends, while the rest of the time it specializes in folk nights, curry nights and a thousand other inventive offerings to lure you here. You can even take a ferry there from the riverside in Beccles – see ⓦbigdogferry.co.uk. April–Oct Mon–Fri noon–2.30pm & 6–9pm, Sat & Sun noon–9pm; Nov–March Thurs–Sat noon–2.30pm & 6–9pm, Sun noon–4pm.

Wherry Inn 7 The Street, NR34 0LB ☎01508 518371, ⓦthewherryinn.co.uk. In the heart of the pretty village of Geldeston, this is a comfy village pub that serves simple but well-cooked and - presented pub food: nothing fancy, but good steaks, burgers, fish and chips and the like. And they host food "theme nights" on the third Thursday of each month. Mon & Wed–Fri noon–2pm & 6–8.30pm, Sat & Sun noon–3pm & 6–8.30pm.

2

The north Norfolk coast

CROMER PIER (P.124)

The north Norfolk coast

About forty miles from one end to the other, the north Norfolk coast is one of the UK's top tourist destinations, attracting a wide cross section of the population to its long sandy beaches and seaside resorts. This stretch of coast begins (or ends) at Cromer, perhaps the most appealing of the larger resorts on account of its handsome setting, perched on the edge of blustery cliffs with its pier poking nervously out into the ocean. A few miles to the west is another well-established resort, Sheringham, though here the shoreline is buttressed by concrete sea defences, and then it's on to Weybourne, smaller and more subdued, but with another slab of sandy beach.

3

Thereafter, and almost without interruption, the shoreline becomes a patchwork of marshes, creeks, sand dunes and shingle spits, which combine to offer a haven to millions of **birds**, both resident and migratory. The small villages backing onto these creeks and marshes – Blakeney, Cley and Brancaster to name but three – were once important sea ports, but the silting up of the coast did for them economically until tourism refloated the local economy in the 1960s. This is north Norfolk at its most beguiling, beginning with a trio of lovely little places: **Salthouse**, which has a superb medieval church; **Cley**, where there is a major nature reserve as well as several smashing food stores; and **Blakeney**, with its beguiling harbour, enticing hotels and excellent restaurants.

Beyond Blakeney is **Wells-next-the-Sea**, a relative giant with a population of 3000, though this swells to nearly 10,000 in the summer months. Wells is at its prettiest on the Buttlands, where Georgian mansions flank an open green, but although its "next-the-sea" tag may have been accurate once, the town now lies about a mile inland from its beach, a magnificent tract of sand bordered by pine-clad dunes. Pushing on from Wells, you soon reach **Holkham Hall**, an imposing eighteenth-century pile set in the middle of an enormous estate, part of which includes the wide, pristine sands of **Holkham Bay**. To the west of Holkham lies the studied gentility of the **Burnhams** – especially **Burnham Market**, a favourite with well-heeled Londoners, and **Burnham Thorpe**, the childhood home of Nelson – and then the coast quietens down, its salt marshes and muddy creeks flanked by the tiniest of hamlets. All of these hamlets give ready access to the coast. There are important nature reserves at **Titchwell** and **Holme-next-the-Sea**, and three of them, **Brancaster Staithe**, **Brancaster** and **Titchwell**, have first-rate hotels. Just to the west of Holme is the kiss-me-quick resort of **Hunstanton** and here the coast veers south to run alongside The Wash, whose wide mud-flats extend as far as King's Lynn (see p.166), passing near the pretty little village of **Snettisham** on the way.

The other major attractions hereabouts are a short distance inland, principally **Little Walsingham**, an ancient village that was the country's most important place of pilgrimage throughout the medieval period, and a charming stately home, the National Trust's **Felbrigg Hall** near Cromer. There's also **Holt**, a lovely little market town with a

HOLKHAM BEACH

Highlights

❶ Cromer pier Battered by the ocean and attacked by molluscs, Cromer pier has somehow managed to survive – walk out along it, high above the waves, and enjoy the views. **See p.124**

❷ Felbrigg Hall Neither grandiloquent nor pompous, this exquisite country house is Jacobean architecture at its finest. **See p.127**

❸ Priory Maze and Garden These delightful themed gardens have a natural feel and the maze is large and suitably puzzling. **See p.130**

❹ Blakeney Point Nudging out into the ocean, this elongated spit is a wild and windy spot famous for its terns and seals. **See p.135**

❺ Cley Smoke House Local seafood smoked in Cley – hard to beat and certainly delicious. **See p.136**

❻ Holkham Bay and beach Wide and inviting bay holding one of Norfolk's finest beach – acres of golden sand set against hilly, pine-dusted dunes. **See p.146**

❼ Holme Dunes National Nature Reserve This gorgeous, pristine stretch of coastline with its long beach and sand dunes attracts birds by the thousand. **See p.158**

HIGHLIGHTS ARE MARKED ON THE MAP ON PP.122–123

top-drawer range of shops and stores, the landscaped grounds of **Sheringham Park**, and the royal estate of **Sandringham**, one of the region's most popular attractions.

GETTING AROUND	THE NORTH NORFOLK COAST

By train There's a regular train service on the Bittern Line (☏08457 484950, ⓦbitternline.com) from Norwich to three major stops on the north Norfolk coast – Cromer, West Runton and Sheringham; trains run hourly.

By bus A battery of local buses traverse north Norfolk, but easily the most useful is the Norfolk Coasthopper bus (☏01553 776980, ⓦcoasthopper.co.uk), which runs along the coast between Cromer and King's Lynn via a whole gaggle of coastal towns and villages, including Blakeney, Sheringham, Wells and the Burnhams. Frequencies vary on different stretches of the route, and there are more services in the summer than in the winter, but on the more popular stretches buses appear every 30min or hourly, less frequently on Sundays. There are lots of different tickets and discounts, but perhaps the handiest is the Coasthopper Rover, which provides unlimited travel on the whole of the route for either one day (£7), three days (£15) or seven days (£30); they can be bought from the driver. For route planning by train and bus, go to ⓦwww .travelineeastanglia.org.uk.

Cromer and around

Dramatically poised on a high bluff, **CROMER** should be the most memorable of the Norfolk coastal resorts, but its fine aspect is undermined by a certain shabbiness in its narrow streets and alleys – an "atrophied charm" as Paul Theroux called it – though

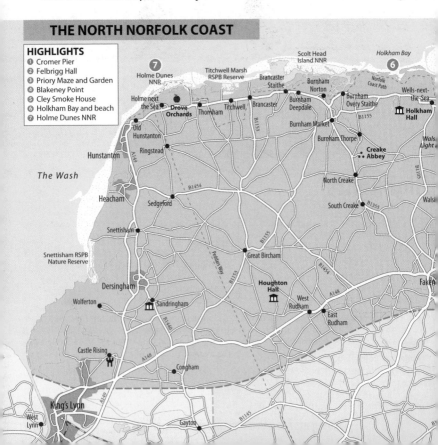

THE NORTH NORFOLK COAST

HIGHLIGHTS
1. Cromer Pier
2. Felbrigg Hall
3. Priory Maze and Garden
4. Blakeney Point
5. Cley Smoke House
6. Holkham Bay and beach
7. Holme Dunes NNR

LONG-DISTANCE FOOTPATHS AND CYCLE ROUTES

For walkers, the **Norfolk Coast Path**, which runs the 46 miles from Cromer to Hunstanton, is an especially fine way of exploring the north Norfolk coast's nooks and crannies as it edges through belts of sand dune, strips along muddy creeks and inches past salt and freshwater marsh. As you might expect from the flatness of the terrain, it's all easy going with barely any inclines along its entire course. The path intersects with the 57-mile **Weavers' Way** (see p.28) at Cromer (see p.122) and with the 47-mile **Peddars Way**, which begins near Thetford, at Holme-next-the-Sea (see p.157). A National Trail guide (ⓦnationaltrail.co.uk) covers the route in detail, otherwise you'll need the appropriate OS Explorer map.

For cyclists, **National Route 1** (ⓦsustrans.org.uk) loops through the area, running from King's Lynn to Ringstead, Burnham Market, Wells and the Walsinghams.

things are on the mend with new businesses arriving to add a touch of flair, while the town council keeps a string of mini-parks and **gardens** in immaculate condition. It's no more than the place deserves: Cromer has a long history, first as a prosperous medieval port and then as a fashionable watering hole after the advent of the railway in the 1880s. The Victorians and then the Edwardians built a bevy of grand hotels along the seafront, but the gloss soon wore off and only the dishevelled *Hotel de Paris* has survived as a reminder of all the bustles and top hats, its imposing red-stone facade

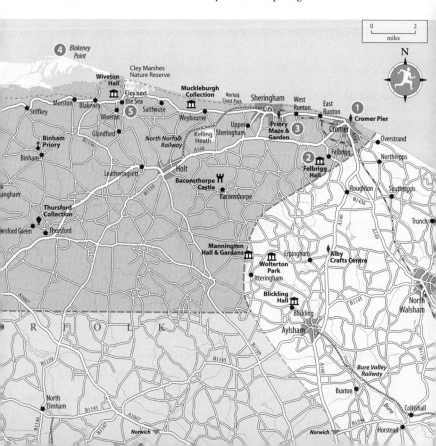

topped by a copper-green cupola. There are three things you must do here: take a walk on the **beach**; stroll out onto the **pier**, and, of course, grab a **crab**. Cromer crabs are famous right across England and several places sell them, cooked and stuffed every which way and reliably fresh (see box, p.126). There are enjoyable clifftop walks too, with top of the pile being the thirty-minute stroll east along the sea cliffs from Cromer to the Overstrand lighthouse, plus a pair of stately homes within easy striking distance inland – **Felbrigg Hall** and **Blickling Hall**.

The Gangway

Cromer doesn't have a natural harbour and from time immemorial local seamen have had to haul their boats in and out of the ocean up and over the shingle beach. Finally, in 1902, the town got round to building a ramp and this, **The Gangway**, survives today, its cobblestones lipped to provide leverage for the horses and mules that once lent a helping hoof moving goods up from the beach to the town.

The Henry Blogg Museum

The Gangway, NR27 9ET • Early April to Sept Tues–Sun 10am–5pm; Oct & Nov Tues–Sun 10am–4pm; Dec Sat & Sun 10am–4pm • Free • ☎ 01263 511294, Ⓦ rnli.org.uk

In the glassy, very modern RNLI building beside The Gangway is the **Henry Blogg Museum**, which takes its name from Cromer's most distinguished lifeboatman. Blogg (1876–1954), the long-time coxswain of the lifeboat, was a volunteer for no less than 53 years, picking up a hatful of medals for his bravery and saving nigh-on nine hundred lives – not that you would have known it from meeting him: Blogg was the most modest of men, quiet to the point of retiring, and never boastful. The museum's main exhibit is the lifeboat on which Blogg undertook most of his missions, but the vintage photos of old lifeboat crews are perhaps more interesting, hinting at a tightly knit world of thick jumpers, big sea boots, flat caps and alarmingly ponderous cork lifejackets. Curiously – and like most of his sea-mates – Blogg never learnt to swim.

Cromer Pier

Pavilion Theatre, Cromer Pier, NR27 9HE • ☎ 01263 512495, Ⓦ cromer-pier.com

From the Henry Blogg Museum, it's a brief stroll over to the **pier**, whose gift shop, café and fast-food joints culminate in the **Pavilion Theatre**, whose light-entertainment treats pull in the crowds with everything from Michael Jackson impersonators to the rather more enticing "Folk on the Pier", a three-day festival of folk music held in May. Behind the theatre is the present **Lifeboat Station**. Over the years, repairs to the pier have cost a small fortune: the first cast-iron pier of 1822 lasted just 24 years before it was swept away in a storm and its wooden replacement came a cropper in 1897 when a coal boat accidentally smashed into it. Four years later, the pier was replaced, but storms and nautical collisions have been a regular handicap – in 1993, for instance, an oil rig bumped into the pier and almost sliced it into two.

Church of St Peter and St Paul

Church St, NR27 9ES **Church** Daily 9am–4.30pm • Free **Tower** Late May to late Sept Mon–Fri 10.30am–4.30pm, Sat 10.30am–2.30pm • £1.50

With its slender buttresses and pinnacled balustrade, the imposing tower of **St Peter and St Paul**, at 160ft the tallest in Norfolk, lords it over the centre of Cromer just as it was supposed to – a declaration by the town's late-medieval merchants that they

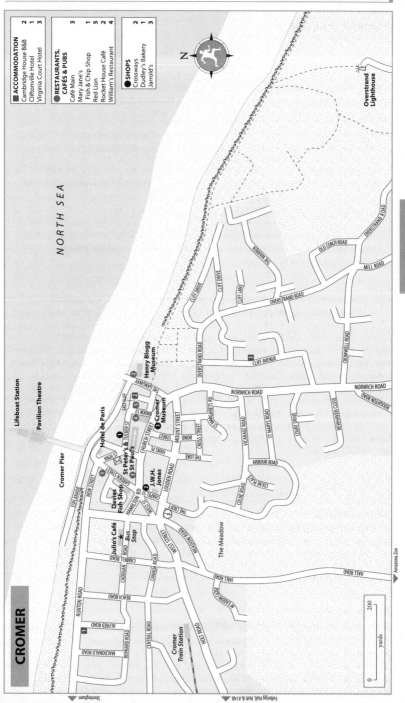

CROMER

3

NORTH SEA

N

Lifeboat Station

Pavilion Theatre

Cromer Pier

Hotel de Paris

Henry Blogg Museum

THE GANGWAY

BATH CLIFF

BOND ST

ST LUCER ST

St Peter's & St Paul's

Cromer Museum

Davies Fish Shop

ESPLANADE

NEW STREET

GARDEN STREET

HIGH ST

HAMILTON RD

CHAPEL ST

WEST ST

J.W.H. Jonas

HANS PL

CHURCH STREET

CROSS STREET

LOUDEN ROAD

MOUNT STREET

ST MARGARETS RD

NORWICH ROAD

NORWICH ROAD

ROUGHTON ROAD

OVERSTRAND ROAD

CLIFF AVENUE

CROMWELL ROAD

NEWHAVEN CLOSE

COURT DRIVE

ST MARY'S ROAD

VICARAGE ROAD

BOND STREET

ARBOUR ROAD

COLNE ROAD

COLNE PLACE

THE CROFT

THE LOKE

WEST STREET

MEADOW ROAD

HALL ROAD

HALL ROAD

MEADOW CLOSE

HOLT ROAD

CENTRAL ROAD

BERNARD ROAD

MACDONALD ROAD

ALFRED ROAD

BEACH ROAD

CADOGAN ROAD

CABBELL ROAD

RUNTON ROAD

CANADA ROAD

Julio's Café

Bus Stop

The Meadow

Cromer Train Station

CLIFF DRIVE

CLIFF DRIVE

CLIFF LANE

OVERSTRAND ROAD

OVERSTRAND ROAD

OVERSTRAND RD

THE WARREN

OLD COACH ROAD

MILL ROAD

Overstrand Lighthouse

▼ Sheringham

▼ Felbrigg Hall, Holt & A148

Amazona Zoo ▶

0   200

yards

3

UNFORCRABBABLE

No one really knows why **Cromer crabs** are so delicious, but there's no shortage of theories: some say it's to do with the quality of the waters off Cromer, others put it down to the skill of the crab fishermen, but perhaps the most likely explanation is the relatively slow speed at which they grow. There are enough crabs to keep a fair-sized industry ticking over in several parts of the UK, but the Minimum Landing Size (MLS) stipulated by EU and UK regulators varies: Cromer crabs can be landed when they reach 4.5 inches, elsewhere it's 5.5 inches, a discrepancy that reflects the Cromer crab's slow rate of growth. This would seem to mean that the flesh of the Cromer crab is a good deal more tender than the faster-growing versions with a higher proportion of white meat to dark. Currently, the Cromer crab fleet consists of around a dozen boats, who tend about two hundred baited crab pots, long-lined together and positioned on the seabed about three miles offshore. The genuine article is reddish-brown in colour with a distinctive pie-crust-shaped edge to its shell (or carapace). The **crabbing season** begins in March and ends in October and, although Cromer crabs are distributed far and wide, there are several key outlets in the town itself:

Davies Fish Shop 7 Garden St, NR27 9HN ☎ 01263 512727. Long-established fishmongers specializing in boxed and dressed crab, not to mention kippers and smoked haddock. They have their own crabbing boat – so they really do know what they are doing.

J.W.H. Jonas 7 Chapel St, NR27 9HJ ☎ 01263 514121. Down an ancient lane, in an ancient courtyard, this cubbyhole of a shop has a daily catch of fresh-from-the-boats fish plus a good supply of crabs.

---

were here to stay. In the event, their confidence was misplaced: the general movement of trade to the ports of western England marooned Cromer and by the 1780s the church was pretty much a ruin, its wardens keeping vermin at bay by employing a small platoon of hedgehogs. The Victorians saved the church, rebuilding the chancel and repairing the **nave**, whose huge Perpendicular windows, with their tinted, lozenge-shaped panes, fill the church with light, while up above a handsome set of angels decorate a magnificent hammerbeam roof. The finest window of them all, at the east end of the south aisle, is by **Edward Burne-Jones** (1833–98), who worked closely with William Morris and did more than anyone else to rejuvenate what was then the dying art of stained-glass making. This particular window, in the full florid flourish of the Pre-Raphaelites, depicts half a dozen Old Testament figures – Enoch, Elijah, Samuel, Moses, Abraham and Abel – among dappled greenery.

Cromer Museum

Church St, NR27 9ES • March–Oct Mon–Sat 10am–5pm, Sun 1–4pm; Nov–Feb Mon–Sat 10am–4pm • £3.40 • ☎ 01263 513543, ⓦ museums.norfolk.gov.uk

Cromer Museum dips and delves into the town's history as a seaport, fishing village and Victorian seaside resort. The particular highlight is its collection of old sepias and, more unusually, an assortment of autochrome colour pictures taken of local scenes and people by the pioneering photographer **Olive Edis** from 1905 onwards. Edis had her studio just along the coast in Sheringham.

Amazona Zoo

Hall Rd, NR27 9JG • April–Oct daily 10am–5pm • Adults £9.90, under-15s £7.90, under-4s free • ☎ 01263 510741, ⓦ amazonazoo.co.uk

An old patch of woodland on the south of Cromer has been recycled to house the **Amazona Zoo**, where most of the animals are native to the Amazon. There are around a dozen featured areas, including a hothouse and a "Feline Forest", home to puma, ocelot and jaguars. Reassuringly, none of the animals here are taken from the wild with most coming from breeding programmes in sister zoos.

East and West Runton

Cromer has a lovely sandy **beach**, but it can get a little crowded and if you're after a little more solitude, you may prefer **The Runtons**, just to the west of Cromer before you reach Sheringham (see p.128). First up along the main coastal road, the A149, is **EAST RUNTON**, where static caravans line up along the sea-bluff and a narrow lane, **Beach Road**, cuts down from the main road to a long strip of sandy beach. Neighbouring **WEST RUNTON** is a little bit larger, and here **Water Lane** cuts off the A149 to weave its way though the village before emerging beside crumbling sea cliffs with another slice of sandy beach extending east back towards Cromer. There's a smashing campsite here too (see p.132).

Felbrigg Hall

Felbrigg, NR11 8PR **House** March–Oct Mon–Wed, Sat & Sun 11am–5pm • £8.30 (includes gardens); NT **Gardens** March–Oct daily 11am–5pm; Nov to mid-Dec Thurs–Sun 11am–4pm • Gardens only £3.90 **Parkland** Daily dawn to dusk • Free • ☎ 01263 837444, Ⓦ nationaltrust.org.uk

3

Felbrigg Hall, situated just a couple of miles southwest of Cromer off the A148, is a charming Jacobean mansion. The main facade is particularly appealing, the soft hues of the ageing limestone and brick intercepted by three bay windows, which together sport a large, cleverly carved inscription – *Gloria Deo in Excelsis* – in celebration of the reviving fortunes of the family who then owned the place, the Windhams. The interior is splendid too, with the studied informality of both the dining room and the drawing room enlivened by some magnificent seventeenth-century plasterwork ceilings and sundry objets d'art. Many of the paintings were purchased by William Windham II, who undertook his Grand Tour in the 1740s – hence the two paintings of the Battle of the Texel by Willem van de Velde the Elder, and the six oils and twenty-odd gouaches of Rome and southern Italy by Giovanni Battista Busiri.

The surrounding **parkland** divides into two, with woods to the north and open pasture to the south. Footpaths crisscross the park and a popular spot to head for is the medieval **church of St Margaret's** in the southeastern corner, which contains a fine set of brasses and a fancy memorial to William Windham I and his wife by Grinling Gibbons. Nearer the house the extensive walled **garden** features flowering borders and an octagonal dove house, while the stables have been converted into particularly pleasant **tearooms**.

ARRIVAL AND INFORMATION   CROMER AND AROUND

By train Somewhat miraculously, Cromer has managed to retain its rail link with Norwich (trains hourly; 50min); from the station it's a 5min walk northeast into the centre.

By bus Buses to Cromer terminate outside *Julio's Café*, on Cadogan Rd, on the western side of the town centre.

Tourist office The North Norfolk Information Centre is on the south side of the town centre on Louden Rd (Jan to late May & Sept–Dec daily 10am–4pm; late May to Aug Mon–Sat 10am–5pm & Sun 10am–4pm; ☎ 0871 2003071, Ⓦ visitnorfolk.co.uk).

Guided walks The tourist office has a good range of local walking maps as well as the details of a varied programme of guided walks around both Cromer and its immediate surroundings (April–Oct; £3).

ACCOMMODATION

Cambridge House B&B East Cliff, NR27 9HD ☎ 01263 512085, Ⓦ cambridgecromer.co.uk. In a hard-to-beat location, with wide views out to sea, this B&B occupies a classic, Victorian terrace house on the clifftop in the centre of Cromer. There are six bedrooms, most en suite, and each has high ceilings and is pleasantly decorated in modern style. Good home-cooked breakfasts too. No cards. £10 reduction for shared facilities. **£76**

Cliftonville Hotel 29 Runton Rd, NR27 9AS ☎ 01263 512543, Ⓦ cliftonvillehotel.co.uk. Among the big old mansions that line up along Runton Rd just west of the town centre facing out to sea, this is the smartest, its grand Edwardian foyer equipped with an impressive double staircase and oodles of wood panelling. After the foyer, the rooms beyond can't help but seem a tad mundane, but they are large and they all have sea views. **£150**

Virginia Court Hotel Cliff Ave, NR27 0AN ☎ 01263 512398, Ⓦ virginiacourt.co.uk. The new owners of this medium-sized hotel are in the process of a thoroughgoing upgrade – and they have started with what's most important: the beds are super comfy, the towels are super thick, the duvets super warm and there's free wi-fi. The hotel dates back to Edwardian times, hence the capacious foyer with its wide, sweeping staircase, and the atmosphere is very much that of a traditional seaside hotel, friendly and relaxed. It's in a handy location too, on a quiet residential street a couple of minutes' walk from the immaculate greenery of North Lodge Park, and the owners are a goldmine of local information. The hotel restaurant (daily 6.30–8.30pm) is excellent with due emphasis on local, seasonal ingredients – try, for example, the roast duckling with an orange and redcurrant jus (one course £13.95; two-course £18.95; three-course £22.95). Accommodation and dinner deals available. **£140**

EATING AND DRINKING

Café Main 50 Church St, NR27 9HH. This popular modern café serves the best coffee in town along with a good line in snacks and cakes. If the sun is out, you can join the scramble for a seat on the mini-pavement terrace. Mon–Sat 9am–5pm.

Mary Jane's Fish & Chip Shop 27 Garden St, NR27 9HN ☎01263 511208. Many Norfolk tourists are fastidious about their fish and chips with allegiances strongly argued and felt. This particular, family-owned place is especially popular, not for the decor (which is very basic), but for lightness of the batter and the freshness of the fish. Eat-in or takeaway. Daily from 11am.

Red Lion Brook St, NR27 9HD ☎01263 514964. Right in the centre of old Cromer, on the ridge facing out to sea, this lively pub has a grand old bar behind which are parked enough spirits to destroy the average liver. A good supply of real ales and above-average pub-grub too. Daily 11am–11pm.

Rocket House Café RNLI building, The Gangway, NR27 9ET ☎01263 519126. Offering sparkling views over the beach, pier and ocean from its giant windows – and outside from its blustery terrace – this café has the best location in town by a long chalk, though the food lacks subtlety – stick to the crabs and the salads. Salads start at just £4.50. Mon–Fri 9am–5pm, Sat 10am–5pm & 6–9pm & Sun 10am–5pm.

William's Restaurant 2 Brook St, NR27 9EY ☎01263 5196199. Right in the centre of old Cromer, this smart little restaurant serves delicious British food with a few Italian flourishes with the likes of slow-roasted pork belly with mash, roasted carrots and kale leading the gastronomic charge. Mains are very reasonably priced at around £13. Out of season: Fri–Sun noon–2.30pm & 6–9pm. In season: Tues–Sat 10am–2pm & 6–10pm.

SHOPPING

Crossways 1 Chapel St, NR27 9HJ ☎01263 513207. For better or worse, you don't see many shops like this any more, a good traditional tobacconist with every sort of cigarette and cigar you can think of, plus snuff, which is – apparently – enjoying something of a revival. Mon–Sat 9.30am–5pm.

Dudley's Bakery 21 Tucker St, NR27 9HA ☎01263 519777. The best bakers in town where a wide range of breads is supplemented by pies, cakes and quiches. Mon–Sat 7am–4pm.

Jarrold's 33 Church St, NR27 9ES ☎01263 512190, ⊕jarrold.co.uk. A branch of the independent Jarrold's department store in Norwich (see p.57), this is easily the best stationers in town with good sidelines in jigsaws and games, local maps and travel guides. Mon–Sat 9am–5.30pm & Sun 11am–3pm.

Sheringham and Weybourne

SHERINGHAM, a popular seaside town with a shingle beach, just four miles west of Cromer, has an amiable, easy-going air, its narrow High Street dotted with souvenir shops, cafés and chip shops. One of the town's more distinctive features is the smooth **pebbles** that face and decorate many of its houses, a flinting technique used frequently in this part of Norfolk. The downside is that the power of the waves, which makes the pebbles smooth, has also forced the local council to spend thousands rebuilding the sea defences, and the resultant mass of reinforced concrete makes for a less than pleasing **seafront** – despite the best efforts of **The Mo**, one of north Norfolk's more enjoyable museums. Sheringham's two main attractions are, however, elsewhere – in the hilly expanses of **Sheringham Park** to the southwest of town and in the volunteer-run **North Norfolk Railway**, whose trains shunt along the five miles of track from Sheringham to Holt (see p.130).

The Mo Museum

Lifeboat Plain, NR26 8BG • Feb–Oct Tues–Sat 10am–4.30pm & Sun noon–4pm • £3.50 • ☎ 01263 824482, Ⓦ sheringhammuseum.co.uk

Spread over two floors, **The Mo** – aka Sheringham Museum – focuses on the town's nautical past, its prime exhibits being a substantial collection of vintage fishing smacks and lifeboats alongside archive film of dramatic sea rescues. There are also displays on old Sheringham, something on wind farms, and a viewing tower offering wide views out to sea. The museum puts on a lively programme of temporary exhibitions and events too, for example a nostalgic look at British seaside holidays and a "Spooky Pirate Treasure Trail" for kids.

Sheringham Park

Upper Sheringham, NR26 8TL • Park daily dawn to dusk; visitor centre mid-March to Sept daily 10am–5pm; Oct Wed–Sun 10am–5pm; Nov to mid-march Sat & Sun 11am–4pm • Free but parking £4.50; NT • ☎ 01263 820550, Ⓦ nationaltrust.org.uk • Reached from Sheringham along the B1157, or from Cromer and Holt along the A148; buses run from Cromer and Sheringham train station

Stretching over a large and distinctly hilly chunk of land just a couple of miles to the southwest of town, Sheringham Park was laid out to a design by **Humphry Repton** (1752–1818), one of England's most celebrated landscape gardeners. Repton professed

---

THE NORTH NORFOLK RAILWAY

Never a big player, the **Midland and Great Northern Joint Railway** (M&GN) served much of Norfolk and Lincolnshire from its establishment in 1893 through to nationalization in the 1940s, though most of its routes were closed not long afterwards. Familiarly known as the "Muddle and Get Nowhere", one of the company's branch lines ran southwest from Sheringham to Holt and this five miles of track was adopted by the volunteer enthusiasts of the **North Norfolk Railway** (NNR; April & Oct most days; May–Sept daily; Nov–March limited service; Sheringham–Holt £10.50 return, £6 on discount days; ☎ 01263 820800, ⓦ nnrailway. co.uk) in 1965 with the first vintage steam trains chugging down the "**Poppy Line**" two years later. The NNR is now a firm fixture of the Norfolk tourist scene, its steam and vintage diesel trains rumbling through the countryside with stations at Sheringham, yards from the ordinary train station (see opposite), Weybourne Heath, within walking distance of Sheringham Park (see p.129), Kelling Halt and Holt (see p.140).

3

himself very pleased with the result – Sheringham Park was "my most favourite work" he proclaimed, though the commission was not without its problems: following a carriage accident in 1811, Repton was confined to a wheelchair which severely limited the number of inspectorial visits he could make. Over the decades, Repton's original design has been modified on several occasions, but the broad principles have survived, most memorably in the several **lookout points** that dot the wooded ridge running across the southern half of the park. Here also, among the Scots pine, sweet chestnut and oak, are two later additions, the magnificent, 50-acre **rhododendron garden**, seen at its best from late May to early June, and the **Gazebo** on top of Oak Wood Hill, where a steep modern stairway leads up to a viewing platform that offers sumptuous views over the coast. Further north, the park gets flatter and more agricultural, culminating in the grassland, which backs on to its honey-coloured **sea cliffs**. There's also an area of heathland on the west side of the park and from here it's an easy stroll through to **Weybourne Heath Station** on the North Norfolk Railway line (see box, above).

From the entrance, three **circular walking trails** are clearly signed: the shortest is the half-mile jaunt to the **Temple**, a modest ornamental folly on top of Temple Hill, and the longest is the five-mile **Ramblers' Route**, which threads its way through woodland and across open farmland to hit the coast and intersect with the Norfolk Coast Path (see p.123). The third, intermediate walking trail, the two-mile **Repton Trail**, uses the carriageway that was originally laid out by Repton before proceeding onto the Gazebo.

Priory Maze and Garden

Cromer Rd, Beeston Regis, NR26 8SF • April–Oct daily 10am–5pm; Nov–Feb Wed–Sun 10am–4pm • £5, children £2.50 • ☎ 01263 822986, ⓦ priorymazegardens.co.uk

Situated next door to the ruins of the thirteenth-century Beeston Priory, on the east side of Sheringham beside the A149, **Priory Maze and Garden** is one of the biggest draws along this part of the coast. It's a beautiful collection of themed gardens, mainly created over the past decade, that have a deliberately natural feel; the **maze** itself is as large and puzzling as any you'll find. There's a plant centre attached, and a really nice café, with plenty of choice and seats out on the lawn. But the real draw is the **gardens** themselves, artfully planned, with a water meadow, a pine plantation, overlooked by the ruins of the thirteenth-century priory, and borders that bloom with colour in summer. There are also plenty of quizzes and activities to keep the kids entertained.

Weybourne

Travelling west from Sheringham, the A149 meanders through a pretty rural landscape offering occasional glimpses of the sea and a shoreline protected by both a slab of marshland and a giant shingle barrier erected after the catastrophic flood of 1953. After about four miles you reach **WEYBOURNE**, whose huddle of houses falls either side of the main road. In the middle of the village, **Beach Lane**, a side road on the right, leaves the A149 to weave its way down to the shoreline, where a large shingle mound protects this part of the seashore and abuts a wide shingle **beach**. Likely as not, you'll spot a handful of anglers with their lines tugging in the surf – the beach shelves straight into the ocean, putting deep water close at hand. This is unusual for Norfolk and raiding Danes took full advantage in the ninth and tenth centuries, grounding their boats here at Weybourne before marching inland. Much later, in Elizabethan times, there was a real local panic when it was thought the Spaniards were heading for Weybourne, but they didn't, leaving the anchorage to a boisterous bunch of pirates, who made a living hereabouts until the late 1800s.

Kelling Heath

Holgate Hill, NR25 7HW • Open access • Free • ⓦ kellingheathwildlife.org.uk

On the other side of the A149, just south of Weybourne, **Kelling Heath** is a protected parcel of heathland that is mostly covered by gorse, heather and bracken, though its northern slopes sustain a mixed woodland. The heath is crisscrossed with walking paths, which are most readily reached from the car park on Holgate Hill – take the Holt Road south from Weybourne and veer right.

The Muckleburgh Collection

Muckleburgh House, Weybourne Rd, NR25 7EG • April–Oct daily 10am–5pm • £7 • ⓣ 01263 588210, ⓦ muckleburgh.co.uk

The vintage tank parked beside the A149 just to the west of Weybourne marks the entrance to the **Muckleburgh Collection**, whose assorted military hardware, much of which dates from World War II, is dotted around what was once an anti-aircraft training camp. Pride of military place goes to the **tanks**, including Soviet, German, US and British examples, and visitors are offered a cross-country ride in an American personnel carrier. If you stump up an extra £100, you can also have a bash at driving a tank for about forty minutes – and great fun it is too, in a very noisy kind of way.

ARRIVAL AND INFORMATION SHERINGHAM AND WEYBOURNE

By train Sheringham has two train stations opposite each other, on either side of Station Rd, a 5- to 10min walk from the seafront down Station Rd and its continuation, High St. The main station, the terminus of the Bittern Line from Norwich (hourly; 1hr), is on the east side of Station Rd. The North Norfolk Railway station, which has been restored to its appearance as of 1963, is to the west.
By bus Buses to Sheringham mostly pull in beside the

North Norfolk Railway station, on Station Approach. In Weybourne, the Norfolk Coasthopper bus (see p.122) uses the bus shelters outside the *Ship Inn*, on the A149 in the centre of the village.
Tourist office Next to the North Norfolk Railway station on Station Approach, NR26 8RA (Easter to June & Sept–Oct daily 10am–2pm; July & Aug Mon–Sat 10am–5pm, Sun 10am–4pm; ⓣ 0871 2003071, ⓦ visitnorthnorfolk.com).

ACCOMMODATION

Cleat House B&B 7 Montague Rd, Sheringham, NR26 8LN ⓣ 01263 822765, ⓦ cleathouse.co.uk. This deluxe B&B, in a sympathetically modernized Edwardian house, a 5min walk from the seafront, offers three, very comfortable, en-suite guest rooms, each of which is decorated in period style. The breakfasts are excellent, there's a summer patio and free wi-fi, plus the overnight rate includes an afternoon cream tea when you arrive. April–Sept minimum two-night stay at weekends.. **£105**
Dales Country House Lodge Hill, Upper Sheringham,

NR26 8TJ ⓣ 01263 824555, ⓦ dalescountryhouse .co.uk. In a superb location, just a couple of miles inland from Sheringham on the edge of Sheringham Park, this manor-house hotel occupies a rambling Edwardian mansion that was designed for a local bigwig – one Commodore Henry Douglas King, MP – in 1910 with the original Victorian rectory as its architectural base. With its tall and slender chimneys, half-timbering, ruddy-coloured stonework and turret, it's an impressive building and much of the interior is impressive too, beginning with the

3

splendid wood-panelled foyer and dining room. Other parts of the house are not so endearing, reflecting its one-time use as a Council residential home, but the best of the 21 guest rooms are captivating, complete with mini-terrace, four-posters, oak furniture and open fireplaces. You can also access Sheringham Park direct from a gate in the hotel grounds. **£160**

Sheringham Youth Hostel 1 Cremer's Drift, Sheringham, NR26 8HX ☎0845 3719040, ⓦyha.org .uk. This well-equipped hostel occupies a large Victorian house on the south side of Sheringham, just beyond the A149 and a 5-to-10min walk from the town's train and bus stations. Among its facilities, there is a cycle store, a self-catering kitchen, free wi-fi, a laundry and a dining room.

There are one hundred beds in two- to six-berth bedrooms and family rooms are available too. Dorm **£20.40**

CAMPING

Beeston Regis Holiday Park Cromer Rd, West Runton, NR27 9QZ ☎01263 823614, ⓦbeestonregis.co.uk. First impressions of this site, which lies just to the north of the A149 and just to the west of West Runton, may not be too favourable – there are a few too many static caravans for that – but campers share a lovely little patch perched immediately behind the sea cliffs; there's even a steep staircase leading down to a small sandy beach. Camping pitch for two, including hook-up **£22**

EATING AND DRINKING

SHERINGHAM

Dales Country House Lodge Hill, Upper Sheringham, NR26 8TJ ☎01263 824555, ⓦdalescountryhouse .co.uk. *The Dales* is a smashing hotel (see p.131) and it also possesses a very competent restaurant. The menu exhibits both flair and imagination: try, for example, confit of wild rabbit for starters, followed by the roast rump of lamb served with parmentier potatoes, herbs, shallots, sautéed courgettes and mint jus; mains start at £15. Daily noon–2pm & 6.30–9.30pm.

Ellies 14 High St, NR26 8JR. Kiosk and simple café selling Norfolk's own Ronaldo's ice cream in a mouthwatering battery of flavours, from chocolate and ginger to cinnamon, pineapple, coconut and lavender. Yum, yum. Daily 11am–5pm, later in season.

No. 10 Restaurant 10 Augusta St, NR26 8LA ☎01263

824400. Many visitors think this is the best restaurant in Sheringham – and it definitely has the prettiest premises, the windows of its Edwardian facade showing off a tasty batch of cakes and scones. The menu is well considered – the cod fillet with spring onion risotto and red pepper sauce (£14.95) is a good example – and they serve snacks too. Meal: Wed–Sat noon–2pm & 6.30–9.30pm; teas, coffees and snacks: Wed–Sat 10am–noon.

WEYBOURNE

The Ship Inn The Street, NR25 7SZ ☎01263 588721. This family-run pub, in a substantial, early twentieth-century building beside the A149, serves up well-above-average bar food with a good range of local produce. A good range of Norfolk ales too. Mains average around £9. Kitchen: Mon–Sat noon–2pm & 6.30–9.30pm; pub: daily 11am–11pm.

ENTERTAINMENT

Sheringham Little Theatre 2 Station Rd, NR26 8RE ☎01263 822347, ⓦsheringhamlittletheatre.com. This popular, 180-seat theatre offers a wide-ranging, all-year programme of music, art, comedy, film and theatre, but

the highlights are the Christmas panto and the Summer Rep of classical and contemporary plays, anything from Wilde to Ayckbourn and running from July until September.

Salthouse

With marshes to the north and heathland to the south, the tiny hamlet of **SALTHOUSE**, just a couple of miles west along the coast from Weybourne, may seem inconsequential today, but its flocks of sheep once provided a rich living for the lord of the manor – quite enough to arouse the ire of the local peasantry during Kett's Rebellion of 1549 (see p.317), when they took the opportunity to polish off one of the family, William Heydon. Today, the main evidence of the wealth and power of the Heydons is the **church of St Nicholas** (daily 9am–3.30pm), stuck on top of a grassy knoll at the insistence of Henry Heydon, its prominent position both a reminder to the faithful and a landmark for those at sea. Mostly dating from the sixteenth century, the church is an imposing structure, its aisle windows tall and slender, its tower squat and strong, but the interior is bare and bleak, even though the handsome timber ceiling does its best to cheer things up. The church also holds the **tomb** of Henry Stanforth, who died in 1751 at the age of 69, his qualities epitomizing all that was ideal in the Georgian gentleman: Stanforth was "An affectionate husband, an indulgent parent and a generous friend". It's also possible to reach the seashore at Salthouse along **Beach Lane**, which leaves the A149 at the east end of the village, but all you'll find at the end of the lane is a shingle hump and a shingle beach.

ARRIVAL AND DEPARTURE   SALTHOUSE

By bus In Salthouse, the Norfolk Coasthopper bus (see p.122) pulls in beside the Green, a small triangular piece of grass beside the A149.

EATING

Cookies Crab Shack The Green, NR25 7XA ☎ 01263 740352. Overlooking the A149, *Cookies* has something of a cult following, not for the decor, which is simple in the extreme, consisting of a tiny shop, a plastic gazebo and a glorified garden shed, but for the freshness and variety of the seafood. Crabs, prawns and smoked fish lead the maritime way, but there's lots more to choose from including samphire, a local delicacy harvested from the surrounding mud flats and salt marshes from late June to mid-September. Daily Oct–March 10am–4pm; April– Sept 9am–7pm.

Salthouse Dun Cow Coast Rd, NR25 7XA ☎ 01263 740467. The only pub in Salthouse, the *Dun Cow* has been refurbished in gastro pub style, its bare-brick walls and wooden beams left intact. The food is strong on local seafood and meat with mains starting at around £14. The pub occupies one side of a courtyard, a second holds two self-catering apartments costing £65 for two people per night with small discounts for longer stays. Food served daily noon–8.30pm.

Cley-next-the-sea

Heading west from Salthouse on the A149, it's about half a mile to the Cley Marshes nature reserve (see p.134) and another three-quarters of a mile to the distinctive windmill at the start of **CLEY-NEXT-THE-SEA**, once a busy wool port but now little more than a row of flint cottages and Georgian mansions set beside a narrow, marshy inlet that (just) gives access to the sea: at high tide, the sea once swept over the marshes, but these were encased behind a new set of sea defences in the 1940s. In medieval times, the tides went much further, which explains why Cley's fine medieval **church** is located

---

ADMIRAL SIR CLOUDESLEY SHOVELL LOSES HIS WAY

A big man with a big wig, **Sir Cloudesley Shovell** (1650–1707) was born in Cley and joined the Royal Navy as a cabin boy at the tender age of 14. Keen to earn promotion, Shovell taught himself navigation and his skilled seamanship then saw him scuttling up through the ranks in smart order. In 1676, Shovell hit the big time, becoming something of a national hero when he led two daring raids against the pirates of North Africa. Over the next twenty years, Shovell was involved in a series of naval battles until finally, in 1704, he was rewarded by his appointment as Rear Admiral of England. So far so good, but Shovell's career came to an untimely end just three years later: sailing from Gibraltar to Portsmouth, Shovell's fleet lost its bearings and struck the rocks off the **Scilly Isles** with the loss of four ships and two thousand men, one of the greatest naval disasters in British history.

 Shovell avoided the ignominy of facing a board of enquiry by dying when the fleet ran aground, though there were some oddities about his death. Shovell's body was found seven miles from where his ship went down, so it seems likely he got away in a rowboat before this itself was wrecked – and the crew drowned – when they tried to come ashore at Porthellick Cove on St Mary's, or so it was assumed. On her deathbed some thirty years later, a certain **Mrs Thomas**, a Scilly islander, confessed that she had discovered the half-conscious Shovell on the seashore and had promptly smothered him for his large emerald ring. Mrs T then produced the ring and gave it to the attendant clergyman, who passed it back to the Shovell family. Meanwhile, after several comings and goings, the admiral's body ended up being buried in Westminster Abbey. There's a small display on Shovell in **Strangers' Hall** in Norwich (see p.46).

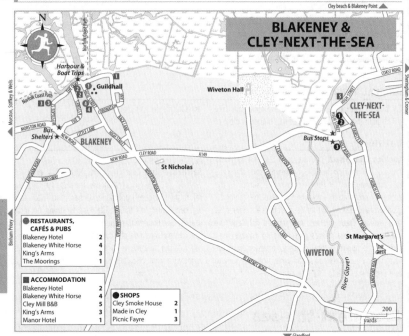

half a mile inland at the very southern edge of the current village, overlooking **The Green**, which was itself once the main harbour. Church apart, Cley's main draws are gastronomic with a pair of excellent shops (see p.136) on the main street, which doubles as the A149.

Church of St Margaret

Holt Rd, NR25 7UD • Daily 9.30am–4.30pm or dusk

Cley's architectural pride and joy is the church of **St Margaret**, whose most striking feature is its entrance **porch**, a two-storey, fifteenth-century extravaganza with the priest's chamber up above and a vaulted chamber down below, complete with a woman chasing a fox in the central boss. There's more unusual – and unusually secular – carving inside, where the arches of the **nave** frame a series of cameos, from a lion gnawing at a bone to St George tackling a distinctly un-frightening dragon, and the bench ends are decorated with the most playful of monster-gargoyles. The nave and the now ruined transepts were completed in the Decorated style in the early fourteenth century and there were plans to rebuild the glum-looking tower and chancel, but these were abandoned when the Black Death reached Cley in 1349, killing over half the population: the village never really recovered.

Cley Marshes Nature Reserve

A149, NR25 7SA • Daily: April–Oct 10am–5pm; Nov–March 10am–4pm • £4 • ☎ 01263 740008, ⓦ norfolkwildlifetrust.org.uk

Roughly midway between Cley and Salthouse along the A149 is **Cley Marshes Nature Reserve**, whose conspicuous, roadside **visitor centre** attracts birdwatchers like bees to a honeypot. Owned and operated by the Norfolk Wildlife Trust (NWT), the visitor centre has displays on local wildlife, sells books on the same, has OS maps, and issues

permits for entering the reserve, whose saltwater and freshwater marshes, reedbeds and coastal shingle ridge are accessed on several **footpaths** and overseen by half a dozen **hides**. You can, however, avoid the £4 charge by walking round the edge of the reserve, but you'll miss out on the hides.

On foot to Blakeney Point

Blakeney Point National Trust information centre: early April to Sept dawn to dusk • Free • No telephone, ⓦ www.nationaltrust.org.uk.

On the west side of the Cley Marshes Nature Reserve – and about 400 yards east of Cley village (see p.133) – is the mile-long byroad that leads to the shingle mounds of **Cley beach**. This is the starting point for the four-mile hike west out along the spit to **Blakeney Point**, a nature reserve famed for its colonies of terns and seals. The **seal colony** is made up of several hundred common and grey seals, and the old **lifeboat house**, at the end of the spit, is now a National Trust information centre. The shifting shingle can make walking difficult, so keep to the low-water mark – which also means that you won't accidentally trample any nests. The less strenuous alternative is to take one of the boat trips to the point from Blakeney or Morston (see box, p.137). The Norfolk Coast Path passes close to Cley beach too, and then continues along the northern edge of the Cley Marshes Nature Reserve (see opposite).

Glandford

From Cley, it's a mile or so south to **GLANDFORD**, a pretty little hamlet whose flint and red-brick cottages were built at the behest of a local landowner, Sir Alfred Jodrell, at the beginning of the twentieth century. Jodrell was well known for his charitable acts, but this does not seem to have extended as far as his political opponents: the story goes that when he asked one of his labourers how he was going to vote, the man rashly told him he was a "Radical", so Jodrell sacked him on the spot. It was the same Jodrell who set up Glandford's **Shell Museum** (Easter–Oct Tues–Sat 10am–12.30pm & 2–4.30pm; £2; ☎01263 740081, ⓦshellmuseum.org.uk) to house his substantial collection of sea-shells and here also are exhibited archeological bits and pieces and semiprecious stones.

Wiveton Hall fruit farm, café and farm shop

Wiveton Hall, NR25 7TE • Café: April to early Nov daily 9.30am–4.30pm • ☎01263 740515, ⓦwivetonhall.co.uk

Wiveton Hall fruit farm, café and farm shop, just off the A149 midway between Cley and Blakeney, casts its gastronomic net as widely as possible. Visitors can pick their own fruit and veg in the fields, buy local produce at the farm shop, and pop into the café, a charming rustic-rural kind of place with a homely feel and offering excellent home-made snacks and meals: the café uses the farm's produce wherever and whenever possible. From the café, it's a few yards to **Wiveton Hall**, a sprawling country house, parts of which, including some of the Dutch-style gables, date back to the seventeenth century. One wing offers self-catering accommodation, but much of the rest is more than a bit of a shambles.

ARRIVAL AND DEPARTURE   CLEY-NEXT-THE-SEA

By bus The Norfolk Coasthopper bus (see p.122) stops outside the Picnic Fayre delicatessen on Cley's main street, which doubles as the A149.

ACCOMMODATION AND EATING

★ **Cley Mill B&B** Cley-next-the-Sea, NR25 7RP ☎01263 740209, ⓦcleymill.co.uk. This outstanding B&B occupies a converted windmill complete with sails and a balcony offering wonderful views over the surrounding marshes and seashore. The guest rooms, both in the windmill and the adjoining outhouses, are decorated in attractive period style and the best, like the Stone Room, have handsome beamed ceilings;

self-catering arrangements are possible as well. At peak times, there's a minimum two-night stay. The *Mill's* smart and very agreeable restaurant specializes in traditional, home-made English cooking. Dinner is served at 7.30pm and a three-course set meal costs £32.50 per person. Advance reservations – by 10am of the same day – are required; open to residents and non-residents alike. **£129**

SHOPPING

★ **Cley Smoke House** High St, NR25 7RF ☎01263 740282, ⓦcleysmokehouse.com. This superb smoke-house sells a wide range of freshly smoked shellfish, fish and cured meats as well as home-made pâtés. Everything is smoked on site and their kippers are near impossible to beat. Mon–Sat 8.30am–5pm, Sun 9.30am–4.30pm.

Made in Cley High St, NR25 7RF ☎01263 740134, ⓦmadeincley.co.uk. Of several fine and applied art shops in Cley, this is the pick. They sell jewellery, prints and modern sculpture, but above all it's for their pottery they are praised, imaginative pieces for domestic use, from oven to tableware, and mostly made of hard-wearing stoneware clay. Next door to the Smoke House. Mon–Sat 10am–5pm, Sun 11am–4pm.

Picnic Fayre The Old Forge, High St, NR25 7AP ☎01263 740587, ⓦpicnic-fayre.co.uk. Squeezed into the old village forge, this long-established deli has been catering to urban – and urbane – tastes since it opened in 1984. Holidaymakers come from miles around to buy the freshly baked bread, dip into the antipasti, and make a selection from a wide range of cheeses, mustards, chutneys, jams and marmalades. Mon–Sat 9am–5pm & Sun 11am–4pm.

GLANDFORD

CleySpy Glandford, NR25 7JP ☎01263 740088, ⓦcleyspy.co.uk. There's everything for the birder here, from monoculars to binoculars, tripods and night-vision gear. Most of the stuff is new, but there are secondhand items too, plus an informed and helpful staff team. Mon–Sat 10am–5pm, Sun 10am–4pm.

Blakeney and around

BLAKENEY, a mile or so to the west of Cley, is delightful. Once a bustling seaport exporting fish, corn and salt, Blakeney even provisioned two ships for the Crusaders and accommodated an émigré colony of Dutch merchants, but that was long before its harbour silted up and nowadays it's a lovely little place of pebble-covered cottages sloping up from the creekiest of harbours. Crab sandwiches are sold from stalls at the quayside, family-run shops flank the winding high street, and footpaths stretch out along the sea wall to east and west, offering long, lingering views over the salt marshes with their deep and sticky mud-banks and abundant birdlife.

The Guildhall

Back Lane, NR25 7NR • Open access • Free; EH • ⓦwww.english-heritage.org.uk.

At low tide, Blakeney harbour is no more than a muddy creek ideal for a bit of quayside crabbing and mud sliding. Here also is one reminder of the village's long history, the medieval **Guildhall**, though the locals were hardly overawed by its antiquity – right up until the 1950s, they grew rhubarb in its dark and gloomy, brick-vaulted undercroft.

The Church of St Nicholas

Wiveton Rd, NR25 7NJ • Daily 9.30am–4.30pm or dusk

Blakeney's second noteworthy building is the **church of St Nicholas**, a large and sterling structure stuck on a grassy hillock beside the A149 at the south end of the village. Dating from the fifteenth century, the church's main tower and nave are made of flint rubble with stone trimmings, the traditional building materials of north Norfolk, but it's the second, smaller, minaret-like **tower** above the chancel that grabs most attention because no one is really sure why it is there: too slender to carry a bell, too angular to have been a stair turret, the usual explanation is that it served as

---

> **BOAT TRIPS TO BLAKENEY POINT**
>
> **Blakeney harbour** is linked to the sea by a narrow channel, which wriggles its way through the salt marshes, and is only navigable for a few hours at high tide. Depending on the tides, there are **boat trips** from either Blakeney or Morston quay, a mile or two to the west, to both Blakeney Point (see p.135) – where passengers have a couple of hours at the point before being ferried back – and to the seal colony just off the point. The main operators advertise departure times on blackboards by Blakeney quayside or you can reserve in advance with **Beans Boats** (☎ 01263 740505, ⊛ beansboattrips.co.uk) or **Bishop's Boats** (☎ 01263 740753, ⊛ norfolksealtrips.co.uk). Both the seal trips and those to Blakeney Point cost £9.

---

a beacon to those out at sea, which seems strange when the main tower is much taller and more conspicuous. The **church's interior** is not exactly riveting, but it does hold a fine oak and chestnut hammerbeam roof and a mildly engaging set of twentieth-century stained-glass windows outlining the early history of Christianity in Britain. The late thirteenth-century chancel is the only survivor from the original Carmelite friary church.

Morston

It's just over a mile west from Blakeney to minuscule **MORSTON**, where the main event is the **quay**, more accessible by boat than its neighbour and a departure point for boat trips to Blakeney Point and its seal colony (see p.135). The National Trust owns Morston Quay and operates an **information centre** here and this has displays on local flora and fauna. There are no fixed opening hours, but the centre is usually open two hours either side of high tide in summer with restricted hours in winter. The quay is also crossed by the Norfolk Coast Path (see p.123).

Binham Priory

Binham, NR21 0DW • Grounds and ruins: access at any reasonable time; church daily: May–Sept 10am–6pm; Oct–March 10am–4pm • Free; EH • ⊛ www.english-heritage.org.uk.

The substantial remains of **Binham Priory** boast a handsome rural setting about four miles southwest of Blakeney, on the edge of the hamlet of **Binham**. The Benedictines established a priory here in the late eleventh century, but long before its suppression in 1540, it had gained a bad reputation, its priors renowned for their fecklessness. One of the worst was William de Somerton, a fourteenth-century figure who funded his dabblings in alchemy by selling the church silverware and then the vestments. Neither were the monks a picture of contentment – one became insane through excessive meditation, so the prior had him flogged and then kept in solitary confinement until his death. Today, the porridge-like ruins focus on the priory church, whose nave was turned into the parish church during the Reformation. Inside, the nave arcades are a beautiful illustration of the transition between the Norman and Early English styles with a triple bank of hooped windows shedding light on the austere interior. Among the fittings, look out for the delicately carved **font** and the poppy-head **bench ends**, worn smooth by the touch of generations of worshippers. Look out also for the remains of the former **rood screen** kept at the back of the church. The Protestants whitewashed the screen and then covered it with biblical texts, but the paint is wearing thin and the saints they were keen to conceal have started to pop out again.

ARRIVAL AND DEPARTURE   BLAKENEY AND AROUND

By bus Buses to Blakeney, principally the Norfolk Coasthopper (see p.122), pull in at the Westgate bus shelter, a couple of minutes' walk from the harbour. The Coasthopper also serves Morston.

3

ACCOMMODATION

BLAKENEY

Blakeney Hotel Blakeney, NR25 7NE ☎01263 740797, ⓦblakeneyhotel.co.uk. *The Blakeney* is one of the most appealing seaside hotels in Norfolk, occupying a rambling building with high-pitched gables and pebble-covered walls – all in a smashing location right down by the quayside. The hotel has a heated indoor swimming pool, a secluded garden, cosy lounges with exquisite sea views and an excellent restaurant (see below). The cheaper rooms can be poky and somewhat airless, so it's worth paying more – up to a maximum of £250 – for one with views out across the harbour and the marshes. Off-season special deals and discounts are legion. **£180**

Blakeney White Horse 4 High St, NR25 7AL ☎01263 740574, ⓦblakeneywhitehorse.co.uk. Recently revamped and thoroughly modernized, this long-established inn, just up from the quayside, holds nine guest rooms kitted out in a bright and cheerful, albeit pared-down version of country-house style with creams, beiges, and blues to the fore. **£100**

King's Arms Westgate St, NR25 7NQ ☎01263 740341, ⓦblakeneykingsarms.co.uk Blakeney's best pub (see below) also offers seven, modest, modern en-suite bedrooms with doubles. **£70**

Manor Hotel Blakeney, NR25 7ND ☎01263 740376, ⓦblakeneymanor.co.uk. This medium-sized hotel occupies an old courtyard complex in a prime location, a few yards to the east of the harbour. The modern rooms are neat and trim, if somewhat dowdy, and there's an attractive garden. **£94**

Quayside Cottages Blakeney ☎01462 768627, ⓦblakeneycottages.co.uk. For longer stays, this efficient company rents out a handful of quaint Blakeney cottages. Advance reservations are strongly recommended – the cottages go quick. Cottage per week in high season (half the price in winter): **£500**

MORSTON

Morston Hall Hotel Morston, NR25 7AA ☎01263 741041, ⓦmorstonhall.com. Deluxe hotel in an immaculately updated country house of traditional flint and brick, which sits pretty beside the A149. The rooms are smart and really rather grand, with heavy drapes and lots of tartan flourishes, and the gardens are kept in tip top order. All this luxury doesn't come cheap, especially as room prices include a four-course set dinner menu at the hotel restaurant (see below). **£310**

EATING AND DRINKING

BLAKENEY

Blakeney Hotel Blakeney, NR25 7NE ☎01263 740797, ⓦblakeneyhotel.co.uk. Outstanding lunches and afternoon teas are served at both the hotel bar and the more formal restaurant, where, in the evenings, a three-course set meal costs £27.50. The restaurant menu is modern British – try, for example, the seared fillet of black bream with sautéed potatoes and confit shallots with chive sauce. Kitchen: daily 12.30–2pm & 6.30–9.30pm.

Blakeney White Horse 4 High St, NR25 7AL ☎01263 740574, ⓦblakeneywhitehorse.co.uk The *White Horse* is noted for its food, which is served either in the bar or in the smarter conservatory. They offer two menus – one a lunchtime snack menu, the other an à la carte supper menu. Dishes include the like of roast partridge with braised red cabbage, mushrooms, sprouts and black truffles and a walnut emulsion (£15.95), and pan-fried halibut with crab cannelloni and Provencal vegetables (£16.95). Kitchen: daily 12.30–2.30pm & 6.30–9.30pm.

King's Arms Westgate St, NR25 7NQ ☎01263 740341, ⓦblakeneykingsarms.co.uk. The best pub in Blakeney by a long chalk, this traditional boozer, with its low, beamed ceilings and rabbit-warren rooms, offers top-ranking bar food,

largely English but with an international zip: try, for example the home-made steak and Adnams ale suet pudding with rich onion gravy (£11.50), or the warm butterbean, blue cheese and tarragon tartlets with roasted red pepper coulis (£9.50). Kitchen: daily noon–2pm & 6–9pm.

The Moorings High St, NR25 7NA ☎01263 740 054. Informal little bistro, painted in bright and cheerful colours, where the menu is strikingly creative and is particularly strong on Norfolk fish and shellfish, though other local foods feature too, including meat, game and vegetables – a typical main course is sautéed lamb kidneys with pancetta and rosemary and white bean ragout (£16.50). Tues–Sat 10.30am–9.30pm, July & Aug also Mon.

MORSTON

Morston Hall Hotel Morston, NR25 7AA ☎01263 741041, ⓦmorstonhall.com. Much-vaunted restaurant, where they work hard to create the most enticing of menus: parmesan terrine with carrot ribbons and brown-bread tuile is a typical starter. It's smart and expensive with their set-menu dinner costing £60, a more affordable £35 at lunch times. Lunches: noon–2pm; dinner sitting at 7.30 for 8pm.

Stiffkey

The main coastal road, the A149, is unkind to **STIFFKEY** (pronounced "Stewkey"): trapped between high flint walls a couple of miles west of Morston, the road narrows to

SCANDAL AT THE VICARAGE

The villagers of Stiffkey had a real shock in the 1930s when the alleged activities of their local clergyman, **Harold Francis Davidson** (1875–1937), hit the national headlines. By all accounts, Davidson was a diligent man, regularly visiting his parishioners and undertaking all sorts of charitable acts. This made him extremely popular with the ordinary folk of the parish, but the local landowners, fearing subversion, did not take to him at all, especially **Major Philip Hamond**, who conspired to bring about his downfall. Hamond recruited a solicitor called **Henry Dashwood**, who looked for scandal in the charity work Davidson did in London, where the rector had taken a particular interest in the poorly paid young girls who worked at Lyons Tea Rooms. Davidson always insisted he was just trying to help the girls, Dashwood said it was much more than that – and the dispute went to a Church of England ecclesiastical court in 1932. The clinching evidence was two photos showing Davidson in close proximity to partly clad girls, though Davidson always insisted they were forgeries. Whatever the truth, Davidson was defrocked, though that was not quite the end of the story: Davidson went on to appear in public entertainments, which traded on his fame. In one, he was placed in a barrel that was apparently being roasted in an oven while a figure dressed as the devil prodded him with a pitchfork, in others he regularly entered a lion's cage where he proclaimed his innocence. In the event, it wasn't a good career choice as one of the lions mauled him and he died shortly afterwards, though this was more the result of medical incompetence than the efforts of the animal. Davidson was buried back in Stiffkey, where attending his **funeral** was, to all intents and purposes, an act of defiance against the authorities: three thousand mourners turned up and his widow wore white. The scandal was revived in **The Prostitute's Padre**, which was performed at Norwich Playhouse in 1997 and in John Walsh's recent novel *Sunday at the Cross Bones*.

a single file, bottling up the traffic and creating long tailbacks throughout the summer. What the locals think of all this congestion is not hard to imagine, especially as Stiffkey is, at least when the cars have gone, a pretty little place whose haphazard string of cottages lies dotted to either side of the meandering River Stiffkey. An ancient village – Stiffkey appears in the Domesday Book of 1086 – it was the Saxons who named the place "island with stumps of trees" after its watery location, and its long history is typical of the villages hereabouts. Generations of agricultural labourers were pretty much at the beck and call of the local landowners, though here at least the labourers could earn a little extra money by gathering cockles from the salt marshes to the north of the village; these "**Stewkey Blues**" are still a delicacy, their shells stained blue by the mud in which they live.

One further curiosity is **Camping Hill**, the wooded rise beside the A149 at the east end of the village: it's not named after "camping" as we know it, but rather the community free-for-all in which two mini-mobs would try to get a ball from one "goal" to another amid black eyes, broken noses and sometimes much worse.

ACCOMMODATION   STIFFKEY

High Sand Creek Campsite Greenway, NR23 1QF ☏ 01328 830235. Signed from the A149 on the west side of Stiffkey, this straightforward, low-key campsite is geared up for tents with its pitches spread over a hedge-sheltered hillside that looks out over the salt marshes. It's also a stone's throw from the Norfolk Coast Path. Open April to Oct. Tent pitches from £12

Stiffkey Red Lion Wells Rd, NR23 1AJ ☏ 01328 830552, ⓦstiffkey.com. Beside the main road, at the

west end of the village, this charming pub has been sensitively modernized, keeping its original low-beamed ceilings, stone floors, cosy rooms and country benches. Immediately behind is a new hotel block, comprising ten modern, chalet-style guest rooms, each of which has either a small terrace and garden or, on the first floor, a private balcony. There are some welcome eco features too, like the sedum roof and the rainwater-flush toilets. £90

EATING AND DRINKING

Stiffkey Red Lion Wells Rd, NR23 1AJ ☏ 01328 830552, ⓦstiffkey.com. The food at this stylish pub is

first-rate, its staple of English dishes varied by the likes of curry and lasagne, though it's hard to beat the fish pie with mixed-leaf salad (£9.95). Kitchen: daily noon–2.30pm & 6–9pm.

Stiffkey Stores Wells Rd, NR23 1QH ☎ 01328 830489. There may be a lot of north London about this shop and café, but although the assorted knick-knacks are distinctly chichi, the cakes really are superb, try, for example, the soft and moist, deliciously tangy almond cake. Also sells cards, gifts, kitchenware, bread and a battery of local farm produce. Mon–Sat 8am–5pm, but closes Wed at 12.30pm, Sun 9am–3pm.

Holt and around

Neat and trim, spick-and-span **HOLT**, just five miles southeast of Blakeney, is the prettiest town in north Norfolk and has long attracted the praise of passing travellers: "Holt is most picturesquely situated, [making] it perfectly charming" wrote one, though grumpy old radical William Cobbett (1763–1835) was less impressed, moaning that it was distinctly "old-fashioned". Most of Holt was burnt to a cinder in a great fire of 1708 and in its place rose the Georgian buildings that characterize the town today, lining up along the attractive **Market Place**. In recent years, Holt has also proved particularly adept at pulling in the tourist money and its streets now boast a string of independent shops and stores – a real retail treat.

Baconsthorpe Castle

Baconsthorpe, NR25 6AB • Open access in daylight hours • Free; EH • ⓦ www.english-heritage.org.uk • Just over three miles from Holt : take the signed country lane running southeast from the A148 on the edge of Holt, go through Baconsthorpe village and then watch for the signed (but easy to miss) turning on the left

Deep in the Norfolk countryside, the extensive ruins of **Baconsthorpe Castle** are a monument to the failed ambitions of the Heydon family, who ruled the local roost for several generations. It was here, in their salad days, that the Heydons built themselves a

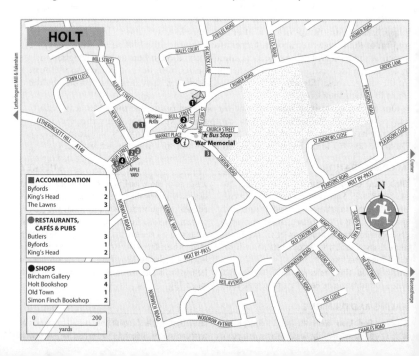

grand moated and fortified manor house, raising the inner gatehouse in the fifteenth century and adding the outer gatehouse not long afterwards. The inner gatehouse was strong enough to shelter the family in times of danger – and it needed to be as these were troubled times and the Heydons were a quarrelsome lot. It all went wrong for the Heydons in the late sixteenth century, when one of the clan – Sir William – fell into debt and thereafter much of the property fell into ruin, though the outer gatehouse was inhabited until 1920. Despite the years of neglect, much has survived, including a slice of the curtain wall and moat, plus the imposing flint walls of both gatehouses, each of which is punctuated by delicately carved stone doorways and window lintels.

Letheringsett Watermill

Riverside Rd, NR25 7YD • Mill operating hours Tues–Sat 1.30–3.30pm; shop: Mon–Fri 9am–4pm & Sat 9am–1pm; self-guided tours of the watermill during shop hours • £4 when the mill is working, £3 when it's not • ☏ 01263 713153, Ⓦ letheringsettwatermill.co.uk

Letheringsett Watermill, a rare example of a fully working watermill, is located in the hamlet of **LETHERINGSETT**, which bunches up on the east bank of the River Glaven, just a mile west from Holt along the A148. There's been a watermill here since Norman times, maybe earlier, but the current imposing and severe, four-storey brick building dates from 1802. The mill still supplies many types of flour and bread to local businesses and there's a shop here too. In Victorian times, Letheringsett was home to a renowned blacksmith, **Johnson Jex**, whose inventiveness endeared him to the local gentry – his speciality was making watches to his own design.

3

ARRIVAL AND INFORMATION

By bus Mon–Sat Sanders Coaches (Ⓦ www .sanderscoaches.com) links Holt with several other towns in Norfolk, including Cromer, Fakenham and Norwich. Holt is also on the route of the Coasthopper (see p.122). Buses arrive and depart from the Market Place.

HOLT AND AROUND

Tourist office In the centre of town on the Market Place, NR25 6BW (Easter to mid-May, Sept & Oct Mon–Sat 10am–2pm; mid-May to Aug Mon–Sat 10am–5pm; ☏ 01263 516096, Ⓦ visitnorthnorfolk.com).

ACCOMMODATION

Byfords 1 Shirehall Plain, NR25 6BG ☏ 01263 711400, Ⓦ byfords.org.uk. Promoting itself as a "Higgledy-piggledy World of Pleasure" may be rather excessive, but *Byfords* attempts to hit all the bases, its substantial town-centre premises holding a deli, a café, a restaurant (see below) and a self-styled "posh B&B" with sixteen guest rooms. Every effort has been made to keep the original character of the building, most of which dates back to the early 1900s – hence the exposed brick and flintwork and oak flooring. Otherwise, it's all high spec, from the Bang & Olufsen TVs to the power showers and underfloor heating. **£140**

King's Head 19 High St, NR25 6BN ☏ 01263 712543, Ⓦ kingsheadholt.org.uk. Upstairs, above the *King's Head*

pub (see p.142), there are three, en-suite B&B rooms, where the somewhat austere modern decor is softened by the exposed beams and antique furniture. Great big beds too. Breakfast is served at *Byfords* (see below), the sister business. **£90**

The Lawns 26 Station Rd, NR25 6BS ☏ 01263 713390, Ⓦ lawnsatholt.co.uk. In a distinctive brick building, complete with an unusual turret tower, this family-owned hotel has eight guest rooms with fairly ordinary furnishings and fittings. The rooms are large and the hotel is a stone's throw from the centre of town, but the public areas are not enticing. More positively, the breakfasts are very good – especially the kippers. **£95**

EATING AND DRINKING

HOLT

★ **Butlers** 9 Appleyard, NR25 6AR ☏ 01263 710790. Tucked away in a mini-shopping precinct just off the High St, this welcoming café-cum-restaurant features a particularly well-balanced mixture of meat and fish dishes on its lunch and dinner menus, with a couple of veggie options thrown in. The breakfasts are excellent too – and in between breakfast, lunch and dinner times, they serve tasty snacks

and appetizers. Everything is fresh and almost everything is home-made. The decor is straightforwardly modern and there's outside seating as well. Mains £9.95–£14.95. Mon–Sat 8.30am–11pm: breakfast 9am–11am; lunch noon–3pm; dinner 6–9pm.

Byfords 1 Shirehall Plain, NR25 6BG ☏ 01263 711400, Ⓦ byfords.org.uk. Extremely popular, the deli here at *Byfords* sells home-made bread, cakes, pies and pre-cooked, frozen dinners. The café and restaurant continue the home-made theme – and visitors queue up for the breakfasts: try, for example, the kippers from Cley Smoke-House (see p.136). The restaurant menu dips into several cuisines, including, for example, a Moroccan aubergine and chickpea casserole (£11.95). There's also live jazz in the evening on the last Wed of each month. Kitchen: daily 8am–10.30pm, last orders 9.30pm.

King's Head 19 High St, NR25 6BN ☎ 01263 712543, ⓦ kingsheadholt.org.uk. Recently refurbished, this busy pub offers a tasty range of local brews as well as pool and darts. The main bar has large flat-screen TVs with sports the main offering, but there's a quieter bar too – plus above-average bar food in both. Kitchen daily: noon–3pm & 6–9pm.

LETHERINGSETT

King's Head Letheringsett, NR25 7AR ☎ 01263 712691, ⓦ kingsheadnorfolk.co.uk. This well-run inn, a member of the Flying Kiwi mini-chain, occupies a distinctive, two-storey brick building a few yards from the A148. The interior has been cleverly kitted out with all sorts of bygones, from old books to countrified furniture, but the open fires are original. The menu is strong on local, seasonal ingredients – they even have their own herd of cattle in an adjacent field – and features the likes of Norfolk duck cassoulet with mixed-leaf salad and vegetable crisps (£16.45). Daily: lunch noon–2.30pm; dinner 6.30–9.30pm.

SHOPPING

Bircham Gallery 14 Market Place, NR25 6BW ☎ 01263 713312, ⓦ birchamgallery.co.uk. Holt has a clutch of art galleries and although some of them verge on the tourist-twee, others are distinctly more up market and this is the pick of the artistic crop, its well-lit premises displaying regularly rotated displays of ceramics, prints, paintings, jewellery, sculpture and glassware. There's a good showing here for local contemporary artists and the gallery is perhaps at its strongest in its prints, many of which feature Norfolk land- and seascapes. Mon–Sat 9am–5pm.

Holt Bookshop Appleyard, NR25 6AR ☎ 01263 715858, ⓦ holtbookshoponline.co.uk. Named in a recent poll as one of the UK's top independent bookshops, this bright and amenable store has more than 12,000 books on its shelves with special attention given to local interest titles of which it has a comprehensive selection. Readings and cultural events too. Mon–Sat 9am–5pm, April–Dec till 5.30pm.

★ **Old Town** 49 Bull St, NR25 6HP ☎ 01263 710001, ⓦ old-town.co.uk. Running the flag up for British manufacturers, this excellent clothes' shop has its own on-site workshop, where they turn out around fifty garments a week using British cottons, woollens and linens wherever possible. The clothes are made to order – as opposed to made to measure – with corduroy and moleskin being two of the most popular, fustian-type fabrics. Tues–Sat 10am–5pm.

Simon Finch Bookshop 3 Fish Hill, NR25 6BD ☎ 01263 712650, ⓦ simonfinchnorfolk.co.uk. Proud to be old-fashioned, this long-established, secondhand and antiquarian bookshop occupies ancient premises, its 20,000-odd books packed into ten rooms spread over three floors. An outlet of Simon Finch Rare Books, Maddox St, London. Mon–Sat 10am–5pm.

Fakenham and around

It's hard to say quite why, but **FAKENHAM**, a medium-sized market town twelve miles southwest of Holt, seems to have missed the tourist money and although its **Market Place** is flanked and fringed by a pleasant assortment of old brick buildings, there's precious little sign of the bijou shops that are such a feature of its smaller neighbour. The town is at its busiest on horse-racing days – **Fakenham Racecourse** (☎ 01328 862388, ⓦ fakenhamracecourse.co.uk) lies just to the south of town – but otherwise it's a quiet sort of place, though it is near several popular attractions, specifically **Pensthorpe Nature Reserve** to the east, the **Thursford Collection** to the northeast, and **Houghton Hall** to the west. There are a trio of good places to stay near Fakenham too – all of them lie to the west of town near the main road, the A148.

Museum of Gas and Local History

Hempton Rd, NR21 7LA • April, May & Oct Thurs 10am–noon; June–Sept Thurs & Sat 10am–3.30pm • Free • ☎ 01328 863150, ⓦ fakenhamgasmuseum.com

Fakenham's main sight is the **Museum of Gas and Local History**, the only surviving town gasworks in the whole of England. It displays all the gear used for the manufacture of gas from coal – retorts, condensers, purifiers – in a technology that was rendered redundant when gas was discovered beneath the North Sea. There are also examples of vintage gas fires, lights, cookers and heaters. It's located a few minutes' walk south of the Market Place.

Pensthorpe Nature Reserve

Fakenham, NR21 0LN • March–Dec daily 10am–5pm; Jan & Feb daily 10am–4pm • £9.50 • ☎ 01328 851465, ⓦ pensthorpe.com

Norfolk's most popular nature reserve, **Pensthorpe** occupies a large slab of land and lagoon about a mile from the centre of Fakenham. A network of footpaths negotiates most of the reserve, where waterfowl gather by the hundred, Norfolk's birdlife supplemented by (clipped-wing) imports from round the world. One part of the reserve is dedicated to declining species – there is a red squirrel hutch and a corncrake breeding programme – and there are also several themed gardens. If you like things a little wilder, there are bird hides on the edge of Pensthorpe where you can observe waterfowl in a less constrained environment.

3

The Thursford Collection

Thursford Green, NR21 0AS (clearly signed from the A148) • Easter to late Sept Mon–Fri & Sun noon–5pm • £8 • ☎ 01328 878477, ⓦ thursford.com

One of Norfolk's biggest attractions, the **Thursford Collection**, about four miles northeast of Fakenham via the A148, holds what the owners claim is the world's largest collection of steam engines and organs with pride of place going to the whopping Wurlitzer, played with pizzazz by the resident organist twice daily. There are also fairground rides, tourist shops, restaurants and a playground, plus regular screenings of old silent films.

Houghton Hall

Houghton, PE31 6UE (signed from the A148) **House** Easter to late Sept Wed, Thurs, Sun & bank hol Mon 1.30–5pm, last admission 4.30pm • £8.80 (includes grounds) **Park and grounds** Easter to late Sept Wed, Thurs, Sun & bank hol Mon 11.30am–5.30pm • £6 • ☎ 01485 528569, ⓦ houghtonhall.com

Built for England's first Prime Minister, Sir Robert Walpole (1676–1745), **Houghton Hall**, some nine miles west of Fakenham, is a grandiloquent, early eighteenth-century pile, whose assorted state rooms include the imperious **Stone Hall**, which comes complete with a bust of Sir Robert dressed up as a Roman and looking distinctly haughty – no one ever accused him of being modest. Perhaps the most appealing room, in a gaudy sort of way, is the **Saloon**, which was kitted out in all its luxury by **William Kent** (1685–1748), the hall's principal architect and designer. Kent was especially fond of classical Greek and Roman allegories – hence the painting of *Apollo driving his Chariot of the Sun* in the ceiling's central octagon. After the house, you can wander the **park** and **gardens** and visit the former **stables**.

ARRIVAL AND DEPARTURE	FAKENHAM AND AROUND

By bus Fakenham is well connected by bus to a hatful of Norfolk towns and villages, including East Rudham, seven miles to the west, where buses halt in front of the *Crown* *Inn* (hourly on Norfolk Green's bus no. #X8). In Fakenham, buses pull in on Oak St, just to the north of the Market Place.

ACCOMMODATION

GRIMSTON

Congham Hall Grimston, PE32 1AH ☎ 01485 600250, ⓦ www.conghamhallhotel.co.uk. In a rural setting just south of the A148 – and thirteen miles west of Fakenham – this deluxe hotel occupies a handsome Georgian mansion surrounded by well-tended gardens and with its own capacious herb garden. The rooms have been decorated in smart-to-lavish period style and there is a fully equipped spa. **£150**

EAST RUDHAM

Crown Inn The Green, PE31 8RD ☎01485 528530, ⓦwww.crowninnnorfolk.co.uk. There's not much going on in the hamlet of East Rudham, but *The Crown* is a real treat of a hotel with half a dozen comfortable bedrooms painted in creams, beiges and greys and equipped with brass bedsteads. A Flying Kiwi inn. **£100**

TATTERSETT

Manor Mews Tattersett, PE31 8RS ☎01485 528204, ⓦwww.manormews.co.uk. This family-run, high-spec conversion of old farm buildings consists of nine spacious cottages for two guests or more and the former farmhouse, which sleeps 22. The owners have chosen to keep things simple and light with wood or stone floors, open fireplaces and the like, plus self-catering facilities. They have thought about energy conservation as well – most of the cottages have ground-source heat pumps. The *Mews* is in a rural setting, just off the A148 a mile or two from East Rudham, in the scattered hamlet of Tattersett. Advance reservations required with a minimum three-night stay. Cottage for two or three nights **£250**

EATING

★ **Crown Inn** The Green, East Rudham, PE31 8RD ☎01485 528530, ⓦwww.crowninnnorfolk.co.uk. This old country pub has been intelligently renovated, its low-beamed ceilings preserved, its interior now decked out with a pot pourri of suitably rustic furniture and fittings – one of the table tops is even a walnut-veneer slice of tree trunk. The daily specials are chalked up on a blackboard above the open fireplace – choose from the likes of tagliatelli with crayfish and walnuts, or sea bass with squash and chorizo risotto. Mains average a very reasonable £15. Daily noon–2.30pm & 6.30–9.30pm.

Wells-next-the-Sea and Holkham

Despite its name, **WELLS-NEXT-THE-SEA**, some eight miles west of Blakeney, is situated a good mile or so from open water. In Tudor times, before the harbour silted up, this was one of the great ports of eastern England, a major player in the trade with the Netherlands. Those heady days are long gone and although it's now the only commercially viable port on the north Norfolk coast, this is hardly a major boast. More importantly, Wells is also one of the county's larger tourist resorts, and even though there are no specific sights among its narrow lanes, it does make a convenient base for exploring the surrounding coastline, especially **Holkham Hall** and **Holkham Bay**, and it's also the terminus of a toy-town tourist train, the **Wells and Walsingham Light Railway**.

The Buttlands and town centre

Wells divides into three distinct areas, starting with the prettiest part of town, **The Buttlands**, where a broad rectangular green is lined with oak and beech trees and framed by an attractive medley of old, mostly Georgian houses and pretty little cottages; the green takes its unusual name from the time it was used for archery practice (a butt being the earthen mound behind the target). North from here, across Station Road, lie the narrow lanes of the **town centre** with Staithe Street, the minuscule main drag, flanked by old-fashioned knick-knack shops, charity shops, ice-cream kiosks and cafés.

The beach and harbour

Staithe Street leads down to **The Quay**, a somewhat forlorn affair inhabited by a couple of amusement arcades and a big old warehouse or two, reminders of the town's previous role as a major port. Beginning here also is the mile-long byroad that scuttles north to the **beach**, a handsome sandy tract backed by pine-clad dunes. The beach road is shadowed by a high flood defence and the tiny, narrow-gauge **Wells Harbour Railway** (Easter to mid-Oct, trains every 20–30min from 10.30am; £1.30 each way), which scoots down to the beach every twenty minutes or so. Overlooking the start of the railway is a **monument** to the **lifeboatmen**, who drowned in the worst disaster ever to

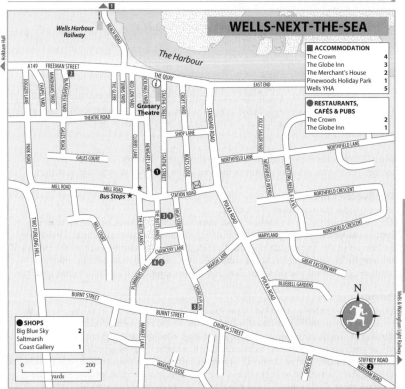

WELLS-NEXT-THE-SEA

ACCOMMODATION

The Crown	4
The Globe Inn	3
The Merchant's House	2
Pinewoods Holiday Park	1
Wells YHA	5

RESTAURANTS, CAFÉS & PUBS

The Crown	2
The Globe Inn	1

SHOPS

Big Blue Sky	2
Saltmarsh Coast Gallery	1

befall the Wells lifeboat: in October 1880, in heavy seas and amid a howling gale, the Wells lifeboat, *The Eliza Adams*, saved the crew of one ship before setting out again to save the men of another. Before the lifeboat could complete this mission, however, it was hit by a freak wave and, even worse, the boat could not right itself after it capsized because its mast had got stuck in a sandbank. Twelve of the crew were washed from the boat and eleven lost their lives, leaving ten widows and 28 children to grieve their passing.

Holkham Hall

Holkham, NR23 1AB • April–Oct Sun, Mon & Thurs noon–4pm • £9 (parking £2.50) • ☎ 01328 710227, ⓦ holkham.co.uk • The Norfolk Coasthopper bus (see p.122) stops beside the *Victoria Hotel* at the north entrance of the Holkham estate, about a mile from the Hall, and at the south end of Lady Anne's Drive, which leads to Holkham Bay

Holkham Hall, three miles to the west of Wells along the A149, is a grand and self-assured (or vainglorious) stately home designed by the eighteenth-century architect William Kent for the first earl of Leicester, whose descendants still own the place in the person of the seventh earl, **Edward Coke**. The severe sandy-coloured Palladian exterior belies the warmth and richness of the interior, which retains much of its original decoration, notably the much-admired **Marble Hall**, with its fluted columns, coffered ceiling and intricate reliefs. The rich colours of the **state rooms** are an appropriate backdrop for a wide selection of paintings, including canvases by Van Dyck, Rubens and Gainsborough, and, if opulence is your thing, you'll be delighted by the resplendent **North State Sitting Room**, which is adorned by four seventeenth-century

---

THE WELLS AND WALSINGHAM LIGHT RAILWAY

The **Wells and Walsingham Light Railway** (WWLR; early April to late Oct 3–5 daily; 30min each way; adult return £8, children £6.50, one-way £6.50/£5; no cards; ☎01328 711630, ⑩wellswalsinghamrailway.co.uk) is proud to be the longest **10¼-inch narrow-gauge steam railway** in the world, its vintage locomotive chugging its way the four miles south from Wells to Walsingham on what was originally a branch line of the Great Eastern Railway. The WWLR opened in 1982 largely thanks to the tireless endeavours of Roy Francis and it's now operated and maintained by a devoted team of volunteers. Wells station is southeast of town, just over a mile from the quayside; the Norfolk Coasthopper bus (see p.122) stops close by.

Brussels tapestries depicting the sun's annual progress through the signs of the zodiac, though – for some obscure reason or another – the summer months are missing.

The Bygones Museum

April–Oct daily 10am-5pm •£4 (combined entry with Hall £11)

The Earl has rustled up a couple of other attractions at Holkham, beginning with the **Bygones Museum**, where an assortment of old cars and agricultural tools and machinery are housed in the former stables of 1860. Here also is an exhibition entitled the **History of Farming** (free), which pays fulsome tribute to the Coke family's pioneering efforts to improve agricultural practices hereabouts in the late eighteenth and nineteenth centuries.

The park

April–Oct daily 7am–7pm; Nov–March Mon, Wed & Fri 7am–7pm or dusk, Tues & Thurs 9.30am–7pm or dusk • Free (parking £2.50)

Holkham's surrounding **parkland** is laid out on sandy, saline land, much of it originally salt marsh. The focal point is an eighty-foot-high **obelisk**, atop a grassy knoll, from where you can view both the hall to the north and the triumphal arch to the south. In common with the rest of the north Norfolk coast, there's plenty of birdlife – Holkham's lake attracts Canada geese, herons and grebes – and several hundred deer graze the open pastures. **Cycle rental** is available from £10 per day and there are also thirty-minute **lake cruises** (April & Oct Sun, Mon & Thurs 11am–5pm; May–Sept Mon, Tues, Thurs Sat & Sun, 11am–5pm; £3.50).

Holkham Bay

Parking at Lady Anne's Drive £5 (arrive before 10am in summer to be sure of a spot)

Much admired, **Holkham Bay** boasts one of the finest beaches on this stretch of coast, its golden sands stretching out into the ocean with pine-studded sand dunes behind. The bay is at its prettiest at high tide, when the sea breaks through the shoreline to create a shallow lagoon, which ripples and glistens in the summer sun. The nearest you can get by car and bike is **Lady Anne's Drive** a half-mile byroad-cum-car park accessed from the A149 opposite the *Victoria Hotel*. The northern end of Lady Anne's Drive intersects with the **Norfolk Coast Path** (see p.123), which heads off in both directions around the edge of the bay (2.75miles to Wells, 3.5miles to Burnham Overy Staithe), or you can stay put and enjoy the **birdlife**: warblers, flycatchers and redstarts inhabit the drier coastal reaches, while waders paddle about the mud and salt flats. In winter, thousands of geese drop by after their long flight from the Arctic and in spring and summer ground-nesting birds such as the lapwing and the avocet congregate here. There are two bird hides a short walk to the west of Lady Anne's Drive.

ARRIVAL AND INFORMATION
WELLS-NEXT-THE-SEA AND HOLKHAM

By bus Buses to Wells-next-the-Sea, including the Coasthopper (see p.122), stop on Station Rd, in between Staithe St and the Buttlands, and some also travel down to

The Quay. For Holkham Hall, the Coasthopper stops beside the *Victoria Hotel* at the north entrance of the Holkham estate and at the south end of Lady Anne's Drive, which leads to Holkham Bay.

Tourist office Wells's seasonal tourist office is a few yards from The Quay on Staithe St, NR23 1AN (late March to mid-May & early Sept to Oct daily 10am–2pm; mid-May to early Sept Mon–Sat 10am–5pm & Sun 10am–4pm; ☎ 0871 2003071, ⓦ visitnorthnorfolk.com).

ACCOMMODATION

WELLS-NEXT-THE SEA

★ **The Crown** The Buttlands, NR23 1EX ☎ 01328 710209, ⓦ crownhotelnorfolk.co.uk. Of the two hotels on the Buttlands, this one has the edge, beginning with the building itself, an especially attractive, three-storey former coaching inn with a handsome Georgian facade. Inside, the first batch of public rooms is cosy and quaint, all low ceilings and stone-flagged floors, and upstairs the dozen guest rooms are decorated in an imaginative and especially soothing style, though opinions are divided on the (very colourful) acrylic designs on the toilet seats. **£145**

The Globe Inn The Buttlands, NR23 1EU ☎ 01328 710206, ⓦ holkham.co.uk/globe. Not perhaps as lively as *The Crown* just along the street, *The Globe Inn* does have seven, very well-appointed guest rooms, each of which is decorated in a light and self-assured, vaguely rural style, complete with oak flooring. Two-night booking policy on most weekends. **£140**

The Merchant's House 47 Freeman St, NR23 1BQ ☎ 01328 711877, ⓦ the-merchants-house.co.uk. Occupying one of the oldest houses in Wells, parts of which date back to the fifteenth century, this deluxe B&B has just two, en-suite guest rooms – one with a four-poster bed. It has a handy location too, just a couple of minutes' walk from the quayside and the dining room, where breakfasts are served, holds a wide supply of information on local sights and walks. Minimum stay of two nights July & Aug. **£80**

Pinewoods Holiday Park Beach Rd, NR23 1DR ☎ 01328 710439, ⓦ pinewoods.co.uk. *Pinewoods* has been welcoming holidaymakers for over sixty years, its popularity based on its location, right behind a long line of pine-clad sand dunes that themselves abut a gorgeous stretch of sandy beach. It's evolved into a sprawling complex that holds touring and static caravans, beach huts, camping pitches and cosy wooden holiday lodges, the latter equipped with kitchen diners. As you might expect, there's a comprehensive range of facilities to cater for the crowds from shops to toilet blocks. *Pinewoods* is a 15min walk from The Quay in Wells or you can take the Wells Harbour Railway (see p.144). The tariff for all the various options available at *Pinewoods* is necessarily complicated, but in high season a three-bed (six-berth) lodge costs around £750 per week. Camp and caravan pitches mid-March to late Oct; lodges mid-March to Dec. Tent pitches from **£11**

Wells YHA Church Plain, NR23 1EQ ☎ 0845 3719544, ⓦ yha.org.uk. Located on the southern side of town, just off the A149, this medium-sized YHA hostel occupies an imaginatively recycled old church hall, which dates back to the early twentieth century. Especially popular with groups, the hostel offers self-catering facilities and 31 beds in two- to four-bunk bedrooms. Reception is open 8am–noon & 5–8pm. Dorms **£18.40**

HOLKHAM HALL

The Victoria Hotel Park Rd, NR23 1RG ☎ 01328 711008, ⓦ www.holkham.co.uk/victoria. Part of the Holkham estate, *The Victoria* boasts a fine location in between Holkham Bay and Holkham Hall, though the streaming traffic of the A149 does take the gloss off things. There are just ten guest rooms here and the general feel is country-house, though lots of the furnishings and fittings have been imported from Rajasthan, which makes the hotel look rather strange – charmingly idiosyncratic some would say. A refurbishment is underway. Minimum two-night stay most weekends. **£130**

EATING

The Crown The Buttlands, NR23 1EX ☎ 01328 710209, ⓦ crownhotelnorfolk.co.uk. *The Crown* hotel prides itself on its food. You can eat in several areas, each with a different atmosphere from the slightly formal to the very relaxed, though the menu is the same throughout. The house speciality is extrapolations on traditional British dishes – try, for example, the trout with black pudding or the steak and beetroot. Prices are very competitive with mains averaging around £15. Kitchen: daily noon–2.30pm & 6.30–9.30pm.

The Globe Inn The Buttlands, NR23 1EU ☎ 01328 710206, ⓦ holkham.co.uk/globe. Well-regarded restaurant featuring meat and vegetables from the nearby Holkham estate (see p.145). Mains begin at £13. Kitchen daily noon–2.30pm & 6.30–9pm.

SHOPPING

Big Blue Sky Warham Rd, NR23 1QA ☎ 01328 712023, ⓦ bigbluesky.uk.com. With the boast that "everything here comes from Norfolk", this large shop specializes in all things idiosyncratic, from sweet-smelling soaps, cups and ceramic coasters through to jute beach bags and wooden jigsaw towers. Can be a tad twee, but good fun all the same. Mid-March to Oct Mon–Sat 10am–5pm & Sun 11am–4pm; Nov to mid-March Wed–Sat 10am–5pm &

3

Sun 11am–4pm.

Saltmarsh Coast Gallery 35a Staithe St, NR23 1AG ☎ 07833 296654, ⓦ saltmarshcoastgallery.co.uk. Wells's main street may have more than its fair share of tourist tat, but this excellent gallery, which showcases the landscape photography of John Gibbs and Gareth Hacon,

really is very good, its prime images being of Norfolk in general and the Norfolk coast in particular. Apart from the photos, there are also art cards, calendars, acrylics and framed prints – all at surprisingly affordable prices: a good-size, framed photo will cost you about £100. Wed, Thurs, Sat & Sun 10am–5pm.

ENTERTAINMENT

The Granary Theatre Staithe St, NR23 1NE ☎ 01328 710193, ⓦ granarytheatre.co.uk. Operated by the volunteer Wells Community Association, the Granary Theatre is in the old maltings building at the foot of Staithe St. It's a tiny affair, with just 69 seats, but it puts on a varied

programme, everything from touring professional theatre companies, cinema screenings and performing arts workshops to individual performances by a mixed bag of artists and musicians.

3

Little Walsingham

For centuries, **LITTLE WALSINGHAM**, five miles south of Wells, rivalled Bury St Edmunds and Canterbury as the foremost pilgrimage site in England. It all began in 1061 when the lady of the manor, one Richeldis de Faverches, was prompted to build a replica of the **Santa Casa** (Mary's home in Nazareth) in this remote part of Norfolk – inspired, it is said, by visions of the Virgin Mary. Whatever the reason, it brought instant fame and fortune to Little Walsingham and every medieval king from Henry III onwards made at least one trip, walking the last mile barefoot. Both the Augustinians and the Franciscans established themselves here and all seemed set fair when Henry VIII followed in his predecessors' footsteps in 1511. Yet, pilgrim or not, it didn't stop Henry from destroying the shrine in the Dissolution of the 1530s, and at a stroke the village's principal trade came to a halt. **Pilgrimages** resumed in earnest after 1922, when the local vicar, a certain Alfred Hope Patten, organized an Anglo-Catholic pilgrimage, the prelude to the building of an **Anglican shrine** in the 1930s – much to the initial chagrin of the diocesan authorities. Nowadays, the village does good business out of its holy connections as well as from the **WWLR** steam railway, which links it with Wells (see p.144).

Common Place and the High Street

Pocket-sized Little Walsingham has an attractive and singularly old-fashioned centre, beginning with **Common Place**, the main square, whose half-timbered buildings surround a quaint octagonal structure built to protect the village pump in the sixteenth century. The **High Street** extends south from here, overlooked by antique brick and half-timbered houses, several of which are given over to religious bookstores. The northern end of the High Street is also overseen by the impressive, if badly weathered, fifteenth-century **abbey gatehouse** of the old priory – look up and you'll spy Christ peering out from a window – though the abbey grounds beyond can only be reached from Common Place (see opposite). At the south end of the High Street is the **Friday Market Place**, a tiny crossroads edged by a pretty medley of very old houses. Beyond here, about 200 yards out on the Fakenham road, is the tumble-down stonework of the old **Franciscan Friary** (no access).

The Anglican shrine

Common Place, NR22 6BP • Open daily • Free • ☎ 01328 820255, ⓦ walsinghamanglican.org.uk

Dotted around Little Walsingham are a number of shrines catering to a variety of denominations – there's even a Russian Orthodox Church – but the main event is the

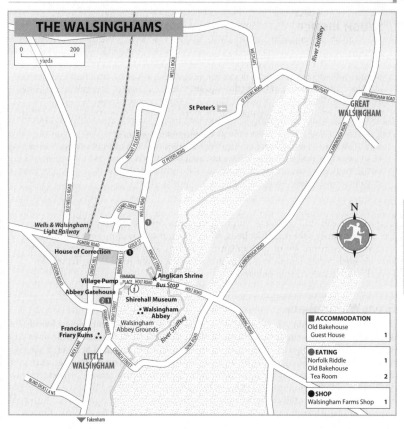

Anglican shrine, beside Holt Road, a few yards to the east of Common Place. Flanked by attractive gardens as well as a visitor centre, where there's a small exhibition on the history of the cult, the shrine is a strange-looking building, rather like a cross between an English village hall and an Orthodox church. The interior holds a series of small chapels and a Holy Well with healing waters as well as the idiosyncratic Holy House – **Santa Casa** – which contains the much revered **statue** of Our Lady of Walsingham.

Shirehall Museum and Walsingham Abbey ruins

Common Place, NR22 6BP • Early Feb to Oct daily 10am–4pm with entry through the Shirehall Museum; abbey grounds only Nov to early Feb Mon–Fri 9am–1pm & 2–5pm with entrance via the Walsingham Estate Office, 10 Common Place • £3.50 • ☎ 01328 820510, ⓦ walsinghamabbey.com

For most of the year, entry to the abbey grounds is via the mildly diverting **Shirehall Museum**, which has modest displays on the history of Little Walsingham, including a section on its role as a centre of pilgrimage. The Shirehall was also the seat of justice hereabouts as recalled by the original **Georgian Court Room** and an old holding cell. In the cell is a crude life-size model of **Rice Gavercoli** (see box, p.150), a local man who was transported to Australia in 1831 for breaking the machines that were threatening his livelihood as a day labourer.

Beyond the museum are the **abbey grounds**, whose lovely landscaped gardens stretch down to the River Stiffkey enclosing the **ruins of Walsingham Abbey**, primarily a large

3

TOUGH JUSTICE

Little Walsingham's **Shirehall** was where generations of Norfolk peasantry felt the full brunt of a legal system that gave short shrift to anyone who dared to attack the property of his or her social "superiors". In 1885, **Horace Pegg**, for one, set fire to a farmer's stack of wheat and barley and was given eighteen months in prison for his pains – but at least he didn't have to go far: Little Walsingham's **House of Correction** was just a few yards away off Bridewell Street (it's still there –but in a dreadful state of repair). However, Pegg and his fellow prisoners may well have preferred to serve their time elsewhere for here in Walsingham the incarcerated experienced at first hand the shifting fashions in punishment. The worst time to be locked up was after 1836 when the authorities introduced the so-called **Pentonville System** of "Separation and Silence": the prisoners were kept in perpetual solitary confinement, and were compelled to wear masks when they took to the exercise yard. This system was founded on the pseudo-scientific theory that defined crime as a contagious disease, but unfortunately for the theorists, the system drove so many prisoners crazy that it was abandoned a few years later.

---

chunk of the east wall complete with its imposing Gothic window. Otherwise, the grounds are famous for their **bluebells**, which burst into flower in early February, signifying the start of spring and, in Christian terms, symbolizing the day, six weeks after his birth, when Joseph and Mary presented the infant Jesus at the Temple in Jerusalem as Jewish custom demanded.

Great Walsingham

If **GREAT WALSINGHAM** was ever "great", it certainly isn't today, comprising a handful of old flint houses scattered on either side of the River Stiffkey just half a mile or so north of Little Walsingham. The main reason to visit is the **church of St Peter**, a squat tumble of a flint building sitting on a grassy knoll just to the west of the river and almost untouched since its construction in the early fourteenth century. The exterior is distinguished by the impressive gargoyles that adorn the tower and by some particularly fancy stone tracery round the windows, while inside pride of place goes to the forest of poppy-head bench ends carved with a menagerie of medieval life from saints, flowers and mythical monsters to real-life creatures including a dog and a chameleon.

ARRIVAL AND INFORMATION

LITTLE WALSINGHAM

By train There are no regular train services to Little Walsingham, but the toy-town trains of the Wells and Walsingham Light Railway (see p.146), linking it with Wells, pull in at the station off Egmere Rd, from where it's a 5min walk south to Common Place: from the station, turn left along Egmere Rd and take the second major right down Bridewell St.

By bus Norfolk Green's (☎ 01553 776980, ⍟ norfolkgreen. co.uk) bus service #29 runs south from Wells to Fakenham via Little Walsingham, pausing outside the Anglican Shrine (Mon–Sat hourly, Sun every 2hr).

Tourist office At the Shirehall Museum, on Common Place, NR22 6BP (same times as museum; ☎ 01328 820510, ⍟ visitnorthnorfolk.com).

ACCOMMODATION AND EATING

Little Walsingham is light on accommodation and during major pilgrimages vacant rooms are almost impossible to find. The same applies on major Christian holidays – Easter being the prime example. The village has one good place to eat and one well-stocked food shop.

Norfolk Riddle 2 Wells Rd, NR22 6DJ ☎ 01328 821903. A combined fish and chip shop and restaurant supplied – and owned – by the local farmers of the Walsingham Farms Shop (see p.152). The restaurant is a bit short of decorative charm, but there's no denying the tastiness of the food and by and large it's all locally sourced – try, for example, the slow-roasted pork belly with apple sauce (£12.50). East Anglian beers and ciders too. Restaurant Wed–Sun noon–2pm & 6–9pm; fish & chip shop daily 11.30am–2pm & 4.30–9.30pm.

FROM TOP BINHAM PRIORY (P.137); OYSTERS AT *THE SHIP*, BRANCASTER (P.159) >

Old Bakehouse Tea Room & Guest House 33 High St, NR22 6BZ ☎01328 820454, ⓦ glavenvalley.co.uk/oldbakehouse. In the centre of the village, this long-established tearoom offers a tasty range of home-made cakes, scones and soups plus top-ranking cream teas (Wed–Sun 10.30am–4.30pm). They also have three commodious, en-suite double rooms – the best in the village – and each is decorated in a reassuringly traditional style. Free wi-fi. **£80**

SHOPPING

Walsingham Farms Shop Guild St, NR22 6BU ☎01328 821877, ⓦ walsinghamfarmsshop.co.uk. Surprisingly large shop-cum-deli showcasing the produce of a raft of local farmers, especially meat, game and veg. They have their own butchers and also a kitchen, where they churn out pies and pâtés, soups, stews and puddings. Tues–Fri 9am–6pm, Sat 9am–5pm & Sun 10am–4pm.

The Burnhams

Heading west from Wells on the A149, it's about five miles to **Burnham Overy Staithe**, a tiny hamlet whose easy ramble of old buildings nudges up against a creeky little harbour. This is the first of the **BURNHAMS**, the handful of villages that occupy this corner of Norfolk, the leading player being the postcard-pretty village of **Burnham Market**, where an attractive medley of Georgian and Victorian houses surrounds a dinky little green with an oh-so-cutesy stream flowing across the road whenever it rains. **Burnham Thorpe**, a mile or so to the southeast, is best known as the birthplace of **Horatio Nelson** while further north **Burnham Deepdale** heralds a stretch of marshy coast that includes **Brancaster Staithe**, access point for the nature reserve on Scolt Head Island.

Burnham Market

BURNHAM MARKET attracts a well-heeled, metropolitan crew, in no small measure because of the *Hoste Arms* (see p.154), an old coaching inn beside the green that offers some of the best restaurant and bar food on the coast. There's quite enough money here to support several chichi shops and food stores (see p.155), but there's only one sight as such, the **church of St Mary**, whose stumpy tower is easy to spot just beyond the west end of the green. Every inch a country church, the interior of St Mary's is of some mild interest for its three-seater sedilia (for the priest, deacon and sub-deacon) on the south side of the chancel and the stained glass of the east window, which was inserted in 1953.

Burnham Thorpe

Straggling **BURNHAM THORPE** was the birthplace of **Horatio Nelson** (see box, p.154), who was born in the village parsonage on September 29, 1758. The parsonage was demolished years ago, but the great man is still celebrated in the village's **All Saints Church**, where the lectern is made out of timbers taken from Nelson's last ship, the *Victory*, the chancel sports a Nelson bust, and the south aisle has a small exhibition on

---

WHAT'S IN A NAME – THE BURNHAMS

There are of course exceptions, but most villages in Norfolk have **Anglo-Saxon names** with many ending in "ham" or "ton". These two endings were largely interchangeable, meaning settlement, though sometimes – as in the case of the Burnhams – "ham" referred to a central habitation with "tons" surrounding it. Thus, **Burnham Market** seems to have been the centre of a Saxon village with outlying settlements at **Norton** (north) and **Overy** (over the river), though – just to complicate matters – the "Thorpe" in **Burnham Thorpe** is thought to be of Scandinavian origin.

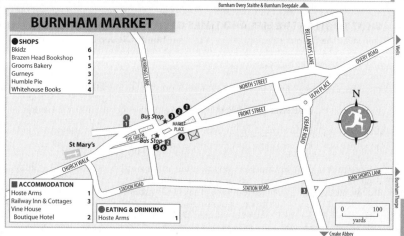

Burnham Overy Staithe & Burnham Deepdale ▲

BURNHAM MARKET

● **SHOPS**
Bkidz	6
Brazen Head Bookshop	1
Grooms Bakery	5
Gurneys	3
Humble Pie	2
Whitehouse Books	4

St Mary's

■ **ACCOMMODATION**
Hoste Arms	1
Railway Inn & Cottages	3
Vine House Boutique Hotel	2

● **EATING & DRINKING**
| Hoste Arms | 1 |

Creake Abbey ▼

3

his life and times. The other place to head for is the village pub (see p.155), where Nelson held a farewell party for the locals in 1793.

Creake Abbey

North Creake, NR21 9LF • Open access daylight hours • Free; EH • ⓦ www.english-heritage.org.uk. • Signed from the B1355 just north of North Creake

Heading south from Burnham Thorpe, it's about a mile to **Creake Abbey**, whose shattered remains occupy a captivating setting near the River Burn amid woods and fields – and just a few hundred yards from Abbey Farm's attractive Courtyard complex (see p.156). A handsome set of Gothic arches support what remains of the abbey's flint walls, but in truth this was never an important foundation, though it did come to a dramatic end: in 1506, the seven remaining monks died of the plague and, in fright, the abbot took flight and no one ever opened it up again.

Burnham Deepdale and Brancaster Staithe

Heading north from Burnham Market, you rejoin the main coastal road, the A149, just a mile or two from minuscule **BURNHAM DEEPDALE**, the home of the assorted holiday facilities of **Deepdale Farm** (see p.155). From here, it's a couple of hundred yards to the beginning of **BRANCASTER STAITHE**, where a strip of housing falls either side of the main road. First impressions of the village are not especially favourable, but it does possess the excellent *White Horse* (see p.155) and it also runs parallel and very close to the marshes of the seashore – and the **Norfolk Coast Path** (see p.123). There are several access points, the most easterly being at the back of the *White Horse* car park. Alternatively, head west from the *White Horse* along the A149 and, after a few hundred yards, you'll spy the *Jolly Sailors* pub (see p.155) on the left. Opposite, on the right, an easy-to-miss unmarked lane leads down to **Brancaster Staithe Quay**, where a tumble of old fishermen's shacks and sheds flank the tiniest of jetties. The quay is now owned and operated by the National Trust, who are upgrading its facilities to cater for up to twenty local fishermen.

Scolt Head Island National Nature Reserve

The narrow creeks and salt marshes that spread north from Brancaster Staithe are protected from the ocean by **Scolt Head Island**, a national nature reserve in the care of

3

SHOT TO BITS – THE LIFE AND TIMES OF NELSON

Born in Burnham Thorpe, the sixth of eleven children, **Horatio Nelson** (1758–1805) joined the navy at the tender age of 12, and was soon sent to the West Indies, where he met and married **Frances Nisbet**, retiring to Burnham Thorpe in 1787. Back in action by 1793, his bravery cost him first the sight of his right eye, and shortly afterwards his right arm. His personal life was equally eventful – famously, his infatuation with **Emma Hamilton**, wife of the ambassador to Naples, caused the eventual break-up of his marriage. His finest hour was during the **Battle of Trafalgar** in 1805, when he led the British navy to victory against the combined French and Spanish fleets, a crucial engagement that set the scene for Britain's century-long domination of the high seas. The victory didn't do Nelson much good – he was shot in the chest during the battle and even the kisses of Hardy failed to revive him. Thereafter, Nelson was placed in a barrel of brandy and the pickled body shipped back to England, where he was laid in state at Greenwich and then buried at St Paul's. It was, however, Nelson's express wish that he should be buried here in Burnham Thorpe, but to no avail – he was too much of a national/imperial hero to ever allow that to happen. In all the naval hullabaloo, Nelson's far-from-positive attitude to the landowners of his home village was soon glossed over too: in 1797, he sent a batch of blankets back to Norfolk to keep the poor warm, railing that an average farm labourer received "Not quite two pence a day for each person; and to drink nothing but water, for beer our poor labourers never taste…".

Natural England (w naturalengland.org.uk). The island, which is gradually growing westward, has four main habitats – sand dune, shingle, salt marsh and inter-tidal mud flats – and these attract a wide range of birdlife, especially breeding terns and wintering wildfowl plus waders like the shelduck, wigeon, teal and curlew. Access is difficult, impossible on foot, but the Deepdale Farm information centre (see below) has the details of local **boat operators** who sally out to the island in the summer or you could try Branta Cruises (see below).

ARRIVAL AND INFORMATION
THE BURNHAMS

By bus The Norfolk Coasthopper bus (see p.122) stops beside the green on the Market Place in Burnham Market. It also travels through Burnham Overy Staithe, Burnham Deepdale and Brancaster Staithe on the A149, but it does not pass through Burnham Thorpe.

Deepdale Farm Information Centre Burnham Deepdale, PE31 8DD (Daily 10am–4pm; ☎01485 210256, w deepdalefarm.co.uk). This useful information centre has details of local walks and boat trips, sells road and hiking maps, has tide times and internet facilities. They also have a campsite and a hostel here (see opposite).

Branta Cruises ☎01485 211132, w brantacruises.co.uk. Organizes a variety of coastal boat trips including excursions to Scolt Head. Most of their tours last about two hours, but longer trips are possible. Two-hour tours cost £20 per person, £30 for three hours; advance reservations are essential.

ACCOMMODATION

BURNHAM MARKET

Hoste Arms Market Place, PE31 8HD ☎01328 738777, w hostearms.co.uk. One of the most fashionable spots on the Norfolk coast, this former coaching inn at the heart of Burnham Market has been sympathetically modernized. The hotel's 35 guest rooms are round the back and range from the small (verging on the cramped) to the much more expensive (and expensive). The decor in the buildings here can verge on the pretentious/preposterous (Zulu shields, would you believe), but there's no denying the buzz of the place. Weekend rates are always higher with two nights usually a minimum stay. **£160**

The Railway Inn Creake Rd ☎01328 738777, w hostearms.co.uk. Burnham Market train station was closed down in the 1950s, but it has been tastefully modernized and converted by the owners of the *Hoste Arms* into a pretty little hotel with one of the rooms in an old railway carriage. Keys from the *Hoste Arms*, from where it is a ten-minute walk. Minimum two-night stay most of the year. Per night from **£100**

Vine House Boutique Hotel The Green ☎01328 738777, w hostearms.co.uk. Boutique hotel in a Georgian townhouse across the green from the *Hoste Arms*, where you get the keys. Seven deluxe guest rooms with all mod cons. **£200**

THE BURNHAMS **THE NORTH NORFOLK COAST** ┃ 155

BURNHAM DEEPDALE

Deepdale Backpackers & Camping Deepdale Farm, Burnham Deepdale, PE31 8DD ☎01485 210256, ⓦ deepdalefarm.co.uk. Full marks for ingenuity go to this lively, youthful and very amiable setup, where they operate a combined campsite, info centre (see p.154), café and eco-friendly, backpackers' hostel in creatively renovated former stables beside the main coastal road. Not only that, but they have also diversified into tipis and yurts. Cheaper midweek. Dorms **£15**, doubles **£60**; 2-person tipi **£80**; 2-person yurt **£95**

BRANCASTER STAITHE

★ **White Horse** Brancaster Staithe, PE31 8BY ☎01485 210262, ⓦ whitehorsebrancaster.co.uk. This combined hotel, pub and restaurant backs straight onto the marshes, lagoons and creeks of the coast – and, even better, the North Norfolk Coast Path runs along the bottom of the hotel car park. The hotel divides into two sections: there are seven, en-suite rooms in the main building, one of which is a split-level room with a telescope thrown in for free, and eight more at the back with grass roofs. The decor is light and airy with a few nautical bits and pieces thrown in for good measure. **£70**

EATING AND DRINKING

BURNHAM MARKET

Hoste Arms Market Place, PE31 8HD ☎01328 738777, ⓦ hostearms.co.uk. At the front, the *Hoste's* antique bar, complete with its wooden beams and stone-flagged floor, is merely a foretaste of the several, chichi dining areas beyond. Throughout, the menu is a well-balanced mixture of "land and sea", anything from wood pigeon with strawberries to cod in beer batter with peas and chips, and main courses range from £15 to £20 in the evening, slightly less at lunch. Kitchen: daily noon–2pm & 6–9pm; cream teas in between: 9am–noon & 3–5.30pm.

BURNHAM THORPE

Lord Nelson Walsingham Rd, PE31 8HN ☎01328 738241. They have kept modernity at bay here at this ancient village pub, from the old wooden benches through to the serving hatch and tiled floor. There's a good range of real ales plus above-average bar food – try, for instance, the Norfolk chicken breast wrapped in ham with a green-herb filling (£14). Pub: Mon–Sat noon–3pm & 6–11pm,

Sun noon–10.30pm; kitchen: Mon noon–2.30pm, Tues–Sun noon–2.30pm & 6–9pm.

BRANCASTER STAITHE

Jolly Sailors Brancaster Staithe, PE31 8BJT ☎01485 210314. Relaxed and easy-going pub, kitted out in traditional style, where they do a good line in pizzas from as little as £6. Also daily specials, including a local speciality, Brancaster mussels, cooked every which way and also from £6. Pub: Mon–Sat noon–11pm & Sun noon–10.30pm; kitchen: Mon–Fri noon–9pm, Sat & Sun noon–10.45pm.

★ **White Horse** Brancaster Staithe, PE31 8BY ☎01485 210262, ⓦ whitehorsebrancaster.co.uk. Brancaster is famous for its mussels and oysters and this is as good a place as any to try them, though the restaurant has all sorts of other temptations from local duck to local beef with main courses averaging around £16. Kitchen: daily noon–2pm & 6.30–9pm; also bar menu daily 11am–9pm.

SHOPPING

BURNHAM MARKET

Bkidz Emma's Court, off Market Place, PE31 8HD ☎01328 738950, ⓦ bkidz.co.uk. This bijou little shop sells a wonderful range of stuff for kids. Toys and clothes are its primary pull, but there's lots more too, including all sorts of games. Mon–Sat 10am–5pm, Sun 10am–4pm.
Brazen Head Bookshop Market Place, PE31 8HD ☎01328 730700, ⓦ brazenhead.org.uk. In antique premises, this top-notch bookshop is especially strong on children's classics and classic novels with a good sideline in local stuff as well. Stocks both new and secondhand titles. Mon–Sat 9.30am–5pm.
Grooms Bakery Market Place, PE31 8HD ☎01328 738289. Top-notch bakery offering a wide range of Italian and French breads plus specialist health-food loaves too – multigrain, low-in-salt and so on. Mon–Sat 8am–4pm.
Gurneys Market Place, PE31 8HF ☎01328 738967, ⓦ gurneysfishshop.co.uk. Outstanding fishmongers

selling smoked and fresh fish and shellfish, including local lobsters and crabs. Has a quaint and old-fashioned appearance too – entirely appropriate in this most gentrified of villages. Mon–Sat 9am–5pm, Sun 10am–4pm.
Humble Pie Market Place, PE31 8HF ☎01328 738581, ⓦ humble-pie.com. Local produce is the big deal here in this excellent, well-established deli, which sells everything from pies and tarts, chutneys, cheeses, chorizo and marmalades through to cakes and biscuits, not to mention all sorts of olives and pre-cooked deli dishes. Mon, Tues, Thurs & Fri 9.30am–1pm & 2–5pm, Wed 9.30am–1pm, Sat 9am–1pm & 2–4.45pm.
Whitehouse Books Market Place, PE31 8HD ☎01328 730270, ⓦ whitehouse-books.co.uk. Enterprising, independent bookshop stocking a wide range of titles as well as cards, CDs and wrapping paper. Also puts on special events and sells OS maps. Mon–Sat 9.30am–1pm & 2–5pm.

3

CREAKE ABBEY
The Courtyard at Creake Abbey NR21 9LF
☎ 07801 418907, ⓦ creakeabbeystudios.co.uk. Here on Abbey Farm, a set of old, stable-like agricultural buildings has been turned into a pleasant little tourist complex.

There's a café and a deli, a therapy suite, children's clothing and an interior design shop – and all very cosy it is too. Farmers' markets are also held here on the first Saturday of each month, except January (9.30am–1pm), and there are vintage fairs too. Tues–Sun 10am–4pm.

Brancaster to Holme-next-the-Sea

From Brancaster Staithe (see p.153), it's a few hundred yards west along the main road to the turning for **Brancaster Harbour**, home to all sorts of sailing boats and the NT's **Brancaster Millennium Activity Centre** (☎ 01485 210719, ⓦ nationaltrust.org.uk/brancaster), where from February to December they organize guided walks across the mud flats, birdwatching rambles, sailing courses and taster days. The harbour is at the east end of the village of **BRANCASTER**, which straddles the A149 within easy walking distance of both the marshes and the Norfolk Coast Path (see p.123). Brancaster once bordered the open sea and it was here that the Romans built a fort – **Branodunum** – but this disappeared centuries ago, the only reminders of its location today being a number of street names – "Roman Way" for example. At the west end of the village, a turning leads the three-quarters of a mile north across the reedy marshes to **Brancaster beach** (£3.50 parking), where the sands are backed by a ridge of dunes; at low tide, the sand flats extend as far as the eye can see to either side of a narrow creek-cum-river. Brancaster may be an uneventful sort of place today, but it was the site of a major scandal in 1833, when the *Earl of Wemyss* ran aground here in a surging storm. Several of the passengers drowned as the result of the incompetence of the captain and several others, washed ashore half-dead, were most likely stripped of their possessions by the villagers – as recorded on the (badly weathered) tombstone of Susan Roche in **Brancaster church graveyard**.

Titchwell

From Brancaster, it's a little less than a mile to the next hamlet along, **TITCHWELL**, where a handful of flint-walled houses plus the enjoyable *Titchwell Manor Hotel* (see p.158) spreads out along the A149. Before its harbour silted up, Titchwell sat right next to the sea, a tiny fishing village whose inhabitants helped themselves to whatever was washed ashore – much to the chagrin of the local landowners, who had wreckage rights if, that is, they could enforce them: as early as 1317, one lord of the manor wrote to the courts accusing some of his tenants of stealing what was rightfully his. The locals were, however, far from lawless, often helping out those pilgrims who trudged through the village on the way to Little Walsingham (see p.148) – and the old **stone cross**, which stands on a grassy mound beside the A149, appears to have been a waymarker on the old pilgrims' route.

Titchwell Marsh Nature Reserve

Titchwell, PE31 8BB • Daily dawn to dusk • Free, but £4 parking • Shop & information centre daily 9.30am–5pm; Nov–March 9.30am–4pm • ☎ 01485 210779, ⓦ rspb.org.uk/titchwell • The reserve is clearly signed from the A149 on the west side of Titchwell

Today, the old sea approaches to Titchwell harbour have become the RSPB's **Titchwell Marsh Nature Reserve**, whose mix of marsh, reedbed, mud flat, lagoon and sandy beach attracts a wide variety of birds, including marsh harriers, bearded tits, avocets, gulls and terns. A series of footpaths explore this varied terrain, there are several well-positioned bird hides, including a super-duper Parrinder hide, and a very helpful shop-cum-information centre.

Thornham

In *The King's England: Norfolk*, published in 1940, good old Arthur Mee got rather carried away when he came to describing **THORNHAM**, the next village along from Titchwell, declaring it had "grown old beautifully by a creek of the North Sea, and trees have risen like friends to shield it from the winds". Elegies apart, Thornham had a brief industrial flurry when the lady of the manor, Edith Ames-Lyde, established an iron foundry here in 1887, but it didn't last long – the factory closed down in the 1920s – and today Thornham is a quiet little place whose brick and flint cottages stretch north from the A149 to the edge of the marshes. On the west side of the village, **Staithe Lane** leads the mile or so north from the A149 to the **harbour**, where a couple of rickety jetties oversee the narrowest of creeks set amid an expanse of salt marsh and mud flat. Walkers can pick up the **Norfolk Coast Path** (see box, p.123) either at the harbour or in Thornham village as the Path returns to the coast here after its detour inland around Titchwell. From the harbour, it takes about thirty minutes to walk along the path to the visitor centre at **Holme Dunes National Nature Reserve**, which stretches as far as Holme-next-the-Sea (see below).

Drove Orchards

A149, PE36 6LS **Farm shop** Daily 10am–5pm; restricted hours in winter – call ahead • ☏ 01485 525652, ⓦ droveorchards.com **Yurt Restaurant** Mon–Sat 10.30am–5pm & 6–9pm, Sun 9am–5pm; restricted hours in winter • ☏ 01485 525108, ⓦ theyurt.co.uk

Beside the main road, just to the west of Thornham, is **Drove Orchards**, an enterprising concern, which started out as an apple orchard, but has now diversified, selling a whole range of home-grown and local meat, cheese, fish, vegetables and fruit at their **Drove Orchard Farm Shop** – or, depending on the season, you can pick your own. Encouraged by the success of the shop, the owners pitched a yurt here and this is now the **Yurt Restaurant**, where again the emphasis is on all things local.

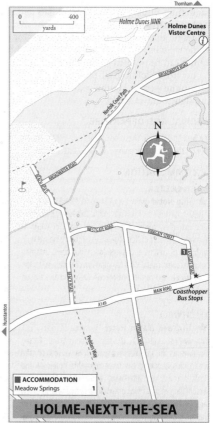

Holme-next-the-Sea

HOLME-NEXT-THE-SEA, about two miles west of Thornham, is the quietest of villages, its gentle ramble of old flint cottages and farm buildings nudging up towards the **sand dunes** of the coast. It's here at Holme that the Norfolk Coast Path (see p.123) intersects with the Peddars Way (see p.206), which follows the route of an old Roman road for most of its course, though it's likely the Romans simply enhanced what was there before: any doubts on the matter were surely quashed when, in 1998, gales uncovered a fascinating prehistoric site in the sands just off Holme, comprising a circle of timber posts surrounding a sort of inverted tree stump. Dated to around 2050 BC, "**Seahenge**", as it soon became known, attracted hundreds of visitors, but fears for its safety, prompted its removal to the Lynn Museum in King's Lynn (see p.170) and there's nothing to see here today.

To get to the junction of the two long-distance trails, go to the north end of **Beach Road** on the western edge of Holme and from here it's a few minutes' walk to the signed intersection on the other side of the golf course. From the intersection, the Norfolk Coast Path heads northeast, crossing the sand dunes of Holme Dunes National Nature Reserve (see below) en route to Thornham (see p.157). On the way, you'll pass within a few yards of the reserve's visitor centre, which can also be reached by car (see below).

Holme Dunes National Nature Reserve

Holme-next-the-Sea, PE36 6LQ **Reserve** daily 10am–5pm, or dusk if earlier • £4 for the reserve's footpaths and bird hides, but you can walk through the reserve on the Norfolk Coast Path for free **Visitor centre** April–Oct daily 10am–5pm; Nov–March Sat & Sun 10am –dusk • ☎01485 525240, ⓦ norfolkwildlifetrust.org.uk • 40min walk to the visitor centre from the nearest Coasthopper bus stop on the A149 at Holme.

Owned and managed by Norfolk Wildlife Trust, the **Holme Dunes National Nature Reserve** stretches along the coast at the point where The Wash meets the North Sea. The extensive sand and mud flats here have long protected the coast and allowed for the formation of a band of sand dunes, which have, in their turn, created areas of salt- and freshwater marsh, reedbeds, and Corsican pine woodland. This varied terrain attracts all sorts of **birds**, with waders such as grey plover, knot, bar-tailed godwit and sanderling zipping across the mud flats and migrant wildfowl like wigeon, brent geese and teal arriving in autumn to graze the marshes. In spring and summer, the shingle ridges on the beach attract nesting birds, for example ringed plover and oystercatchers, while lapwing, redshank, snipe and avocet breed on the marshes. The reserve's **visitor centre** can be reached on foot from Thornham via the Norfolk Coast Path (3miles) and by car from Holme-next-the-Sea (see p.157): from the A149, turn down Beach Road just to the west of Holme-next-the-Sea and, near the end of the road, turn right down the signed gravel track.

ARRIVAL AND DEPARTURE   BRANCASTER TO HOLME-NEXT-THE-SEA

By bus The Norfolk Coasthopper bus (see p.122) travels along the A149 stopping at Brancaster, Titchwell, Thornham and Holme-next-the-Sea.

ACCOMMODATION

BRANCASTER

★ **Ship Hotel** Main Rd (A149), PE31 8AP ☎01485 210333, ⓦ shiphotelnorfolk.co.uk. This lovely pub offers nine extremely pleasant guest rooms, each of which is decorated in a sort of New Age-meets-country-house style with lots of creams and greys, lovely big beds, Ottoman bedside tables, metal stars hanging like chandeliers, tartan stair carpets and tartan bedspreads. Great fun and a good night's sleep. **£145**

TITCHWELL

★ **Titchwell Manor Hotel** Titchwell (A149), PE31 8BB ☎01485 210221, ⓦ titchwellmanor.com. Facing out towards the salt marshes that roll down towards the ocean, this is one of the most enjoyable hotels on the Norfolk coast, an intelligent and extremely creative remodelling of what was originally a fairly modest, albeit large Victorian brick building. There are nine guest rooms in the main building with more in the contemporary-style,

courtyard complex round the back, some of which are dog-friendly. Everything is high spec, from the top-quality duvets to the bespoke furniture. **£130**

THORNHAM

Lifeboat Inn Ship Lane, PE36 6LT ☎01485 512236, ⓦ maypolehotels.com. In ancient premises facing the fields just to the north of the A149, this rambling hotel possesses a particularly striking main hall, which comes complete with a whopping open fire and an assortment of stuffed animal heads. There are thirteen guest rooms here and the pick are decorated in a sort of country-house style and have views out towards Thornham harbour. The hotel restaurant is open daily 7–9.30pm. **£140**

HOLME-NEXT-THE-SEA

Meadow Springs 15 Eastgate, PE36 6LL ☎01485 525279, ⓦ meadowsprings.co.uk. Holme is a little short of accommodation, but this pleasant B&B, in a modern brick house amid substantial gardens, helps fill the gap, its two guest rooms traditionally decorated and with their own entrance, independent of the family home. **£70**

EATING

BRANCASTER

★ **Ship Hotel** Main Rd (A149), PE31 8AP ☎01485 210333, ⓦshiphotelnorfolk.co.uk. Long a Brancaster landmark, the *Ship* once welcomed customs officers in search of smugglers and shipwrecked mariners in need of care and attention. Nowadays, as one of the Flying Kiwi mini-chain, it offers simply delicious restaurant and bar food with oysters, mussels and crab to the fore. The bar is low-ceilinged, warm and friendly, the restaurant relaxed and kitted out with all sorts of incidental bygones. If the weather is good, you can also eat out in the garden. A typical main course is seared sea-bass fillets with crab mash, baby fennel and shallot dressing (£16.95). Daily: lunch noon–2.30pm; dinner 6.30–9.30pm.

TITCHWELL

★ **Titchwell Manor Hotel** Titchwell (A149), PE31 8BB ☎01485 210221, ⓦtitchwellmanor.com. This hotel (see opposite) boasts an outstanding restaurant as well as a couple of bar-like eating areas. The decor is appealing throughout – bright, sunny and somehow rather nautical. The menu is very British with traditional dishes superbly prepared – anything from fish and chips with mushy peas (£12) through to lobster thermidor with new potatoes (£18) – and the service is fast and efficient. Kitchen: daily noon–2.30pm & 6.30-9.30pm, plus snacks and light meals in between times.

SHOPPING

★ **Fish Shed** Brancaster Staithe, PE31 8BY ☎01485 210 532, ⓦfishshed.co.uk. On the main coastal road, a couple of hundred yards west of the *White Horse* (see p.155), the Fish Shed is just how it sounds – a shed with fish in, but what a range: there's cod and haddock, mullet and brill, tuna and trout, but the place specializes in Norfolk stuff, most memorably lobsters, cockles, crabs, mussels, oysters, whelks and samphire. Daily 10am–5pm, but restricted opening hours in winter.

Hunstanton and around

The north Norfolk coast pretty much ends (or begins) at **HUNSTANTON**, a popular seaside resort positioned just where the coastline turns south to run along beside the wide and stumpy Wash. The now-defunct railway reached here in 1862 and thereafter Hunstanton grew by leaps and bounds, sprouting scores of good-looking Victorian houses that are still a feature of the town, though today you'll be just as struck by the sheer awfulness of the modern development that has scarred the centre. The main attraction remains the **beach**, a lovely sandy tract backed by the stripy, **gateau-like cliffs** for which Hunstanton is well known, comprising a layer of red sandstone set beneath a band of white chalk. Beach and cliffs stretch north to **Old Hunstanton**, the site of the original fishing village and the place where a large and grassy park-cum-car park backs onto the sea cliffs offering panoramic ocean views.

Heacham

From Hunstanton, it's the briefest of drives south to **HEACHAM**, whose semi-suburban tangle of narrow streets lies just inland from an army of static caravans that line up along The Wash. In 1929, the town was accidentally propelled into newspaper headlines when Mercedes Gleitze swam ashore here, becoming the first woman to swim across The Wash – accidental because she was actually aiming for Hunstanton. Similarly accidental is Heacham's connection with **Pocahontas** (c.1595–1617), a Native American from present-day Virginia, who helped the early English colonists in their assorted travails. Her relationship with the settlers was not straightforward – at one time the English held her captive – but she did end up marrying one of them, **John Rolfe**, whose family home was here in Heacham and this was where he brought his wife during her extended visit to England. Pocahontas was presented at court, though quite how well she was received – as an honorary guest or freakish curiosity – is a matter of

3

debate and, in the event, she never managed to get back home from England, dying on the return journey shortly after the boat set sail.

Norfolk Lavender

Beside the A149, on the eastern edge of Heacham, PE31 7JE • **Norfolk Lavender** Daily 9am–5pm • Free • ☎ 01485 570384, ⓦ norfolk-lavender.co.uk **Farmer Fred's Adventure Play Barn** Mon–Fri 9.30am–6pm, Sat & Sun 10am–6pm • 1- to -4 year olds £4.50, 4 years plus £5.50 • ☎ 01485 579526, ⓦ farmerfredsplaybarnnorfolk.co.uk

The only real reason to visit Heachem today is **Norfolk Lavender**, a popular tourist attraction, where the big pull is the lavender gardens and the lavender plant sales, though there are also a couple of gift shops, a rare breed animal centre, a farm shop and a large, indoor play area for kids – **Farmer Fred's Adventure Play Barn** – with slides, climbing frames, a maze and so forth.

Sedgeford

Heading inland from Heacham, it's a couple of miles to **SEDGEFORD**, whose flint cottages and old agricultural buildings spread out along the main road. There's no strong reason to hang around here, but there is an excellent **B&B**, *Magazine Wood* (see opposite), a little less than a mile to the east of the village beside the Peddars Way long-distance footpath (see p.206). Sedgeford was also home to the redoubtable **Sir Holcombe Ingleby** (1854–1926), onetime mayor and Conservative MP for King's Lynn, who was tried – but found innocent – of bribing his way into office by scattering free rabbits among the voters. It was the same Ingleby who, in World War I, became convinced that west Norfolk was infested with German spies after the first of several **zeppelin** bombing raids had hit the county. No spies were ever found, but the raids did create a real panic among the locals, one of whom described the zeppelin in true agricultural style as being "the size of a bullock, but sounding like a bee".

Great Bircham Windmill

Great Bircham, PE31 6SJ • April–Sept daily 10am–5pm • Windmill £3.85, otherwise free • ☎ 01485 578393, ⓦ birchamwindmill.co.uk

Pressing on from Sedgeford, it's a little over three miles east to **Docking**, where you turn right along the B1153 to get to **GREAT BIRCHAM**, or more specifically **Great Bircham Windmill**, which stands in a field to the west of the village – just follow the signs. There were once dozens of windmills dotted over the Norfolk countryside and this is a rare survivor, a sturdy, grey-yellow brick structure with a white top and sails dating from the nineteenth century. The windmill is in full working order and you can clamber up inside for a good look around and afterwards you can wander round the huddle of little outhouses, where there's a café, a bookshop, a milking parlour and a cheese shop; you can also buy bread made from flour ground here at the windmill's bakery.

ARRIVAL AND INFORMATION
HUNSTANTON AND AROUND

By bus Hunstanton bus station is on Westgate, a couple of minutes' walk from the seafront Promenade. There are regular services from King's Lynn and to the rest of the Norfolk coast with the Norfolk Coasthopper (see p.122).
Tourist office In the Town Hall just off Cliff Parade – and

beside the wide sloping green that serves as the resort's focal point (daily: April & May, Sept & Oct 10.30am-4.30pm; June–September 10am–5pm; Nov–March 10.30am–3pm; ☎ 01485 532610, ⓦ visitnorthnorfolk.com).

ACCOMMODATION

HUNSTANTON

Neptune 85 Old Hunstanton Rd, Old Hunstanton, PE36 6HZ ☎ 01485 532122, ⓦ theneptune.co.uk. Well away from Hunstanton's tourist tat, on the main coastal road as it cuts through Old Hunstanton, this agreeable hotel occupies

a tastefully modernized old coaching inn, its six modern guest rooms equipped with all mod cons and white "New England-style" furniture. It's really known for its restaurant, however (see opposite). **£120**

SEDGEFORD

Magazine Wood Peddars Way, PE36 5LW ☎ 01485 570422, ⓦ magazinewood.co.uk. This deluxe B&B, deep in the Norfolk countryside, is strong on luxury with each of the spacious guest rooms decorated in an attractive modern style with king-size double beds, plasma-screen TVs, and superb bathrooms. Every room has a private terrace with wide views and each has a separate entrance independent of the main house/family home. Breakfasts are outstanding too. Note that sat navs will take you to Magazine Cottage, a distinctive flint and stone building beside the main road, the B1454, just to the east of Sedgeford; *Magazine Wood* is a short distance to the north along Peddars Way. Minimum two nights' stay on weekends; three nights on bank holiday weekends. **£95**

EATING

Neptune 85 Old Hunstanton Rd, Old Hunstanton, PE36 6HZ ☎ 01485 532122, ⓦ theneptune.co.uk. Well-regarded restaurant, where the modern British menu is the work of husband-and-wife team Kevin and Jacki Mangeolles: pan-fried gurnard, smoked aubergine, red pepper, wild garlic puree and spinach (£23.95) is a typical main-course dish. Reservations are well-nigh essential. Kitchen: Tues–Sun 7–9pm, plus Sun noon–1.30pm.

SHOPPING

The World of Fun St Edmund's Terrace, PE36 5EH ☎ 01485 532016, ⓦ jokes-online.co.uk. Laugh till you weep – or just weep – this is supposedly the largest joke shop in the world, stocking everything from the innocent and the harmless to the dubious and positively strange (a pecker whistle, would you believe). It's been going strong since 1978 with such perennial favourites as wigs, whoopee cushions, sneeze powder and joke sweets. Daily: May–Sept 9am–7pm; Oct–April 9am–5.30pm.

Snettisham and around

The A149 bypasses **SNETTISHAM**, a mile or two to the south of Heacham, and this has saved the village's pint-sized centre from excessive development, its pleasant collection of old stone houses fanning out from the old-fashioned stores and shops of the **Market Place**. The village's main draw is the *Rose and Crown Hotel* (see p.162), but it is also a stone's throw from **Sandringham** (see p.162) and home to the handsome **church of St Mary** (usually closed; ask for keys at the post office, yards from the Market Place at 11 Alma Rd), whose mighty stone tower and stone nave, perched on a grassy knoll on the east side of the village, are most unusual in Norfolk, where almost all the churches are built of flint. Dating from the fourteenth century, St Mary's was meant to impress and the highlight of the interior is the splendid stained glass of the west window, though the finely crafted eagle lectern also deserves a second look. Snettisham is also famous for the **Snettisham Treasure**, unearthed by a ploughman in 1948 and the richest Iron Age hoard ever found in the UK; the key finds are now displayed in the British Museum in London.

Snettisham Nature Reserve

Beach Rd, PE31 7RA • Open access • Free • ☎ 01485 542689, ⓦ rspb.org.uk

From Snettisham, it's about three miles to the shores of The Wash – take Beach Road west from the A149 and keep going. As you near the coast, you'll pass the signed gravel byroad that leads south to the RSPB's **Snettisham Nature Reserve**, which stretches along the mud flats of The Wash and includes the long and slender lagoons immediately behind. Footpaths negotiate the reserve and there are four, strategically placed bird hides, with most birdwatchers timing their visit to coincide with the hour before high tide when thousands of **wading birds** are pushed off their feeding grounds out in The Wash onto the banks and islands in front of the RSPB's hides. The higher the tide, the greater the concentration of waders – ring ahead for advice on local conditions. From mid-November to late January, the reserve is also a superb spot to see **pink-footed geese** flying overhead in formation from their nesting grounds out in The Wash to their feeding grounds inland at dawn, the other way round at dusk. It is, however, best to avoid the three or four days either side of the full moon as the geese are not as reliable as normal on these days.

Beyond the turning to the nature reserve, **Beach Road** pushes on towards the coast, coming to a halt at a large car park immediately behind the seashore with static caravans and seaside chalets stretching away to the south. From the car park, you can wander out onto the mud flats or stroll along the sea wall.

Sandringham House

Sandringham Estate, PE35 6EN • Daily late April to Oct, but closed for one or two weeks in late July or early Aug; house 11am–5.30pm, last entry 4.45pm; museum 11am–5pm; gardens 10.30am–5.30pm • House, museum & gardens £11, museum & gardens £7.50 • Visitor centre & shop daily: late April to Oct 9.30am–5.30pm; rest of year 9.30am–4.30pm • ☎ 01485 545408, ⊚ sandringhamestate.co.uk • Bus #41 from King's Lynn to the visitor centre every hour or so during opening hours

Famous as the Christmas hidey-hole of Queen Elizabeth II, **Sandringham House,** off the A149 about three miles south of Hunstanton – and six miles northeast of King's Lynn - was built in 1870 on land purchased by Queen Victoria for her son, the future Edward VII. The house is billed as a private home, but few families have a drawing room crammed with Russian silver and Chinese jade and neither do many homes hold a substantial collection of oriental arms and armour, this particular lot being brought back from the Far East and India in 1876. The **museum**, housed in the old coach and stable block, contains an exhibition of royal memorabilia from dolls to cars, but much more arresting are the beautifully maintained **gardens**, a mass of rhododendrons and azaleas in spring and early summer. The estate's sandy soil is also ideal for game birds, which was the attraction of the place for the terminally bored Edward, whose tradition of posh shooting parties is still followed by the royals of today. For lovers of royalty, the **gift shop** sells all manner of "royal" trinkets, including tea towels and mugs.

Wolferton

Queen Victoria rarely did things by half, so when she bought Sandringham, she also opened the royal family's own train station at **WOLFERTON**, a tiny but incredibly prim-and-proper estate village a couple of miles to the west of the main house on the other side of the A149. Neither was this all: there's no way the royals were going to loaf around on the station platform, so the queen had a set of elegant waiting rooms built as well and, although the station was closed in the 1960s and has subsequently become a private home, the old mock-Tudor train station, the station platform and the old railway crossing gates have survived.

| **ARRIVAL AND DEPARTURE** | **SNETTISHAM AND AROUND** |

By bus Buses to and from Snettisham pull in beside the Market Place at the centre of the village – and a couple of minutes' walk from the *Rose & Crown*.

ACCOMMODATION AND EATING

★ **Rose & Crown** Old Church Rd, PE31 7LX ☎ 01485 541382, ⊚ roseandcrownsnettisham.co.uk. If you are looking for a prime example of exactly how to update a traditional village pub, this must be it. The owners have kept all the good parts, from the low ceilings, wooden beams and log fires through to the cosy little rooms, but added a sunny and attractive conservatory and upgraded sixteen guest rooms with sleep-deep beds and bright and cheerful decor. The food, which is served in all of the three dining areas, is excellent too – try, for example, the Norfolk venison sausages with braised puy lentils, cavolo nero (£10.75). As if this wasn't

enough, they also serve an excellent range of local ales on draft. Kitchen: Mon–Fri noon–2pm, Sat & Sun noon–2.30pm; Sun–Thurs 6–9pm, Fri & Sat 6–9.30pm. **£110**

Twitchers' Retreat 9 Beach Rd, PE31 7RA ☎ 01485 543581, ⊚ twitchers-retreat.co.uk. In a modern house, 2.3 miles west along Beach Rd from the A149, this friendly B&B has just three guest rooms decorated in a bright and breezy modern style. As you'd expect from the name, birdwatching is the big deal here – and the breakfasts will definitely set you up for wandering the shores of The Wash. Usefully, their website has a tide table. Minimum two-night stay. **£75**

Castle Rising

Minuscule **CASTLE RISING**, roughly midway between King's Lynn and Sandringham, is a prosperous kind of place, its comfortable suburban streets fanning out from the substantial remains of its twelfth-century **castle**, which sits on top of a grassy mound at the centre of extensive earthworks.

The castle

Low Rd, Castle Rising, PE31 6AH • April–Oct daily 10am–6pm or dusk if earlier • £4; EH • ⓦ www.english-heritage.org.uk.

Towering over the surrounding flatlands, **the castle** is a powerful, imposing structure, some of whose finer architectural details have survived, most notably its precise blind arcading and interior galleries gouged out of the original defensive walls. An important medieval stronghold, it was here that **Queen Isabella** (1295–1358) lived during the last decades of her eventful life. Born in France, the young Isabella was married off to King Edward II of England, an unhappy match if ever there was one – they may have had four children, but Edward was almost definitely bisexual and, more importantly, he destabilized the throne by showering his male favourites with money and honours. Isabella eventually tired of all these shenanigans, deposing Edward and probably having him murdered, though the legend that he was killed by having a red-hot poker stuck up his back passage is most likely untrue. Isabella ruled as regent with her lover, Mortimer, until her son, **Edward III**, deposed the two lovers in 1330. The new king was not, however, bent on revenge: he did have Mortimer executed, but he spared his mother, who moved to Castle Rising, where she received a generous allowance – quite enough for her to hire a veritable army of Norfolk minstrels, grooms and huntsmen. Courtiers as well as the king himself regularly visited Isabella, who lived here for the rest of her life, developing her many interests – in religion, astrology and geometry.

The Church of St Lawrence

Low Rd, Castle Rising, PE31 6AH • Daily 9am–4.30pm

Below the castle, the **village** holds a quadrangle of immaculately kept, seventeenth-century **almshouses**, whose elderly inhabitants still go to church in orange-red cloaks and pointed black hats, the colours of the original benefactor, the Earl of Northampton. The church in question is **St Lawrence**, of medieval foundation, but much mucked about by the Victorians, who added the conspicuous tower with the saddle-shaped roof that now rises above the central crossing. The church's finest features are the Norman dog-tooth decoration round several of the doorways and windows plus the Norman font with its three cats' faces.

ARRIVAL AND DEPARTURE   CASTLE RISING

By bus Norfolk Green's bus #11 (ⓦ norfolkgreen.co.uk) links King's Lynn bus station with Hunstanton via Castle Rising – you want to get off at the village's *Black Horse* pub. Services are frequent Mon through Sat, but patchy on Sunday (every 2hr).

EATING

Unique Tea Rooms 28 Lynn Rd, PE31 6AG ☎ 01553 631211. There's not much choice in Castle Rising, but this cosy tearoom, in what was formerly the village post office, hits the mark, serving up traditional English food, mostly home-made and including whopping scones. Eat either inside or in the large garden at the front. Daily 8am–5pm, Tues–Sat till 9pm in summertime.

SHOPPING

Unique Castle Farm Barn & Unique Hats Lynn Rd, PE31 6AG ☎ 01553 631500, ⓦ uniquegiftsandinteriors. co.uk. An old barn packed to the rafters with assorted furnishings and fittings from this Norfolk-based homes and gardens chain. The adjacent Unique Hats holds an extensive collection of hats, fascinators and costume jewellery. Mon–Sat 9.30am–6.00pm, Thurs till 8.00pm, Sun 10.30am–4.30pm.

King's Lynn and the Fens

DENVER WINDMILL

King's Lynn and the Fens

Norfolk's third largest town, King's Lynn is an ancient port that prospered on the back of its easy access to seven English counties, its position straddling the canalized mouth of the Great Ouse river a mile or so before it slides into the Wash. It's not the most obvious holiday destination, but it does have a cluster of handsome old riverside buildings, and its lively, open-air markets attract large crowds. Many visitors head north from King's Lynn to the North Norfolk Coast, but there is interest, too, to the east and south of the town, in the part of the country known as the Fens, the smallest section of which lies in Norfolk. To the west you can follow the Peter Scott Walk to his former home near Sutton Bridge, and explore the medieval churches of the tiny communities here, while to the south, Downham Market is a base for a number of enticing villages, and waterland attractions like the Denver Windmill, the Welney Wetland Centre and Wicken Fen, across the border in Cambridgeshire. Also in Cambridgeshire, make time for Ely, whose imposing cathedral – the so-called Ship of the Fens – is the Fens' major historical attraction.

King's Lynn

KING'S LYNN was once one of the major ports of England. A member of the powerful Hanseatic League during the late Middle Ages, the town's merchants grew rich importing fish from Scandinavia, timber from the Baltics and wine from France, while exporting wool, salt and corn. The good times came to an end when the focus of maritime trade moved to the Atlantic seaboard, but its port struggled on until it was reinvigorated in the 1970s by the burgeoning trade between the UK and its EU partners. Much of the old centre was demolished during the 1950s and 1960s to make way for commercial development, and as a result most of Lynn – as it's known locally – is not especially enticing. But in its historic core, around the waterfront, between the Purfleet and Millfleet inlets and around the so-called Saturday Market and Tuesday Market places, the medieval streets are remarkably untouched and the quaysides retain something of the feel of a seventeenth-century trading port.

The Custom House

Purfleet Quay, PE30 1HP • April–Sept Mon–Sat 10am–4.30pm, Sun noon–4.30pm; Oct–March Mon–Sat 10.30am–3.30pm, Sun noon–3.30pm • Free • ☎ 01553 763044

Right on Purfleet Quay, the splendid **Custom House** overlooks a short and stumpy harbour once packed with merchant ships. It was erected in 1683 in a style clearly influenced by the Dutch, with classical pilasters, petite dormer windows and a rooftop

The Peter Scott Walk and the Fens River Way p.171
The Fens p.175

Opium eating in the nineteenth century p.176

ELY CATHEDRAL

Highlights

❶ King's Lynn waterfront An amazingly overlooked slice of life from mercantile medieval England. **See p.169**

❷ The Peter Scott Walk The blustery, evocative, coastal trek to the naturalist's Fenland hideaway. **See p.171**

❸ The Wiggenhalls This group of villages and their churches are easily Fenland's most alluring corner. **See p.175**

❹ Welney Wetland Centre Perfect all year round for novices and lazy twitchers. **See p.178**

❺ Ely Cathedral Rising magisterially out of the Fens, this is one of England's largest and most magnificent medieval cathedrals. **See p.180**

HIGHLIGHTS ARE MARKED ON THE MAP ON P.168

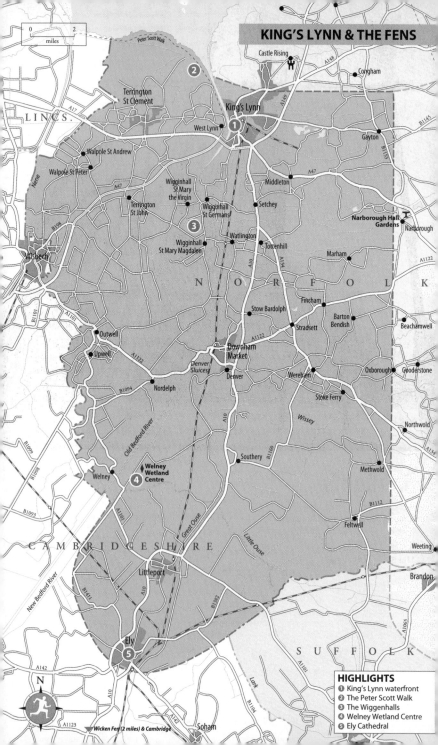

0 | 2
miles

Peter Scott Walk

Castle Rising

Congham

A148

A149

LINCS.

Terrington
St Clement

King's Lynn

West Lynn

Gayton

B1145

A17

Walpole St Andrew

A149

Middleton

A47

B1153

Walpole St Peter

Nene

Wigginhall
St Mary
the Virgin

Setchey

Narborough Hall
Gardens

Narborough

A47

Terrington
St John

Wigginhall
St Germans

Watlington

Tottenhill

Marham

A1122

B198

Wigginhall
St Mary Magdalen

A134

A10

Wisbech

N O R F O L K

Fincham

Barton
Bendish

Beachamwell

Stow Bardolph

Outwell

A1101

A1123

Stradsett

Oxborough

Gooderstone

Upwell

Downham
Market

Denver
Sluices

Denver

Wereham

Stoke Ferry

Northwold

A1122

Nordelph

B1094

Wissey

B1160

A10

A134

B1098

Old Bedford River

Southery

Methwold

B1093

Welney

Welney Wetland
Centre

B1112

Great Ouse

Little Ouse

Feltwell

Weeting

C A M B R I D G E S H I R E

B1382

Brandon

New Bedford River

B1411

Littleport

A10

A1065

A142

Ely

S U F F O L K

A1101

N

A1123

Wicken Fen (2 miles) & Cambridge

Soham

Lark

B1104

HIGHLIGHTS
❶ King's Lynn waterfront
❷ The Peter Scott Walk
❸ The Wigginhalls
❹ Welney Wetland Centre
❺ Ely Cathedral

balustrade, but it's the dinky little cupola that catches the eye, and its all-round elegant proportions – Pevsner called it "one of the most perfect buildings ever built". The Custom House was in use until 1989, since when it has served as the tourist office (see p.172), and a couple of upstairs rooms have displays on the port and its heritage, including a number of matchstick models of the town's principal buildings. Out on the quayside giant boat-chains and a statue of King's Lynn native George Vancouver, scroll in hand, best known for mapping the west coast of America in the late eighteenth century, are further reminders of the town's maritime past.

The waterfront and around

The **waterfront** stretches west of the Custom House, as far as **Millfleet Quay**, and is a beautifully preserved area, its Georgian and earlier frontages sliced through with evocative old alleys that lead back into the centre of town. Most of the buildings along here are given over to other purposes these days, and not accessible to the public, but take a look at the country's most intact Hanseatic-era warehouse – now the **Green Quay Discovery Centre** (daily 9am–5pm; free; ☎01553 818500, ⓦthegreenquay.co.uk) and café – the most evocative of the medieval buildings that survive along the quayside. Built around 1475, its half-timbered upper floor juts unevenly over the cobbles of St Margaret's Lane and contains revolving exhibitions alongside a permanent exhibit on The Wash.

Saturday Market Place

4

Behind the waterfront, the **Saturday Market Place** is one of the focal points of the old town, a thin triangle that is the older and smaller of the town's two marketplaces. It's home to Lynn's main parish church, St Margaret's, and, across the square, its prettiest building, the **Trinity Guildhall**, which has a wonderful, chequered flint-and-stone facade dating from 1421 and repeated in the Elizabethan addition and the Victorian town hall immediately to the left.

St Margaret's

Saturday Market Place, PE30 5EB • ☎ 01553 772858, ⓦ stmargaretskingslynn.org.uk.

The Saturday Market Pace is dominated by the hybrid church of **St Margaret's**, a large and dignified building (one of the largest churches in the county) with an eighteenth-century organ and choir stalls covered with images of the Black Prince and Edward III. The monarch is also remembered by the two medieval bronzes in the south aisle: the Walsoken brass, adorned with country scenes, recalling in particular the Peacock's Feast that was thrown for Edward when he visited the town in 1349, and the Braunche brass, named after a certain Robert Braunche, mayor of Lynn at the time and shown with his two wives.

King Street

Beyond the Custom House, **King Street** continues where Queen Street leaves off, and is the town's most elegant thoroughfare, lined with Georgian buildings and eulogized by none other than John Betjeman (a fan of Lynn, by all accounts) as one of the best walks in England. On the left, just after Ferry Lane, **St George's Guildhall** dates from 1410 and is one of the oldest surviving guildhalls in England. It was a theatre in Elizabethan times and is now part of the **King's Lynn Arts Centre** (see p.174), a much-loved local facility which has just been rescued from a threatened closure.

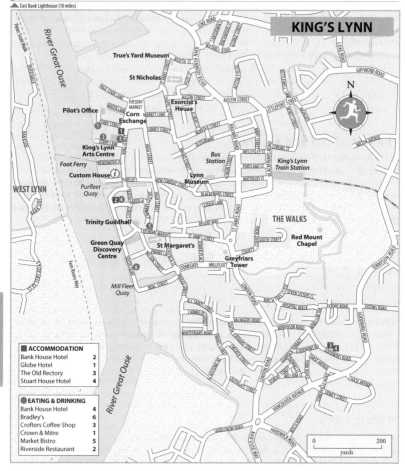

ACCOMMODATION

Bank House Hotel	2
Globe Hotel	1
The Old Rectory	3
Stuart House Hotel	4

EATING & DRINKING

Bank House Hotel	4
Bradley's	6
Crofters Coffee Shop	3
Crown & Mitre	1
Market Bistro	5
Riverside Restaurant	2

Tuesday Market Place and the Pilot's Office

The **Tuesday Market Place** is a handsome square by any standards, still surrounded by a good sprinkling of Georgian buildings and with the Rococo pastel-pink *Duke's Head Hotel*, dating from 1689, facing the plodding, Neoclassical **Corn Exchange** (now a theatre), on the far side. It's home to King's Lynn's main market on Fridays and, yes, Tuesdays.

Wander down to the riverfront, two minutes from the square, where the nineteenth-century **Pilot's Office**, with its octagonal brick tower, still does service as the King's Lynn Conservancy Board, looking after the port and harbour. A notice board outside still displays the expected arrivals of ships from all over Europe to the docks just beyond.

Lynn Museum

Market St, PE30 1NL • Tues–Sat 10am–5pm • £3.30; free audioguide • ☎ 01553 775001, ⑩ museums.norfolk.gov.uk

Housed in the old Union Chapel by the bus station, bang in the centre of town, much of the refurbished **Lynn Museum** is given over to "Seahenge", a circle of 556 oak timbers, preserved in peat, that were found at low tide at Holme-next-the-Sea in 1998 (see p.158). The timber circle is reckoned to be around four thousand years old and was moved here amid much controversy in 2008, and is housed in an atmospheric gallery that showcases the timbers themselves, their original position and possible purpose, along with the giant upturned tree stump that stood in its centre – emphasizing what is thought to be its ritualistic purpose. The rest of the museum, in the wooden-beamed chapel, has displays on every aspect of life in Lynn and the region, including medieval times, World War II, the sea and the working lives of ordinary people, and there's a lot of good stuff for kids too.

True's Yard Museum and the North End

North St, PE30 1QW • Tues–Sat 10am–4pm • £3 • ☎ 01553 770479, ⓦ truesyard.co.uk

The **True's Yard Museum** is housed in some of the last remaining cottages in the heart of King's Lynn's North End district, once a hardcore fishing community, with the museum pretty much its only memorial. It's all very convincingly done, an affectionate commemoration of life in the old days, with lots of old photos. The two cottages in the yards behind have been restored to how they were in the 1920s, when a family of seventeen lived there – as neat and prim as it must have been crowded, with more than a dozen layers of wallpaper uncovered and photos on the walls of its former occupants. An old smokehouse and smithy with more displays complete the picture.

St Nicholas

True's Yard Museum holds the key to the nearby chapel of **St Nicholas**, an enormous structure that stood at the heart of the town's old North End neighbourhood, and is now part of the Churches Conservation Trust. The spire was added by Gilbert Scott in the nineteenth century, but inside the church is pure medieval Gothic, with a fifteenth-century wooden roof and lots of seventeenth- and eighteenth-century memorials to the seafarers who built King's Lynn. The gabled seventeenth-century building outside the churchyard is rather scarily known as the **Exorcist's House**, while **Pilot Street**, which winds around the back of the church, gives the best indication of how North End looked before the bulldozers moved in.

Greyfriars Tower and the Red Mount Chapel

Just outside the centre of Lynn, the brick and stone **Greyfriars Tower** is all that's left of a Franciscan friary that once stood here, and it's recently been restored after an appearance on TV's *Restoration*. **The Walks**, across the road, is the town's main city

---

THE PETER SCOTT WALK AND THE FENS RIVER WAY

The **Peter Scott Walk** runs along the other side of the Ouse from the centre of town from the West Lynn Ferry jetty for ten miles to the **East Bank Lighthouse** on the River Nene, where the conservationist lived from 1933 to 1939. From the lighthouse you can make the two-mile walk up the Nene to pick up the bus at Sutton Bridge back to King's Lynn (there's parking there too, if you want to do the walk the other way around). The first stretch, along the river, isn't that interesting, but once at the mouth of the river the views over The Wash and salt marshes are glorious, as are those inland over the Fenland that used to be under the sea.

If you don't fancy the full North Sea blow, or just don't want to walk so far, **the Fens River Way** runs in the opposite direction from the ferry jetty, following the river to the first bridge and back into town along the other side – a 45-minute walk in all. There are good views of the town across the river, and on a sunny summer's day it can be almost picturesque. To get to the start of either take the **West Lynn ferry** from Ferry Lane (daily 6.45am–6pm; 70p each way).

centre park, and features another restored building, the **Red Mount Chapel**, a café and a children's playground.

ARRIVAL AND INFORMATION — KING'S LYNN

By train King's Lynn's train station is a short walk east of the town centre across Railway Rd, the principal north–south thoroughfare that borders the centre's eastern edge, and down Waterloo St. It's at the end of the main line from London King's Cross, via Cambridge, Ely and Downham Market. A branch line also runs roughly hourly up to Hunstanton and Wells-next-the-Sea.

By bus The bus station is right in the centre, amid the main shopping area about 150m west of Railway Rd; there are regular buses from here south and west into the Fens, north to Hunstanton (30min) and the north Norfolk coast, and west to Swaffham (40min), Dereham (1hr 10min) and eventually Norwich (2hr).

Tourist office By the river in the Custom House on Purfleet Quay (Mon–Sat 10am–5pm, Sun noon–5pm; t 01553 763044, w visitwestnorfolk.com).

Walking tours One of the best ways to delve in Lynn's historical corners is to take one of the excellent walking tours that run regularly – choose from "Historic Lynn", "Pubs and Mansions"' or the intriguingly titled "Darker Side of Lynn", among many others. All walks start at 2pm unless otherwise stated and last approximately 2hr; tickets cost £4 and are available from the tourist office.

ACCOMMODATION

★ **Bank House Hotel** King's Staithe Square, PE30 1ED t 01553 660492, w thebankhouse.co.uk. One of North Norfolk's best boutique-style hotels, and offering a chance to enjoy this fantastic Georgian merchant and banker's house, right on the quay in the heart of King's Lynn's historic district. There's a choice of eleven distinctive rooms, and a great bar and restaurant that make it almost a destination in itself. Room rates vary according to size and levels of sumptuousness, but they all enjoy marvellous views over the river, although the large Captain's Room and Bath Room are definitely the ones to go for if you can. Owned by the Goodriches, who cut their teeth on the excellent *Rose & Crown* in Snettisham (see p.162), the hotel is very friendly and also organizes guided walks around old King's Lynn with a local historian. Rates include first-class breakfast. **£100–140**

Globe Hotel Tuesday Market Place, PE30 1EZ t 01553 668000, w jdwetherspoon.co.uk/home/pubs/globe-hotel. Slightly bland but comfortable rooms in this busy Wetherspoon's hotel and pub. Breakfast is served in the pub downstairs, and in typical Wetherspoon' s style is cheap but quite cheerful. **£54**

The Old Rectory 33 Goodwins Rd, PE30 1QX t 01553 768544, w theoldrectory-kingslynn.com. Small and agreeable B&B whose bedrooms are decorated in a reassuringly modern, cosy style, though the house itself dates back to the 1840s. Goodwins Rd is on the southern side of town, east of London Rd, a southerly extension of Railway Rd. Breakfast included. **£60**

Stuart House Hotel 35 Goodwins Rd, PE30 5QX t 01553 772169, w stuarthousehotel.co.uk. Small hotel just a 5min walk from the town centre that has a busy restaurant and bar with a good selection of real ales. The rooms are nice enough but can be a bit noisy if there's a function on downstairs – doubles go up to £130; family rooms are also available for £120. **£92**

EATING AND DRINKING

★ **Bank House Hotel** King's Staithe Square, PE30 1ED t 01553 660492, w thebankhouse.co.uk. The warm, flickering lights of the *Bank House*'s bar and restaurant are wonderfully inviting from the relative darkness of King's Lynn's waterfront, and it's a very comforting feeling to be sitting in its elegant restaurant while the brown, sluggish Ouse lumbers by outside. Choose starters like salt-and-pepper squid and ham hock terrine, for £5.95, and mains like Lowestoft plaice, guinea fowl with bacon and cabbage and some confidently simple big salads, gammon steaks and burgers, for £9.95–14.95. House wine from £13.50 a bottle. Breakfast Mon–Fri 7.15–9.15am, Sat & Sun 7.30–10am; lunch Mon–Sat noon–2.30pm, Sun noon–3.30pm; dinner Mon–Thurs 6.30–9pm, Fri 6.30–9.30pm, Sun 7–9pm.

Bradley's 10 South Quay, PE30 5DT t 01553 819888, w bradleysbytheriver.co.uk. Occupying an elegant quayside mansion, *Bradley's* is the cosiest place to have a drink in town. Its downstairs wine bar resembles an upscale Victorian drawing room, and has a really good selection of wines and champagnes by the glass; there's also draft beer and cider and a bar menu featuring home-made pies, fish cakes, filled baguettes with chunky chips and suchlike. The upstairs restaurant puts on more style, though again of a rather old-fashioned variety, with a refined and traditional menu that changes seasonally – think broccoli soup with truffle oil (£5.50), followed by sea bass in vermouth sauce (£16.95). Bar: Mon–Fri noon–2.30pm & 5.30–10.30pm, Sat noon–11.30pm, Sun noon–4pm; restaurant: Mon–Sat noon–2pm & 6.15–

FROM TOP WIGGENHALL ST GERMANS (P.175); KING'S LYNN WATERFRONT (P.169) >

9.15pm, Sun noon–2.30pm.

Crofters Coffee Shop 29 King St, PE30 1ET ☎01553 765565. Part of the Arts Centre complex, located in the undercroft of the St George's Guildhall, this serves as good a breakfast or light lunch as you'll find in central King's Lynn, with a menu of sandwiches, salads and quiches. Mon–Sat 9.30am–5pm.

Crown & Mitre Ferry St, PE30 1LJ ☎01553 774669. A traditional cosy pub down by the water, with food – either on its riverside terrace or in its dining room with a roaring log fire. Basic pub grub – steaks, gammon, liver and bacon – in generous portions; and a good selection of real ales. Daily noon–2pm & 6–9pm.

★ **Market Bistro** 11 Saturday Market Place, PE30 5DQ ☎01553 771483. Boosted by an appearance on *Ramsey's Kitchen Nightmares*, this once under-performing restaurant seems to have cracked it with superb food and service in a stripped-down bistro environment. The food is hearty rather than refined, using locally sourced ingredients in an inventive and thoroughly up-to-date way – the menu includes specials such as seared scallops with home-made black pudding, locally foraged cep risotto, slow roast pork belly with mash and greens, along with simple classics like burgers, fish and chips, ham and eggs, rib-eye steak. A well-chosen wine list too, from £12.50 a bottle. Mon–Sat noon–2pm & 6.30–9.30pm.

Riverside Restaurant 27 King St, PE30 1ET ☎01553 773134. Housed in a handsomely converted, fifteenth-century warehouse overlooking the river at the back end of the St George's Guildhall Arts Centre; this is a decent venue for either lunch or dinner, with a good, varied menu featuring everything from warm ciabattas to ham and eggs and burgers at lunchtime and more refined fare in the evening, with Gressingham Duck, beef fillet and rack of lamb from £13.95. Mon–Sat noon–2pm & 6.30–9.30pm.

ENTERTAINMENT

King's Lynn Arts Centre 29 King St, PE30 1ET ☎01553 764864, ⓦkingslynnarts.co.uk. Stages a wide range of performances and exhibitions both here and in several other downtown venues, including the old Corn Exchange, on Tuesday Market Place.

4

South and east of King's Lynn

The Fens is an amazing part of the country in many ways, but nowhere more so than the villages immediately to the **south and east** of King's Lynn where you'll find some of the finest medieval ecclesiastical architecture and art in Britain. The countryside is distinctive and oddly hypnotic: wide, endless fields of arable crops, split by drainage ditches and the slow-moving rivers of the Great and Little Ouse, the Nene and the Bedford – majestic thoroughfares that once carried convoys of commercial river traffic (hidden by dykes, you only become aware of them once you're upon them). With much of the land reclaimed from fen and marshland, there's naturally a Dutch feel to the landscape, as well as a captivating prettiness, especially around the **Wiggenhalls** and the villages to the south. The settlements to the north, closer to King's Lynn, are more pedestrian sprawls of bungalows and workyards, scattered across the thunderous arterial roads of the A47 and A17, and interspersed between fields of crops – a hint, to some extent, of what is to come across the border in Lincolnshire.

Terrington St Clement

St Clement, Churchgate Way, PE34 4LZ • ⓦtsc-church.org.uk

Four miles east of King's Lynn, **TERRINGTON ST CLEMENT** is the closest Fenland settlement with something worth seeing, a dull village on the whole but with an enormous parish church – **St Clement** – whose nave is the longest of any in the county (get the key from the house to the left of the church gate). In the north aisle, the massive wooden font cover was added in the sixteenth century, and inside has paintings of the four Evangelists added about a hundred years later; open the doors to peek in and look.

The Walpoles

In the far west of north Norfolk, just a stone's throw from the Lincolnshire border, the conjoined villages of **WALPOLE ST ANDREW** and **WALPOLE ST PETER** are nothing special

THE FENS

One of the strangest of all English landscapes, **the Fens** cover a vast area of eastern England from just north of Cambridge right up to Boston in Lincolnshire. For centuries, they were an inhospitable wilderness of quaking bogs and marshland, punctuated by clay islands on which small communities eked out a livelihood cutting peat for fuel, using reeds for thatching and living on a diet of fish and wildfowl. Piecemeal land reclamation took place throughout the Middle Ages, but it wasn't until the seventeenth century that the systematic draining of the fens was undertaken – amid fierce local opposition – by Dutch engineer **Cornelius Vermuyden**. This wholesale draining had unforeseen consequences: as it dried out, the peaty soil shrank to below the level of the rivers, causing frequent flooding, and the region's **windmills**, which had previously been vital in keeping the waters at bay, compounded the problem by causing further shrinkage. The engineers had to do some rapid backtracking, and the task of draining the Fens was only completed in the 1820s following the introduction of **steam-driven pumps**, leviathans which could control water levels with much greater precision. Drained, the Fens now comprise some of the most fertile agricultural land in Europe.

in themselves, but the church of **St Peter** is known as the "Cathedral of the Fens" for its size, grandeur and fine proportions, as well as the host of features that reside within. There is a wealth of woodcarving – nothing incredible, but check out the animals and saints in the choir, which mostly date from the fifteenth century, as well as the faded saints on the chancel screen. Look too at the more low-key details at the western end: a sentry box used by ministers during rainy funerals, and a fine old table dating from the early seventeenth century. The Walpoles' sister church of **St Andrew** is a slightly more run-down version of St Peter, and is now owned by the Churches Conservation Trust – pick up the key from the house next door, 5 Kirk Rd. Inside it's strangely empty and rather damp, but a wonderful example of the period nonetheless.

The Wiggenhalls

A short way to the south of King's Lynn, just off the main A10, the group of villages known as the **WIGGENHALLS** offer the most appealing glimpse of fens close to the town. Right on the river, the church at **Wiggenhall St Germans**, next door to the **Crown & Anchor** pub boasts a fine set of carved choir stalls and enjoys a perfect riverside position next to the Great Ouse. You can follow the riverside path from here two miles downstream to **Wiggenhall St Mary Magdalen** and the lovely brick church of **Magdalen**, rebuilt in the fifteenth century by the same architect as the one at Walpole St Peter. It's a light, well-proportioned building with a beautiful wooden roof, though it's best known for the mid-fifteenth century stained glass in the north aisle – mostly representations of saints and martyrs from the early Christian church.

St Mary of the Virgin

Church Rd, Wiggenhall, PE34 3EJ • ⓦ visitchurches.org.uk

Of all the Wiggenhall churches, and despite not being right on the river, **St Mary the Virgin** enjoys the best position, outside the village surrounded by fields and with a resoundingly peaceful churchyard. Now part of the Churches Conservation Trust (you can pick up the key from Wiggenhall House in front of the church), it also holds quite a haul of treasure for such a remote site, not least a set of fifteenth-century pew carvings that are reckoned to be the finest examples of their kind in England. They're much larger than you usually find, often with two figures at each end and another in a niche below, and are in a marvellous state of preservation, full of everyday details and observances. There's also an elaborate alabaster tomb in the aisle, with the life-sized effigies of a local aristocrat and his wife, who died in the early seventeenth century, together with beautifully realized and rather sad carvings of their children at the end,

---

OPIUM EATING IN THE NINETEENTH CENTURY

The Fens have always been poor, but a century ago, when the area was still prone to frequent inundations by water and all the problems associated with this, they were dirt poor, and unhealthy to boot, with those who lived here prone to debilitating "ague" and rheumatism brought on by the marshy environment. There wasn't much in the way of medical help, and many here turned to **opium** to enhance their frequently miserable existence. As a result opium usage in the Fens was way above the national average in the nineteenth century and infiltrated all sectors of the population. It was given to children (thereby exacerbating an already high infant mortality rate), dropped into beer in the pub, and added to tea at home; and it wasn't unusual to see labourers asleep at their plough in the fields or bumping into the crowds on market day – indeed chemist's shops were often the busiest places when the rural poor came into town. As the Fens were drained, and the region in effect joined the rest of society, so opium usage declined, but there were still instances of it in the early part of the twentieth century.

---

who apparently died before them. Check out, also, the beautifully coloured rood screen in the choir, with four saints on each side, which would alone be enough to draw you to the church.

Watlington

WATLINGTON is a pretty village centred around a large village green, and with a church – **St Peter and St Paul**, which has fine old medieval bench-end carvings of the seven deadly sins – and a pub, the **Angel**, which offers a warm welcome and does roasts on Sunday (see below).

Beers of Europe

Garage Lane, Setchey, PE33 0BE · ☏ 01553 812000, ⓦ beersofeurope.co.uk

Situated just off the A10, in Setchey, about four miles south of King's Lynn, **Beers of Europe** is basically a large warehouse stacked full of beers you won't find elsewhere in Britain, and especially good on Belgian and German ales, together with the glasses to drink them from. There's an international selection of ciders, wines and weird spirits too, but as the name suggests beer is the thing here, and the selection of local ales is also strong.

ARRIVAL AND DEPARTURE

SOUTH AND EAST OF KING'S LYNN

By bus Around 6 buses a day leave King's Lynn for Wisbech (#64) via the Walpoles, reaching Walpole St Peter's church in about 40min. There are also roughly half-hourly buses (#505) from King's Lynn to Spalding in Lincolnshire which stop off at Terrington St Clement (20min) and Sutton Bridge just beyond – for the Peter Scott Walk (see p.171). Bus #47 runs hourly down to Watlington to Downham Market (45min) and Ten Mile Bank beyond (1hr), while bus #37 will drop you at Setchey for Beers of Europe (15min).

ACCOMMODATION AND EATING

Andel Lodge 48 Lynn Rd, Tottenhill, PE33 0RH ☏ 01553 810256, ⓦ andellodge.co.uk. A good selection of double and twin rooms, all individually furnished, and a handy location midway between King's Lynn and Downham Market. There's not much to Tottenhill itself but the hotel has its own restaurant serving a good selection of steaks, duck, chicken and veggie options for £10–15. **£77**

Angel 41 School Rd, Watlington, PE33 0HA ☏ 01553 811326. Good local pub, right on the village green in Watlington that does food all week and roasts on Sunday. A warm welcome, and regular karaoke and quiz nights too. Food served Mon 5–11pm, Tues–Thurs noon–2.30pm & 4.30–11pm, Sat & Sun all day.

Crown & Anchor 16 Lynn Rd, Wiggenhall St Germans, PE34 3EY ☏ 01553 617340. A homely riverside pub that does a basic menu of pies, hot pots and burgers for £6–8, and traditional desserts like jam roly-poly and spotted dick. Tues–Sat noon–2pm & 6–8.30pm, Sun noon–3.30pm.

Downham Market and around

Fifteen minutes by train south of King's Lynn, **DOWNHAM MARKET** is the gateway to the Norfolk Fens, and, although not much in itself, is a well-placed and pleasant base, within easy reach of some of the most alluring Fenland villages, and also compelling natural attractions like the **Welney Wetland Reserve** and **Wicken Fen**. It's also within twenty minutes' drive or so of some of the best villages and attractions in the Brecks – **Oxburgh Hall**, **Gooderstone Water Gardens** and even **Thetford Forest** (see p.208).

The Market Place and Heritage Centre

Heritage Centre • Tues 9.30am–11.30am, Fri & Sat 10am–noon • Free • ⓦ downhamheritage.org.uk

Downham Market gathers around its **Market Place**, at the intersection of High Street and Bridge Street, marked by the town's iconic Victorian **clock tower**, a dinky cast-iron structure with a weather vane on top. There are weekly Friday and Saturday markets here. Just off the main street, the **Downham Market Heritage Centre**, upstairs at the town hall, tells the story of the area with the usual array of old maps, photos and trinkets.

Holy Trinity, Stow Bardolph

A couple of miles north of Downham Market, just off the A10, **Stow Bardolph** is a pretty village that is home to the church of **Holy Trinity**, a late twelfth-century church whose main feature is a chapel off the choir which is full of memorials to the local Hare family, who occupied nearby Stow Hall (the local pub, the *Hare Arms*, is named after them too). There are memorial tablets to Hugo and Nicholas Hare, who died in 1597 and 1619 respectively, a large monument to Susanne Hare (1741) by the sculptor of Shakespeare's tomb in Westminster Abbey, and a reclining figure of Thomas Hare as a Roman general (1697), but most spooky is the wax effigy of Thomas Hare's daughter Sarah, who died in 1744 and chose to have her likeness forever captured in wax. Check out, too, the accomplished sixteenth-century carvings of hares (geddit?) at the far end of the choir stalls.

4

Church Farm Rare Breeds Centre, Stow Bardolph

Stow Bardolph, PE34 3HU • Mid-Feb to Oct daily 10am–5pm • £7, children £6, family tickets £24 • ☎ 01366 382162,
ⓦ churchfarmstowbardolph.co.uk

Almost next door to the church in Stow Bardolph, **Church Farm Rare Breeds Centre** is an unashamedly child-focused attraction, a small farm with sheep and lambs, Gloacestershire Old Spot pigs, a couple of Suffolk Punch horses and tractor rides, along with a large kids' play area (inside and out), although much of the focus is on the busy café and toyshop.

St Mary's, Barton Bendish

Boughton Long Rd, Barton Bendish, PE33 9DN • ⓦ visitchurches.org.uk

About seven miles east of Downham Market, **Barton Bendish** is more of a Breckland than a Fenland village, and has an interesting church – **St Mary's** – on its outskirts, which is now under the care of the Churches Conservation Trust and usually open during the day. Thatched, and without a tower, Pevsner called its west door "one of the best Norman doors in England", and its interior is one of Norfolk's finest too – wonderfully peaceful and with the traces of an ancient and mysterious painting of a woman on a cartwheel on the wall of the nave. The village also has a great pub, the **Berney Arms** (see opposite).

Denver Mill

Sluice Rd, Denver, PE38 0EG • Daily 10am–5pm • £2 • ☎ 01366 384009, ⓦ denvermill.co.uk

About a 25-minute walk from the centre of Downham Market, on the far side of the pretty village of Denver, **Denver Mill** is a working windmill that grinds – and sells – its own flour in the shop downstairs; you can also eat its bread in the excellent tearoom. The great thing about the mill is that you can see it in operation, as it's used more or less every day if there's enough wind and it's not under repair (the engine room downstairs houses the sparklingly preserved diesel engine that was used on days without wind). You can view the wheels and shafts moving at the top, the grinding floor and the bags of flour at the bottom – and the Fenland views are glorious, though be warned that the steps to reach each floor are very steep.

Denver Sluices

Sluice Rd, Denver, PE38 0EG • ⓦ environment-agency.gov.uk

Twenty minutes' walk from Denver Mill, through an unspoilt Fenland landscape, **Denver Sluices** spread across the intersection of various channels of the Great Ouse and its drainage cuts. The first sluice was constructed here in 1651 by the great Dutch engineer Cornelis Vermuyden, and contributed greatly to the initial draining of the Fens, although it has been replaced and added to over the centuries. The complex is still a working one, and under the auspices of the Environment Agency, who host occasional drop-in events to explain how the sluices work and contribute to flood management in the area. Oddly, most of the water here is diverted way down south to Essex where they are more short of the stuff.

Welney Wetland Centre

Hundred Foot Bank, Welney, PE14 9TN • March–Oct daily 9.30am–5pm; Nov–Feb Mon–Wed 10am–5pm, Thurs–Sun 10am–8pm • £7.10, children £3.50, families £18.95 • ⓦ wwt.org.uk/visit-us/welney

Almost the perfect location for the novice or lazy twitcher, the **Welney Wetland Centre** occupies a complex of expensively assembled, cedar-clad and eco-friendly buildings astride the road and the marsh land in between the New and Old Bedford rivers, about ten miles northwest of Ely and about a mile and a half outside the village of Welney.

Twitchers aside, it can be a tremendously peaceful place, and is sensitively done, with total regard given to the birds' habitat. There's a variety of observation points along a linear trail sandwiched between the river and fen, ranging from basic one-man hides to the large centrally heated suite at the centre of the complex, where reference books are laid out for your edification and – if you've forgotten your binoculars – you can zero in on the best bits with hand-controlled CCTV. You can also rent binoculars for £5 and free wellies are on hand if it's muddy. And it may be: one of the most popular events at Welney is the migration and feeding of winter swans (though you can also observe this most evenings in floodlit comfort).

ARRIVAL INFORMATION
DOWNHAM MARKET AND AROUND

By train Downham Market's train station is a 10min walk west of the centre of town – from the station just follow Railway Rd then Bridge St and you will come eventually to the Market Place. There are regular connections to King's Lynn (20min), Ely (30min) and Cambridge (45min).
By bus Buses pull up on just off Bridge St, close by the

Downham Fryer; there are half-hourly services to King's Lynn (45min).
Tourist office Next door to Tesco in the council offices on Priory Rd (Mon–Thurs 8.45am–5.15pm, Fri 8.45am–4.45pm; Easter to mid-Sept also Sat 9am–noon; ☎01366 387770).

ACCOMMODATION

DOWNHAM MARKET

Castle Hotel High St, PE38 9HF ☎01366 384311, ⓦcastle-hotel.com. Recently upgraded, the twelve en-suite doubles here vary quite a bit, with a mixture of four-posters, double and twin beds. Breakfast included. **£95**

Crown Hotel 12 Bridge St, PE38 9DH ☎01366 382322. Right in the heart of town, this creaky old coaching inn has simply furnished en-suite doubles. Owned by the same folk who run the *Jenyns Arms* and *Foldgate Inn*. Breakfast costs £6. **£50–70**

★ **Dial House** 12 Railway Rd, PE38 9EB ☎01366 385775, ⓦdialhousebnb.co.uk. Halfway between the station and the town centre, this is your chance to stay in a real gingerbread house. Run by Bob and Jaquie, this small B&B is beautifully kept inside and out, with three double rooms each named after the sisters who used to run a school for young gentlemen here. Look for the sundial on the side of the house. Excellent breakfast included. **£60**

DENVER

★ **Berney Arms** Church Rd, Barton Bendish, PE33 9GF ☎01366 347995, ⓦtheberneyarms.co.uk. Long-running village pub that has offered good food and accommodation in various incarnations over the years. There are five recently converted doubles in the stable block, and a suite in the old forge; they also accommodate children under 12 for free on put-up beds. Excellent value, with a great breakfast and the only thing that's lacking is wi-fi in the rooms, though it's no great hardship to stroll across the drive to hook up in the excellent pub-restaurant (see below). Rooms **£50**, suite **£70**

Denver Mill Sluice Rd, Denver, PE38 0EG ☎01366 384009, ⓦdenvermill.co.uk. The miller's house at Denver Mill (see opposite) has been converted to three self-catering holiday cottages, each sleeping three to four people, and what better place to stay than here, bang in the middle of Fenland, with the mill's home-baked bread on your doorstep for breakfast? One week in summer **£350–450**

EATING AND DRINKING

DOWNHAM MARKET

Downham Fryer 38 Bridge St, PE38 9DH ☎01366 383029. Good fish and chips and lots of seating inside. Mon–Sat 11am–9pm, Fri & Sat till 10pm.

The Railway Arms and Fenland Express Downham Market train station, PE38 9EN Old-fashioned café and pub nestled into the train station, with a bar and two cosy rooms with comfy armchairs to sink into. Shelves and shelves of secondhand books too, all of which are for sale – just pop the money into the box. Mon–Fri 5.30am–5.30pm, Sat 7am–5.30pm.

STOW BARDOLPH

★ **Hare Arms** Lynn Rd, PE34 3HT ☎01366 382229,

ⓦtheharearms.co.uk The village pub is also named after the family, and is a popular place, serving food that's a cut above average pub grub, with a large menu featuring good sausages, burgers, chicken and pork dishes – all locally sourced and beautifully cooked. There's a posher dinner menu, too, and a pleasant beer gardens, full of peacocks. Bar Mon–Sat noon–2.30pm & 6–11pm, Sun noon–10pm; restaurant Mon–Sat 7–11pm.

DENVER

Jenyns Arms Denver Sluice, PE38 0EQ ☎01366 383366, ⓦjenyns.co.uk. Right by the sluices outside Denver village, the *Jenyns Arms* enjoys a perfect position by the river, and a garden to enjoy it from. There's also basic pub grub,

4

including sausage pie, fish and chips, shepherd's pie, along with salads and sandwiches. Mon–Fri & Sun noon–2pm & 7–9.30pm, Sat noon–2.30pm & 6–9.30pm.

BARTON BENDISH

★ **Berney Arms** Church Rd, PE33 9GF ☎01366 347995, ⊕theberneyarms.co.uk. Run by the always welcoming husband-and-wife team of Phil and Sue Hirst, this village inn has long been a tremendously popular choice for food and drink, with a room focused on drinking one side and a gastropub restaurant on the other. There's a great, regularly changing menu, featuring the likes of breast of pheasant, belly of pork, home-made fishcakes

and haunch of venison, much of it sourced from the surrounding estate. Moderately priced too, considering the quality – starters £5.95–7.95, mains around £13.95. Mon–Sat noon–2pm & 6–9pm.

WELNEY

Lamb & Flag Main St, PE14 9RB ☎01354 610242, ⊕lambandflagwelney.co.uk. Large pub that does good food from a short menu of burgers, steaks and other staples – try the Fenman's steak pie – from around £7.95. Usually a blackboard of specials too. They also have a few rooms upstairs. Mon 6.30–8.30pm, Tues noon–2.30pm & 6.30–8.30pm, Sun noon–3.30pm.

Ely and around

Perched on a mound of clay above the River Great Ouse, about fifteen miles south of Downham Market, the attractive little town of **ELY** – literally "eel island" – was indeed an island until the draining of the Fens in the seventeenth century. Up until then the town was encircled by treacherous marshland, which could only be crossed with the help of the local "fen-slodgers" who knew the firm tussock paths. In 1070, Hereward the Wake turned this inaccessibility to military advantage, holding out against the Normans and forcing William the Conqueror to undertake a prolonged siege. Centuries later, the Victorian writer Charles Kingsley resurrected this obscure conflict in his novel *Hereward the Wake*, presenting the protagonist as the last of the English who "never really bent their necks to the Norman yoke" – a heady mixture of nationalism and historical invention that went down a storm. The reason you come to Ely, however, is for its magnificent Norman **cathedral**, a towering structure visible for miles across the flat Fenland landscape that is a worthwhile destination in its own right – although you may also want to take in the National Trust's **Wicken Fen**, nearby, which is as close to a rare chunk of undrained and unmolested Fenland as you can get.

The High Street and Riverside

Ely is a pleasant and pretty small town, but apart from the cathedral is hardly compelling. To the immediate north of the church, the **High Street** is a slender thoroughfare lined by old-fashioned shops, cafés and charity shops. East of the dinky Market Place it becomes Waterside, which leads down to the river at **Riverside** – a relaxing stretch with a large antique centre, a marina, a riverside footpath, a tearoom or two, a small art gallery and an entertainment complex housed in the splendidly restored **Old Maltings**.

Ely Cathedral

June–Sept daily 7am–7pm; Oct–May Mon–Sat 7am–6.30pm, Sun 7am–5pm • £6.50 Mon–Sat, free on Sun ; includes a ground-floor tour, Octagon tours cost an extra £5.50 (best reserved in advance) • ☎01353 667735, ⊕elycathedral.org

Dating mainly from the late twelfth century, **Ely Cathedral** is one of the largest and most impressive churches in England, but outside at least it's also one of its most unsymmetrical, with only one transept – the other collapsed in a storm in 1701. The remaining transept is an imposing sight, its dog-tooth windows, castellated towers and blind arcading possess all the rough, brutal charm of the Normans. Inside, the nave is the fourth longest in the country at 538ft, its procession of plain late-Norman arches leading to the architectural feature that makes Ely so special, the **octagon**, built in 1322 to

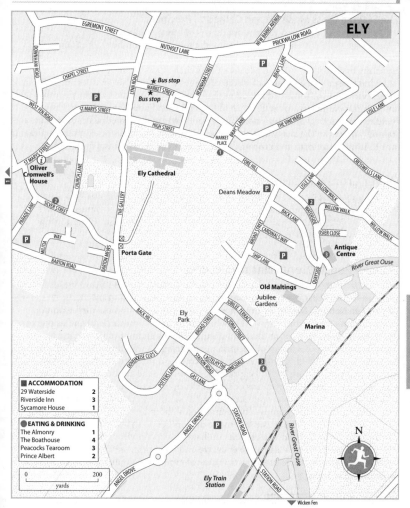

ELY

ACCOMMODATION

29 Waterside	2
Riverside Inn	3
Sycamore House	1

EATING & DRINKING

The Almonry	1
The Boathouse	4
Peacocks Tearoom	3
Prince Albert	2

replace the collapsed central tower. Its construction, employing the largest oaks available to support some four hundred tons of glass and lead, remains one of the wonders of the medieval world, and the effect, as you look up into this Gothic dome, is breathtaking.

The first three bays of the **choir** were rebuilt at the same time as the octagon in the Decorated style – in contrast to the slightly plainer Early English of the choir bays beyond. A commemorative plaque here marks the site of the shrine of **St Ethelreda**, founder of the abbey in 673, who, despite being twice married, is honoured liturgically as a virgin. The shrine once attracted pilgrims from far and wide, but it was destroyed during the Reformation. At the far east end of the cathedral, the thirteenth-century **presbytery** has two medieval **chantry chapels**, the more intricately carved of which (on the left) is an elaborate Renaissance affair dated to 1488. The other marvel to see is the **Lady Chapel**, a separate building accessible via the north transept: it lost its sculpture and its stained glass during the Reformation, but its fan vaulting remains, and is an exquisite example of the late English Gothic style.

The Stained Glass Museum and Cathedral Precincts

Mon–Sat 10.30am–5pm, Sun noon–6pm, till 4.30pm Nov to Easter • £4 • ⓦ stainedglassmuseum.com

Close to the main entrance of the cathedral the south triforium holds the **Stained Glass Museum**, exhibiting examples of this applied art from 1200 to the 1970s, including some especially fine work by William Morris and his circle. Outside, the **Precincts** of the cathedral boast a fine ensemble of medieval domestic architecture, an assortment of old stone, brick and half-timbered buildings that runs south from the Infirmary complex, abutting the presbytery, to the Prior's buildings near the Porta Gate. Many of the buildings are used by the King's boarding school – where the cathedral's choristers are trained – others by the clergy, but although you can't go in any of them, it's still a pleasant area to stroll; a free map and brochure are available from the cathedral itself.

Oliver Cromwell's House

29 St Mary's St, CB7 4HF • April–Oct daily 10am–5pm; Nov–March Mon–Fri & Sun 11am–4pm Sat 10am–5pm • £4.50

Northwest from the cathedral is **Oliver Cromwell's House**, a timber-framed former vicarage, which holds a small exhibition on the Protector's ten-year sojourn in Ely, when he was employed as a tithe collector.

Wicken Fen National Nature Reserve

Lode Lane, Wicken CB7 5XP • Nature Reserve: daily 10am–5pm or dusk if earlier; dragonfly centre end-May to end-Sept Sat & Sun 11am–4pm; cottage April–July & Sept–Oct Sat & Sun 2–5pm, Aug Wed, Sat & Sun 11am–5pm • £5.99; NT • ☎ 01353 7202734, ⓦ wicken.org.uk

4

Wicken Fen National Nature Reserve, nine miles south of Ely, has the distinction of being Britain's first nature reserve (Darwin used to collect insects here) and as one of the few remaining areas of undrained Fenland remains an important wetland habitat. It owes its survival to a group of Victorian entomologists who donated the land to the National Trust in 1899. The seven hundred acres are undrained but not uncultivated – sedge and reed cutting are still carried out to preserve the landscape as it is – and the reserve is easily explored by means of several clearly marked footpaths, the easiest of which is a three-quarter-of-a-mile stroll along a boardwalk, passing one of the last surviving Fenland wind pumps. The reserve holds about ten birdwatching hides and is also one of the best places in the UK to see dragonflies, with a summer **Dragonfly Centre**, full of displays and with experts on hand to explain what you're looking at. At the main entrance, there's also a **visitor centre** and an antique Fenland thatched **cottage**. The visitor centre organizes a variety of events and guided walks – call ahead or go online for details.

ARRIVAL AND INFORMATION ELY

By train Ely lies on a major rail intersection, receiving direct trains from as far afield as Liverpool (4hr), Norwich (every 30min; 50min) and London King's Cross (hourly; 1hr 20min), as well as from Cambridge, just to the south (every 15–20min; 15min). From the train station, it's a 10min walk to the cathedral, straight up Station Rd and then Back Hill before veering right along The Gallery.

By bus Buses, including hourly services from Cambridge, stop on Market St immediately to the north of the cathedral.

Tourist office A couple of minutes' walk northwest of the cathedral in what was once Oliver Cromwell's House at 29 St Mary's St (April–Oct daily 10am–5pm; Nov–March Mon–Fri & Sun 11am–4pm, Sat 10am–5pm; ☎ 01353/662062, ⓦ visitely.eastcambs.gov.uk). They issue free town maps and will help with accommodation

ACCOMMODATION

29 Waterside B&B 29 Waterside, CB7 4AU ☎ 01353 614329, ⊜ info@29waterside.org.uk. Down near the river, this cosy B&B occupies a pair of pretty little brick cottages dating back to the 1750s. Several of the original features have been preserved, especially the beamed ceilings, and the remainder has been sympathetically modernized. If the sun is out, breakfast is taken in the cottage garden. __£66__

Riverside Inn 8 Annesdale, CB7 4BN ☎ 01353 661671, ⓦ riversideinn-ely.co.uk. Ely is noticeably short on hotels, but the *Riverside* does its best to remedy matters, its three guest rooms decorated in a pleasing version of country-house-meets-boutique style. All the rooms here overlook the marina and are competitively priced. **£90**

Sycamore House 91 Cambridge Rd, CB7 4HX ☎01353 662139, ⓦsycamoreguesthouse.co.uk. In a well-maintained detached house on the southwest edge of town, the *Sycamore* has three en-suite, guest rooms and all are decorated in an agreeable, vaguely retro style. Tasty home-cooked breakfasts too. **£80**

EATING AND DRINKING

The Almonry 36 High St, CB7 4JU ☎01353 666360. Good café in a great location, with lovely views of the cathedral, albeit with a fairly pedestrian array of sandwiches and snacks. Daily 10am–5pm.

The Boathouse 5 Annesdale, CB7 4BN ☎01353 664388, ⓦtheboathouseely.co.uk. The best restaurant in Ely, a modern, bistro-style place down by the river, its menu features local, seasonal ingredients, in a firmly British style, with the likes of pheasant, skate, mutton and – the house speciality – sausages and mash. Mains average £14, but the sausages cost just £11. Daily noon–2.30pm, plus Mon–Thurs 6.30–9pm, Fri & Sat 6.30–9.30pm & Sun 6.30–8.30pm.

★ **Peacocks Tearoom** 65 Waterside, CB7 4AU ☎01353 661100, ⓦpeacockstearoom.co.uk. Down by the river, this popular tearoom serves a delicious range of cream teas, salads, sandwiches, soups and lunches with the odd surprise: try, for example, the chocolate courgette cake. Its also has an enormous choice of teas from every corner of the globe. Wed–Sun 10.30am–5pm.

Prince Albert 62 Silver St, CB7 4JF ☎01353 663494. This traditional, neighbourhood joint has a good selection of guest ales on tap, and a handy location too – a short stroll from the cathedral. Pub grub too. Food daily noon–3pm & 6–9pm.

4

Central and southern Norfolk

CYCLISTS IN THETFORD FOREST

5

Central and southern Norfolk

A large and diverse area, central and southern Norfolk includes both some of the most scenic and some of the lesser-known parts of the region – the Brecks and the Waveney Valley. These areas cross the borders of the two counties, and although they lie mostly in Norfolk, the forests and heaths of Breckland dip a toe into Suffolk, and the Waveney River forms the meandering border between the two counties, dividing two of their nicest small towns, Diss (in Norfolk) and Beccles (in Suffolk): the land in between counts as one of Norfolk's most beautiful stretches of countryside.

At the heart of the region, **Breckland** is a notoriously dry area of forest and heathland that provides fine countryside for walking and a host of attractions, not to mention a series of pleasant market towns to rest up in at the end of the day. **Swaffham** is the best placed of these, but **Thetford**, to the south, has its moments, and there are villages with pubs scattered across the countryside that are among the prettiest in East Anglia. Above all, try to make some time to visit **Thetford Forest**, whose pine woodland and heath is one of Norfolk's hidden secrets, full of well-marked trails that are ideal for walking, biking and even husky racing. To the west Breckland fades into the low-lying landscapes of the **Fenland** (see p.175), while to the east there is the valley of the **Waveney River**, where you can spend some time adjusting to the slower pace of life of the towns that straddle the border: **Diss**, **Harleston** and **Bungay** all repay a visit – precisely for what it is hard to say, but their small-town charm is undeniably appealing. The same applies to **Beccles**, at the far end of the Waveney Valley and the furthest southern point of the Broads; it's the area's most handsome and thriving town, and a perfect place from which to explore.

Swaffham and around

It's hard to believe now, but like a lot of Breckland towns, **SWAFFHAM** was once a large and relatively important place, the centre of an agricultural area that was as rich as anywhere in England during medieval times. Later it was a favourite haunt of Lady Hamilton and various Nelsons, and although those days are long gone, it's still a pleasant town, famously used as the fictional market town of Market Shipborough in the Stephen Fry TV series, *Kingdom* (Fry himself lives nearby). Swaffham is also brilliantly placed for a number of outlying attractions, including **Beachamwell Forest** and **Swaffham Heath** immediately to the southwest, crisscrossed by countless numbered paths and trails, and Oxburgh Hall beyond.

The Market Cross

Swaffham's central area focuses on the triangular **Market Cross**, appropriately graced by a statue of Ceres, Roman goddess of wheat and the harvest. There's a good market here on Saturday mornings, and not much goes on in Swaffham that can't be viewed from here.

OXBURGH HALL

Highlights

❶ Strattons Hotel, Swaffham Eat, drink and sleep at one of the best small hotels in the county. **See p.193**

❷ Oxburgh Hall East Anglia is stuffed with glorious stately homes, but this fine moated manor is in the top three. **See p.194**

❸ Castle Acre Priory These represent some of Norfolk's most evocative abbey ruins, and are situated in one of its most picturesque small villages. **See p.196**

❹ Thetford Forest This isn't an ancient woodland by any means, but it is maybe the jewel in Breckland's crown of heaths and forests. **See p.208**

❺ Bressingham Gardens and Steam Museum These beautiful gardens are supplemented by a marvellous steam museum (with, incidentally, a great section on *Dad's Army*). Plus you can stay the night. **See p.211**

HIGHLIGHTS ARE MARKED ON THE MAP ON PP.188–189

CENTRAL & SOUTH NORFOLK

HIGHLIGHTS
1. Stratton's Hotel, Swaffham
2. Oxburgh Hall
3. Castle Acre Priory
4. Thetford Forest
5. Bressingham Gardens & Steam Museum

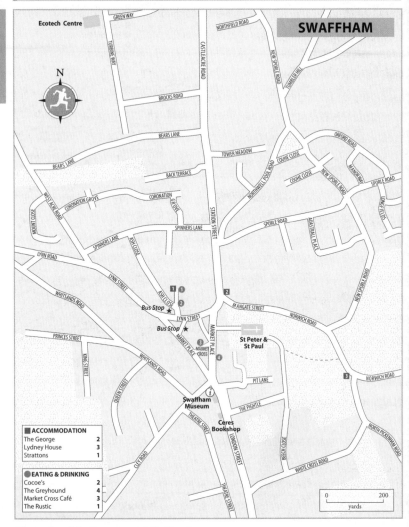

Church of St Peter and St Paul

Market Place, PE37 7AB • ⓦ swaffham.churchnorfolk.com

Just across the road from the Market Cross, Swaffham's church of **St Peter and St Paul** was built in the late fifteenth century. Its gorgeously preserved chestnut hammerbeam roof is the attention-grabber here, and there's a mirror in the nave to aid viewing of the 192 carved angels, all in immaculate condition, that decorate it. But there's much else to see besides: the church's good state of preservation may be down to the fact that Catherine Stewart, Oliver Cromwell's maternal grandmother, is buried here, and remembered by a memorial at the head of the south aisle. Other features include the 500-year-old wooden pews, which depict John Chapman, church warden in the fifteenth century, the so-called Pedlar of Swaffham (see box, opposite). Chapman funded the building of the unusually fancy tower and of the north aisle, where these pews used to rest, and he's depicted with his faithful dog, while his wife is shown opposite, with a rosary, behind the counter of a shop. Chapman and his family also appear in the tops of the windows in the north aisle – the only original stained glass. The church has a large and ancient churchyard that stretches way back beyond the church, where you might see the odd gambolling rabbit.

Swaffham Museum

4 London St, PE37 7DQ • Feb–Dec Tues–Sat 10am–4pm • £2.50 • ☎ 01760 721230, ⓦ swaffhammuseum.co.uk

Housed in the town hall alongside the tourist office, **Swaffham Museum** has the usual jumble of locally gathered artefacts – Bronze Age to medieval coins, weapons and domestic implements – but it also more entertainingly focuses on the bizarre personal collections of local people – baked-bean-tin wrappers, gadgets, toby jugs and cigarette cards. Upstairs is a model of the town in 1935, made by the cousin of Howard Carter, the Egyptologist who lived in Swaffham as a child. Carter has his own display, detailing his early life, along with his Tutankhamun discoveries, including a few Egyptian figurines and other objects – and Egyptian dressing-up clothes for kids.

Ecotech Centre

Turbine Way, PE37 7HT • Mon–Fri 10am–4pm, plus Sat & Sun during Aug • Free; guided tours £6, children £4 • ☎ 01760 726100, ⓦ ecotech.org.uk

On the eastern edge of town, ten minutes' walk from the Market Cross, Swaffham's **Ecotech Centre** showcases alternative energy and sustainability with displays, a café and a shop. You can see the "Green Bird", a sort of giant sportscar that's officially the fastest wind-powered vehicle on earth, having clocked up to 126mph in 2009, an organic vegetable garden and an impressive rebuilding of the base of a typical Norfolk flint tower – and there are activities for children in the main building, all free. However, the main event is the wind turbine that towers above the complex, which you can climb if you're lucky enough to coincide with a tour. If not, just standing at its base is a fairly awesome experience.

Narborough Hall Gardens

Narborough, PE32 1TE • May–Sept Sun 2–5pm • £4 • ☎ 01760 338827, ⓦ narboroughhallgardens.com

About six miles northwest of Swaffham, at the centre of the village of **Narborough**, is the elegant country house of **Narborough Hall**. Joanne Merrison moved here just over eight years ago and has been reinvigorating the gardens, establishing new borders close to the house and renovating much of the rest of the grounds. It's great for children, with inventive trails and a treehouse overlooking the lake, paths along the tiny Nar River, which runs through the estate, and a walled fruit and vegetable garden that provides the ingredients for Joanne's culinary creations – served in the courtyard café. There are also regular events and art exhibitions inside the house. Altogether it's a beautiful spot, laboured over with love, and only let down by its restricted and variable opening times – check before you go.

THE PEDLAR OF SWAFFHAM

A local legend tells the tale of the **Pedlar of Swaffham**, a poor man called **John Chapman**, who, having dreamt he went to London and made his fortune, decided to go to London to see what happened. Nothing much occurred, but he met a man who ridiculed him for following his dreams, telling him of a dream he had had that he'd found treasure under an old oak in a Norfolk town called Swaffham but wouldn't be so stupid as to go there to find it. Chapman of course went right back to Swaffham, found the oak, and dug up the treasure, making his fortune overnight and funding the rebuilding of the church and so many other civic projects that he's remembered throughout the town, most prominently on the town sign in the middle of the Market Cross.

5

BRECKLAND: BRITAIN'S ATACAMA?

The Brecks – or **Breckland**, – is one of Britain's most unusual lowland areas. Largely in Norfolk though partly in Suffolk too, it stretches roughly from Swaffham in the north, across to Brandon and Mildenhall (both in Suffolk) in the west and to Watton in the east, and down to just south of Thetford in the south. It's officially the driest place in Britain, with a more continental climate than the rest of the country, colder in winter and hotter in summer than the British average; incredibly, annual rainfall is on a par with Jerusalem. Its landscape, too, is distinctive, with sandy heaths and thick forests, that are home to a variety of **wildlife** not readily found in other parts of the UK – woodlarks, stone curlews and nightjars are common here, as are various species of deer and muntjac. As such, the Brecks are a great place for active, **outdoor activities**: there are numerous footpaths for hiking, most spectacularly in Thetford Forest, but copious paths crisscross the entire region, and there's no better place in the country for biking and horseriding. It's a great place to camp too, though its main towns of Swaffham and Thetford provide excellent bases, as do a number of other villages in between.

Beachamwell

A short way southwest of Swaffham is the small village of **BEACHAMWELL**, whose unusual thatched church of **St Mary** anchors the village green. It's around a thousand years old, Saxon in origin, with a round tower topped with a hexagonal turret that was added a couple of hundred years later. Inside – you have to get the key from Beachamwell Cottage across the road – is graffiti that dates back to the building of the church, scratched on a pillar at the back, including a depiction of a horned figure – the so-called Beachamwell devil.

Iceni Village, Cockley Cley

Cockley Cley, PE37 8AG · April–Oct daily 10am–5pm; July & Aug till 5.30pm · £5 · ☎ 01760 724588, ⓦ icenivillage.com

About five miles southwest of Swaffham, the small village of **Cockley Cley** is not much in itself but is home to a good pub, a partially collapsed round-towered church, and the **Iceni Village** – a collection of attractions that just about fits together. Started by a Sheffield industrialist on his country estate, and still owned by the family, its focus is a re-creation of an Iceni tribal homestead from the first century BC, with a circle of mocked-up village buildings inhabited by various figures – the Iceni lived in this area around 2000 years ago and their most famous denizen was Boudicca (see p.313). Beyond here there's a nature trail around a reedy lake (with a birdwatching hide part of the way round), while across the car park a number of fairly run-down barns house steam engines and threshing machine, ploughs and other farm implements along with a collection of carriages. The most impressive features, though, are the seventeenth-century **cottage** across the road, and the **Saxon church** in the woodland beyond. The latter was only discovered in the 1950s, when it was (unknowingly) lived in as a cottage. It's believed to have been built on the site of a pagan temple, and hosts a Roman lead coffin from 350 AD, found nearby, and a flinty apse and thick walls that feel very ancient indeed.

Gooderstone Water Gardens

The Street, Gooderstone, PE33 9BP · Daily 10am–5.30pm; Nov–March till 4pm; tearoom Easter to end Sept only · £4.75, children £1.50 · ☎ 01603 712913, ⓦ gooderstonewatergardens.co.uk

Beyond Cockley Cley, the **Gooderstone Water Gardens**, just outside the village of the same name, are very much a family affair, and all the better for it – dug out on a whim by a local farmer thirty years ago, and lovingly restored by his daughter Coral in 2002, who still oversees it (her brothers farm the adjoining land). It's a truly tranquil spot, its ponds and channels traversed by little bridges and fringed by majestic willows, offering splendid vistas at every turn, while its nooks and corners absorb visitors with ease.

Follow the paths to the river and cross over for a nature trail through the woodland, or settle down in the bird hide to spot kingfishers on the lake – all before enjoying tea and Coral's home-made cakes in the tearoom. There are plant sales, too, by the entrance.

ARRIVAL AND INFORMATION
SWAFFHAM AND AROUND

By bus Buses stop in the centre of town, close to the junction of London St and the Market Place near *Strattons Hotel*; the town is on the regular #X1 (every 30min) line between King's Lynn (35min), East Dereham (35min) and Norwich (1hr25min). There are also less regular connections to Fakenham (1 hr).

Tourist office Small office in the town hall and museum building, 4 London St (Tues–Sat 10am–4pm; ☎01760 724988).

ACCOMMODATION

SWAFFHAM

The George Station St, PE37 7LJ ☎01760 721238, ⓦarlingtonhotelgroup.co.uk. Don't be too put off by the "two-for-one" and "Sunday Carvery" signs outside, the *George* is quite a lot nicer than you might think, with thirty comfortable if slightly characterless double rooms. There's parking too, a nice bar downstairs that serves food all day, and the *Green Room* restaurant serving lunch and dinner. The best rooms are in the old building, at the front. **£75**

Lydney House Norwich Rd, PE37 7QS ☎01760 723355, ⓦwww.lydney-house.demon.co.uk. Just across the meadow from the churchyard, on the edge of Swaffham town centre, this mid-eighteenth-century Georgian house has eight bedrooms, most of them decently if a little uninspiringly furnished, some with recently refurbished bathrooms. The welcome is warm, there's free wi-fi, and a downstairs bar. Includes breakfast. **£80**

★ **Strattons** Ash Close, PE37 7NH ☎01760 723845, ⓦstrattons-hotel.co.uk. Vanessa and Les Scott opened *Strattons* twenty years ago, and either they were remarkably ahead of the curve, or they have adapted it to be almost the epitome of a new breed of British boutique hotel, with an attractive historic building, a great restaurant and comfortable rooms that make the most of their location but are also contemporary and welcoming. There are eight rooms in the main house, and half a dozen slick suites in a converted printworks across the garden, all decorated with an impeccable eye for detail. Wi-fi free throughout, although a bit erratic in the annexe. Double **£155**, suite **£260**

BEACHAMWELL

Great Danes Country Inn The Green, Old Hall Lane, PE37 8BG ☎01366 328443, ⓦcountryinns.co.uk. Much smaller than its rather grand title would suggest, and all the better for it – a privately owned hotel with just six rooms in the converted annexe, simply but cosily furnished. There's a welcoming restaurant and bar too. **£60**

EATING AND DRINKING

SWAFFHAM

Cocoe's 2 Ash Close, PE37 7NH ☎01760 723845, ⓦcocoes. co.uk. Part of *Strattons* hotel just behind, this stylish café and deli does good coffee, great all-day breakfasts and light lunches – tapas platters, posh pies and salads – and is licensed too. Free wi-fi. Mon–Thurs 9am–5pm, Fri 9am–6pm, Sat 8am–6pm, Sun 11am–4pm.

The Greyhound 97 Market Place, PE37 7AQ ☎01760 725468. Swaffham isn't great for pubs, but the *Greyhound*, right on the main street, is a good locals' spot that doubled as the *Startled Duck* in Stephen Fry's TV series *Kingdom*. Daily 11am–3pm & 6pm–midnight.

Market Cross Café Market Place, PE37 7AB ☎01760 336671. This homely café, with comfy seating upstairs and an outside terrace that overlooks most of what passes for life in central Swaffham, serves a quirkily individual lunch menu that ranges from stilton rarebit to whitebait and Cajun spiced chicken. Great salads and filled ciabattas too, and home-made cakes. The food is fresh and good, portions generous, and the service excellent, and it's licensed. Mon–Wed 10am–6pm, Thurs–Sat 10am–9pm (evening meals from 7pm), Sun 10am–4pm.

★ **The Rustic** Ash Close, PE37 7NH ☎01760 723845, ⓦstrattons-hotel.co.uk. Located in the basement of *Strattons* hotel, this restaurant has a sense of occasion, though is still relaxed, and its modern British menu is both traditional and inventive, with starters like pigeon pastrami and Brancaster mussels, and mains like stargazy (rabbit and crayfish) pie, or just fish and chips or hanger steak – all very well priced at £12 a main, and with a big emphasis on local suppliers. Mon–Sat 6.30–9pm, Sun noon–2.30pm & 6.30–9pm.

COCKLEY CLEY

Twenty Churchwardens Cockley Cley, PE37 8AN ☎01760 721439. A cosy local, dog-friendly and with a wood-burning stove in winter, and easy chairs and walls lined with books. The food is basic – mostly predictable pub grub – but they do a good line in home-made pies; try the churchwarden's pie – filled with pork, veg and mildly spiced with chilli. Mon–Sat noon–2pm & 7–9pm, Sun noon–2pm.

5

Ceres Bookshop 20 London St, PE37 7DG ☎01760 722504, ⓦceresbookshopswaffham.co.uk. A few doors past the Swaffham Museum, the Ceres Bookshop is an excellent, large and well-stocked secondhand bookstore (though with a few new books too) with a tearoom at the back that does excellent home-made cake. Mon–Sat 9am–5pm, tearoom till 4pm.

Oxborough and around

About six miles southwest of Swaffham, the small village of **OXBOROUGH** sits in the middle of glorious if unspectacular countryside – very rural, very pretty, and rather off the beaten track. The main thing to see here is the National Trust property, Oxburgh Hall but it's also worth taking the time to visit the church of **St John**, next door.

Oxburgh Hall

Oxborough, PE33 9PS • End Feb to mid-March & Oct Mon–Wed, Sat & Sun 11am–4pm; mid-March to end Sept Mon–Wed, Sat & Sun 11am–5pm; school hols & Aug also open Thurs & Fri 11am–5pm; gardens also Sat & Sun Nov–Feb • House & garden £8.20, garden only £4.30; NT • ☎01366 328258, ⓦnationaltrust.org.uk/oxburghhall

Dominating the heart of the village, **Oxburgh Hall** was the family home of the Bedingfield family from 1482, and is now in the hands of the National Trust. It's an impressive sight from the outside, a moated manor house at the end of a long drive, and inside has a wealth of features – a "priest hole" in which a priest would hide in the event of a raid during the Reformation (the Bedingfields were a devout Catholic family), and a series of wall hangings stitched by Mary Queen of Scots while in captivity, although the building itself is the real star – that, and the gardens which you can appreciate on a series of guided trails and woodland walks.

St John

Oxborough's fourteenth-century **Church of St John** on Oxborough Road was an impressive construction until 1948, when its spire collapsed and destroyed most of the building, leaving only the choir intact. The church was never rebuilt, and its churchyard, and the open ruined nave, make for a peaceful and bucolic spot, while the choir serves as the village chapel. Take a look at the Bedingfield Chapel on the right, full of memorials to the family, in particular two carved terracotta tombs from the late fifteenth century which seem almost French in style, and point to the Catholic devoutness of the family. Next door, the main body of the choir has another pre-Reformation treasure – a brass lectern in the shape of an eagle, with slits in the beak to receive donations to the Church of Rome – so-called "Peter's Pence".

Castle Acre

One of west Norfolk's most immediately appealing villages, **CASTLE ACRE** sits on a bluff above the Nar valley about five miles north of Swaffham. Its centre is an improbably picturesque cluster of flint cottages set around a rectangular green, at the top of a steep hill, framed by the old bailey gate of the village's castle. It's a small place, with a population of less than a thousand, but punches far above its weight in terms of attractions, principally because the land here was gifted by William the Conqueror to one of his generals, Earl William de Warenne, who adopted it as his country seat and made it an important local powerbase for centuries to come. It's a stop on the Peddars Way long-distance footpath, so gets its fair share of walkers stopping off at one of its excellent accommodation choices.

CASTLE ACRE PRIORY >

5

St James

Priory Rd, PE32 2AE • W narvalleygroup.org.uk

Castle Acre's church of **St James**, at the far end of the village green, backs onto the ruins of the town's more famous priory, and is a large, three-aisled fifteenth-century Perpendicular-style church in classic Norfolk style: Inside is a soaring Gothic font cover and a beautiful painted rood screen featuring the Apostles – each shown with their symbolic emblem: St Thomas with a spear, St Batholomew with a knife, Andrew with a saltire – and a hexagonal pulpit decorated with the figures of the church, dating from 1440.

Castle Acre Priory

Priory Rd, PE32 2XD • April–Sept daily 10am–5pm; March & Oct Mon & Thurs–Sun 10am–4pm; Nov, Jan & Feb Sat & Sun 10am–4pm; Dec Sun 10am–4pm • £5.60, children £3.40, family tickets £14.60; EH • ☎ 01760 755394, W www.english-heritage.org.uk

Although you can't move for ruined monasteries in Norfolk, Castle Acre's **Priory** is one of the finest, the best-preserved Cluniac monastery in the country, with extant ruins spread across a fairly large and atmospheric site. Founded by the Earl of Warenne in 1077, it has a well-preserved Norman frontage to the ruins of the church, and slices of Norman decoration throughout. At its height the priory was home to around 35 monks, though this was down to just ten by the time Henry VIII dissolved the monastery in 1537. There are displays showing how it would have originally looked in the entrance buildings, and a good free audioguide that helps to bring the place alive as you stroll around. Also, unusually, you can access the quarters of the prior himself – a bedroom and an attached chapel – which are still intact and overlook the cloister, and would have been very grand.

Castle Acre Castle

Open at all times • Free; EH • W www.english-heritage.org.uk/daysout/properties/castle-acre-castle-and-bailey-gate

Castle Acre's **Castle**, on the opposite side of the centre to the priory, is the village's most ancient feature: it fell into disrepair in the twelfth century, just as the priory rose to prominence, and there's not much of it left. But its position high up on a couple of mounds, looking over the very gently rolling countryside to the south, is superb both scenically and defensively, and it's a fun place to clamber about among the ruins. The keep is semi-intact, and there are walkways and wooden steps to help you on your way.

ARRIVAL AND DEPARTURE

CASTLE ACRE

By bus To get to Castle Acre by bus you need to change in Swaffham, from where there are buses every couple of hours and it's a 10min journey. Buses stop on the corner of Town Lane and Massingham Rd, just a minute from the village green.

ACCOMMODATION

Church Gate Tearooms Willow Cottage, Stocks Green, PE32 2AE ☎ 01760 755551, W churchgatecastleacre .co.uk. On the green, right by the churchyard, this has four comfy rooms, all en suite, not over-large but cosily furnished with TVs, and including breakfast, and a holiday cottage out the back for those who prefer self-catering. **£65**

Old Red Lion Bailey St, PE32 2AG ☎ 01760 755557, W oldredlion.org.uk. The cheap, alternative place to stay in Castle Acre, a former pub with a mix of dormitory accommodation and private rooms. It's a great, friendly place, with an artsy, vibe, and offers weekly yoga classes, painting and drawing tuition and veggie food. Dorms **£20**, doubles **£70**

The Ostrich Stocks Green, PE32 2AE ☎ 01760 755398, W ostrichcastleacre.com. This welcoming pub does a good job as a hotel restaurant while still being a desirable village pub, with wood-burning stoves and a cosy main bar and five very well-finished en-suite double rooms and a couple of family rooms. Free wi-fi too. **£75**

EATING AND DRINKING

Church Gate Tearooms Willow Cottage, Stocks Green, PE32 2AE ☎ 01760 755551, W churchgatecastleacre .co.uk. They serve a simple menu here, of sandwiches and baguettes (from £3.40), jackets and omelettes and salads, as well as hot dishes like Welsh rarebit and poached eggs on toast (£4–5), in a traditional English tearoom setting. Tues–Sun 10.30am–4.45pm.

★ **The Ostrich** Stocks Green, PE32 2AE ☎ 01760

755398, ⓦostrichcastleacre.com. *The Ostrich* is a good place to stay, but it's also a great place to eat, with thoughtful and beautifully cooked modern British starters from £5.95 and mains from around £11.95 – think potted pigeon, pancetta and capers followed by calves' liver and bacon, game hot pot or beer-battered fish and chips. Or just have one of their gourmet sandwiches. Always lots of variety, and several daily specials, including veggie options. Mon–Sat noon –3pm & 6–9pm, Sun noon–3pm.

East Dereham and around

About fifteen miles west of Norwich, **EAST DEREHAM** – sometimes known simply as "Dereham" – is as close to the centre of Norfolk as you can get, a pleasant market town that is a good base for much of the county, although arguably this close to Norwich you may just as well stay in the city. Dereham has an attractive small-town feel and is close to lots of worthwhile attractions – not only Gressenhall, but many of the places close to Swaffham, too.

St Nicholas

Church St, NR19 1DN • ⓦdereham.churchnorfolk.com

Dereham's parish church of **St Nicholas** was founded on the site of a shrine to a seventh-century Saxon saint, Withburga, whose body lay here until it was stolen in the tenth century and a spring erupted from her grave – you can see the well outside the west door, at the centre of a small overgrown grotto. The church itself is fifteenth century, with a separate sixteenth-century bell tower, and there are a number of items of interest inside: the highly polished eagle lectern, made in Liège in the late 1400s; the finely carved font of 1468, showing the seven sacraments – baptism up to unction; and a painted screen enclosing a chapel in the south transept which dates from 1488 and shows St Withburga herself, among other saints.

Opposite, in the north transept, there's a memorial to local poet **William Cowper**, who is buried in the church, and a stained-glass window from 1905 showing Cowper alongside quotes from his work and two pet hares that were given to him to alleviate (it's said) a bout of deep depression. Cowper wasn't the most pious of souls, and had a long-standing affair with one Mary Unwin, whose wish to be buried near her lover was frowned upon in local Dereham society – hence the ultra-plain black slab that marks her final resting-place in the north aisle.

Bishop Bonner's Cottage

Church St, NR19 1ED • May–Sept Tues & Thurs 2–4.30pm, Fri 11am–1.30pm, Sat noon–3pm; Oct Sat noon–3pm • £1

Just outside the church of St Nicholas, a crooked old thatched flint cottage houses **Bishop Bonner's Cottage**, which has displays on Dereham's history and lots of photos and archeological bits and pieces. As for Bishop Bonner, this was indeed his home, and he had a fearsome reputation in the mid-sixteenth century, first as rector of Dereham and later as Bishop of London under "Bloody" Queen Mary, when he took it upon himself to rid the country of anti-Catholic "heretics". Not a nice man by all accounts.

Gressenhall Farm and Workhouse

Gressenhall, NR20 4DR • Mid-March to end Oct daily 10am–5pm • £8.90, children £5.90 • ☎01362 869263, ⓦmuseums.norfolk.gov.uk

About two miles north of Dereham, the **Gressenhall Farm and Workhouse**, one of only three Victorian workhouses in the UK open to the public, is essentially a museum of rural life in Victorian England, but its best displays focus on its time as a workhouse. You can see the claustrophobic dungeon, where inmates were sent if they transgressed the strict rules, plus other rooms and artefacts, from here and other workhouses – like

5

the wedge-shaped iron beds that allowed them to squeeze in more people, the laundry, with its original steam-powered machines and drying racks, and the men's exercise courtyard, complete with inmates' graffiti. On the first floor the workhouse's original clock ticks away, as it has done since the building opened in 1777, alongside display cases that contain all manner of objects relating to rural Norfolk life – tools, toys, bottles and crockery. Perhaps the most interesting items are the photographs of Norfolk locations and people that you can browse through. Outside you can visit the chapel and schoolroom, and mock-ups of village businesses – the post office, general store, blacksmith's. There's also a decent adventure playground, and a working farm run on traditional lines by volunteers, with rare breeds, a barn full of old farm implements and the chance to jump on Gressenhall's own tractor-pulled trailer. The farmhouse itself is kitted-out as it would have been in Victorian times, and the walks you can do across the fields or down by the river are lovely.

ARRIVAL AND DEPARTURE   EAST DEREHAM

By train Dereham no longer has a main-line station, but its old railway buildings on the edge of the town centre survive and house the northern terminus of the Mid-Norfolk Railway, which runs both steam trains and diesel locomotives down to Wymondham (see box, opposite).

By bus Buses stop in the centre of Dereham at several locations, most centrally outside Specsavers on the High St. Regular services to Norwich (every 30min; 1hr), Swaffham (every 30min; 35 min) and Kings' Lynn (every 30min; 1hr 10min). For most other places you need to travel to Norwich and change.

ACCOMMODATION

EAST DEREHAM

George Hotel Swaffham Rd, NR19 2AZ ☎01362 696801, ⓦthegeorgehoteldereham.co.uk. Right in the town centre, the *George* has a comfy downstairs bar and restaurant and ten comfortable en-suite double rooms, each decorated in a different style. Free wi-fi and parking. **£75**

Romany Rye Church St, NR19 1DL ☎01362 654160, ⓦjdwetherspoon.co.uk/home/pubs/the-romany-rye. Right by the church, this newly opened Wetherspoon's pub and hotel is a much-needed refurbishment of a previous hotel, and boasts 22 double rooms that have been very nicely done and are excellent value even if prices don't include breakfast. The downstairs pub follows the usual Wetherspoon's formula of well-priced drink and food. **£64**

NORTH ELMHAM

Park House Brisley Rd, NR20 5DL ☎01362 668933, ⓦparkhousebedandbreakfast.co.uk. About five miles north of Dereham, this B&B is very handy for the Gressenhall Museum – and a cut above the competition, with three nicely furnished suites, one in the main Georgian property and the others in a converted stable block next door. Breakfast is excellent, with homemade jam and home-laid eggs. **£95**

WENDLING

Greenbanks Hotel Swaffham Rd, NR19 2NA ☎01362 687742, ⓦgreenbankshotel.co.uk. Country hotel about five miles west of Dereham that has cosy doubles, an indoor pool and a good restaurant that emphasizes fresh produce and veggie options. **£60**

YAXHAM

Nature's Path Dereham Rd, NR19 1RF ☎01692 671834, ⓦnaturespathtipis.co.uk. Whether you prefer a wigwam or a yurt, or even just a regular tent, this super-organized site enjoys a great lakeside location and excellent facilities, including a shop, café and children's playground. The yurts and tipis are the thing though, complete with comfy beds and enough room for 4 to 5 people. One week high season from **£300**

Yaxham Mill Norwich Rd, NR19 1RP ☎01362 288185, ⓦyaxhammill.com. This converted old mill has six double rooms and a handful of holiday cottages too, all comfortably furnished and well priced, with rates including an excellent breakfast in the attached restaurant. Rooms and cottages **£60**

EATING AND DRINKING

EAST DEREHAM

The Bull 25 High St, NR19 1DZ ☎01362 697771. Decent town-centre pub with a well-priced and extensive pub menu that has plenty for around a fiver. Plus the kitchen is open all day every day. Daily 11am–8.45pm.

Lottie's George Hotel, Swaffham Rd, NR19 2AZ ☎01362 696801, ⓦthegeorgehoteldereham.co.uk.

Maybe the town centre's classiest place to eat, with a varied menu that takes in everything from Thai prawn curry and lasagne to sausage and mash, steaks and racks of ribs, as well as having an interesting "pick-and-mix"' take on veggie dishes. You can also eat in the bar if you prefer. Most mains £10–12. Tues–Thurs 7–9.30pm, Fri–Sun noon–3pm & 7–9.30pm.

Tall Orders 2 Market Place ☎01362 697676. Friendly café serving teas, coffees, panini and jackets. Mon–Sat 9am–4pm.

NECTON
The Windmill 15–17 Mill St, PE37 8EN ☎01760 722057, ⓦthenectonwindmill.co.uk. A friendly pub

midway between Swaffham and Dereham, just off the A47, that does good pub food from around £9.95 – sausage and mash, liver and bacon, steaks and fish and chips – served in the bar or the slightly posher restaurant next door. Mon–Sat noon–2pm & 6.30–9pm, Sun noon–3.30pm.

Wymondham

Just nine miles southwest of Norwich, **WYMONDHAM** (pronounced "Wind'um") is a small town with plenty of character, once notorious for its connection with Robert Kett, a local landowner who led a peasants' revolt against enclosures of common land in Norwich in 1549, and was later executed along with his brother William. In 1615, Wymondham burned to the ground and had to be almost entirely rebuilt. Later it made its fortune as a weaving centre before declining in the nineteenth century. You'd be hard-pressed to find a good reason to stay in Wymondham with Norwich so near, but the abbey is certainly worth the journey, and there are a couple of good pubs – in town and nearby – if you're on the hunt for lunch.

The Market Cross

Wymondham's main street leads up to the market square and the early seventeenth-century **Market Cross,** raised up on stilts to protect documents and other valuables from floods and other perils; indeed live rats used to be nailed onto its sides to deter vermin – until, that is, someone died after being bitten by one.

Wymondham Abbey

The main thing to see in Wymondham are the ruins of the town's Benedictine **Abbey**, at the other end of the high street from the Market Cross. Spread across green meadows the site is dominated – as indeed is the town – by its twin-towered church, a twelfth-century construction whose nave is arguably the most beautiful in the county, with two rows of Norman arches in soft grey Normandy stone supporting a wooden beamed roof decorated with over seventy carved angels. The neo-Gothic screen in the chancel is a memorial to the local casualties of World War I, while outside Robert Kett's brother, William, was strung up on the tower – a plaque marks the spot. From here there are some lovely riverside **walks** beyond the abbey, along the banks of the Tiffey River and across the bridge from the station.

Wymondham Heritage Museum

10 The Bridewell, NR18 0NS • March–Oct Mon–Sat 10am–4pm, Sun 2–4pm • £3 • ☎01953 600205
Not far from the Market Cross, the **Wymondham Heritage Museum** has displays on its

---

THE MID-NORFOLK RAILWAY

Wymondham is the eastern terminus of the **Mid-Norfolk Railway**, which runs re-conditioned steam and diesel trains to **East Dereham** (p.197) from a station near the abbey, taking in **Thuxton** (the main stop) and unmanned stations at **Yaxham** and **Kimberley Park**, although they're hoping to extend this north to North Elmham and County School before long. The journey from Wymondham to Dereham takes 1 hour 40 minutes (3–4 services a day April–Oct Sat & Sun; also Aug Tues–Thurs; June, July & Sept Wed & Thurs; May & Oct Wed; see ⓦmnr.org.uk for timetable; £10 return steam, £7 return diesel).

5

time as a House of Correction, with a basement dungeon and remand cell upstairs, complete with recorded background and dialogue. There is also an exhibit on brush-making – for around two hundred years one of the town's major industries – and almost every other aspect of life in Wymondham that you could think of, including Robert Kett's Rebellion.

ARRIVAL, INFORMATION AND ACTIVITIES — WYMONDHAM

By train Wymondham's train station is just outside the centre across London Rd – about a 10min walk from Market Cross – and is quaint enough to have been used as the backdrop for Warmington-on-Sea's station in the 1970s series, *Dad's Army*. It also has a good restaurant (see below). Wymondham is on the main line between Cambridge, Ely and Norwich and there are roughly hourly services to Attleborough (8min) and Thetford (25min). You can also reach East Dereham on the Mid-Norfolk Railway (see box, p.199).

By bus Buses stop on Bridewell St, a minute's walk from the Market Cross: services to Norwich (every 20min; 30min); Attleborough (every 20min; 20min) and Thetford (roughly hourly; 40min).

Tourist information In the Market Cross (Easter to Oct Mon–Sat 10am–4pm; Nov to Easter Mon, Fri & Sat 10am–4pm; ☎ 01953 604721).

Balloon rides Wymondham is one of the launch sites for Virgin's balloon flights (☎ 0871 6630063, ⓦ virginballoonflights.co.uk), which leave from Wymondham rugby club on Tuttles Lane, just north of the town centre. Flights cost £109–129 and last about an hour.

ACCOMMODATION

WYMONDHAM

Abbey Hotel 10 Church St, NR18 0PH ☎ 01953 602148, ⓦ the-abbeyhotel.com. Friendly small hotel, if slightly lacking character, in a nice location right by the abbey grounds, with twelve rooms with sleigh beds – the best overlook the abbey. Its restaurant, *L'Auberge*, has a short menu of vaguely French food served every night. **£70**

Elm Lodge Downham Grove, NR18 0SN ☎ 01953 607501, ⓔ elm.lodge@btinternet.com. Just north of the town centre off the B1172 Norwich road this B&B is has comfy, well-equipped rooms and lovely, huge gardens. **£60**

Green Dragon 6 Church St, NR18 0PH ☎ 01953 607907, ⓦ wymondhamgreendragon. This ancient pub has three plain but homely double rooms, with en-suite bathrooms and wi-fi; breakfast £5. **£45**

BARNHAM BROOM

Barnham Broom Hotel Honingham Rd, NR9 4DD ☎ 01603 759393, ⓦ barnham-broom.co.uk. This sprawling country-house hotel about five miles north of Wymondham fancies itself as one of the best places to stay around Norwich, and with some reason – it's got fifty-odd comfortable rooms, golf courses, a swimming pool and full fitness facilities. The restaurant is pretty decent too. Overall maybe not quite as good as it thinks it is. **£125**

EATING AND DRINKING

WYMONDHAM

Brief Encounter Wymondham Station Approach, NR18 0JZ ☎ 01953 606433. A spick-and-span café-restaurant that would look old-fashioned enough on its own, even without the ancient railway memorabilia decor. The menu is a short and deliberately simple roster of classics, from lasagne and steak and kidney pudding to chicken curry and sweet and sour chicken. Mon–Sat 8.30am–3pm, Fri & Sat 6–9pm, Sun noon–2.30pm.

Courtyard Coffee Shop 6 Wharton Court, NR18 0UQ ☎ 01953 604436. Just off Market St, this handy lunch stop does a menu of jackets and sandwiches and always has a board of hot lunch specials for around £4.95. It's licensed and has a pleasant and busy outside terrace. Mon–Sat 9am–5pm.

Green Dragon 6 Church St, NR18 0PH ☎ 01953 607907, ⓦ wymondhamgreendragon.co.uk. Timbered old pub, tucked away off the end of Market St, near the abbey, cosy and welcoming and something of a locals' joint, with a beer garden and basic pub classics alongside grander choices like rack of lamb and beef and chorizo lasagne – all served in hearty portions. Food served all day Sat & Sun & Mon–Thurs noon–3pm & 5.30–8.30pm.

WRENINGHAM

The Bird-in-Hand Norwich Rd, NR16 1BJ ☎ 01508 489438, ⓦ birdinhandwreningham.com. A couple of miles east of Wymondham, this country pub on the edge of the village serves relatively upscale pub food local in its cosy main bar or adjacent dining room – everything from sausage-and-mash and steak-and-ale pie for £10–12 to salade niçoise, grilled sea bass and savoury bread-and-butter pudding. Mon–Thurs 10am–noon & 6–9pm, Fri noon–2.30pm & 5.30–10pm, Sun noon–9pm.

Lotus cars

Potash Lane, Hethel, NR14 8EZ • Factory tours Wed at 2pm • £39; driving days and tours from £399 • ☎ 01953 608547l, ⓦ lotusdrivingacademy.com

Just outside Wymondham, a couple of miles east of the A11, is the headquarters of **Lotus cars**, which, despite many changes of ownership over the years, remains a Norfolk business through-and-through – and indeed one which has enjoyed something of a resurgence in recent years as the demand for its iconic, handmade sports cars has increased. You can view some of its products in the car park, or better still join one of their Wednesday afternoon tours of the plant, which take in the full construction process from the chassis-build to the paint shop. If money is no object, join one of their track days when, as well as the plant tour, they offer expert tuition from one of their drivers out on their test track.

Attleborough and around

Halfway up the A11 between Thetford and Norwich, **ATTLEBOROUGH** has the feel of a village, its centre grouped around a small green – Queen's Square. There's not all that much to see here, but the town does have a good, contemporary hotel, and is the closest base for the Snetterton motor-racing circuit, just to the south, and one or two other nearby attractions.

St Mary

Right in the centre of Attleborough, the church of **St Mary** is a short, wide flint Gothic structure for the most part, although sections – like the tower – date back to Norman times; indeed, there was a church here as early as 856. The major feature, however, is the faded but still beautiful Gothic rood screen that fills the entire width of the building, decorated with images of saints and the coats of arms of the cathedral towns of England in the 1400s. Behind are the remains of a remarkably well-preserved fresco showing an Annunciation and various angels.

Peter Beale's Roses

London Rd, NR17 1AY • Mon–Sat 9am–5pm, Sun 10am–4pm • Free • ☎ 01953 454707, ⓦ classicroses.co.uk

The well-known specialist rose gardener Peter Beales regularly wins awards at the Chelsea

---

LOTUS: NORMAL FOR NORFOLK?

Think of Norfolk and supercharged, state-of-the-art sports cars don't necessarily come to mind, yet the British sports car maker **Lotus** has been associated with the county for almost half a century, when the company and its inspirational founder, **Colin Chapman**, took over part of the old RAF base at Hethel just east of Wymondham in 1966. They built a factory here, and used the disused runways as test tracks. Chapman was something of a Sixties legend, a flamboyant character and brilliant engineer who not only produced some of the design icons of the age (the Lotus Elan, was driven by Emma Peel of *The Avengers*, and Roger Moore drove a submersible Lotus Elise in *The Spy Who Loved Me*, a decade or so later), but also built Lotus into the top British Formula 1 team of the age, winning half-a-dozen championships with state-of-the-art cars driven by great drivers like Jim Clark. Clark died in an accident in 1968, and although fatalities weren't that unusual then, Lotus came under fire for designing cars that were considered too fast and too fragile. Later drivers included Jochen Rindt, Emmerson Fittipaldi and Mario Andretti, who won Lotus's last championship in 1978. However, the company declined in the 1980s – a process perhaps accelerated by Chapman's untimely death from a heart attack in 1982. The ensuing years were mixed, with changes of ownership and mounting debts, and finally a withdrawal from Formula 1 in the mid-1990s. Recent years have been kinder, with fresh injections of cash from the Far East and a reappearance on the Formula 1 scene with two teams, Renault and Team Lotus. Lotus is also enjoying record sales for its successful road cars – the seminal boys' toy, the Elise, the Exige and the sleek Evora.

Flower Show and this is his home garden, with three acres of variations on the rose, from large old-fashioned varieties to ramblers and small shrubs, set amid arches and pergolas. It's open all summer, along with a garden centre and café that are open all year.

Snetterton Circuit

Snetterton, NR16 2JU • Tickets £15–30; driving experiences £99–185 • ☎ 01953 887303, ⓦ motorsportvision.co.uk/snetterton

Just off the A11 near Attleborough, the circuit at **Snetterton** was fashioned out of a series of USAF runways shortly after the war. It has just undergone a major revamp, redesigning its shape, with more corners and faster straights to become a virtually three-mile track. It hosts F3 and the British Superbike championships, among other events, and tickets are reasonably easy to come by, but in between major race meetings no one will stop you driving in and having a look around the paddock and pit lane. You could grab lunch at *Tyrrels* restaurant, or maybe even purchase one of their "driving experiences" and take to the track yourself in a single-seater or super car.

Model and Toy Expo

Snetterton Park, NR16 2JU • Daily 9am–5pm • ☎ 01953 887878

Right next door to Snetterton, you can drop into the **Model and Toy Expo**, which sits alongside – a series of large warehouses that house the largest toy store for miles around – well worth a browse, with giant Lego dinosaurs, huge train set layouts and vast Playmobil lands. There's also a regular car boot sale outside on Sundays.

St George's Distillery

Harling Rd, Roudham, NR16 2QW • Daily 10am–4pm; tours on the hour • £5 • ☎ 01953 717939, ⓦ englishwhisky.co.uk

Just off the A11 between the villages of of Roudham and East Harling, **St George's Distillery** lays claim to being the only whisky producer in England, the first in the country for a century, set up by local farmer Andrew Nelstrop and his father in 2006. It released its first product in December 2009 (whisky has to be in the barrel for three years), and their products have so far been well received; they hope to scale up to 120,000 bottles a year in time (by way of comparison, Glenfiddich makes over ten million). The hour-long tour starts with a brief talk and short film, before you're taken around the plant and the distilling process is explained in more detail. It's all very well done, and there's a tasting at the end in which their single malts hold their own – a fact demonstrated by the well-stocked shop, which is chock-full of high-end Scottish malts. They also run world whisky tours once a month, taking in the distillery tour but also tasting lots of whiskies from different parts of the world.

Old Buckenham

Just a couple of miles southeast of Attleborough, **OLD BUCKENHAM** is a small, pretty village, but as it's home to the largest village green in England it can take a while to walk from one side to the other. Luckily there's a pub on each side to help you on your way – the traditional and very friendly **Ox & Plough** and the foodier, more upscale **Gamekeeper**. Next door to the *Ox & Plough*, **All Saints** church has a flint hexagonal tower and a font carved with cheeky faces under the bowl – although the church's real treasures are the choir stalls, carved with Old Testament prophets.

New Buckenham

Two miles east of its sister village of Old Buckenham, **NEW BUCKENHAM** is not new at all, having been founded in the twelfth century. It focuses on a much smaller village green distinguished by a shabby medieval loggia supported by wooden columns – a pleasant spot, though sadly the village pub is currently closed. On the edge of the village, towards Old Buckenham, a path leads off from a bend in the road to follow the overgrown bastions of a twelfth-century fortress – a popular spot for blackberry picking.

Banham

Roughly halfway between Attleborough and Diss, **BANHAM** centres on a rectangle of village green backed by its church of **St Mary the Virgin**, a typical Gothic Norfolk church that's home to a thirteenth-century wooden memorial effigy of local squire Sir Hugh Bardolph, painted to look like stone.

Banham Zoo

Kenninghall Rd, Banham, NR16 2HE • Daily: April–July & Oct 9.30am–5pm; Aug–Sept 9.30am–6pm; Nov–March 9.30am–4pm • Low season £10.95, children £7.95, high season £14.95, children £10.95 • ☎ 01953 887771, ⓦ banhamzoo.co.uk

Set in thirty acres of sumptuous grounds, **Banham Zoo** is a thriving small zoo and one of the most popular family attractions in south Norfolk, dating back to the late 1960s, when it opened as a monkey and ape sanctuary. Apes and monkeys are still some of the biggest attractions, but the zoo has expanded and hosts good collections of big cats (in particular snow leopards), giraffes (which you can get up close to by means of a unique walkway) and one of the best groupings of owls in the UK. Add in all the associated paraphernalia of train rides, targeted kids' activities and regular feeding sessions with commentary, and it makes for a pretty good family day out.

ARRIVAL AND INFORMATION

By train The station is just off Station Rd, 200m south of the *Mulberry Tree*, and is on the main line between Cambridge (1hr 30min), Ely and Norwich (50min), with connections to Thetford and Wymondham every hour.

By bus Buses stop on Church St and there are services to Norwich (every 30min; 45min), Wymondham (every

ATTLEBOROUGH AND AROUND

20min; 15min), Thetford (every hr; 40min) and Banham (3 daily; 20min).

Tourist office In the town hall on Queen's Square (Mon–Wed 9.30am–1.30pm, Thurs 9.30am–3pm, Fri 9.30am–12.30pm, Sat 9.30am–11.30am; ☎ 01953 456930).

ACCOMMODATION

ATTLEBOROUGH

★ **Mulberry Tree** Station Rd, NR17 2AS ☎ 01953 452124, ⓦ the-mulberry-tree.co.uk. On the edge of the centre not far from the station, this boutique hotel feels a bit out of place in humdrum Attleborough, but it's a great place to stay, with five slickly decorated double rooms and a cool bar and restaurant to boot. **£95**

Sherbourne House 8 Norwich Rd, NR17 2JX ☎ 01953 454363, ⓦ sherbourne-house.co.uk. Just outside the centre, *Sherbourne House* is a lovely Georgian mansion with eight spacious rooms (seven doubles, one single).

Free wi-fi throughout and a very warm welcome – for pets too. It also has a small restaurant and bar. **£85**

LARLING

★ **The Angel** Larling, NR16 2QU ☎ 01953 717963, ⓦ angel-larling.co.uk. Despite being right by the roaring A11, the *Angel* is a cosy, peaceful and very friendly place to stay, with seven en-suite double rooms, wi-fi throughout and good food on site; plus it has a campsite in the adjacent meadow (April–Sept; £10 per pitch). **£80**

EATING AND DRINKING

ATTLEBOROUGH

Mulberry Tree Station Rd, NR17 2AS ☎ 01953 452124, ⓦ the-mulberry-tree.co.uk. On the edge of the town centre not far from the station, this is the place to eat and drink in Attleborough, a sleek boutique hotel with a contemporary restaurant serving a modern British menu (starters from £6.95, mains £15–16), and sandwiches and lighter meals at lunchtime in the bar,

which has an outside terrace. Mon–Sat noon–2pm & 6.30–9pm.

Steffijon Gelateria Queen's Square, NR17 2AF ☎ 01953 459731, ⓦ www.steffijongelateria.net. Next door to the tourist office in the centre of Attleborough, this Italian sandwich shop and gelateria does great ciabatta sandwiches and excellent Italian ice cream. Mon–Fri 9am–5pm, Sat 10am–5pm.

5

OLD BUCKENHAM

★ **The Gamekeeper** The Green, NR17 1RE ☎01953 860397, ⓦthegamekeeperfreehouse.com. The village's gastropub, with a cosy bar out front and a room given over to eating at the back – plus a beer garden. As you would expect, food is the focus here, and it's good, with options ranging from hot steak or pork sandwiches (£6.95), through pub classics like fish and chips, burgers, mussels and sausage and mash, to more elaborate evening options like rump of lamb with rosti and chicken with rosemary and gnocchi and chorizo salad. Mon–Sat noon–2.30pm & 6–9pm, Sun noon–3pm.

Ox & Plough The Green, NR17 1RN ☎01953 860004. A dog-friendly locals' joint, with tables outside and a very warm welcome. No food though. Daily noon–11pm.

NEW BUCKENHAM

La Maison 3 King St, NR16 2AF ☎01953 860713. This dinky interiors and homewares shop also has a small tearoom which does sandwiches and cream teas, soups and jackets and platters of cheese and crackers. Tues–Sat 10am–5pm.

LARLING

The Angel Larling, NR16 2QU ☎01953 717963, ⓦangel-larling.co.uk. This family-owned, seventeenth-century coaching inn, which has is a great mix of a drinker's pub and a food venue, and was deservedly CAMRA's Norfolk "pub of the year"' in 2010. Very friendly, with a big menu of home-cooked food – steaks (£14.95), steak-and-kidney pie and fish and chips (£9.95), as well as specials from grilled cod to lamb korma; lighter stuff too – burgers, omelettes, Welsh rarebit. It also has rooms and camping facilities, and hosts a popular August beer festival. Daily noon–9.30pm.

TACOLNESTON

★ **The Pelican** 136 Norwich Rd, NR16 1AL ☎01508 489521, ⓦthe-pelican-inn.co.uk. Welcoming, family-run pub that serves a good choice of ales (some for sale in the pub's shop) and great food in the pub and dining room – from hearty open sandwiches and fish and chips to beef bourguignon and confit of duck. Mains from £10. A large garden and rooms available. Daily noon–2pm & 6–9pm.

Watton and around

WATTON lies at the centre of a region known as **Wayland**, situated on the far eastern edge of the Brecks. It's a small, fairly undistinguished market town (with a weekly general market and monthly farmers' market), whose small thirteenth-century parish church of **St Mary** (Tues–Thurs 9am–1pm), accessible by foot by way of an avenue of truncated pines from near the Thetford crossroads, has an unusual round tower – although inside is almost entirely Victorian. It does, however, retain a donations box from 1640, charmingly carved in the likeness of the vicar at the time. On the long, busy high street, check out the town's seventeenth-century **clock tower**, sandwiched between the terraces opposite the town sign which commemorates the sad tale of Babes in the Wood.

Wayland Wood

Always open • ⓦwww.norfolkwildlifetrust.org.uk/Wildlife-in-Norfolk/Reserves/Wayland-Wood.aspx

Just a mile or so south of Watton, **Wayland Wood** is one of the largest forested areas in south Norfolk, and is said to have been the original inspiration for the fairy tale, "Babes in the Wood", in which a boy and his sister are left to die in a hostile forest. It's a less hostile place now, and managed by the Norfolk Wildlife Trust, with coppiced glades of oak and ash, interspersed with wild flowers – perfect for a walk that's easy on the feet and the eyes, with well-marked trails and bridleways leading through the trees.

Hingham

A large village about six miles to the east, **HINGHAM** is more immediately appealing than Watton, with a much larger parish church and two almost conjoined triangular greens either side, picturesquely fringed by Georgian houses and thatched cottages. The fourteenth-century church of **St Andrew** (April–Oct daily 9am–5pm; Nov–March 10am–2pm) is a huge, cathedral-like structure with a high tower and a churchyard that spreads all the way around the church, although the large and majestic interior was – like Watton's St Mary's – revamped in the nineteenth century. There are some remnants of the original church in the choir – a piscina and sedilia – along with some elegant sixteenth-century stained glass. In the north aisle there's a bust of **Abraham Lincoln** of all people – his ancestor, Samuel Lincoln, was baptized in this church before emigrating to the New World in 1637.

Breckles

Right in the heart of Wayland, the village of **BRECKLES** (or Breccles) is home to the church of **St Margaret**, which has a Saxon tower topped by a chequerboard hexagon section in the fifteenth century. Inside has changed a lot over the years, but the font is one of the oldest in Norfolk, and unusual in its square shape, carved in the eleventh century with foliage, heads and figures.

East Wretham Heath

Always open • ⓦ www.norfolkwildlifetrust.org.uk

About seven miles south of Wayland Wood, towards Thetford, **East Wretham Heath** is another NWT property, a mixture of cratered heath and woodland of old Scots Pines, through which paths wind around a couple of "meres" – fed by springs and shallow in winter, deeper in summer, and home to various birdlife that complements the gangs of gambolling rabbits (dogs need to be kept on a lead).

ARRIVAL AND INFORMATION

By bus Buses stop on the High St, opposite *The Crown*, and run to Wymondham (every 30min; 30min), Dereham (hourly; 30min), and Hingham (every 30min; 15min).

WATTON AND AROUND

Tourist office At Dragonfly Gallery, Wayland House, High St (summer only Mon–Fri 9am–4pm, Sat 9am–1pm).

ACCOMMODATION

Broom Hall Richmond Rd, Saham Toney, IP25 7EX ☎01953 882125, ⓦ broomhallhotel.co.uk. Just to the north of Watton, this hotel is situated in a stately Victorian house at the centre of extensive gardens. It's fairly traditional, but the welcome is warm and the service helpful, and there's an in-house restaurant too. There are fourteen en-suite double rooms; free wi-fi. **£95**

Willow House 2 High St, IP25 6AE ☎01953 881181, ⓦ thewillowhouse.co.uk. Their moniker, "a little piece of countryside in the town", is hardly necessary, as it's at the end of Watton High St – not the most metropolitan location in the world. But it's a welcoming place, with deliberately simple and comprehensively refurbished double rooms. It also has a restaurant. **£70**

EATING AND DRINKING

★ **The White Hart** 3 Market Place, Hingham, NR9 4AF ☎01953 850214, ⓦ whitehartnorfolk.co.uk. The most recent addition to chef Chris Couborough's small Norfolk-based chain of restaurants and hotels, and a very welcome one, occupying a distinctively grand building and serving a good menu of well-executed British and continental dishes – everything from Italian caponata to slow-cooked brisket and mash – in a contemporary environment that sits well with the beams and fireplaces of this old coaching inn.

Moderately priced too – starters from £5.95, mains from £11.95. Daily noon–2.30pm & 6.30–9.30pm.

Willow House 2 High St, IP25 6AE ☎01953 881181, ⓦ thewillowhouse.co.uk. Hotel-restaurant that serves an uncomplicated menu of steaks, duck breast and fillets of sea bass (there's mushroom stroganoff for veggies); starters £5.90, mains average around £15. Plus there's a bar menu serving sandwiches, jackets and ploughman's. Mon–Sat noon–3pm & 7–9pm, Sun noon–3pm.

Thetford

The small town of **THETFORD** enjoys a poor reputation across the rest of Norfolk, populated mainly by rough èmigré Londoners, with around five thousand arriving here since the end of the last war, and as one of the few towns in the county with a large immigrant population – mostly Portuguese who have arrived in the past two decades (indeed around a quarter of the town's 20,000 population speak Portuguese as their mother tongue). It's a pity, because it's not a bad place, and although the

5

centre has its share of charity shops and boarded-up shopfronts, there's a lively atmosphere, and its riverside location (the Little Ouse runs right through the centre) provides pleasant walks along its banks. It's also an ancient place, the home of Queen Boudicca during Roman times and later various Saxon royals – indeed a hoard of Saxon treasure was discovered here and is on show at the British Museum. It was also the birthplace of US radical and reformer Thomas Paine, no less, though its biggest claim to fame is its role in *Dad's Army*, when it doubled as Warmington-on-Sea in the popular 1970s British TV comedy series – a connection the town quite naturally makes the most of. All that said, the town's modest charms are soon exhausted, and there's no real reason to stay over, apart from its handy location for visiting Thetford Forest and the southern reaches of the Brecks. You can follow the riverside path from the centre of Thetford to Brandon in the heart of **Thetford Forest**, a roughly two-hour journey.

King Street and around

The centre of Thetford is small and bisected by the Little Ouse River, quite pretty, despite a slightly frayed-around-the-edges appearance. The **bridge** over the river marks the centre of town; close by you'll notice a well-realized statue of **Captain Mainwaring** sitting pertly on a bench. From the bridge, pedestrianized **King Street** cuts through the centre, past the church of **St Peter**, on the corner, next door to which, in front of the so-called **Kings House**, is a statue of the town's most famous son, **Thomas Paine**, who was educated at nearby **Thetford Grammar** back across the river.

The Ancient House

21–23 White Hart St, IP24 1AA • Tues–Sat 10am–5pm • £3.70 • ☎ 01842 752599

Around the corner from the church, the timbered **Ancient House** dates from 1490 and is home to the **Museum of Thetford Life**, which has displays on Thomas Paine and Duleep Singh, the last Sikh ruler of the Punjab during the British Raj, who settled at nearby Elveden Hall in 1863 (see p.209), and whose statue can be seen in the park on Bittern Island, on the river just beyond the bridge (he's buried in Elveden churchyard). There's also the obligatory old kitchen and displays on who may have lived in the house, including one Betty Radcliffe, landlady at the *Bell*, who lived here in the early nineteenth century and still haunts one of the rooms at the inn. However, the star attraction is the building itself – well preserved and properly ancient, with bare timbered walls and a distinctive rickety old charm.

Thetford Priory

Water Lane, IP24 2AZ • Daily 10am–5pm • Free; EH • ⓦ www.english-heritage.org.uk/daysout/properties/thetford-priory

Beyond the Ancient House, across the main road and accessible by subway (follow Minstergate from the bridge), **Thetford Priory** was one of the richest medieval monasteries in Norfolk, and its extensive ruins, including a very well-preserved fourteenth-century gatehouse (accessible through a private garden), are a peaceful and evocative spot for a stroll and a picnic lunch.

THE PEDDARS WAY

The **Peddars Way** national footpath (ⓦ nationaltrail.co.uk/PeddarsWay) runs through the heart of the Brecks, starting in Kettishall Heath just to the southeast of Thetford, and running north towards Swaffham before continuing on to meet the North Norfolk Coast Path at Holme-next-the-Sea. It's a gentle route, much of it suitable for cyclists, and easiest to get a taste of from Castle Acre, just to the north of Swaffham, which it passes right through.

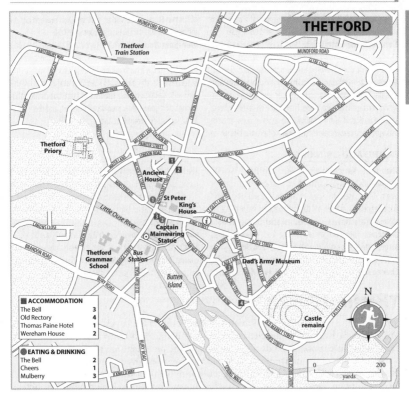

▮ ACCOMMODATION	
The Bell	3
Old Rectory	4
Thomas Paine Hotel	1
Wereham House	2

● EATING & DRINKING	
The Bell	2
Cheers	1
Mulberry	3

Dad's Army Museum

Cage Lane, IP24 2DS • April–Nov Sat 10am–4pm • Free • ⓦ dadsarmythetford.org.uk

On the far side of Market Place at the town's **Dad's Army Museum** photographs from the series are displayed alongside all kinds of official memorabilia – and, for those who are really keen, there are monthly walking tours, led by a Captain Mainwaring lookalike, which take in all the key locations. Inevitably there's a shop, in which you can buy tea towels, mugs and even a replica of Pike's "stupid boy" scarf.

ARRIVAL AND INFORMATION

By train The station is 300m north of the centre, at the far end of Station Rd, which spears left off London Rd near the top of White Hart St. Thetford is on the main line from London, Cambridge and Ely to Norwich, with regular trains (every hr) to Attleborough and Wymondham.

By bus The bus station is by the river. There are irregular

services to Mundford (25min) and Brandon (30min), as well as regular connections with Attleborough (hourly; 25min), Wymondham (hourly; 40min) and Norwich (every 20min; 1hr).

Tourist office 20 King St on the left (Mon–Fri 9am–5pm, Sat 9am–4pm; ❼01842 751975).

ACCOMMODATION

The Bell King St, IP24 2AZ ❼01842 754455, ⓦwww .oldenglishinns.co.uk/thetford. This old, much expanded coaching inn by the river is under new management, and once again makes a nice place to stay, with comfortable rooms and free wi-fi. The rooms with most character are in the old building, and a couple – those facing onto King St

– are said to be haunted, one of them by the ex-landlady of the hotel, who is commemorated in the Ancient House. **£59**

Old Rectory 30 Raymond St, IP24 2EA ❼01842 765419, ⓦbedandbreakfast-thetford.co.uk. Commodious old building two minutes' walk from King St, with three good-sized, well-kept rooms, simply but comfortably furnished

5

– one family room with en-suite bathroom, the other two sharing a bathroom. Includes breakfast, and wi-fi. **£50**

Thomas Paine Hotel White Hart St, IP24 1AA ☎01842 750372, ⓦthethomaspainehotel.co.uk. At the top of White Hart St, this place used to have a terrible reputation but it has since been refurbished and has large double rooms with en-suite bathrooms, and a decent bar and restaurant too, serving well-priced Italian food. There's free wi-fi throughout, and the back end of the building, made up of three ancient cottages, has a reasonable claim to having been the birthplace

of Thomas Paine – he's said to have watched proceedings on the nearby scaffold from his attic room. **£97.50**

Wereham House 24 White Hart St, IP24 1AD ☎01842 761956, ⓦwerehamhouse.co.uk. Right in the heart of town, and run by a husband-and-wife team with years in the hotel business, this elegant old building at the top of White Hart St has eight en-suite rooms, not huge but comfortable enough and good value. Breakfasts are great, and there's also a bar, free wi-fi throughout and parking. **£79**

EATING AND DRINKING

The Bell King St, IP24 2AZ ☎01842 754455, ⓦoldenglishinns.co.uk/thetford. The cast and crew of *Dad's Army* used to stay at the *Bell*, and the hotel understandably trades on the association, with function rooms, bars and restaurants named after characters from the series. The food served in the bar – sandwiches, burgers, steak – passes muster for lunch and dinner, with mains from £6.95 to £10.95. Daily noon–10pm.

Cheers 3a White Hart St, IP24 1AA ☎01842 750170.

The town's most central Portuguese restaurant with a short menu specializing in steaks and great fish and seafood. A good Portuguese wine list too. Try the steak on a stone – cooked at your table. Tues–Fri 6–11pm, Sat & Sun noon–3pm & 6–10.30pm.

Mulberry 11 Raymond St, IP24 2EA ☎01842 824122. Thetford's classiest place to eat, serving modern British cuisine in a cosy setting. Mains for £15–20, a great wine list, and excellent service too. Tues–Sat 6–9pm.

Thetford Forest

Straddling the Norfolk–Suffolk border, **Thetford Forest** is the largest stretch of low-lying forest in the UK. It's not an ancient woodland, only having been created after World War I to replace timber used during the war, and the pines here are not indigenous – indeed much of the native Breckland landscape was destroyed when the forest was created. Nonetheless it's a beautiful area, and the network of walking and cycle trails is second to none, providing an outlet for all manner of hobbyists, including bikers, hikers and one of the largest contingents of husky-racing teams in the UK. The most central settlement for the forest is the small town of **Brandon** in Suffolk, but there's not much to it apart from its train station, either in terms of sights or facilities, and you might be better off using Thetford or Mundford or even places further afield as a base.

High Lodge Forest Centre

Thetford Forest, B1107, IP27 0AF • Daily: March & Nov–Feb 9am–5pm; April, Sept & Oct 9am–6pm; May–Aug 9am–7pm • ☎01842 815434, ⓦwww.forestry.gov.uk/highlodge

High Lodge Forest Centre is the best place to start if you're exploring Thetford Forest for the first time, with a good position well away from the main road, plenty of parking, a shop and café, and bike rental from **Bike Art** (daily 9am–5pm, July & Aug till 6pm; Nov–March till 4pm; ☎01842 810090, ⓦbikeartthetford.com). There are several loop walks from here, ranging from one to three miles, and cycle trails suitable for families and more serious mountain bikers from six to ten miles. High Lodge is also home to the tree-top rope-and-ladder outfit **Go Ape** (☎0845 643 9146, ⓦgoape.co.uk).

Brandon Country Park

IP27 0SU • March–Oct Mon–Fri 10am–5pm, Sat & Sun 10am–5.30pm • Nov–Feb daily 10am–4pm • Free • ☎01842 810185, ⓦbrandonsuffolk.com/brandon-country-park.asp

Just outside Brandon, **Brandon Country Park** is another place to easily experience Thetford Forest, which has a visitor centre with maps, books and information, together with a café, kids' playground and walled garden. From the centre you can do a variety of marked walks, lasting anything from thirty minutes to three hours, and there's a well-marked four-mile mountain bike loop.

Elveden Estate

London Rd, Elveden, IP24 3TQ • Shops open Mon–Fri 9.30am–4.30pm, Sat 9.30am–5pm, Sun noon–5pm

On the edge of Thetford Forest, close to the junction of the Brandon road and the A11 – and across the border in Suffolk – the **Elveden Estate** was bought by the ex-ruler of the Punjab, Maharajah Duleep Singh in 1849, on his exile from India. He rebuilt Eleveden Hall, and lived here until 1886, shortly after which the estate was bought by the earls of Iveagh, aka the Guinness family, who have owned it ever since and developed it into a considerable agricultural and commercial concern. The hall is empty, and not open to the public, but you can visit the parish church of **St Patrick and St Andrew**, which has the graves of the Iveagh dynasty in its churchyard, although it's also often closed and most people just stop to visit the estate's complex of **shops**, including a high-end food shop selling produce from the estate, a cookware store and toyshop, and a really good café-restaurant serving breakfasts and lunches (see p.210).

Weeting

Castle always open • Free; EH • ⓦ www.english-heritage.org.uk/daysout/properties/weeting-castle

Just across the river from Brandon, and in Norfolk, the village of **WEETING** has a village green boasting one of the longest thatched terraces you've ever seen – a full ten eyebrow windows long. On the edge of the village, **Weeting Castle** is not a castle at all but the remnants of a twelfth-century moated manor house, home of the De Plais family, who were tenants of Castle Acre's de Warennes. It's an imposing ruin, but nothing more, although its location, surrounded by the peaceful fields and shaded by mature trees is pretty much the perfect summer picnic spot. Next door, the round-towered village church of **St Mary** cuts an elegant figure, but it's usually locked.

Weeting Heath

Weeting, IP26 4NQ • April–Sept daily 7am–dusk, visitor centre April–July daily 10am–4pm • £4 • ⓦ www.norfolkwildlifetrust.org.uk

Weeting Heath, a mile outside the village, is an NWT reserve that occupies a pretty stretch of woodland housing several hides, from which you can spot the stone curlews that breed here in summer; you can also do a three-mile loop through the woods.

Grimes Graves

Lynford, IP26 5DE • March & Oct Thurs–Mon 10am–5pm; April, June & Sept daily 10am–5pm; July & Aug daily 10am–6pm • £3.30; EH

About three miles northwest of Thetford, at the end of a long track, the forest opens out to a vast and open grassy moonscape known as **Grimes Graves**, the earliest significant industrial site in Europe, dating from around 2000 BC. The craters are the result of Neolithic flint mines, one shaft of which you can descend by ladder 100ft down if you don a hard hat, from where galleries burrow deep into the ground in all directions. The mines were not identified as such until they were excavated in the 1870s, although they owe their collective moniker to the Anglo-Saxons, who named them after one of their gods, Grim.

Mundford

Approaching it from the main A134 from Thetford, the village of **MUNDFORD** doesn't look up to much at all, but beyond the cricket pitch it's one of the prettiest villages in the area, with a main street of flint and thatched cottages and a small triangular green that's home to the **Crown Inn** (see p.210).

5

Iceni Brewery

Foulden Rd, Ickburgh, Mundford, IP26 5HB • Shop Mon–Fri 8.30am–4.30pm, Sat 9am–3pm • ☎ 01842 878922, • ⓦ icenibrewery.co.uk

Just north of Mundford on the edge of Thetford Forest, the **Iceni Brewery**, is just a tiny affair, with a shop in a small hut selling their various ales. You can either phone in advance to request a tour, or on quiet days they'll show you round the plant anyway – it's doesn't take long to see the whole place.

ARRIVAL AND DEPARTURE
THETFORD FOREST

By train Trains run to Brandon station, just outside the centre of town across the river, on the main line from London and Cambridge (trains hourly), and from Thetford (hourly; 8min), Ely, Attleborough, Wymondham and of course Norwich where trains terminate.

By bus Brandon and Mundford are connected by infrequent buses, but really the way to get around the forest is to walk or bike.

ACCOMMODATION

Colveston Manor Mundford, IP26 5HU ☎ 01842 878218, ⓦ colveston-manor.co.uk. A farm-based B&B with four generously proportioned rooms (two doubles, one twin, one single) furnished in traditional style and with breakfast using ingredients from the farm. It's a lovely, remote spot; you can wander the farm to your heart's content – and it couldn't be in a better position for the forest. Bear in mind, though, that without a car you are a good half-hour walk from the village, although they will provide dinner if arranged in advance. **£60**

The Crown Crown Rd Mundford, IP26 5HQ ☎ 01842 878233, ⓦ the-crown-hotel.co.uk. This seventeenth-century village pub couldn't be in a more picturesque location, right in the heart of Mundford village, and has 38 large, attractive rooms in the beamed main building and the separate converted barn next door, as well as a large self-catering house for rent. Breakfasts are excellent, and you can eat lunch and dinner here too (see below). **£74.50**

EATING AND DRINKING

The Crown Crown Rd, Mundford, IP26 5HQ ☎ 01842 878233, ⓦ the-crown-hotel.co.uk. There's a slightly confusing array of menus at this pub-restaurant-hotel, and the food is filling rather than refined. But the bar menu standards are reliable and good, and the T-bone steaks, sea bream and steak-and-mushroom pie they serve both in the pub and restaurant certainly hit the spot, and there are always a few vegetarian options. All mains cost £7.95–13.95. Daily noon–3pm & 6.30–10pm.

Eleveden Estate London Rd, IP24 3TQ ☎ 01842 898068, ⓦ www.elveden.com. A rather brilliant all-rounder, the Eleveden Estate restaurant serves great breakfasts until 11.15am and lovely lunches until 3.30pm. It's a bright, modern environment, the service is top-notch and the food delicious, whether you're sampling one of their excellent burgers or fishcakes or tucking into their Sunday roast lunches. Always lots of tempting specials too. Mon–Fri 9.30am–4pm, Sat 9.30am–5pm, Sun 10am–5pm.

Diss and around

Right on the southern border of Norfolk, at the western end of the Waveney Valley **DISS** is as appealing a market town as you could wish for, unusually built around a lake – the Mere – and much admired by the poet John Betjeman, who typically gloried in its unremarkableness in his 1960s poem *A Mind's Journey to Diss*, which famously proclaimed to Harold Wilson's wife Mary how it would be "bliss, to go with you by train to Diss". These days Diss is still rather proud of its ordinariness, and like Aylsham further north joined the Cittaslow movement in 2006 (ⓦ www.cittaslow.org.uk) to help promote and protect its quality of local life. But the best thing that you can do is experience the bliss that is Diss for yourself – not to mention the various attractions around: **Banham Zoo**, the **Buckenhams** and the excellent **Bressingham Steam Museum and Gardens**.

The Market Place

Diss's central **Market Place** forms a triangle at the top of the main street, Mere Street, and is home to a busy weekly market on Fridays. Housed in a wooden hut on the Market Place, **Diss Museum** (mid-March to Oct Wed & Thurs 2–4pm, Fri & Sat 10am–4pm; May–Aug also 2.30–4.30pm; free) has displays on the town, the Mere, and John Skelton, sometime poet laureate and rector of the church of **St Mary the Virgin**, at the top end of the square. The church is a very dignified building from the outside, although most of its originally fifteenth-century interior was refurbished in the nineteenth century.

The Mere

Mere Street leads as you would expect to the **Mere**, a picturesque spot surrounded by willows and with a spouting fountain at its centre. It's a natural lake, deeper than you might think (it reaches 65ft in places), and carpeted by thick mud so noxious that in times gone by eels were said to throw themselves out to die on the banks rather than live there. Happily the eels are long gone, and you can safely sit on the benches at the so-called **Mere's Mouth** and feed the ducks, or take a stroll through the park on the far side, where there's also a children's playground.

Fair Green

Beyond the Mereside park, Denmark Street leads down to the main road through town, across which is **Fair Green** – the prettiest part of Diss, with clapboard and timbered houses set around a village green. The river is just beyond, and a path alongside leads a mile or so to **Roydon Fen**, a small nature reserve maintained by the Suffolk Wildlife Trust (ⓦwww.suffolkwildlifetrust.org).

Bressingham Gardens and Steam Museum

Bressingham, IP22 2AA • End March to Oct daily 10.30am–5pm, closes 5.30pm July & Aug • Entry including steam train rides (Wed–Sun only) £12.50, children £8.50; including diesel rides £10/£6.50; entry only £8.50/£5 • ☎ 01379 686903, ⓦ bressingham.co.uk

This is two attractions in one, both of them the vision of one man, Alan Bloom, who

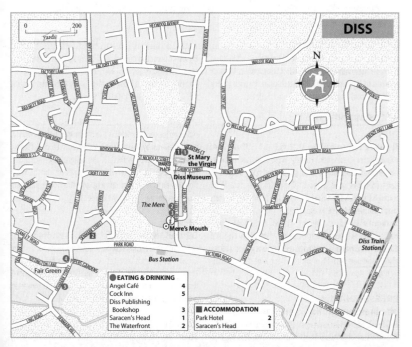

● EATING & DRINKING	
Angel Café	4
Cock Inn	5
Diss Publishing Bookshop	3
Saracen's Head	1
The Waterfront	2

■ ACCOMMODATION	
Park Hotel	2
Saracen's Head	1

5

bought **Bressingham Hall** in 1946 and indulged his two passions – collecting old steam engines and gardening. The result is a large complex encompassing the enormous Blooms **garden centre**, the **gardens** of Bressingham Hall and a **museum** of steam engines. Bloom's legacy has been continued by his sons, one of whom still lives in the grounds.

The **museum** is housed in several engine sheds, some of which have some very fancy engines indeed, including the former royal coaches of both the current Queen and Edward VII. You can peer in to see the sumptuous period fixtures and fittings. Another shed houses the collection of the **Dad's Army Appreciation Society**, and its homage to the series, most of which was filmed in the area, is a rival to Thetford's better-known but much less accessible museum (see p.207). There are mock-ups of Jones the Butchers and Captain Mainwaring's bank, numerous photos of the Norfolk locations used, not to mention a portrait of actor Bill Pertwee by former England wicketkeeper Jack Russell. You can tour the gardens and the adjacent nursery on regularly running mini steam and diesel **trains**, and there's a carousel and other rides. As for the **gardens** themselves, they are a magnificent sight, best enjoyed during spring or summer. They consist of Alan Bloom's original "Dell" garden in front of the house, and his son Adrian's Foggy Bottom garden behind – a perfect counterpoint to the steam trains, though in their way no less man-made.

100th Bomb Group Memorial Museum

Thorpe Abbotts, IP21 4PH • May–Sept Wed, Sat & Sun 10am–5pm; March, April & Oct Sat & Sun 10am–5pm • Free • ☎ 01379 740708, ⓦ 100bgmus.org.uk

Just outside the village of Thorpe Abbotts, the airfield buildings of the **100th Bomb Group Memorial Museum** commemorate the US airmen of the 100th Bomb Group – "the bloody hundredth", as they were known – who fought alongside the RAF in World War II for over two years. It's an evocative place, no less so for its seemingly remote location among the sweeping fields of south Norfolk, and its photos, uniforms and personal effects – including a mock-up of the gun turret of a "Flying Fortress" – form a haunting, small collection.

ARRIVAL AND INFORMATION

By train The station, 500m east of the centre off Victoria Rd, is on the main line from London Liverpool St. Services also run to Norwich (every 30min; 20min), Ipswich (every 30min; 20min) and Stowmarket (hourly; 10min).

DISS AND AROUND

By bus Buses stop on Park Rd. Hourly services to Harleston (30min), Bungay (50min) and Beccles (1hr 30min).
Tourist office In a kiosk on Mere St, by the Mere's Mouth (Mon–Sat 10am–4pm; ☎ 01379 650523).

ACCOMMODATION

DISS

The Park 29 Denmark St, IP22 4LE ☎ 01379 642244, ⓦ parkhotel-diss.co.uk. Twenty well, if rather blandly, furnished double rooms with good-sized bathrooms and flat-screen TVs, and a reasonable restaurant too. Walk through the park from the far side of the Mere and turn left onto Denmark St. Free wi-fi. **£65**

Saracen's Head 75 Mount St, IP22 4QQ ☎ 01379 652853, ⓦ saracensheaddiss.co.uk. The plain en-suite doubles here provide good value for money, and there's also the added benefit of an excellent breakfast in their restaurant downstairs. **£50**

BRESSINGHAM

★ **Bressingham Hall** Bressingham, IP22 2AA ☎ 01379 687 243, ⓦ bressinghamgardens.com/bed_ breakfast.php. A couple of miles west of Diss, *Bressingham*

Hall is no longer occupied by the Bloom gardening dynasty, but it's still run by them, or at least by Jason Bloom's father-in-law, Ian, as a posh B&B, in the delightfully unchanged Bloom home, complete with family photos on the wall. Doubles are simple but homely, and the house naturally has gorgeous views over the gardens. **£95**

BROME

Cornwallis Hotel Rectory Rd, IP23 8AJ ☎ 08444 146524, ⓦ oxfordhotelsandinns.com/ourhotels/cornwallis. Five minutes by car from Diss, just over the border in Suffolk, this country-house hotel set in large grounds has big, old-fashioned double rooms. The historic building has been well converted with a pleasant bar and an excellent restaurant. **£95**

SCOLE

Scole Inn Ipswich Rd, IP21 4DR ☎ 01379 740481,

ⓦ scoleinn.co.uk. A mile or so east of Diss, on the main A1066 in the small village of Scole, this is an old Georgian coaching inn with 22 good-sized rooms, half of which are in the converted stable block out the back. The business has been through multiple changes of management in recent years and it shows in the unevenness of the service and – literally – of the building itself, which is creaking with age. Downstairs it's a cosy old pub with a swanky restaurant next door. **£85**

PULHAM MARKET
Old Bakery Church Walk, IP21 4SL ☎ 01379 676462, ⓦ www.theoldbakery.net. This deliberately upscale B&B is the sort of place where no expense has been spared and nothing is too much trouble. The building is indeed an old bakery, and its four rooms are individually furnished, and well worth the money. Breakfasts too are top-notch and wi-fi is free. A pity, then, that children aren't welcome. **£75**

EATING AND DRINKING

DISS

Angel Café 1 Fair Green, IP24 4BQ ☎ 01379 640758. A hippy-dippy local favourite, which does good cooked breakfasts and lunches, with home-made soups and quiches and lots of veggie options. Mon–Sat 10am–4pm.

Cock Inn Lower Denmark St, IP22 4BE ☎ 01379 643633, ⓦ cockinndiss.co.uk. Right on Fair Green, this is the town centre's best pub, with good, rotating choice of ales, food every day from a determinedly simple and well-priced menu (most mains under £10, and lunchtime sandwiches for £5), and live music most Saturday nights. Food served daily noon–3pm & 6–9.30pm.

Diss Publishing Bookshop 40 Mere St, IP22 4AH ☎ 01379 642047. Next door to the tourist office, this is a great independent bookshop with a café backing onto the Mere that does coffee, sandwiches, soup and hot lunches. Mon–Sat 8.45am–5.15pm.

Saracen's Head 75 Mount St, IP22 4QQ ☎ 01379 652853, ⓦ saracensheaddiss.co.uk. Pub at the top end of the high street that serves a fairly meaty menu of burgers, steaks, and much more besides, with lunchtime mains starting at £5.95, and in the evening around £11.95. Daily noon–2pm & 7–9.15pm.

The Waterfront 43 Mere St, IP22 4AG ☎ 01379 652695. A decent and very popular high street boozer that does pub grub all day from £5.99 – burgers, salads and all the usual standards – and has the added bonus of a terrace overlooking the Mere. Food served daily 11am – 9pm.

BROME

Cornwallis Hotel Rectory Rd, IP23 8AJ ☎ 08444 146524, ⓦ oxfordhotelsandinns.com/ourhotels/cornwallis. This low-key country house is a destination in itself for food, with a bar that does hot dishes from £9.95, as well as sandwiches and ploughman's, and a posher restaurant with a regularly changing menu of half a dozen starters (around £5) and mains (£10.95–13.95) – excellent quality, modern British food. Daily 12.30–2.30pm & 6.30–9.30pm.

BURSTON

★ **The Crown** Mill Rd, IP22 5TW ☎ 01379 741257, ⓦ burstoncrown.com. Classic village pub that's both a cosy boozer with a garden and a food destination in its own right, with a menu – cooked up by Steve, ex-chef to U2 and Bruce Springsteen – that aims to be a notch above your average pub offering. There's an all-day bar menu that includes sandwiches, excellent home-made burgers, steak-and-kidney pie and the like (£9–12), and more refined dishes served in the separate restaurant lunchtime and evenings – rib-eye steak, sea bass fillet, for £12–15. Mon–Sat noon–2pm & 6.30–9pm, Sun noon–3.30pm.

SCOLE

Scole Inn Ipswich Rd, IP21 4DR ☎ 01379 740481, ⓦ oxfordhotelsandinns.com/OurHotels/ScoleInn. Old inn with rooms that serves a great bar menu – mains £6.95–8.95 (Cromer crab, Norfolk pork sausages, chicken curry) – much better value than the fussier fare in the adjoining restaurant. Daily noon–2.30pm & 6–9pm.

THE SAINTS

To the southwest of Bungay, and northeast of Halesworth, the flattish farmland of **The Saints** feels somehow off the map, a bleakish, windswept region that is crisscrossed by footpaths and byways. It's named for the numerous small villages named after a saint – either with the prefix "Ilketshall" or the suffix "South Elmham" – and although none are especially worth stopping at, the area has a unique feel, and of course there is always a medieval church to go with each saint. It's a good area to cycle through, and you can do a sixteen-mile loop from Bungay that takes in the villages of **Ilketshall St Andrew** and **St Lawrence**, before crossing the main Halesworth road – the A144 – to visit the **Elmham** villages and finish up at St Peter's Brewery, just between **St Peter South Elmham** and **Ilketshall St Margaret**. It's worth taking a picnic and making a day of it if you can, maybe stopping off at the eleventh-century ruins of **South Elmham Minster**, which hide among the trees in the grounds of South Elmham Hall farm.

5

Bungay and around

"Welcome to Bungay, a fine old town", proclaim the signs, and it's hard to disagree that **BUNGAY**, just south of the border in Suffolk, would be a nice place to live. But there's not all that much to bring you here, beyond a possible change in lifestyle. Clasped in a meander of the River Waveney, it's an odd mix of the well-to-do and shabby (Earsham Street is its most upscale stretch), but otherwise it's a smallish market town with a handful of low-key attractions and a couple of good gastropubs. A great place, in short, to just loaf about, before heading off to explore the countryside around.

St Mary

St Mary's St, NR35 1AF • ⓦ bungay-suffolk.co.uk/community/worship.asp

The centre of Bungay isn't very big, and focuses on the Butter Cross and Market Place intersection, and the bulky fifteenth-century church of **St Mary**. Formerly part of a priory, the remains of which – the nun's choir – you can see outside, and badly damaged by a seventeenth-century fire, it's now owned and run by the Churches Conservation Trust.

Bungay Castle

NR35 2AF • Free • ⓦ bungay-suffolk.co.uk/activities/castle.asp

Across the road from the church, Bungay's **Castle** was built by Hugh Bigod in 1165, and, after it was destroyed by Henry II, rebuilt a hundred years later by his descendant Roger. The Bigods were a powerful Norman family hereabouts, and Hugh in particular was a vicious tyrant who by all accounts wasn't much admired by the local populace, eventually dying in Syria after embarking on the Crusades. There's certainly not much left of his edifice now, just the gateway and the grassed-over ruins of the keep, accessible through *Jester's Café*, just off the Market Place.

Harleston

There are a number of Norfolk (and Suffolk) towns that seem to survive in a self-contained bubble, doing very nicely despite the encroachment of out-of-town shopping and the lure of bigger urban centres. Swaffham is one, Framlingham and Halesworth in Suffolk are others, and **HARLESTON**, about eight miles down the Waveney from Bungay, yet another, with an attractive and relatively thriving main street that ends at the inevitable market-place and not all that much to see or appreciate apart from the enjoyable small-town vibe. There are lots of timbered houses, and you can stroll the town centre in twenty minutes, before dropping into the town centre's best pub for a well-earned pint.

St Peter's Brewery

St Peter's Hall, South Elmham, NR35 1NQ • **Tours** Sat & Sun 11am–3pm on the hour • £4.50 **Shop** Mon–Fri 9am–5pm, Sat & Sun 11am–4pm • ☎ 01986 782322, ⓦ stpetersbrewery.co.uk

Bang in the centre of the Saints, the buildings of **St Peter's Brewery** were an abandoned

---

BUNGAY'S BLACK DOG

St Mary's is best known for the legend of the **black dog of Bungay** – when in a terrible storm of 1577 a black dog ("black shuck") appeared and attacked the congregation, before descending on Blythburgh church (see p.264), leaving many dead and the locals terrified. Many speculated that the dog was an incarnation of the evil local landowner Hugh Bigod, who had terrorized the town three hundred years earlier, others felt it was an appearance by Satan himself. Whatever the truth, the black dog lives on – not least in Bungay's coat of arms.

farm until the mid-1990s, when John Murphy – the founder of the multinational brand consultancy Interbrand – developed the brewery here. Murphy has done a great job in producing an excellent selection of mainly bottled ales – around a dozen varieties in all – that have won a number of awards, although the real key (as he has acknowledged) was in bringing his marketing background to the fore and putting his products in distinctive and well-designed oval-shaped bottles that helped distinguish them from other small brewers who have sprung up in the last twenty years, particularly in East Anglia. You can take a **tour** of the plant, taste some beer and, of course, buy more of it in the **shop**. Across the courtyard, **St Peter's Hall** houses a bar and restaurant (see below).

ARRIVAL AND INFORMATION
BUNGAY AND AROUND

By bus Bungay doesn't have a train station; buses either stop opposite the Butter Cross or on Trinity St, and there are services to Beccles (roughly hourly; 30min), Diss (hourly; 50min), Harleston (hourly; 20min) and Halesworth (hourly;

30min), South Elmham (hourly; 30min) and Ilketshall St John (hourly; 10min).
Tourist office In the centre of town on Broad St (Mon–Thurs 9am–4.30pm, Fri 9am–4pm; ☎01986 892716).

ACCOMMODATION

BUNGAY

Castle Inn 35 Earsham St, NR35 1AF ☎01986 892283, ⓦthecastleinn.net. The accommodation at this restaurant is the best option in the centre of Bungay, with four simple yet comfortable en-suite rooms. **£85**

King's Heads and Queen's Jules 2 Market Place, NR35 1AW ☎01986 893583, ⓦkingsheadandqueensjules. co.uk. Long-established town centre pub now under the new management of the ebullient Jules. The rooms are simple but there's a friendly welcome, the bar is convivial and cosy and they're trying to establish their marvellous back rooms as regular live music venues. **£65**

EARSHAM

Earsham Park Farm Earsham, NR35 2AQ ☎01986 892180, ⓦearsham-parkfarm.co.uk. Very friendly B&B in a working farmhouse just outside Bungay which has four en-suite rooms and serves convivial breakfasts. Lovely gardens, too, full of the proprietress's sculptures. **£82**

HARLESTON

JD Young 2–4 Market Place, IP20 9AD ☎01379 852822, ⓦjdyoung.co.uk. This coaching inn offers eleven en-suite rooms – recently refurbished with satellite TV – and a popular bar and restaurant that's very much the hub of the town. **£95**

EATING AND DRINKING

BUNGAY

★ **Castle Inn** 35 Earsham St, NR35 1AF ☎01986 892283, ⓦthecastleinn.net. Bright, almost antiseptically restored old pub run by London escapees Mark and Tanya that focuses squarely on food, and does so with some style. There are classic pub options and sandwiches at lunch as well as a good-value two-course menu for £14 (noon–2.30pm), featuring the likes of beef bourguignon, Norfolk sweetcorn chowder and roasts on Sundays. Evening menus (£13.50–15) have a Mediterranean flavour with mains such as Bungay rabbit, pigeon and parma ham-wrapped cod fillet. Delicious, locally sourced food, very friendly and welcoming service, and a wine list that includes a white from nearby Fressingfield. Food: Mon–Fri noon–2.30pm & 6–9pm, Fri & Sat noon–2pm & 6–9.30pm, Sun noon–4.30pm.

BROOME

The Artichoke 162 Yarmouth Rd, NR35 2NZ ☎01986 893325, ⓦtheartichokeatbroome.co.uk. Homely pub in an otherwise nondescript village just outside Bungay that has a focus on food – pub food, really, but a cut above, and

not expensive. Lunchtime mains go for £7–8, and there are plenty of veggie options, alongside home-made pies, lamb's liver and sausage and mash. The evening menu focuses on steaks (£11–15) and a short menu of meat and fish dishes, again with at least one veggie option. Tues–Sat noon–2.30pm & 6.30–9pm, Sun noon–2.30pm. Closed Mon.

HARLESTON

JD Young 2–4 Market Place, IP20 9AD ☎01379 852822, ⓦjdyoung.co.uk. This revamped old pub has a busy bar and an attractive book-lined dining room, and serves a good choice of food all day – adventurous sandwiches and burgers, beef-and-ale pie, Thai chicken curry (£7.95–10.95), and an excellent-value three-course lunch special. Mon–Fri 11am–9.45pm, Sat & Sun 11am–10pm.

SOUTH ELMHAM

St Peter's Hall NR35 1NQ ☎01986 782288, ⓦstpetersbrewery.co.uk. Restaurant attached to the brewery, serving steak-and-ale pie for £9.95 among other things; it also hosts live music. Daily noon–3pm & 6–11pm.

Ipswich and Felixstowe

CHRISTCHURCH MANSION, IPSWICH (P.221)

Ipswich and Felixstowe

Situated at the head of the Orwell estuary, Ipswich is the largest town in Suffolk by some way, twice the size of its nearest rival, Lowestoft, although most people would struggle if you were to ask them to name a reason to visit. Certainly it's not seen as an alluring destination in its own right – in the way, say, Norwich might be; it's not even technically a city, and has a reputation for seediness that most ports are saddled with, though one without any attendant glamour. However, the town is both a more appealing and more historic destination than you might think, with any number of reasons to make a trip, not least the waterfront development, which on a good day is as nice a place to shoot the harbourside breeze as any in England.

Thirteen miles southeast, at the end of the Orwell estuary, **Felixstowe** is the port that stole Ipswich's thunder, and the most southerly town on the Suffolk coast. It too is not the county's most appealing corner but is certainly its most economically productive, a powerhouse of a port that handles much of the container traffic for southern England – hence the parade of trucks that continuously thunders up and down the A14. Even Felixstowe has its good bits, though, and for the most part it's a decent resort with a long sandy beach and the tiny satellite village of Felixstowe Ferry to tempt you to stay a little bit longer.

Ipswich

IPSWICH is one of the oldest towns in the country, the Saxon stronghold of Raedwald, ruler of East Anglia in the seventh century, whose burial site was at Sutton Hoo (see p.239). The town became a rich trading port in the Middle Ages, exporting the fruits of the Suffolk textile industry to the rest of Europe, it was home to one of the most popular medieval shrines, and to one of its least popular figures, Cardinal Wolsey, who was born here and made the town his power base. Later, Thomas Gainsborough lived and worked in Ipswich, and Tolly Cobbold established their brewing dynasty here.

The port declined at the beginning of the twentieth century and the town has a rather tawdry reputation today, its **centre** has the usual pedestrianized precincts and chain stores and there's been some poor postwar redevelopment. However, the city is as vital and dynamic as any provincial British town, and is certainly more handsome than you might expect. The redevelopment of the waterfront only adds to the confident and resurgent impression. There are a couple of good local museums, including **Christchurch Mansion**, with its collection of Gainsboroughs and Constables, and there's plenty to see nearby, not least **Constable Country**, a series of pretty villages and countryside in between down towards the Essex border where the early John Constable lived and worked (see p.278).

Come on you Tractor Boys! p.221   On the river p.224
Harvest at Jimmy's p.223

A CONTENTED RESIDENT OF JIMMY'S FARM

Highlights

❶ Christchurch Mansion Ipswich's most handsome building, and with an art collection that features work by local boys Gainsborough and Constable. **See p.221**

❷ The Waterfront One of the most successful dockside developments you'll find – don't come to Ipswich without seeking it out. **See p.223**

❸ Jimmy's Farm "As seen on TV", and a perfect attraction for kids, and also featuring a great

farm shop and restaurant too. **See p.224**

❹ Landguard Fort This historic fort is by far the best venue from which to appreciate Felixstowe's unique port and harbour. **See p.229**

❺ Felixstowe Ferry Felixstowe – indeed Suffolk – at its best, and you could be a million miles away from the docks, with fresh fish stalls, a couple of places to eat and the ferry across the river to Bawdsey. **See p.230**

HIGHLIGHTS ARE MARKED ON THE MAP ON P.220

Cornhill and around

If Ipswich has a focal point then it's **Cornhill**, a central square at the end of the town's main Tavern Street, flanked by a bevy of imposing Victorian edifices – the Italianate **Town Hall** (Tues–Sat 10am–5pm), now a venue for exhibitions of contemporary and local art, the old Neoclassical post office next door, and on the other side of the square the pseudo-Jacobean Lloyds Building. Cut through from here to the end of the town's other main drag, Buttermarket, and the **Giles Statue**, which remembers the *Daily Express* cartoonist, Carl Giles, with a representation of "Grandma" from the popular strip which ran in the newspaper from 1945 until the early 1990s. The cartoon followed the daily fortunes of an ordinary family, of which Grandma was perhaps the most memorable member, although, as Giles himself claimed, her conversation amounted only to "ailments, horseracing and little else". With her dog at her feet, Giles' Grandma looks up to the building opposite where the cartoonist had his studio, while in the opposite direction the *Swan* pub on King Street is apparently where he often used to wind up after work (see p.228).

The Ancient House

On the corner of Buttermarket and St Stephen's Lane, Ipswich's most renowned building is the **Ancient House**, whose stuccoed exterior was decorated around 1670 in an extravagant style that makes it one of the finest examples of Restoration artistry in the country. There are plasterwork reliefs of pelicans and nymphs as well as representations of the four continents (that were known about at the time) – Europe symbolized by a Gothic church, America a tobacco pipe, Asia an Oriental dome and Africa by a native astride a crocodile.

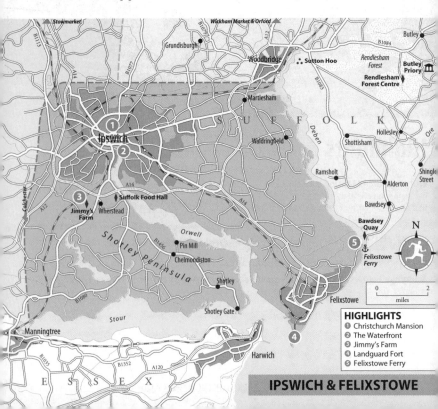

HIGHLIGHTS
1. Christchurch Mansion
2. The Waterfront
3. Jimmy's Farm
4. Landguard Fort
5. Felixstowe Ferry

IPSWICH & FELIXSTOWE

The house is now a branch of the Lakeland homewares chain, and as such you're free to take a peek inside to view yet more of the decor, including its hammerbeam roof.

St Mary-le-Tower

Tower St, IP1 3BE • Mon–Sat 9am–5pm, Sun 8am–12.30pm & 6.30–7.30pm • ☎ 01473 289001, ⓦ stmaryletower.org.uk

Ipswich is not a city, so doesn't have a cathedral, and the nearest it gets is in the church of **St Mary-le-Tower**, whose spire is a familiar landmark wherever you are in the town centre. Although it's not even close to being on a par with Norwich's cathedral, and has been hugely updated over the years, it's an important symbol of the town, and there are some aspects of it that locals can be proud of – not least its size, which is vast and atmospheric. The font is a typical example from the fifteenth century, decorated with lions and human heads, and the pews at the back of the church have finely carved ends showing devout monks and dragons, while in the north aisle you can see memorials to the local Cobbold brewing dynasty. Look also for the painted memorial in the north aisle to William Smart MP; it shows Ipswich as it would have looked when he died in 1599.

6

Ipswich Museum

High St, IP1 3QH • Tues–Sat 10am–5pm • Free • ☎ 01473 433550, ⓦ ipswich.gov.uk

On the edge of the town centre, the **Ipswich Museum** is an old-fashioned museum of the very best kind, with a wonderful main gallery full of traditional glass display cases, stuffed birds and animals from the Victorian era – a giraffe, zebra and plenty more, including a very charming mock-up of a life-sized woolly mammoth. The gallery above concentrates on the history of Ipswich to the present day, and there's a great archeological section, with locally found Roman jewellery, tableaux of life in the fields and in a Roman villa, and a good array of Egyptian artefacts, well exhibited with children in mind. The ethnographic section, too, has costumes and weapons and day-to-day items from the developing world, and a series of galleries focus on life in the town during World War II – again, really well thought out and great for kids.

St Mary-at-the-Elms

Probably Ipswich's quaintest town-centre church, **St Mary-at-the-Elms**, is distinguished by its red-brick Tudor tower, although this was damaged by a fire in 2010. Dating back to the thirteenth century, the church is linked to the shrine of **Our Lady of Grace** which once stood nearby – its site, on Lady Lane, is marked by a plaque – and was second only to Walsingham in stature until it was suppressed by Henry VIII in the 1530s. Today the church houses a copy of the wooden statue of the Virgin that used to reside in the shrine and somehow ended up in Nettuno, Italy.

Christchurch Mansion and Wolsey Art Gallery

Soane St, IP4 2BE • Daily 10am–5pm • Free • ☎ 01473 433554, ⓦ cimuseums.org.uk

A few minutes' walk north of the town centre, Christchurch Park is worth a stroll in itself, but it's also home to **Christchurch Mansion**, a handsome if much-restored Tudor building

---

COME ON YOU TRACTOR BOYS!

Ipswich Town FC are struggling to get back to their glory days under Bobby Robson in the 1960s and 1970s but still enjoy solid support locally, and of course loathe their East Anglian rivals Norwich City. They play at Portman Road, a 30,000-capacity stadium on the western edge of the town centre, five minutes' walk from Cornhill and the train station, and ten minutes' from the Waterfront. For information and tickets see ⓦ itfc.co.uk.

6

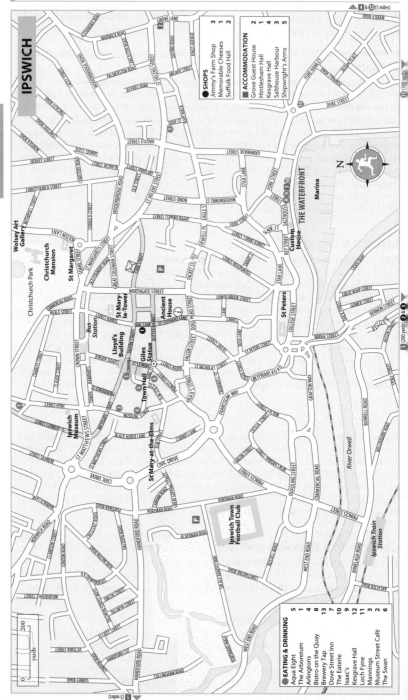

IPSWICH

● SHOPS
Jimmy's Farm Shop   3
Memorable Cheeses   1
Suffolk Food Hall   2

■ ACCOMMODATION
Grove Guest House   2
Hintlesham Hall   1
Kesgrave Hall   4
Salthouse Harbour   3
Shipwright's Arms   5

● EATING & DRINKING
Aqua Eight   5
The Arboretum   1
Arlingtons   4
Bistro on the Quay   8
Brewery Tap   13
Dove Street Inn   7
The Eaterie   10
Isaac's   9
Kesgrave Hall   12
Loch Fyne   11
Mannings   3
Museum Street Café   2
The Swan   6

sporting seventeenth-century Dutch-style gables, attached to the **Wolsey Art Gallery** behind. It was built in the sixteenth century on the grounds of a priory seized for the crown by Cardinal Wolsey and later occupied in its eighteenth- and nineteenth-century heyday by the wealthy Fonnereau family, who added the various wings and extensions. There's quite a lot to see, starting in the impressive arcaded Great Hall in the Jacobean core, and finishing up in the Victorian wing, with its downstairs kitchen and servants' quarters – all sensitively and effectively filled with period furniture, paintings and other displays, including one of vintage toys and dolls' houses. There are paintings throughout, including one by the Dutchman Adriaen van Ostade in the library, various Tudor and Stuart portraits and landscapes by nineteenth- and twentieth-century Suffolk artists including the entertaining *Felixstowe to Ipswich Coach* by Russell Sidney Reeve. Perhaps most unusual, though, are the early seventeenth-century Horstead Panels, which occupy a room to themselves and were based apparently on an elegy by John Donne; they were painted on the death of one of the daughters of the family, and each depicts a different thought or prayer.

The attached **Wolsey Art Gallery** displays a collection of mostly Gainsborough and Constable paintings – the largest outside London, and a homage to the area's most renowned painters. You'll find early landscapes and portraits of local eighteenth-century dignitaries by Gainsborough – notably one of the local MP at the time, William Wollaston – and landscapes and family portraits by Constable, including a wonderfully verdant painting of his father's vegetable garden.

The Waterfront

Ipswich's wet dock or **Waterfront** dates from the nineteenth century, when its mills and warehouses were the focal point of the town's Victorian docks, which were the largest in Europe when they opened in 1845. Like inner-city port areas across the country, it fell into disrepair some time ago and is now in the process of being transformed into one of the city's most exciting and dynamic new neighbourhoods, with a busy marina and a barrage of cool apartment and office buildings, bars, restaurants and hotels; it's also been the home campus of the University of Suffolk since 2008. The area is something of a work-in-progress, but already its quayside main drag has been pretty successful in creating an almost Mediterranean ambience – squint across the masts of the marina on a summer's evening and you could almost believe you were in St Tropez. The cafés and restaurants along the water's edge certainly make a good fist of aping life on the Riviera, none more so than the slick *Salthouse Harbour Hotel* (see p.225), while the stolid Neoclassical **Customs House**, provides a reminder of yesteryear, complete with a grand portico and a wide double stairway.

St Peter's by-the-Waterfront

College St, IP1 1XF • Mon–Fri 10am–3.30pm • ☎ 01473 225269, ⓦ stpetersbythewaterfront.com

Just outside the Waterfront development, across the main road, is the church of **St Peter's-by-the-Waterfront** and the so-called **Wolsey Gate** next door. There has been a church here since the eleventh century and the current building dates from the 1500s when Cardinal Wolsey made it his own private chapel. It's a community arts centre these days, and hosts all sorts of events, and you can either attend one of these or just drop by to see its marble font and medieval roof, and a display on Wolsey and his times, as well as admiring the extensive nineteenth-century renovation.

HARVEST AT JIMMY'S

If you can, check out **Harvest at Jimmy's**, a great food and music festival held in early September that is co-hosted with Alex James' place in Oxfordshire. It blends appearances from top chefs and food writers with a decent music line-up, and somehow pulls it off. You can go for just a day or camp and stay for the full weekend – more information at ⓦ harvestatjimmys.com.

Ipswich Transport Museum

Cobham Rd, IP3 9JD • March–Nov Sun 11am–4pm, plus additional weekdays 1–4pm during Easter, school and bank hols.• £4.50, children £2.50, family tickets £13 • ☎ 01472 715666, ⓦ ipswichtransportmuseum.co.uk

About a mile down Felixstowe Road from central Ipswich, the **Ipswich Transport Museum** isn't a must-see, but its vintage trams and buses, fire engines and related items – the self-proclaimed largest collection of transport vehicles in the country derived from just one town – may provide respite from the weather, or indeed satisfy the eager public transport buff in your family.

Jimmy's Farm

Pannington Hall Lane, IP9 2AR • Daily 9.30am–5.30pm; butterfly House April–Oct only • £4.50, children £3.50, family tickets £15 • ☎ 0844 493 8088, ⓦ jimmysfarm.com

The domain of Jimmy Doherty, farming's answer to Jamie Oliver (in fact the two are close friends), **Jimmy's Farm** focuses on rare breeds and has a great farm shop (see p.228). You're not likely to see its celebrity owner or his wife Michaela, although they're both still pretty active around the place, but pigs, turkeys and chickens and goats abound, alongside "ferret world", a guinea pig village and a lovely hothouse full of butterflies. There are also well-marked walks through the surrounding woodland, where your charges can make dens from timber that's left invitingly strewn around, and a good restaurant, fashioned out of a wonderful beamed old barn and partly supplied by the farm, including Michaela's nearby vegetable patch – a well-tended spread if ever there was one.

The Shotley Peninsula and Pin Mill

The **Shotley Peninsula** is an unusual if not especially endearing mix of farmland and semi-suburban industry and housing that extends to the southeast of Ipswich, and culminates in the village of **Shotley Gate**, where you can observe the container port that dominates Felixstowe (see p.228), just across the river. Halfway there, pushed in tight against the muddy banks of the River Orwell, the tiny village of **Pin Mill** hogs a marshy inlet, its huddle of old houses edging a busy boatyard, whose vintage boats creak and groan with the tides. Once the haunt of smugglers, Pin Mill is a peaceful, very nautical place today, and you can stroll along the riverbank or hoof it up to the National Trust's **Cliff Plantation** (always open; free), where a network of footpaths crisscross the hilly woodland that runs roughly parallel to the river. In Pin Mill itself, take time out at the riverside **Butt and Oyster** pub (see p.226).

ARRIVAL AND DEPARTURE   IPSWICH

By train The station is on the south bank of the river, about a 15min walk from Cornhill along Princes St, and is very well connected to the rest of East Anglia.
Destinations Beccles (hourly; 1hr 20min); Bury St Edmunds (hourly; 35min); Cambridge (hourly; 1hr 20min); Diss (every 30min; 25min); Felixstowe (hourly; 30min);

London, Liverpool St (every 30min; 1hr 10min); Lowestoft (hourly; 1hr 30min); Newmarket (hourly; 55min); Norwich (every 30min; 40min); Oulton Broad (hourly; 1hr 25min); Saxmundham (hourly; 40min); Stowmarket (every 30min; 15min); Woodbridge (hourly; 15min).
By bus Buses arrive at and leave from various places

ON THE RIVER

Orwell River Cruises (☎ 01473 258070, ⓦ orwellrivercruises.co.uk) run trips aboard the *Orwell Lady* from their berth on the eastern side of the Waterfront. One trip goes to **Pin Mill** (see above), which lasts 2hr 30min, and another – 1hr longer – further downriver to **Harwich**, while other options include cream tea cruises and themed evening cruises. The Harwich trips run 3 to 4 days a week, and several times each day, during summer, and cost £13 per person (family tickets £32); Pin Mill cruises are less frequent – usually just one day a week – and cost £10 per person (family tickets £26).

around the town centre: the Old Cattle Market bus station, the Tower Ramparts bus station on Crown St, from Turret Lane, a southerly extension of St Stephen's Lane. Destinations include Felixstowe (from the Old Cattle Market station; every 15min; 40min); Framlingham (from the corner of Northgate St and Great Colman St; every 30min; 45min).

By car Driving's not easy as traffic flows are carefully managed to avoid the city centre proper; there are centrally placed car parks just off Tacket St at Cox Lane, just south of Tavern Lane, and at the junction of Alf Ramsey Way and Portman Rd, right by the football ground.

INFORMATION AND TOURS

Tourist office St Stephen's Lane, IP1 1DP (Mon–Sat 9am–5pm; ☎01473 258070, ☞visit-suffolk.org.uk). Very centrally placed in the converted flint St Stephen's Church with its vaulted wooden ceiling.

Walking tours There are regular guided walks around the city centre, starting at the tourist office (usually Tues & Fri at 2.15pm; 90min; £3).

6

ACCOMMODATION

IPSWICH

Grove Guest House 14 Grove Lane, IP4 1NR ☎01473 221014, ☞acguesthouse.co.uk. Fairly centrally located B&B with four comfortable rooms, two of which are en suite and each furnished differently. Follow St Helen's Lane to the end and make a right, or walk up from Fore St across Alexandra Park – both about ten minutes' walk. **£49**

Salthouse Harbour Neptune Quay, IP4 1AX ☎01473 226789, ☞salthouseharbour.co.uk. Housed in an imaginatively converted old warehouse, down on the quayside of the Waterfront, this is the city's best choice if you can afford it, with seventy large, modern and minimalist-style rooms whose floor-to-ceiling windows look out over Ipswich's yacht harbour. It's not Antibes, or even Dartmouth, but it's undeniably nice, and not necessarily what you thought Ipswich would be like – especially if you are enjoying the view from your bath while listening to music on the room's iPod dock. **£125**

Shipwright's Arms 55–61 Wherstead Rd, IP2 8JJ ☎01473 602261, ☞theshipwrightsarms.co.uk. Friendly place just south of the centre, where the service can be variable but is usually well intentioned. They'll pick up and drop off for free from the train or bus station, the rooms are all en suite and very comfortable, with satellite TV and free wi-fi, and although it's not in the best part of town, it's easy walking distance from the Waterfront. **£65**

KESGRAVE

Kesgrave Hall Hall Rd, IP5 2PU ☎01473 333741, ☞milsomhotels.com/kesgravehall. On the furthest eastern edge of Ipswich, an ex-private school, and also once owned by the Tolly Cobbold brewing dynasty, this is a boutique hotel with a contemporary feel. Part of the small, mainly Essex-based Milsoms group, it has 23 rooms, around half of which are in the main house while the rest are in the former headmaster's quarters and various outbuildings. The rooms are sumptuous but not old-fashioned, kitted out with sound systems, flat-screen TVs and free wi-fi; the bar and lounge is relaxed rather than stuffy; and the restaurant stays open all day (see p.226). **£125**

HINTLESHAM

Hintlesham Hall Hintlesham, IP8 3NS ☎01473 652334, ☞hintleshamhall.co.uk. Country-house hotel west of Ipswich with large and very well-appointed rooms and service that is of the nothing-is-too-much-trouble variety. Outdoor pool and health club, and a very grand restaurant, fuelled with herbs from the hotel garden. The à la carte prices here fit the surroundings, but the table d'hôte fixed-price menus, served during the week, are excellent value. **£160**

EATING AND DRINKING

Ipswich has a fairly ordinary nightlife but an excellent selection of restaurants and places to drink for a town of its size, both in the immediate centre and down on the Waterfront, where you can sit outside if the weather is kind. Also, don't rule out some of the upscale hotels on the outskirts (*Kesgrave Hall* and *Hintlesham Hall*), which provide excellent quality and are easy to get to with your own transport.

CAFÉS AND RESTAURANTS

Aqua Eight 8 Lion St, IP1 1DQ ☎01473 218994. Very cool Asian fusion restaurant right in the heart of town. Most mains go for £10–12 but you could push the boat out and try the Alaskan black cod with miso sauce for £18.50; you won't regret it. It also has a great bar serving oriental-style meze and finger food. Tues–Thurs noon–2.30pm &

7–10pm, Fri & Sat noon–2.30pm & 5.30–11pm, Sun 5.30–10pm.

Arlingtons 13 Museum St, IP1 1HE ☎01473 230293, ☞arlingtonsbrasserie.co.uk. Big, airy restaurant, formerly home to the Ipswich Museum. At the upstairs brasserie mains go for £8.75–14.75, and are mainly tried-and-tested French favourites like beef bourguignon, cassoulet and steak frites, with some English standbys – fish pie, fish and chips and the inevitable burgers. Service can be a bit chaotic, but the food and ambience should make up for it. The downstairs café does great coffee, bagels and croissants, as well as a delicious breakfast for £5.95, and a simple lunch menu of gourmet sandwiches (£4.65), big salads (Greek, Caesar, etc) and jackets. Daily: brasserie 10am–10pm; café 8am–5.30pm.

Bistro on the Quay Wherry Quay, IP4 1AS ☎01473 286677, ☻bistroonthequay.co.uk. This restaurant epitomizes the revitalization of the Waterfront, with its clean modern interior and big windows looking out onto the water. The food too, is a contemporary take on some deliberately simple classics, with things like skate wing, monkfish fillets, lamb shank and dauphinoise potatoes predominating. Mains go for around £12.95, but there are good-value menus on offer too – £16.95 for three courses, less at lunchtime – and you can also get light lunch specials for just £6.95. Mon–Sat noon–2pm & 6.30–9.30pm, Sun noon–2.30pm.

The Eaterie Salthouse Harbour Hotel, Neptune Quay, IP4 1AX ☎01473 226789, ☻salthouseharbour.co.uk/eaterie. The restaurant lives up to the hotel's high standards, with curvy banquettes and a low-lit, New York warehouse feel that they pull off rather well – much like the rest of the Waterfront district in fact. The food is hearty rather than healthy, but always served with a flourish and a keen eye for detail – think crispy squid and octopus served on a slate with herby leaves, followed by venison steak with mash and bourguignon sauce. There are usually a few specials on the board too; generally starters go for £5.95–8.95, mains £12.95–16.95; there are lots of wines by the glass and by-the-bottle prices start at £15–17. Not bad for the coolest location east of, er, Bury St Edmunds. Daily noon–5.30pm & 6–10pm.

Kesgrave Hall Hall Rd, Kesgrave, IP5 2PU ☎01473 333741, ☻milsomhotels.com/kesgravehall. Despite the relative grandeur of the surroundings, *Kesgrave Hall's* restaurant is busy and relaxed at the same time, with stripped pine tables, an open kitchen and a quirky way of ordering: just jot what you want on a pad and they come and take it away. There are always daily specials, or you can order à la carte, choosing "ample" (starter-size) or "generous" (main-course size) portions in some cases. Prices are keen: starters are £5.75–7.95 and mains £9.95–18.95 (though most at the bottom end of that range), wine starts at £16 a bottle. Daily noon–9.30pm, Fri & Sat until 10pm.

Loch Fyne 1 Duke St, IP3 0AE ☎01473 269810, ☻lochfyne.com. A chain, but a good one, and in a handy location, just off the Waterfront. The menu features the usual well-prepared selection of fish and seafood. Moderately priced too with most starters at around £5–6,

mains £12–15. Sun–Thurs noon–10pm, Fri & Sat noon–10.30pm.

Museum Street Café Westgate House, Museum St, IP1 1HQ ☎01473 232393. Great café right in the heart of town, serving a regularly changing menu of really tasty vegetarian delights from pumpkin soup and butternut squash lasagne to sweet potato tortillas. Great value, and justifiably busy at lunchtime, it will be a hit even with your carnivore friends. Mon–Sat noon–2.30pm.

PUBS

The Arboretum 43 High St, IP1 3QL ☎01473 222177, ☻the-arboretum.net. At the top of the High St near the Ipswich Museum, this newly reopened pub has an appealing local feel and serves some excellent British food from a blackboard menu – lamb tenderloin, sardines, steak and celeriac mash, fish and chips – in a buzzy, pubby atmosphere. Mon–Sat noon–2.30pm & 6–9pm, Sun noon–3pm.

Brewery Tap Cliff Rd, Cliff Quay, IP3 0AT ☎01473 225501, ☻thebrewerytap.org. Just beyond the showy developments of the Waterfront, the *Brewery Tap* is almost the perfect boozer – a dockside pub, plumb by the entrance to what's left of the town's port, with a warm welcome, lots of space and great food. Mains go for £9–12 and include such delights as pork belly and polenta and venison sausages and onion gravy, and more pickled eggs than you're ever likely to see. It also hosts live music and serves a great selection of beers, including Suffolk Calvors lager and their own Cliff Quay brews. A real haven in a pretty unappealing part of town, though only a 10min walk from the more obvious bars and restaurants of the Waterfront district. Mon 6–9.30pm, Tues–Sat noon–2.30pm & 6–9.30pm, Sun 10.30am–8pm.

Butt and Oyster The Quay, Pin Mill, IP9 1JW ☎01473 780764, ☻debeninns.co.uk/buttandoyster. This quarry-tiled seventeenth-century pub has a great riverside location up the estuary from central Ipswich, and is well worth the short drive out of the town, not least because it serves food all day – decent pub grub mainly, and great sharing platters. Some people of a certain age might recognize it from the TV series, *Lovejoy*, in which it starred as the Three Ducks. Daily noon–9.15pm.

Dove Street Inn 76 St Helens St, IP4 2LA ☎01473 211270, ☻dovestreetinn.co.uk. Just outside the city centre, this is one of Ipswich's best locals, deceptively large inside, with a back room and courtyard and a cosy bar in the front. Lots of real ales (they host regular beer festivals), and an unusually wide choice of bottled beers too. They and also serve a hearty menu of home-made chilli, curries, beef and ale stew for £5–6, and a great cheese and crackers plate for £6. Daily noon–11.45pm.

Isaac's 7 Wherry Quay, IP4 1AS ☎01473 259952,

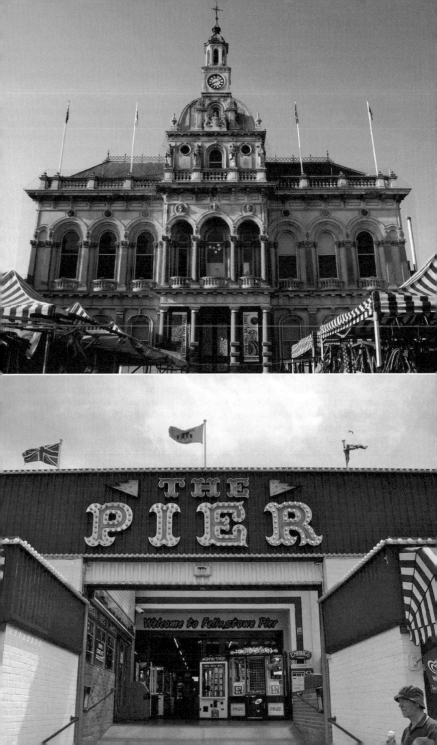

ⓦisaaclord.org. Waterfront café and pub with tables outside on the quay. Its various levels and huge courtyard can be party central some evenings. Food ranges from hearty cooked breakfasts to club sandwiches, steaks, burgers and more. Daily noon–6pm; adjoining café daily 7.30am–6pm.

Mannings 8 Cornhill, IP1 1DD ☎01473 254170. Well-established city-centre pub from whose accommodating yet unpretentious sixteenth-century interior you can watch the comings and goings on the square. Some outside seating, too, and a garden at the back. If you're hungry, feast on their doorstep sandwiches or bowls of chips with various toppings. Mon–Sat 11am–11pm, Sun noon–5pm.

The Swan King St, IP1 1EG ☎01473 252485. Long-running pub which is one of the better city centre venues for a drink, but is also one of the best night-time venues for music, with regular live bands – big with students. Mon–Wed noon–11pm, Thurs noon–midnight, Fri & Sat noon–1am, Sun 4–10.30pm.

SHOPS

Cornhill, right in the centre of Ipswich, hosts a regular, mainly food market (Tues, Thurs, Fri & Sat).

Jimmy's Farm Shop Pannington Hall Lane, IP9 2AR ☎0844 493 8088, ⓦjimmysfarm.com. One of the best farm shops you'll find, selling all manner of meat and poultry, sausages and bacon, from the farm's rare-breed pigs, as well as fruit and veg – and only a 10min drive from the centre of town. Daily 9.30am–5pm.

Memorable Cheeses 10 Dial Lane, IP1 1DL ☎01473 257315, ⓦmemorablecheeses.co.uk. There's not a great deal of competition, but this is the town centre's most well-stocked deli by a mile, with an excellent choice of chocolates, jams and chutneys, wine and beer and, of course, cheese. Mon 9am–4pm, Tues–Sat 9am–5.15pm.

Suffolk Food Hall Wherstead, IP9 2AB ☎01473 786610, ⓦsuffolkfoodhall.co.uk. It's a fair way out of the centre of Ipswich, in the shadow of the Orwell bridge, but the Suffolk Food Hall is probably the best one-stop shop for local produce, with a butcher's, deli, wet fish shop, bakery and much more besides. They host lots of foodie events, too. Mon–Sat 9am–6pm, Sun 10.30am–4pm.

Felixstowe

Like Ipswich, **FELIXSTOWE** perhaps gets a worse press than it deserves. It's the largest container port in the UK, and one of the biggest in Europe, the target destination of the giant trucks and lorries that travel in convoys down the A14. But it's also a well-developed seaside resort, and while it's not the most glamorous place on the Suffolk Coast, it's not the worst either, with a pier and seafront promenade backed by subtropical gardens that edges a long shingle beach, and a pleasant town centre on the cliff above. There's not all that much to see once you've strolled the prom and gone to the end of the pier or taken a dip in the sea, but you certainly wouldn't be aware of its port activities if you just stayed in this part of town, apart from the distant cranes on the skyline. Bear in mind too the waterside village of Felixstowe Ferry, where you can take a foot ferry across the Deben river mouth to Bawdsey on the far side.

The seafront and town centre

Felixstowe's **seafront** is a fairly traditional English affair, with well-tended gardens and a promenade lined by mainly Edwardian hotels and B&Bs along Sea Road and Undercliff Road West. There's a run-down **pier** and a hideous but occasionally useful leisure centre, but none of the seaside tack you'll find in, say, Yarmouth, and there's even a hut selling fresh fish not far from the pier. Close by the *Alex* restaurant, Bent Hill winds up to the **town centre** above – similarly ordinary, focused on the one main shop-lined street of Hamilton Road, and giving way to a quiet suburban network of Edwardian streets that spreads out on both sides.

The port

Bus #77 from Felixstowe Station

Most of Felixstowe's sights – such as they are – are in the area around the **port**, an area

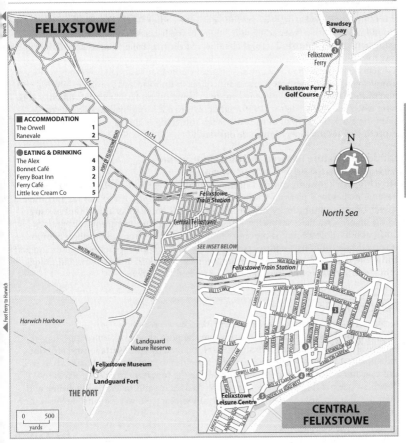

that has its own unique appeal. You can watch the ships pass by from a viewpoint right by the docks, in the shadow of giant dockside cranes, joining the locals to gaze out across the channel to Essex while sipping tea from the car park tea hut. You can also take the foot ferry to Harwich from here, visit the port's old fort and tramp through the duney grasses of the nearby nature reserve.

Felixstowe Museum

Viewpoint Rd, IP11 7JG • June–Sept Wed & Sun 1–5.30pm; otherwise just Sun and bank hols 1–5.30pm • £1 • ☎ 01394 674355, ⓦ felixstowe-museum.co.uk

Right by the main channel, **Felixstowe Museum** is an enthusiastically run local museum that focuses on nearby Landguard Fort and both the seafaring and wartime history of the town, with model aircraft and ships, paintings and other bits and pieces that help to paint a picture of Felixstowe past and present.

Landguard Fort

Viewpoint Rd, IP11 3TW • April–Oct daily 10am–5pm, June–Sept till 6pm • £3.50; EH • ☎ 07749 695523, ⓦ landguard.com

The pentagon-shaped **Landguard Fort** guards the estuaries of the Orwell and Stour, and dates mainly from the first part of the eighteenth century, although there were fortifications at least two hundred years before that. Originally ordered by Henry VIII,

6

it was on active service most of the time until the end of World War II. You can wander around at will with a free audioguide, taking in the barrack rooms, soldiers' washrooms, the long corridors and chambers of the magazine stores that run right the way round the fort, and the bastions up above, which give a good idea of how effective a defensive position the fort enjoys. The great thing about Landguard, though, is its untouched quality: there are a few mannequins in uniform and a small exhibition and film of its history, but otherwise its empty, echoing rooms have been left much as they were when the soldiers left in 1956, right down to a few original sticks of furniture. Even the clock on the wall of the outer keep still works – almost as if they were expecting to resume operations here one day.

Landguard Nature Reserve and Bird Observatory

Viewpoint Rd, IP11 3TW • Open all the time • ☎ 01394 673782, ⓦ lbo.org.uk

Stretching back towards central Felixstowe from Landguard Fort, **Landguard Nature Reserve** makes for a pleasant stroll after the claustrophobic corridors of the fort itself, a stretch of grassy, hummocky shingle and sand that's home to an array of interesting edible plants – sea kale, sea rocket – and a variety of spring and autumn migratory birds, and in summer ringed plovers, which you can view from a bird observatory here. It's an odd location, part nature reserve, part military dumping ground, full of concrete and metal detritus from the nearby fort complex, but it's an atmospheric and unique spot – and shows yet another side to multi faceted Felixstowe.

Felixstowe Ferry

Buses #172 and #173 (8 daily; 10min from Great Eastern Square) to Woodbridge drop off at Felixstowe Ferry

On the opposite side of central Felixstowe to the port, the town's most appealing enclave is the tiny village of **Felixstowe Ferry**, marked by two Martello towers about a mile north of Felixstowe proper, a huddle of houses, beach huts and boatyards as well as a café and a pub (see opposite). You can take the **foot ferry** from here across to Bawdsley (see p.239), where the *Boatyard Café* does tea and snacks at lunchtime and there are also a couple of stalls by the boatyard selling fresh wet fish and shellfish, for example **Springtide Fish**.

ARRIVAL AND DEPARTURE

FELIXSTOWE

By train Felixstowe's train station is a 5min walk from the top end of Hamilton Rd; to get there turn left onto High Rd West and it's on the left. It's the end of the line so the only connections are with Ipswich (hourly; 25min).

By bus Buses stop outside the train station, at Great Eastern Square, opposite the *Orwell Hotel*, on Hamilton Rd, and just to the north on High Rd West.
Destinations include Felixstowe Docks and Felixstowe Ferry (both every 40min); Ipswich (every 15min; 40min); Woodbridge (every 2hr; 35min).

By boat Perhaps the nicest way to arrive in Felixstowe is by foot ferry – either from Bawdsey just across the river from Felixstowe Ferry (every 30min: April & Oct 10am–5pm; May–Sept 10am–6pm; £1.80 one-way, £2.50 return, with bike £3.50 & £5; ☎ 07709 411511) or from Harwich across the river from Felixstowe Docks (May–Aug daily every 2hr; 9.45am–5pm; Easter & Sept weekends only; £4 one-way; bikes £2; ☎ 07919 911440, ⓦ www.harwichharbourferry .com).

INFORMATION AND TOURS

Tourist office On the seafront next door to the town hall at 91 Undercliff Rd West (Mon–Fri 9am–5.30pm, Sat 9am–5pm; ☎ 01394 276770).

Tours The Old Smokey mini train goes up and down the promenade every day in school holidays; otherwise weekends only (10am–5pm; £2, children £1.50).

ACCOMMODATION

The Orwell Hamilton Rd, IP11 7DX ☎ 01394 285511, ⓦ theorwellhotel.co.uk. At the top end of the high street, this resolutely traditional hotel, housed in a grand red-brick

building 5–10min walk from the seafront, has sixty nice en-suite double rooms. With palatial and beautifully maintained public areas, a clubby bar and restaurant, the hotel is perfectly in tune with the Edwardian ambience of this part of Felixstowe. Free wi-fi throughout. **£56**

Ranevale 96 Ranelagh Rd, IP11 7HU ☎ 01394 270001, ⓦ ranevale.co.uk. This homely B&B is just a 5min walk from Hamilton Rd in Felixstowe town centre's peaceful Edwardian core. It's both human- and pet-friendly, with comfy and clean double rooms, and serves a fine full English breakfast. **£70**

EATING AND DRINKING

The Alex 123 Undercliff Rd West, IP11 2AF ☎ 01394 282958, ⓦ alexcafebar.co.uk. Ever-popular seafront café and restaurant serving excellent food all day in its downstairs café (try the eggs Benedict and smoked salmon at £5.95) and posher, more substantial fare in its upstairs brasserie – skate wings, mussels, steaks – for around £5 a starter, £9 a main. There's always a crowd, and it's the buzziest place in Felixstowe by some way. Café daily 9.30am–9.30pm; brasserie Wed–Sun 11am–9.30pm.

Bonnet Café 1b Hamilton Rd, IP11 7AX ☎ 01394 282310, ⓦ bonnetcafe.co.uk. Right on the main street in the upper part of Felixstowe, this posh bakery does sandwiches and baguettes and really good hot lunches (11.30am–3pm): bangers and mash, shepherd's pie, good salads – as well as great cakes and afternoon tea. It also sells handmade chocolates. Mon–Sat 10am–4pm.

Ferry Boat Inn Felixstowe Ferry, IP11 9RZ ☎ 01394 284203, ⓦ ferryboatinn.org.uk. This fifteenth-century inn sits picturesquely on the village green facing the sea wall. It's a cosy pub, with a low-beamed interior and lots of different nooks and corners, fine for a drink but also very popular for food, with a large menu featuring every kind of fish and chips for around £10, pies and steaks, chicken curry and – when in season – mussels; baguettes and ploughman's complete the picture. Tables on the green outside in summer. Mon–Sat noon–2pm & 6.30–9pm, Sun noon–2pm & 6.30–8.30pm.

Ferry Café Felixstowe Ferry, IP11 9RZ ☎ 01394 276305. This immaculately painted and very popular shack by the ferry quay in Felixstowe Ferry does good fish and chips, breakfasts, burgers and the like. Daily 9am–5pm.

Little Ice Cream Co 59–61 Undercliff Rd West, IP11 2AD ☎ 01394 670500, ⓦ littleicecream.co.uk. On the seafront opposite the leisure centre this coffee shop (with one other branch in Colchester) does home-made ice cream in loads of flavours as well as cakes, pancakes, waffles, sandwiches and coffee. Sun–Fri 10am–5.30pm, Sat 10am–8pm.

6

The Suffolk coast

THE SCALLOP, ALDEBURGH BEACH (P.250)

The Suffolk coast

The Suffolk coast feels a little detached from the rest of the county: the road and rail lines from Ipswich to Lowestoft funnel traffic a few miles inland for most of the way, along the busy A12, while patches of marsh, heath and woodland make the separation still more complete. It's a wilder region than you might expect, but it's also home to established resorts like Aldeburgh and Southwold, whose worldly charms are an appealing contrast to the more remote delights of Shingle Street and Dunwich, and the nature reserves at Dunwich Heath and Minsmere. There are other, cultural highlights too – the earthen mounds of Sutton Hoo, the medieval delights of Blythburgh and Framlingham and the Cold War spookiness of Rendlesham Forest. But the entire coast and its hinterland repays a visit: it's one of Britain's most diverse and untouched regions.

7

The coast really starts with **Felixstowe** (see p.228), partly because you can go no further without taking the first of the Suffolk Coast's many foot ferries across the Deben River. Across the river, **Bawdsey** is famous as the home of the last war's radar efforts, and is just a few miles from the unashamedly parochial town of **Woodbridge** – which is close to the Anglo-Saxon burial mounds of **Sutton Hoo** and the wilds of **Rendlesham Forest**. Further north, there's the relative isolation of tiny **Orford** and the nature reserves you can reach from its harbour, and beyond here the upmarket resort of **Aldeburgh**, famed for its links with Benjamin Britten and the **Aldeburgh Festival** – East Anglia's most compelling cultural gathering, which takes place every June at nearby **Snape Maltings**.

North of Aldeburgh, **Thorpeness** is an odd, purpose-built Edwardian resort village, while nearby **Leiston**, just inland, adds a dose of grit to the coast's predominantly genteel pleasures, a small town that punched far above its weight during the nineteenth-century Industrial Revolution and now supports the power station at nearby **Sizewell**, where two nuclear facilities are oddly plonked among the dunes and woods of Sizewell beach (and they're thinking of adding a third). Nearby **Saxmundham** is a pleasant town and major rail hub, while **Framlingham**, a few miles west of the A12 artery, is the region's most alluring market town, with a fantastic castle and a pleasantly prosperous centre with a handful of enticing places to eat. Back on the coastal strip, between Sizewell and Southwold, lies the most appealing stretch of Suffolk's coast, a wildish area of heath, marsh and woodland around the RSBP reserve at **Minsmere** and the National Trust-owned **Dunwich Heath** – great walking country at any time of year.

ALDEBURGH SEAFRONT

Highlights

❶ **Sutton Hoo, Woodbridge** One of the country's most evocative and best Anglo-Saxon sites, well preserved and explained by the National Trust. **See p.239**

❷ **Framlingham** A few miles inland from the coast, this market town represents the essence of provincial Suffolk, and has a couple of great attractions to boot. **See p.244.**

❸ **Fish huts, Aldeburgh** There's nothing quite like choosing and buying fish from the seafront at Aldeburgh and going home and cooking it up for tea. **See p.248**

❹ **Minsmere** This RSPB reserve gets busy, but somehow soaks up people into its glorious mixture of reedbeds, woodland and heath. **See p.258**

❺ **Holy Trinity, Blythburgh** This landmark building is one of Suffolk's finest churches, with wonderfully preserved medieval features. **See p.264**

❻ **Oulton Broad** Lowestoft's watery heart, and a perfect introduction to the glories of the Broads further north. **See p.270**

HIGHLIGHTS ARE MARKED ON THE MAP ON P.236

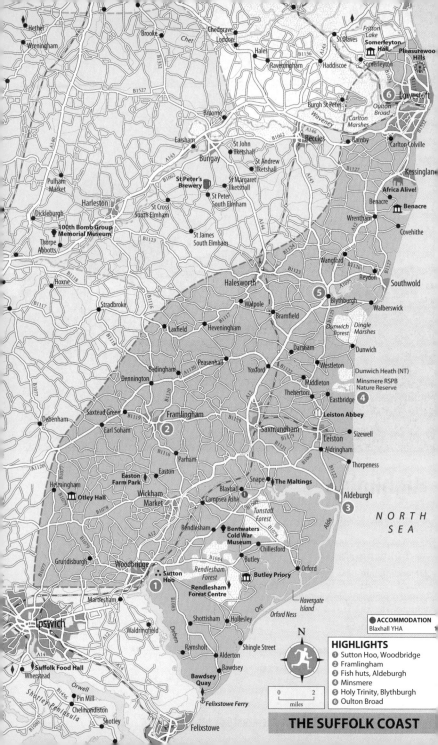

THE SUFFOLK COAST

HIGHLIGHTS
1 Sutton Hoo, Woodbridge
2 Framlingham
3 Fish huts, Aldeburgh
4 Minsmere
5 Holy Trinity, Blythburgh
6 Oulton Broad

ACCOMMODATION
Blaxhall YHA

N

NORTH SEA

0   2
miles

Dunwich itself was the Felixstowe of the Middle Ages, but got swallowed up by the sea long ago and now lies mostly beneath the waves. But it's a lovely spot, and is only an hour or so's walk along the coast from the pretty village of **Walberswick**, popular for its beach, its yearly crabbing festival and the foot ferry to the outskirts of **Southwold**. This is Suffolk's largest and most popular resort, with the most all-round metropolitan vibe of the entire coast, full of Londoners dreaming of relocating and some decent hotels and restaurants. Just inland, at the head of the deep Blyth estuary, **Blythburgh**'s church, with its enormous tower, is a landmark for miles around, and the most impressive medieval monument along the coast. Further inland still, **Halesworth** is, like Framlingham, the epitome of the self-sufficient Suffolk market town, while further up the coast grim reality takes over in **Lowestoft**, where the fishing industry limps on manfully alongside the town's ailing resort business, neither with a great deal of conviction. However, even Lowestoft is not entirely without interest, with a number of attractions both in and around the town, and up towards the Norfolk border. It's also the jumping-off point for **Oulton Broad** and the Broads in general (see p.270).

7

Woodbridge and around

If you came to England for the first time and only went to **WOODBRIDGE**, you would go away with a skewed but not entirely false sense of modern Britain. The town claims to be the best place to live in the country (though it has a few rivals for that in Suffolk alone); it was voted among the top foodie destinations in the UK by *Country Living* magazine recently; and it generally wins praise and plaudits for the easy-going, locally focused pace of life. Naturally, the folk of Woodbridge want to keep all this to themselves, and it's a better place to live than to visit, with a small and low-key selection of things to see. But its small centre is unspoilt and walkable, with an array of independent shops and cafés, good pubs and a couple of excellent places to stay, and an enticing riverside area down by the much-photographed Tide Mill. It's also within easy reach of **Sutton Hoo**, the most important Anglo-Saxon archeological site in the country.

Market Hill and around

The centre of Woodbridge focuses on the main shopping street of the **Thoroughfare** and, at the top of Church Street, **Market Hill**, a small square gathered around the Dutch-looking **Shire Hall**, built by Thomas Seckford in 1575. This now houses a small **museum** devoted to the Suffolk Punch, a heavy-working-horse breed that was revived in the 1960s (Easter to end Sept Tues, Thurs & Sat 2–5pm; £2).

Woodbridge Museum

5a Market Hill, IP12 4AU • Easter to end Oct Thurs–Sun 10am–4pm, daily during school hols • £1 • ☎ 01394 380502

Opposite the Shire Hall, **Woodbridge Museum** is just a couple of rooms really, with Anglo-Saxon finds from nearby excavations at Butley and a case of displays on Sutton Hoo, with replicas of the finds and a model of the ship, plus exhibits relating to Thomas Seckford – sometime adviser to Elizabeth I, local benefactor and the builder of

---

ELECTRIFY YOUR TRIP

LEV are a Suffolk-based company that specialize in importing **electrically powered bikes** from Holland. They're based in Leiston, 5–7 Valley Rd (Mon–Sat 9am–5pm; ☎ 01728 830817, ⦿ electricbikehire.co.uk), and they rent their bikes from here and other locations up and down the coast – usually hotels and guesthouses – including Woodbridge, Aldeburgh, Thorpeness, Saxmundham and Southwold. Rates are £24.50 a day or £96 a week.

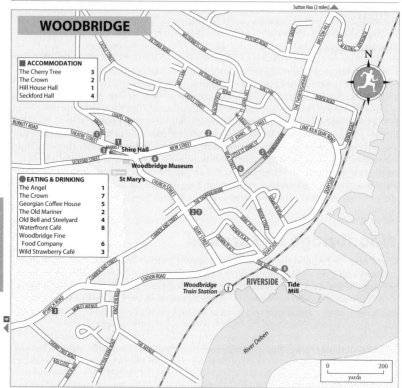

7

nearby Seckford Hall. There are also sections on the war years, and the second half of the twentieth century, when Woodbridge became, in the words of the museum "the perfect place to live".

St Mary's

11 Market Hill, IP12 4LU • ⓦ stmaryswoodbridge.org

At the top of Church Street, just off Market Hill, Woodbridge's parish church of **St Mary** is a flint Gothic building from the mid-fifteenth century. Inside it has an octagonal font decorated with reliefs depicting the seven sacraments plus one of the Crucifixion, which sits in the corner with the painted wooden panels from the church's original rood screen, now preserved behind glass.

Riverside

Woodbridge is situated on a river, the Deben – in days gone by its main industry was shipbuilding – but you could spend a day here and not know it. The **Riverside** lies apart from the centre, on the far side of the railway tracks. It's no less picturesque for that, and serves as a marina for Woodbridge's yachties, but has managed to avoid being overly spruced up, despite the refurbished white bulk of the clapboard **Tide Mill** (May–Sept daily 11am–5pm, plus Easter & weekends April & Oct; £2.50), which houses a small museum about the mill machinery plus other local displays and artworks.

Sutton Hoo

Tranmer House, IP12 3DJ • Jan, Feb, Nov & Dec Sat & Sun 11am–4pm; March Wed–Sun 10.30am–5pm; April–Oct daily 10.30am–5pm •
£7.20, tours £2.50; NT • ☎ 01394 389700, ⓦ nationaltrust.org.uk/main/w-suttonhoo

Just outside Woodbridge, off the Orford road on the far side of the River Deben,
Sutton Hoo – "hoo" means promontory or headland in ancient local dialect – is one of
the most important Anglo-Saxon archeological sites in the country. Now owned by the
National Trust, it was discovered by local landowner Edith Pretty and amateur
archeologist Basil Brown in 1939, who excavated a number of burial mounds in the
remote countryside here, unearthing the forty-oar burial ship of an Anglo-Saxon
warrior king, packed with his most valuable possessions, from a splendid iron and
tinted-bronze helmet through to his intricately worked gold and jewelled ornaments.
It's now believed to be the tomb of Redwald, king of East Anglia, who died in 625.

The focus is the **exhibition hall**, where a very well-mounted series of displays includes
a mock-up of how they think the king may have been laid in his ship, although sadly
there's not much in the way of treasure, as most of this is kept in the British Museum
(including the famous helmet you see on all the Sutton Hoo posters). A short film tells
the story of the finds and the Anglo-Saxons in general, and there are details of what was
found in the other mounds, including another young warrior buried with his weapons
and his horse next to him – his sword, belt buckles, even a comb, are on display. Next
door to the exhibition hall, a **visitor centre** houses a ticket office, shop and café.

The **site** itself, just a short walk from the visitor centre, is very atmospheric, and there
are a couple of viewing platforms, one right by the mound where they discovered the
ship (which would have been hauled up from the river, several hundred metres below).

Bawdsey

To the south of Sutton Hoo, the village of **BAWDSEY** sits almost at the end of the main
road, and as such feels like the back of beyond – a mood only enhanced by the shady
churchyard of its church, **St Mary the Virgin**. Inside are memorials to the local Quilter
family, who lived in nearby Bawdsey Manor, and the Cavells who occupied Bawdsey
Hall, including a short spiel on Edith Cavell (see p.44). Look also at the Bawdsey altar
frontal, embroidered with figures of God, Jesus and various saints in thirteenth-century
Flanders (though the bolder stitching is Victorian).

Bawdsey Manor

Just outside the village, **Bawdsey Manor** looks older than it is, a Victorian Gothic mansion
that was built in the 1870s by William Quilter as a lavish holiday home, and which in 1936
became the secret Ministry of Defence research establishment that developed radar under
Robert Watson Watt – an invention without which, arguably, World War II would have been
lost. It occupies a fantastic location, hugging a gorgeous stretch of the coast and overlooking
the Deben estuary, but unfortunately it's now used for conferences and functions and is pretty
much off-limits to the public – although you can see the main house and extensive gardens
on the occasional guided tour (under the ⓦ invitationtoview.co.uk network).

A WALK ALONG THE DEBEN ESTUARY AT RAMSHOLT

About five miles south of Woodbridge, **Ramsholt** is not so much a village as a handful of
houses above a riverside pub. You can do a great shortish **walk** (45min–1hr) from the
Ramsholt Arms (see p.242) following the estuary inland from the pub and then up into the
woods after about a mile. Bear right in the woods, keeping the sandy quarry to your left, before
joining a farm track to the round-towered church of **All Saints**. Turn right here, back towards
the river and then edge the fields and then turn right, following the signs through the woods
and a few houses to join up with the main road above the *Ramsholt Arms*.

The concrete bunker of the original **transmitter block**, which played a crucial role in the Battle of Britain, is open on sporadic Sundays and Mondays throughout the summer (12.30–4pm; £3, children free; ☎07821 162879, ⊛bawdseyradar.org.uk).

Bawdsey Quay

A mile or so from the village of Bawdsey, **Bawdsey Quay** is no more than a strip of houses, a small visitor centre and the grounds of Bawdsey Manor looking across the mouth of the Deben River to old Felixstowe. You can take the foot ferry to the other side, though you may need to hail the boatman from the quay, and there is car parking on the quay and in the woods behind, and meals at the **Boathouse Café** (see p.242).

Rendlesham Forest

Rendlesham Forest Centre, IP12 3NF • Daily dawn–dusk • Car park £3.10

Immediately east of Woodbridge, **Rendlesham Forest** is a Forestry Commission-owned stretch of coniferous woodland and heath – a beautiful area that's great walking, cycling and indeed camping country. The forest hit the national headlines in 1980 when there were a series of UFO sightings here that have since passed into the folklore of conspiracy theories, partly because it is near Bentwaters USAF base and RAF Woodbridge.

The **Rendlesham Forest Centre** has parking and a small information centre with leaflets detailing "UFO Trails", bike rental and forest camping nearby, and is a convergence point for bike trails and footpaths (there are three detailed circular trails you can do from here) – although the forest has any number of other car parks and clearings where you can park up and hike off into the woods.

LIGHTS IN THE NIGHT: THE RENDLESHAM FOREST AFFAIR

No one outside of Suffolk would have heard of Rendlesham Forest if it wasn't for the events of December 1980, when on an evening before Christmas a number of air-force personnel witnessed strange lights in the trees and a "craft" or "object" with triangular landing gear. Since dubbed "**Britain's Roswell**", it was at first thought that an aircraft had crashed in the trees. The police were called but apparently could find no evidence of anything much, claiming that the lights must have been those from nearby Orford Ness lighthouse. The site was re-visited on Boxing Day and then again two days later, when scorch marks were discovered on the trees, higher levels of radiation recorded and more lights were seen, but again nothing was done – and nothing was reported or revealed about the sightings until a couple of years later, when a memo by a local base commander, Colonel Charles Halt (the so-called "Halt Memo") was made public. It referred to the sightings in quite a lot of detail, mentioning how long the lights remained in the air (several hours) and the depressions that were found where the craft was said to have landed. Halt clearly felt that something unusual had been going on, and couldn't explain what it was.

To this day the incident has not been officially investigated, and this has of course allowed the conspiracy theories to flourish, but it's worth noting that as recently as 2010 Colonel Halt, now retired, defended his memo, claiming that the sightings had been deliberately covered up by the MOD, USAF and the local police. There are many who believe that it was the cover-up of some sort of secret military exercise rather than UFOs, and it hasn't helped that the MOD recently admitted that a number of files relating to the incident had "disappeared". What really happened in Rendlesham will probably never been known, but there's no doubt that it's fun to speculate, and many do – see ⊛ianrobpath.com/ufo/rendlesham.htm or ⊛uk-ufo.org/condign/rendsec.htm, if only to see just how long a story like this can run, and run, and run, and take one of the UFO trails that run through the woods from the Forest Centre (see above).

Bentwaters Cold War Museum

Building 134, Bentwaters Park, Rendlesham, IP12 2TW • End April to early Oct Sat & Sun 10am–4pm • £5 • ☎ 07588 877020, ⓦ bcwm.org.uk

Housed in the former control tower, bang in the middle of the airfield that formerly served both the USAF and RAF Woodbridge, the **Bentwaters Cold War Museum** only serves to enhance the atmosphere of military secrecy that hangs over this part of Suffolk. Here you'll find operations rooms, mostly fitted with original equipment, that not only functioned during World War II and the Cold War but also as recently as 1986, when the US bombed Colonel Gaddaffi's complex in Libya, and during the first Gulf War.

Shingle Street

About eight miles southeast of Woodbridge, across the marshes on the far side of the village of Hollesley, **SHINGLE STREET** is a very desolate place. Its name is a misnomer as it's probably the only settlement in Suffolk without streets of any kind – just a long line of bungalows and cottages facing directly onto the beach and the North Sea. Until a series of top secret documents were declassified in 1992, well before their official 2021 expiry date, all sorts of rumours circulated about Shingle Street, most luridly that around three thousand German soldiers, part of an attempted invasion force, were killed in a firefight here. Most of this has proved to be wartime propaganda, and what happened during World War II was not that remarkable though a little scandalous: it was forcibly evacuated in 1940 in anticipation of a German invasion, and three years later was a venue for the testing of new, experimental bombs. After the war it was deemed uninhabitable because of the number of mines that had been laid on its beach, and it wasn't until the late 1940s that these were cleared and people began to drift back. It has never regained the prosperity it once had, and is now mainly made up of holiday homes. You may find its eerie isolation compelling and even addictive, but without a holiday home of your own there's not much to keep you here, and you may be glad to head back inland to relative civilization.

7

ARRIVAL AND INFORMATION

WOODBRIDGE AND AROUND

By train Woodbridge is on the main Ipswich–Lowestoft line, and its train station is down in the riverside part of the centre.

Destinations (trains hourly): Ipswich (15min); Lowestoft (1hr 15min); Oulton Broad (1hr); Saxmundham (40min); Wickham Market (10min) .

By bus Buses stop at the so-called "Turban Centre", close by the Thoroughfare, and there are bus connections with Ipswich (lots of alternatives), Wickham Market (#62), Framlingham (#63), Aldeburgh, Leiston and Saxmundham (# 64), Orford (#71) and Rendlesham (#65).

Tourist office In Woodbridge train station (Mon–Fri 9am–5.30pm, Sat 9am–5pm; ☎ 01394 382240).

ACCOMMODATION

The Cherry Tree 73 Cumberland St, IP12 4AG ☎ 01394 384627, ⓦ www.thecherrytreepub.co.uk. Friendly, family-run pub on the edge of the centre, serving well-cooked pub food lunchtime and evenings and with three really nicely furnished rooms fashioned out of a clapboard barn in the back garden, one of which is large enough for a family. Flat-screen TVs, free wi-fi and parking, a 5min walk from Market Hill. **£90**

★ **The Crown** Thoroughfare, corner of Quay St, IP12 1AD ☎ 01394 384242, ⓦ thecrownatwoodbridge .co.uk. This updated pub, hotel and restaurant has ten double bedrooms, each individually designed with fresh and simple colours and a deliberately coastal, almost New England feel. There's a great restaurant and comfy bar downstairs, too, which serves a very good breakfast. **£145**

Forest Camping Butley, IP12 3NF ☎ 01394 450707, ⓦ forestcamping.co.uk. Lovely, dog-friendly campsite with good facilities, yet surrounded by the forest. Two people, car and a tent **£17**

★ **Hill House Hall** 30 Market Hill, IP12 4LU ☎ 01394 383890, ⓦ hillhousehall.com. Right on the main square, this hotel has the town's best and certainly most central location, and is certainly its most historic, a thirteenth-century building that was upgraded in Tudor times. There are three rooms in all – a double and family suite in the main building, and a double in a converted barn in the garden – and its beams and rickety floors are lovingly watched over by owner Sarenka Knight, who will tell you all about the building. Free wi-fi. **£75**

Seckford Hall Near Woodbridge, IP13 6NU ☎ 01394

385678, ⓦseckford.co.uk. Just outside town across the A12, Seckford Hall was the home of Thomas Seckford, a high-ranking official at the court of Elizabeth I and a local philanthropist, and his marvellously preserved sixteenth-century seat was converted some time ago to a four-star country-house hotel that does a good job of retaining the building's age and atmosphere while providing a decent degree of comfort. There's a lovely wood-panelled sitting room, the guest rooms are comfortable, with well-equipped and recently refurbished bathrooms, and there's free wi-fi throughout. There are also gardens to stroll through and a decent indoor pool in a separate complex. The main restaurant is a formal affair, serving a two-course menu for £31.50, but there's a more relaxed "Club" restaurant which does sandwiches and salads and a short menu of simple mains for £10–12. Breakfast extra; check online for deals. **£140–160**

EATING AND DRINKING

The Angel 2 Theatre St, IP12 4NE ☎01394 382660, ⓦtheangelwoodbridge.co.uk. Newly renovated pub with an area of comfy sofas and another, more pubby section, where you can enjoy its simple menu of fish and chips, sausage and mash, steaks and a few veggie dishes – easy stuff, but all locally sourced and beautifully cooked, for £9 a main dish. There is usually an interesting special or two on the board as well. Mon–Sat noon–2.30pm & 6–9pm, Sun noon–2.30pm.

Boathouse Café The Quay, Bawdsey, IP12 3AZ ☎07900 811826, ⓦwww.boathousecafe.co.uk. There's no better place to enjoy lunch than on the veranda of this homespun café, looking out over the Deben River, and serving home-made soups, sandwiches and full meals made with produce from the fish stalls across the river. March, April & Nov Fri–Sun 11am–5pm; May–Oct Thurs–Mon 11am–5pm.

★ **The British Larder** Orford Rd, Bromeswell, IP12 2PU ☎01394 460310, ⓦbritishlardersuffolk.co.uk. *The British Larder* is the epitome of the British gastropub, stripped down and spruced up and serving thoughtful and delicious, locally sourced menus – one a lunchtime list of deli platters, sandwiches and light hot meals for £11–12, the other a slightly more serious dinner menu with starters for about £7 and mains for £15. The service is lovely, and the cooking and presentation of a very high quality. Try the Orford smoked eel to start, followed by pan-roasted hake, braised pork belly or rump of lamb, or the Dingley Dell Platter, which is served both for lunch and as a dinnertime starter – heaven on a plate. Mon–Thurs noon–3pm & 6–9pm, Fri noon–3pm & 6–9.30pm, Sat noon–3.30pm & 6–9.30pm, Sun noon–3.30pm & 6–9pm.

★ **The Crown** Thoroughfare, corner Quay St, IP12 1AD ☎01394 384242, ⓦthecrownatwoodbridge.co.uk. Really good, well-established hotel-restaurant – the style is modern British, with a passionate attachment to English traditions and local suppliers. Considering the quality, it's not expensive either, with starters from £6.50 and mains from £15. Rightly listed as one of the country's top fifty gastropubs in the *Independent* in 2011. Kitchen: daily noon–3pm & 6–10pm; brunch served 10am–noon Sat & Sun.

Georgian Coffee House 47a Thoroughfare, IP12 1AH ☎01394 387292, ⓦgeorgiancoffeehouse.co.uk. Small café in the heart of town that's nothing special but makes for a handy place for light lunches, jackets and sandwiches. Mon–Sat 9am–5pm.

Old Bell and Steelyard 103 New St, IP12 1DZ ☎01394 382933, ⓦyeoldebellandsteelyard.co.uk. Great old timbered pub in a crooked building dating from 1549, with good beer, a garden and a games room out the back with everything from bar billiards to Trivial Pursuit. A good, simple menu, too, with pub grub staples from £8.95 and ploughman's, sandwiches and cheese platters from £3.95. Ask about the daily specials, and bear in mind that this place and the *Angel* are about the only places in Woodbridge serving food on a Monday night. Mon–Sat noon–2pm & 6–9pm, Sun noon–2pm & 7–9pm.

The Old Mariner 26 New St, IP12 1DX ☎01394 382679. Cosy old pub that serves food lunch and evening and usually has a wide choice of ales to enjoy in an interior of old quarry-tiled floor and ochre, nicotine-stained walls covered with rugby and nautical memorabilia. Food served noon–2pm & 7–9pm.

Ramsholt Arms Dock Rd, Ramsholt, IP13 3AB ☎01394 411229. About five miles south of Woodbridge, this riverside pub at Ramsholt (see box, p.239) sits right on the Deben estuary, with big picture windows overlooking the water, a homely, dog-friendly place with a large terrace and decent food – lots of fish dishes for around £10, a children's menu and more besides. Mon–Fri noon–2.30pm & 6–9pm, Sat & Sun noon–3pm & 6–9pm.

Waterfront Café The Granary, Tide Mill Way, IP2 1BY ☎01394 610333, ⓦwww.woodbridgefinefoodcompany.co.uk. Right opposite the Tide Mill in an old granary, this is a perfect place for tea and cake, or something more substantial from their full menu, which is crammed with locally sourced dishes – home-smoked salmon, rustic fish soup, local rabbit hotpot, fresh local crab, duck pâté or just a burger (most mains around £12.95). The same people run the Woodbridge Fine Food Company deli at 2a New St (Mon–Sat 9am–5pm; ☎01394 610000). Daily 10am–5pm.

Wild Strawberry Café 19a Market Hill, IP12 4LX ☎01394 388881, ⓦwildstrawberrycafe.co.uk. Good coffee, breakfasts and lunches are served in this bright modern café right on Woodbridge's main square. Mon–Fri 8am–5pm, Sat 9am–4pm; breakfast 8am–noon, lunch noon–2.30pm.

Wickham Market and around

Not much more than a large village really, **WICKHAM MARKET** lies just off the A12, a few miles to the north of Woodbridge, and has a pretty main square that's home to most of the town's commercial activity, and its spiritual too, in the shape of the nearby church of **All Saints**, with its spired hexagonal tower. There's little else to Wickham Market, but just outside are two of the finest examples of sixteenth-century country houses in the UK – **Otley Hall** and **Helmingham Hall** (though these are often inaccessible), and the family attraction of **Easton Farm Park**.

Easton Farm Park

Easton, IP13 0EQ • Mid-March to Sept daily 10.30am–6pm, half-term daily 10.30am–4pm, Christmas hols daily 11am–3pm; farmers' markets 4th Sat of the month • £7.95, children £6.75, family tickets £28 • ☎ 01728 746475, ⓦ eastonfarmpark.co.uk

Just a few miles outside Woodbridge on the far side of the A12, this kid-friendly farm is a popular day out for families, with goats, sheep and rare breed cattle, Suffolk Punch horses, train and cart rides. It's a full-on affair for the most part, but does also have attractive trails through the meadows by the river.

Otley Hall

Hall Lane, Otley, IP6 9PA **Gardens** May–Sept Wed noon–5pm • £2.50 **House** Selected days throughout the summer (see website) or groups by appointment • £7.50 • ☎ 01473 890264, ⓦ otleyhall.co.uk

About four miles west of Wickham Market, **Otley Hall** is a sixteenth-century moated manor house, set in well-groomed gardens, which is perhaps the county's best example of late-medieval architecture – although it's privately owned and only occasionally open to visitors. If you can't coincide with the dates of one of its tours, make do with the gardens, which stretch to ten acres and include various Elizabethan garden horticultural specialities – for example a "knot garden", a "herber" and other eighteenth- and nineteenth-century-style terrains.

Helmingham Hall

Helmingham, IP14 6EF • May to mid-Sept Tues, Wed, Thurs & Sun noon–5pm • £6 • ☎ 01473 890799 • ⓦ helmingham.com

Almost midway between Wickham Market and Stowmarket, **Helmingham Hall** has been the home of the Tollemache family for around five centuries, a brewing dynasty who threw in their lot with the Cobbolds of Ipswich to create the Suffolk Tolly Cobbold business (although this too sadly no longer exists). You can't visit the house, but the estate and its gardens are open during the summer months and are vast – a fabulous mixture of borders, orchards and artfully planned walks and vistas. They also run cookery courses throughout the summer in the hall's kitchens.

ARRIVAL AND DEPARTURE

WICKHAM MARKET AND AROUND

By train Wickham Market's station is on the branch line from Ipswich and Lowestoft and is situated three miles outside the town in the village of Campsea Ashe.

By bus Plenty of buses from Ipswich and Woodbridge.

ACCOMMODATION

Easton Farm Holiday Cottages Easton, IP13 0EQ ☎ 01728 746475, ⓦ eastonfarmpark.co.uk/accommodation. Three beautifully converted holiday cottages of varying sizes, all well furnished and homely, plus another at the Aldeburgh end of the beach at Thorpeness. One week **£950**

The Old Rectory Campsea Ashe, IP13 0PU ☎ 01728 746524, ⓦ theoldrectorysuffolk.com. This boutique B&B, housed in a beautiful Georgian house in the village of Campsea Ashe, is very handy if you're travelling by train, as it's walking distance from Wickham Market's station. It's also equidistant between Woodbridge and Orford and equally convenient for both. It has seven imaginatively furnished double bedrooms – prices depend on room and day of the week, and rates include a gorgeous breakfast. Pleasant gardens too, where the converted coach house is a wonderful family option. **£90**

Orchard Campsite 28 Spring Lane, IP13 0SJ ☎ 01728 746170, ⓦ orchardcampsite.co.uk. Just outside Wickham Market, this was judged "campsite of the year" in 2010 by *Camping Magazine*, and quite right too – it's a great, family-orientated place, run by the same people for twenty years, and set among both meadows and woodland which stretch down to the river. It allows campfires, and will even sell you the wood to start your own. It also has a gypsy caravan for rent, and there's free wi-fi that works across much of the site. All in from **£16**

EATING AND DRINKING

Revetts 81 High St, IP13 0RA ☎ 01728 746263. Fantastic local butcher and deli that also sells cakes, pastries and a great selection of French wine. Mon & Wed 7.30am–1pm, Tues & Thurs 7.30am–1pm & 2–4.30pm, Fri 7.30am–1pm & 2–5pm, Sat 7am–1pm.

Teapot Tearoom 46 The Hill, IP13 0HE ☎ 01728 748079. Right on the main square, this is the perfect place for a cup of coffee or a light lunch, a buzzy place full of locals that has cakes, sandwiches, jackets and salads for £4–6. Mon–Sat 9am–5pm.

7

Framlingham and around

FRAMLINGHAM, or "Fram", as it's known to locals, is small-town Suffolk *par excellence*, grouped around a triangular market square and with an enticing, parochial feel typical of this part of the county. For once, this is matched by a couple of heavyweight attractions at the top of its main street – the castle and parish church.

Framlingham Castle

Church St, IP13 9BP • April–June, Sept & Oct daily 10am–5pm; July & Aug daily 10am–6pm; Nov–March Mon & Thurs–Sun 10am–4pm • £6, children £3, family tickets £15; EH • ☎ 01728 724819, ⓦ www.english-heritage.org.uk

The crenellations of **Framlingham Castle** cut a classic shape at the top of Church Street. The castle dates from the twelfth century, and was the seat of the dukes of Norfolk. It's little more than a shell inside, but the curtain wall, with its thirteen towers, has survived almost intact, a splendid example of medieval military architecture, topped by ornamental Tudor chimney stacks. Unfortunately nothing remains of the castle's Great Hall, where Mary Tudor was proclaimed Queen of England in 1553; Mary was responsible for freeing the Duke Of Norfolk, Thomas Howard, from the Tower (see opposite). You can get good views of the castle from the outside by following the footpaths that lead around the moat and down to and around the lake or "mere" below, where you can see across the valley to Framlingham College.

St Michael's Church

Fore St, IP13 9BJ • ⓦ www.onesuffolk.co.uk/StMichaelsChurchFram

The large thirteenth-century church of **St Michael** is extraordinary, not because of the building, although this is impressive enough, but for the sepulchral monuments of the **Howard family**, perhaps the finest array of monumental sixteenth-century sculpture in the country, and also a brilliant snapshot of court life and relationships during the time of the Tudors.

The church has other highlights before you get to the tombs: the fourteenth-century font in the north aisle, a seventeenth-century organ, one of only two still in use in the UK, and the roof, whose carved fan vaulting fitted around the nave windows is ingenious, and contemporary with the church. But it's the **tombs** that steal the show, at the far eastern end of the church, in a chancel that was enlarged to accommodate them in the 1400s. To the right of the high altar, the tomb of Thomas Howard, Duke of Norfolk, is surrounded by the twelve Apostles, and the niches they stand in support the praying effigies of Thomas and his wife Anne, the daughter of Edward IV. Thomas Howard lived dangerously: he was a rival to Thomas Cromwell, and indirectly sent the latter to the gallows, shortly after which Henry VIII wedded his niece Katherine. Later he had the chancel enlarged to accommodate the family tombs, and he was lucky to survive to see its completion, for in 1546 he was charged with treason and would have been executed but for the death of the king and an eleventh-hour pardon. Not so lucky was Henry Howard, in the coloured alabaster tomb on the far left, who was executed by Henry for the same offence – hence the coronet which rests by his side, not on his head. To the left of the altar is the tomb of Henry Fitzroy, an illegitimate son of Henry VIII (the only one the king ever acknowledged), who married Thomas Howard's daughter, Mary, in 1533.

Dennington

A couple of miles north of Framlingham, **Dennington** is a tiny place but is home to an intriguing church in **St Mary's**, whose medieval benches and pews sport a fantastical series of carvings showing wild and folkloric figures and beasts. In particular there is a rare representation of a sciapod, a mythical creature that avoided sunlight by shading itself with its one, large foot – according to legend, sciapods would die if they smelt contaminated air, so they carried sniffable fresh fruit around with them everywhere. Elsewhere, and equally unusual, is a rare pyx canopy over the altar (pyx was the vessel in which the Holy Sacrament was kept), one of only two such surviving canopies in Europe.

7

ARRIVAL AND DEPARTURE   FRAMLINGHAM AND AROUND

By bus Buses stop on Bridge St in the centre of Framlingham and there are regular connections (every 30min–1hr) to Ipswich (1hr 20min) and to Woodbridge (2hr; 30min).

ACCOMMODATION

The Crown Market Hill, IP13 9AN ☎01728 723521, ⓦframlinghamcrown.co.uk. Right in the centre of town, this sixteenth-century coaching inn, all flagstones, oak beams and creaky floors has fourteen rooms. They are decently furnished and nice enough, and there's a cosy bar downstairs and a pleasant courtyard in which to while away summer evenings. **£100–130**

EATING AND DRINKING

Dancing Goat Café 33 Market Hill, IP13 9BA ☎01728 621434. Popular joint during the morning and at lunchtimes when locals sip coffee and munch cakes, sandwiches and panini outside on the main square. Mon–Sat 8.45am–5pm.

Lemon Tree 3 Church St, IP13 9BE ☎01728 621232, ⓦthelemontreebistro.com. Somewhat upscale café with a contemporary menu focused on locally sourced ingredients, with starters for £5–6, mains mostly £10–15. Think rump of local lamb, rib-eye steak, sea bream with crushed new potatoes, or crab and chilli linguini. Pizzas too. Tues–Sat 10am–2pm, Wed–Sat also 6–9pm, Sun 11am–2pm.

★ **Station Hotel** Station Rd, IP13 9EE ☎01728 723455, ⓦthestationhotel.net. Not much from the outside, but this old pub, next door to a workshop specializing in British bikes, is a real haven on the inside, with a stripped-down interior that caters for local drinkers and foodies alike. The lunch menu features Irish stew, kedgeree, mussels, burgers and more for £8–10 (roasts on Sundays). The evening menu is less rustic and slightly more expensive (£6–8 starters, £10–16 mains) – venison fillets, lamb rump, pork belly, sea bass, oysters. Really good food and service, with the atmosphere of a home cook's front room. Small garden out the back. Food served Mon–Sat noon–2pm & 6.30–9pm, Sun noon–3pm & 7–9pm.

Orford and around

Some eight miles north of Woodbridge, in one of the most secluded parts of Suffolk, the tiny, eminently appealing village of **ORFORD** was, like many of the Suffolk coastal towns, a working port in the Middle Ages. Like Woodbridge, its focus now is slightly inland, its centre a generously proportioned rectangle of houses between the castle and church, while half a mile away the harbour looks out to its most famous feature, the

---

WALKS AROUND ORFORD

One of the best of the many walks around Orford is the five-mile hike **north** from Orford Quay along the river wall that guards the west bank of the River Alde, returning via Ferry Road, a narrow country lane that enters the village by the *King's Head* pub.

Alternatively, you can head off in the opposite direction from Orford Quay, **south** along the north bank of the Ore, turning inland after about a mile and following the path across country to the top end of the village from where you can either turn right into the village (about 3 miles in all), or continue on and do a loop around the fields, also returning back into Orford by way of Ferry Road (about six miles).

National Trust-owned nature reserve of **Orford Ness** – the largest shingle spit in Europe – which you can reach by boat.

Orford Castle

Orford, IP12 2ND • April–June & Sept daily 10am–5pm • July & Aug daily 10am–6pm; Oct daily 10am–4pm; Nov–March Mon & Thurs–Sun 10am–4pm • £5.60; EH • ☎ 01394 450472, ⓦ www.english-heritage.org.uk/daysout/properties/orford-castle

Orford's most impressive historic building is the twelfth-century **castle**, which lies just off the main square, built on high ground by Henry II, and under siege within months of its completion from his rebellious sons during the revolt of 1173–74. Most of the castle disappeared centuries ago, and it's only the lofty keep that remains, although its impressive stature hints at the scale of the original fortifications. Today, the castle offers wide views over Orford Ness from its battlements and also holds a pocket-sized museum, which puts some flesh on local bones, describing the various uses the castle has been put to over the years and hosting displays of local archeological finds.

St Bartholomew's

Church St, IP12 2LW

Besides its castle, Orford's other medieval edifice is **St Bartholomew's church**, on the other side of the main square, where Benjamin Britten premiered his most successful children's work, *Noye's Fludde*, as part of the 1958 Aldeburgh Festival (see p.254). St Bart's is mainly fourteenth-century but has been much messed about with since, and the original church here was a Norman construction – the arched remains of which you can see outside the church's east end, and also on the left side of the choir inside.

Orford Ness National Nature Reserve

April–June & Oct Sat 10am–2pm; July–Sept Tues–Sat 10am–2pm; last ferry back 5pm • £7.50, NT members £4 • ☎ 01394 450900

Lying tight against the coast, and linked to the mainland at Aldeburgh to the north, **Orford Ness National Nature Reserve** is a six-mile-long shingle spit that has all but blocked Orford from the sea since Tudor times. The spit's assorted mud flats and marshes nourish sea lavender beds, which act as prime feeding and roosting areas for wildfowl and waders. The National Trust runs boat trips across to the Ness from Orford Quay, and a five-mile hiking trail threads its way along the spit. En route, the trail passes a string of abandoned military buildings: some of the pioneer research on radar was carried out here, but the radar station was closed at the beginning of World War II for fear of German bombing – although the military stayed on here until the 1980s.

Havergate Island

Boats first Sat of each month at 10am, returning at 3pm; 20min • £15 • ⓦ www.rspb.org.uk/reserves/guide/h/havergate/index.aspx

The second of the two places you can visit by boat from Orford harbour is the RSPB reserve at **Havergate Island**, best in spring and summer when you can see its colonies of avocets, wheatears and terns, and pintails and wigeons in autumn and winter, as well as hares, rabbits and other creatures. There's just one trail on the island, which runs for around a mile and a half to several bird hides, but no other facilities. If you can't coincide with a trip, you can always content yourself with a one-hour trip around the island on the passenger boat, *Regardless*, which runs regularly from the harbour during the summer (£8 per person; ☎01394 450169).

ARRIVAL AND DEPARTURE   ORFORD AND AROUND

By bus Buses pull up on the central square and connect 4-5 times daily with Melton, Sutton Hoo and Woodbridge.

There is also one bus a day to Ipswich.

ACCOMMODATION

Butley Priory Butley ☎01394 450046, ✆butleypriory. co.uk. This fourteenth-century priory – or, at least, what's left of it, the gatehouse and a bit of the original church – is now gorgeous self-catering accommodation, which sleeps fourteen. It's not cheap, but the building, its gardens and above all the location, deep in the forest between Orford and Woodbridge, are stunning. Three nights £2000, one week £3000

★ **Crown & Castle** Market Square, IP12 2LJ ☎01394 450205, ✆crownandcastlehotel.co.uk. There's no better place to stay overnight and enjoy Orford's gentle and unhurried air than at this excellent, revamped pub, whose

modest-looking exterior doesn't quite do justice to the eighteen stylishly simple guest rooms within and in the outbuildings behind. It has a good restaurant too, and standards generally are top-notch – as you would expect from TV hotel inspector Ruth Watson's place. They offer a lot of good value, dinner-included breaks if you plan to stay more than one night. £125

Jolly Sailor Quay St, IP12 2NU ☎01394 450243, ✆thejollysailor.net. The village's best place for a drink, but with rooms as well – three doubles and one twin, well fitted out with en-suite bathrooms, and a camping area out the back. £70

EATING AND DRINKING

Butley Orford Oysterage Market Square, IP12 2LH ☎01394 450277, ✆butleyorfordoysterage.co.uk. An institution for many years in Orford and indeed for miles around. Great fish and seafood, much of it caught and smoked locally by the family themselves, served in a simple café-restaurant environment. No trip to Orford is complete without eating here, and they also have a shop, **Pinney's**, on Quay St near the harbour, a slick operation which has fresh and smoked fish and seafood. Mon–Fri 10am–4.30pm, Sat 9am–4.30pm, Sun 10am–4pm.

★ **Crown & Castle** Market Square, IP12 2LJ ☎01394 450205, ✆crownandcastlehotel.co.uk. An outstanding restaurant, where the emphasis is on local ingredients. Good lunchtime specials for around £10 and evening main courses in the range of £16–20. Think rump of Suffolk lamb, Orford skate, sea bass fillet niçoise – all delicious. Daily 12.15–2pm & 6.45–9pm.

Froize Inn Chillesford, IP12 3PU ☎01394 450282, ✆froize.co.uk. A couple of miles outside Orford, the *Froize Inn* is known for well-prepared modern British food that's all locally sourced – good on meat dishes especially, using local lamb, beef and venison, and great home-made pies too. Starters from £6.95, mains around £16, and plenty of blackboard specials. Tues–Sun noon–2pm, Thurs–Sat noon–2pm & 7pm–midnight.

Jolly Sailor Quay St, IP12 2NU ☎01394 450243, ✆thejollysailor.net. Really cosy, dog-friendly pub just

back from the harbour, which is great for a drink, with a wood-fired stove in winter, and does excellent food, too – giant bowls of mussels, skate, halibut and smoked fish from Pinney's across the road, as well as decent steaks, Barnsley chops and burgers. Most things go for £10–12. There's a kids' menu, too, and lots of good desserts and a cheeseboard. Or you can just grab one of their hot filled baguettes. Daily 11am–3pm & 6–9pm.

Penny's Café Pump St, IP12 2LZ ☎01394 450219. Just off the main square, this relatively new addition to Orford's food scene does sandwiches, home-made pies and sausage rolls, and great meat, cheese and fish platters for £6.95. Mon–Sat 8am-4.45pm, Sun 8am–3.45pm.

Pump Street Bakery 1 Pump St, IP12 2LZ ☎01394 459829, ✆www.pumpstreetbakery.com. The bread at this renowned local bakery is wonderful, as are the lunches and weekend brunch dishes, but it's not open every day. Wed–Sat 9am–4pm, Sun 10am–4pm.

★ **Richardson's Smokehouse** Baker's Lane, IP12 2LH ☎01394 450103, ✆richardsonssmokehouse. co.uk. Just behind the *Butley Orford Oysterage*, and not to be confused with it, Richardson's has been going for over two decades, and you can smell it before you see it – a couple of old sheds that between them are used as a smokehouse and shop. And not just fish, either – there's everything from kippers and mackerel to poultry and game – it's hard to leave Orford without buying something from

7

here. Daily 10am–4pm, Wed closes 2.45pm.
Riverside Tearooms Orford Quay, IP12 2NU ☎01394
459797, ⓦriversidetearoom.co.uk. Run by the folk who
run the *Regardless* passenger boat, this is housed in one of

the huts on Orford's quayside, and does good breakfasts
and lunches, with seating on the terrace decking. Jan &
Feb Sat & Sun only 10am–4pm; April–Oct daily
10am–5.30pm; March & Nov Wed–Sun 10am–4pm.

Aldeburgh and around

Well-heeled **ALDEBURGH**, a small seaside town of just three thousand people situated
just north of the meandering Alde River, is one of Suffolk's most popular coastal towns,
and has a buzzy, prosperous vibe that draws visitors from far and wide. It's also known
for its annual arts festival, the brainchild of composer Benjamin Britten, who lived here
for many years, and nowadays the town has a small fishing fleet selling its daily catch
from wooden shacks along the pebbled shore. But in essence it's a seaside resort, and an
increasingly gentrified one at that, with a high street featuring a handful of national
chains alongside an array of bijou local businesses. There are good hotels and B&Bs,
and some of Suffolk's best places to eat – Aldeburgh pretty much has it all if you're
looking for somewhere to stay for a while on the East Anglian coast.

The High Street and around

Aldeburgh's centre is clearly defined by its wide **High Street** which runs parallel to the
seafront and the narrow side streets that run off at right angles, but this was not always
the case: the sea swallowed much of what was once an extensive medieval town long
ago. Nowadays the side streets run down to the pedestrianized seafront and the large
stony **beach** beyond, the top end of which is lined with **huts** selling fresh fish.

Aldeburgh Lifeboat Station

Crag Path, IP15 5BP • Daily 10.30am–4.30pm • Free • ⓦ aldeburghlifeboat.org.uk

The spanking new Aldeburgh lifeboat is poised and ready to launch in the recently
built **lifeboat station** on the beach. You can peek inside for a look – the boat is

---

BENJAMIN BRITTEN

Born in Lowestoft in 1913, **Benjamin Britten** was closely associated with Suffolk for most of
his life. He started composing music as a boy, and attended the Royal College of Music in 1930,
where he wrote his first major work, a *Sinfonietta* for chamber ensemble. By the close of the
1930s he was an established composer of some renown, and had met his lifelong partner, the
tenor, **Peter Pears**, with whom he enjoyed both a loving and creative relationship for the rest
of his life. Pears and Britten fled Britain for the US in 1939, as conscientious objectors, and
stayed there until 1942, when they returned to Aldeburgh. They lived in Crag House, at 4
Crabbe St, on the seafront next to the boating pond, until 1957, when they supposedly grew
tired of fans peering through the windows, and moved to the grander Red House, about a
mile out of town on the road to Leiston. The work of the nineteenth-century Suffolk poet
George Crabbe formed the basis of the libretto of Britten's best-known opera, *Peter Grimes*,
which premiered in London in 1945 (with Peter Pears in the main role) to great acclaim. It was
followed a year later by Britten's *Young Person's Guide to the Orchestra*, igniting a burst of
creative energy that led to a flood of operas and choral music – *Billy Budd, The Turn of the Screw*
(his masterpiece for children), *Noye's Fludde*, a *Midsummer Night's Dream* and finally his last
opera *Death in Venice*. He died in 1976, aged just 63, after undergoing heart surgery. Peter
Pears outlived him by over a decade and continued to live in Aldeburgh until his death in
1986. He was buried next to Britten in the local churchyard, but their best memorial must really
be the **Aldeburgh Festival**, which they founded in 1948 and which is bigger and stronger
today than it has ever been (see p.254).

surrounded by photos and memorabilia, including details of all recent rescue operations – and afterwards pop into the RNLI shop, whose cards, stationery and gifts make good Aldeburgh souvenirs.

St Peter and St Paul

Church Close, IP15 1DY • ⓦ www.aldeburghparishchurch
.org.uk

The fourteenth-century flint church of **St Peter and St Paul** sits on a hill just off one end of the High Street, a large and very well-looked-after church – as you would expect in a place like Aldeburgh. Inside there's a small display on Britten and Pears, and a memorial to the eighteenth-century poet George Crabbe, who also lived in the town. But most Britten devotees make their way to the pair's simple slate headstones at the far end of the large churchyard, where they are buried – just in front, as it happens, of their close friend the conductor and composer Imogen Holst, the only child of Gustav, who lived in Aldeburgh for much of her life until she died in 1984.

Aldeburgh Museum

Moot Hall, IP15 5LE • Easter to end April Sat & Sun & bank hols 2.30–5pm; May, Sept & Oct daily 2.30–5pm; June–Aug daily noon–5pm • Free • ☎ 01728 454666, ⓦ aldeburghmuseumonline.co.uk

A creaky timbered edifice, with a sundial on its side, sixteenth-century **Moot Hall**, Aldeburgh's oldest building, began its days in the centre of town, but with the erosion that has swallowed half of the town centre over the centuries, it now finds itself almost on the beach. Inside, beneath its venerable beams, it houses the **Aldeburgh Museum**, whose displays take in all aspects of the town's history, including its prosperous years as a port, the lifeboats, its growth as a holiday resort and the war years.

The boating pond and Snooks

Next door to the Moot Hall is the **boating pond**, donated to the town by Elizabeth Garrett Anderson and a focus for families during summer who gather here to eat ice cream and watch the boats. Beside the pond is a statue of **Snooks** – the much-loved

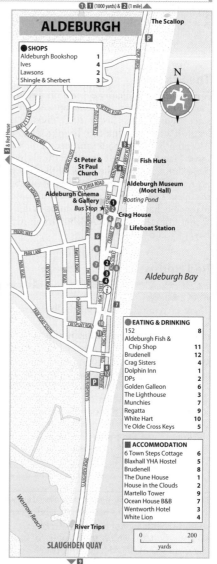

ALDEBURGH

The Scallop

● SHOPS

Aldeburgh Bookshop	1
Ives	4
Lawsons	2
Shingle & Sherbert	3

N

St Peter & St Paul Church

Fish Huts

Aldeburgh Cinema & Gallery

Aldeburgh Museum (Moot Hall)

Boating Pond

Bus Stop

Crag House

Lifeboat Station

Aldeburgh Bay

● EATING & DRINKING

152	8
Aldeburgh Fish & Chip Shop	11
Brudenell	12
Crag Sisters	4
Dolphin Inn	1
DPs	2
Golden Galleon	6
The Lighthouse	3
Munchies	7
Regatta	9
White Hart	10
Ye Olde Cross Keys	5

■ ACCOMMODATION

6 Town Steps Cottage	6
Blaxhall YHA Hostel	5
Brudenell	8
The Dune House	1
House in the Clouds	2
Martello Tower	9
Ocean House B&B	7
Wentworth Hotel	3
White Lion	4

0 ——— 200
yards

River Trips

SLAUGHDEN QUAY

dog of a local doctor that is something of a symbol for the town, especially since the original statue was stolen in 2003. The current *Snooks* is a replacement, funded by locals chipping in after much public outcry.

The Scallop

A memorial to Benjamin Britten, on the northern end of Aldeburgh's beach, Maggi Hambling's 13ft-high steel **Scallop** sculpture has caused quite a rumpus in Aldeburgh since it was first unveiled in 2003, dividing opinion in the town between those who loathe it and would like it to be moved and those who feel it's a fitting tribute to Aldeburgh's most famous son, sited in the midst of the landscape that inspired him most. Hambling herself described the sculpture as a conversation with the sea, and it is pierced through with the words of the George Crabbe poem – *The Borough*, a grisly portrait of the life of the fishermen of Aldeburgh – that inspired Britten to compose the opera *Peter Grimes*. It's designed, apparently, to induce a contemplative state, which it arguably has some chance of doing in this location – although it's more often used to shelter from the wind on Aldeburgh's blustery beach, and sadly of late has become a target for anti-*Scallop* graffiti.

Red House

Golf Lane, Aldeburgh, IP15 5PZ • Closed in 2012 but usually open for guided tours July & Aug Tues 2.30pm; tours 90min • £7 • ☎ 01728 451700, ⍟ brittenpears.org

There are reminders of Benjamin Britten and his partner Peter Pears all over Aldeburgh, but the one that resonates most is the house in which they spent the last three decades of their lives together, the **Red House**, now home to the Britten-Pears Foundation. Britten and Pears moved here in 1957, when their home in the centre of town became too public and they agreed to swap homes with their good friend Mary Potter. Britten and Pears were extraordinarily happy here, and the house has been preserved more or less as it was when Britten died in 1976 – although Pears lived on here until his own death in 1986, and tours – led by volunteers – take in all sorts of bits and pieces, not least the great man's piano, various manuscripts and a revolving selection of correspondence with the greats of the music world. But above all they reveal some of the minutiae of the composer's life and the circle of creative friends that gathered here. A pity, really, that it's not open more regularly.

Snape Maltings

Bridge Rd, Snape, IP17 1SR • April–Oct daily 10am–5.30pm; Nov–March 10am–5pm • ☎ 01728 688303, ⍟ snapemaltings.co.uk

Just off the main road between Aldeburgh and the A12, **Snape** is more or less a straggle of houses with a good pub – the *Golden Key* – just off the main drag. However, the village is best known for the complex of former malthouses known as **Snape Maltings,** the main site of the Aldeburgh Music Festival and home to one of the finest concert venues in the country and much more besides; indeed the Maltings has grown into quite a commercial behemoth in recent years, with various craft shops and galleries, a

---

ALDE RIVER TRIPS

At the far southern end of town, Aldeburgh's High Street gives way to the unmade surface of **Slaughden Quay**, where you can take one-hour **river trips** down the mouth of the Alde River and back again on the *Sandpiper* (May to mid-Sept hourly from 11am; £8, £4 children; ⍟ aldeburghrivertrips.co.uk). The same company also runs a ferry between Orford and Aldeburgh every Saturday from mid-July to August, which is the most direct way of getting from one to the other (1hr one-way from Orford at 10am & 2.30pm; £10 one-way, £15 return, plus £1 landing fee).

> ## WALKS AROUND ALDEBURGH
>
> Several **footpaths** radiate out from Aldeburgh, with the most obvious trail leading two miles north along the beach to **Thorpeness**, where you can pick up the Suffolk Coast Path towards Sizewell, a lovely passage along the cliffs through heathy landscapes almost as far as Sizewell, turning inland just by Sizewell Hall and cutting across the woodland and heath of the so-called Aldringham Walks back to Aldeburgh – an easy five miles (2–3hr walk) in all. You can also pick up the coastal path in the opposite direction, off the main road out of town beyond the golf course, which leads across country to Snape and through the reeds to the Maltings (about 3 miles).

food hall, a couple of cafés and a pub, the *Plough & Sail*. It's a pleasant place, and you could easily spend a couple of hours strolling around, afterwards maybe taking a walk along the river through the reedbeds to nearby **Iken** and its church – about two miles in all, and an easy, partly boardwalked route. The Maltings also hosts a farmers' market on the first Saturday of each month, and an annual food festival in September – ⊛www.aldeburghfoodanddrink.co.uk.

7

Thorpeness

A couple of miles north of Aldeburgh, a bracing thirty-minute walk along the beach, **THORPENESS** is a slightly peculiar place, with a toy-town quaintness reminiscent of the 1960s TV show *The Prisoner*. Formerly a tiny fishing village, it was bought up in its entirety in 1910 by (ironically) a Scottish lawyer called Stuart Ogilvie, who was determined to re-create a retreat that was English to the core, and turned it into his private holiday village, with a country club and golf course and an estate of mock-Jacobean and Edwardian holiday homes, some of which fringe Thorpeness's most distinctive and central feature, the Meare. The **Meare** was created as a boating lake with the help of Ogilvie's friend J.M. Barrie, who mocked up several Peter Pan-type locations on the islands in the middle, and you can still tour the deliberately shallow lake by rowing boat, canoe or sailing dinghy (April–Oct daily 10am–5pm; £7/30min; ☎01728 832523). There's a shop and a café nearby, the **Meare Shop & Tearoom** (see p.253). As for the rest of the village, a series of tracks lead through its centre to the sea, among which nestles a local pub, the *Dolphin Inn* (see p.253), while the *Thorpeness Hotel and Golf Club* continues to this day, now owned by the people behind the *Brudenell* and *White Lion* in Aldeburgh, and very much *the* place to stay.

ARRIVAL AND INFORMATION

ALDEBURGH AND AROUND

By bus Buses pull in along the High St and at Fort Green, near to Slaughden Quay, and there are hourly connections to Leiston (12min) and the nearest train station at Saxmundham (25min). The same service also runs on to Wickham Market (40min), Woodbridge (1hr) and Ipswich (1hr 30min).

By car You can park along the seafront by the Moot Hall, on

the High St, or there's a pay-and-display car park at the far end of the High St close to Slaughden Quay.

Tourist office 152 High St (Mon–Sat 9am–5.30pm, plus June–Sept Sun 10am–4pm; ☎01728 453637, ⊛www .suffolkcoastal.gov.uk/tourism). The tourist office has local bus timetables and can book accommodation.

ACCOMMODATION

Aldeburgh is solid second-home territory, so the number of hotels and B&Bs is relatively low, and a number of places are only available as self-catering, and rentable by the week. During the festival (see p.254) you'll need to reserve well in advance.

6 Town Steps Cottage 6 Town Steps, IP15 5AT; book through Best of Suffolk, Lime Tree Farm, Badingham ☎01728 638962, ⊛bestofsuffolk.co.uk. One of Aldeburgh's prettiest self-catering cottages, an immaculately refurbished haven just off the High St. The kitchen is well equipped, there's a patio area at the rear and

two bedrooms. Weekend deals are commonplace; one week high season £725

Brudenell The Parade, IP15 5BU ☎01728 452071, ⊛brudenellhotel.co.uk. This seafront hotel has been refurbished and updated relatively recently and is part of the same local hotel family as the *White Lion* at the other

7

end of town and the *Thorpeness Hotel*. It's very comfy, with a yachty feel that sits very well with the Aldeburgh vibe. There's a cosy sitting room downstairs in which you can sip tea and look out over the sea, free wi-fi throughout, and the rooms are thoughtfully if not imaginatively furnished. Service is excellent, and there's a good ground-floor restaurant with outside terrace. **£170**

Martello Tower Slaughden Rd, IP15 5NA ☎01628 825925, ⓦlandmarktrust.org.uk. This heavily fortified Martello tower, right on the edge of the ocean about half a mile south of the centre of Aldeburgh along Slaughden Quay provides the town's most distinctive accommodation, with two bedrooms, a roof terrace and parking nearby. Four-nights from **£500**, seven nights **£1000–1500**

Ocean House B&B 25 Crag Path, IP15 5BS ☎01728 452094, ⓦoceanhousealdeburgh.co.uk. In a prime location, this immaculately maintained Victorian dwelling right on the seafront in the centre of town has just three guest rooms, including a top-floor suite. All the rooms are en suite and are decorated in traditional style complete with period furnishings. The full English breakfasts, with home-made bread, are delicious too. **£90**

Wentworth Hotel Wentworth Rd, IP15 5BD ☎01728 452312, ⓦwentworth-aldeburgh.com. With its series of Edwardian half-timber gables, this is a lovely seafront hotel, old-fashioned but briskly and efficient, with elegant public areas and 35 lovely rooms, the best of which overlook the boats and fish huts on the beach. There is free wi-fi throughout and a slightly fusty restaurant serving two-course menus for £17.50. The welcome is professional rather than warm, but all in all the *Wentworth* nails the traditional British seaside hotel experience perfectly. **£169**

White Lion Market Cross Place, IP15 5BJ ☎01728 452720, ⓦwhitelion.co.uk. Recently upgraded, and now making much better use of its perfect position on the seafront right by the Moot Hall, with a reception area that flows through into the hotel's popular restaurant and bar.

It's basically the slightly less upscale sister of the *Brudenell* at the other end of the seafront, and the cheaper and less refined rival to the *Wentworth*, a few doors down. **£95**

BLAXHALL

Blaxhall YHA Hostel Heath Walk, Blaxhall, IP12 2EA ☎0845 3719305, ⓦyha.org.uk. This very tranquilly situated hostel is housed in the old village school at Blaxhall, a tiny hamlet a couple of miles beyond Snape Maltings. It has forty beds in two- to six-bedded rooms, a self-catering kitchen, a café and a laundry. Dorms **£16**; doubles **£50**

THORPENESS

The Dune House Aldeburgh Rd, IP16 4NR no phone ⓦliving-architecture.co.uk. Situated right on the beach between Aldeburgh and Thorpeness, *Dune House* is the brainchild of the writer Alain de Botton and a firm called Living Architecture, whose aim is to introduce ordinary folk to the delights of modern architecture in amazing settings. Designed by a renowned firm of Norwegian architects, it makes the most of its big-skied beach location: all glass on the ground floor and with views in all directions, it almost invites the beach inside the house. A great place to stay, and the prices, while not within reach of everyone, are relatively modest considering the location and size – its five bedrooms sleep up to nine people. Four-night stay **£760**

House in the Clouds Uplands Rd, IP16 4NQ ☎020 7724 3615, ⓦhouseintheclouds.co.uk. Thorpeness's best established unusual self-catering option, situated in the most prominent of Stuart Ogilvie's creations, is a five-storey pitched-roof clapboard tower bang in the centre of the village. You can't take your eyes off the views from its top-floor galleried games rooms, and the four double/twin bedrooms are suitably baronial to make the high prices seem like pretty good value. One week **£2100–3200**

EATING AND DRINKING

152 152 High St, IP15 5AX ☎01728 454594, ⓦ152aldeburgh.com. Long-standing restaurant whose popularity ebbs and flows with the nearby tides. It's almost on the beach, and has a nice menu, with skate wing, local sea bass or basic fish and chips for £10.95–17.95, and usually lots of specials to choose from. They do two courses for £12.95 during the week. Daily from 10am for breakfast and coffees; food served noon–3pm & 6pm–late.

Aldeburgh Fish & Chip Shop 226 High St, IP15 5DJ ☎01728 452250. Aldeburgh's two almost world-renowned fish and chip shops are owned by the same people, and they do mostly justify their huge reputations. This one, at the southern end of the High St, just does takeaways and you can expect to queue most evenings

– there's a webcam perpetually trained on the queue if you want to pick the best moment (ⓦchipshopqueue.co.uk). Mon–Thurs noon–2pm & 5.30–8pm, Sat noon–8pm.

Brudenell The Parade, IP15 5BU ☎01728 452071, ⓦbrudenellhotel.co.uk. The restaurant of the hotel (see p.251) has good sea views and a deliberately short menu (half a dozen starters and mains) that focuses on dishes with simple ingredients. Though some of the dishes try a bit too hard, and the portions could be a bit more generous, the food is pretty good – try the smoked eel and scrambled egg starter, followed by fillet of beef or fillet of halibut; they also do oysters – simply, at £15 a dozen, or as angels on horseback at £17 a dozen. Otherwise starters go for around £6.95, mains £12.95–18.95. Mon–Fri noon–2.30pm & 6.30–9pm, Sat & Sun noon–3pm & 6–10pm.

ALDEBURGH CINEMA AND GALLERY

Wouldn't you just know it, but opposite its fantastic local bookshop Aldeburgh has its own **gallery and cinema** complex, a dinky, toy-town affair at 152 High St (☎01728 452996, ⓦaldeburghcinema.co.uk) that has been screening films since 1919. It's a fairly small space, and one which was only saved from demolition in the 1960s when Benjamin Britten and other concerned locals clubbed together to save it – a very Aldeburgh sort of fate – and it's to the town's credit that it's still going. Plus, of course, the Gallery hosts regular exhibitions by local artists.

Cragg Sisters 110 High St, IP15 5AB ☎07813 552181, ⓦcraggsisters.co.uk. Busy serving tea in the same location since the days of Britten and Pears, and doing as good a job as ever. Mon–Sat 11am–5pm, Sun 11am–4.30pm.

DPs 106–108 High St, IP15 5AB ☎07854 920332. Short for David's Place, this is a handy local bar right on the high street that does decent home-made food – tapas-style snacks, kebabs and burgers, and even the fish you bought from one of the fish huts (£5 a head) – as well as hosting popular quiz nights. Very convivial.

Golden Galleon 137 High St, IP15 3AR ☎ 01728 454685. If you want to sit down for your fish and chips, or to swap queues, try *Aldeburgh Fish & Chip Shop*'s sister establishment, which has a restaurant upstairs, the "Upper Deck". Mon–Thurs noon–2pm & 5–8pm, Fri & Sat noon–2.30pm & 5–8.30pm.

★ **The Lighthouse** 77 High St, IP15 5AU ☎01728 453377, ⓦlighthouserestaurant.co.uk. Perhaps Aldeburgh's best restaurant, this locals' favourite on two floors is a relaxed and informal place that serves lunch and dinner seven days a week. The menu favours locally sourced ingredients and good, simple home-cooked food, with everything from excellent fish and chips, liver and bacon and burgers to pan-fried scallops and venison tagine with couscous. Mains go for £10.95–14.95. Always busy. Daily from 10am for coffee, lunch noon–2pm, dinner 6.30pm–late.

Munchies 163 High St, IP15 1AN ☎01728 454566, ⓦaldeburghmunchies.co.uk. With another branch in Southwold, this is one of the best places in town for a coffee and a pastry or gourmet sandwich (£2.60–6.95). Daily 8am–4.30pm.

Regatta 171 High St, IP15 1AN ☎01728 452011, ⓦregattaaldeburgh.com. One of Aldeburgh's longest established restaurants, and still a reliable choice, with a range of daily specials on a blackboard – local sprats for starters, followed by spicy cod loin couscous – and a creative menu with a British base, especially strong on seafood. Mains average about £14. Daily noon–2pm & 6–10pm.

White Hart 222 High St, IP15 5AJ ☎01728 453205. Good locals' joint, a very friendly small pub with one big main room in which everyone mucks in together. Another side of Aldeburgh. Daily 11am–3pm & 6pm–midnight.

Ye Olde Cross Keys Crabbe St, IP15 5BN ☎01728 452637, ⓦaldeburgh-crosskeys.co.uk. Cosy pub popular with a good portion of Aldeburgh's youth, who spill out into its sea-facing courtyard in the summer months. Daily 11am–3pm & 5pm–midnight; all day during summer.

THORPENESS

Dolphin Inn Peace Place, Thorpeness, IP16 4NA ☎01728 454994, ⓦthorpenessdolphin.com. Thorpeness's local is no ordinary boozer, as you might expect, but a stripped-down modern pub serving a good haute pub food from a blackboard menu – skate wing, fish and chips, sausage and mash, mussels for £10–14 – and with a number of bright en-suite doubles rooms upstairs. It's the home of the village store, too. Daily noon–2.30pm & 6–9pm.

Meare Shop & Tearoom Thorpeness, IP16 4NW ☎01728 452196, ⓦmeareshop.co.uk. Right by the Meare in the centre of Thorpeness, this hut-based shop and café does sandwiches, home-made quiche and ice creams and sells newspapers and basic provisions

SHOPS

★ **Aldeburgh Bookshop** 42 High St, IP15 5AB ☎01728 452389, ⓦaldeburghbookshop.co.uk. Great independent bookshop that would grace the high street of a much larger town, let alone one the size of Aldeburgh. Good on local titles, biography and new fiction, and a layout that encourages you to pick up and browse. Quite a good children's section too. Mon, Tues & Thurs–Sat 9.30am–6pm, Wed 9.30am–5.30pm, Sun 10.30am–5.30pm.

Ives 160 High St, IP15 5AQ ☎01728 452264. *The* place to go for an ice cream on the High St, but be prepared to

queue in summer. April–Oct Tues–Sun 10am–5pm (schools hols open daily 10am–6pm); Nov–March Sat & Sun 10am–4pm.

Lawsons 138 High St, IP15 5AQ ☎01728 454052, ⓦlawsonsdelicatessen.co.uk. This sleek and refined deli continues to win awards for being one of the best of its kind in Suffolk, and it's pretty good, selling a thoughtful selection of deli goodies, although being in Aldeburgh it doesn't stand out as much from the crowd as it would in most places. Not cheap. Mon–Sat 9am–5pm, Sun 10am–2pm.

7

ALDEBURGH: FESTIVAL TOWN

When Benjamin Britten launched the **Aldeburgh Festival** in 1948, in part as a showpiece for his own works and those of his contemporaries, he didn't know what he had started: Aldeburgh and its hinterland has since turned into a major festival venue in its own right, and Britten's festival in particular has grown exponentially. By the mid-1960s, it had outgrown the parish churches in which it began, and moved into a collection of disused malthouses, five miles west of Aldeburgh on the River Alde, just south of the small village of Snape (see p.250). The festival now takes place every June and lasts two and a half weeks. Core performances are still held at the Maltings, but a string of other local venues are pressed into service as well,. Throughout the rest of the year, the Maltings hosts a wide-ranging programme of musical and theatrical events, including a three-day Britten Festival in October. For more information, contact Aldeburgh Music (☎01728 687110, ⓦaldeburgh.co.uk), which has box offices at Snape Maltings and on Aldeburgh High Street alongside the tourist office. Tickets for the Aldeburgh Festival itself usually go on sale to the public towards the end of March, and sell out fast for the big-name recitals.

But it's not just Britten's festival that brings visitors to Aldeburgh these days: the **Aldeburgh Food and Drink Festival** (ⓦaldeburghfoodanddrink.co.uk) takes place during the last weekend in September at the Maltings and at a variety of venues across east Suffolk, from Orford to Woodbridge and as far afield as Framlingham. There's also the **Aldeburgh Carnival** (ⓦaldeburghcarnival.com) which has been held across the third weekend in August for over half a century, and gives this normally relatively buttoned-up town the chance to let its hair down, with a parade, firework display and Chinese lantern procession.

Shingle & Sherbert 158 High St, IP15 5AQ ☎01728 454308. Part of the craze for old-style sweets that's sweeping Britain, this is Aldeburgh's very own old-fashioned sweetshop. Mon–Sat 10am–5pm.

Leiston and around

It's just inland from the Edwardian fantasy village of Thorpeness, but the gritty, grounded town of **LEISTON** couldn't be more different – indeed aside from the tourist industry Leiston has been the area's main source of employment for years, first with the innovative Garrett works during the nineteenth and early twentieth centuries, and since the 1960s with the nuclear power station at the village of Sizewell – on what is in effect Leiston's beach. Leiston is also the home of Summerhill School, which was founded on the edge of town by A.S. Neill in the 1920s, a democratic institution in line with Neill's philosophy "to make the school fit the child instead of making the child fit the school", that is still going strong today.

The Long Shop Museum

Main St, IP16 4ES • End March to Oct Mon–Sat 10am–5pm • £5 • ☎01728 832189, ⓦ www.longshopmuseum.co.uk

Right in the centre of Leiston, the **Long Shop Museum** was originally the site of the Leiston Works, which was founded by Richard Garrett in 1778 as a maker of agricultural tools and went on to become a pioneer of steam-driven machinery and equipment, employing over two thousand staff and exporting its products all over the world. The Garretts were quite a dynasty: Richard Garrett's granddaughter, Elizabeth Garrett Anderson, was a nineteenth-century feminist and the first woman to qualify as a doctor in the UK, while her younger sister, Millicent Fawcett was an early campaigner for women's suffrage and founder of the feminist organization now named after her.

As for the museum, there is a steam engine – the *Sirapite* – in a separate shed, and threshing machines and old fire engines in another, and lots of fine details – not least the job vacancy cards from 1887, looking for "sober and hardworking boilermakers and engine erectors to travel to all parts of the British Empire, Austro-Hungarian

Empire and Russia". But the heart of the displays are in the **Long Shop** itself, a giant vaulted engine shed, with traction engines and steam tractors and various other bits of machinery, including the dry-cleaning machines the Garretts manufactured towards the end of their days here. The gallery upstairs takes you through the finer points of the steam process, as well as later sources of energy, including the building of Sizewell A in 1966, then B in the 1990s, which replaced the Garretts as the lifeblood of the town.

Leiston Abbey

Abbey Rd, IP16 4TD • Always open • Free; EH • ⓦ www.english-heritage.org.uk

About half a mile outside Leiston are the ruins of **Leiston Abbey**, built in the fifteenth century as a replacement for a thirteenth-century abbey in Minsmere, and constructed from some of the stones from the previous complex. It met its fate a century or so later when it was dissolved under Henry VIII, but the ruins are reasonably substantial, and you can still make out the refectory, with its large Gothic window, the cloister space next door and the abbey church. It's all part of a large complex incorporating a training academy for young musicians and a wedding and conference operation housed in the nearby thatched medieval barns, and, just beyond, the rebuilt guesthouse from the original abbey.

7

Sizewell

A couple of miles out of Leiston, right on the sea, the village of **Sizewell** amounts to no more than a handful of houses, but its name has a notoriety that belies its modest size, home as it is to two of southern Britain's largest nuclear power stations, both of which dominate the coastal landscape for miles around. The southernmost and older of the two, the Magnox **Sizewell A** reactor, has been recently de-commissioned, but its sister reactor to the north, **Sizewell B**, with its distinctive white golfball dome, is Britain's only functioning PWR reactor, and one of the most modern in the UK, completed in 1995. A third reactor, **Sizewell C**, is planned, and work may well start in the next couple of years. There used to be a visitor centre at Sizewell but it closed a few years back over security fears, but you can get up closer than you might expect on the beach.

Theberton

There's not much to the village of **THEBERTON**, a couple of miles north of Leiston, but its church of **St Peter** is a very elegant-looking building, with a long main body and a lovely thatched roof, and a handsome crenellated hexagonal tower. Just inside the porch is a large fragment of a German zeppelin which came down in a nearby field in June 1917, killing all sixteen aircrew, who are remembered (but no longer buried) by a rudimentary plaque in the graveyard on the other side of the road. Otherwise the church is an ancient building, originally Norman and with a few remaining features from that time, along with a fifteenth-century font carved with angels and wild men with clubs – so-called woodwoses – and a pulpit from the same period.

ACCOMMODATION

LEISTON AND AROUND

Cliff House Park Sizewell Common, IP16 4TU ☎ 01728 830724, ⓦ cliffhousepark.co.uk. A lovely campsite, well positioned above the beach and across the road from Sizewell Hall and the Aldringham Walks (though of course also virtually in the shadow of the power station). It also has good facilities, a bar and café and games room. Pitches **£25**

EATING AND DRINKING

Sizewell Beach Café Sizewell Gap, IP16 4UH ☎ 01728 831108. Right by the beach and in the shadow of the power station, this is a great little café that does breakfasts and lunches and has books and newspapers to browse – cosy inside and with tables outside during summer. Daily 9am–5pm.

Saxmundham and around

Just off the A12, about six miles inland from Aldeburgh, **SAXMUNDHAM** retains a pleasant small-town vibe, helped no doubt by the presence of its main-line station, which provides a lifeline for the towns and villages around, but hindered somewhat by the recent dumping of a giant Waitrose right in the middle of town. It's more upmarket than Leiston, but doesn't have the cachet – or indeed the cash – of, say, Framlingham. However, there are worse places to wind up, with a couple of things to help you pass the time and it's a base too for some of the area's most desirable villages and countryside.

Church of St John

Church St, IP17 1EP

Right opposite Waitrose's car park, the church of **St John** is a flint-built edifice of the thirteenth century, though with parts dating back much earlier. It boasts a lovely wooden hammerbeam roof and a well-preserved font carved with images of the club-wielding "old man of Suffolk" – common hereabouts, and known as woodwoses.

Saxmundham Museum

49 High St, IP17 1AJ • April–Sept & last week of Oct Mon–Sat 10am–1pm • Free • ☎ 01728 663583

Situated on the high street right by the railway bridge, **Saxmundham Museum** is the most obvious local attraction, with several rooms containing an old-fashioned station booking office, and a number of good displays on the town and its history, including plenty of local anecdotes.

Yoxford

Straddling the A12 just north of Saxmundham, the large and very sought-after village of **YOXFORD** was an important stopover in times gone by, occupying a key point not only on the London–Yarmouth road but on the road to Dunwich too, when the seaside town was one of the most important ports in the land. There's evidence in the form of a nineteenth-century road **sign**, pointing the way to Framlingham, Yarmouth and London, in the centre of the village. Right by the sign, the spired church of **St Peter** is the site of many memorials to the Blois family, who occupied the adjacent **Cockfield Hall**, the grounds of which back onto the village. Lady Jane Grey's younger sister Catherine was held here for the last two weeks of her life in 1568. She died, aged 27, after spending most of her adult life in captivity (she was regarded, like her sister, by Elizabeth I as having a potentially legitimate claim on the throne). You can see her memorial in the church, and gain access to at least a little bit of the grounds by taking the path by the gatehouse opposite the church.

Peasenhall

Travelling up the A1120 from the A12 and Yoxford, you soon reach **PEASENHALL**, which has fair claim to being the prettiest village in a region of exceptionally pretty villages, its main street lined by alluring cottages and the sunken stream of the River Yox, crisscrossed by occasional footbridges. It no longer has a village pub, which is a pity, but it more than makes up for this with its village store and tearoom, **Emmets**, on the main street (see opposite), another good tearoom, *Weavers*, at the other end of the village on the green, and, opposite, an excellent local butcher, **J.R. Creasey**. All in all not a bad place to find yourself, especially if you're hungry and/or self-catering.

FOOD SAFARI

One of the best local businesses in this part of Suffolk is **Food Safari** (☎01728 621380, ✉polly@foodsafari.co.uk, ⬤foodsafari.co.uk), which organizes cookery courses and demonstrations and visits to food producers, artisans and eateries. The emphasis is on **local produce** and the people who make a living out of it, with events devoted to all aspects of the food process, typically starting with a visit to a farm, a spot of butchery, and ending up with a cookery demonstration – after which you eat the results. Themes include free-range pork farming, butchery and cookery, bread-making, game preparation, foraging for mushrooms, smokehouse visits and more. Their events are not cheap (reckon on around £150 a head for a full day, £75 for a half-day), but you do usually get to take something home for tea.

ARRIVAL AND DEPARTURE

SAXMUNDHAM AND AROUND

By train Saxmundham's train station is right in the centre of town just off the main street – follow Station Approach from Market St – and is connected every hour with Ipswich to the south (40min) and Lowestoft to the north (50min).

By bus Buses stop on the High St and there are hourly buses between Ipswich, Woodbridge, Wickham Market, Aldeburgh and Saxmundham, and much more infrequent connections to Yoxford and Halesworth.

ACCOMMODATION

SAXMUNDHAM

Alde Garden Low Rd, Sweffling, IP17 2BB ☎01728 664178, ⬤aldegarden.co.uk. Fantastic small campsite that's perfect for people who don't really like camping, with a couple of yurts, a tipi and even a gypsy caravan. There are pitches available too if you have your own tent, and a small cottage which you can rent by the week for about £300. Yurts, tipis and caravans **£50–60**

The Bell 31 High St, IP17 1AF ☎01728 602331, ⬤www.bellhotel-saxmundham.co.uk. Under new management, and being quirkily refurbished by the new owners, who are making the most of the *Bell*'s ten large double rooms. The location is a winner, just a few minutes' walk from the main-line station; the flagstones and offbeat decoration of the lobby create a timeless yet contemporary vibe, and the restaurant is atmospheric and elegant. Its bar, too, is one of the nicest places to drink in town. **£110**

EATING AND DRINKING

SAXMUNDHAM

Bistro at the Deli 26a High St, IP17 1AB ☎01728 605607, ⬤thedeli.biz. Deli and café in one, offering coffee and tea, breakfasts, panini and deli delights like Greek salads and antipasti, from about £5. Cream teas, too. Mon–Fri 9am–5pm, Sat 9am–2pm.

The Butterfly The Bell, 31 High St, IP17 1AF ☎01728 602331, ⬤bellhotel-saxmundham.co.uk. Excellent hotel-restaurant – all white with flickering candles at night – whose menu is admirably short and seasonal, and usually features classics alongside more inventive dishes– think steak and chips, fillet of bream with pak choi or tenderloin of pork with rosti – and always includes a veggie dish or two. Not especially cheap – starters £6–7, mains around £15–16, plus sides – but it's a nice place to eat and their two-course lunch specials for £14 are a bargain. Tues–Sat noon–2pm & 6.30–9pm, Sun & Mon noon–2pm.

YOXFORD

Mains High St, IP17 3EU ☎01728 668882, ⬤mainsrestaurant.co.uk. Spick-and-span modern restaurant serving an imaginative – and short – menu of modern British food using local ingredients; think parsnip and lemon soup followed by slow roast shoulder of lamb and colcannon, skate with caper butter or roast pheasant with cep gravy. Moderately priced. Tues–Sat from 7pm.

PEASENHALL

Emmett's The Street, IP17 2HJ ☎01728 660250, ⬤emmettsham.co.uk. Great village store which cures its own bacon and stocks all manner of deli goodies and fruit and veg, including Spanish products like chorizo and Serrano ham. It also has a small tearoom next door, in which you can sample many of its wares. Mon–Fri 8.30am–5.30pm, Sat 8.30am–5pm.

Weavers The Knoll, IP17 2JE ☎01728 660548. Peasenhall's tearoom occupies a classic village green location and serves coffee, sandwiches, cream teas and hot lunches. Well worth the stop in this village of foodie delights. Daily except Wed 10am–5pm.

7

Dunwich and around

Tiny **DUNWICH**, just over twelve miles up the coast from Aldeburgh, is probably the strangest and certainly the eeriest place on the Suffolk coast. The one-time seat of the kings of East Anglia, a bishopric and formerly a large port, Dunwich peaked in the twelfth century, since when it's been downhill: over the last millennium, something like a mile of land has been lost to the sea, a process that continues at the rate of about a yard a year. As a result, the whole of the medieval city now lies under water, including all twelve churches, the last of which toppled over the cliffs in 1919.

Greyfriars monastery

The only things that survive from medieval Dunwich are the fragments of the **Greyfriars monastery**, which originally lay to the west of the city and now dangles near the sea's edge. You can access them from the Westleton road out of town, and although there's not much to see, it's an evocative sight, and one that brings home not only how grand a place Dunwich once was, but also just how close to obliteration the village has been for centuries.

Dunwich museum

St James St, IP17 3DT • March Sat & Sun 2–4.30pm; April–Sept daily 11.30am–4.30pm; Oct daily noon–4pm • £1 donation

Dunwich's dinky **museum**, located just down from the *Ship* pub, and recognizable by the giant anchor outside, gives a potted history of the town, and has an interesting section on those many locals who decided to emigrate to Canada, including the grandmother of Lucy Maud Montgomery, the author of one of the most popular children's books of all time, *Anne of Green Gables*.

Dunwich Heath

March to mid-July & mid-Sept to Dec Wed–Sun 10am–4pm; mid-July to mid-Sept daily 10am–5pm • Free, parking £4.40; NT

From Dunwich car park, it's possible to walk south along the seashore and then cut inland up and over the dunes to National Trust-owned **Dunwich Heath**, where heather and gorse spread over a slab of upland. You can also drive here – the turning is clearly signed on the more southerly of the two byroads to Dunwich. At the end of this turning, on the heath immediately behind and above the coast – the views are fantastic – the old **coastguard cottages** accommodate a shop and tearoom, and are available for self-catering (see opposite).

Minsmere RSPB Nature Reserve

Reserve daily 9am–9pm or dusk **Visitor centre** daily 9am–5pm, Nov–Jan till 4pm • £5 • ⓦ rspb.org.uk

A narrow lane off the main road into Dunwich branches off to the **Minsmere RSPB Nature Reserve**, a varied terrain of marsh, woods and heathland, and in the autumn a gathering place for wading birds and waterfowl, which arrive here by the hundred. It's best known for marsh harriers and avocets – the latter familiar from the RSPB's logo – and the reserve is also home to a small population of notoriously shy bitterns. It's a glorious place, and very well managed, with well-marked trails and hides, and even a place you can stay over, a huge car park and visitor centre, and a shop selling everything you could think of to do with birdwatching. There's a decent café too, serving hot food at lunchtime and snacks, tea and coffee all day.

Dunwich Forest

St Helena, IP17 3ED • Open all year • ⓦ suffolkwildlifetrust.org/reserves-and-visitor-centres/dunwich-forest

Just outside Dunwich, **Dunwich Forest** is co-managed by the Forestry Commission and

---

A MINSMERE CYCLE CIRCLE

Using the *Eel's Foot Inn* (see below) as your base, you can do a **walk** right around Minsmere reserve, taking in all of the forest, heath, marsh and coastal habitats without actually entering the reserve itself – five miles in all, and a good way of working up an appetite for a meal at the pub. You can do pretty much the same walk starting from the NT tearoom and visitor centre at Dunwich Heath. Alternatively **Eastbridge Cycle Hire** offers another good way of touring the area (☎07828 113279, ⓦ theeastbridgecyclehirecompany.co.uk), with good-quality bikes for £12.50 a day.

---

the Suffolk Wildlife Trust and is home to loads of bike and walking trails, and you can link up with the trails to Dingle Marshes, which stretch towards Walberswick. It's a lovely spot, which is being gradually returned to its traditional state, with the coniferous trees that currently predominate being harvested and replaced by native deciduous woodland and pasture, much of which is grazed by a small herd of recently introduced Dartmoor ponies.

Westleton

On the seaward side of the A12, a couple of miles north of Saxmundham, a turning off the main road towards the sea leads a few miles to **WESTLETON**, a pretty village built around a large green and with the thatched fourteenth-century church of **St Peter's**, though very unusually for Norfolk and Suffolk, it lacks a tower, as it was destroyed by a World War II bomb. Though there's not much to see in the church, the churchyard is a pleasant spot.

ARRIVAL AND DEPARTURE
DUNWICH AND AROUND

By bus There are buses every two hours to Dunwich from Leiston, Darsham train station, Westleton and Theberton.

By car A sprawling, seashore car park gives easy access to both the village and this stretch of the coast.

ACCOMMODATION

The Crown The Street, Westleton, IP17 3AD ☎01728 648777, ⓦ westletoncrown.co.uk. This pub-restaurant has 34 en-suite bedrooms, either in the main building or dotted about the various converted barns outside. They're all beautifully finished, and are quirkily and confidently classified as "good", "better", and "best", which they are, with even the cheapest rooms recently refurbished with TV, wi-fi and well-fitted bathrooms. **£120**

Coastguard Cottages IP17 3DJ ☎0870 4584422, ⓦ nationaltrustcottages.co.uk. The cottages at the Dunwich Heath National Trust centre have been converted to two very comfortable one-bedroom apartments and are available for rent, with a minimum two-night stay. One week around **£700**

Eel's Foot Inn Eastbridge ☎01728 830154, ⓦ theeelsfootinn.co.uk. Just a few miles inland from Dunwich in the tiny village of Eastbridge, this old smugglers' haunt is a popular base for twitchers, with not only good pub food and drink at lunchtimes and in the evening, but also a blackboard detailing recent sightings. Very friendly too, and with six en-suite double rooms. **£70**

The Ship IP17 3DT ☎01728 648219, ⓦ shipatdunwich. co.uk. Owned by the same people as the *Crown* at Westleton, the refurbished, fairly simple rooms here make it well worth staying over in Dunwich, as it's only in the dead of night that the peace and spookiness of the place really strikes home. **£115**

EATING AND DRINKING

★ **The Crown** The Street, Westleton, IP17 3AD ☎01728 648777, ⓦ westletoncrown.co.uk. Long-standing pub that has been well updated, with a stripped-down bar and a light-filled dining room out the back, which serves an upscale but deliberately hearty British menu. Starters – £5.50–6.50 – include smoked haddock tart and mussels, while the mains – £13.95–19.95 – take

in pan-fried bream, saddle of venison, Gressingham duck and fish and chips. They also serve a lunch menu of sandwiches and light dishes – try the smoked chicken hash with poached egg – and lunch specials for £10 a main. Daily noon–2.30pm & 6.30–9.30pm.

Floral Tea Rooms Dunwich Beach ☎01728 648433. Right by the beach in Dunwich, this is a Suffolk coast

---

MIDDLETON'S ALTERNATIVE TO BOXING DAY TELLY

A pretty village grouped around a green off the main road just south of Westleton, and with a pub, *The Bell*, **Middleton** is known for its **cutty wren festival**, an old English ritual that takes place every year on St Stephen's Day, more prosaically known as Boxing Day (December 26). It's an ancient event, dating back to times when people thought the wren to be the "king of all birds". Historically a wren was caught and killed and paraded around the village; nowadays it's a carved wooden effigy, but the ceremony still takes place, having been revived about twenty years ago. It begins after dark, when the participants blacken their faces with soot and dance around the village with the bird on a stick, finishing up at the village pub, where there's more dancing and the wren is ceremonially buried. What you might make of it is anybody's guess, but if you're in the area on Boxing Day, why not stop by and have a look?

---

institution, basically a large hut serving big plates of excellent fish and chips, pies, burgers and salads to an assortment of birdwatchers, hikers and anglers. Outside seating too. Daily 11am–5pm.
The Ship IP17 3DT ☎ 01728 648219, ⓦ shipinndunwich

.co.uk. With its low wooden beams and open fire, this is a cosy, traditional pub serving good food made with locally sourced pork, lamb and fish. Try their fish and chips, fried in their secret-recipe batter. Daily noon–3pm & 6–9pm.

Southwold and around

Perched on the cliffs just to the north of the River Blyth, **SOUTHWOLD** is a small town of around 1500 people that competes with Aldeburgh for the London tourist and second-homer trade. It was Suffolk's busiest fishing port in the sixteenth century, but in time lost most of its fishing industry to Lowestoft, just up the coast, and today, although a small fleet still brings in herring, sprats and cod, the town its primarily a seaside resort, a genteel and eminently appealing little place with fine old buildings, a long sandy **beach**, open heathland, a dinky harbour and even a little industry in the shape of the Adnams brewery. It's a gentility that wasn't to the liking of George Orwell, who lived for a time at 36 High St (a plaque marks the spot) with his parents. He heartily disliked the town's airs and graces, and soon fled to live more cheaply and "have less temptation from the world, the flesh and the devil".

Market Place and the Greens

The centre of Southwold is its triangular, pocket-sized **Market Place**, framed by attractive, mostly Georgian buildings, which sits at one end of the town's busy **High Street**. One of the great things about Southwold is that its centre is dotted with green spaces, left as firebreaks after the town was gutted by fire in 1659. The two most central are **East Green**, where you'll find the Adnams Brewery, and **South Green**, the largest, which looks out to sea and down across the fields towards the harbour. **North Green** is a smaller open space at the top of the High Street. But Southwold is a pretty green place all round, with common land stretching out west from the centre of town behind the High Street.

Adnams Brewery

Sole Bay Brewery, IP18 6JW • Tours usually 2–3 daily during summer • £10, including a bottle of beer to take home • ☎ 01502 727225, ⓦ brewerytours.adnams.co.uk

North from Market Place, **East Green** is the site of the **Adnams Brewery** its various buildings filling the air with vaguely malty fumes throughout much of the day. Adnams has been here for well over a century and not surprisingly remains an important local employer. But what's admirable about Adnams is the way it has turned a successful local business into a nationwide (and even international) one, investing in the latest brewing methods and cannily extending into the catering trade, with a number of wholly owned pubs and hotels and a great local chain of wine merchant and kitchen stores, Cellar & Kitchen (see p.267). You can take a tour of the brewery, viewing the state-of-the-art brewing process and finishing up with a tutored tasting and a trip to their store to taste wine.

The Lighthouse

Stradbroke Rd, IP18 6LU • Mid-April to late July & Oct Wed, Sat & Sun 2–4pm; late July to Sept Wed–Sun 11am–1pm & 2–4pm; also 11am–1pm & 2–4pm on bank holiday weekends • £3.50, children £2.50, family tickets £10 • ☏ 01502 724729, Ⓦ trinityhouse.co.uk

On the opposite side of East Green to the Adnams brewery, is Southwold's famous white **Lighthouse**, built in 1887 and open to the public on guided tours, which take you right the way up to the lantern, around 100ft high. Tours last twenty minutes and are not for those nervous about heights or confined spaces.

St Edmund

Bartholomew Green, IP18 6AH • Daily 9am–4pm, July–Aug till 6pm

Just off East Green, right in the centre of Southwold, the large church of **St Edmund** is a light and very handsome mid-fifteenth-century church whose solid symmetries are balanced by a long sequence of elegantly carved windows. Inside there are lots of neo-Victorian additions and renovations, but some original features too, not least a rood screen that goes the full width of the building, painted with images of

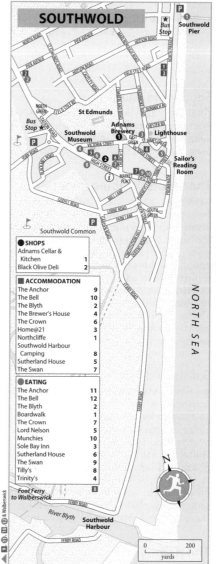

angels on the left, Apostles in the centre and Old Testament prophets on the right. Cromwell's troops hacked off their faces in the mid-seventeenth century – a similar fate befell the original font at the other end of the church. Beyond the rood screen, the choir stalls carry finely fashioned human and animal heads as well as grotesques, not least a depiction of a man in the throes of toothache. Look out also for "Southwold Jack", a brightly painted, medieval effigy of a man in armour nailed to the wall beside the font; he was once part of a clock, nodding belligerently as he struck the hours.

> **BOUTIQUE BEACH HUTS**
>
> Southwold's sandyish **beach** is backed by row upon row of candy-coloured huts which face out towards the ocean. Beach hut rental costs £15–18 a day, £90–108 a week (☎07842 528164, ⓦbeachhutsouthwold.co.uk), or you can bite the bullet and buy your own for around £50,000.

Southwold Museum

9–11 Victoria St, IP18 6HZ • Easter–Oct daily 2–4pm, Aug also 10.30am–noon • Free • ☎01502 726097, ⓦsouthwoldmuseum.org

Just across the road from the town's parish church, **Southwold Museum** covers an awful lot in a relatively small space, from the rise and fall of the local fishing industry to the town's latter-day gentrification – all very well displayed following a recent renovation.

The Sailors' Reading Room

East Cliff, IP18 6EL • Daily 9am–5pm; Oct–March till 3.30pm • Free

From the lighthouse, follow the seafront path right to the curious **Sailors' Reading Room**, built in 1864 in memory of a local Captain Rayley, one of Nelson's officers at the Battle of Trafalgar who had died the previous year. It's a peaceful haven, open to anyone, which serves as – yes – a reading room where only the ticking of the clock can disturb your browsing of the morning papers, boating magazines and Lloyds ship registers that are left on the tables. There's also a make-do Southwold **maritime museum**, with models of old ships, an array of painted figureheads from ships long since sunk and photos of the various local salts who helped to fund and build the place. The late W.G. Sebald, in his book, *The Rings of Saturn*, regarded it as his favourite haunt in Southwold, "better than anywhere in the long winter months for looking out on the stormy sea as it crashes on the promenade".

Southwold Pier

Mon–Fri 9am–6pm, Sat 8.30am–7pm, Sun 8.30am–6pm; Under the Pier Show Mon–Fri & Sun 10am–6pm, Sat 10am–7pm • ⓦwww.southwoldpier.co.uk

Southwold Pier is the latest incarnation of a structure that dates back to 1899. Built as a landing stage for passenger ferries, it has had a troubled history – repeatedly damaged by storms, hit by a sea-mine and then partly chopped up by the army as a protection against German invasion in World War II. Recently revamped and renovated, it's nowadays delightfully retro, with deliberately low-key attractions and almost classy gift shops in rows of humdrum white huts. Be sure not to miss the **Under the Pier Show**, full of Tim Hunkin's off-the-wall handmade games, the most popular of which is unsurprisingly "Whack-a-banker", although you might also like to try "Rent-a'-Dog", "Autofrisk" and "My Nuke". Afterwards relax at the *Boardwalk* restaurant (see p.266).

The Harbour

Just below the Market Place, **South Green** is the largest and prettiest of Southwold's greens, and you need to cross this to reach both Ferry Road and the ferry footpath that lead down to the **harbour**, at the mouth of the River Blyth – a ten-minute walk. It's an idyllic spot, where fishing smacks rest against old wooden jetties and nets are spread out along the banks to dry. From the mouth of the river, a footpath leads west to a tiny passenger **ferry** (early April & June–Sept daily 10am–12.30pm & 2–5pm; late April, May & Oct Sat & Sun 10am–5pm; 90p; ⓦwalberswick.ws/ferry.php), which shuffles across the river to Walberswick (see p.264). If you're heading back towards Southwold, however, keep going along the river until you pass the *Harbour Inn* and then take the

path that leads back into town across **Southwold Common**. The whole circular walk takes about thirty minutes.

Walberswick

Just across the River Blyth from Southwold lies the pretty little village of **WALBERSWICK**, another once-prosperous port now fallen (or risen) into well-heeled tranquillity. For many years it was the home of the English Impressionist painter Philip Wilson Steer (1860–1942), and, warming to the same theme, it's now a seaside escape with an arty, sometime celebrity undertow. There's not much to see as such, though you can stroll south along the coast to Dunwich (see p.258) and its annual crabbing festival is a popular event – too popular in recent years as it was cancelled in 2011 because of the sheer numbers attending.

Blythburgh

The small village of **BLYTHBURGH** lies at the end of the Blyth estuary, which reaches inland from Southwold's harbour. Its church of **Holy Trinity** is known as the "cathedral of the marshes", and with good reason – its tower can be seen long before you reach the village, and it's an enormous church even by East Anglian standards. Inside it's a high, open structure, with a prominent shining beamed ceiling decorated with carved angels, as well as other details to seek out, such as the so-called "poppyhead" carving at the end of the pews, each one depicting one of the seven deadly sins, and the Jack o' Bell in the choir, who originally rang his bell every hour but now only does so to signal the arrival of the priest. Look also at the north door at the back of the church, scorched black in 1577 by the devil or "Black Shuck" – the ghostly black dog thought to roam East Anglia in the Middle Ages, who appeared the same night in Bungay (see p.214) – and the restored priest's room above the porch, which is a haven of contemplation, if you can manage the stairs.

Covehithe

Just under five miles north of Southwold, **COVEHITHE** is technically at the end of the road, although the "end" keeps changing as coastal erosion causes the nearby cliffs to fall into the sea. That's not the reason the church of **St Andrew** is mostly a ruin; the once enormous church was deemed unviable in the seventeenth century and they let it fall apart while building the thatched edifice you see today, only keeping the church's massive tower. There's nothing much to see inside, apart from a beamed ceiling and medieval font, but the location, and especially the ruins, are uniquely atmospheric – although sadly a number of signs warn against proceeding any further due to the instability of the cliffs beyond.

ARRIVAL AND INFORMATION

SOUTHWOLD AND AROUND

By bus Buses pull in on the High St, yards from the tourist office, and there are regular connections with the nearest train station at Darsham (every 2hr; 50min). The same bus goes onto Yoxford, Saxmundham, Leiston and Aldeburgh,

---

STRIKING OUT FROM COVEHITHE: BENACRE BROAD

There's a great, shortish walk (about 2hr) you can do from **Covehithe** that takes in the lagoon-like **Benacre Broad** to the north and then comes full circle back down the coast – about five miles in all, and pretty easy. Walk back up the road inland from St Andrew's church and take a path off to the right after about half a mile, alongside a section of wood. This leads across country and after about a mile and a half links up with the Suffolk Coast Path, which leads right back down to the coast, where it heads south, skirting the edge of Benacre Broad and finally finishing up at Covehithe.

OUT ON THE WATER

Coastal Voyager (☎07887 525082, ⓦcoastalvoyager.co.uk) operates a variety of sea and river trips from Southwold. You can choose from a gentle 3hr 30min cruise up the Blyth River (£25, children £12.50, families £66), drop-offs at Dunwich beach or Blythburgh church for walks back to Southwold, or 30min out on the sea on their 400hp powerboat (£20, children £10, families £54). You can also opt to drive the powerboat yourself if you have £220 to spare.

and there are also buses every hour to Lowestoft (50min) and every 2hr to Halesworth (25min).

By car There are two central car parks in the town, both free – one just off the common, close to the *Red Lion* pub, the other at the other end of the High St just off York Rd, on the way to the water tower. There's also a pay-and-display car park just north of the pier.

Tourist office 69 High St (April–Oct Mon–Fri 10am–5pm, Sat 10am–5.30pm, Sun 11am–4pm; Nov–March Mon–Fri 10.30am–3pm, Sat 10am–4.30pm; ☎01502 724729, ⓦwww.visit-sunrisecoast.co.uk).

ACCOMMODATION

7

The tourist office has a reasonably long list of local accommodation, but the number of vacant rooms can get mightily thin on the ground in high season.

SOUTHWOLD

The Blyth Station Rd ☎01502 722632, ⓦblythhotel. com. On the edge of the town centre, but just a 5min walk from the High St, the thirteen rooms here are cosily decorated in country style and there's a good bar and restaurant downstairs. Free wi-fi throughout, and dog-friendly. **£110**

The Brewer's House 56 Victoria St, Southwold, IP18 6JQ ☎01502 722186, ⓦadnams.co.uk. The double-fronted Victorian former home of the Adnams head brewer is centrally placed and very comfortable, and has been beautifully refurbished by the brewery. It sleeps 6–8. One week **£1500**

The Crown 90 High St, IP18 6DP ☎01502 722186, ⓦadnams.co.uk. The less upmarket – and cheaper – of Adnams' two hotels in Southwold, with fourteen rooms above a bar-restaurant. Most of the rooms are large and have been recently refurbished, decorated in a contemporary style. **£100**

Home@21 21 North Parade, IP18 6LT ☎01502 722573, ⓦhomeat21northparade.co.uk. Near the pier, this seafront guesthouse occupies a well-maintained Victorian terrace house, whose rooms have been sympathetically updated and opened out. Three rooms, two en suite and two sea-facing. **£75–95**

Northcliffe 20 North Parade, IP18 6LT ☎01502 724074, ⓦnorthcliffe-southwold.co.uk. Of several guesthouses that line up along the seafront promenade, this is one of the nicest, with three en-suite guest rooms decorated in comfortable if undramatic style. **£90**

Southwold Harbour Camping Ferry Rd, IP18 6ND ☎01502 722486. Great family site down by the river and harbour, and as such a 10min walk from the centre of town. The plus is it's close to the beach and to Walberswick across the river. Pitches around **£25**

Sutherland House 56 High St, IP18 6DN ☎01502 724544, ⓦsutherlandhouse.co.uk. The three rooms above this smart restaurant are all very comfy, but the pick is the room that James II slept in when he was the grand old Duke of York, although the more expensive top-floor suite, with its adjoining sitting room is perfect if you're staying a while or you're a family. Free wi-fi throughout, and DVD players in all the rooms. **£180**

★ **The Swan** Market Place, IP18 6EG ☎01502 722186, ⓦadnams.co.uk. Delightful hotel which occupies a splendid Georgian building right at the heart of Southwold. Some of the guest rooms are in the main building, which is a real period piece, its nooks and crannies holding all manner of Georgian details, others occupy the more modern, blander garden annexe at the back – the "Lighthouse Rooms" – which are a bit cheaper. **£140–220**

WALBERSWICK

The Anchor The Street, IP18 6UA ☎01502 722122 ⓦanchoratwalberswick.com. Best known for its food, but also offering a choice between the old-fashioned cosiness of its three doubles and one single in the main building and the more contemporary comforts of its six cedar-clad garden chalets outside, half of which are dog-friendly. Hardly a better place to stay on the coast. **£110**.

The Bell Ferry Rd, IP18 6TN ☎01502 723109, ⓦthebellwalberswick.wordpress.com. Under new management, this local pub has six double rooms that are simple rather than spectacular. Includes breakfast. **£100–120**

EATING AND DRINKING

SOUTHWOLD

The Blyth Station Rd, IP18 6AY ☎01502 722632,

ⓦblythhotel.com. The restaurant here has a more contemporary feel than the upstairs rooms, and has

7

LATITUDE FESTIVAL

Local lad George Orwell may have hated Southwold, but he might well have approved of the town's music festival, **Latitude**, which began in 2006 and now spreads over four days in the middle of July with happy campers grubbing down in Henham Park about five miles west of town, just across the A12. It bills itself as a festival with a literary and dramatic bent, and is deliberately a lot more family-friendly than the multitude of other British summer music fests. Tickets generally go for £170 including camping for the full long weekend; more from ⊛ latitudefestival.co.uk.

two-course menus starting at £22.95 as well as a separate menu served in the bar next door, although you can mix and match the two. The food is good enough, and choices are deliberately kept simple – things like steak, leg of duck and sea bass fillets, and sausage and mash and fish pie in the bar. Mon–Sat noon–2pm & 6–9pm, Sun noon–5pm.

Boardwalk Southwold Pier, IP18 6BN ☎ 01502 722105. The pier's restaurant is a great spot for tea and cake or fish and chips but you'll also find less obvious stuff too, like roasted sea bream, pan-fried local herrings and grilled swordfish as typical daily specials. Mussels, too, when in season, all for around £10 a main course. It's licensed as well. Daily 10am–8pm; lunch 11.30am–4pm, dinner 5–8pm.

The Crown 90 High St, IP18 6DP ☎ 01502 722186, ⊛ adnams.co.uk. Deluxe bar food featuring local, seasonal ingredients, all washed down with Adnams ales. Mains here average around £16 and tables are allocated on a first-come, first-served basis, in *The Crown*'s wood-panelled back-bar or restaurant. Mon–Fri noon–2.30pm & 6–9pm, Sat & Sun noon–2.30pm & 6.30–9.30pm.

Lord Nelson East St, IP18 6EJ ☎ 01502 722●079, ⊛ thelordnelsonsouthwold.co.uk. A lively neighbourhood pub of low-beamed ceilings just back from the seafront. There's an emphasis on food, with a really good, locally inspired menu featuring herring, "Nelson smokies" (smoked haddock and cod in sauce), dressed crab and local sausages. Food served daily noon–2pm & 7–9pm.

Munchies 2 East St, IP18 6EH ☎ 01502 725651. Just off the Market Place, this is the sister to the Aldeburgh outfit of the same name, and the slightly larger of the two, with a deli out the front and a spacious café out the back, serving home-made soup, sandwiches and toasties from £3.95, all-day breakfast baps, good coffee and cakes and big salads. Daily 8am–4.30pm.

Sutherland House 56 High St, IP18 6DN ☎ 01502 724544, ⊛ sutherlandhouse.co.uk. Classy, modern British restaurant presided over by the ebullient Peter Banks that's housed in one of Southwold's oldest buildings, home to the admiralty in days gone by. There's a strong local emphasis to the menu – main courses range from

£11–18 – and they have a helpful food-miles chart attached. Daily noon–2.30pm & 6.30–8.30pm; closed Mon in winter.

Sole Bay Inn 7 East Green, IP128 6JN ☎ 01502 723736, ⊛ solebayinn.co.uk. This couldn't help but be an Adnams pub, based as it is right opposite the brewery, and it's a convivial, one-bar place, with a stripped-back interior, that's popular with locals as well as tourists and serves decent pub food, with most mains – chicken curry, minute steak, fishcakes, lamb chops – £9–10. Mon–Wed & Sun lunch only, Thurs–Sat lunch & dinner.

The Swan Market Place, IP18 6EG ☎ 01502 722186, ⊛ adnams.co.uk. Southwold's best hotel offers its most upscale, if old-fashioned dining experience, with great food served in an elegant dining room overlooking the Market Place which always feels like a treat. It's moderately priced too, considering the environment and quality, and service is excellent. The menu is old-school, French-influenced dining (starters £6–8, mains £14–18) nothing very original but beautifully executed: start with smoked breast of duck or seared scallops, and follow with baked halibut, sea bass, or roast loin of beef. Mon–Sat noon–2pm & 7–9pm, Sun 12.30–2.30pm.

Tilly's 51 High St, IP18 6DJ ☎ 01502 725677, ⊛ tillysofsouthwold.co.uk. The pick of Southwold's many teashops – the service is electric fast and they do a great line in sandwiches and home-made cakes both inside and outside in the walled garden. Daily 9am–7pm.

Trinity's 54 High St, IP18 6DN ☎ 01502 722888. Popular and convenient café and tearooms right on the High St that does good breakfasts and hot and cold lunches. Daily 10am–4.30pm.

WALBERSWICK

The Anchor The Street, IP18 6UA ☎ 01502 722122, ⊛ anchoratwalberswick.com. This place strives to be both a village local and a gastropub, and succeeds pretty well at both, with a convivial bar that always boasts a great choice of draught beers and lunch and dinner menus that focus on Norfolk and Suffolk fish and seafood, local game and even local flour with which they make their home-made bread, It's a great place, never

> **THE SOUTHWOLD CIRCULAR**
> You can do a three-mile circular **walk** all the way around Southwold, by following the path to the harbour and then right up the Blyth River and across the marshes, and then back across the main road down to the coast just north of the pier. You can also follow the river all the way up to Blythburgh church (see p.264), about four miles in all, either then coming back the same way or having the *Coastal Voyager* pick you up or drop you off (see p.265).

better than when serving its excellent Saturday brunch, or one of its summer Sunday lunchtime barbecues. Mon–Fri noon–3pm & 6–9pm, Sat & Sun noon–10pm.

The Bell Ferry Rd, IP18 6TN ☎01502 723109, ⓦthebellwalberswick.wordpress.com. Close to the beach and river, *The Bell* is a rabbit warren of a place, with all sorts of ancient nooks and crannies, and a separate dining room. Daily noon–2.30pm & 6–9pm.

SHOPS

Adnams Cellar & Kitchen 4 Drayman Square, Victoria St, IP18 6EW ☎01502727 244. Large store around the corner from the brewery that's typical of this great local chain, with a fantastic choice of wine and of course Adnams beer, kitchenware and a café out the back. Mon–Sat 9am–6pm Sun 10am–4pm.

Black Olive Deli 80 High St, IP18 6DP ☎01502 722312. Great deli right on the High St that has all the usual deli favourites but has a particularly good selection of fish and seafood products, home-made pies and, of course, olives. Mon–Sat 9am–5pm, Sun 10am–4pm.

Halesworth and around

The archetypal small Suffolk town of **HALESWORTH** is a self-sufficient sort of place rooted in the local farming community but one that has done a good job of updating itself, with a slightly artsy edge these days. Its pedestrianized main street – the **Thoroughfare** – is a bustling mix of low-key local businesses that leads to the *Angel Hotel* (see p.268) and small **Market Place** opposite, from which a path leads through to the precincts of the parish church of **St Mary**. Once you've seen these you've pretty much seen Halesworth, although there are pleasant walks to be done by the **river** and in the meadows just south of the centre known as **Millennium Green**.

St Mary the Virgin

1 Steeple End, IP19 8LL • ⓦblythvalleychurches.org.uk

At the centre of Halesworth, the stout flint church of **St Mary the Virgin**, surrounded by a pleasant triangle of timbered and Georgian houses, was built on much earlier foundations, as evidenced by the so-called "Dane Stone" in the choir, a Saxon carving sunk into the wall and showing arms reaching out to clasp branches and leaves. At the back of the church, the font, with its carvings of woodwoses is a more conventional feature.

Halesworth Museum

Halesworth Station, IP19 8BZ • May–Sept Tues–Fri 10am–12.30pm also Sat in July & Aug; Oct–April Tues–Thurs 10am–12.30pm • Free • ☎01986 873030, ⓦhalesworth.ws/museum

Halesworth Museum, just out of the centre in the train station, has displays on local industry and local characters, including the re-creation of a local tailor's workshop and the collections of Haleworth botanist Sir William Hooker, who was the first director of Kew Gardens.

Bramfield

The village of **BRAMFIELD**, a couple of miles south of Halesworth, is home to the *Queen's Head* pub and the church of **St Andrew**, a well-kept thatched church with a round tower, though one which is unusually separate from the main body of the church. Inside it has one of the best-preserved rood screens in Suffolk, with rich and clear paintings showing various saints. Look, too, at the seventeenth-century memorial for a certain Arthur Coke in the choir, a beautifully carved piece of work, which shows his wife lying by him with her baby daughter at her side (she died, apparently, in childbirth).

Laxfield

About six miles southwest of Halesworth, the pretty village of **LAXFIELD** feels quite remote, situated as it is in the no-man's-land between Halesworth and Framlingham. Its centre is marked by the timbered **Guildhall**, built in 1515 on the site of an earlier building, and home to a small museum (Easter & May–Sept Sat & bank hols 2–5pm; free), with various exhibits relating to rural life in the area. Directly opposite, **All Saints** church is a fourteenth-century building that's unusual for its exceptionally wide timber roof, which covers an equally broad single aisle. It also has an impressive large font from the early sixteenth century, with carvings of the seven sacraments (although it could be in better repair), some early sixteenth-century pews carved with various creatures, and a giant fifteenth-century chest – that used to hold church records.

ARRIVAL AND INFORMATION — HALESWORTH AND AROUND

By train Halesworth is on the main Ipswich to Lowestoft line and its train station is just outside the town centre off London Rd.

Tourist office occupies a room in the *Angel Hotel* on the Thoroughfare.

ACCOMMODATION

Angel Hotel Thoroughfare, IP19 8AH ⓣ 01986 873365, ⓦ angel-halesworth.co.uk. At the far end of the Thoroughfare, the *Angel* is a bit of a hub, holding as it does the town's tourist office, a bar that's popular for both morning coffee and evening drinks, and a well-patronized restaurant. It's also a really cosy old coaching inn, with seven decently furnished en-suite doubles upstairs. £75

Rendham Hall Rendham, IP17 2AW ⓣ 01728 6634409, ⓦ rendhamhall.co.uk. This homely B&B, based on a working dairy farm just outside Halesworth, has just two rooms – a family room and double, both en suite. Very friendly, and in a beautiful location that's great for kids. £58

EATING AND DRINKING

Baytree Bistro 6 Thoroughfare, IP19 8AH ⓣ 01986 874119, ⓦ baytreebistro.co.uk. Good place for a coffee or a cooked breakfast, and also serving sandwiches, omelettes, sausages and mash and jackets and various lunchtime specials later in the day – most from around £6.95. It's licensed too, and has a small garden out the back. Mon & Tues 9am–5pm, Wed–Sat 9am–9pm. Closed Sun.

Cleone's Thoroughfare, IP19 8AH ⓣ 01986 873365, ⓦ angel-halesworth.co.uk. The restaurant of the *Angel Hotel* has a very Italian flavour, with pizzas, pasta courses from £5 and mains from about £9 on a short and pretty authentic, if slightly fussy, menu. Sun–Thurs noon–2pm & 7–9pm, Fri & Sat noon–2pm & 6.30–9.30pm.

King's Head Gorams Mill Lane, Laxfield, IP13 8DW ⓣ 01986 798395, ⓦ laxfieldkingshead.co.uk. Below the church, across the stream that runs through the village, this was proclaimed "Adnams Pub Of The Year" in 2010, and is unusual in that it has no bar – just a room full of barrels that staff disappear into to get your order while you make yourself comfy in one of the pub's wood-panelled little rooms. There is also food, served in a separate dining room – home-made pies, steaks, liver and bacon, etc. Very friendly, and especially cosy on a winter's night. Daily noon–3pm & 7–9pm.

Singtong Neeyom 37 Thoroughfare, IP19 8LE ⓣ 01986 873737, ⓦ singtongthairestaurant.co.uk. Virtually opposite the church, and housed in the old town police station, this is the place to go if you're tired of modern British food made with locally sourced ingredients. Good Thai cooking, and a welcoming environment to enjoy it in. Tues–Sat 6.30–9.30pm.

Lowestoft

Suffolk's second-largest town, **LOWESTOFT** is known for two things: fish and the seaside, two industries which to say the least are in decline – a fact that's unfortunately evident pretty much everywhere you look. The heart of the town, close by the **harbour**, is a down-at-heel mix of chain and Poundstretcher stores, while the harbour itself is a workaday fishing port that is a shadow of its former self. The southern end of the town's centre is its most alluring stretch, focusing on the **beach**, which is undeniably fine, a long strip of golden sand kept in immaculate condition and lined by a typically English seaside blend of Victorian terraces, pristinely planted gardens and beach huts. There's a small **pier**, and the East Point Pavilion close to the harbour houses the tourist office, but to be honest there's not a great deal to be gained in hanging around here unless you're going to the beach. There are things to see in Lowestoft, but the town's best attractions lie beyond the centre, either on the northern and southern edges of the centre by the sea, or amid the bypasses and roundabouts that encircle the town – specifically Oulton Broad, which provides the town's most alluring destination by some way.

The Mincarlo

Royal Plain, NR33 0AQ • Easter to Oct Tues–Thurs 10.30am–3.15pm • Free • ☎ 01502 565234, ⓦ lydiaeva.org.uk

Moored by the South Pier, the **Mincarlo**, the last sidewinder trawler to be built in Lowestoft, offers a glimpse of life on board Lowestoft's fishing fleet at its height, fitted out much as it was when it was built in 1960.

Maritime Museum

Sparrow's Nest, Whapload Rd, NR32 1XG • May–Sept daily 10am–5pm • £1 • ☎ 01502 561963, ⓦ lowestoftmaritimemuseum.org.uk

Lowestoft's **Maritime Museum** is north of the town centre, just below the

ACCOMMODATION
Ivy House	1
Victoria Hotel	3
Winelodge	2

EATING & DRINKING
Coast	3
Crooked Barn	1
Winelodge	2

town's lighthouse, facing the beach. It's a good local museum, crammed with artefacts pertaining to the fishing, shipbuilding and World War II among other things. There are models of sailing and steam drifters, mock-ups of the cabin of a drifter and the bridge of a trawler and lots of background on the fishing industry here in general, much of whose story is told in some constantly running short films – though the most tangible relic from the town's fishing past are the rows of wooden racks across the road outside, which were once used for drying nets.

East Anglia Transport Museum

Chapel Rd, Carlton, Colville, NR33 8BL • July & Aug Tues, Thurs & Sat 2–5pm, Sun 11am–5pm; June & Sept Thurs & Sat 2–5pm, Sun 11am–5pm; April & May Thurs 2–5pm & Sun 11am–5pm • £7, children £5 • ☎ 01502 518549, ⦿ eatm.org.uk • Buses every 15min from the train station to Beccles Rd, from where it's a 5–10min walk

The **East Anglia Transport Museum** is not the Suffolk coast's most vital attraction. But this open-air museum of old trams, trains and buses does a great job of showing the development of mass transport over the past century or so. You can ride on trains, buses and trams and afterwards stop for a cup of tea at the museum's café.

The Carlton Marshes Nature Reserve

Always open; office Mon–Fri 9am–5pm • Car parking available

On Lowestoft's western edges, close to Oulton Broad, **Carlton Marshes** gives a hint of the Broadland landscape that lies just beyond, a wide-skied expanse of marshy grazing land, reeds and water. It's crisscrossed by paths that you can wander through on circular walks or walk to Oulton Broad in about twenty minutes. Various birds are often spotted here – marsh harriers, kestrels, golden plovers, reed and sedge warblers and others, along with a number of different kinds of dragonfly.

Oulton Broad

Lowestoft's most compelling attraction, **Oulton Broad**, where the town takes on a riverside rather than seaside feel, is effectively the southern gateway to the Broads National Park. There's a gathering of shops and restaurants around the eastern end at **Mutford Lock,** where you can either take a **cruise** around the Broad on the *Waveney Princess* (1hr; £4.50) or up the Waveney to Burgh St Peter (1hr 30min; £8). The Broad itself is fringed by the grass and trees of Nicholas Everitt Park, where the **Lowestoft Museum** (April–Oct daily 1–4pm; free) is hosted by the crenellated flint Broad House and has displays of eighteenth-century Lowestoft porcelain, others pertaining to Lowestoft local luminaries including Benjamin Britten, and of course the fishing industry, and mock-ups of old living rooms, shops and suchlike. Or you can just sit and nurse a coffee at the ramshackle **Quays Café** and watch dayboaters and yachtsmen try to make land at the nearby free moorings. It's busy here during summer, and summer evenings can be great fun, especially when the Broad hosts motorboat racing every Thursday evening.

Africa Alive

White's Lane, Kessingland, NR33 7TF • Daily: mid-March to end July 9.30am–5pm; end July to mid-Sept 9.30am–6pm; mid-Sept to Oct 9.30am–5pm; Oct to mid-March 9.30am–4pm • £14.95–16.95, children £10.95–12.95 • ☎ 01502 740291, ⦿ africa-alive.co.uk

A slice of tropical savannah transplanted to Suffolk, the **Africa Alive** zoo and adventure park focuses on Africa and has giraffes, rhino, cheetahs, zebras and other animals roaming its enclosures, along with lemurs and other creatures you can get a bit closer to. Zulu warriors and the like top it all off. It's a decent, if expensive day out, and one of Lowestoft's relative highlights, for families at least.

Pleasurewood Hills

Leisure Way, Corton, NR32 5DZ • End July to early Sept daily 10am–6pm; end June to end July daily 10am–5pm; April to mid-June & Sept Sat & Sun 10am–5pm, also Easter hols and Oct half-term daily 10am–5pm • £17, children £15 slightly cheaper and family tickets online • ☎ 01502 586000, ⊛ pleasurewoodhills.com

This theme park just north of the centre of town has been around for a while, and it shows a bit, but there are a couple of scary roller coasters and a vicious a waterslide as well as gentler attractions aimed at younger children – boat rides, racing cars, a gentler roller coaster and more. Disneyworld it ain't, but there are worse ways of spending a cloudy day in Lowestoft.

ARRIVAL AND INFORMATION   LOWESTOFT

By train Lowestoft's train station is right in the centre of town by the harbour; there are also stations on the other side of the town centre at Oulton Broad North and Oulton Broad South, and all three stations are connected roughly hourly with Ipswich (1hr 30min–1hr 50min) and stations on the way – Darsham, Saxmundham and Woodbridge, among them. Lowestoft is also connected by rail with Norwich roughly ever hour, taking in stops at Haddiscoe, Reedham, Acle and Brundall.

By bus The bus station is also centrally placed, a short walk north of the main train station on Gordon Rd, just behind the Britten Centre. The most useful bus is the #X1, which leaves every half an hour for Great Yarmouth (30min), travelling from there right across Norfolk via Acle, Norwich,

Dereham, Swaffham and King's Lynn as far as Peterborough (4hr 30min away). There are also regular buses – ever half-hour – to Norwich via Beccles (35min) and Loddon (1hr), and half-hourly services to Yarmouth and Hemsby and Caister beyond.

By car The most central car parks are those on Denmark Rd by the train station and across the river from here by the East Point Pavilion – both pay-and-display. However, there are often spaces free along Kirkley Cliff Rd.

Tourist office In the East Point Pavilion right on the seafront near the station and harbour (April–Sept daily 9.30am–5pm; Oct–March Mon–Fri 10.30am–5pm, Sat & Sun 10am–5pm; ☎ 01502 533600).

7

ACCOMMODATION

Ivy House Ivy Lane Oulton Broad, NR33 8HY ☎ 01502 501353, ⊛ ivyhousecountryhotel.co.uk. More of an upmarket motel than the country house hotel it calls itself, but it's undeniably a nice place to stay, with twenty comfy rooms in a series of barn conversions and other buildings that back onto the marshes and Oulton Broad. Free wi-fi throughout. It has a good restaurant too. **£130**

Victoria Hotel Kirkley Cliff, NR33 0BZ ☎ 01502 574433, ⊛ thehotelvictoria.co.uk. An elegant old building, reasonably well refurbished, with lovely views over South

Beach and lots of good-sized rooms facing the sea, although service is patchy. That said, it's one of the better places to stay in Lowestoft, and enjoys a good location a 10min walk from the train station and main pier. **£120**

Winelodge 1 Victoria Terrace, NR33 0QJ ☎ 01502 512777, ⊛ winelodge.co.uk. Simple but nicely furnished in this arch-contemporary hotel-restaurant concept that also has a branch by Oulton Broad. Prices are deliberately keen and offer excellent value especially the family room that sleeps four. **£65–90**

EATING AND DRINKING

Coast Kirkley Cliff, NR33 0BZ ☎ 01502 574433, ⊛ thehotelvictoria.co.uk. The restaurant of the *Victoria Hotel* has perfect views over the beach from its sea-facing dining room, and a thoughtful and not overlong menu that includes lots of Norfolk and Suffolk produce – Brancaster mussels, Adnams beer-battered cod, Suffolk ham and the like. Mains go for £12–18, starters £5–6, and, although the cooking is only average to good, it's one of the town's pleasantest places to eat. **Mon–Fri noon–2.30pm & 6.30–9pm, Sat & Sun noon–9pm.**

Crooked Barn Ivy Lane, Oulton Broad, NR33 8HY ☎ 01502 501353, ⊛ ivyhousecountryhotel.co.uk. The restaurant of the *Ivy House* hotel offers Lowestoft's best

chance of a slap-up gourmet experience, and isn't that expensive either, with a two-course lunch option for £15.95 and a three-course dinner menu at £37.50. And the room itself is a lovely, eighteenth-century beamed affair, full of character. **Daily noon–1.45pm & 7–9.30pm.**

Winelodge 1 Victoria Terrace, NR33 0QJ ☎ 01502 512777, ⊛ winelodge.co.uk. The dining room of the hotel is cool and aspirational in feel; the menu is a slightly less classy affair, kind of a spin on the J.D. Wetherspoon's concept, with something for everyone, from lamb shanks to Thai red curry to all-day breakfasts. Jackets, pizzas and steaks too, and all extremely well priced, with mains from £5–10. **Daily noon–9pm.**

Inland Suffolk

FLATFORD MILL

Inland Suffolk

Stretching forty-odd miles north from the Essex border, inland Suffolk is deeply rural, its myriad hamlets and villages linked by an intricate network of country lanes. At first glance, the landscape changes very little, but change it does, from the valley meadowlands in the south through rolling farmland and on up to the plateau claylands of what is sometimes called High Suffolk. The River Stour weaves its way through the southern reaches of the region, creating the verdant vistas much admired by the painter John Constable – hence the tourist moniker "Constable Country". The National Trust's Flatford Mill celebrates the life and times of the painter, but otherwise it's the prettiness of the villages that remains the main draw hereabouts with Stoke-by-Nayland and Dedham leading the picture-postcard charge. The River Stour also runs through Sudbury, a pleasant little town that boasts an excellent museum devoted to the work of another highly regarded English artist, Thomas Gainsborough, and from here it's another short hop to another small town, Long Melford, home to a pair of stately homes and a particularly splendid church.

Sudbury, Long Melford and the other villages and towns dotted along the River Stour and its tributaries were once busy little places at the heart of East Anglia's medieval **weaving trade**. By the 1490s, the region produced more cloth than any other part of the country, but in Tudor times production moved on and, although most of the smaller places continued spinning cloth for the next three hundred years or so, their importance slowly dwindled. Bypassed by the Industrial Revolution, the southern reaches of inland Suffolk had, by the late nineteenth century, become a remote rural backwater, an impoverished area whose decline had one unforeseen consequence: with few exceptions, its settlements were never prosperous enough to modernize, and the architectural legacy of medieval and Tudor times survived. The two best-preserved villages are **Lavenham** and minuscule **Kersey**, both of which hold a battery of ancient, rickety half-timbered buildings, many painted in the bright yellows and pinks popular hereabouts – though they both heave with sightseers on summer weekends.

Moving north, **Bury St Edmunds** can boast not just the ruins of its once-prestigious abbey, but also some fine Georgian architecture on its grid-plan streets, and nearby **Newmarket** is different again, a one-industry, mono-culture town devoted to the racehorse with 16,000 people and 3000 horses. Both Bury St Edmunds and Newmarket are on the **A14**, which slices across inland Suffolk, and the scattering of hamlets to the north of this main thoroughfare are the quietest of places, the two

LAVENHAM

Highlights

❶ Flatford Mill Take a peek at the land- and riverscape that inspired one of England's greatest painters, John Constable. **See p.278**

❷ Sudbury The home town of one of England's finest portraitists, Thomas Gainsborough, whose rich talents are celebrated in the Gainsborough House gallery. **See p.282**

❸ Long Melford In a county that seems to drizzle superb medieval churches, Holy Trinity is one of the most beautiful, if not the most beautiful of all. **See p.285**

❹ Lavenham With a small army of antique, half-timbered buildings, this lovely town is the cream of the scenic crop. **See p.289**

❺ Kersey Few would argue that this isn't the prettiest village in Suffolk – there's hardly an architectural hair out of place. **See p.292**

❻ Bury St Edmunds Atmospheric old town, whose star turn is the crumbly ruins of its once-mighty abbey. **See p.299**

HIGHLIGHTS ARE MARKED ON THE MAP ON PP.276–277

Brandon Country Park
High Lodge Forest Centre
Thetford Forest
Ely
Norwich
Thetford
A1066
Little Ouse
B1382
B1106
B1107
A11
B1106
Elveden Estate
Elveden
A134
A1088
Mildenhall
B1112
Lark
A1101
Icklingham
Anglo-Saxon Village
West Stow
Ingham
Ixwo
Barton Mills
B1101
A11
Tuddenham
A1101
A143
Soham
A142
B1104
Kennett
B1085
Pakenham
Thurston
B1102
Kentford
A14
Cambridge
B1506
B1085
6
Bury St Edmunds
A14
Newmarket
B1063
B1061
Cheveley
Ickworth House
B1066
Bradfield Combust
A134
C A M B S.
Ditton Green
B1063
Denston
Hartest
A1304
A143
Boxted
Lavenham
B1066
B1052
B1001
Stour
A1307
Kedington
Nether Hall
Kentwell Hall
Melford Hall
Clare
Cavendish
A1092
3
B1064
Long Melford
B1071
Haverhill
B1057
Stoke by Clare
2
Sudbury
B1054
B1508
N
E S S E X
A1307
A131
Bures

HIGHLIGHTS
1. Flatford Mill
2. Sudbury
3. Long Melford
4. Lavenham
5. Kersey
6. Bury St Edmunds

0   2
miles

INLAND SUFFOLK

Braintree
Halstead & Braintree

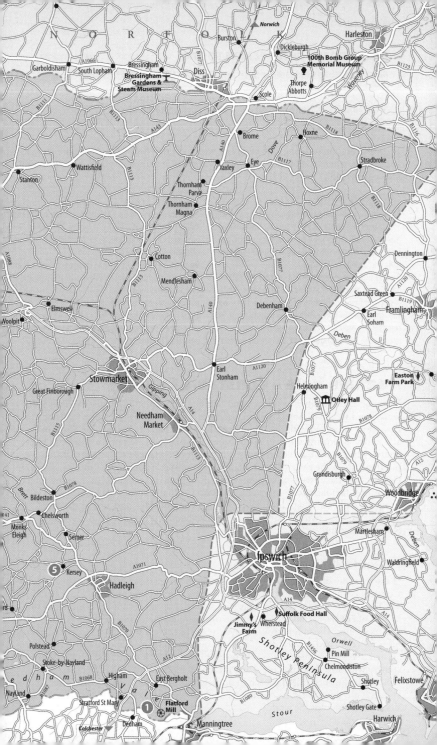

HALF A DOZEN GREAT PLACES TO STAY

Black Lion Hotel Long Melford. See p.287
Great House Hotel Lavenham.
See p.291
Swan Hotel Lavenham. See p.291

Old Cannon B&B Bury St Edmunds.
See p.305
The Bildeston Crown Bildeston. See p.293
Ickworth Hotel Ickworth House. See p.305

---

particular highlights being **Eye**, complete with its battered castle and splendid church, and **Hoxne**, where one of the most popular saints of medieval England, King Edmund, met a grisly end.

GETTING AROUND

By train The main train line hereabouts links Ipswich with Stowmarket, Needham Market, Bury St Edmunds and Newmarket and you can also get to Sudbury, which is on a branch line off the London Liverpool Street–Colchester main line; change at Marks Tey.

By bus Bus services between the villages are patchy – and almost nonexistent in the evenings and on Sundays – so you'll find it difficult to get away from the towns. The situation isn't helped by the multitude of bus companies, though Chambers (⑩ chamberscoaches .co.uk), one of the largest, does operate an especially

useful service linking Bury St Edmunds, Lavenham, Long Melford and Sudbury (Mon–Sat hourly, 8am–6pm). For bus timetable information, go to ⑩ suffolkonboard.com or ⑩ travelineeastanglia.org.uk.

On foot For walkers, footpaths crisscross the area, with some of the most enjoyable being in the vicinity of Lavenham and Long Melford. All the local tourist offices sell easy-to-use walking leaflets. The main long-distance route is the Stour Valley Path, which runs for sixty miles, linking Dedham Vale with Sudbury and ultimately Newmarket.

Dedham Vale – Constable Country

Forming the border between Essex and Suffolk for much of its length, the **River Stour** weaves and wends its way through a handsome, quintessentially English landscape of farms and woodland with the thick grassy banks of the river keeping the Stour in check and at bay. Following the river inland from its estuary, the first major port of call is Sudbury (see p.282), but on the way it negotiates **Dedham Vale**, undoubtedly the prettiest part of the river valley and famous as **Constable Country**, for this was the home of John Constable (see box, opposite), one of England's greatest artists, and the subject of his most famous works. Inevitably, there's a Constable shrine – the much-visited complex of old buildings down by the river at **Flatford Mill** – and among the area's assorted hamlets, two are extremely pretty, **Dedham**, just over the border in Essex, and **Stoke-by-Nayland**.

Flatford Mill

"I associate my careless boyhood to all that lies on the banks of the Stour", wrote John Constable, who was born in East Bergholt, nine miles northeast of Colchester in 1776. The house in which he was born has long since disappeared, so it has been left to the hamlet of **FLATFORD MILL**, down by the river a mile or so to the south, to take up the painter's cause. The mill here was owned by his father and was where Constable painted his most celebrated canvas, *The Hay Wain* (now in London's National Gallery), which created a sensation when it was exhibited in Paris in 1824: Constable rendered his scenery with a realistic directness that infuriated many of his contemporaries, but typically he justified this approach in unpretentious terms, observing that, after all "no two days are alike, nor even two hours; neither were there ever two leaves of a tree alike since the creation of the world".

Bridge Cottage and around

Flatford Mill, CO7 6UL • Jan & Feb Sat & Sun 11am–3.30pm; March Wed–Sun 11am–4pm; April daily 11am–5pm; May–Sept daily 10.30am–5.30pm; Oct daily 11am–4.30pm; Nov & Dec Wed–Sun 11am–3.30pm • Free, except for parking; NT

The **mill** itself – not the one he painted, but a Victorian replacement – is not open to the public and neither is neighbouring Willy Lott's Cottage, which does actually feature in *The Hay Wain*, but the National Trust has colonized several local buildings, principally **Bridge Cottage**, which was familiar to Constable and is now packed with Constabilia. None of the artist's paintings is displayed here, but there's a pleasant riverside tearoom to take in the view. Many visitors are keen to see the **sites** associated with Constable's paintings and, although there is something a tad futile about this – so much has changed – the National Trust does organize **guided walks** (☎01206 298260) to these locations; the nearest are the remains of the dry dock next to Bridge Cottage and the *Hay Wain* view itself. Rather more rewarding, however, is the easy, two-mile stroll over to Dedham village – cross the bridge beside Bridge Cottage, veer right and keep going along the riverbank. Alternatively, you can rent a rowing boat from beside this same bridge and potter along peacefully to your heart's content.

Dedham

Constable went to school in **DEDHAM**, just upriver from Flatford Mill and one of the region's prettiest villages, its wide and lazy main street graced by a handsome medley of old timber-framed houses and Georgian villas. The main sight as such is **Dedham Parish Church of St Mary** (daily 9am to dusk; ⓦdedham-parishchurch.info), a large

8

THE EPITOME OF SINCERITY: JOHN CONSTABLE

The son of a well-heeled miller and corn merchant, **John Constable** (1776–1837) was born in **East Bergholt**, a village just to the north of Flatford Mill. His father wanted him to continue the family business, but in 1799 the young Constable persuaded his father to release him from his obligations, citing the successful sketching trips he had been making out into the Suffolk countryside. Constable then went on to train at the Royal Academy in London and it was here that he first encountered both the Old Masters and the new, from Rubens to Gainsborough. For several years thereafter, the artist spent the winter in London, returning to paint in and around East Bergholt during the summer, though from 1811 onwards he also made regular visits to – and painted many pictures of – Salisbury, a city that was very much to his liking.

It's impossible to weigh and weight the various influences Constable absorbed at the Royal Academy, but with remarkable fortitude he broke with the Romantic, Italianate landscape tradition that was then in vogue, opting instead for finely detailed and observed landscapes that were reminiscent of the Dutch Realists of the seventeenth century. Perhaps even more remarkably, he introduced a startling freshness of light and colour to his paintings, capturing sunlight in blobs of yellow and white, storms with rapid and broken brushwork. Constable's inspiration was quite simply his delight in his rural surroundings – as he summed it up himself "The sound of water escaping from mill dams, willows, old rotten planks, slimy posts and brickwork, I love such things".

Initially at least, matters both financial and matrimonial were difficult for Constable: his paintings were poorly received and the family of his proposed bride, Maria Bicknell, was dead set against the match. In 1816, however, his father died, which both secured his finances and enabled the marriage to take place. The next few years were the best of times for Constable. His paintings became increasingly popular and Maria, very much the love of his life, produced a fair brood of children. In 1828, the high times ended abruptly with the death of Maria, a shock from which he never really recovered, always being "prey to melancholy and anxious thoughts". He lies buried alongside his wife in Hampstead.

Constable is often considered as the most English of painters and it comes as a surprise to realize his influence was actually far greater in France, where he inspired both the Barbizon School and the French Impressionists.

and well-proportioned structure with a sweeping, sixteenth-century nave that is adorned by some attractive Victorian stained glass in the style of the Pre-Raphaelites. Constable painted the church on several occasions and today it holds one of the artist's rare religious paintings, *The Ascension*, but frankly it's a good job Constable concentrated on landscapes – his figure of Christ floating in the sky manages to be both trite and unconvincing. Dedham is also popular with day-trippers, who arrive here by the coach-load throughout the summer, and one of the results has been the creation of the **Dedham Art and Craft Centre** (daily 10am–5pm; free; ☎01206 322666, ⓦdedhamartandcraftcentre.co.uk), housed in a converted church just along the main street from St Mary's. The centre holds over thirty stores, selling everything from clothes and furniture to photography, ceramics, jewellery and garden gubbins.

Sir Alfred Munnings Art Museum

Castle House, CO7 6AZ • April–Oct Wed, Thurs, Sat & Sun 2–5pm • £5 • ⓦ siralfredmunnings.co.uk

In front of the Art and Craft Centre, Dedham's main street swings right for the mile-long journey to the **Sir Alfred Munnings Art Museum**, in Castle House, an expansive country villa set in its own grounds. Barely remembered today, Munnings (1875–1959) was a major figure and President of the Royal Academy in the 1940s. He earned his artistic spurs as a poster artist for Caley's Chocolates of Norwich, but made a name for himself as an official war artist attached to the Canadian cavalry in 1918. It was then that he discovered his penchant for painting horses – with and without their riders – a skill that brought him scores of aristocratic commissions, though today his

8

DASTARDLY DEEDS IN POLSTEAD

There's no strong reason to visit the hamlet of **Polstead**, a couple of miles north of Stoke-by-Nayland, but the village was on everyone's lips in the 1820s on account of the **Red Barn Murder**, which shocked and titillated the whole of England. At first glance, it was a simple tale: a young mole-catcher's daughter by the name of **Maria Marten** had arranged to meet her lover **William Corder** at the Red Barn, a local landmark, from where they were to elope to Ipswich. Unluckily for Marten, Corder killed her instead and although he subsequently sent letters to her family purporting to come from Maria, the game was up when the authorities found her body buried in the barn – no one could say Corder was a master of subterfuge. Corder was quickly tracked down in London – where he had married someone else, a certain Mary Moore – brought back to Suffolk, and then tried and hanged in front of a huge crowd in Bury St Edmunds in 1828.

In itself the murder might have passed without too much attention, but during and after the trial, all sorts of details emerged which were bizarre and riveting in equal measure: to start with, Maria had already had two children, one with William's older brother, Thomas, and one with William himself – and, for that matter, there were persistent rumours that William and Maria had murdered their own child the year before. Neither was their elopement a secret: William had suggested to Maria that they meet at the Red Barn in the presence of Maria's stepmother, Ann Marten, who was probably having an affair with William herself. To add to this heady mix of infanticide and sexual shenanigans, there was also the gore: despite lengthy and detailed proceedings, the exact cause of Maria's death could not be ascertained – she was either shot, strangled or stabbed, or a combination of all three, but no one was sure. William Corder's guilt was, however, not in doubt, and his sentence exemplary: "…That you be hanged by the Neck until you are Dead; and that your body shall afterwards be dissected and anatomized". Cambridge University students did the honours, concluding – in the mumbo-jumble style of the phrenologists of the period – that Corder's skull showed strong signs of "secretiveness and destructiveness". Bits and pieces of Corder ended up at Moyse's Hall Museum in Bury St Edmunds (see p.303), as did a book giving an account of the murder bound in the poor bugger's tanned skin.

The Red Barn itself suffered for its notoriety too: literally thousands of sightseers visited Polstead, stripping the barn down for souvenirs and even turning its plank walls into toothpicks; the remains burnt down in 1842.

paintings of rural East Anglia rest more easily on the eye. It was Modernism that did for Munnings: as President of the Royal Academy, he savaged almost every form of modern art there was, creating enemies by the score and ensuring he was soon ridiculed as old-fashioned and out of touch. The museum displays a comprehensive range of Munnings's paintings and posters and although few would say they were inspiring, seeing them is a pleasant way to fill a (rainy) afternoon. A clearly signed **footpath** leads from the village cross beside the church to the museum – allow about fifteen minutes.

Stoke-by-Nayland and Nayland

North from Dedham, the B1029 dips beneath the A12 on its way to **Higham**, where you pick up the road to **STOKE-BY-NAYLAND**, four miles further west. This is the most picturesque of villages, where a knot of half-timbered and pastel-painted cottages cuddle up to one of Constable's favourite subjects, **St Mary's Church** (daily 9am–5pm), with its pretty brick and stone-trimmed tower. The doors of the church's south porch are covered by the beautifully carved if badly weathered figures of a medieval **Jesse Tree** (purporting to show the ancestors of Christ) and, although the interior is sombre and severe, it does boast a beautifully carved medieval font and a pair of splendid, seventeenth-century alabaster tombs, one each in the south and north chancel chapels. The village also has a pair of appealing pub-restaurants (see below).

Travelling southwest from Stoke-by-Nayland, it's two miles back to the River Stour at **NAYLAND**, a workaday little place whose most distinctive feature is the **church of St James** (daily 9am–5pm), whose square tower and copper-green spire poke high into the sky. Inside, behind the high altar, Constable's *Christ Blessing the Bread and Wine* is one of only three attempts he made at a religious theme – and, dating from 1809, it was completed long before he found his artistic rhythm.

8

GETTING AROUND · DEDHAM VALE

By train The nearest station is Manningtree, on the Colchester to Norwich line, from where it's a couple of miles gambol northwest to Flatford Mill.

By bus Exploring Dedham Vale by public transport is problematic – distances are small, but buses between the villages are generally infrequent. The best you'll do is the reasonably frequent bus service from Colchester to Dedham and Stoke-by-Nayland and Nayland. For timetable details, go to ⓦ suffolkonboard.com.

By car Drivers will find Flatford Mill well signed from the B1070, which links the A12 and the A137. The Mill is located at the end of a country lane, which is itself a dead end. Note that it's a circuitous drive of around 5km from Flatford Mill to Dedham (see p.279) via the A12.

On foot For walkers, footpaths crisscross the area, with some of the most enjoyable being in the vicinity of Dedham village. All the local tourist offices sell easy-to-use walking leaflets.

ACCOMMODATION AND EATING

FLATFORD MILL

The Granary B&B Flatford Mill, CO7 6UL ☎01206 298111, ⓦ granaryflatford.co.uk. In the annexe of the old granary that was once owned by Constable's father, this appealing B&B has a real cottage feel with its beamed ceilings and antique furniture. There are two ground-floor guest rooms here, both en suite and both opening onto a garden that borders the River Stour. **£58**

DEDHAM

The Sun Inn High St, Dedham, CO7 6DF ☎01206 323351, ⓦ thesuninndedham.com. Among Dedham's several pubs, the pick is *The Sun*, an ancient place, which has been sympathetically modernized. The menu is strong on local ingredients and offers a tasty range of both Italian

and British dishes, all washed down by real ales; main courses average around £13. The Sun also has five en-suite rooms decorated in a creative blend of country-inn and boutique hotel, from four-poster beds through to billowy, caramel-cream curtains. **£145**

STOKE-BY-NAYLAND

The Angel Inn Polstead St, CO6 4SA ☎01206 263245, ⓦ angelinnsuffolk.co.uk. A recent change of ownership means that things are on the move at this agreeable country pub with its bare-brick walls and rustic beams. The menu is firmly British – steak-and-ale pie, fish and chips – with mains averaging around £13. *The Angel* also has half a dozen comfortable en-suite guest rooms, each of which is pleasantly kitted out in a sort of country house style with lots of creams. **£100**

The Crown Polstead St, CO6 4SE ☎01206 262001, ⓦ crowninn.net. *The Crown* may fancy itself just a little too much, but there's no disputing the quality of the food or the inventiveness of the menu, which features such delights as venison chop with horseradish and mustard butter, watercress and chips, with mains starting at £12.

The decor is appealing too, with the open-plan restaurant spreading over several separate areas and decorated in a sort of low-key, country house style with flowery wallpaper and so forth. The same decorative approach has been followed in the eleven bedrooms, which are all kept in tiptop condition. **£95**

Sudbury

With a population of around twelve thousand, **SUDBURY** has doubled in size in the last forty years, to become by far the most important town in this part of the Stour Valley. A handful of timber-framed houses recalls wool-trade prosperity, but its salad days were underwritten by another local industry, silk weaving, which survives on a small scale even now. Sudbury's most famous export, however, is **Thomas Gainsborough**, the leading English portraitist of the eighteenth century, whose statue, with brush and palette, stands on the traffic-choked triangle of **Market Hill**, the town's predominantly Victorian marketplace. A superb collection of the artist's work is on display a few yards away in the house where he was born – Gainsborough's House. Sudbury also saw service as a major staging post on the journey north to Norwich and it was here that a young reporter by the name of **Charles Dickens** came to observe the general election of 1836, a process whose assorted corruptions he described in *The Pickwick Papers*, with Sudbury rebranded to obvious effect as the fictional *Eatanswill*.

Gainsborough's House

46 Gainsborough St, CO10 2EU • Mon–Sat 10am–5pm • £4.50, free Tues 1–5pm • ☎ 01787 372958, ⓦ gainsborough.org

Kept in excellent order, **Gainsborough's House** possesses an outstanding collection of the artist's work distributed over a couple of main floors. The house also offers a lively programme of **temporary exhibitions**, has a café and a garden, and organizes lessons and demonstrations in its Print Workshop, which is lodged in what was originally the coach house. As for the man himself, **Thomas Gainsborough** (1727–88) was the son of a Sudbury cloth merchant, who left his home town when he was just thirteen, moving to London where he was apprenticed to an engraver. Nevertheless, it seems he was soon moonlighting and the earliest of his surviving portrait paintings – his *Boy and Girl*, a remarkably self-assured work dated to 1744 – is displayed here in two pieces as someone, somewhere chopped up the original. In 1752, Gainsborough moved on to Ipswich, where he quickly established himself as a portrait painter to the Suffolk gentry with one of his specialities being wonderful "conversation pieces", so-called because the sitters engage in polite chitchat – or genteel activity – with a landscape as the backdrop. Stints in Bath and London followed and it was during these years that Gainsborough developed a fluid, flatteringly easy style that was ideal for his well-heeled subjects, who posed in becoming postures painted in soft, evanescent colours. Examples of Gainsborough's **later work** on display include the *Portrait of Harriet, Viscountess Tracy* (1763) and the particularly striking *Portrait of Abel Moysey, MP* (1771). In his last years, the artist also dabbled with romantic paintings of country scenes – as in *A Wooded Landscape with Cattle by a Pool* – a playful variation of the serious landscaping painting he loved to do best; the rest, he often said, just earned him a living. Gainsborough never bothered with assistants, with one exception, his nephew **Gainsborough Dupont** (1754–97), who has a room devoted to his work on the top floor.

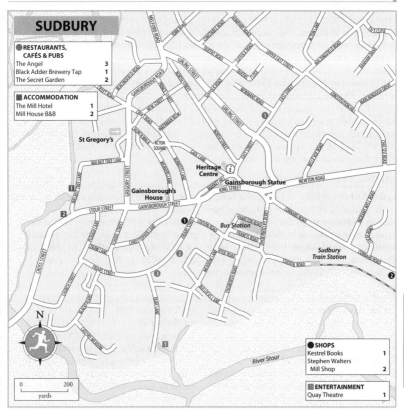

RESTAURANTS, CAFÉS & PUBS
The Angel	3
Black Adder Brewery Tap	1
The Secret Garden	2

ACCOMMODATION
| The Mill Hotel | 1 |
| Mill House B&B | 2 |

SHOPS
| Kestrel Books | 1 |
| Stephen Walters Mill Shop | 2 |

ENTERTAINMENT
| Quay Theatre | 1 |

8

Sudbury Heritage Centre and Museum

Gaol Lane, off Market Hill • Mon–Sat 10am–4pm • Free • ⓦ sudburysuffolk.co.uk/heritagecentre

Adjoining the tourist office, at the back of the Town Hall, the **Sudbury Heritage Centre and Museum** may be small and a tad short of exhibits, but its explicatory panels are well written and together they present a clear and concise history of the town. There are particularly good sections on the silk-weaving factories that kept the town going in the nineteenth century and the arrival of the **USAF in World War II**. The Americans began to arrive in numbers in 1943, congregating at a hastily prepared airstrip beside the tiny hamlet of Chilton Street, a few miles west of town. By the following year, there were no less than three thousand stationed in the vicinity of Sudbury, much to the delight of many local women, who found them much more attractive than the local men – they were generally bigger, better paid and had better teeth. Predictably, Suffolk men were less enamoured, coining various wry-to-bitter jokes about their predicament.

St Gregory's Church

Gregory St, CO10 2BJ • Daily 8.30am–5.30pm • Free • ⓦ stgregoryschurch.org.uk

There are three medieval churches in Sudbury, but the only one of any real interest is the church of **St Gregory**, a large flint, rubble and stone-trimmed structure whose heavily buttressed tower pokes high into the sky on the west side of the town centre.

Highlights of the interior include the painted ceiling of the chancel, the Victorian stained-glass windows, and more particularly the cover of the font, an extraordinarily ornate wooden structure dating from the fifteenth century. In an alcove, there's also a display on Richard II and his henchman **Simon of Sudbury**, one-time Papal nuncio and Archbishop of Canterbury. Simon was appointed Lord Chancellor of England in 1380 and this was to cost him his life during the Peasants' Revolt, which convulsed much of southern England the following year. Taxation was the immediate cause of the rebellion and when the insurgents stormed the Tower of London, they caught and beheaded Simon, holding him responsible for the poll tax of 1381. The revolt was brutally suppressed and afterwards Simon's body went to Canterbury Cathedral, but his **skull** was sent here to St Gregory's: it's locked away in the vestry, but the church custodian is more than happy to show it to you if you ask.

ARRIVAL AND INFORMATION SUDBURY

By train Sudbury train station is a 5–10min walk from the centre via Station Rd. There are hourly services to and from Marks Tey, on the London to Colchester line.

By bus The bus station is on Hamilton Rd, just south of Market Hill; it doesn't win any beauty contests, but a refurbishment is planned. The main local bus company is H.C. Chambers (☎01787 227233, ⓦwww.chamberscoaches

.co.uk), who – among a batch of services – link Sudbury with Colchester.

Tourist office At the back of the Town Hall on Gaol Lane, just off Market Hill (Mon–Fri 9am–5pm, plus April–Sept Sat 10am–4.45pm; Oct–March Sat 10am–2.45pm; ☎01787 881320, ⓦsudburytowncouncil.co.uk).

ACCOMMODATION

The Mill Hotel Walnut Tree Lane, CO10 1BD ☎01787 375544, ⓦthemillhotelsudbury.co.uk. Near the river on the west side of town, this distinctive hotel occupies an intelligently recycled, Victorian mill, whose four floors rise high above their surroundings. The hotel has its original flagstone floors and water wheel, now enclosed within a glass case, but of its 56 rooms, those in the main building are more appealing than those in the adjoining annexe –

specify if you book. **£100**

Mill House B&B Cross St, CO10 6DS ☎01787 882966, ⓦmillhousesudbury.co.uk. This old house and cottage, whose exterior walls are painted terracotta, has a couple of comfortable, en-suite guest rooms, but its prime appeal is its conservatory and garden, which stretch down towards the River Stour. Central location and home-made breakfasts. **£70**

EATING AND DRINKING

Perhaps surprisingly, Sudbury's café and restaurant scene is distinctly pedestrian with only one, maybe two places worth a second look. Enjoyable or at least distinctive pubs are similarly thin on the ground, though there is one notable exception.

The Angel 43 Friars St, CO10 2AG ☎01787 882228. This traditional boozer has been refitted and refurbished in slick modern style – all high-back chairs and wood floors – but the food can be unreliable. Probably a better bet for lunch than dinner with the likes of venison, dauphinoise potatoes in a thyme jus costing in the region of £15. Mon–Sat noon–2pm & 6–9.30pm, Sun noon–3pm.

Black Adder Brewery Tap 21 East St, CO10 2TP. Not much in the way of decorative finesse here, but who cares when the big deal is the beer – a rotating selection of eight real ales on draught, but always including something from Mauldons, a local brewer who produce, among several

offerings, the sterling Black Adder stout. There's a courtyard patio out at the back, pub grub and occasional jazz gigs too. Mon–Thurs 11am–11pm, Fri & Sat 11am–midnight, Sun noon–10.30pm.

The Secret Garden 21 Friars St, CO10 2AA ☎01787 372030. Independent tearoom with bells, where the menu has lots of French flourishes and they do their best to source locally. For lunch, you might try their ham, spinach and cheddar cheese salad for just under £10. Cosy, antique premises too. Mon–Sat 9am–5pm, plus Fri & Sat 7–9.30pm.

ENTERTAINMENT

Quay Theatre Quay Lane, CO10 2AN ☎01787 374745, ⓦquaytheatre.org.uk. Sudbury's main performance venue covers all the bases, from country to comedy, soul to

skiffle. There's classical music too, plus jazz – Jacqui Dankworth has appeared here – and a good film programme organized by the town's Cinema Club.

SHOPS

Kestrel Books 10 Friars St, CO10 2AA ☎01787 372735. Enterprising, independent bookshop that stocks both new and secondhand titles. Also does sidelines in cards and jigsaws, road maps and local hiking maps. Mon–Sat 9.30am–5pm.

Stephen Walters Mill Shop Cornard St, CO10 2XB ☎01787 466189, ⓦ www.stephenwalters.co.uk. This factory shop – the mill (not open to the public) is next door – sells handbags and cushions as well as roll upon roll of fabric. The company moved here from London in 1894 and it was in Sudbury that they established a flourishing silk-weaving business, producing such items as parasols and black mourning crepe. They now focus on high-quality furnishing fabrics, with silk to the fore, as well as men's and women's clothing, again with silk the principal material. The shop is located a 5–10min walk from the town centre. Tues 10am–3pm, Wed–Fri 10am–4.30pm, Sat 10am–3pm.

Long Melford

From Sudbury, it's just three miles to **LONG MELFORD**, which dates back to the Iron Age, though its heyday was as a cloth town in the fifteenth century. The village may share the same industrial history as its neighbours, but it looks very different, its northern approaches dominated by a long and very conspicuous triangular **green**, which is itself flanked by **Melford Hall and Park**, one of Suffolk's most popular country houses. Beyond the green, the village is not much more than one long street, variously the High Street, Hall Street and Southgate, and this is flanked by a pleasing mix of architectural styles, from Georgian villas to Victorian red brick. The main street is also overlooked by the splendid **church of the Holy Trinity** and lined by a good selection of shops, pub-restaurants and a couple of hotels. There's a second country house on the northern edge of the village, **Kentwell Hall** – altogether quite enough to pull in the tourists by the coachload.

8

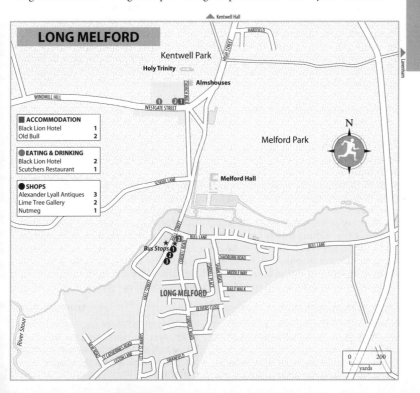

Melford Hall

Hall St, CO10 9AA • April & Oct Sat & Sun 1.30–5pm; May–Sept Wed–Sun 1.30–5pm • House and garden £6; garden only £3; NT • ⓦ nationaltrust.org.uk

The pepper-pot turrets and slender chimneys of **Melford Hall** were built on the orders of William Cordell, a prominent Elizabethan lawyer and Speaker of the House of Commons in the 1550s. The house goes round three sides of a courtyard, with its entrance set away from the village to face the garden. The general shape of the house may be Elizabethan, but much of the detail is not – cue the Georgian sash windows – and neither is the **interior**, which was badly damaged by fire in the 1940s. Highlights here include the splendid main staircase, the long gallery on the second floor and the Rococo fireplace in the drawing room, though most visitors are more interested by the **Beatrix Potter Room**, which features a selection of the author's watercolours and drawings. Potter (1866–1943), who was related to the Hyde Parkers, the long-time owners of Melford Hall, slept in the **Victorian Bedroom** when she stayed here, as she often did, bringing with her a travelling menagerie of toy animals.

Holy Trinity church

High St, CO10 9DN • Daily: April–Oct 10am–6pm; Nov–March 10am–4pm • Free

One of the finest churches in the whole of Suffolk, **Holy Trinity** occupies a gentle ridge on the northern edge of Long Melford, opposite Melford Park. Mostly dating from the 1490s, the church's long and lovely nave, with its high pointed windows, marches up to a squat, square tower, which is topped by a set of elongated pinnacles. Inside, the first eight windows of the north aisle hold some especially beautiful, late-medieval **stained glass**, including – in the second frame from the left in the most westerly window – the figure of Elizabeth Talbot, said to be the inspiration for the original illustration of the Duchess in Lewis Carroll's *Alice in Wonderland*. At the east end of the north aisle is the **Clopton Chantry Chapel**, named after the former owners of Kentwell Hall and distinguished by a rare example of a **Lily Crucifix window** depicting Christ crucified on the leaves of a lily – most were destroyed during the Reformation. In the adjacent **Sanctuary** are the assorted tombs of another powerful family, the Cordells, with one of the clan, Sir William, lying there in his armour beneath a fancy set of columns and coffered arches.

Kentwell Hall

High St, CO10 9BA • Opening times vary – check website • £9.95, garden & farm £7 • ☎ 01787 310207, ⓦ kentwell.co.uk

Approached along an avenue of lime trees just to the north of the village, moated **Kentwell Hall** has an impressive red-brick facade whose long line of gables is topped off by a pair of dinky, copper-green cupolas. A fire in the 1820s took care of most of the original interior and the house was pretty much a ruin when the present owners moved in during the 1970s, since when they have re-invented it as a major tourist attraction, creating, for example, a two-dimensional, brick-paved maze; a camera obscura fabricated from an old gazebo; and a rare breeds farm. They have also restored the old ice house and installed the strange vessel-cum-prop that was designed by Terry Gillian for the 1988 film *The Adventures of Baron Munchausen*. These specific attractions are also supplemented by a lively programme of shows and special events, from medieval banquets to sheepshearing.

ARRIVAL AND DEPARTURE   LONG MELFORD

By bus Buses pull in along the main street and there are reasonably frequent services to Sudbury, Bury St Edmunds, Colchester and Ipswich.

By foot Perhaps the happiest way to reach Long Melford is on foot from Lavenham (see p.289), four miles to the northeast. For the most part, the footpath follows the old railway line, which was closed down in 1961. In Long Melford, the main path emerges on the north side of the village opposite the entrance drive to Kentwell Hall.

ACCOMMODATION AND EATING

Black Lion Hotel The Green, CO10 9DN ☎01787 312356, ⓦblacklionhotel.net. Quite simply the best place to eat and sleep in Long Melford, this small, privately owned hotel occupies a good-looking Georgian building a few yards from the church of the Holy Trinity. The interior is kitted out in an attractive, country house style and each of the ten bedrooms has luxurious, heavy drapes and iron bedsteads. Guests can eat in the restaurant, which is smart and fairly formal, or in the bar – less formally and more economically. They are strong on local food – partridge pâtè and Suffolk pork for example – and the menu offers some interesting variations on traditional English dishes as well as more straightforward favourites like shepherd's pie (for £13). Daily: lunch noon–2pm, afternoon tea 2–5pm & dinner 7–11pm. **£125**

Old Bull Hall St, CO10 9JG ☎01787 378494, ⓦoldenglishinns.co.uk. One of a largish chain, Old English Inns, this medium-sized hotel occupies a handsome half-timbered building that was originally built for a wealthy cloth merchant in the fifteenth century. Many of the original features have survived, from the squeaky wooden floors and open fireplaces through to the heavy oak beams in the foyer, but the 25 guest rooms are suitably modern, furnished and fitted in a pleasant and unfussy style. **£100**

Scutchers Restaurant Westgate St, CO10 9DP ☎01787 310200. Smart and intimate restaurant offering a short but finely judged menu that features the likes of plaice fillet on a crab mash with a lemon butter sauce. Save space for a dessert – if it's on, their vanilla panacotta with a compote of cherries is especially delicious. Mains average around £15. The restaurant is a few yards west of the *Black Lion Hotel*. Tues–Sat noon–2.30pm & 7–10pm.

SHOPPING

Alexander Lyall Antiques Belmont House, Hall St, CO10 9JF ☎01787 375434, ⓦalexlyall.ndo.co.uk. Upmarket, antique furniture shop whose forte is top-quality Georgian and Victorian mahogany, rosewood and walnut pieces, for example dwarf and revolving bookcases, pedestal desks, dining tables, corner cupboards, chest of drawers and chairs. Also do promising side lines in mirrors, cameos and ceramics. Near the *Old Bull*. Mon–Sat 10am–5.30pm.

Lime Tree Gallery Lime Tree House, Hall St, CO10 9JF ☎01787 319046, ⓦlimetreegallery.com. Of the several fine and applied art shops in Long Melford, this is arguably the pick, specializing in contemporary paintings and glassware. They are particularly keen on Scottish artists and they also organize several exhibitions each and every year. Close to the *Old Bull*. Mon–Sat 10am–5pm.

Nutmeg 8 Hall St, CO10 9JF ☎01787 311842, ⓦnutmeglongmelford.co.uk. Chic women's fashion shop, which specializes in smart, casual wear from an eclectic mix of designers – Lauren Vidal, Sahara, La Bottega di Brunella and Mouse. Particularly good for separates, but there's also a good selection of dresses and accessories. A few doors down from the *Old Bull*. Mon–Sat 9.30am–5pm.

8

The Upper Stour River Valley

Heading west from Long Melford, the **A1092** stays close to the River Stour as it cuts a meandering route through meadows and farmland, acting as the county boundary between Suffolk and Essex at the same time. En route, the road slips through several little villages, among which **Cavendish** and **Clare** are the most appealing. The other village of some interest hereabouts is **Hartest**, which lies six miles north of Long Melford along narrow country lanes.

Cavendish

CAVENDISH is a tiny place, but it does have a whopping **green**, a sloping slab of grass framed by an attractive mix of old houses from Georgian villas to terracotta-painted cottages. The village looks prosperous, and it most certainly is, and it also has one real claim to fame as the final resting place of **Leonard Cheshire** (1917–1992) and his wife **Sue Ryder** (1924–2000), the joint founders of a highly regarded charity that cares for people with terminal and/or incurable illnesses both in the UK and abroad. The couple's good deeds are recalled by the pocket-sized **Sue Ryder Shop** (Mon–Sat 9am–5pm; ☎01787 282591), which overlooks the green. Nearby is the **church of St Mary** (daily 9.30am–5pm or dusk), a handsome medieval structure where pride of place goes to an exquisite Flemish alabaster of the Crucifixion dating to the sixteenth century and now positioned on the north wall of the nave. St Mary's may look the picture of peace and tranquillity, but there were bloody goings on here during the Peasants' Revolt of 1381. The local bigwig, a certain John Cavendish, was chased through the village by the rebels and managed to get to the church doors, where he grabbed the knocker and claimed sanctuary – but to no avail as the peasants chopped him up anyway: the **knocker** is still there, worn thin by thousands of hands over hundreds of years.

Clare

Small and pretty, the tiny town of **CLARE** was fast out of the municipal blocks: as early as the eleventh century, it had a sizeable number of merchant-landowners and by the thirteenth it was a major cloth-producing town, churning out heavy-duty broadcloth by the cartload for export far and wide. Like the rest of Suffolk, it hit the economic buffers in the sixteenth century with the decline of the wool trade, but the townsfolk diversified and **Daniel Defoe**, for one, remarked on the number of turkeys in Clare, though he did not like the place at all: it was he said in his *Tour Thro' the Whole Island of Great Britain*, written in the 1720s, "a poor town and dirty".

Clare Castle Country Park

Malting Lane • Daylight hours • Free

To protect his real estate in the 1070s, the local lord of Clare built a wooden motte and bailey castle down near the River Stour and the keep was, in its turn, replaced by a stone structure a couple of centuries later. Perched high on an earthen mound, the battered ruins of this **castle** are now incorporated within **Clare Castle Country Park**, which also holds the remains of another era – the railway age, with the old station, the station house and the shed of the former goods yard nestling among the greenery. There's also an unsigned footpath leading west along the river from the Country Park to **Clare Priory**, a modern pink-stone structure inhabited by Augustinian monks and built on the site of the medieval monastery, which was suppressed during the Reformation.

Ancient House Museum

26 High St, CO10 8NY • Easter to Sept Thurs, Fri & Sun 2–5pm, Sat 11.30am–5pm • £1 • ⊕ clare-ancient-house-museum.co.uk

From Clare Castle Country Park, it's a couple of minutes' walk to the town's main crossroads, from where the High Street proceeds north to the **Ancient House Museum**, which holds a series of mildly diverting displays on the history of the town, though frankly the exterior of the building is the main pull on account of its fancy plasterwork (or pargeting).

Church of St Peter and St Paul

High St, CO10 8PB • Daily 9.30am–5pm or dusk • Free

The Ancient House faces out towards Clare's finest building, the **church of St Peter and St Paul**, whose exterior, with its turrets, mighty windows and castellated tower, looks both dignified and serene. The interior is similarly imposing and a menagerie of medieval faces peer down from the upper reaches of the nave. Also in the nave is a large and really rather dramatic Stuart **gallery-pew** that looks like an opera box – the lords of Clare may have been equal before God with their fellow worshippers, but not that equal.

Hartest

Distinguished by its lovely old houses, the hamlet of **HARTEST**, deep in the Suffolk countryside, frames an expansive green, where the war memorial stands proud and solitary. Hartest is located in what is sometimes called "High Suffolk", an area of rolling agricultural land very different from the flatter heaths, forests and fens to the north and east, though the village was once surrounded by thick woodland as recalled by its sign, which features a stag standing tall against a boulder – the so-called Hartest stone. A narrow country lane – Hartest Hill – leads southeast from the village to **Giffords Hall vineyard** (☎01284 830799, ⓦgiffordshall.co.uk), which was planted about twenty years ago and now produces some of the region's best-regarded wines. They organize regular open days and tastings throughout the season – call ahead or check their website for details.

ACCOMMODATION AND EATING
THE UPPER STOUR RIVER VALLEY

CAVENDISH

The George The Green, CO10 8BA ☎01787 280248, ⓦthecavendishgeorge.co.uk. Smart and very amenable country pub-cum-restaurant, where the lively menu often surprises – try, for example, the whole roasted quail, butternut squash, olive and hazelnuts (£13). *The George* occupies a very old building, many of whose features have been preserved and conserved. It also has four en-suite guest rooms decorated in soothing colours and with lots of period flourishes. Kitchen open: Mon–Sat noon–2pm & 6–9.30pm, Sun noon–3pm. £75

CLARE

Number One Delicatessen & Café 1 High St, CO10 8NY ☎01787 278932, ⓦnumberonedeli.co.uk. This café and delicatessen, in the old village post office, serves a tasty line in sandwiches and light lunches. Mon–Sat 9am–5pm.

HARTEST

The Crown The Green, IP29 4D ☎01284 830250. Hartest may be small, but here, unlike many other villages the pub has survived. A sprawling affair situated just off the green. It's one of the Greene King chain, so the beers are reliably good, and there's a pleasant and well-kept garden. Daily noon–11pm.

8

Lavenham

LAVENHAM, some eight miles northeast of Sudbury, was once a centre of the region's wool trade and is now one of the most visited villages in Suffolk, thanks to its unrivalled ensemble of perfectly preserved half-timbered houses. In outward appearance at least, the whole place has changed little since the demise of the wool industry, owing in part to a zealous local preservation society, which has carefully maintained the village's antique appearance by banning from view such modern frivolities as advertising hoardings. Such a setting has attracted the occasional film producer – though not perhaps as many as you would have thought: Stanley Kubrick used the Guildhall (see below) for several scenes of *Barry Lyndon*; parts of *Harry Potter and the Deathly Hallows* were filmed here in 2010; and, much more bizarrely, John Lennon and Yoko Ono made a short film in Lavenham in 1969, peering out from big black capes as a hot air balloon was launched from the Market Place in *Apotheosis 2*. Lavenham's musical connections don't end there: "Twinkle, Twinkle Little Star" was written by Jane Taylor, the daughter of the Reverend Isaac Taylor in the early 1800s, shortly after the poor old reverend had been driven out of his village by locals angry at his French revolutionary sympathies.

Guildhall

Market Place, CO10 9QZ • March Wed–Sun 11am–4pm; April–Oct daily 11am–5pm; Nov Sat & Sun 11am–4pm • £4; NT • ☎01787 247646, ⓦnationaltrust.org.uk

Lavenham is at its most beguiling in the triangular **Market Place**, an airy spot flanked by pastel-painted, medieval dwellings whose beams have been bent into all sorts of wonky angles by the passing of the years. It's here you'll find the village's most celebrated building, the lime-washed, timber-framed **Guildhall of Corpus Christi**, erected in the sixteenth century as the headquarters of one of Lavenham's four guilds. In the much-altered interior (used successively as a prison and

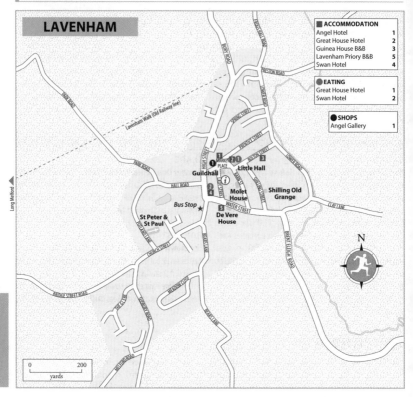

workhouse), there are modest exhibitions on timber-framed buildings, medieval guilds, village life and the wool industry, though most visitors soon end up in the walled garden or the teashop next door.

Little Hall

Market Place, CO10 9QZ • April–Oct Mon 11am–5.30pm; Wed, Thurs Sat & Sun 2–5.30pm • £3 • ☎ 01787 247019, ⌨ littlehall.org.uk

From the Guildhall, it's a few yards across the Market Place to another handsome timber-framed building, **Little Hall**. Dating from the 1390s, but expanded and modified in Tudor times, the Hall had become something of a ruin by the 1920s when the Gayer-Anderson brothers rode to the rescue, repairing and reviving the place and installing the objets d'art that are on display today.

Back outside, the **view** down Prentice Street from beside the *Angel Hotel* is one of Lavenham's most exquisite – a line of creaky timber-framed dwellings dipping into the deep green countryside beyond.

Church of St Peter and St Paul

Church St, CO10 9QT • Daily 8.30am–4pm • Free

Be sure to spare some time for the Perpendicular church of **St Peter and St Paul**, which, with its gargoyle water spouts and carved boars above the entrance, is sited a short walk southwest of the centre, at the top of Church Street. Local merchants endowed the church with a nave of majestic proportions and a mighty flint tower, at 141ft the highest for miles around, partly to celebrate the Tudor victory at the Battle of Bosworth in 1485, but mainly to show just how wealthy they had become. Inside, the nave is suitably wide and high and the nave aisles hold two splendid Chantry chapels, whose screens are simply exquisite, their delicate and intricate carving a wonderful illustration of sixteenth-century craftsmanship. In the floor, look out also for the tiny and really rather mournful **brass** of a baby in swaddling clothes, who died just ten days old sometime in the seventeenth century.

ARRIVAL AND INFORMATION   LAVENHAM

By bus Buses to Lavenham pull in at the corner of Water and Church streets, a 5min walk from the Market Place. Chambers bus #753 (Mon–Sat hourly; ⓦ chamberscoaches. co.uk) links Lavenham with Sudbury, Long Melford, Bury St Edmunds and Colchester.

Tourist office Just south off the Market Place on Lady St (mid-March to Oct daily 10am–4.45pm; Nov to mid-Dec daily 11am–3pm; Jan to mid-March Sat & Sun 11am–3pm;

ⓣ 01787 248207, ⓦ southandheartofsuffolk.org.uk). They sell a detailed, street-by-street walking guide and can help with accommodation – there's plenty of choice but rooms still get mighty tight in the high season. They can also advise on – and sell maps of – local walking routes, with the most obvious stroll being the four-mile jaunt southwest to Long Melford (see p.285), mostly along the old railway line.

ACCOMMODATION

Angel Hotel Market Place, CO10 9QZ ⓣ 01787 247388, ⓦ maypolehotels.com. One of a small chain, the *Angel* has just eight guest rooms decorated in a spick-and-span modern style, though some are enlivened by period flourishes – exposed beams, old open fires and so forth. The popular bar-restaurant cooks up a good range of English dishes and prices are reasonable – the lemon sole, for instance, costs just £11. __£130__

★ **Great House Hotel & Restaurant** Market Place, CO10 9QZ ⓣ 01787 247431, ⓦ greathouse.co.uk. Charming, family-run hotel bang in the centre of the village. There are five guest rooms here and each is decorated in a thoughtful and extremely tasteful manner, amalgamating the original features of the very old house with the new. Deeply comfortable beds and a great breakfast to round it all off. __£95__

Guinea House B&B 16 Bolton St, CO10 9RG ⓣ 01787 249046, ⓦ guineahouse.co.uk. In a dinky little house a short walk from the Market Place, this well-established

B&B has two low-beamed, folksy-meets-cosy guest rooms. No credit cards. __£75__

Lavenham Priory B&B Water St, CO10 9RW ⓣ 01787 247404, ⓦ lavenhampriory.co.uk. The most luxurious B&B in Lavenham, this deluxe place occupies a handsome, half-timbered complex of buildings that began life as a priory. There are half-a-dozen en-suite guest rooms here, each decorated in a fancy version of period style – four-poster beds are (almost) de rigueur. __£120__

★ **Swan Hotel** High St, CO10 9QA ⓣ 01787 247477, ⓦ theswanatlavenham.co.uk. One of a small chain, this excellent hotel is a veritable rabbit warren of a place, its various nooks and crannies dating back several hundred years. There's a lovely – and very traditional – lounge to snooze in, especially in winter when the fire is stacked high with logs, a courtyard garden, an authentic Elizabethan Wool Hall, and a wood-panelled bar with mementoes of the American servicemen who hunkered down here in World War II – it's likely that the band leader Glenn Miller

8

A LAVENHAM WALKING TOUR

The centre of Lavenham is packed to the gunnels with historic buildings, several of which are of particular interest. The village peaked as a centre of the wool trade during the reign of Henry VIII, but there was a second spurt of industrial activity in Victorian times, when Lavenham factories turned out coconut matting and horsehair fabric. An especially fine example of a Tudor clothier's dwelling, **Molet House**, stands just off the Market Place on Barn Street, its splendid doorway set beneath a triple overhang of black and white timbers. Nearby **Shilling Street** boasts the finest assortment of Tudor facades in Lavenham, though the most conspicuous building – **Shilling Old Grange** – is a bit of a fraud as its lower floor was '"invented" in the 1920s. Shilling Street connects with Water Street, the site of a former horsehair factory and the distinctly bendy **De Vere House**, whose odd angles and thick mullion windows look decidedly Dickensian. Just along the street is *The Swan Hotel* (see above), which incorporates the old Wool Hall, reopened after a thorough refit in 1965 by, bizarrely enough, the then Miss World, Ann Sydney.

popped in for a pint or two. The guest rooms are very comfortable and aesthetically pleasing, and most have lots of original features – low wooden beams etc. **£180**

EATING AND DRINKING

★ **Great House Hotel & Restaurant** Market Place, CO10 9QZ ☎01787 247431, ⓦgreathouse.co.uk. This hotel restaurant specializes in classic French cuisine, with a three-course set meal costing £21 at lunch, £32 at night; you can also opt for à la carte. With such delights as belly of Suffolk pork confit and duck in cider, they have garnered rave reviews all over the place, so book ahead. Wed–Sun noon–2.30pm & Tues–Sat 7–10.30pm.

Swan Hotel High St, CO10 9QA ☎01787 247477, ⓦtheswanatlavenham.co.uk. The *Swan's* restaurant is first-rate, attracting what is by and large an older clientele, drawn here by the imaginative British-based cuisine with the likes of roasted wood pigeon and puy lentils. Mains start at around £13. Main restaurant is open daily 7–9pm, the brasserie daily noon–2.30pm & 5.30–9.30pm.

SHOPPING

Angel Gallery Market Place, CO10 9QZ ☎01787 248417, ⓦangelgallerylavenham.co.uk. Lavenham has more than its fair share of antique and souvenir shops – though, as befits such a prosperous village, there's certainly no tourist tat – and in the last few years several artists have moved here too. You may be able to catch sight of their work at the Angel Gallery, whose assorted paintings, sketches, ceramics and sculptures are displayed in an ancient wool merchant's house dating from the fifteenth century. Mon–Sat 10am–5pm.

Kersey, Hadleigh and around

Among the assorted towns and villages within easy striking distance of Lavenham, the prettiest is **Kersey**, where an impossibly picturesque main street of timber-framed houses seems to have dodged just about every historical bullet since the seventeenth century. Neighbouring **Hadleigh** is larger and more mundane, though it does have one or two interesting old buildings, while straggling **Bildeston** is home to one of the county's most enjoyable country hotels.

Kersey

Minuscule **KERSEY**, nine miles southeast of Lavenham off the A1141, is one of the most photographed villages in Suffolk. Another old wool town, it now comprises little more than one exquisite street of rickety old houses, which dips in the middle to cross a ford that's inhabited by a family of fearless ducks. Kersey's more populous past is recalled by the large parish **church of St Mary** (daily 9am–4.30pm or dusk; free), visible for miles around, perched on high ground above the village. The tower is classic Suffolk – square, heavy and strong – but the south **porch** is unusually grand and indeed it may not have been built for the villagers at all, but for pilgrims visiting the miracle-making shrine of Our Lady of Kersey, which was chopped up during the Reformation. The interior is a bit of a disappointment, though six painted panels from the old rood screen dado have somehow managed to survive, including a picture of St Edmund holding an arrow to represent his martyrdom (see p.301).

Hadleigh

From Kersey, it's two and a half miles southeast to the market town of **HADLEIGH**, whose long and really rather workaday **High Street** runs parallel to – and just to the east of – the River Brett. Locals from the surrounding villages pop in here to do their shopping, but for the passing visitor there are only a couple of buildings worth a second look, clustered close together, just west of the High Street and best reached via the elegant Georgian terrace that makes up **Queen Street**. Here, at the end of Queen Street, stands **St Mary's church** (daily: May–Sept 9am–5.30pm; Oct–April

---

DOWN ON THE FARM

Getting into the real swing of the tourist market, 140-acre **Hollow Trees Farm** (Semer, IP7 6HX; Mon–Sat 8.30am–5.45pm & Sun 9am–5pm; ☎01449 741247, ⓦhollowtrees.co.uk) offers "a farm experience that will delight all of your senses, from the noise of our busy farmyard to the smell of fresh baked bread". The shop sells their own vegetables and meat, there are a couple of clearly marked **farm trails**, and visitors can feed the animals in the livestock barn. Hollow Trees is located just north of Hadleigh in the hamlet of Semer.

9am–3.30pm), which mostly dates from the fifteenth century, being a good-looking replacement for several earlier versions. Legend asserts that Guthrum, the Danish chieftain and arch-rival of Alfred the Great, was buried underneath the south aisle in 889, but his remains have never been definitively identified. Opposite the church, across the graveyard, is the half-timbered **Guildhall**, every bit as immaculate as Lavenham's, with the earliest sections dating to the 1430s. Behind the church is the ornate brickwork of the **Deanery Tower**, a fifteenth-century gatehouse whose palace was never completed. In the garret room at the top of the tower, the Oxford Movement, which opposed liberal tendencies within the Anglican Church and sought to promote Anglo-Catholicism, was founded in 1833 by local rector Hugh Rose.

Bildeston

From Hadleigh, it's about four miles northwest to the hamlet of **BILDESTON**, whose long and narrow High Street strings along the shallow valley of the River Brett. The original village actually started out on higher ground a few hundred yards to the west, but the villagers opted for a more sheltered location in the thirteenth century, though the church was never moved, which is why the **church of St Mary Magdalene** occupies a solitary location among fields a five- to ten-minute walk from the High Street along Church Road. The church is a substantial affair, complete with an elaborate entrance porch, but the tower is new – the old one collapsed in 1975. Bildeston also possesses an outstanding hotel (see below).

8

ARRIVAL AND DEPARTURE   KERSEY, HADLEIGH AND AROUND

By bus Hadleigh is easy to reach by bus with regular services from the likes of Sudbury, Lavenham, Ipswich and Colchester, though Sundays can be a bit tricky. Buses pull into the bus station on Magdalen Rd, immediately to the east of the High St. From Hadleigh, there are buses to both Kersey and Bildeston, but only once or twice a day and not on Sundays.

ACCOMMODATION

KERSEY
Primrose Cottage The Street, IP7 6DY ☎01787 211115, ⓦgrove-cottages.co. It's not big and it's certainly not cheap, but *Primrose Cottage*, which dates from the sixteenth century, does do a little to fill the accommodation gap in Kersey. The decor may be a little traditional for some tastes, but the lounge with its open fireplace is especially cosy. One bedroom, sleeps two. Minimum stay two nights. **£225**

BILDESTON
★ **Bildeston Crown** High St, IP7 7EB ☎01449

740510, ⓦthebildestoncrown.com. Village hotels don't come much better than this lovely place, which occupies an immaculately maintained, mustard-painted half-timbered building – plus adjoining annexe – at the heart of Bildeston. The hotel has around a dozen rooms, where top-of-the-range facilities – wide-screen TVs, a/c, luxuriant bathrobes etc – are complemented by well-chosen furnishings, sometimes antique, sometimes modern: one room, for example, has an open fire and exposed beams, another has a four-poster bed. **£150–250**

EATING AND DRINKING

KERSEY
Bell Inn The Street, IP7 6DY. In ancient beamed premises

dating from the thirteenth century if not before, the village pub is strong on real ales with both Adnams and Greene

King represented. Filling bar food and snacks are available too. Tues–Fri 11.30am–3pm & 6–11pm, Sat 11.30am–11.30pm, Sun noon–10.30pm.

HADLEIGH

Crabtree's Café-Bar 66 High St, IP7 5EF ☎01473 828166, ⓦcrabtreescafebar.co.uk. Easily the liveliest place in Hadleigh, *Crabtree's* does a good line in coffee and cakes (the coffee is excellent), offers up tasty lunches and even has "disco'" nights in the bar. There's a garden terrace too. Mon–Sat 8am–6pm, Fri till 11pm, Sun 10am–3pm. Food served daily until 3.30pm.

BILDESTON

★ **Bildeston Crown** High St, IP7 7EB ☎01449 740510, ⓦthebildestoncrown.com. *The Crown's* restaurant is outstanding, its attractive modern decor respecting and including all sorts of period flourishes. The menu is modern British with added vim and gusto, featuring the likes of fish stew, saffron potato, aioli and rarebit croutons; mains average around £17. They also have special seven-course tasting menus, a real feast that lasts a good couple of hours with game a particular speciality. Daily noon–3pm & 7–10pm, 9.30pm on Sun.

SHOPPING

Kersey Pottery The Street, Kersey, IP7 6DY ☎01473 822092, ⓦkerseypottery.com. Occupying former stables, this bijou pottery features the stoneware of Fred Bramham and Dorothy Gorst. They employ a spectrum of glazes and regularly experiment with materials, for example fish-smokers' wood ashes. Also on display are the etchings of local artist Glynn Thomas. Tues–Sat 10am–5.30pm, plus occasional Sun and Mon 11am–5pm.

Stowmarket and around

Northeast of Bildeston lies the market town of **STOWMARKET**, which, with a population of around 16,000 is a relative giant hereabouts, though it has been badly mauled by the developers, a fate that has also befallen its near neighbour, **Needham Market**. Just outside Stowmarket is the hamlet of **Great Finborough** and it's here that the **DJ John Peel** holed up for several decades – and lies buried in the churchyard.

Museum of East Anglian Life

Lliffe Way, Stowmarket, IP14 1DE • Late March to Oct Mon–Sat 10.00am–5pm & Sun 11am–5pm; rest of year, open access to the museum site and the woodland walks • Late March to Oct £6.50, rest of year £2 • ☎01449 612229, ⓦeastanglianlife.org.uk

The main attraction in Stowmarket is the **Museum of East Anglian Life**, comprising a series of relocated old buildings moved here to a large site that features nearly two miles of woodland and riverside nature trails. Salvaged buildings include an old blacksmith's forge, a watermill, a grocer's, a Victorian schoolroom, a barn, an engineering workshop, a wind-pump and a carpentry workshop. There's also a "Tin Tabernacle", the simplest of structures where the Nonconformist residents of Great Moulton once gathered to hear the word of God. The museum also owns a substantial collection of antique objects, photographs and books illustrating life and work in East Anglia in the nineteenth and early twentieth centuries and organizes special exhibitions and events, anything from beer festivals to arts and crafts.

Cotton Mechanical Music Museum

Blacksmith's Rd, Cotton, IP14 4QN • June–Sept Sun 2.30–5.30pm • £5 • ☎01379 783350, ⓦmechanicalmusicmuseum.co.uk

The hamlet of **COTTON**, about five miles north of Stowmarket on the B1113, holds one real surprise, a **Mechanical Music Museum**, where a miscellany of fairground organs, barrel organs and such like are topped off by a mighty Wurlitzer cinema organ, all crowded into tiny premises. It may all be a bit eccentric, but it is certainly good fun.

FROM TOP ICKWORTH (P.303); BURY ST EDMUNDS (P.299) >

Needham Market

No one could accuse **NEEDHAM MARKET**, five miles southeast from Stowmarket, of being excessively picturesque, but its long and workaday main street does have one real surprise, the **church of St John the Baptist** (daily 9.30am–4pm or dusk; free), which possesses one of the county's finest hammerbeam roofs – not that you'd guess it from the outside, as the church looks a bit of a mess: there's no tower and no churchyard and the original exterior has been clumsily amended. There is, however, no disputing the architectural virtuosity of the roof, its delicately carved horizontal timbers decorated by a veritable herd of angels, exquisite creatures whose wings are open and closed alternately.

Debenham

The moisture-retaining clay soils around **DEBENHAM**, some ten miles east of Stowmarket, produce some of the largest yields of barley and wheat in the UK, so it's no surprise that the village retains an agricultural air – especially when the giant-sized tractors, combines and harvesters of today rumble along the elongated High Street. The street is lined by a fetching mix of brick cottages, pastel-painted timber-framed houses and Georgian villas, though the grandest building, a Neoclassical stone pile built for – and carrying the moniker of – the Ancient Order of Foresters has ended up as a vintage bathroom store. The village gets its name from the River Deben, which flows beside and beneath the main street. Incidentally, neither river nor town was responsible for the name of the Debenhams department chain, though **William Debenham** (1794–1863), the founder of the store, was a Suffolk man, born just outside Lavenham.

ARRIVAL AND DEPARTURE

STOWMARKET AND AROUND

By train Stowmarket and Needham Market both have train stations. From Needham Market, there are regular services to and from Bury St Edmunds (hourly; 30min), Ipswich (hourly; 15min), and Norwich (hourly; 1hr, change

---

JOHN PEEL AND GREAT FINBOROUGH

Born as Robert Parker Ravenscroft near Liverpool, but a long-time resident of Suffolk, **John Peel** (1939–2004) was a key figure in the evolution of popular musical taste from the late 1960s until his death from a heart attack while on a working holiday in Peru. His main platform was as a DJ on BBC Radio 1, a station he broadcast on for several decades. His honest, sometimes confessional, warmly laconic style made him immensely popular among both his general listeners and professional musicians, many of whom he counted as friends. Many more were eternally grateful to him (or in some cases ungratefully not) for launching their careers – and Peel developed a peerless reputation for playing the obscure and the new: he was, for example, one of the first DJs to play reggae, psychedelic rock and punk, and he always championed the unusual, from Captain Beefheart to his favourite band of all, The Undertones. No wonder young hopefuls bombarded him with demo tapes and discs.

In the 1970s, Peel and Sheila, his wife, moved to a cottage – "Peel Acres" – in **Great Finborough** just west of Stowmarket. In his later years, Peel broadcast many of his shows from a studio in this house, which also had room enough for live performances. In 2003, Peel was persuaded to write his autobiography, but in the event he died before he could finish it, and the book was left to his wife to finish off, with the **Margrave of the Marshes** finally published in 2005. Typically, Peel had often spoken wryly of his death: "I've always imagined I'd die by driving into the back of a truck while trying to read the name on a cassette and people would say, 'He would have wanted to go that way'. Well, I want them to know that I wouldn't."

Over a thousand people attended his funeral in Bury St Edmunds and, in accordance with his wishes, he was buried at St Andrew's church in Great Finborough, his tombstone engraved with a line from his favourite song, "Teenage Kicks" by The Undertones: "Teenage dreams, so hard to beat".

at Stowmarket). From Stowmarket, there are also trains to Bury St Edmunds (2 hourly; 20min), Ipswich (2 hourly; 15min), and Norwich (hourly; 30min). Stowmarket train station is just to the east of the town centre – and about a 20min walk from the Museum of East Anglian Life. From Needham Market train station, it's a couple of minutes' walk to the High St – turn right for the 5min stroll to the church of St John the Baptist.

By bus In Stowmarket, there's no bus station as such, but two main bus stops – one on Bury St (for Ipswich and points south and east), the other on Ipswich St (for Bury St Edmunds and points west), both in the centre. In Needham Market, most buses pull in along the High St as they do in Debenham.

EATING

The Garden of Debenham 6 High St, Debenham, IP14 6QJ ☎ 01728 860190. This pleasant little place is a flower shop with bells – the bells being an unassuming café, where the Illy coffee is reliably good and the snacks and cakes are home-made. The bonus is that you can eat and drink amid and among the scent of the flowers. Mon, Wed, Thurs & Fri 9am–5pm, Tues & Sat 9am–1pm.

SHOPPING

Alder Carr Farm Creeting St Mary's Rd, Needham Market, IP6 8LX ☎ 01449 720820, ⓦ aldercarrfarm .co.uk. The flood plain of the River Gipping, the slender parcel of land between Needham Market High St and the A14, has been left pretty much exclusively for agricultural use – and it's here among the orchards that the enterprising owners of Alder Carr Farm have established a farm shop and deli, both stuffed to the rafters with local produce. There's pick your own in season too, as well as a nature trail, farmers' markets, craft shops and a play area. Mon–Sat 9am–5pm & Sun 10am–4pm.

Eye and around

8

It may be within easy striking distance of Diss (see p.210), just over the border in Norfolk, but the pocket-sized town of **EYE**, around fifteen miles northeast of Stowmarket, can't help but feel remote, a rural fastness that was once surrounded by water and marshland – hence its Saxon name, literally "island". Eye has the tiniest of main squares and it's here you'll find a conspicuous stone **memorial** to **Viscount Sir Edward Clarence Kerrison** (1821–86), long-time Conservative MP for Eye and a paternalist of the first rank, who was commonly described as a "great friend of the agricultural labourer". He also burnished his local credentials by having Eye connected to the rail network, but this particular branch line was closed in 1931. In the immediate vicinity of Eye is the lovely little village of **Hoxne**.

Church of St Peter and St Paul

Church St • Daily 9.30am–5pm or dusk, except during services • Free

Eye is at its prettiest on **Church Street**, whose handsome medley of old cottages ambles down from the main square to both the **Guildhall**, an attractive timber-framed structure dating back to the fifteenth century, and the adjacent **church of St Peter and St Paul**, whose beautiful tower soars high above its surroundings, its contrasting panels, alternately stone and flint flushwork, an exercise in the Perpendicular. Inside, the most interesting feature is the fifteenth-century **rood screen**, whose dado sports a series of remarkably well-preserved, albeit naive – almost doll-like – saints, including St Ursula, who shelters her acolyte-virgins, and St Barbara with a miniature representation of the tower in which she was, according to legend, imprisoned by her father.

Eye Castle

Castle Hill, off Castle St • Easter to Oct daily 9am–7pm or dusk • Free

From the church, it's easy to spot the prominent bramble-covered mound on which are perched the battered remains of **Eye Castle**, reached by clambering up a long wooden stairway in the castle grounds on Castle Hill, just off Castle Street – which itself adjoins Church Street. The original motte and bailey fortress was erected in the eleventh century, but later fell into disrepair. A windmill was built here in the sixteenth century and a mansion was added in the reign of Queen Victoria, but the remains of both have vanished leaving the crumbly stone walls of today. The ruins may be scant, but the wide views over the surrounding countryside are compensation.

Thornham Estate

Thornham Magna, IP23 8HH • Daily: April–Oct 9am–6pm; Nov–March 9am–4pm • Free, parking £2, £3 on Sun • ☎ 01379 788345, ⓦ thornham.org.uk

From Eye, it's a mile or two west to the **Thornham Estate**, where the **Thornham Walks** comprise over twelve miles of waymarked footpaths leading through woods, parkland and water meadows. There's also a photographers' gallery, a walled garden, two cafés and a programme of special events with kids very much in mind, from bat evenings to den building. Maps of the estate are available at the entrance.

St Mary's Church, Thornham Parva

Daily 9.30–4pm or dusk • Free

On the northeast edge of the Thornham Estate, the scattering of houses that make up **THORNHAM PARVA** includes **St Mary's church**, a solitary affair, long bereft of its surrounding houses, whose ancient rubble walls are topped off by a splendid thatched roof. The simple, aisle-less interior bears witness to all sorts of historical tinkering – for a start there are both Saxon and Norman windows – and the faded wall paintings tell the tale of St Edmund (see p.301), but pride of place goes to the painted, fourteenth-century **retable** in which eight saints flank the Crucifixion. Saved from Thetford Priory during the Reformation, it's a beautiful work of art with a soft, sinuous quality: St Catherine, for example, holds the Catherine' wheel on which she was martyred, her face gripped with a look of determined piety. Look out also for the engraved window on the south side of the nave, the work of the poet and artist **Laurence Whistler** (1912–2000) in tribute to his friend, the improbably named Lady Osla Henniker-Major.

Hoxne

The pretty little village of **HOXNE** (pronounced "Hoxon"), about six miles northeast of Eye, has one major claim to fame for it was here in 869 AD that the Anglo-Saxon ruler of East Anglia, **King Edmund**, came a cropper. A victim of excessive polishing, legend asserts that, after a defeat in battle, Edmund was hiding from his enemies, the Danes, beneath Hoxne's **Goldbrook bridge** when a local couple, who were on their way to church to get married, spotted the reflection of his glistening spurs in the river. They informed the Danes, who promptly captured him, tied him to a tree and shot him full of arrows – but not before Edmund laid a hex on the bridge, cursing any bride and groom who would ever use it in the future. Well into the nineteenth century, betrothed locals went to considerable trouble to avoid the bridge and, unpleasant curse or not, Edmund still ended up the most popular **saint** in East Anglia after various miracles were attributed to his body (see box, p.301).

Today, a **plaque** on the Goldbrook bridge, at the south end of the village, remembers Edmund's betrayal and capture, and a clearly signed **Heritage Walk** begins here too, covering all the historical sites in the village and its immediate surroundings, including the spot where St Edmund's first chapel was erected and the place where he died. Maps of the walk are available at the car park on the far side of the Goldbrook bridge.

There's also a small display on Edmund in the **church of St Peter and Paul** (daily 9am–4pm or dusk; free), at the top of the village beside the B1118. This display is supplemented by old photos of the village and information on the Hoxne hoard, a large collection of Roman coins found here in 1992 – and subsequently transferred to the British Museum.

ARRIVAL AND DEPARTURE

EYE AND AROUND

By bus Some buses to Eye pull in beside the Town Hall, on Broad St, from where it's a few yards to the minuscule main square and Church St, but most use Bellands Way, off Victoria Hill, about 5min walk north along the main street (the B1077). Among a limited range of services, there are buses to Ipswich (Mon–Sat every 1–2hr; 1hr); Diss (Mon–Sat every 1–2hr; 30min); and Hoxne (Mon–Fri 3 daily, Sat 1 daily; 15min). In Hoxne, buses pull in opposite the Goldbrook bridge, on Abbey Hill, though services are few and far between and there's pretty much nothing in the evenings and on Sundays.

ACCOMMODATION AND EATING

EYE

Beards Deli, Café and B&B 39 Church St, IP23 7BD ☎01379 870383. In a neat and trim, two-storey, eighteenth-century house, *Beards* offers a good range of luxury foods as well as all sorts of local stuff from pork to asparagus. They also have two double and one single guest rooms – nothing too extravagant, but very cosy. Deli: Mon 8.30am–6pm & Wed–Sat 8.30am–5.30pm. __£60__

HOXNE

Swan Inn Low St, IP21 5AS ☎01379 668275, ⓦhoxneswan.co.uk. In a good-looking half-timbered building, this excellent country pub has preserved many of its oldest features, from the plank floor to the open fire. They offer a tiptop selection of brews and delicious home-made food – try, for instance, their silverside served on root vegetable mash with a red-wine gravy costing £15. Kitchen is open Mon–Sat noon–2pm & 6.30–9.30pm, Sun noon–3.30pm & 6.30–8.30pm.

8

Bury St Edmunds and around

One of Suffolk's most appealing towns, **BURY ST EDMUNDS**, ten miles north of Lavenham, started out as a Benedictine monastery, founded to accommodate the remains of **Edmund**, the last Saxon king of East Anglia. Edmund had been buried in Hoxne, where the Danes had killed him, but later on he was dug up and re-interred in Bury, where his shrine became a major point of pilgrimage. (see box p.301). Almost two centuries later, England was briefly ruled by the kings of Denmark and the shrewdest of them, **King Knut** (Canute), made a gesture of reconciliation to his Saxon subjects by granting the monastery a generous endowment and building the monks a brand-new church. It was a popular move and the abbey prospered, so much so that before its dissolution in 1539, it had become the richest religious house in the country, attracting hundreds of pilgrims eager to seek divine assistance via the mouldering bones of **Saint Edmund**.

Most of the **abbey** disappeared long ago, and nowadays Bury is better known for its graceful Georgian streets, its lovely public gardens and its clutch of enjoyable bars and restaurants. The town also acts as a supply centre for the surrounding villages, which means it has a fairly good selection of shops, and is home to the **Greene King brewery**, though Bury's good looks are spoiled by the hulking sugar-beet plant just outside the town centre.

Bury St Edmunds sits pretty with rolling farmland stretching away towards every point in the compass except to the northwest where the A1101 is flanked by wooded heathland. Dotted over this rural terrain are several attractions, the pick of which is **Ickworth House**, the ancestral home of one of the aristocracy's oddest families, the Herveys, and you could also squeeze in detours to **Pakenham Mill**, the **Wyken Estate** and the recreated Anglo-Saxon Village at **West Stow**.

The town centre

Bury **town centre** has preserved much of its Norman street plan, a gridiron in which **Churchgate** was originally aligned with – and sloped up from – the abbey's high altar. It was

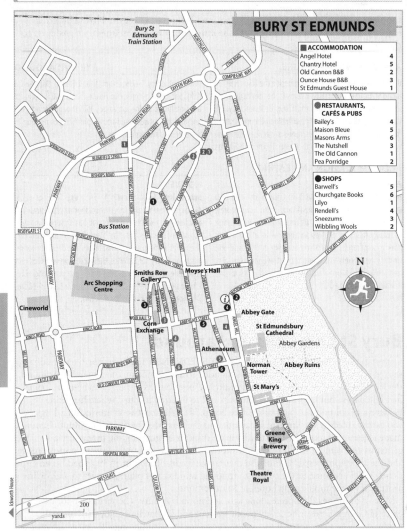

the first planned town of Norman Britain and, for that matter, the first example of urban planning in England since the departure of the Romans. At the heart of the town is **Angel Hill**, a broad, spacious square partly framed by Georgian buildings, the most distinguished being the ivy-covered **Angel Hotel**, which features in Dickens' *Pickwick Papers*. Dickens also gave readings of his work in the **Athenaeum**, the Georgian assembly rooms at the far end of the square. A twelfth-century wall runs along the east side of Angel Hill, with the bulky **Abbey Gate** forming the entrance to the abbey gardens and ruins beyond. An imposing structure dating from the middle of the fourteenth century, the gate's strong lines are emphasized by its castellated parapet and surly gargoyles – for make no mistake the gate was designed to overawe the locals: in 1327, the townsfolk had attacked the monastery, angered by its excessive power and wealth, and afterwards the abbot had this new gate built both to show exactly who was in control and to make sure it would never happen again.

Abbey Gardens and ruins

Abbey Gardens, off Angel Hill, IP33 1LS • Mon–Sat 7.30am–dusk, Sun 9am–dusk • Free

Ensconced within the immaculate greenery of the **Abbey Gardens**, the abbey **ruins** are themselves like nothing so much as petrified porridge, a rambling assortment of incidental remains with little to remind you of the grandiose Norman complex that once dominated the town. Thousands of medieval pilgrims once sought solace at St Edmund's altar and the cult was of such significance that the barons of England gathered here to swear that they would make King John sign their petition – the Magna Carta of 1215. A **plaque** marks the spot where they met beside what was once the high altar of the old abbey church, whose crumbly remains are on the far (right) side of the abbey gardens behind the cathedral.

St Edmundsbury Cathedral

Angel Hill, IP33 1LS • Daily 8.30am–6pm • Free, but donation requested • ⓦ stedscathedral.co.uk.

On Angel Hill, the Anglican **St Edmundsbury** Cathedral is a hangar-like affair, whose most attractive features are its Gothic lantern tower and its beautiful painted roof. The tower was completed in 2005 as part of the Millennium Project, a long-term plan to improve the church, which has also involved the installation of a vaulted ceiling under the tower and the reconstruction of the cloisters. St Edmundsbury was only granted cathedral status in 1914, though it was close call: many clergy would have preferred to see the neighbouring (and more interesting) church of **St Mary's** (see below) upgraded, but that church holds the tomb of Mary Tudor, the sister of Henry VIII and one-time Queen of France – and that was quite enough to put the church authorities off.

Next door to the cathedral stands the twelfth-century **Norman Tower** (no access), a solitary structure whose rounded arches, blind arcading and dragon gargoyles once served as the main gatehouse into the abbey.

8

St Mary's church

Crown St, IP33 1RT • Mon–Sat 10am–4pm, 3pm in winter • Free

St Mary's church, just along the street from the cathedral, is a handsome structure that dates from the twelfth century, though most of what you see today is the result of an extensive revamp carried out in the 1430s. The revamp was not without its mishaps: the congregation was mumbling away one dark and stormy evening when the tower collapsed, narrowly missing the worshippers below, but covering them in dust and

---

EDMUND: SAXON SAINT AND HERO

Before the pagan Danes killed him in Hoxne (see p.298), **Edmund**, the last Saxon king of East Anglia (c.840–869) allegedly refused to save his life by abjuring his Christian faith and, in the way of would-be saints, his death was accompanied by miracles: the Danes threw his head into a wood, where the Anglo-Saxons discovered it guarded by a wolf, and when head and body were reunited, they miraculously re-attached themselves. Edmund was canonized early in the tenth century, the speed of his elevation no doubt influenced by the stirring account of his death provided by the **Anglo-Saxon Chronicle**, which recorded the history of the Anglo-Saxons at considerable length: "The heathens then became brutally angry because of Edmund's beliefs… They shot then with missiles, as if to amuse themselves, until he was all covered with their missiles as with bristles of a hedgehog, just as [Saint] Sebastian was. Then Hinguar, [the Danish chieftain], saw that the noble king did not desire to renounce Christ, and with resolute faith always called to him; Hinguar then commanded to behead the king and the heathens thus did. While this was happening, Edmund called to Christ still. Then the heathens dragged the holy man to slaughter, and with a stroke struck the head from him. His soul set forth, blessed, to Christ."

grime. St Mary's boasts an especially wide and well-lit nave, whose tall and slender pillars rise up towards a simply magnificent **hammerbeam roof**, where a full set of angels preside over the proceedings below, their wings unfurled as if ready for take-off. The central arch also catches the eye, not so much for its height but because of the richly coloured stained-glass window depicting the martyrdom of the saint-king Edmund. The window is cut in the shape of the original pilgrim's badge and was the work of **Thomas Willement** (1786–1871), a once famous stained-glass artist and dedicated medievalist. Beside the high altar, two badly weathered table tombs commemorate local bigwigs – the delicately carved, tasselled cushions beneath the wife of Robert Drury are particularly delightful – and nearby, behind the altar at the far end of the church, is the simple **tomb of Mary Tudor** (1496–1533), the favourite sister of Henry VIII, after whom he named his leading warship, the *Mary Rose*; Mary was originally buried in the abbey, but her remains were moved here after the Reformation. Mary Tudor may have been Henry's favourite sister, but it didn't save her from being shipped off to France to be married to the ailing King of France, Louis XII, who – at 52 – was 34 years her senior. Louis did not last long, so Mary's time as Queen of France was limited to just a few months and afterwards she hotfooted it back to England to marry the Duke of Suffolk.

Greene King brewery

Westgate St, IP33 1QT• Guided tours: Sun, Mon & Tues 1 daily, Wed–Fri 2 daily, Sat 3 daily • £8 • ☏ 01284 714297, ⓦ greeneking.co.uk

From St Mary's church, it's a couple of minutes' walk south along Crown Street to the **Greene King brewery**, where the visitor centre sells tickets for guided tours of the museum and the adjacent brewery. The tour is finished off by a pit stop at the Brewery Tap, where you can wet your whistle on the full range of their products with **Old Speckled Hen** being their most celebrated brew.

Theatre Royal

Westgate St, IP33 1QR • Guided tours: Tues, Thurs, Sat & Sun 1 daily; 1hr 20min • £6, NT members £5 • ☏ 01284 769505, ⓦ theatreroyal.org

Across the street from the brewery stands the **Theatre Royal**, an attractive building of 1819 which is owned by Greene King, but leased to the National Trust, who in their turn have rented it out to a theatre company (see p.306). Sympathetically restored to its Regency appearance, the interior is the most intimate of auditoria and comes complete with a painted frieze and a painted ceiling plus a sweeping circle of dinky little boxes.

Corn Exchange

Bury's main commercial area lies just to the west of Angel Hill up along Abbeygate. There's been some intrusive modern planning here, but sterling Victorian buildings flank both the L-shaped Cornhill and the Buttermarket, the two short main streets, as well as the narrower streets in between. The dominant edifice is the **Corn Exchange**, whose portico is all Neoclassical extravagance with a whopping set of stone columns and a carved tympanum up above. Perhaps the Victorian merchants who footed the bill decided it was too showy after all, for they had a biblical quote inscribed up above the columns in an apparent flash of modesty – "The Earth is the Lord's and the Fulness Thereof".

Smiths Row

Smiths Row, Cornhill, IP33 1BT • Tues–Sat 10.30am–5pm • Free • ☏ 01284 762081, ⓦ smithsrow.org

From the Cornmarket, it's a few yards up along the Cornhill to **Smiths Row**, an airy, well-lit gallery that features a lively programme of temporary exhibitions focusing on contemporary fine and applied art. They also have workshops of various descriptions and a shop selling British crafts.

Moyse's Hall

Cornhill, IP33 1DX • Daily 10am–5pm • £4 • ☎ 01284 706183, ⓦ moyseshall.org

Across the Cornhill from Smiths Row is **Moyse's Hall**, a modest museum lodged in an early medieval building, whose twin gables give the exterior the appearance of a church. It's likely that the abbot owned the hall, but it's possible it was built for a wealthy member of the small Jewish community that lived in Bury in the twelfth century. Frankly, the interior is a bit of a yawn, but there is a mildly interesting section on the Suffolk Regiment, which was amalgamated with the Norfolk Regiment in 1959, and another on "Witchcraft and Superstition", which includes examples of the poor old cats that were habitually interred inside the walls of houses to ward off the evil eye. In the same room is a motley collection of instruments of torture plus one or two mementoes of William Corder, the **Red Barn Murderer** (see p.280), principally his death mask, his desiccated scalp and, most gruesome of the lot, a book bound with his skin.

Guildhall Street

The streets to the south of the Cornhill are lined by an attractive medley of architectural styles, from elegant Georgian townhouses to Victorian brick terraces. You'll see the best by strolling along **Guildhall Street** and turning left down Churchgate, which brings you back to Angel Hill.

Ickworth House

Horringer, IP29 5QE • House: March–Oct Mon, Tues & Fri–Sun 11am–5pm; park: daily 8am–8pm; gardens: March–Oct daily 10am–5pm; Nov–Feb daily 11am–4pm • House, park & gardens £9.55; park & gardens only £3.60; NT • ☎ 01284 735270, ⓦ nationaltrust.org.uk

Surrounded by acres of parkland, **Ickworth House** is distinguished by its huge stone **rotunda**, which was commissioned by **Frederick Hervey**, the Bishop of Derry and Earl of Bristol in the 1790s. The Earl-Bishop loved all things Italian, hence the design of the rotunda, but when he died in 1803, his new palace-home was far from completed and his successors, lacking their ancestor's architectural enthusiasms, never really made a full fist of it, though two wings were subsequently attached to the rotunda with the East Wing becoming the family home in the 1820s, the other now turned into an excellent hotel (see p.305).

On public display in the **house** are paintings by a number of leading artists, most notably Velázquez, Titian, Gainsborough and Reynolds, as well as a fine collection of Georgian silver and Regency furniture. There's also the iconic *Death of Wolfe* by Benjamin West (1738–1820). The British general James Wolfe inflicted a crushing defeat on the French outside Québec City in 1759, but was killed during the battle. West's painting transformed this grubby colonial conflict into a romantic extravagance,

---

THE HERVEYS OF ICKWORTH

The Sixth Marquess of Bristol, **Victor Frederick Cochrane Hervey** (1915–85) gave **Ickworth House** and its grounds to the National Trust in the 1950s in lieu of death duties with the proviso that the Herveys could continue to live in the East Wing. The Herveys had a long-standing reputation for eccentricity, but the Sixth Marquess trumped his predecessors by masterminding the activities of a gang of jewel thieves – he was sent down for three years in 1939 – before amassing a fortune in various business activities. Neither does he appear to have been a good father and his son, **Frederick William John Augustus Hervey** (1954–99), the Seventh Marquess of Bristol, had a particularly troubled life, whittling away a vast fortune in a frenzy of cocaine, heroin and rent boys. At Ickworth, the antics of the seventh marquess antagonized his landlord, the National Trust, who just about bit his hand off when he offered to sell his remaining rights to them in 1998. The Herveys no longer have any connection with Ickworth, though the hotel (see p.305) displays photos of this unloveable brood.

with the dying general in a Christlike pose, a pale figure held tenderly by his subordinates. West presented the first version of his painting to the Royal Academy of Arts in 1771 and it proved so popular that he spent much of the next decade painting copies. After the house, most visitors proceed to ramble round the **park**, pausing at the so-called Fairy Lake and popping into the walled garden.

West Stow Country Park and Anglo-Saxon Village

Icklingham Rd, West Stow, IP28 6HG • Daily 10am–5pm • £7, children £5 • ☎ 01284 728718, ⓦ weststow.org

This unusual attraction, located among wooded heathland seven miles northwest of Bury St Edmunds via the A1101, comprises around a dozen recreated **Anglo-Saxon houses** on the site of what was originally a late Iron Age village, whose layout was fully excavated in the 1960s. The attached **visitor centre** examines the nature of Anglo-Saxon society and explores the various controversies surrounding the houses: it's agreed they were thatched, but the key debate is whether the Anglo-Saxons lived in pits or on wooden floors. The village is popular with school parties and there's a programme of special events and displays, while the adjacent **Country Park** provides pleasant wooded walks and has a lake with bird hides.

Pakenham Mill

Water Mill Farm, Mill Rd, Pakenham, IP31 2NB • Early April to late Oct Sat & Sun 1.30–5pm & Thurs 10am–4pm; milling on the first Thurs morning of each month • £3.50 • ☎ 01284 724075, ⓦ pakenhamwatermill.co.uk

On the edge of the village of **PAKENHAM**, about seven miles northeast of Bury St Edmunds via the A143, stands **Pakenham Mill**, the last working water mill in Suffolk. Visitors can wander around the old workings, examine the antique bread oven and brewing vat, and finish off with a cuppa and a cake at the tearoom.

Wyken Estate

Wyken Rd, Stanton, IP31 2DW **Garden** Late March to late Sept daily except Sat 2–6pm; £3.50 **Restaurant, café and shop** Daily 10am–6pm, plus Fri & Sat 7–10pm • ☎ 01359 252372, ⓦ wykenvineyards.co.uk

Deep in the countryside, nine miles northeast of Bury St Edmunds, the **Wyken Estate** is an exercise in diversification with something for just about everyone: there are woodland walks; a flock of Shetland sheep and a small herd of Red Poll cattle on the farm; a well-regarded vineyard; a restaurant in the old barn that specializes in meat, game and vegetables from the estate; formal gardens surrounding the Elizabethan manor house; an excellent farmers' market (Sat 9am–1pm); and a very good arts, crafts and gifts country store.

ARRIVAL AND INFORMATION

BURY ST EDMUNDS AND AROUND

By train Bury St Edmunds' train station is on the northern edge of the centre, a 10min walk from Angel Hill via Northgate St. There are trains to Cambridge (hourly; 45min); Ely (every 2hr; 30min); Ipswich (hourly; 40min); Newmarket (hourly; 20min); and Stowmarket (hourly; 20min).

By bus The town bus station is on St Andrews St North, from where it's a couple of minutes' walk south to the Cornhill. Principal destinations include Long Melford

(Mon–Sat hourly; 1hr) and Thetford (Mon–Sat hourly; 20–40min).

By car The A14 skirts the eastern edge of Bury St Edmunds and on-street parking is rarely a problem.

Tourist office In the centre of town at 6 Angel Hill (Easter to Oct Mon–Sat 9.30am–5.30pm, plus May–Sept Sun 10am–3pm; Nov to Easter Mon–Fri 10am–4pm, Sat 10am–1pm; ☎ 01284 764667, ⓦ stedmundsbury.gov.uk).

ACCOMMODATION

Bury St Edmunds is especially popular with day-trippers, but there's still enough overnight trade to support a good range of hotels and B&Bs either in or very close to the centre. If you're on a tight budget, stick to the B&Bs, if you're after luxury make a beeline for the **Ickworth Hotel**.

Angel Hotel 3 Angel Hill, IP33 1LT ☎01284 714000, ⓦtheangel.co.uk. Long-established former coaching inn whose public areas have been remodelled in an ungainly contemporary style. Beyond are over seventy comfortable bedrooms, some with a country house feel, others with a more modern complexion. Great location, a few yards from the abbey gardens. **£115**

Chantry Hotel 8 Sparhawk St, IP33 1RY ☎01284 767427, ⓦchantryhotel.com. There are seventeen guest rooms here in this privately owned hotel and they occupy the Georgian house at the front and the annexe behind. The decor is retro with big wooden beds and even the odd four-poster, though the bathrooms are routinely modern. A handy, central location too, but note that Sparhawk St can get very busy with speeding traffic. **£110**

★ **Ickworth Hotel** Horringer, IP29 5QE ☎01284 735 350, ⓦickworthhotel.co.uk. This superb hotel occupies an extraordinary location – the East Wing of Ickworth House (see p.303), its imposing stonework and high-ceilinged corridors added to the house's original rotunda in the early nineteenth century. The facilities are outstanding – there's a basement spa and a pool – and, although the rooms vary, the finest are stunning, with the commodious "Grand Tour" room big enough to accommodate a magnificent antique bed, two fine old sofas, a splendid chandelier and a capacious built-in wardrobe. Add to this a large bathroom and views out across the surrounding parkland and it's hard to imagine somewhere much better. Breakfast is taken in the conservatory and the hotel restaurant is a fine affair as well – try, for instance, the Horringer pheasant with saute potatoes, spinach and roasted pumpkin puree. Mains average around £19 and hotel guests are advised to make advance reservations. **£240**

★ **Old Cannon B&B** 86 Cannon St, IP33 1JR ☎01284 768769, ⓦoldcannonbrewery.co.uk. Arguably Bury's most distinctive B&B, there are a handful of neat and trim modern guest rooms here, all en suite, in an intelligently recycled brewhouse, which is itself attached to a micro-brewery, restaurant and bar (see below). Over in the bar, the brews are strong – so you might be glad your bed is near at hand. Cannon St is on the north side of town, a 5min walk from the centre: to get there, take Northgate St from Angel Hill and watch for the (hard) turning on the left. **£90**

Ounce House B&B 14 Northgate St, IP33 1HP ☎01284 761779, ⓦouncehouse.co.uk. Upmarket B&B in a large, three-storey Victorian house a couple of minutes' walk from the centre. Each of the well-equipped guest rooms has antique furniture, a flat-screen TV, free wi-fi, an ironing board and that most mysterious of items, the trouser press. All are en suite. **£125**

St Edmunds Guest House 35 St Andrews St North, IP33 1SZ ☎01284 700144, ⓦstedmundsguesthouse .net. Browns and creams with oak furniture are the order of the day in this pleasant B&B, which has nine, en-suite guest rooms. Occupies a straightforward, three-storey brick house on the west side of the centre, a 5–10min walk from Angel Hill. Free wi-fi and a full English breakfast. **£68**

EATING AND DRINKING

Bailey's 5 Whiting St, IP33 1NX. This cosy, modern place just off Abbeygate is the best teashop in town – no argument. The food is fresh, the service fast and the menu extensive, but look no further than the toasties (£5–6) – lip-smackingly good. Mon–Sat 9am–4pm.

Maison Bleue 31 Churchgate St, IP33 1RG ☎01284 760623. Slick and sleek seafood restaurant noted for its outstanding (French-influenced) menu, covering everything from crab and cod through to sardines and skate. Main courses average £16. Tues–Sat noon–2.30pm & 7–9.30pm.

Masons Arms 14 Whiting St, IP33 1NX ☎01284 753955. This pub-cum-restaurant, with its traditional interior, occupies a very old building, though the weatherboarding that covers the outside is entirely Victorian. The food is above-standard pub grub, featuring the likes of chilli con carne and roast beef. Mains average around £13. Mon–Sat 11am–11pm, Sun noon–3.30pm & 7–10.30pm; kitchen open daily noon–2.30pm & Mon–Sat 5.30–8.30pm.

★ **The Nutshell** The Traverse, IP33 1BJ. At the top of Abbeygate, *The Nutshell* claims to be Britain's smallest pub and it certainly is small – it's only sixteen feet by seven, big enough for twelve customers or maybe fifteen, provided they can raise a pint without raising their elbows, though on one splendid occasion in the 1980s no less than 102 drinkers managed to squeeze inside on a charity gig. As you might expect, successive landlords have warmed to the theme of size and the antique interior, with its wood panelling, benches and gnarled bar, has at one time or another held the world's smallest dartboard and snooker table. As if that was not enough, the desiccated body of a cat hangs from the ceiling, but this is not the origin of the phrase "Not enough room to swing a cat", but rather the result of a traditional custom in which builders walled in cats behind the fireplace to ward off the evil eye; the cat was found during renovations. The pub is owned by Greene King (see p.302), which provides some sterling beers, including the full-bodied Abbot Ale and Old Speckled Hen, a ruddy ale with a tangy zip. Daily 11am–11pm.

★ **The Old Cannon** 86 Cannon St, IP33 1JR ☎01284 768769. This enjoyable and very relaxing place hits all the spots: with a B&B (see above) in the adjoining brewhouse, the large and softly lit restaurant-bar offers a superb range of daily specials with due prominence given to local ingredients – Norfolk mussels, Suffolk pork, Lowestoft cod

8

and the like. Even better, main courses are competitively priced at around £12. The restaurant-bar also holds two brewing vats, evidence of the on-premises microbrewery, whose assorted brews include the award-winning, dark ale Gunner's Daughter. Outstanding service too. Kitchen: Mon–Fri noon–2pm, Sat & Sun noon–3pm, plus Tues–Sat 6–9.15pm; Bar: Mon–Fri noon–3pm & 5–11pm; Sat noon–11pm & Sun noon–10.30pm.

Pea Porridge 28 Cannon St, IP33 1JR ☎01284 700200. In a small, terrace house just across the street from the *Old Cannon* (see p.305), this small and intimate restaurant has a homely feel and an inventive, thoughtful menu with mains averaging around £17. One delicious choice is pigeon with beetroot and fondant potato in an artichoke jus. Tues–Sat noon–2pm & 6.30–9.30pm.

ENTERTAINMENT

Cineworld Parkway, IP33 3BA ☎0871 2002000, ⓦcineworld.co.uk. Bury's main cinema is big enough to cater to both mainstream and art-house tastes, and is handily located to the rear of the Arc Shopping Centre beside the inner ring road. Tickets from £6.60.

Theatre Royal Westgate St, IP33 1QR ☎01284 769505, ⓦtheatreroyal.org. Bury's principal performing arts venue offers a year-round programme of cultural events, from Shakespeare to pantomime.

SHOPPING

Bury St Edmunds possesses a reasonably good range of small, independent shops though they are under pressure from the glitzy new **Arc Shopping Centre** that has sprung up on the site of the old Cattle Market, just off St Andrews St. The town also has a busy and popular open-air provisions **market** held on Wednesdays and Saturdays on and around the Cornhill and the Buttermarket area of the town.

Barwell's 39 Abbeygate St, IP33 1LW ☎01284 754084, ⓦbarwellsfood.com. Something of a local institution, Barwell's has been supplying this part of Suffolk with meat, game, poultry and pies since 1860. They take great trouble to ensure their suppliers abide by the highest standards of animal welfare – so full marks to them for that. Mon–Sat 9am–5pm, Sun 11am–4pm.

Churchgate Books 47 Churchgate St, IP33 1RG ☎01284 704604, ⓦchurchgatebooks.co.uk. In quaint old premises in the old part of town, this enterprising, independent bookshop carries a wide selection of secondhand and antiquarian books. Is particularly strong on local stuff – East Anglian history and so forth – and they even make a range of hand-crafted blank books in their own bindery. Mon–Sat 9.30am–5pm, and often Sun afternoons during summer.

Lilyo 77b St John's St, IP33 1SQ ☎01284 766330, ⓦlilyo.com. Unusual little shop whose speciality is

freshwater pearls placed in all sorts of creative designs by the owner, Lily Daly, and her team. The pearls are often interspersed with Swarovski crystals and semiprecious stones. Prices range from the very affordable to top-end luxury. Mon–Sat 10am–5pm.

Sneezums 10 Cornhill, IP33 1BH ☎01284 752634, ⓦsneezums.co.uk. Not, as you might expect from the name, a supplier of snuff, but rather an independent shop selling an excellent range of watches, cameras, binoculars and telescopes with a tasty sideline in jewellery. Mon–Sat 9am–5.15pm.

Wibbling Wools 24b Angel Hill, IP33 1UZ ☎01284 749555, ⓦwibblingwools.co.uk. Self-proclaimed, one-stop shop for all your yarn and pattern choices, including Sublime, Debbie Bliss and Louisa Harding. Rack upon rack of balls of wool plus classes and a weekly coffee morning on Thursdays at 10am. Mon 11am–3pm & Tues–Sat 9.30am–5pm.

Newmarket

NEWMARKET, just fifteen miles from Bury St Edmunds, is dedicated to the **racehorse** – or more specifically the flat (fence-less) horse racing season, which runs from April to October. There are farriers, betting shops and bloodstock agents, two racecourses, stud farms and stables, saddlers and jockey-barracks, plus vets galore and nigh on three thousand horses. As you approach the town its equine credentials are announced with a wide sweep of carefully maintained, grassy-green **heathland** and it's here that the country's leading racehorses are put through their paces – and have been since horserace-loving King Charles II put the place on the map, moving his court to Newmarket once or twice a year. Nowadays, the Dubai Royal Family is the dominant economic force here, but they don't control the training grounds – that's down to the

EATING
Bedford Lodge	1
Coffee & Co	2

ACCOMMODATION
Bedford Lodge	2
The Jockey Club Rooms	3
Norfolk House B&B	4
Tuddenham Mill	1

NEWMARKET

Jockey Club, whose 120 members gather in discreet premises in the centre of town. Otherwise, Newmarket's centre is really rather undistinguished, but make no mistake, there's big money here, though it's all tied up with the horses: a top **thoroughbred** can go for £2 million and every aspect of the animal's life is carefully (and expensively) monitored, from the food they eat and the mares the stallions mate with (or "cover") through to each horse's exercise regime. This ultra-scientific approach is part of an attempt to cut the odds, reduce the uncertainties, but in the end it's all a gamble and a flutter – and that's the thrill. The casual visitor is kept very much on the outside of the racing, but there are ways to gain an insight: the obvious ploy is to drive out along the **Heath Road** to watch the horses training on **The Gallops**, the wide heath just to the east of the town centre that is latticed with white posts and rails; the horses have right of way till 1pm, when the heath reverts to common land. You can also go to the races (see box, p.308), take a guided tour (see box, p.309), pop into the **Horse-racing Museum** and, although access is limited, visit the **National Stud** and the **Jockey Club**

National Horseracing Museum

99 High St, CB8 8JH • March–Dec daily 10am–5pm • £6.50 • ☎ 01638 667333, ⦿ nhrm.co.uk

The **National Horseracing Museum** dips and delves into every aspect of the sport, beginning with an intriguing section on the "Origins of Racing 1600–1900", which includes paintings and prints, a stuffed horse's head or two and examples of early jockey gear. There's also a fascinating display on the evolution of the **thoroughbred**: remarkably enough, all are descendants of just three, early eighteenth-century "**Foundation Sires**" (Darley Arabian,

---

HORSERACING IN NEWMARKET

Newmarket has two racecourses, Rowley Mile and July Racecourse. They share the same website and box office (☎0844 5793010, ⓦnewmarketracecourses.co.uk). There are five classic flat races every year:

1000 Guineas Early May, Newmarket
2000 Guineas Early May, Newmarket
The Oaks Early June, Epsom Downs Racecourse

The Derby First weekend in June, Epsom Downs Racecourse
St Leger September, Doncaster Racecourse

Godolphin Arabian and Byerley Turk), Arabian stallions noted for their speed and agility, which were bred with English mares, renowned for their strength and courage. Other sections of the museum include a Jockeys' Hall of Fame, a selection of racehorse paintings and the skeleton of one of the most successful sires of all time, "**Hyperion**", who galloped off into the stable in the sky in1960; there's a statue of him outside the Jockey Club next door. Finally, the museum has a small hands-on section aimed at kids, who can dress up in racing silks and weigh themselves before mounting a (vigorous) horse simulator. Plans are afoot to develop and expand the museum, funds permitting.

The Jockey Club

101 High St, CB8 8JH • Teas & tours by advance reservation only: Sun pm once monthly • £25 • ☎01638 663101, ⓦjockey-club-estates.co.uk

Founded in 1750, the **Jockey Club** has precious little to do with jockeys, but a lot to do with those wealthy enough to own Newmarket's racehorses. For most of its history, the club controlled the sport, but these regulatory functions were surrendered a few years ago and passed to the newly founded **British Horseracing Authority** in 2007. Since then, the Jockey Club has been free to concentrate on its commercial interests and the operation of its extensive estate – in particular the club owns Newmarket's large and extensive horse-training grounds. A little tentatively, the club has also opened its doors to outsiders for weddings, special events and **teas and tours**. Tea is taken in the Coffee Room, a handsome Georgian salon with leather benches, discreet little alcoves, lots of horsey paintings and heavy drape curtains. The tour includes a scoot through a series of rooms, including the portrait gallery, card room and boardroom – all spiced up with tales of horses and their riders.

National Stud

Newmarket, CB8 0XE (off the A1304) • Guided tours daily mid-Feb to Sept 11.15am & 2pm; Oct 11.15am only; 90min • £7 • ☎01638 663464, ⓦnationalstud.co.uk • Two miles southwest of Newmarket, next to the July Racecourse: at the Racehorse Statue roundabout take the same exit as for the July Racecourse and follow the signs

Owned and operated by the Jockey Club, the **National Stud** was established in 1916 to ensure that the British cavalry had decent horses to ride – just as the poor animals were being slaughtered in their hundreds during World War I. **Tours**, which are by bus and on foot, last about ninety minutes and include visits to the foaling unit, the nursery paddocks, the stallion house, and a peek inside the covering (mating) shed. The economics of the Stud dwarf the prize money offered to the winners of the races: a top-ranking stallion can cover 120 mares per year at a rate of £65,000 per session.

Devil's Dyke

The finest surviving Anglo-Saxon earthwork in East Anglia, the **Devil's Dyke** cuts a dead-straight line across the chalky downs to the west of Newmarket, running northwest the eight miles from **Ditton Green to Reach**. A **footpath** runs along the top of the dyke, providing wide views over the surrounding countryside – and making a pleasant and easy day-long excursion. You can join the footpath at its midway point just outside Newmarket: turn right off the main road at the Racehorse Statue roundabout and keep going right to the end of the road (200 yards or so) and you'll spot the Devil's Dyke sign.

ARRIVAL AND INFORMATION NEWMARKET

By train Newmarket train station is on the south side of the town centre, a 10–15min walk from the National Horseracing Museum. Services run to Bury St Edmunds (hourly; 20min), Cambridge (hourly; 25min) and Ipswich (hourly; 1hr).
By bus Most buses pull into the bus station inside The Guineas shopping centre abutting Fred Archer Way.

Principal services include Cambridge (Mon–Sat hourly, Sun every 2–3hr; 40min); Ipswich (every 2hr; 1hr 40min).
Tourist office Part of the District Council offices on the east side of The Guineas shopping centre (Mon–Thurs 9am–5pm, Fri 8.30am–4.30pm & Sat 10am–4pm; ☎ 01638 719749, ⓦ forest-heath.gov.uk).

ACCOMMODATION

Bedford Lodge 11 Bury Rd, CB8 7BX ☎ 01638 663175, ⓦ bedfordlodgehotel.co.uk. The best hotel in Newmarket, the *Bedford Lodge* occupies a former stables in substantial grounds a 10min walk east of the town centre. There are 55 spacious guest rooms and suites here, each decorated in an attractive modern style with lots of pastel shades. There's a fitness suite too. **£110**
The Jockey Club Rooms 101 High St, CB8 8JL ☎ 01638 663101, ⓦ jockey-club-estates.co.uk. Members of the Jockey Club have been staying in deluxe accommodation at the back of the main building, just across the immaculate lawn, for many decades, but these eighteen bedrooms are now available to the general public. Each is decorated in an easy-going and really rather genteel country house style, with extravagant bathrooms, and the setting is as tranquil as tranquil can be. Advance reservations are recommended and note that some periods are reserved for club members. **£160**

Norfolk House Bed and Breakfast 141 High St, Cheveley, CB8 9DG ☎ 01638 730424, ⓦ www .norfolkhouse.biz. Deluxe B&B with two well-appointed guest rooms, one en suite, in an appealing Georgian country home. Price includes a cup of tea and a piece of cake on arrival and use of the outdoor swimming pool during the summer. In the village of Cheveley, about three miles southeast of Newmarket via the B1063. **£80**
Tuddenham Mill High St, Tuddenham, IP28 6SQ ☎ 01638 713552, ⓦ tuddenhammill.co.uk. This deluxe hotel is sited in a sympathetically renovated old water mill about eight miles northeast of Newmarket in the village of Tuddenham. No luxury has been skimped on in the fifteen smart guest rooms, which come complete with walk-in showers, whopping baths, Italian contemporary furniture and, de rigueur for this sort of boutique hotel, fine Egyptian cotton bed linen. **£205**

EATING

Bedford Lodge 11 Bury Rd, CB8 7BX ☎ 01638 663175, ⓦ bedfordlodgehotel.co.uk. Excellent hotel restaurant, where the fusion menu includes dishes like braised shin of beef with a red-wine glaze and horseradish creamed potato, or more adventurously venison with a chocolate sauce. Mains average around £15. Kitchen: daily noon–

2pm & 7–9pm, but closed Sat lunchtimes.
Coffee & Co 12–14 Palace St, CB8 8EP ☎ 01638 611000. This pleasant, brightly decorated little café serves up scrumptious light meals, snacks and sandwiches. Very friendly too. Mon–Fri 8.30am–5.30pm, Sat 8.30am–6pm & Sun 10.30am–2.30pm.

HOOFBEATS GUIDED TOURS

One sure-fire way of getting a handle on Newmarket's **horse racing culture** is to take a guided tour with **Hoofbeats** (☎ 01638 578628, ⓦ hoofbeats.co.uk), not least because the owner-guide is an experienced horse trainer with his own stables. The standard minibus tour lasts four hours, costs **£35 per person** (minimum of 2 people), and starts at the National Stud (see opposite), though this is negotiable as is the itinerary if visitors have a special interest. The itinerary can also vary depending on what's happening and what's open, but usually it includes time watching the horses on The Gallops and visits to a stable and horse-training yard, an equine swimming pool, the British Racing School, where young jockeys learn their skills, and, on occasion, **Tattersalls** horse auctions (ⓦ tattersalls.com), whose world-famous horse auctions take place on about sixteen days a year in their large premises in the town centre. On the tour, you'll also have chance to see the various sorts of training track – the most sophisticated are of sand fibre doused in hot Vaseline. Advance reservations are required.

BLACK-TAILED GODWIT

Contexts

History

On the map, Norfolk and Suffolk look something like a sack on the back of the rest of England, a sack that pushes out into the North Sea. This hints at the region's isolation, but doesn't tell the whole story as the forests of Essex to the south and the sticky marshes of the Fens to the west pretty much cut the two counties off until the seventeenth century – and it was another one hundred years before the journey overland from London to Norwich looked more tempting than the sea cruise. It was the incoming Angles who gave the counties their names (the North Folk and the South Folk) and they threw in the name of the region too (East Anglia), though nowadays no one can agree as to what exactly constitutes East Anglia: some add Lincolnshire, Cambridgeshire and Essex.

The stone ages

Norfolk and Suffolk have been inhabited for over half a million years and although the earliest archeological evidence is necessarily scant, an assortment of Old Stone Age (Palaeolithic) bones and flint tools has been found in coastal deposits near **Happisburgh** in northeast Norfolk. The comings and goings of these migrant peoples were dictated by the fluctuations of several ice ages. The last spell of intense cold began about 17,000 years ago, and it was the final thawing of this last **Ice Age** around 5000 BC that caused the British Isles to separate from the European mainland. Perhaps surprisingly, the sea barrier did nothing to stop further migrations of nomadic hunters into the region, the main magnet being the game that inhabited its forests. These Middle Stone Age (Mesolithic) people needed tools and weapons, and the easy-to-work surface flint of Norfolk and Suffolk was ideal. One of the richest Mesolithic sites in East Anglia is Kelling Heath, near Weybourne, where a scattering of around one hundred Mesolithic flint artefacts have been discovered.

In about 3500 BC, a new wave of colonists reached England from the continent, probably via Ireland, bringing with them a **New Stone Age** (Neolithic) culture based on farming and the rearing of livestock. These tribes were the first to make some impact on the environment, clearing forests, enclosing fields and constructing defensive ditches around their villages. They were also the first to mine flint from the subterranean seams of chalk, the prime example being Grime's Graves near Thetford (see p.209), where these early miners sank shafts through no less than 10ft of sand and clay before quarrying a 20ft band of chalk, a remarkable effort given the crudeness of their tools. In most of England, the most profuse relics of this Neolithic culture are their graves, usually stone-chambered, turf-covered mounds (called **long barrows**), but here in agricultural Norfolk and Suffolk almost all were lost to the plough ages ago, a rare exception being the two barrows at Broome Heath, near Bungay in Suffolk.

6000 BC	2500 BC	2050 BC	55 BC
End of the last Ice Age; the sea separates Britain from the continent	Beginning of the Bronze Age	Construction of Seahenge in Norfolk	Chickens reach Norfolk – courtesy of Julius Caesar

The Bronze Age

The transition from the Neolithic to the **Bronze Age** began around 2500 BC with the importation from northern Europe of artefacts attributed to the **Beaker Culture** – named from the distinctive cups found at many burial sites. In East Anglia as elsewhere, the spread of the Beaker Culture along established trade routes helped stimulate the development of a comparatively well-organized social structure with an established aristocracy. Many of Britain's stone and timber circles were completed at this time, including Stonehenge in Wiltshire, while many others belong entirely to the Bronze Age, including Norfolk's remarkable **Seahenge**, which was discovered on the coast at Holme-next-the-Sea in 1998 – and transferred to a King's Lynn museum a few years later (see p.170). Dated to around 2050 BC, the Seahenge was almost certainly some kind of ceremonial site, perhaps with astronomical significance, though some have argued that this was where the dead were brought to speed the process of decay.

The Iron Age

Covering the period from about 700 BC to the Roman conquest beginning in 43 AD, the British **Iron Age** saw the consolidation of a relatively sophisticated farming economy with a social hierarchy that was dominated by a druidic priesthood. These early Britons gradually developed better methods of metal working, forging not just weapons but also coins and ornamental works, thus creating the first recognizable indigenous art – as famously demonstrated by the wonderfully crafted, gold neck ring – or Great Torc – found at Snettisham and now displayed in the British Museum. The tribes' principal contribution to the landscape was a network of **hillforts** and other defensive works stretching over the entire country, and there are the remains of such fortifications at a dozen or so places in Norfolk and Suffolk, including Clare, Narborough, South Creake, Holkham and Thetford. These earthworks suggest endemic tribal warfare, a situation further complicated by the appearance of bands of Celts, who arrived in numbers from central Europe in around 600 BC. In Norfolk and Suffolk, the origins of the dominant tribe, the **Iceni**, are open to debate: some have argued they were a Germanic people, others that they were invading Celts from France and Belgium, yet others insist they were descendants of the prehistoric inhabitants of the region – or a combination of all three. Whatever their origins, the Iceni – the "People of the Horse" – traded widely: they were familiar with Mediterranean artefacts and the long-distance Icknield Way, running south from their tribal heartland to the Chiltern Hills and Berkshire, was named after them.

Roman conquest and resistance

The Roman invasion of Britain began hesitantly, with small cross-Channel incursions led by **Julius Caesar** in 55 and 54 BC. Almost a century later, in **August 43 AD**, the Romans warmed to the task, landing a substantial force in Kent, from where they fanned out, soon establishing a base along the estuary of the Thames. Joined by a menagerie of elephants and camels for the major battles of the campaign, the Romans soon reached Camulodunum (Colchester) – East Anglia's most important city – and within four years were dug in on the frontier of south Wales. Inter-tribal rivalries

43 AD	60 AD	630	840
The Romans invade Britain and overrun East Anglia	Boudicca and her Iceni ravage Essex	Mass baptisms after Sigebert, the king of East Anglia, opts for Christianity	Danish Vikings invade East Anglia; fear and panic spread

BOUDICCA

Among the many tribes of Iron Age Britain, the **Iceni** were one of the more powerful. By the first century BC, they had settled most of Norfolk and Suffolk, but their tribal heartland was just outside what is now Bury St Edmunds in and around Ixworth, Icklingham and West Stow (see p.304). In 43 AD, **Prasutagus**, the chief of the Iceni, allied himself to the Romans during their conquest of Britain. Initially, this suited the Iceni very well, but just five years later, when the Iceni were no longer useful, the Romans attempted to disarm them and, although the tribe rebelled, they were soon brought to heel. Rubbing salt into the wound, the Romans confiscated the property of Prasutagus upon his death and when his wife, **Boudicca** – aka Boadicea – protested, they flogged her and raped her daughters. Enraged, Boudicca determined to take her revenge, quickly rallying the Iceni and their allies before setting off on a rampage across southern Britain in 60 AD.

As the ultimate symbol of Roman oppression, the Temple of Claudius in Colchester was the initial focus of hatred, but, once Colchester had been razed, Boudicca soon turned her sights elsewhere. She laid waste to London and St Albans, massacring over seventy thousand citizens and inflicting crushing defeats on the Roman units stationed there. She was far from squeamish, ripping traitors' arms out of their sockets and torturing every Roman and Roman collaborator in sight. The Roman governor Suetonius Paulinus eventually defeated her in a pitched battle, which cost the Romans just four hundred lives and the Britons untold thousands. Boudicca knew what to expect from the Romans, so she opted for suicide, thereby ensuring her later reputation as a patriotic Englishwoman, who died fighting for liberty and freedom – claims that Boudicca would have found incomprehensible.

among the Britons dampened resistance, but the Romans did come a military cropper when they tangled with the Iceni under their queen **Boudicca** – or Boadicea – in 60 AD (see box, above).

The Romans ruled England for over three centuries. For the first time, the country began to emerge as a clearly identifiable entity with a defined political structure and, in general terms at least, peace brought prosperity. Commerce flourished, cities prospered and Latin became the language of the Romano-British ruling elite, though local traditions were allowed to coexist alongside imported customs. The benefits of the Roman occupation were, however, largely lost on the Iceni, whose lands were traduced when their rebellion was crushed. It took decades for the region to recover and East Anglia long remained peripheral to the Roman interest, though the legions did keep a beady eye on the Iceni, running two military roads into their heartland from the garrison town of Camulodunum (Colchester): one followed the route of today's **Peddars Way** (see p.206), the other, the Pye Road, went to **Venta Icenorum**, an administrative centre whose scant remains lie just outside Norwich in the village of Caistor St Edmund.

The Anglo-Saxon onslaught

By the middle of the third century AD, the **Roman Empire** was in trouble with frequent collapses of central authority, its military commanders ever more inclined to act independently. And there was the problem of the **Germanic Saxons**, who had begun to raid England's eastern shore. In response, the Romans built a series of coastal defences, which were known as the **Saxon Shore**, stretching along the coast from Norfolk to the

869	1066	1072	1085
Edmund, the last Saxon king of East Anglia, comes to a sticky end	King Harold, the last Saxon king of England, also comes to a sticky end	Rebellion in Ely: Hereward the Wake resists the Normans, but is defeated	The Normans compile the Domesday Book, which details who owns what, does what and lives where

Isle of Wight and including forts at Brancaster and Burgh Castle. These strongholds, holding mixed garrisons of soldiers, sailors and cavalry, frustrated the Saxons for sixty years or more, but by the end of the fourth century England had become irrevocably detached from what remained of the Roman Empire and by then the **Saxons** – and the **Angles**, also from northern Germany – had begun settling England themselves. By the end of the sixth century, the Angles and the Saxons had all but eliminated Romano-British culture and England was divided into the **kingdoms** of Northumbria, Mercia, East Anglia, Kent and Wessex. So complete was the Anglo-Saxon domination of England, through conquest and intermarriage, that some ninety percent of English place names today have an Anglo-Saxon derivation.

Anglo-Saxon East Anglia

Little is known for sure about the Anglo-Saxon kingdom of **East Anglia**, but it seems to have been created in about 520 AD by the Germanic Angles, who had dispossessed or absorbed the Iceni. One of its early kings was an obscure figure by the name of **Wuffa**, who established a dynasty – the Wuffingas – in the late sixth century. His grandson, **Raedwald**, who died in about 624, appears to have extended his authority well beyond the region and is generally regarded as being the chieftain commemorated by the principal ship burial at **Sutton Hoo** (see p.239). The treasures of Sutton Hoo proclaim the wealth and power of the warrior aristocracy who ruled East Anglia, hanging around their communal halls, drinking mead and listening to the lyre. Life for their subjects was, predictably enough, much harsher with most of them eking out a precarious living in small farming communities like the re-created Anglo-Saxon village in **West Stow** (see p.304). It was a barter economy – there was no money – and effectively an illiterate one too, until, that is, the church introduced the elite to Latin. Raedwald flirted with Christianity, but it was **Sigebert**, his stepson, who turned East Anglia **Christian**, welcoming the services of Felix, a priest-evangelist, whom he installed as bishop in Dunwich.

For decades, the marshy fenlands of Lincolnshire and Cambridgeshire had protected East Anglia from the rival kingdom of Mercia to the west, but the most powerful of the Mercian kings, **Offa**, overcame this natural barrier and conquered the region in about 794. Thirty years later, the warrior aristocracy of East Anglia rebelled, but although they defeated the Mercians, their independence did not last long for the Danes were about to arrive in numbers.

The Danish onslaught

After the death of Offa in 796, Wessex gained the upper hand among the Anglo-Saxon kingdoms, and by 825 the kings of Wessex had conquered or taken allegiance from all the other English kingdoms, including East Anglia. Their triumph was, however, short-lived. Carried here by their longboats, the **Vikings** – in this case mostly Danes – had started to raid the east coast towards the end of the eighth century and, emboldened by their success, these raids soon turned into a migration. By 870, the Danes had conquered Northumbria, Mercia and East Anglia, where, in 869, they murdered King Edmund at Hoxne (see p.298). Thereafter, the Danes set their sights on Wessex, whose new king was the exceptionally talented **Alfred the Great**. Despite

1096	1190	1256	1349
Work begins on Norwich Cathedral – stonemasons hit the good times	King Richard complains that in England it is "cold and always raining," and joins the Third Crusade	The calendar is getting out of sync, so a decree installs a leap year – one leap day every four years	The Black Death reaches Norfolk and Suffolk; Hunstanton gets a dose first

the odds, Alfred successfully resisted the Danes and eventually the two warring parties signed a truce, which fixed an uneasy border between Wessex and Danish territory, the so-called **Danelaw**, which lay to the north of a line drawn between London and Chester – and included East Anglia. Alfred died in 899 and his successor, **Edward the Elder**, capitalized on his efforts, establishing his supremacy over the Danelaw to become the de facto overlord of all England. The relative calm continued until the Vikings returned in force to milk the king of Wessex for all the money they could, though the ransom – the **Danegeld** – paid brought only temporary relief and, in 1016, the Danes took control of the whole of England.

Danish rule and Norman conquest

The first Danish king of England was **Canute**, a shrewd and gifted ruler, who took a gamble – or paid off some military indebtedness – when he appointed Thorkell the Tall to be the Jarl of East Anglia in 1017. It didn't work. Thorkell's relationship with Canute broke down irretrievably when the jarl's wife was found guilty of poisoning his son by his first marriage with the help of a witch – heady stuff even by Viking standards. Neither did Canute's carefully constructed Anglo-Scandinavian empire last much beyond the king's death, soon brought to ruin by his two disreputable sons. Thereafter, the Saxons regained the initiative, putting **Edward the Confessor** on the English throne in 1042. On Edward's death, **Harold**, the Earl of Wessex, became king, but it was a disputed succession, the end result being the invasion of William, Duke of Normandy, who famously routed the Saxons – and killed Harold – at the **Battle of Hastings** in 1066.

Norman East Anglia

William I imposed a Norman aristocracy on his new subjects, rewarding his leading retainers with vast estates – within a decade ten of William's relatives owned thirty per cent of English land. In Norfolk, the Bigod and Warenne families led the territorial charge and the Bigods were large landowners in Suffolk too. Other beneficiaries included Richard Fitzgilbert, who ended up with 95 lordships in Suffolk, where he made Clare his base, and Robert Malet, who accrued 221 Suffolk holdings with his headquarters in Eye. What was left of the Anglo-Saxon aristocracy must have viewed all this with a mix of horror and trepidation, but William crushed any acts of resistance – like Hereward the Wake's rebellion in Ely (see p.180) – with great brutality. William and his Norman successors also overawed their new subjects with a series of strongholds – the **castles** at Norwich, Eye, Castle Rising and Castle Acre are prime examples – and encouraged the establishment of **monasteries** like those at North Creake, Binham and Little Walsingham. There were, however, exceptions to the usual pattern of dispossession and castellation, principally in Bury St Edmunds, where the Normans did not erect a castle and also permitted Abbot Baldwin, who had been a physician to Edward the Confessor, to stay in post. Perhaps the single most effective controlling measure, however, was the compilation of the **Domesday Book** between 1085 and 1086, which recorded who owned what and where. The Domesday Book paints a rosy picture of Norwich, one of the country's largest and most important towns with no less than 1320 burgesses, indicating a population of about 10,000 inhabitants.

1381	1549	1605	1642
Peasants' Revolt convulses East Anglia	More discontented peasants: Kett's rebels occupy Norwich	Gunpowder Plot: the Catholic Guy Fawkes plans to blow up the Houses of Parliament, but fails	The English Civil War begins; most of Norfolk and Suffolk supports Parliament against the king

Medieval tribulations

William I died in 1087, but his kingdom was soon wracked by **civil war** as rival sets of feudal barons slugged it out for control of the English throne. This bitter conflict lasted for several centuries during which, in 1214, a large group of disgruntled barons gathered in the abbey church of Bury St Edmunds to swear to bring King John to heel. The following year they famously forced John to accept the **Magna Carta**, a charter guaranteeing their rights and privileges, but, charter or not, the struggle between central and local power rumbled on for decades. The whole balance of medieval society was, however, much more profoundly affected by the **Black Death**, which reached Norwich in 1349. It's impossible to know what percentage of the Norfolk and Suffolk population died from the Black Death, especially as its ravages varied from parish to parish, but it's likely that most towns and villages lost between twenty and fifty percent of their inhabitants. Further visitations of the plague followed shortly afterwards and the scarcity of labour that followed gave the peasantry more economic clout than they had ever had before. Predictably, the landowners attempted to restrict the concomitant rise in wages, thereby provoking the widespread rioting that culminated in the **Peasants' Revolt of 1381**, though the immediate spark was lit by the imposition of a swingeing poll tax. In Norfolk, the peasantry seized Norwich and proceeded to take bloody revenge on their oppressors. Their leader, a dyer by the name of Geoffrey Litster, even installed himself in the castle, making four gentlemen knights wait upon him while he banqueted. Unluckily for Litster, his feasting did not last long: in London, the Peasants' Revolt was crushed after the murder of its leader, Wat Tyler, and, with the forces of reaction rallying, Bishop Henry Despenser, marched on Norwich and crushed the revolt forthwith; the **Despenser Reredos** in Norwich Cathedral (see p.42) celebrated his success.

The fifteenth to early seventeenth centuries

Throughout most of the fifteenth century, the kings of England were preoccupied with the Anglo-French **Hundred Years' War** (effectively till 1454) and the **Wars of the Roses**, a protracted civil war between two rival sets of barons – the Yorkists and the Lancastrians – which only ended with the death of Richard III at Bosworth Field in 1485. One result was the dislocation and transformation of the wool trade with Flanders (see box, opposite), another was Richard III's replacement by **Henry VII**, the first of the **Tudors**, which was when England began to assume the status of a major European power. After Henry VII came **Henry VIII**, who is best remembered for his separation of the English Church from Rome and his establishment of an independent Protestant church – the **Church of England**. Famously, Henry's motives were all to do with his quest to divorce Catherine of Aragon for her failure to provide him with a son, rather than any doctrinal issues – Henry was never a Protestant himself – but his break with Rome in the **Reformation** shattered the traditional alliance of church and state that had dominated medieval England: pope and bishops, kings and dukes were supposedly the representatives of God on earth, and Henry's schism stood the country on its intellectual head. The whole of England was convulsed by religious debate, nowhere more so than in Norfolk and Suffolk where the seeds of **Protestantism** had already fallen on fertile ground among both the

1645	1660	1734	1754
Cromwell creates the formidable New Model Army; East Anglians are its backbone	The Restoration: Charles II takes the throne – and digs up the body of Oliver Cromwell to prove his point	Work starts on Holkham Hall	Charles Wesley tours Norfolk; Methodism takes root

THE WOOL TOWNS OF NORFOLK AND SUFFOLK

Since the thirteenth century, the wool trade, which involved the export of raw wool from England to the weavers of Flanders, had become a mainstay of the English economy. In **East Anglia** as elsewhere, the main beneficiaries were the owners of the flocks, often the monasteries, and the wool merchants, few in number but extraordinarily rich. During the fifteenth century, however, protectionist tariffs, war and taxation combined to boost domestic cloth-making and the towns of **southern Suffolk** – Lavenham, Hadleigh, Kersey for instance – flourished. Helped by refugee Flemish weavers, Suffolk's cloth workers learnt how to produce top-quality, short-fibre woollens (rather than the traditional, long-fibre worsteds) in a complex cottage industry that involved at least six separate procedures: washing, sorting, scouring and soaking in oil; carding; spinning; weaving; fulling and bleaching; dyeing and finishing. It was a dynamic industry too, with each village developing its own speciality – Lavenham's was blue broadcloth – but one in which the workforce was soon in thrall to the wool and cloth merchants, a perennial source of bitterness and discontent. In the event, the success of the Suffolk cloth industry was short-lived as its products could not compete with the lighter, stronger "new draperies" developed elsewhere in England and, although the industry survived for another hundred years or so, its salad days were over by 1550. In **Norwich**, the textile industry lasted longer, partly as a result of a further influx of Flemish weaver refugees, who fled here from the Spanish Netherlands to avoid the tender mercies of the Inquisition in the 1560s.

region's merchants, whose burgeoning wealth and independence had never been easy to accommodate within a rigid caste society, and their employees, the skilled cloth workers and their apprentices, who had a tradition of opposing arbitrary authority.

In the late 1530s, one of the consequences of Henry's break with Rome was the **Dissolution of the Monasteries**, which gave both king and nobles the chance to get their hands on valuable monastic property. This was a windfall for the large landowners, many of whom had already started expanding their estates by summarily fencing in common land to graze their flocks of sheep, acts of **enforced enclosure** which threatened the very livelihood of their poorer neighbours. Out of fear and anger, a great concourse of country folk gathered outside Norwich in 1549 under the general leadership of **Robert Kett**. Here they engaged in a sort of prototype sit-down strike, the "rebels" organizing themselves into a rudimentary mini-state, holding Protestant religious services and buying supplies before ultimately occupying Norwich itself. They were convinced that the obvious justice of their cause would persuade the government to punish the land grabbers, but they were wrong: instead, the government dispatched an army of mercenaries, who butchered the rebels; Kett was hung over the walls of Norwich castle, his death purposefully prolonged as an example to all.

The crushing of Kett's rebellion gave the green light for further acts of enclosure and East Anglia seethed with discontent, especially at the treatment of one of the region's most popular Protestant preachers and pamphleteers, **William Prynne** (1600–69). In punishment for his assorted diatribes against church and state, Prynne had already had his ears cropped, but that did not deter him at all and in 1636 his *Newes from Ipswich* had him up in court again: at something of a loss as to how to punish him, the judge ordered the remaining stumps of his ears be chopped off – and the crowds cheered and threw flowers in front of Prynne as he approached the place of punishment.

1846	1862	1902	1915
Opening of Ipswich train station. General delirium	Royal family buys Sandringham; locals delighted (mostly)	First football game between Ipswich and Norwich – beginning of the "Old Farm derby"	German Zeppelins bomb Norfolk: little damage; light casualties; great fear

The English Civil War

Elizabeth I steered a skillful course between the religious factions that might have stretched her authority, but her successors - **James I and Charles I** - were much less prudent, clinging to an absolutist vision of the monarchy – the divine right of kings – that was totally out of step with the Protestant leanings of the majority of their subjects. It was a recipe for disaster – and sure enough disaster came with the outbreak of the **English Civil War** between Parliament and king in 1642. The Royalist forces ("Cavaliers") were initially successful, but afterwards key regiments of the Parliamentarian army ("Roundheads") were completely overhauled by **Oliver Cromwell** (1599–1658). The kernel of the **New Model Army** that Cromwell created came from the small freeholders and skilled craftsmen of Norfolk and Suffolk – butchers, weavers, dyers, shoemakers and men like Philip Skippon, a minor gentleman from West Lexham in Norfolk, who became a major general. Well drilled and well trained, the New Model cut its teeth at the Battle of Naseby and thereafter simply brushed the Royalists aside, the end result – after endless royal shenanigans – being the **king's execution** in January 1649. For the next eleven years, England was a **Commonwealth** – at first a true republic, then, after 1653, a **Protectorate** with Cromwell as the Lord Protector and commander in chief. The turmoil of the Civil War and the pre-eminence of the army unleashed a furious legal, theological and political debate in every corner of the country, but especially in Norfolk and Suffolk. This milieu spawned a host of proto-communist sects, the most notable of whom were the **Levellers**, who demanded wholesale constitutional reform, as well as a battery of **Nonconformist** religious groups, including the **Quakers**, who established a dissenting tradition that long remained a feature of Norfolk and, to a lesser extent, Suffolk life. There was a less palatable side to all this religious fervour too, most notably the New Model's savage treatment of Irish Catholics and, in East Anglia, the multiple denunciations of witchcraft which fed the "trials" of the so-called **Witchfinder General**, Suffolk's own Matthew Hopkins (c.1620–1647), who managed to kill around three hundred "witches" in just a couple of years.

Cromwell died in 1658 and two years later the monarchy was restored in the shape of **Charles II**, the exiled son of the previous king: the dissenting Protestants of Norfolk and Suffolk knew what was coming next – the return of the old regime, and lots more enforced enclosures.

The eighteenth century

With the decline of the cloth trade (see p.317), Norfolk and Suffolk had become much more reliant on **agriculture** and by the 1750s East Anglia was providing London with much of its wheat and meat. A buoyant agricultural sector encouraged the region's larger landowners to enclose yet more tracts of common land and between 1792 and 1815 no less than one million acres were lost to East Anglia's landless labourers, tenants and lease holders, who were no longer allowed to graze their animals, collect firewood or do pretty much anything else on land they had used (but not legally owned) for centuries. It was, as E.P. Thompson declared in his seminal *The Making of the English Working Class*, "a plain enough case of class robbery". With their newly enlarged estates, the big landowners of Georgian East Anglia could get down to some serious money-making and in this they were helped by two of their number who pioneered ways of improving the fertility of the land. First up was Raynham's second **Viscount Townshend** (1674–1738)

1920s	1942	1946	1950
Mass unemployment; work schemes create a string of urban parks in Norwich and Ipswich	German air force bombs Norwich in the so-called Baedeker raids	Bernard Matthews leaves school; turkeys frightened	Soap rationing ends in Britain – a general clean-up follows

– aka "Turnip Townshend"– who spent the last years of his life experimenting with all things agricultural, one of his most important innovations being a four-year rotation of crops – wheat, turnips, barley and clover - which helped stop soil exhaustion and increased yields. The second great pioneering figure was Holkham's **Coke of Norfolk** (1754–1842), who, among much else, imported new machinery, experimented with pig breeding and improved the quality of the sandy soils of his estate with marl (a crumbly mixture of clays, calcium and magnesium carbonates). Inevitably, not all the region's landowners were so "agricultural", most notably **Robert Walpole** (1676–1745), generally regarded as England's **first prime minister**, who built himself a real show-off pile, Houghton Hall, and stuffed it with paintings and assorted treasures – not much interest in turnips there then.

The nineteenth century

Powerful aristocrats like Coke, Townshend and Walpole gave eighteenth-century East Anglia a lot of clout, but the situation was transformed by the **Industrial Revolution**, which gathered pace after the defeat of Napoleon at the Battle of Waterloo in 1815. In the space of a few decades, England turned from an agricultural to a manufacturing economy and the cities of the Midlands and the North mushroomed, while East Anglia was effectively marooned, becoming little more than a rural backwater. There were, of course, exceptions – Cromer became a fashionable resort, Ipswich built a huge new dock, and much of the region was linked to the railway network in the 1840s and 1850s – but these developments went against the general tide.

Even worse, the prolonged agricultural **depression** that hit England in the mid-1870s stretched the finances of large and small landowners alike, its effects deepened by the availability – and importation – of cheap grain from North America. Neither did the introduction of **death duties** in 1894 do the big estates any favours and as a result many landowners sold up and several hundred country houses were simply demolished. The situation of the agricultural labourers as a whole was even worse, though there was something of a fightback with the establishment of the **National Agricultural Labourers' Union** in 1872. At its high point, the union had over 86,000 members, over one-tenth of the farm workforce in England, and in 1885, their leader, a farm labourer by the name of **Joseph Arch**, became the MP for Northwest Norfolk, which was to remain a union stronghold for several decades.

The twentieth century

As was the case in most of Europe, the outbreak of **World War I**, was greeted by cheering crowds in both Norfolk and Suffolk, but the reality was grim: both counties lost hundreds of men in the war, the effects compounded by them joining up as groups of "pals" – the "Sandringham Company", which recruited from the King's estate at Sandringham, was, for example, badly mauled at Gallipoli. More unusually, a squadron of German ships bombarded Lowestoft and Great Yarmouth to limited effect in 1916 and there were periodic Zeppelin bombing raids on the likes of Norwich, Harwich and Ipswich.

There was precious little cheering in the early days of **World War II**, especially as many believed that the Germans would invade England via Norfolk or Suffolk. As a result,

1953	1959	1970s	1990
Freak weather conditions bring flooding to the Norfolk coast; many die	BBC *Look East* begins; regional news boosted?	Great Yarmouth booms on the back of North Sea oil	In Norfolk, Mrs Thatcher praises "the common sense of the housewife with her food"; turkeys still frightened (see 1946)

there was a frantic effort to protect the coastline, for example at Shingle Street (see p.241): hundreds of mines were laid offshore, the shoreline was festooned with barbed wire and anti-tank traps, and dozens of concrete pillboxes were constructed just inland. In the event, the Germans never arrived, but the **American air force** did, occupying around 700 hastily constructed air strips from where they could fly off to bomb the continent. In 1943, the airmen were joined by thousands of American soldiers in the lead-up to D-Day and the effect of this amicable invasion on the East Anglian population was quite striking – in particular the Americans went down well with many local women, who found them a breath of fresh air.

In many ways it was the **1970s and the 1980s** that proved to be the decisive decades for Norfolk and Suffolk: the ports of the east coast, particularly Felixstowe, boomed as trade moved from England's west coast to the east; small electronics companies moved into East Anglia by the dozen; commuters could speed their way to the capital with the electrification of the London–Norwich rail line in 1987; Norwich's University of East Anglia began to establish an academic name for itself; and, partly as a result of EU subsidies, big farmers made big profits with fewer men – the agricultural workforce was reduced to a fraction of what it had once been. The aristocracy got into the act too when they realized they no longer had to bulldoze their country houses as uneconomic, but could turn them into tourist attractions instead – and the Queen duly obliged by opening Sandringham up to the general public in 1977.

Norfolk and Suffolk today

Amid all the good news in the 1970s and 1980s, there were two major problems: as **property** prices spiked with the incoming tide of commuters and second-home owners, so local families had to move away, leaving many villages strangely deserted, almost husk-like – with the appearance of a village, but not much else, "pastiche suburbia" in the words of one commentator. This remains a problem today, though a scattering of charitable housing trusts does provide affordable housing across the region. The other issue was **agriculture**. By the mid-1990s, hundreds of hedgerows had been uprooted, acres of marshland drained, scores of ditches and ponds filled, pesticides and nitrates had affected water quality, and fields had been consolidated as never before, creating the so-called "prairie farming" that scars some of the region today. Here the news is better, the future rosier than before as concerted efforts by conservationists are slowly turning back the agricultural clock, the most obvious sign to the visitor being the scores of restaurants that serve organic produce, often seasonal and usually local. Now that is indeed good news.

1994	1996	2007	2010
Channel Tunnel opens to traffic – continent no longer isolated	Delia Smith and husband become majority shareholders in Norwich City Football Club	Smoking banned in enclosed public places in England and Wales	Bernard Matthews dies

Wildlife

With barely a ridge, never mind a mountain in sight, Norfolk and Suffolk are low-lying, but this does not mean they are uniform – far from it. The two counties hold a real mix of habitats from farmland and forest, through to salt marsh, mud flat, sand dunes, sandy beaches, pebble beaches and the occasional sea cliff – think Cromer and Hunstanton. These varied habitats support a varied wildlife, though it's for its birds that the region wins most acclaim.

Mammals

In common with most of rural England, **mammals** such as foxes, hedgehogs, badgers, stoats and weasels are relatively common. The region's rivers support a wide range of mammals too, including otters and water voles, though these are threatened by an alien species, the mink. Similarly, grey squirrels, originally, from America, have pretty much wiped out the native **red squirrel**, though Pensthorpe Nature Reserve (see p.143) near Fakenham is doing its best to protect and conserve some of the reds. There is a significant **bat** population in East Anglia, with the pipistrelle and brown long-eared the most common, and a 200-strong breeding colony of **Daubenton's Bat** in the Broads. The area also has more than half the UK population of the very rare **barbastelle bat**.

Common seals

The Wash and its neighbouring coastline has the largest population of **common seals** in Europe. They are distinguished from the more populous **grey seal** by the V-shaped slant to their nostrils. Lumpen and ungainly on land, their grey or brown dappled fur clearly visible, these large mammals look sleek and streamlined once in the water. They can remain underwater for up to ten minutes at a time, are able to dive to a depth of 160ft, and can swim 30 miles just to feed. They frequently stay out at sea for several days, only heading for land to rest, give birth, suckle their young and moult. The males play no part in rearing pups, opting instead to fight with other males to guarantee their opportunity to mate again. Females give birth to a single pup in the summer, their rich milk allowing the pup to double in weight in three to four weeks. Females live for around 30 years, males usually peg out ten years earlier.

Harbour porpoises

At around 6ft long, **harbour porpoises** are one of the smallest ocean mammals. Grey-backed, but paler underneath, they are round-headed and they make regular appearances along the Norfolk coast, particularly between January and April. Much smaller than their dolphin relatives, they are hard to spot, especially as they are also shy and rarely break the surface for long, and your best chance of a good sighting is in shallow waters.

Reptiles

The pride of East Anglia's reptilian crew is the endangered **natterjack toad**, which is found in the coastal dunes and salt marshes of Norfolk, especially Holme Dunes National Nature Reserve. With yellow-or red-coloured warts covering its brown or green skin, it's most easily distinguished by the yellow stripe down its back. It's not a great swimmer and walks rather than hops. The male's rasping mating call can be heard for miles between April and June, in the evenings and after rain. The region's coastal

THE TOP SIX BIRDWATCHING SIGHTS

NWT Cley Marshes (see p.134). The best known of the NWT's reserves and one of the oldest reserves in the country, where the shingle beach, saline lagoons, grazing marsh and reedbeds attract wintering and migrating water birds. Spring and autumn are best to see these visitors arriving and departing but there's good birding all year round.

NWT Hickling Broad Nature Reserve (see p.84). Overlooking the Broads' largest area of open water, the reedbeds, water meadows and woodland of this excellent reserve provide a rich habitat for bittern, bearded tit, water rail, marsh - and hen – harriers and cranes. Boat trips – which take you to hides only accessible by boat – are available from April to September.

RSPB Minsmere (see p.258). Up to thirty percent of the UK's breeding population of bittern are to be found at Minsmere, where they are most easily spotted in winter. The reserve is also of particular importance for its populations of marsh harrier, pied avocet, bearded tit and reed bunting.

RSPB Snettisham (see p.161). In the winter, the inter-tidal mudbanks and salt marshes of The Wash receive the UK's largest influx of visiting water birds, over 300,000 waders and wildfowl – waders arriving ahead of the wildfowl (ducks and geese). The RSPB reserve at Snettisham provides a perfect place to spot them in number and, as the tide rises and their feeding grounds recede, you can expect amazing flight displays.

RSPB Strumpshaw Fen (see p.111). To catch a glimpse of a kingfisher, bearded tit or hear the song of sedge and reed warblers, head for this RSPB reserve, part of its Fen Restoration Project which removes scrub to encourage bitterns and other fenland wildlife. Best in spring and autumn.

RSPB Titchwell Marsh (see p.156). Spring is perhaps the best time to visit Titchwell with migrating waders arriving by the hundred in April and May and marsh harriers performing their dancing displays, but there's good birding all year given the range of habitats.

heaths also hold a small population of **adders**, a mildly venomous snake with a brown skin and a lozenge pattern down its back. They slither off if they sense people coming, but can sometimes be spotted basking on warm rocks in sunny weather.

Birds

No argument, Norfolk and Suffolk provide the best birding in the UK. The region's long and varied coastline, its inland waterways, estuary, fen, heathland, grazing marshes, woodland, fields and hedgerows all combine to offer an outstanding variety of habitats for a wonderful range of birds, both resident and migratory. There are three main agencies concerned with the preservation of these habitats, the **Norfolk Wildlife Trust** (NWT; ⓦwww.norfolkwildlifetrust.org.uk), which has thirty reserves; the **Suffolk Wildlife Trust** (SWT; ⓦwww.suffolkwildlifetrust.org), with over fifty reserves; and the **Royal Society for the Protection of Birds** (RSPB; ⓦwww.rspb.org.uk) with seventeen reserves across both counties. In addition, the **National Trust** (ⓦwww.nationaltrust.org.uk) protects and conserves certain key locations – for example, Blakeney Point – as does **Natural England** (ⓦwww.naturalengland.org.uk), which is, for instance, responsible for Scolt Island and the Holme Dunes National Nature Reserve. Finally, the **Broads** have been designated a (sort of) National Park (ⓦwww.broads-authority.gov.uk) with all the wildlife protections that that involves.

GLOSSARY OF SELECTED BIRDS

ALL-YEAR RESIDENTS

Avocet A distinctively patterned, black-and-white wader, long-legged with a long upturned bill. Likes shallow, slightly saline water and mud. Found among the coastal lagoons of the east coast during the summer. Emblem of the RSPB.

Barn owl Instantly recognizable large white owl, which is generally seen hunting across open country. Can appear in car headlights as a ghostly apparition. Best seen at dusk but sometimes also seen during the day floating across farmland. Very common across rural Norfolk and Suffolk.

Bearded tit Tawny-brown tit with a grey head, black

moustache and bright yellow eye. A beautiful bird found entirely in reedbeds and localized to the east and south coasts of England. While commonly known as a tit, it is in fact more closely related to the parrot bill family. To add further confusion, it is also sometimes referred to as a bearded reedling. Patience and calm weather are needed to spot this bird as it can be hard to locate in the reeds, but it is a sociable and noisy creature that is easily identified by a loud pinging call.

Bittern A secretive and rare member of the heron family with a stripey, mottled-brown plumage. The bittern relies on the shelter and deep water of the reeds to hunt for fish. Hard to spot, it's often most easily sighted in winter when it leaves the reeds to find areas of water that have not frozen over. The bittern is one of the most threatened species in the UK. Listen for the booming calls in spring as they enter the breeding season. Restricted to a single habitat of wet reedbeds.

Black-tailed godwit Large, handsome wader characterized by exceptionally long legs. Usually stands tall and upright. The summer plumage is very bold and colourful with a coppery-red head and breast; the winter plumage is grey and dull. From autumn to late winter it can be found in flocks in small sheltered muddy estuaries.

Common crane Very large, long-legged and long-necked bird with a 6ft wingspan. Has a grey body with thick black legs. Found in reedbeds, lakes and marshy areas. Large groups will gather in spring for graceful dancing courtship displays. Most readily seen in the Norfolk Broads, where there is a small resident population.

Common crossbill Member of the finch family, looks quite chunky and parrot-like with a distinctive hooked bill, dark wings with bright pink/red rich rump. It uses its bill to prise seeds, insects, buds and berries from cones and twigs. Found in spruce, larch and pine trees. Needs easy access to pools for frequent bouts of drinking.

Dunlin Common small wader with a dull-grey brown head and back with long tapered very slightly curved black bill and short black legs. When in a large flock, it's often seen dashing and sweeping out at sea and back to shore again in spectacular manoeuvres.

Goldeneye Very shy but strikingly beautiful black and white duck. It has black markings on a dazzling white body and a black head with a large distinctive white spot between a yellow eye and a short black beak. Widespread in winter on lakes and estuaries.

Knot Larger and stockier than the dunlin, the knot is a sociable wader with winter plumage of a pale grey back and shortish bill. Summer plumage is a reddish brown coppery head, back and underparts. Often found in huge numbers mingling with dunlins to form dense packs when roosting at high tide and dramatically swarming over mud flats to feed.

Lapwing Comical-looking, pigeon-sized wader with a black cap and wispy crest. Plumage is dark green and purple and it has a white chest. The wings are broad and rounded and distinctly flappy in flight. Also known as the peewit due to its distinctive call. Found predominantly around farmland and in open countryside.

Little egret Stunning small white heron with long black legs. Generally solitary bird of marshy, flooded grassy areas. Spends much of its time standing still or wading in shallow water hunting for prey.

Oystercatcher Medium-sized wader with striking black and white body with a vivid orange bill. Often gathers in large and noisy flocks. Found on sandy, muddy and rocky beaches.

Redshank A medium-sized, very abundant, grey-looking wader. It has long red legs and a long straight bill. Tends to congregate away from other waders and can be distinctly noisy. Probes and picks at mud searching for insects, worms and molluscs. Found on estuaries, salt marshes and freshwater pools.

Ringed plover Small wader with a brown back, white chest, black and white ring around neck and orange bill with a black tip. Fairly common and generally found in coastal areas, particularly shingle and gravel beaches.

Ruff Medium-sized wader appearing in mid-autumn on wetland areas. Has a very plain brown/grey winter plumage, but in the spring the male transforms and has a stunning broad feathery ruff of varying colours. Can appear quite sedate compared with other waders. Males often display in groups to females with mock battles.

Snow bunting Beautiful little bunting with a snowy plumage. Bright white chest and grey/brown back. Most commonly seen in the winter on coastal sites on shingle seashore.

Stonechat Has a black head, rust-red chest and white patch on the side of the neck. Likes open places with gorse, heather and bushes around coastal areas and dunes. Will often be found perching on top of bushes and has a very distinct call which sounds like two stones being bashed together.

Teal The smallest of the ducks. The male has stunning plumage with a bright green patch on hind wings and a black yellow triangle under the tail, while the female is pretty drab-looking with no distinct features. The teal is a surface-feeding duck and can be regularly found among the reeds or well-vegetated shore.

Turnstone Similar size and shape to a dunlin but with a short tapered bill and beautiful black, white and chestnut coloured upperparts and a vivid white underside with bright orange legs. Uses bill to turn over stones and pebbles.

Woodlark A small pretty lark, which has a long white stripe over the eye to the back of the neck. Spends most of its time feeding or standing on the ground. Found in open woodland areas and sandy heaths.

MIGRATORY BIRDS

Brent goose More duck-sized than goose, with a black

head and black chest with a brown underside and a white patch on the neck. Has a distinctive but pleasant growling call. Often behaves more like a duck by upending on the water to feed. Found on salt marshes and estuaries from late autumn through to early spring. Winter resident.

Golden oriole A striking bird with vivid yellow and black plumage and a bright pink-red bill. Can be secretive and will often hide in dense foliage preferring oak, poplar and chestnut trees. Only seen in the UK from April to Sept.

Little tern Smaller and whiter than the common tern with a sharp yellow bill, white forehead, black cap and pale grey body. A small, quick, agile coastal bird often roosting in noisy colonies – breeding on sand and shingle beaches. Seen in the UK April to Oct.

Marsh Harrier Distinguishable from other harriers by its large size. Holds wings in an obvious V while gliding over reedbeds and marshes performing breathtaking courtship displays in spring. A small population is resident all year round, but most are summer visitors.

Nightingale A plain brown rather dull-looking bird with a truly remarkable song. Slightly larger than a robin. A very secretive bird, which sings from deep within bushes. Summer visitor.

Pink-footed goose Pinkish-grey body, small bill with pink band, and pink feet and legs. Breeds in Scandinavia but large numbers spend the winter here in East Anglia, where it feeds in fields, farmland and river estuaries. Winter resident.

Pintail Elegant, dabbling duck with a long black tail, yellow brown body with a brown head and distinctive white stripe on the neck and breast. Can be found on both salt and fresh water but generally quite rare. Found in the UK from Sept to April.

Sand martin The smallest of the swallow and swift family with a stockier body, all brown upperparts with white underparts. Lacking the longer tail feathers of the swallow and swift, it appears weaker in flight. It bores holes into earth cliffs, sandy riverbanks or soft sandstone to breed in large colonies from April till July. Summer visitor.

Scarlet rosefinch A brown finch with cherry-red head, chest and rump with a brown back. Sporadic breeding in deciduous woodland often near wetland areas. May to Oct.

Spoonbill Unmistakeable large heron-like white wader with large spatula shaped black bill, which turns black with age. Wades through water sweeping its bill side to side hunting for prey. Found on marshes and lakes. Seen in the UK April to Sept.

Spotted flycatcher Plumage is very plain and grey with a streaked forehead. A sharp-eyed and alert little bird that inhabits edges of clearings, where it will sit on a perch and fly out to catch insects mid-air. Summer visitor.

Stone Curlew Very distinctive-looking bird with long yellow legs, dark streaky body – which is perfect for camouflage – and round yellow eyes which are well adapted for nocturnal foraging for insects and worms. A bird of the open countryside it visits the UK between April and Sept.

Wryneck Member of the woodpecker family. At a distance may appear fairly brown and dull but closer inspection will reveal a complex and intricate set of colours and markings. Often appears camouflaged against the bark of the tree. Seen April to Oct.

Books

Dozens of writers of all descriptions have lived or worked in Norfolk and Suffolk – the list below just skims the surface. For specialist, regional publications, Halsgrove (ⓦwww.halsgrove.com) are good – we've mentioned one of their Norfolk and Suffolk titles below (Burnham History Group), but they have about twenty books about East Anglia currently in print. Both counties also have websites cataloguing which writers did what, where and when – check out ⓦliterarynorfolk.co.uk and ⓦliterarysuffolk.paperviewer.co.uk.

TRAVEL AND GENERAL

William Cobbett *Rural Rides*. Adventurer, journalist, soldier, traveller and radical, Cobbett (1763–1835) bemoans the death of rural England and rails against the treatment of the poor as he rides across the shires of England, dropping by Norfolk and Suffolk to see how the locals are getting on.

Daniel Defoe *Tour Through the Whole Island of Great Britain*. When he wasn't thinking about desert islands, Daniel Defoe (1659–1731) had other things to do, including this gambol round much of England – including parts of East Anglia – observing the current state of play, both spiritual and economic, in what turned out to be the last years before the Industrial Revolution hit its stride.

Henry Rider Haggard *A Farmer's Year: Being His Commonplace Book for 1898*. Haggard (1856–1925) may once have been famous for his swashbuckling tales of imperial derring-do, but he was also a Norfolk squire (who preferred writing novels to toiling the land) and these are his assorted reminiscences.

★ **J.B. Priestley** *English Journey*. The Bradford-born playwright, broadcaster and author's record of his extensive travels around England in the 1930s, including time in East Anglia, may say nothing about contemporary England, but

in many ways its quirkiness, and eye for English eccentricity, formed the blueprint for the later Brysons and Therouxs.

Peter Sager *East Anglia: Norfolk, Suffolk and Essex*. Sager doesn't half know his East Anglian onions and it shows in this deeply reflective, studied travel guide/travelogue, which draws on many sources. At risk of sounding churlish, however, he does seem a little too pleased with himself when he is speaking to milords and miladies. A Pallas guide last published in 2003.

W.G. Sebald *Rings of Saturn*. Intriguing, ruminative book that is a heady mix of novel, travel and memoir, focusing ostensibly on the author's walking tour of Suffolk – and including several plum historical accounts of those that have lived there, including Joseph Conrad. A UEA academic and highly regarded writer, Sebald (1944–2001) died in a car crash near Norwich in 2001.

Henry Williamson *The Story of a Norfolk Farm*. Published in 1927, *Tarka the Otter* made its author, Henry Williamson (1895–1977), a household name, which made his liking for Hitler all the more conspicuous to his new neighbours when he bought a farm at Stiffkey in 1936. Williamson only stayed in Norfolk for two years, but he did have time to record his time there in what amounts to a rural lament.

HISTORY, SOCIETY AND POLITICS

Ronald Blythe *Akenfield: Portrait of an English Village*. First published in 1969, this much acclaimed book, a surprising bestseller, is a thoroughly researched investigation into the comings and goings, habits and economics of a Suffolk village on the cusp of change. There's no village of "Akenfield" per se, but the odds are it was based on the author's researches in the hamlets of Akenham, near Ipswich, and Charsfield, near Wickham Market. Peter Hall amplified the book's success by making the film *Akenfield* five years later.

Burnham History Group *The Book of the Burnhams: The Story of the Seven Burnhams by the Sea*. Long before the metropolitan tourists arrived by the Porsche load, the Burnhams had a long and unusual history – and this book gives the low-down. Lavishly illustrated with more than

three hundred photographs. A title in the Halsgrove Community History Series.

Helen Castor *Blood & Roses: The Paston Family & the Wars of the Roses*. Norman Davis's book (see below) may have published the Paston letters, but Castor gets stuck into their interpretation.

Norman Davis *The Paston Letters*. Before the family died out in the early eighteenth century, the Pastons were major Norfolk landowners and, unusually, a great treasure-trove of their late medieval letters have survived – and this book prints a selection from 1430 to 1485, when England was wracked by the Wars of the Roses.

Nigel Heard *Wool: East Anglia's Golden Fleece*. The only readily available book on this subject, though it was published in the 1970s. Thoroughly researched.

David Hoare *Standing Up to Hitler: The Story of Norfolk's Home Guard and Secret Army, 1940-44*. Enjoyable account of Norfolk's Home Guard plus the so-called "secret army", which was trained to delay and sabotage the German army if, as was feared, it landed on the east coast.

Charlotte Paton *The King of the Norfolk Poachers: His Life and Times*. East Anglia's Charlotte Paton became intrigued by the life of Fred Rolfe (see below) and her investigations – as revealed in this book – show the man in all his complexity.

Arthur Patterson *Wild Fowlers and Poachers*. Born in the Yarmouth Rows, the youngest of nine children, Patterson (1857–1935) was passionate about wildlife and spent much of his spare time teaching himself about the plants and animals of Breydon Water. At the age of 71, he wrote this memoir of his lifetime on Breydon – celebrating the punt-gunners, fishermen, wildfowlers, eelers, smelters and poachers that he had known.

Fred Rolfe *I Walked by Night: Being the Philosophy of the King of the Norfolk Poachers, Written by Himself*. When Fred Rolfe, an elderly mole-catcher, had his memories/memoirs published in the 1930s, they proved extremely popular

– lost rural days perhaps, but intriguing all the same. He was greatly helped in his task by the daughter of Rider Haggard, Lilias.

Diana Souhami *Edith Cavell: Nurse, Martyr, Heroine*. The execution of Norfolk's Edith Cavell in World War I did much to embitter Anglo-German relations as well as making Cavell a national hero. Her life and death have been trawled over several times, most recently by Souhami, in this detailed book which also looks at the role of late nineteenth-early twentieth-century women in general.

★ **Craig Taylor** *Return to Akenfield: Portrait of an English Village in the 21st Century*. Well written and well researched, Taylor interviews all and sundry to get the flavour of the village today – powerful stuff and certainly not reassuring. Last edition published in 2007.

★ **E. P. Thompson** *The Making of the English Working Class*. A seminal text – essential reading for anyone who wants to understand the fabric of English society – tracing the birth of the working class between 1780 and 1832, a key period in the history of Norfolk and Suffolk. Outstanding description of the agricultural enclosures.

ART AND ARCHITECTURE

Anthony Bailey *John Constable: A Kingdom of his Own*. An in-depth look at Constable's life, times and art; no stone is left unturned in what is the best book on its subject.

Malcolm Cormack *The Paintings of Thomas Gainsborough*. Published in the early 1990s, this well-written book is especially strong on the influences that moulded Gainsborough's approach to his art.

Nicholas Groves *The Medieval Churches of the City of Norwich*. Every ecclesiastical nook and cranny is explored in this extensively researched book. Groves clearly loves his churches – and it's an enthusiasm he communicates well.

★ **Simon Jenkins** *England's Thousand Best Churches*; and also *England's Thousand Best Houses*. Two lucid, immaculately researched volumes describing the pick of England's churches and houses, divided by county and with a star rating. Jenkins does, however, seem to struggle to notch up the 1000 houses – why else would he have included Suffolk's Anglo-Saxon Village (see p.304).

Matthew Rice *Building Norfolk*. A welcome new book with three hundred watercolour illustrations of most of the county's key buildings with separate sections on just about everything you can think of – inns, barns, country houses, farmhouses etc.

FICTION

George Borrow *Lavengro*. Born near East Dereham, George Borrow (1803–81) spent much of his youth in Norwich before starting his extensive travels as a representative of the Bible Society, distant wanderings that were greatly assisted by his remarkable skills as a linguist – though he did return to settle near Lowestoft. Unusually for the day, Borrow felt a great affinity for gypsies as reflected in both his most famous work, *Romany Rye*, and the semi-autobiographical *Lavengro*, with its gentle evocation of Norwich.

George Crabbe *The Borough; The Village*. Born in Aldeburgh, the poet George Crabbe (1754–1832) had a particularly hard life and largely as a result his poetry packs a gritty punch, whether it's describing the swamps, mud flats and shingle banks of his home town, the furious roll of the sea or the harsh conditions endured by his fellow townsfolk. His poetry inspired Benjamin Britten – *Peter*

Grimes is drawn from *The Borough*.

Roald Dahl *The Mildenhall Treasure*. In 1942, a ploughman by the name of Gordon Butcher unearthed a valuable hoard of Roman silverware, "The Mildenhall Treasure". By all accounts, he seems to have been conned out of his just rewards by the man he worked for and Dahl tells the tale – mostly fact, but some conjecture.

Elly Griffiths *The House at Sea's End*. Griffiths has a real liking for Norfolk and this crime novel, her latest, makes good use of its coastal Norfolk setting, where human skeletons turn up as a sea cliff is worn away…and hey presto, here comes forensic archeologist Ruth Galloway to clear things up. If you like this one, try the same author's *The Crossing Places*, where the dastardly deed calling for Galloway's attention has been done on a remote Norfolk beach.

L. P. Hartley *The Go-Between*. Famous book, famous film, all to do with class and sexual desire in Edwardian Norfolk – rural Norfolk at that. Inspired by Hartley's stay at Bradenham Hall, near Thetford, in 1909.

P. D. James One of the UK's most popular writers, P. D. James has a long association with both Norfolk and Suffolk and several of her crime novels are set here – for example ★ *Unnatural Causes* (Minismere and Dunwich); *Death in Holy Orders* (Covehithe); and ★ *Devices and Desires* (the Norfolk coast).

Jim Kelly *Death Wore White*. King's Lynn may seem a fairly safe place to go, but not in this detective novel, which starts with two bodies and lots of suspects. Appealing descriptions of the north Norfolk coast too.

Arthur Ransome *Coot Club*. Ransome (1884–1967) spent several years living in south Suffolk on an around the River Stour, but Breydon Water served as the setting for the dramatic climax to this particular story: the Hullaballoos

are shipwrecked here, leaving Mrs Barrable and the children safe, albeit run aground in the fog.

Ruth Rendell (aka Barbara Vine). A long-time Suffolk resident, Rendell features the county in many of her top-selling crime novels, including *Make Death Love Me*, which begins with a robbery at a Suffolk bank; *The Brimstone Wedding* (Bury St Edmunds); *A Fatal Inversion* (Polstead and Nayland); and *Gallowglass* (Sudbury). In the early 1990s, she also compiled *Ruth Rendell's Suffolk*, in which a handsome set of photographs illustrated her favourite places.

★ **Graham Swift** *Waterland*. Written in 1983, *Waterland* is essentially a family saga set in East Anglia's fenlands – excellent on the subtle appeal of this wide-skied, unerringly eerie landscape. The book went down a storm when it was published and a decade later it was turned into a film, *Waterland*, starring Jeremy Irons.

Small print and index

A ROUGH GUIDE TO ROUGH GUIDES

Published in 1982, the first Rough Guide – to Greece – was a student scheme that became a publishing phenomenon. Mark Ellingham, a recent graduate in English from Bristol University, had been travelling in Greece the previous summer and couldn't find the right guidebook. With a small group of friends he wrote his own guide, combining a highly contemporary, journalistic style with a thoroughly practical approach to travellers' needs.

The immediate success of the book spawned a series that rapidly covered dozens of destinations. And, in addition to impecunious backpackers, Rough Guides soon acquired a much broader readership that relished the guides' wit and inquisitiveness as much as their enthusiastic, critical approach and value-for-money ethos.

These days, Rough Guides include recommendations from budget to luxury and cover more than 200 destinations around the globe, as well as producing an ever-growing range of eBooks and apps.

Visit **roughguides.com** to see our latest publications.

ABOUT THE AUTHORS

Phil Lee Like many a Midlander, Phil has been holidaying in Norfolk since he was knee-high and he was delighted to be asked to help prepare this new book. Phil has been writing for Rough Guides for well over twenty years. His other books in the series include Canada, Norway, Belgium & Luxembourg, Bruges, Amsterdam, Mallorca and Toronto. He lives in Nottingham, where he was born and raised.

Martin Dunford is one of the founders of the Rough Guides and has worked in travel publishing for over 25 years. He is the author of more than ten guidebooks and is a consultant to the travel websites ⓦtripbod.com and ⓦcoolplaces.co.uk. He lives in Blackheath, London, with his wife and two daughters, and in Norfolk, where he goes with his family to canoe, sail and mess around on the beach.

Acknowledgements

Martin Dunford Thanks to my editors, Andy Turner and Alice Park, to Ed Wright and Katie Lloyd-Jones for some superb maps, and my co-author, Phil Lee, for good company, effortless decision-making and happy times in Horning and elsewhere. Thanks to Russell and Sarah Abrahams, for use of their wonderful house and happy days in Suffolk and Norfolk over many years. Also to Paul Dickson of ⓦvisitnorfolk.co.uk, Richard Ginger, Ros Green and Brigit Parker of ⓦchoosesuffolk.com, and Emma French of ⓦvisiteastofengland.com, all of whom were a huge help; and to all the hoteliers and small business owners who helped make travelling around both counties such a pleasure. Finally, special thanks are due to Caroline, Daisy, Lucy and Sonny the dog, for memorable trips to the beach, dunes, Bewilderwood, and, er, accompanying me around all those churches!

Phil Lee would like to thank his editors, Andy Turner and Alice Park, for their diligent attention to detail during the preparation of this new Rough Guide to Norfolk and Suffolk. Special thanks also to Martyn and Chris Livermore for bags of local information and top tips; Pat Edgar of PR Matters; Pamela Farrell of the White Horse, Brancaster Staithe; the indefatigable Squeak of Flying Kiwi Inns; Katherine McGarr of the Ickworth Hotel; Rebecca Scott for comments and opinions; and the cheerful conversation of Delysia Hart. My gratitude also to the ever-helpful Melanie Cook of Visit Norwich; the extraordinarily efficient Paul Dickson; and to Friederike Franck of Choose Suffolk. And cheers to my fellow author, Martin: I couldn't wish for a better colleague/comrade.

Rough Guide credits

Editors: Andy Turner, Alice Park
Layout: Sachin Gupta
Cartography: Katie Lloyd-Jones, Ed Wright
Picture editor: Mark Thomas
Proofreader: Karen Parker
Managing editor: Keith Drew
Assistant editor: Prema Dutta
Production: Rebecca Short
Cover design: Nicole Newman, Sachin Gupta
Photographer: Diana Jarvis
Editorial assistant: Eleanor Aldridge

Senior pre-press designer: Dan May
Marketing, Publicity & roughguides.com: Liz Statham
Design director: Scott Stickland
Travel publisher: Joanna Kirby
Digital travel publisher: Peter Buckley
Reference director: Andrew Lockett
Operations coordinator: Becky Doyle
Operations assistant: Johanna Wurm
Publishing director (Travel): Clare Currie
Commercial manager: Gino Magnotta
Managing director: John Duhigg

Publishing information

This first edition published May 2012 by
Rough Guides Ltd,
80 Strand, London WC2R 0RL
11, Community Centre, Panchsheel Park,
New Delhi 110017, India
Distributed by the Penguin Group
Penguin Books Ltd,
80 Strand, London WC2R 0RL
Penguin Group (USA)
375 Hudson Street, NY 10014, USA
Penguin Group (Australia)
250 Camberwell Road, Camberwell,
Victoria 3124, Australia
Penguin Group (NZ)
67 Apollo Drive, Mairangi Bay, Auckland 1310,
New Zealand
Rough Guides is represented in Canada by Tourmaline
Editions Inc. 662 King Street West, Suite 304, Toronto,
Ontario M5V 1M7
Printed in Singapore by Toppan Security Printing Pte. Ltd.
© Martin Dunford and Phil Lee, 2012

Maps © Rough Guides
Contains Ordnance Survey data © Crown copyright and
database rights 2012
No part of this book may be reproduced in any form
without permission from the publisher except for the
quotation of brief passages in reviews.
336pp includes index
A catalogue record for this book is available from the
British Library
ISBN: 978-1-84836-606-0
The publishers and authors have done their best to
ensure the accuracy and currency of all the information
in **The Rough Guide to Norfolk & Suffolk**, however,
they can accept no responsibility for any loss, injury, or
inconvenience sustained by any traveller as a result of
information or advice contained in the guide.
1 3 5 7 9 8 6 4 2

Help us update

We've gone to a lot of effort to ensure that the first edition
of **The Rough Guide to Norfolk & Suffolk** is accurate
and up-to-date. However, things change – places get
"discovered", opening hours are notoriously fickle,
restaurants and rooms raise prices or lower standards.
If you feel we've got it wrong or left something out, we'd
like to know, and if you can remember the address, the
price, the hours, the phone number, so much the better.

Please send your comments with the subject line
"**Rough Guide Norfolk & Suffolk Update**" to ✉ mail
@uk.roughguides.com. We'll credit all contributions and
send a copy of the next edition (or any other Rough Guide
if you prefer) for the very best emails.

Find more travel information, connect with fellow
travellers and book your trip on ⊕ roughguides.com

Photo credits

All photos © Rough Guides except the following:
(Key: t-top; c-centre; b-bottom; l-left; r-right)

p.1 Getty Images, Dave Porter
p.2 4Corners, Richard Taylor
p.4 Getty Images, Panoramic Images
p.9 Alamy, Ernie Janes (c); Michael Juno (t)
p.10 Getty Images, Jon Gibbs
p.11 Alamy, Clynt Garnham (b); Getty Images: Gary Smith (t)
p.13 Alamy, Jon Gibbs (t); Ernie Janes (b)
p.14 Alamy, David J. Green (t)
p.15 Alamy, BL Images Ltd (b); Getty Images, Jon Gibbs (c)
p.16 Alamy, Charlie Gray (b); Getty Images, Chris Everard (cr)
p.60 Alamy, Jon Gibbs

p.85 Alamy, Tim Oram (b); Travelib (t)
p.187 Alamy, The National Trust Photolibrary
p.195 Alamy, Mike Booth
p.227 Alamy, geogphotos (t)
p.235 Alamy, Les Polders
p.275 Alamy, Jon Arnold Images Ltd
p.295 Alamy, The National Trust Photolibrary
p.310 Alamy, Nigel Pye

Front cover Southwold beach huts; Alamy, Philip Hall
Back cover Turf Fen, Alamy; Chris Herring (t)

Index

Maps are marked in grey

Map symbols

The symbols below are used on maps throughout the book

✈ Airport	🔦 Lighthouse	🍾 Distillery
★ Bus/taxi stop	⛳ Golf course	🍺 Brewery
⚓ Ferry stop	🏞 Country park	⊗ Watermill
🚢 Boat	⊙ Statue	🍎 Orchard
ⓘ Tourist infomation	🏛 Abbey/monastery	Marsh
✉ Post office	∴ Archeological site/ruins	Park
♦ Museum	🏰 Castle	+ Cemetery
♦ Place of interest	🐘 Zoo/wildlife park	Beach
P Parking	🎡 Amusement park	Building
⊠ Gate	🏁 Racing circuit	♦ Church
🏛 Stately home/historic house	T Public gardens	Stadium

Motorway
Dual carriageway
Road
Railway (& stop)
Private/light railway (& stop)
Footpath
Ferry route
Wall

Listings key

■ Accommodation

● Eating and drinking

■ Club/venue

● Shop